*Also by Gananath Obeyesekere*

Land Tenure in Village Ceylon:
A Sociological and Historical Study

Medusa's Hair:
An Essay on Personal Symbols and Religious Experience

The Cult of the Goddess Pattini

Buddhism Transformed:
Religious Change in Sri Lanka *(with Richard Gombrich)*

The Work of Culture:
Symbolic Transformation in Psychoanalysis and Anthropology

The Apotheosis of Captain Cook:
European Mythmaking in the Pacific

# IMAGINING KARMA

COMPARATIVE STUDIES IN RELIGION AND SOCIETY

Mark Juergensmeyer, editor

1. *Redemptive Encounters: Three Modern Styles in the Hindu Tradition*, by Lawrence A. Babb
2. *Saints and Virtues*, edited by John Stratton Hawley
3. *Utopias in Conflict: Religion and Nationalism in Modern India*, by Ainslee T. Embree
4. *Mama Lola: A Vodou Priestess in Brooklyn*, by Karen McCarthy Brown
5. *The New Cold War? Religious Nationalism Confronts the Secular State*, by Mark Juergensmeyer
6. *Pious Passion: The Emergence of Modern Fundamentalism in the United States and Iran*, by Martin Riesebrodt, translated by Don Reneau
7. *Devi: Goddess of India*, edited by John Stratton Hawley and Donna Marie Wulff
8. *Absent Lord: Ascetics and Kings in a Jain Ritual Culture*, by Lawrence A. Babb
9. *The Challenge of Fundamentalism: Political Islam and the New World Disorder*, by Bassam Tibi
10. *Leveling Crowds: Ethnonationalist Conflicts and Collective Violence in South Asia*, by Stanley J. Tambiah
11. *The Bridge Betrayed: Religion and Genocide in Bosnia*, by Michael A. Sells
12. *China's Catholics: Tragedy and Hope in an Emerging Civil Society*, by Richard Madsen
13. *Terror in the Mind of God: The Global Rise of Religious Violence*, by Mark Juergensmeyer
14. *Imagining Karma: Ethical Transformation in Amerindian, Buddhist, and Greek Rebirth*, by Gananath Obeyesekere

# IMAGINING KARMA

## Ethical Transformation in Amerindian, Buddhist, and Greek Rebirth

GANANATH OBEYESEKERE

University of California Press Berkeley Los Angeles London

University of California Press
Berkeley and Los Angeles, California

University of California Press, Ltd.
London, England

In chapter 4, "The Buddhist Ascesis," the author has drawn on his article "Taking the Myth Seriously: The Buddha and the Enlightenment," in *Bauddhavidyāsudhākaraḥ: Studies in Honour of Heinz Bechert on the Occasion of His Sixty-fifth Birthday,* ed. Petra Kieffer-Pülz and Jens-Uwe Hartmann, 473–82. Swisttal-Odendorf: Indica et Tibetica, 1997.



Library of Congress Cataloging-in-Publication Data

Obeyesekere, Gananath.
Imagining karma : ethical transformation in Amerindian, Buddhist, and Greek rebirth / Gananath Obeyesekere.
p. cm. — (Comparative studies in religion and society ; 14)
Includes bibliographical references and index.
ISBN 0-520-23220-8 (alk. paper) —
ISBN 0-520-23243-7 (pbk. : alk. paper)
1. Reincarnation (Buddhism).
2. Reincarnation—Comparative studies.
3. Religious ethics—Comparative studies.
I. Title. II. Series.
BQ4485 .O24 2002
291.2'37—dc21 2001008252

Manufactured in the United States of America

11 10 09 08 07 06 05 04 03 02
10 9 8 7 6 5 4 3 2 1

The paper used in this publication is both acid-free and totally chlorine-free (TCF). It meets the minimum requirements of ANSI/NISO Z39.48–1992 (R 1997) (*Permanence of Paper*).⊗

*For Ian and Roslin Goonetileke,*
*celebrating fifty years of a cherished friendship*

# CONTENTS

# ILLUSTRATIONS

# PREFACE

In this book I examine three eschatologies that until now have not been put together in any kind of systematic comparative perspective: the rebirth doctrines of small-scale societies in various parts of the world, such as West Africa, Melanesia, the Northwest Coast Amerindians, and the Inuit (Eskimo); those in the Buddhist, Jaina, and other religions that flowered in the Ganges valley around the sixth century B.C.E.; and those of the Greeks of the Pythagorean tradition of roughly the same period, which culminated in the soteriological and cosmological thought of Plato and of Plotinus in later times. I maintain that this material can be read at several levels. The comparative perspective can apply to each of three broad substantive domains that I deal with here. The rebirth theories of small-scale societies discussed in chapter 2 have structural similarities that derive to a considerable extent from their smallness. Take two ideas common to virtually all of these societies: first, a dead person will circle back to the same kin group; and second, a neonate can be identified as a specific ancestor returned. I show that although the first feature is applicable to every small-scale society in my sample, the second feature is absent among one of them, the Trobrianders. I demonstrate in my analysis that among Trobrianders it is meaningless to so identify the neonate, given this society's notion of ancestors as mostly anonymous beings. It would be logically and structurally impossible for Trobrianders to get interested in the issue of the identity of the neonate. I also show that among the small-scale societies mentioned in this work there is a fundamental difference between the Amerindians and the rest, that is, West Africans and Melanesians: the presence of animal rebirth in the former and its absence in the latter. The presence of animal rebirths in Amerindian-Inuit societies permits us to establish an important link, methodologically speaking, with both the Buddhist and Greek worlds, which share that same propensity; and it helps us isolate Amerindian and Inuit forms of rebirth in our sample of preliterate societies as the ones most significant for comparative purposes.

As in the small-scale societies mentioned above, Buddhist and Greek doctrines of rebirth also permit internal comparisons such that the Indic religions exhibit close similarities and differences, as do the Greek ones. However, the main point of this work is not to demonstrate internal similarity and difference but to examine structural similarities and variations across the great cultural divides that separate Amerindian, Buddhist, and Greek rebirth doctrines. This may seem a hopeless task at first glance because anyone knows that on the substantive level the actual ethnographic or historical accounts of rebirth theories are vastly different, and there is little to connect Buddhist, Greek, and Amerindian rebirth. Yet this work will show that underlying these vast differences are important structural similarities and variations based on a shared belief in reincarnation, which I show has an unvarying "elementary structure." Hence the methodological thrust of this book: I can demonstrate how transformations can occur on the basis of this common elementary structure, which permits me to depict and compare limited "topographical models" of rebirth theories across great cultural divides. But the structural models are not anchored to universalist theorizing as in Lévi-Strauss's structuralism; rather they have been constructed in the manner of "ideal types" geared to my specific research interest. Thus, this book is an attempt to demonstrate that, although one must eschew universalistic lawlike theories modeled on the natural sciences, one must also reject the contemporary fascination in my own discipline for ethnographic particularity and a rejection of theory unless it shows that no theories are possible outside descriptive specificity. In this work I make the claim, and demonstrate as best I can, that limited comparison and theorizing are possible in the human sciences.

The topographical models I have constructed simplify the complexity of eschatologies on the ground, as it were, permitting us to focus primarily on specific issues of structural similarity and transformation rather than on substantive content. Still, any idea of structure is senseless without the substantive content that permits the construction of simplified models. Once the models are constructed, one can infer some "expectable" features of content in the empirical record. For example, I show that from a structural point of view one could expect societies with rebirth doctrines to show a preoccupation with "endoanthropophagy" (endocannibalism). In reality some do, and some don't; but once one isolates the structural problem of endoanthropophagy, it is possible to adduce reasons for the absence of this phenomenon in specific cases, such as in Buddhism, or, failing that, to at least describe the absence in a specific cultural context. In other instances even these operations may not be possible because of the paucity of relevant sociological and historical data.

The preceding remarks may suggest that I have ventured into abstract realms of little concern to Indologists and classical scholars. Although I primarily address anthropologists, historians of religion, and other inquisitive intellectuals, I try to present my argument in a fashion intelligible to those outside the human sciences. Moreover, readers who are put off by abstractions and who are unsympathetic to my theory of ethical and structural transformation might find provocative my descriptions and incomplete interpretations of specific rebirth eschatologies and cosmologies from different regions of the world.

The comparative information might also surprise many scholars and lay readers who have been prejudiced into thinking that such doctrines are the exclusive preserve of the religions of India. My initial rationale for embarking on this project was to justify decentering India as the home and ground of rebirth. But I go beyond my Buddhist prejudice to a vision of a larger purpose: I explore the common fate of those societies that through historical accident or through the circulation of ideas or through independent invention have come to believe in reincarnation as an integral part of their larger eschatological and cosmological belief systems. In the more abstract arguments presented in this work I explore the implications of that common fate. Another, related, major theme pertains to general epistemology, namely, how thought is constrained within the frame of preexisting knowledge structures—what Foucault called "epistemes"—and the freedom and leeway for innovation and debate permitted to the individual virtuoso or layperson.

This book had a very modest beginning. The problem of the ethical transformation of a previously "amoral" eschatology into a more complex karmic doctrine was one of my early intellectual concerns, but at that time I framed my concern in terms of the origin of the karma theory. I first presented these ideas in Edmund Leach's seminar at King's College, Cambridge, in 1964 and subsequently published them in "Theodicy, Sin, and Salvation in a Sociology of Buddhism."[1] In this first paper I had little information on rebirth theories outside of the Indic area, but I soon discovered the Trobriand eschatology. In 1971, at the 28th International Congress of Orientalists in Canberra, I presented a paper with the deliberately facetious title "Why Is There No Buddhism in the Trobriand Islands?" (which even I did not have the temerity to publish!). In 1980 I followed this paper with "The Rebirth Eschatology and Its Transformations: A Contribution to the Sociology of Early Buddhism," an essay that brought in data from Igbo, Trobriand, and Pythagorean and Orphic religions.[2] However, fascinating and crucial data from the Northwest Coast Indians and the Inuit were absent. Until I read papers by Antonia Mills, I was ignorant, like many others, that Amerindians possessed theories of reincarnation. I participated in a seminar organized by Mills and wrote a foreword for her collection of seminar papers, subsequently published under the title *Amerindian Rebirth: Reincarnation Belief among North American Indians and Inuit.* In that foreword I relate Amerindian rebirth theories to those theories found on the Indian subcontinent.[3] Amerindian rebirth provoked me to rethink the problem of karma, not so much in terms of its origins but in relation to structural and ethical transformations. Nevertheless my early bias toward Buddhism is reflected in the present work. Some of my most important theoretical findings—including the central concept of "ethicization"—are a product of my engagement with early Buddhism. Yet my engagement with rebirth eschatologies of small-scale societies has in turn affected my understanding of both Buddhist and Greek rebirth doctrines.

I was able to rethink these early interests during my sabbatical in Sri Lanka as a Fulbright scholar during the 1993–94 academic year. As always, Sri Lanka, in spite of the violence in which it was enmeshed, inspired my creativity, and during the course of that year I wrote a preliminary draft of this book, focusing on the Amerindian and Indian material but excluding the Greek. The reason was simple: I found my foray into the Greek world in my 1980 paper shallow and unsatisfactory. I therefore decided, somewhat reluctantly, to ignore it. My sabbatical culminated in a marvelous stay at the Rockefeller Center in Bellagio, where I had hoped to put the finishing touches to the book. During my leisure hours at Bellagio I began to reread Plato and whatever was available on the Presocratics at the Bellagio library. I soon recognized that I had no choice but to use the Greek material because, like the Indic and the Amerindian, it included the notion of animal rebirths, a notion crucial to my comparative perspective.

Thus the Greeks came to stay in my book. The Presocratic Greek material was especially difficult for me owing to its fragmentary nature, and this difficulty was compounded by the fact that classical scholars sometimes address their own circles with little serious comparative or theoretical thinking. The task was rendered even more difficult because two writers, H. S. Long and M. Peris, who dealt with this topic explicitly, did not always render the Greek into English.[4] Fortunately, I soon invented my own rationale for bringing in the Greek material, and it can be briefly stated as follows: Contemporary scholars and intellectuals in the West quite rightly see the Greeks as the fountainhead of Western culture, and this view has resulted in a special take toward ancient Greece, one, for example, that highlights Greek rationality and its "enlightened" thought. In this scheme Plato is a key figure, the epitome of the Western speculative philosopher, whose thinking has come down through the Neoplatonists into later Christian theology. Yet Europe as we now understand it scarcely existed in Plato's time or in the time of the Pythagoreans that are the foci of my study. Although European thinkers see the Greeks as their intellectual forebears, the Greeks themselves looked toward the East for the sources of true wisdom—to Egypt, Persia, and, during the early centuries of the common era, India. Thus tradition has it that early Greek thinkers traveled East in their quest for knowledge. Pythagoras, for example, is said to have wandered into Egypt and later to have sat at the feet of Zoroaster. These traditions might not be based on fact, but they do illustrate the reality that Greeks saw the East as the source of knowledge, in much the same way that modern Europeans relate to the ancient Greeks.

This should not surprise those of us who believe that the ancient world, not just Eurasia, was an open one. Along trade and caravan routes and in military campaigns ideas traveled vast distances, borne by merchants, soldiers, early voyagers in flimsy ships, and itinerant religious specialists and wanderers. Recent studies by scholars such as M. L. West, W. Burkert, and P. Kingsley have shown that the idea of Greeks looking to the East is not pure fantasy and that they were influenced by a multitude of ideas stemming from those regions. Kingsley's work, which I read only after this book was nearly completed, is especially interesting because he shows that Pythagoreanism, and this includes Plato's cosmology, was directly influenced by West Asian and Near Eastern thought and ritual structures and that forms of Pythagoreanism filtered into later hermeticism and alchemy in Europe. Nevertheless, I think that Kingsley's own work, contrary to his avowed intention, generates a more or less uniform stream of Pythagoreanism instead of multiple life-forms exhibiting epistemic breaks and differences beneath family resemblances.[5]

Looking at Greek thinkers from my particular approach meant taking their rebirth eschatologies seriously. Although classical scholars do recognize the importance of rebirth doctrines among the Presocratics such as Pythagoras and Empedocles, they rarely do for Plato. But to me Plato's thinking must be seen in terms not of a then-nonexistent European tradition but of existing thinkers in the then-known philosophic world, not just in the Greek world but the known contemporary world of which Greece was a part. In this work I am not primarily interested in the classicists' version of Plato as a philosopher or as a political and ethical thinker. I am concerned rather with Plato as a rebirth theorist and soteriologist who had a spiritual affinity with those of the Indian subcontinent, especially the Buddha. Those who have read the dialogues of the Buddha must surely be aware of their stylistic resemblance to Plato's dialogues, even though the Buddha was not interested in secular polity as Plato was. One does not have to posit actual contact between early Greece and India, although this was both possible and likely. Methodologically, however, given the mode of analysis employed in this book, one has only to recognize that Plato and the Buddha made sense in respect to their times and, given the power of their thought, affected human thought in general. Adopting this perspective I began to see Plato's rebirth eschatology as central to his cosmology and soteriology, not external or peripheral to it. The overwhelming majority of classical scholars, however, tend to treat Plato's rebirth theories as an allegorizing tendency or to simply ignore them. Yet it is interesting to note that Plato's disciple Plotinus treats his master's rebirth theories as literally true and imputes to Plato that same belief. Therefore I am in rather distinguished company in thinking that Plato himself probably believed in the truth of rebirth! However, I should not have been surprised that scholars have more or less ignored this aspect of Plato's thought because such myopia characterizes the work of ethnographers who have barely noticed rebirth eschatologies among the many groups they studied in the past century.

So it is with Plotinus: most contemporary scholars who have written on Plotinus recently barely refer to his reincarnation theory, even though they agree that both Plotinus and his fellow Neoplatonists personally believed in it. Lloyd Gerson puts the matter somewhat equivocally: "I have argued that decline from a discarnate state has no meaning for Plotinus. This is not to say, however, that reincarnation is an essential part of his eschatology. Nevertheless, the evidence strongly suggests that Plotinus did in fact believe in reincarnation."[6] Commitments to such beliefs were so strong that Proclus (412–85 C.E.), a famous Neoplatonic commentator, believed himself an incarnation of Nicomachus (c. 150 C.E.), the author of a work entitled *Theological Arithmetic*.[7] I find it hard to believe that such deeply held commitments were only peripherally relevant for understanding Neoplatonic mysticism and gnosis.

Even more surprising is that the same lacuna exists in contemporary ethnographic accounts of Bali. I, as a native Buddhist, can go to Bali and find no difficulty whatever in carrying on a serious conversation about rebirth in English with educated Balinese, but little information on Balinese rebirth is available in the ethnographic literature by Western scholars. As I show in this book, this is because ethnographers are often not attuned to seeing and responding to views that are thoroughly alien to their own traditions.

Indeed, Buddhists and Hindus find it difficult to converse on such matters with European intellectuals unfamiliar with the subcontinent. For example, for a human being to be reborn as a monkey or a bird or even as an insect or a worm is something flagrantly outrageous or funny. Hence Walter Burkert could say that for the Greeks the doctrine of reincarnation is in essence "not *theologia* but anthropology, fantastic and yet recalling alleged experiences and predicting future ones."[8] He also tells us that reincarnation beliefs "remained a kind of foreign body in the framework of Greek religion."[9] These attitudes are but part of a larger theme that recurs in the classicists' version of Greek history and thought: a rarefied and reified distinction between a rational Milesian tradition, which represents the Greek civilization at its best, and a tradition of Western Greeks, who were influenced by a variety of "oriental" beliefs and also orgiastic rites associated with Orphic and Dionysian mysteries. Hence the cynical comment of Marcel Detienne: "the Greeks aren't like the others."[10] I have little sympathy for the orientalism that condemns oriental beliefs in this fashion, and I hope that this work will help to confirm that Greeks in some significant ways are very much like the others.

Reincarnation beliefs not only enlink the Greeks in a larger chain of being but they were also not "fantastic" for those Greeks who believed in their reality. Hence, like Plotinus, I take seriously Plato's view that hardworking bourgeoisie could be reborn as industrious creatures such as ants and bees. Plato could be as ironic as the Buddha was about such matters, but irony did not exclude commitment to the truth of these beliefs. The fact that thinkers such as the Buddha and Plato allegorized some myths and deconstructed others did not mean that they did not believe in some and invent new ones, just as present-day deconstructionists do. In any case, looking at Plato through the models constructed in this work might throw a different perspective on that great thinker's soteriology. If, with the Presocratics, I rely heavily on the interpretations of classical scholars writing in English, such is not the case with Plato. There was no way that I could master the voluminous research and commentaries on Plato's work. I therefore took the bold and perhaps foolish step of reading Plato in my own fashion, giving my own slant to his eschatological and soteriological vision. This orientation further implies that whether one is dealing with Platonic myths or Buddhist ones or those of small-scale societies, the analytical strategy should remain consistent. Even so, much of my presentation of Plato's thought might seem obvious to Greek scholars but not to my primary readership. Yet Greek scholars ought to recognize, I think, the importance of focusing on the neglected area of Greek rebirth seen within a larger cross-cultural context.

The problem I have with Greek thought is true to a lesser degree with the other rebirth eschatologies I discuss in this work, with the exception of Theravada Buddhism. I can relate to Buddhism both from the inside, as someone socialized in it (albeit very imperfectly), and from the outside, as a scholar looking at texts, contexts, and practices. But what do I know of Amerindian or West African or Melanesian thought and texts? Once more I have to rely on the work of ethnographers who most certainly will disagree with some of my interpretations. Ethnographic prejudice virtually takes for granted that one cannot understand another culture unless one has done fieldwork in it. I do not buy this argument at all, but I am acutely aware of the shortcomings in my knowledge of these ethnographic areas. I ask ethnographers to withhold judgment until they have read the book in its totality because I hope that, in hermeneutical fashion, the exploration of one area will circle into another in a back-and-forth fashion. This book is not meant for someone primarily interested in area studies; it must be read as a totality to be properly appreciated. Breaking down areal barriers also meant breaking down barriers that separate scholarly disciplines and area studies from one another. These barriers, as we all well know, can be jealously guarded.

Areal barriers can be broken only by comparative analyses and theoretical thinking, and comparison is possible only if one moves away from the purely substantive domain to delineating structures, ideal types, or topographical models and their transformations. It is true that this book deals systematically for the first time with theories of rebirth cross-culturally; but "systematicity" is strictly methodological, geared to structural transformations and not toward a complete or exhaustive description of the world's rebirth eschatologies or, for that matter, of the eschatologies of any particular region or religion. Such exhaustiveness is impossible for several reasons. First, as mentioned earlier, rebirth theories have been poorly documented. Second, even where they have been well documented, one has to employ some delimiting principles to write a manageable book. Third, there is no way that any human being could, without spending a lifetime of research, produce an exhaustive study of rebirth in any of the areas that appear in this book. And some likely rebirth eschatologies, for example, that of the Australian "aborigines" or the ancient and present-day religions of Siberia and Inner Asia, hardly appear in this work. My study is substantively incomplete in this sense. This is true even in respect to Buddhism, the religion I know best. I have focused almost exclusively on Theravada rebirth, ignoring for the most part the many fascinating Mahayana karmic eschatologies. Greek scholars will complain that I have neglected the mystery religions and Orphic tablets. Although these sources do contain references to rebirth, I cannot but heed the cautionary voices that tell me that Orphic mysteries "did not include a 'theory of transmigration' but instead consisted of a journey of the soul to another world from its prison-house in the body."[11] This claim has been refuted by Robert Parker, who makes a point that "early Orphism" did possess rebirth theories and a vegetarian diet but that it is impossible to reconstruct the details of Orphic rebirth with any degree of certainty.[12] M. L. West, however, has boldly and speculatively done so, and my very brief references to Orphism are based on his work.[13]

Delimitation does not pertain exclusively to the theme of topographical models and structural change. As with Lévi-Strauss's work, structural models also tie in with much broader issues pertaining to the generation of knowledge, including soteriological knowledge. For example, my discussion of Indic and Greek rebirth focuses on thinkers or systems of thought given to understanding life and the world, existence and the universe, in terms of abstract concepts. I give the unsatisfactory label "conceptualism" (borrowed from European medieval philosophy) to designate this mode of thinking. I believe that Theravada Buddhism is ideally suited for this larger purpose, and it fits nicely with the broad stream of "Pythagoreanism" that I delimit, this being the tradition of thought that stems from Pythagoras and the Pythagoreans to Empedocles, Plato, and Plotinus—all driven by "conceptualism." Hence a further methodological justification for excluding those ecstatic and passionately devotional forms of religious life labeled "Orphism." They are not animated by conceptualism and hence are not necessary for the methodological operations ("imaginary experiments") I perform in this work.

I now want to acquaint the reader very briefly with some stylistic devices I employ. I begin the book with the old problem of origins of Indic rebirth and karma doctrines. An early American Indologist, W. D. Whitney, says that the origin of rebirth is "one of the most difficult questions in the religious history of India," and this view is shared by many modern scholars.[14] Yet there is an inherent difficulty in studying old texts such as Sanskrit and Greek texts (or for that matter ethnographic ones) that are fragmentary and sometimes downright inadequate for reconstituting lost eschatologies. To put it differently: the pre-Buddhist and Presocratic data do not permit reasonably accurate reconstructions of the past, only informed guesswork. Perhaps a structural argument might bring to bear on old texts a certain level of methodological and argumentative rigor. It should not surprise the reader that, as my argument proceeds, the issue of origins drops out of the picture and the larger thesis of ethical transformation begins to emerge. I take the reader along with me to a developing argument, not a finished one.

In general the technical terms I use will be clearly defined in the body of this work, with one proviso. Scholars often use the term *transmigration* as a synonym for *reincarnation* or *metempsychosis*. I use *transmigration* in a more limited sense, to designate an eschatology where the soul at death migrates to another form of sentient existence and stays there without seeking reincarnation. This usage will be made clear in my discussion of Igbo eschatology in chapter 2.

Now to the vexing problem of translations and other technical matters. Translation is something virtually every ethnographer has had to face because ethnographies are never written in local languages, and it is rare that native texts enter into the body of an ethnography. We often have to read ethnographies on faith; there is no way that I could check whether Malinowski's Trobriand ethnography (or for that matter any of the ethnographies used in chapter 2 of this book) is based on an "adequate" knowledge of the local language. This ethnographic laxity will find few defenders among Indologists and classicists whose studies have been intensive and highly focused, based generally on the expert knowledge of one language and most often confined to a very limited historical period. I cannot claim that kind of expertise, and I have had to rely exclusively on translations.

The translations I use for Theravada Buddhism are mostly from the Pali Text translation series, supplemented by some new translations of a few texts, particularly that of the *Dīgha Nikāya* (Long discourses) by Maurice Walshe.[15] These translations are available in any major library. Since the first version of this book was written, I have seen one important new translation of the *Majjhima Nikāya* (Middle length discourses) by Bhikkhu Ñāṇamoli and Bhikkhu Bodhi; I have not been able to use this work as much as I would have liked to.[16] I started with several translations of the Upanishads but soon replaced them with Patrick Olivelle's new translation, *Upaniṣads.*[17] For my initial understanding of the Presocratics my guide has been volumes 1 and 2 of W. K. C. Guthrie's magisterial work *A History of Greek Philosophy.*[18] As far as the important fragments by Empedocles are concerned, I relied mainly on M. R. Wright, *Empedocles: The Extant Fragments,* supplemented by the new translation by Brad Inwood, *The Poem of Empedocles.*[19] Whereas Wright adopts the older view that Empedocles wrote two poems, Inwood thinks he wrote a single poem and rearranges the fragments accordingly. Because I had written most of this book before I read Inwood, I simply continued to use the traditional distinction. I do not think the debate over whether Empedocles wrote one poem or two matters very much for my argument. I also use both editions of *The Presocratic Philosophers* because although the second edition contains extensive changes, I found many useful ideas in the earlier edition.[20] I am also aware that use of these works skews my discussion of Empedocles toward the older English tradition represented by John Burnet and those who followed him. I hope, however, that I have presented my arguments clearly enough to allow scholars to disagree with them. I have used extensively Thomas Taylor's classic nineteenth-century translations *Iamblichus' "Life of Pythagoras"* and *Porphyry on Abstinence from Animal Food.*[21] I have supplemented Taylor's with Gillian Clark's translation and the more recent annotated translation by John Dillon and Jackson Hershbell.[22] I simply used those translations I thought read best. For Plotinus I have used two major translations: the older one by Stephen MacKenna and the new standard edition and translation by A. H. Armstrong.[23] Although Armstrong's is the more scholarly translation, MacKenna, I think, writes with feeling and perhaps touches the spirit of Plotinus's work.

I had some difficulty regarding the transliteration of unfamiliar words in Sanskrit and Pali. For convenience I use the well-known Sanskrit forms such as *karma* and *nirvana* instead of the Pali *kamma* and *nibbāṇa* unless I am quoting from a text. I have, however, retained the Pali *Dhamma* instead of the more popular Sanskrit *Dharma* because the Pali word often has a more restricted meaning of "the Buddha's teaching" rather than the much more extended Sanskrit meaning of "the moral order." I have sometimes used simple renderings of Sanskrit words (for example, *Upanishads*) instead of a strict Sanskrit transliteration unless, once again, I am quoting some source. I have simply added the letter *s* to indicate the plural form of Indic terms. After the first instance I have not italicized technical terms and proper nouns that are commonly employed in this text, and some familiar terms such as *nirvana* are also used without diacriticals. So also with Amerindian and Greek terms, which I try to render simply rather than try for strict transliteration.

In the process of writing this book I have incurred debts to many friends and colleagues who generously gave their time and advice. For the Greek material I owe much to the unstinting help of my colleague at Princeton Richard Martin, who urged me to push ahead with this line of exploration, and to Susan Lape, who helped me track down sources. Others read parts or the whole of the manuscript: William Cobb at the College of William and Mary; Anthony A. Long, whose sympathetic reading for the University of California Press forced me to rethink and rearrange the Presocratic material; Deborah Kamen, who rechecked the Greek material for factual and spelling errors; and my friend Merlin Peris, the Sri Lankan classical scholar, who was always there for advice. In Indological studies I have been blessed with good friends, *kalyāna mitra:* Patrick Olivelle, who helped me with the Vedic and Upanishadic material and corrected some horrendous mistakes, Paul Courtright, for his enthusiastic review for the Press, and Wendy Doniger, who read the original manuscript, prior to my Greek incursions. I must also record my appreciation for the help of H. L. Seneviratne, Henk Bodewitz, Joel Brereton, Deborah Cordonnier, and Sunil Goonesekera. As always I have learned much from Richard Gombrich, such that I do not always know when my ideas begin and his end! I only know that none of my friends and colleagues are responsible for some of the irrepressible thoughts expressed in this book. In my study of small-scale societies I have received similar unstinted support from Antonia Mills, who read the whole manuscript through, and in various ways from Michael Harkin, James Matlock, James Lorand Matory, Betsy Strick, Simon Ottenberg, Alma Gottleib, Sergei Kan, and Flora *Edouwaye* S. Kaplan. Although not all were directly interested in the themes of this book, I have derived much intellectual challenge and stimulation from friends and colleagues in the anthropology department at Princeton, most particularly from Hildred Geertz and John Mac Dougall, for their knowledge of Balinese rebirth, and Carol

Zanca, our department manager, for her unfailing support. Special thanks to Mark Juergensmeyer, who urged me to submit this book for the series Comparative Studies in Religion and Society that he edits for the University of California Press; to Reed Malcolm, the acquisitions editor, for his enormous enthusiasm for the project; to his assistant, Cindy Wathen; to the unfailing courtesy of the staff of the Press, especially my manuscript editor, Rachel Berchten; and to the indefatigable and conscientious copy editor Joe Abbott. This book would never have seen the light of day but for my wife, Ranjini, who continually encouraged me to finish a seemingly interminable project. Many of my ideas were initially presented in several seminars in Paris in June 1992 when I was directeur d'études at the École des Hautes Études en Sciences Sociales. I thank the participants in those seminars for their insightful comments and Eric Meyer, who made this visit possible. These initial ideas were further developed in the seminars I presented at the International Centre for Ethnic Studies in Colombo, with which I was affiliated as a Fulbright scholar in 1993. I must place on record my affection for my many friends there, in particular Radhika Coomaraswamy, Sithie Thiruchelvam, Regi Siriwardene, and the many participants of those intellectual evenings, and for S. Varatharajan, who generously gave his time and help to a computer illiterate. It is with anguish and dismay that I record the tragic death in 1999 of my dear friend Neelan Thiruchelvam, the director of the Centre, as I was engaged in fieldwork in the Uva-Vellassa region of Sri Lanka. And it is with further dismay and sorrow that I record the sudden death of Destry Muller, a talented young photographer who took many pictures for me. He was killed on December 29, 2001, when the motorbike he was riding was hit by a bus on Sri Lanka's murderous roads. He was only twenty-one.

Finally, a word of thanks for other institutions that supported this research at different times: the Fulbright Hays Fellowship, for providing me the opportunity to write the first draft during my 1993 sabbatical; the Rockefeller Center at Bellagio, for its inspirational setting; Princeton University, for faculty grants in times of want (which were many); and last, but not least, the International Institute for Asian Studies at Leiden and its director, Wim Stokhof, and his colleagues. I cannot think of a better place than the beautiful city of Leiden for putting together a satisfactory first version of a work that to me remains an unfinished one.

*Kandy, Sri Lanka*
*February 2002*

# ABBREVIATIONS

| | |
|---|---|
| B | Malinowski, "Baloma: The Spirits of the Dead in the Trobriand Islands" |
| *BP* | Fienup-Riordan, *Boundaries and Passages: Rule and Ritual in Yup'ik Eskimo Oral Tradition* |
| BR | Besterman, "Beliefs in Rebirth of the Druzes and Other Syrian Sects" |
| *Bṛhad. Upan.* | *Bṛhadāraṇyaka Upaniṣad,* trans. Patrick Olivelle |
| CDT | Goulet, "Reincarnation as a Fact of Life among Contemporary Dene Tha" |
| *Chān. Upan.* | *Chāndogya Upaniṣad,* trans. Patrick Olivelle |
| CWC | Mills, "A Comparison of the Wet'suwet'en Cases of the Reincarnation Type with Gitksan and Beaver" |
| *Dial.* | Rhys Davids, *Dialogues of the Buddha* (3 vols.) |
| DL | Connor, "In Darkness and Light: A Study of Peasant Intellectuals in Bali" |
| *Enn.* | Plotinus, *Enneads,* MacKenna trans. |
| *FPP* | Malinowski, *The Father in Primitive Psychology* |
| *Grg.* | Plato, *Gorgias* |

| | |
|---|---|
| *HD* | Basham, *History and Doctrines of the Ājīvikas* |
| IEC | Strick, "Ideology and Expressive Culture in the Druze Family" |
| *ISN* | Uchendu, *The Igbo of Southeast Nigeria* |
| *KEM* | Henderson, *The King in Every Man* |
| *LKA* | Strong, *The Legend of King Aśoka* |
| *MLS* | Horner, *Middle Length Sayings* (3 vols.) |
| *MM* | Haimendorf, *Morals and Merit: A Study of Values and Social Controls in South Asian Societies* |
| *MSE* | de Laguna, *Under Mount Saint Elias: The History and Culture of the Yakutat Tlingit* |
| *NIE* | Fienup-Riordan, *The Nelson Island Eskimo: Social Structure and Ritual Distribution* |
| *OGR* | Guthrie, *Orpheus and Greek Religion* |
| *OP* | West, *The Orphic Poems* |
| *PA* | Taylor, *Porphyry on Abstinence from Animal Food* |
| *Phd.* | Plato, *Phaedo* |
| *Phdr.* | Plato, *Phaedrus* |
| *PSP* | Schmithausen, *The Problem of the Sentience of Plants in Earliest Buddhism* |
| *Rep.* | Plato, *Republic* |
| RKI | Mauze, "The Concept of the Person and Reincarnation among the Kwakiutl Indians" |
| RM | Ottenberg, "Reincarnation and Masking: Two Aspects of the Self in Afikpo" |
| *RP* | Keith, *The Religion and Philosophy of the Vedas and Upanishads* |
| SI | Uchendu, "The Status Implications of Igbo Religious Beliefs" |
| *SLS* | Malinowski *The Sexual Life of Savages* |
| *SR* | Weber, *The Sociology of Religion* |

| | |
|---|---|
| *SU* | Olivelle, *Samnyasa Upaniṣads: Hindu Scriptures on Asceticism and Renunciation* |
| *Symp.* | Plato, *Symposium* |
| *TC* | Stevenson, *Twelve Cases in Lebanon and Turkey* |
| TI | Austen, "Procreation Beliefs among the Trobriand Islanders" |
| *Ti.* | Plato, *Timaeus* |
| *Upan.* | Olivelle, *Upaniṣads* |

# 1 KARMA AND REBIRTH IN INDIC RELIGIONS

## *Origins and Transformations*

The major problem that I investigate in this work is the manner in which the "rebirth eschatologies" of small-scale societies are transformed in two large-scale historical developments: in the "karmic eschatologies" that one associates today with religions such as Buddhism and Hinduism and in the Greek religious traditions that could be broadly defined as "Pythagorean."

I will begin with Hinduism and the problem of origins. The association between karma and rebirth is not at all clear in the earliest texts and discourses on Indic religions. There are virtually no references to rebirth or to an ethical notion of karma in the *Vedas* or in the *Brāhmaṇas,* the oldest texts belonging to the Hindu tradition.[1] The first significant references appear in an early Upanishad, the *Bṛhadāraṇyaka Upaniṣad,* probably composed sometime before the sixth century B.C.E., followed by the *Chāndogya* and the *Kauṣītaki.*[2] A hundred years or more later these theories appear in full bloom in the so-called heterodox religions—particularly in Buddhism and Jainism—that have karma and rebirth at the center of their eschatological thinking. Soon afterward these ideas surface in mainstream Hinduism itself and become an intrinsic part of the eschatological premises of virtually all Indic religions.

Deeply embedded in these religions is the notion of the "unsatisfactoriness of existence," or *dukkha,* often rendered in English as "suffering." Suffering is primarily generated through karma, the law of ethical recompense that governs existence, or samsara *(saṃsāra).* It is karma that fuels rebirth in hells, heavens, and the realms of animals and inferior spirits, returning the subject to earth for a good or bad human existence. Rebirth in these various spheres of existence is endless and is conceptualized as samsara. The aim of salvation is to achieve nirvana, or *mokṣa,* which entails freedom from the rebirth cycle (samsara), stopping the flow of karma and ongoing existence as we normally understand it. The foregoing eschatological premises revolve around the idea of rebirth; karma as ethical compensation and reward is intrinsically associated with rebirth; samsara is the endless cycle of rebirths; and mokṣa, or nirvana, is the cessation of rebirth. The word *karma,* which etymologically means "action," has the meaning of "ritual action" in Vedic (pre-Buddhist and pre-Upanishadic) thought, where it is neither fundamentally ethical nor related to rebirth. By contrast, in Buddhism *karma* refers to intentional ethical action that determines the nature and place of rebirth, and this definition of *karma* has influenced the many Hinduisms that came after.

Let me first present my critique of the Indological examination of the problem of karma and rebirth. Indologists generally assume that it is only necessary to explain karma; rebirth is simply a by-product of the karma theory. With the exception of T. W. Rhys Davids not a single Indologist, as far as I know, has noted that theories of rebirth are found in many parts of the world without being associated with a doctrine of ethical causation such as karma.[3] In one instance at least—that of the Druze of Syria, Lebanon, and Israel and related Ismā'īlī sects—rebirth is uneasily linked to a form of monotheism. Most scholars assume, along with the generality of the educated public, that rebirth and karma are uniquely Indic constructs, invented and perpetuated in that tradition. The most common strategy is to examine the "history" of the word *karma* and trace its evolution from the beginnings of Vedic thought to the *Brāhmaṇas* and the Upanishads and then to Buddhism and other religions of the Ganges valley.

Adopting a different stance, historian A. L. Basham argues that karma is conspicuous by its absence in the Vedas and that only brief references are found in the aforementioned early Upanishads.[4] However, scholars of early Indic thought seem to agree with Eric Frauwallner and J. C. Heesterman that there is a straight line of development of the karma doctrine from the Vedas down to the period of Buddhism, as, for example, *Ṛg Veda* 19.16.3, which shows "incipient elements of the latter karma doctrine." "May your eye go to the sun, your life's breath to the wind. Go to the sky or to earth, as is your nature; or go to the waters if that is your fate. Take root in the plants with your limbs."[5] Yet even a most liberal interpretation of this text would not warrant reincarnation; not a trace of the karma doctrine of ethical recompense is found here either. At best the text might refer to transmigration, a form of religious belief widespread in the cross-cultural record and existing independent of rebirth theories. If one raises the issue of "incipient beliefs" of whatever kind, one can, I think, find them in any religious tradition.

I think it impossible to find a tradition of thought that does not refer back to its antecedents. Even when one makes a radical shift away from a prior tradition, one must refer to it, often explicitly or sometimes implicitly, justifying one's own break with that tradition or arguing for or against it. So it is with the word *karma;* the word is found as "ritual practice" in the early Vedic traditions. In fact, as Patrick Olivelle has shown, this early idea of karma continues into later, post-Buddhist, Upanishadic texts dealing with Hindu doctrines of renunciation.[6] Buddhists, as well as some early Upanishadic thinkers, took the word from the preexisting tradition and gave it a new and sometimes opposed meaning.[7]

This referral back to tradition, even as one moves from it, is common to argumentative discourse, and the human sciences exemplify it all the time. Thus Weber borrowed terms like *charisma* and *theodicy* from Christian theology and then gave each term a different conceptual significance. Such borrowing can certainly lead to confusion. In anthropology itself Radcliffe-Brown's notion of *structure* is quite different from Lévi-Strauss's, and my usage differs from both. But insofar as we all use the same word, it is possible to find some similarities and then make the unwonted inference that, let us say, Lévi-Strauss's structuralism represents a straight line of development from Radcliffe-Brown's. So it is with *karma:* the fact that the word appears in a variety of texts might indicate continuity of an idea. On the other hand it might not, and ethical thinkers in the Buddhist tradition have poured into the term a new set of ideas that break with previous traditions.

J. C. Heesterman, an influential scholar of early Hinduism, affirms the unitary nature of the Vedic tradition. He says that outside influences have caused no break in the development of ritual thought. "They seem rather to have fitted themselves into the orthogenetic, internal development of Vedic thought."[8] Nevertheless, one can also view that tradition from a different perspective as a composite of diverging ideational systems, each of which exhibits continuity of debates and arguments on religious matters with others located in the same broad tradition. Yet as a consequence of these debates, an ideational system will exhibit breaks, shifts, disjunctions, and discontinuities in relation to the others that scholars are arguing against; and some of these shifts might be more significant than others. The continuity of *terms* from a previous ideational system gives the illusion of the continuity of ideas. Sometimes the implied continuity of a term can serve as a deliberate rhetorical strategy to seduce the reader or listener into believing that there has been no real ideational change. At other times it is not so, and different or even opposed ideas might be invested in the old terms.

Indologists have suggested that the first shift in the Vedic idea of karma as "ritual action" to that of ethical action in relation to rebirth appears in the *Bṛhadāraṇyaka Upaniṣad.* The relevant part is 3.2.12–13, where Yājñavalkya and Arthabhāga, two Upanishadic sages, converse on the nature of the senses. Their conversation ends with a discussion of death and the afterlife:

> "Yājñavalkya," Arthabhāga said again, "tell me—when a man dies, what is it that does not leave him?" "His name," replied Yājñavalkya. "A name is without limit, and the All-gods are without limit. Limitless also is the world he wins by it."
>
> "Yājñavalkya," Arthabhāga said again, "tell me—when a man has died, and his speech disappears into fire, his breath into the wind, his sight into the sun, his mind into the moon, his hearing into the quarters, his physical body into the earth, his self [*atman*] into space, the hair of his body into plants, the hair of his head into trees, and his blood and semen into water—what then happens to that person?" Yājñavalkya replied: "My friend we cannot talk about this in public. Take my hand, Arthabhāga; let's go and discuss this in private."
>
> So they left and talked about it. And what did they talk about?—they talked about nothing but action [*karman*]. And what did they praise?—they praised nothing but action. Yājñavalkya told him: "A man turns into something good by good action and into something bad by bad action." (*Bṛhad. Upan.,* 3.2.12–13)[9]

Most scholars, following such eminent ones as Hermann Oldenberg, Paul Deussen, and Surendranath Dasgupta, have seen this passage as proof of the entry into the Vedic tradition of the novel ideas of karma and rebirth.[10] This is correct, although the text itself does not warrant the idea that karma here means "ethical action." As for rebirth it is at least implicit. One argument is that this text is still rooted in the Vedic tradition, clearly indicated by the description of the fate of the dead person. Thus, it is said that the good and bad karma mentioned here refers to the correct and incorrect performance of the sacrifice in the orthodox tradition of the *Brāhmaṇas* rather than the classic karma doctrine that "relates the fact of rebirth to the moral efficacy of an individual's deeds."[11] Yet this also is not clear from the text; and one must reserve judgment. The text implies that Yājñavalkya is postulating a new idea, perhaps the doctrine of rebirth, including the notion that the name does not perish at death, a conception found in other rebirth eschatologies outside the Indic orbit. Yājñavalkya then takes his friend by the hand and says that this question should not be discussed in public. It is as if he is considering an idea that he has invented or borrowed and is trying to articulate it within the frame of the preexisting ritualistic tradition. Herman Tull, however, following Heesterman, Gonda, and others, argues that the *Bṛhadāraṇyaka Upaniṣad* interiorizes the idea of the sacrifice, such that, parallel with the old idea that the efficacy of the sacrifice lies in the correct performance of the ritual, there is another idea that the sacrifice is something within one's own self. He then adds that passage 4.4.3–5 in the same Upanishad is also ambiguous, as far as karma and rebirth are concerned, and shows its affinity with the preexisting Vedic tradition.[12]

Here Yājñavalkya tells King Janaka what happens to the unliberated soul after death, employing the metaphor of the caterpillar or leech (one that became very popular in later Buddhist texts):

> It is like this. As a caterpillar, when it comes to the tip of a blade of grass, reaches out to a new foothold and draws itself onto it, so the self [*atman*], after it has knocked down this body and rendered it unconscious, reaches out to a new foothold and draws itself onto it.
>
> It is like this. Just as a weaver after she has removed the coloured yarn, weaves a different design that is newer and more attractive, so the self, after it has knocked down this body and rendered it unconscious, makes for himself a different figure that is newer and more attractive—the figure of a forefather [*pitaraḥ*], or of a Gandharva, or of a god, or of Prajāpati, or of *brahman,* or else the figure of some other being. (*Bṛhad. Upan.,* 4.4.3–4)

This text is clearer than the one previously quoted. It says that the "spirit," or "self," can be reborn in various spheres, and it highlights "good rebirths" but recognizes the possibility of being born "as some other being"; another recension of this Upanishad states that the spirit could also be reborn as a man or some other creature.[13] Yājñavalkya adds that this self, or spirit, is conditioned by good, and bad actions, or karma:

> What a man turns out to be depends on how he acts and how he conducts himself. If his actions are good, he will turn into something good. If his actions are bad, he will turn into something bad. . . . On this point there is the following verse:
>
> A man who's attached does with his action
>     to that very place to which
>     his mind and character cling.
> Reaching the end of his action,

of whatever he has done in this world—
From that world he returns
back to this world,
back to action. (*Bṛhad. Upan.*, 4.4.7)

Yājñavalkya's view here indicates that good and bad action, or karma, results in rebirth; the cause of rebirth is karma, which is conditioned by desire. By contrast, for the person who is without desire, "his vital functions *[prāna]* do not depart. *Brahman* he is, and to *brahman* he goes" (*Bṛhad. Upan.*, 4.4.7). Thus there are two crucial karmic trajectories: those without desire who go to Brahman, which is the goal of the Upanishadic quest, and those (presumably the majority) who, caught up in desire, continue to be reborn in different forms. The former are "wise men, knowers of *brahman,* the doer of good, the man of light," who go to the heavenly world and then to Brahman. And the latter?

Into the blind darkness they enter,
people who worship ignorance;
And to still blinder darkness,
people who delight in learning.

"Joyless" are these regions called,
in blind darkness they are cloaked;
Into them after death they go,
men who are not learned or wise. (*Bṛhad. Upan.*, 4.4.10–11)

I doubt whether the "joyless regions" refer to the otherworldly hells of later Indic eschatology; the context suggests that this is the fate of those who take the second path, those who are trammeled in desire, and this includes those who desire learning (probably a snide reference to the ritualists of the *Brāhmaṇas*). But the joyless place is not the world into which one is reborn, that idea that was developed in later Indic thought as samsara. Rather it is some place to which the "self" descends at death preparatory to rebirth, perhaps the rebirth process itself, very much in the spirit of the Greek eschatology of Empedocles, who mentions a "joyless place" of unmitigated pain and darkness (see p. 226).

A further development of the two paths is found in a later section of the same Upanishad. In 6.2.2–8 there is a fascinating dialogue between the king of the Pañcālas, Pravāhaṇa Jaivali, and Śvetaketu, the young Brahmin, and later with Śvetaketu's father, Gautama, also known as Uddālaka Āruṇi. The king asks Śvetaketu certain questions that the latter does not understand. The basic question is set forth at the beginning, and it pertains to rebirth:

> [The king asks] "Do you know how people, when they die, go by different paths?"
> "No," he replied.
> "Do you know how they return to this world?"
> "No," he replied.
> "Do you know how the world beyond is not filled up, even as more and more people continuously go there?"
> "No," he replied. (*Bṛhad. Upan.*, 6.2.2)

The young Brahmin is also ignorant of two paths of ascent of the soul at death, one that leads to the Fathers and one that leads to the gods (devas). From the way the text frames the Brahmin's responses, it seems that the king is raising an issue that is not known to the peevish young Brahmin.

The king asks Śvetaketu several other related questions that he fails to answer. Annoyed, Śvetaketu complains to his father, Gautama. "That excuse for a prince asked me five questions and I didn't know the answer to a single one of them" (*Bṛhad. Upan.*, 6.2.3). Gautama is more open-minded and decides to go to the king himself, announcing that he is coming as his pupil, an unusual action for a famous Brahmanic sage. This action of Gautama's has been anticipated earlier, in section 2.1.15 of the same Upanishad, where Gargya, the Brahmin, comes as a pupil to Ajātaśatru, the Kṣatriya, and the latter says: "Isn't it a reversal of the norm for a Brahmin to become the pupil of a Kṣatriya?" A member of the Kṣatriya order (royalty) has begun to expound unorthodox ideas, and Brahmin sages are made to listen to them.[14]

The first part of Jaivali's exposition deals with the doctrine of the five fires, originally a Vedic idea but now given extended symbolic and interiorized meaning.[15] This exposition, as Richard Gombrich shows, was taken up much later by another Kṣatriya sage, the Buddha, in his famous "fire-sermon."[16] For present purposes let me refer to the first and the last fires:

> A fire—that is what the world up there is, Gautama. Its firewood is the sun; its smoke is the sunbeams; its flame is the day; its embers are the quarters; and its sparks are the intermediate quarters. In that very fire gods offer faith, and from that offering springs King Soma. . . .
> A fire—that's what a woman is, Gautama. Her firewood is the vulva; her smoke is the pubic hair; her flame is the vagina; when one penetrates her, that is her embers; and her sparks are the climax. In that very fire gods offer semen, and from that offering springs a man.
> He remains alive as long as he lives, and when he finally dies, they offer

> him in the fire. Of that fire, the fire is the fire itself; the firewood is the firewood; the smoke is the smoke; the flame is the flame. . . . In that very fire gods offer man, and from that offering springs a man of brilliant colour. (*Bṛhad. Upan.*, 6.2.9–13)[17]

The king now expounds to Gautama his doctrine of rebirth. The central idea remains that of the two paths mentioned earlier. Those who know the truth of the fire doctrine will take the path of the gods. They pass from the flame into the day, from the day into fortnights of the waxing and the waning of the moon, and from there to the world of the gods. After an undetermined stay there, they enter the region of lightning. "A person consisting of mind comes to the regions of lightning and leads him to the worlds of *brahman.* These exalted people live in those worlds of *brahman* for the longest time. They do not return" (*Bṛhad. Upan.*, 6.2.15).[18] But what about those who take the second path? The king says:

> The people who win heavenly worlds, on the other hand, by offering sacrifices, by giving gifts, and by performing austerities—they pass into the smoke, from the smoke into the night, from the night into the fortnight of the waning moon . . . [and then] to the world of the fathers, and from the world of the fathers to the moon. Reaching the moon they become food. There the gods feed on them, as they say to king Soma, the moon: "Increase, Decrease!" When that ends, they pass into this very sky, from the sky into the wind, from the wind into the rain, from the rain into the earth. Reaching the earth they become food. They are again offered in the fire of man and then take birth in the fire of a woman. Rising up once again to the heavenly worlds, they circle around in the same way.
>
> Those who do not know these two paths, however, become worms, insects, or snakes. (*Bṛhad. Upan.*, 6.2.16)

It is impossible to give a definitive interpretation to these early Upanishadic texts because we know very little about the social and cultural background of this period. On one level the preceding text is reasonably clear. There is an attempt to bring the idea of rebirth into the "Vedic" scheme of things. Thus the path of the Fathers is for those who follow the traditional sacrificial practices enjoined in the *Brāhmaṇas*, whereas the way of the gods has been given symbolic meaning—presumably the fire sacrifice is a spiritual condition within one's own self.[19] Those who take the path of the gods, through the complicated route described in the text, enter into Brahman, and they do not return. Those who take the conventional Vedic path to the world of the Fathers, the *pitṛyāna,* are reborn in this world and keep going round and round in a cycle. Underlying the two paths is the assumption of rebirth and Brahmanic ethics.

For those who unite with Brahman, the rebirth cycle has stopped, but this is not so for those who go to the world of the Fathers. In classic Vedic and Brahmanic thought those who go to the world of the Fathers remain there. But a new eschatological principle has intervened, namely that of rebirth, such that the soul at death is brought back to the human world. But there is a feature that is left ambiguous: when the soul that achieves a human incarnation eventually dies, it repeats the previous cycle, which means that there is no provision in this text for punishment for those humans who have done wrong.

Although rebirth is the accepted reality for King Jaivali, this is not so for the two Brahmins (father and son), who are represented as being ignorant of it. But this is not all: there is another aspect of this rebirth theory that stipulates that those who are ignorant of either path will be reborn as "worms, insects, or snakes." This refers to an inferior rebirth among lower creatures, but it is not caused by the operation of an ethical law of karma. Rather, it is because of ignorance of *two* legitimate paths to salvation: one enunciated by the Upanishadic thinkers (atman = Brahman) but adapted to a theory of rebirth (unity with Brahman eliminates rebirth), the other path enunciated by the preceding tradition of the Brahmanic sacrifice but now downgraded somewhat. Those who adopt this path continue to be reborn in a desirable way, yet they have missed the terminal bliss of union with Brahman. With Upanishadic thought the idea of salvific knowledge has come to the fore. Truth is the knowledge that "*atman* is Brahman," formulated in the famous phrase "thou art that." But because this knowledge is unavailable to all, the sage king formulates a lesser knowledge that is contained in the previous tradition of the sacrifice but with the proviso that those who sacrifice continue to be reborn and therefore cannot obtain any finality of bliss. This *is* a remarkable shift and suggests that in interiorizing the sacrifice (giving it symbolic values), denying salvation to those who perform sacrifices (downgrading the sacrifice), introducing the new theory of rebirth, and articulating all of this to the general Upanishadic idea of the unity of *atman* and Brahman, this text has made a crucial departure from the whole of the previous Vedic tradition.

But obviously there are people who do not accept (or otherwise realize) the lower path of the Fathers either; they are the ones relegated to an inferior existence. One is tempted to say that this is an implicit reference to the Śūdras in the Hindu fourfold *varṇa* classification.[20] This reference to the Śūdras is possible even though the *Bṛhadāraṇyaka* has a benign view of the four *varṇa* categories; it actually says that the Śūdra "is the very earth, for it nourishes the whole world, it nourishes all that exists" (*Bṛhad. Upan.,* 1.4.13). Note that hell is not mentioned in this scheme, only an inferior rebirth. It seems that the king, Pravāhaṇa Jaivali, is using a familiar idea that states that at death a person may be reborn as a human being or as an animal or similar creature. This is clearly not part of the older Vedic tradition because rebirth is not recognized there. That is why the text presents the two Brahmin sages, who embody Brahmanic thought, as ignorant of this new knowledge. It needs the Kṣatriya sage to tell the Brahmin Gautama "This knowledge has never before been in the possession of a Brahmin" (*Bṛhad. Upan.,* 6.2.8).

This fascinating discourse on rebirth is repeated with some modification in another key Upanishad, the *Chāndogya* (5.3–10). Here also Śvetaketu goes to the assembly of the Pañcālas, whose king is Pravāhaṇa Jaivali, and once again the king asks five questions, more clearly posed than before: how people when they die go by different paths; how they return to this world; why the world beyond is not filled up although more and more people go there; when the oblation of water takes on a human voice and speaks;[21] and what one must do to get to the path of the gods or the Fathers. As before Śvetaketu goes to his father, Gautama, who confronts Jaivali to find out what he told his son. The king replies as before but with an important qualification pertaining to knowledge as power in a very literal sense: "Gautama, let me tell you that before you this knowledge had never reached the Brahmins. *As a result in all the worlds government has belonged exclusively to royalty [Kṣatriya]*" (*Chān. Upan.,* 5.2.7, my italics).[22] Jaivali then discourses with much greater clarity than in the *Bṛhadāraṇyaka* on the fate of the soul at death, expounding on what Eric Frauwallner has called the "water-doctrine."[23] The water-doctrine is simply a further development of the doctrine of the five fires: the previous text says in fact that the fire is the rain cloud that progressively produces lightning, thunder, hail, and rain.

The *Chāndogya* repeats the familiar distinction between the two paths. The nobler path of the gods attracts a minority, "the people here in the wilderness" who believe that "austerity is faith" (5.10), and implies a recognition of both withdrawal into the forest and asceticism. As before, the soul that follows the way of the gods goes into Brahman after sojourning in the realm of the gods. However, some interesting clarifications are found in respect to the second path, that is, the soul's journey into the realm of the Fathers. The text refers to "villagers" who believe that "gift-giving is offerings to gods and to priests." At death the souls of these good folk take the same route as in the previous text, and having gone to the realm of the Fathers, they do not remain there. They take the same route back to earth as in the previous text, initially becoming the food of the gods and eventually coming down as rain or with the rain. "On earth they spring up as rice and barley, plants and trees, sesame and beans, *from which it is extremely difficult to get out.* When someone eats that food and deposits the semen, from him one comes into being again" (*Chān. Upan.,* 5.10.3, my italics). Having been reborn in this unusual fashion, people live good or bad lives, which in turn culminate in a good or bad rebirth. This is a very important ethical movement in the history of Indic rebirth because, unlike the previous text, this clearly says that those who have been reborn will do good and bad and that those ethical actions will condition their next reincarnation: "Now, people whose behavior is pleasant can expect to enter a pleasant womb, like that of the Brahmin, the Kṣatriya or Vaiśya class. But people of foul behavior can expect to enter a foul womb, like that of a dog, a pig, or an outcaste woman" (*Chān. Upan.,* 5.10.7).

The preceding desirable and undesirable states are for those whose conduct has been pleasant and foul respectively. But there is another group of people who do not proceed in either of these two paths: "they become the tiny creatures revolving here ceaselessly. 'Be born! Die!'—that is the third state" (*Chān. Upan.,* 5.10.8). Here again is an intriguing third class of people who presumably are insects incapable of achieving a human rebirth.

Now we can answer an important question posed to Śvetaketu in both these Upanishadic texts, namely, why the upper realms of the gods and the Fathers never get filled up with denizens. First, those who take the path of the gods do not remain there but eventually merge with Brahman, which is a mystical condition and not a place. As a result, the realm of the gods does not get filled with the departed. Second, owing to the new theory of rebirth those who reach the realm of the Fathers do not remain there but achieve a reincarnation on earth. Third, those humans who come down to earth become herbs and trees, and it is difficult for their souls to escape from them except via food. This means that they do not necessarily go back to the realm of the Fathers, or they return to it in a delayed or sporadic fashion. Fourth, there are those human beings who become tiny creatures and then continue to die and get reborn in that very state, having little or no chance of entering either of the preceding realms. Fifth, there is, I think, a further implicit answer to the problem of the peopling of the upper realms. Those who have taken the road of the Fathers and get reborn on earth via trees and food and semen can then perform foul deeds that will ensure their *next* rebirth in a foul womb, such as that of a dog, a pig, or an outcaste woman. Given their lifestyles, it is not likely that these creatures have much chance of changing their status either; those born from an outcaste's womb might, but others will surely end up in their next rebirth either in their present forms as animals or even further downgraded into "tiny creatures," once again ensuring that the upper realms do not get crowded. This text, like the previous ones, mentions only the crowding of the upper realms; there is no mention of any *lower* realms.

The *Chāndogya* text clearly articulates the rebirth theory with Vedic thought and brings the *varṇa* scheme into the picture. As before, some Brahmanic ethics operate here: those who venerate gift giving to gods and priests (Brahmins) go the way of the Fathers. Those whose conduct has been pleasant are reborn as the "twice born" classes; those whose conduct has been foul become inferior domestic animals and "outcastes." The "pleasant" and "foul" conduct of the text does not necessarily imply the ethics of karma, as later Buddhist and Jaina thinkers understood it. The text refers to the proper behavior generally expected of the three higher classes *(varṇa)* of Indian society, that is, to an ordained way of life in which pluralistic ethics operate. Once again it is presumably the ignorance of the two paths rather than morality per se that condemns the last residual category of humans into an endlessly repeating cycle of rebirth as "creatures." Following this is a verse that indirectly indicates what one must do to avoid this last condition:

> A man who steals gold, drinks liquor,
> and kills a Brahmin;
> A man who fornicates with his teacher's wife—
> these four will fall.
> As also the fifth—he who consorts with them. (*Chān. Upan.*, 5.10.9)

The early Upanishads have a highly speculative character as sages engaged in discourses with their students, generally in a one-to-one relationship, discuss a variety of topics, the most significant being the soteriological one regarding the nature of the self and the union of *atman* with Brahman. These eschatological ideas are not elaborated in the excerpts that I have cited. Instead they contain a sophisticated adaptation of rebirth to a Vedic eschatology. It therefore seems to me that there is a hidden discourse in the text; Pravāhaṇa Jaivali, the sage king, is implicitly having an argument with *another* tradition or traditions that seem to believe that after death one can be reborn in the human world or in a subhuman one. He does not invent that theory; he creatively incorporates it into an Upanishadic scheme of things. I will deal with the structure of that somewhat unusual rebirth theory and its associated ethics later on.

These (along with a brief reference in *Kauṣītaki Upaniṣad* 1.2) are virtually all the references to karma and rebirth in the Upanishads. The vast body of the early Upanishadic literature is unaffected by it. The problem that I now pose is this: where did the tradition of rebirth represented in these texts come from?

I think there are three reasonable answers. The first possibility is the view that I have already argued against, namely that it must have been invented de novo by the Upanishadic thinkers themselves. Second, most scholars claim that these ideas already existed in the early Vedic tradition, at least incipiently, and that the texts exhibit a continuous line of development. Third, they must have come from some other tradition, outside the Vedic-Upanishadic. Let me now address the second and third positions.

The scholarly position that the doctrine of rebirth came in unilinear fashion from the Vedas down to the Upanishads and into the later Gangetic religions like Buddhism must confront a difficult and, I think, unresolvable paradox. It assumes that the extant texts accurately represented the empirical reality of the religious situation in ancient India. This assumption is not correct because the texts that we have for ancient India are those that happened to be preserved in an oral tradition committed to memory by special religious virtuosos. It is an accident of history that these traditions and not others were preserved. For example, we know very little of the religions of the Indus valley; and the Ṛg Vedic texts themselves mention the existence of a variety of religious cults, the most famous being that of the *munis,* the silent ones. We know virtually nothing about the beliefs of these munis even though their beliefs and practices were influential enough for the name *muni* to be given to later sages like the Buddha. To put it differently: ancient India must surely have had a multiplicity of religions that would inevitably have influenced one another. It is the case that scholars must make do with what they have; it is absurd to expect them to deal with data that have vanished out of existence! Yet valid as this argument may seem, it does pose a problem when it concerns the question of origins: *one cannot construct the origins or history of a particular set of beliefs in a linear fashion from a body of data or a tradition of beliefs that could not possibly have had that linear quality at all.* To situate the issue in terms of the question of rebirth beliefs: these ideas could have come from a variety of sources, including popular culture. After all, it is easy to demonstrate from the history of religions the influence of popular beliefs on the so-called high religions. If I am right, then any attempt to trace the history of the idea of rebirth from texts that exist only through the accident of history is by definition futile.

To come to the third issue: several scholars have resisted a linear interpretation. One such scholar is G. C. Pande: "It is . . . impossible to see a linear and simple evolution from the Brahmanic views regarding afterlife to the theory of transmigration [rebirth] found at places in the Upanishads."[24] His solution is to see rebirth as a development from an ancient non-Vedic tradition of the munis. And D. D. Kosambi tries to trace this and other ideas to the Indus valley civilizations.[25] There is no serious evidence to support any of these assertions, however, so the scholar must chase one will-o'-the-wisp after another. Methodologically speaking, both positions only displace the issue slightly; they introduce another antecedent condition ignoring the multiple religious realities that would have existed in ancient India. The rebirth eschatology could have emerged from any one or more of them! Another possible strategy is to look for rebirth in the "little traditions" of India, based on the assumption that the post-Vedic religions would have picked up these ideas from peasant or tribal peoples. But this strategy has limited efficacy because these "little traditions" have often been contaminated by the high religions around them. Consequently, one might be able to argue that the only defensible methodological strategy is to ignore the question of origins or the history of a difficult eschatological problem, a position that some anthropologists might favor. After all, origins are not important; what matters, anthropologists tend to argue, are the existent realities of any belief system. Yet this stance seems a bit dated because the "genealogies" of ideas have come into prominence recently owing to the resurgence of Nietzsche's thought.

I think it reasonable to ignore the problem of origins owing to the methodological impossibility of finding them but not on a priori grounds that the problem of origins is not significant. It is true that there is no way to trace the history of the theory of rebirth backward, but there is a methodological way out by examining how it *might* have originated. This requires the foolhardy methodological postulate that tells us to "forget India" and to look instead for similar forms of life from the cross-cultural ethnographic record of non-Indic societies. Fortunately, one can demonstrate the existence of "rebirth eschatologies" *without the theory of karma* in many small-scale societies all over the world. These societies are located in the most diverse places—in the vast circumpolar region stretching from eastern Siberia to the Northwest Coast of North America, in many parts of West Africa, among the Trobriand Islands in Melanesia, and in Australia.

Thus the first implication of the ethnographic data is that India is *not* the exclusive ground and home of rebirth doctrines because it is quite impossible that such doctrines could have diffused from India to all of these diverse regions and then eventually come to be accepted by the local populations. The second implication is that although these rebirth eschatologies show considerable substantive differences even within a single region, they also show considerable similarity across regions. The reason for such similarity is that a rebirth eschatology has an inescapable logical form: the individual at death has to be reborn in the human world either immediately or after a temporary sojourn in some other world, and this cycle must go on repeating itself. Without these minimal conditions one cannot have a rebirth theory. One can give some flesh and blood to this minimal logic of a rebirth eschatology by spelling it out at greater length and adding some important motivational elements:

1. The fundamental idea of reincarnation is that at death an ancestor or close kin is reborn in the human world whether or not there has been an intermediate sojourn in another sphere of existence or afterworld. I may die and go to some place of sojourn after death, but eventually I must come down and be reborn in the world I left. Transmigration without eventual return to the human world does not qualify for inclusion.

2. The motivational basis is also reasonably clear: the dead kinsperson or ancestor has only temporarily left his or her mortal body; at some point she will come back because something in her survives and affects continuity. There is a powerful wish or desire to bring the dead kinsperson back into the world of human association.

3. Other conditions overdetermine the prevalence and perpetuation of rebirth (or reincarnation) eschatologies, particularly the power and influence attributed to ancestors. Perhaps it goes without saying that the worlds of deceased ancestors can exist without rebirth theories, but rebirth theories are strongly associated with them.

4. The motivation to preserve the ancestor must, in most instances, have its parallel in the concomitant wish to have him or her in a congenial place. The most obvious place is in one's own family or group or in closely related ones. Rarely would one want one's kinsperson to be born among strangers or hostile peoples! If rebirth beliefs are associated with unilineal descent groups, there might be further motivation to have the ancestor incarnated in the same clan or lineage.

The preceding analysis suggests that there is an elementary form of rebirth theory: a person after dying returns to the world he or she has left behind, sometimes sojourning in an intermediate world located in the space between death and rebirth. This elementary form lies at the heart of any eschatology of rebirth, irrespective of the larger culture in which it is enveloped. I have represented it topographically below (see fig. 1). The parentheses indicate a few basic and expectable features one might want to add to this model.

All substantive differences in empirically existent rebirth eschatologies have to be worked around this model although these empirical variations are also finite and could also be presented topographically, as I will do after I have described actual cases. For the moment let me merely affirm that several finite topographical models of rebirth theories could be constructed on the basis of the elementary form.

Models of the sort I construct in this work are simplifications of the complex empirical data and are therefore never exactly replicated in reality. They are what Max Weber called "ideal types," constructs that re-present in topographical form the world of empirical reality. Because of their artificial nature Weber called them utopian and "one-sided," this one-sidedness often a result of the position taken by the analyst.[26] For example, there is no intrinsic reason why rebirth eschatologies have to be represented as cycles; they could be represented lineally, triangularly, or in some other shape or form. However, for my (one-sided) purpose I present them in circular form, which, incidentally, fits nicely with the way they are imagined in Indic cultures, among Northwest Coast Indians, and by ancient Pythagorean Greeks (although not necessarily elsewhere). To put it differently: topographical representations permit us to shuttle back and forth from model (ideal type) to "reality" and from reality back to the model. Following Weber one can argue that the phenomenal world (reality) can never be replicated in our work; our descriptions of *any* phenomenon must of necessity be ideal typical. But

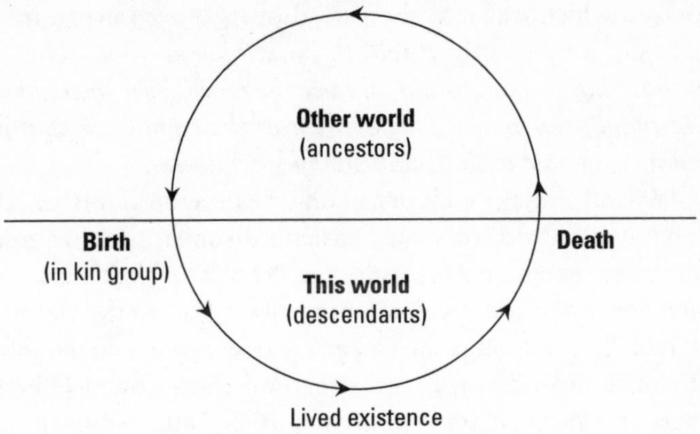


Figure 1. Elementary form of a rebirth eschatology, showing circulation of souls.

there are different degrees of abstraction possible; a topographical model in my usage is an abstract representation of the world based on extant ideal typical descriptions, in this case descriptions of a variety of existent rebirth eschatologies.

Now let me shuttle back to the empirical issue at hand. I will use the term *rebirth eschatology* to refer to theories of rebirth in societies that have no theory of karma, and I will use the term *karmic eschatology* for those that combine rebirth with karma. An overwhelming number of societies the world over have "rebirth eschatologies"; "karmic eschatologies" are found only in Indic religions. Greek Pythagorean and Platonic eschatologies have intermediate forms that I will discuss later. Further, I will demonstrate that even for India discourses on karma and rebirth can exist separately or that at the very least one can have a rebirth theory without karma. These two ideas are empirically and conceptually separable. Finally, rebirth eschatologies must have been invented for the most part independently of each other because they can be found in regions that do not seem to have had mutual contact. Hence the methodological leap that I want to make: because rebirth eschatologies are empirically widespread and perhaps prior to karmic eschatologies, India might well have had similar (rebirth) eschatologies before it developed its karmic ones. The rebirth eschatologies that I describe at length are found in small-scale village or "tribal" societies. I assume that they existed in similar small-scale societies in India also. After all, India was nothing but a conglomerate of small-scale societies (villages and tribes) prior to the period of Buddhism, which was also the period of its second urban transformation. To put it differently: *if rebirth eschatologies (those rebirth doctrines without karma) are found all over the world, it is likely that they existed in India prior to the development of the complex eschatologies that we now associate with Buddhism and Hinduism.*

The analytical strategy I adopt can now be developed further. The rebirth eschatologies I describe have structural similarities that could be topographically represented in an ideal model of a "rebirth eschatology." I will then depict the historical conditions that lead to the transformation of a rebirth eschatology into a karmic one. From a methodological point of view I am concerned with structural change, namely how one model gets transformed into another and the intervening historical processes (rather than causal variables) responsible for this transformation. This is a kind of "imaginary experiment" tentatively formulated by Max Weber.[27] Although all experiments are imaginary (that is, constructed in the imagination), experimentation in the human sciences is exclusively imaginary rather than partially constructed and tested in a laboratory. In my thinking all models of structural transformation, including those employed by Lévi-Strauss, are imaginary experiments, although they are never recognized as such by their proponents! I will deal in the conclusion of this book with the differences between my idea of structural transformation and that of Lévi-Strauss and other structuralists. For the moment let me say that I do not have an "epistemological" view of structure, namely a preconception that the nature of the world is such that it could be interpreted totalistically as a system of signs. I favor a more ad hoc notion of structure heuristically geared to a specific research problem in the Weberian style and, more recently, in the style of Braudel. Braudel says: "By *structure,* observers of social questions mean an organization, a coherent and fairly fixed series of relationships between realities and social masses. For us historians, a structure is of course a construct, an architecture, but over and above that it is a reality which time uses and abuses over long periods. Some structures, because of their long life, become stable elements for an infinite number of generations: they get in the way of history, hinder its flow, and in hindering it shape it."[28]

# 2 NON-INDIC THEORIES OF REBIRTH

## WEST AFRICA

Although it is well known that rebirth beliefs exist in Africa, especially in West Africa, their ethnographic documentation is meager. West African eschatology needs the kind of rethinking done by the authors of *Amerindian Rebirth* in their studies of Northwest Coast and Inuit religions.[1] In the African situation ethnographers were sensitive to religious and magical practices with which they were familiar, especially those resonating with their own European traditions, or they recorded customs exotic in the extreme if only to show the hidden rationality of seemingly irrational beliefs and practices. These were such things as African theism or pantheism or practices such as shamanism, spirit possession, witchcraft, and sorcery. Africa was also the locus of that custom known by anthropologists as "ancestor worship," which was penetratingly criticized by Igor Kopytoff.[2]

Whether one likes or dislikes the invented ethnographic category "ancestor worship," there is little doubt that the dead person continues to exist in association with ancestors and to influence what goes on in the human world. Given the importance of ancestors in African thought, one would expect ethnographers to show a parallel interest in reincarnation because only through reincarnation can an ancestor be brought back to the world of the living and reincorporated into one's kin group. To put it differently: if the soul of a dead ancestor is brought back after death into the world of human association and this process is continued, one has a rebirth eschatology. It will soon be clear that once a rebirth eschatology is invented, it takes ontological and ontic meanings vastly different from that of the more typical "ancestor cults" where the dead go to an afterworld without any reincarnation in the human.

The category term *reincarnation* suffered a different fate from the category "ancestor cult." Ethnographers of Africa produced rich descriptions of the latter phenomenon. *Reincarnation,* however, was narrowly defined as the entry of the soul from the world of the ancestors back to the earthly lineage structure, rather than a complex of beliefs intrinsically related to ancestors. Early ethnographers did record some of these reincarnation beliefs, but in the most cursory fashion.[3] Even classic studies of West African religion such as that of Melville Herskovits refer only briefly to reincarnation, although there are elaborate descriptions of the great gods and the worship associated with them.[4] And it might be too late for ethnographers to study African reincarnation beliefs on the ground today because they might have declined owing to the influences of Christianity and Islam, religions generally hostile to reincarnation.

Let me give the reader a feel for reincarnation beliefs from contemporary ethnographic fieldwork from West Africa with a preliminary account of reincarnation among the Benin of Nigeria by Flora Kaplan:

> The newborn infant is critically studied by the parents and other relatives to ascertain his or her resemblance to a deceased relative, who is then said to have "come back" in this or that child. Their judgement finds expression in the naming ceremony for a child, which customarily takes place seven days after it is born, and fourteen days after birth if it is a child of the royal family. Everyone is believed to come back (to be reincarnated in another person) fourteen times. Of course, no one is sure which of the fourteen times is represented by any one reincarnation.
>
> The belief in reincarnation based on shared characteristics with a deceased relative serves to create strong ties with the ancestors and the familial past in each generation. The ideas of individual uniqueness and of continuity with the past are expressed also in the naming ceremonies of the Obas [kings] prior to being crowned. For example, after the 1897 British military assault and "interregnum" in Benin City that lasted till 1914, the heir to Benin's throne took the name "Eweka II" in a traditional ceremony that involved divination. In so doing, Oba Eweka II called attention to the antiquity of kingship in Benin and the continuity of the eight-hundred-year-old dynasty founded by "Oba Eweka I."[5]

One is grateful to Kaplan for this concise and valuable description, which also presents key Benin ideas related to their rebirth eschatology, ideas such as their concept of "predestiny," their eschatology of heaven, their sodalities of ancestors, their naming rituals, and their sacred kingship itself. Yet Kaplan's essay is primarily about Benin kingship, and much about the beliefs of ordinary people is missing in this and other accounts.

Fortunately, fuller accounts of West African reincarnation are available for the Igbo of southeastern Nigeria owing to the work of Richard Henderson, of Victor Uchendu, and of Simon Ottenberg.[6] Henderson studied the Onitsha Ibo on the northern and western part of Igboland on the banks of the Niger. Ottenberg worked diametrically east in Afikpo, and Victor Uchendu studied in a third location, south and east of Afikpo. Henderson presents a detailed and fascinating account of Onitsha cosmology that frames its reincarnation ideology, mostly reconstructed from historical and ethnographic sources and applicable to the period before 1880. I will focus on the material relevant for understanding Onitsha rebirth eschatology and refer the reader to Henderson's work for details.

A critical Igbo conception is *chi,* that is, "life conceived as an animate self" and is manifested in the individual "as a spiritual essence of the living self that guides and determines the course of that person's life from birth to death."[7] When a person decides to "enter the world," that is, achieve a reincarnation, he or she makes a pact with the *chi* and selects a length of life and future activities. At any point in a person's this-worldly existence he can find out from his *chi,* presumably with the help of a diviner, what these choices were and "then affirm or adhere to these choices, or attempt to modify them if he regards them as undesirable" (*KEM,* 107). Because each person has his or her own *chi,* there are as many *chi* as there are people.

This brings us to the critical Igbo idea that the universe itself possesses a "great *chi,*" known as Chi-ukwu or Chukwu, who, paralleling the individual *chi,* orders "the course and character of the universe as a whole." This essence of the universe is conceived of in different ways as "great *chi,* the creator," as "*chi* in heaven," and as "divinity who supports the world." Chi-ukwu made all physical, terrestrial, and celestial phenomena and gave them energy, direction, and purpose. When individuals die, their personal *chi* returns to the ground of all being, the Universal Self, or the "great *chi.*" Thus the great god is the source from which the particular essences, or *chi,* of individuals originate (*KEM,* 107–8).

*Chi,* or "personal god," as Henderson translates the term, is the Igbo version of the "spirit helper" or "guardian spirit" found in many religions, including the Amerindian and Greek. Among the Onitsha this aspect of *chi* is represented by five wooden sticks called "seeds of the *chi*" and kept in the "vessel of the *chi.*" Four of these sticks represent the essences of the ancestral worlds of the father, the mother, the father's mother, and the mother's mother. The fifth stick represents a man's nonancestral comrades and his age group. Attached to this fifth stick is the figure of a man with a ram's horns on his head holding a machete; this is *ikenga,* "the essence of a man's will to success" (*KEM,* 112), a common aspiration in this nation of entrepreneurs. In the neighboring Nri-Awka Igbo a single stick, known as the *okposi,* cut from the egbo tree *(Newbouldia laevis)* represents a single ancestor determined by a diviner as the objectified guardian spirit. In both places, when a man dies, the *okposi* sticks of the *chi* are discarded because the guardian spirit no longer exists. But in the Onitsha "the senior son of the deceased person will then 'bring his father into the house' by collecting four large egbo sticks," also called *okposi,* along with the father's *ikenga* image. This, I surmise, is a symbolic recognition of the hope that the father will eventually be reincarnated in the same house or lineage and continue to possess his "will to success" (*KEM,* 111–13).

The *chi* therefore is lost at death and is replaced by what Henderson translates as "ghost." The ghost is released to the multiple worlds (four, seven, or eight according to different views), the lands of the dead that constitute the universe. Henderson does not deal with details of these other worlds except as places where the dead are incarnated and from which they depart to get reincarnated as humans. Those who cannot be reincarnated are the "bad dead," living nowhere but not causing trouble to humans either. The living in turn exhort the dead "to return as infants and, periodically, in other forms."[8]

The worlds of the dead are physically near the places where the dead were buried, and "it is believed that the closer a person was buried to a house, the more likely that he or she will choose to reincarnate there as an offspring of its occupants" (*KEM,* 110). Those buried thus may be invoked by their descendants to occasionally appear in their physical forms as the "incarnate dead" to judge the community and demand that social norms be upheld. Their essences can also be invoked to infuse objects, and these objects can then be "venerated and prayed to, and thanked for their spiritual assistance in maintaining long lives for their children and bringing more children into this world" (*KEM,* 110).

As one of the incarnated dead, an ancestor upholds the moral order; as a "ghost" he or she decides to return from the otherworld into the human one. The ghost reaches a liminal space, the crossroads where the two worlds intersect. There it meets its personal or guardian god, or *chi,* and makes a pact with that being or entity regarding the ghost's future life choices on earth. Thus a person who descends into the human world is not only the ghost or soul of a specific ancestor who wishes to be reincarnated; he also has his own *chi,* or guardian spirit, that constitutes another element of being. As I noted earlier, that guardian is in turn composed of the spirit essences of other ancestors (symbolized in the four sticks) and comrades (one stick). This eschatology produces an interesting notion of "individuality": the ancestor reborn is not a replica of a specific dead kinsperson; through his *chi* he is also constituted of the essences of indeterminate others, thus giving cultural recognition to people as different individuals. This formal cultural recognition of individual complexity is obviously not found in the Nri-Awka Igbo, with their single *okposi* stick, but they might have other ways of achieving the same end, perhaps through naming, as with the Amerindian communities to be discussed later.

At the human end conception occurs when the man's "child seed" enters the womb. If the seed is in good condition, conception will occur with repeated intercourse. The ghost, with the help of the guardian spirit, enters the body of the infant at birth, "becoming the 'seeds of the heart' which provide the motive force underlying life, and the body emerges into the world as a living infant whose personal god [guardian] has marked the lines of his destiny enigmatically into his hand" (*KEM,* 110–11). The identity of the neonate is determined by physical and psychological characteristics, but parents hope that it is an ancestor buried nearby, "one (or more) of the deceased fathers, mothers, father's mothers or other ancestor[s] who had observed local community life from the nearby subterranean locality, found it good, and has chosen to return" (*KEM,* 111).

This excellent account of Onitsha Igbo cosmology is given vividness and immediacy by Victor Uchendu, an Igbo anthropologist who was raised in Nsirimo, a small village on the eastern side of the River Imo. The formal eschatology of Nsirimo seems close enough to the Onitsha's, although there are minor variations, but what makes Uchendu's study especially interesting is the narration of his own rebirth history.

According to Uchendu, Nsirimo have a pantheon with multiple nature spirits, a benevolent earth mother known as Ala (not mentioned by Henderson but found among the Awka Igbo as Abwala), a strong ancestor cult that constitutes the invisible segment of a person's patrilineage, and a high god known as Chineke (or Chi-Okike), who, unlike the Onitsha Chi-ukwu, is somewhat otiose, perhaps having retreated owing to the impact of the strongly Christian orientation of the Igbo society in which Uchendu was raised.[9] Here also the guardian spirit *chi* "determines one's fate on earth. On it is blamed one's failures. It is *chi* who leads him in the exercise of this choice."[10] Uchendu adds, "Reincarnation is cardinal in the religious belief of the Igbo. Its chief role is to give hope to those who feel they have failed to achieve their status goal. In the next reincarnation, it is strongly believed, a man has a chance to achieve his objectives. Transmigration, on the other hand, is conceived as the greatest punishment for the incestuous, the murderer, and the witch" (SI, 34).

Let me briefly present Uchendu's description of the Igbo rebirth eschatology.[11] The Nsirimo Igbo are fully aware that conception occurs through sexual intercourse, "but other factors are also involved in pregnancy and are much more important: the consent of the deities and willingness of dead lineage members and other friendly spirits to reincarnate themselves. The absence of either of these two agents renders conception impossible, the Igbo say" (ISN, 57). Accordingly, the ancestral soul is reincarnated in the womb of a woman generally of the same patrilineage.[12] As in other rebirth eschatologies, the Igbo diviner helps to identify the exact kin of the neonate in his or her previous incarnation. Uchendu gives a superb description of his own previous-life persona:

> My name, Chikezie ("May God Create Well") is symbolic of what I meant to them. My family's confidence was doubled when the diviner returned his verdict that I was Ufɔmadu reincarnated. Ufɔmadu was my father's immediate older brother, the third of the four sons of my father's mother. On his death bed, he had advised my father to marry quickly for "he was coming back to him." The diviner's verdict could not be doubted: I have "birth marks" (three black spots on the right side of my belly) to vindicate it! It is claimed by my father that my "birth marks" resulted from the marks made on Ufɔmadu *postmortem* for the purpose of vindicating his "personality" in the next cycle of life, which I now represent. (*ISN*, 6)

The identity of the reincarnated individual affects interpersonal behavior. Uchendu says this about his father's oldest brother, Ogbonna, the leader of the compound (minimal lineage): "Ogbonna loved me. Probably he had no choice: I was not only his brother's son, but his brother during my last cycle on earth" (*ISN*, 7).

Once born, the Igbo individual traverses through his normal earthly existence. Africa's dominant entrepreneurs, the Igbo aspire to status and wealth. "It is a fair assessment of the Igbo world to say that the most important commodity it offers and for which the Igbo strive is the title system. The Igbo are status seekers. To use a market metaphor, they believe that the world is a marketplace where status symbols can be bought" (*ISN*, 16). At death, the Igbo "soul" bargains with the creator regarding the soul's status in the afterworld. Death and rebirth give a person an opportunity to fulfill unrealized status aspirations, so even a low-status person has a chance to improve his or her position in the next rebirth. "A person's social position is such an important thing that even on his deathbed the individual Igbo thinks more of his status in the hereafter than of his death" (*ISN,* 16). At death the soul, guided by the guardian spirit, *chi,* confronts the creator, who presents the soul with two parcels, one containing "the desired social positions that the individual predicted during his *Ebibi* (prereincarnation social position that the individual predicts during his lifetime on earth)" (*ISN,* 16), presumably through the agency of his *chi.* Those who fail to make the right choice by bargaining with the creator need not despair, for they can be reborn on earth again "and hope for better luck during the next cycle" (*ISN,* 17). Further, unless a person has violated a taboo, the Igbo need not fear the otherworld because they have no conception of hell. Thus, if he or she has made a poor bargain with the creator, an Igbo can well afford to wait another lifetime.

What briefly is the nature of the Nsirimo afterlife? Igbo have no heaven and hell as places where retribution and reward are meted out. The soul joins the world of the ancestors, and this invisible society is more or less a continuation of the lineage structure of the earthly society. "In the Igbo conception, the world of the 'dead' is a world full of activities; its inhabitants manifest in their behavior and their thought processes that they are 'living'" (*ISN,* 12). Thus the ancestors live in a society that is organized in terms of patrilineages similar to those on earth.

> For the Igbo death is a necessary precondition for joining the ancestors, just as reincarnation is necessary for peopling of the temporal segment of the lineage. But since the young as well as the old die, death is received with mixed feelings. Death is personified and dealt with as a powerful spirit which gains mastery over Ndo, the life giving principle from the human corporeal body. Without death, there will be no population increase in the ancestral households and correspondingly, no change in social status for the living Igbo. (*ISN,* 12)

The Igbo afterworld, as depicted by Uchendu, is a reified version of the mundane social structure. After a sojourn in the afterworld Igbo are reborn in the earthly social structure, except for those who have violated taboos. The latter have an inferior rebirth; they "are born feet first, or with teeth, or as members of a twin set—all of which are in themselves taboo" (*ISN,* 58). As with the Onitsha, the failure to be reborn at all is regarded as the worst type of punishment and is the fate of the incestuous, the murderer, the witch and the sorcerer. "May you not reincarnate in human form is a great curse for the Igbo" (*ISN,* 102).

Although Uchendu's account is fascinating, it misses much, especially information on women and their rebirth trajectories and aspirations, and this is true of Henderson's account also. Although Uchendu speaks of Igbo reincarnation, his is in fact a description of the beliefs prevalent in his own natal group. Simon Ottenberg presents a different vision of an Igbo rebirth eschatology from Afikpo, consisting of a cluster of twenty-two villages in eastern Nigeria. Here too the data are incomplete but complement Uchendu's and Henderson's and suggest that on the substantive level multiple rebirth eschatologies are found even within a single ethnic group like the Igbo.

Afikpo have double unilineal descent with localized patrilineal groupings constituting the main building blocks of the society; these coexist with "non-residential corporate matrilineal groupings which are the principal landholders."[13] This means that each person has a "father's side" and a "mother's side," and this is reflected in their rebirth eschatology. "Every individual has two reincarnated spirits with him or her, one from each side. The balance of descent groups is thus expressed in the reincarnation beliefs. For a male both reincarnators are male, for a female they are female, expressing the gender of a person" (RM, 1). Yet this is not totally deterministic. Some choice exists: a man, for example, can have his mother's father reincarnated in him. It seems that Ottenberg's data implicitly critique the classic social anthropological position that sees religious beliefs as refractions of the unilineal kinship structure. For although descent is important, says Ottenberg, it is not as significant for reincarnation as the parental sides, generally kinfolk from the grandparents' or great-grandparents' generation. "People very much like the idea that someone they have known, or their parents knew, has reincarnated in their child. It is pleasing, comforting" (RM, 2). It is likely that there are much more specific and powerful motivations at work, but these require detailed and contextualized case studies. In any case, in Afikpo, as with other Igbo groups and with the Amerindian cases to be discussed below, the identification of the previous-life persona is through divination, physical marks, or behavioral similarities.

In addition to the ancestor or ancestors inhabiting the male neonate's body is another spirit, *owa,* "which represents him spiritually, and is closest to our conception of the self" (RM, 2). *Owa* is an extremely important concept that gives recognition to the fact that for Afikpo a person is not simply a replica of a dead ancestor or ancestors. The *owa* relates to individual identity; it is a key component of the masculine "self," as Ottenberg translates it. This notion of uniqueness defies the stereotypic Western view of native peoples as lacking individuality. "When young his father places a pot in the patrilineal ancestral shrine for him, and it is this spirit which, when he dies, if the pot has been established and proper funeral rites are done, can reincarnate" (RM, 2). For example, I may be a vehicle for the soul of my paternal grandfather, but I am not simply my grandfather returned to the patrilineage. According to Ottenberg the ancestral pool is pretty much fixed; thus, although I am my ancestor incarnate (and beyond that to previous ancestors of the paternal line) I am myself also, a distinct person. This distinctiveness is epitomized in my *owa.* What gets reborn is not simply the inherited spirit of my grandfather coming from a pool of spirits but me, my *owa.* When I die I become reincarnated in the body of a descendant, but that descendant is both a continuing ancestral spirit and a distinct person with *his* own *owa.* This means that a male is a composite of incarnated ancestral spirit(s) and his own *owa.* Thus, even though there is a fixed population of souls, there is no fixed population of persons. Further, Afikpo can explain population increase through the idea that "an ancestor can reincarnate in more than one person."[14]

Ottenberg says that there is no female equivalent of the male *owa.* The *egero* is the spirit shrine that is established in the girl's parental home when she is young, and this goes with her throughout her life, but effectively it is replaced by a different shrine, *ci,* at marriage. When she dies, her eldest daughter establishes another shrine, *adudo,* to ensure that the mother's spirit reincarnates. Ottenberg thinks that the three female shrines, which take the place of the single male *owa,* relate "to her mobility in life, marrying several times and moving here and there in Afikpo through time, while the male remains at home in his patrilineal group, always living near his *owa* shrine."[15] However, I think that the woman's *adudo* shrine, founded by her daughter, effectively recognizes her individuality, if only postmortem, and ensures that she reincarnates as *herself* rather than as the spirit(s) of her reincarnating ancestor(s).

According to Ottenberg the reincarnating ancestor acts as a person's conscience, in both its negative and positive aspects. Because reincarnators can bring prosperity to an individual, one must propitiate them with sacrifices. "To fail to do so is believed to cause anger, particularly of one or both reincarnators, which is thought to lead to illness and other misfortunes falling on the person."[16] Ancestors mirror parental attitudes and the values of the lineage, and they may punish with misfortunes those who violate various sexual and behavior codes. Ottenberg, however, does not mention what Uchendu says of the Nsirimo Igbo: that "the ancestors can be scolded as if they were still living . . . and can be reprimanded for failing in their duty to their children, by closing their eyes to the depredations of evil spirits which cause death in the family, cause crop failure, and make trade unprofitable" (*ISN,* 102).

There are remarkable convergences and differences in the three ethnographic accounts, the closest resemblances being between the Onitsha and Nsirimo Igbo. But all three have the basic notion that at death the spirit of a reincarnated ancestor returns to known kinfolk, often but not always into the same patrilineal group. This ancestral spirit is not a simple replica of a dead ancestor; the neonate becomes an individual in his or her own right, or, as Uchendu puts it, there is a kind of "individualism rooted in group solidarity" (*ISN,* 103).

None of the three ethnographies mentions "naming" as a critical feature in reincarnation, as it is with the Benin and the Ga people studied by Field[17] and with the Amerindian communities to be discussed later. However, a missionary ethnographer working among the eastern Igbo, perhaps the Awka, in the 1900s says:

> The Igbo believes that all children are reincarnations of beings who have already passed through a lifetime in this world; hence a man will point to a little girl and gravely inform you that she is his mother reborn into the world. The child will consequently be *given the name of the relative* it is supposed to resemble, and as such will receive a joyful welcome back to earth. It is a time of great rejoicing and feasting, and large quantities of palm-wine are consumed in celebrating the occasion.[18]

## THE TROBRIAND MODEL

> Socrates: We can take [the soul's immortality] as proved. And if so, it follows that the same souls have always existed. Their number cannot be decreased, because no soul can die, nor can it increase; any increase in the immortal must be at the expense of mortality, and if that were possible, everything would in the end be immortal.
>
> —Plato, *The Republic,* book 10.611

Although the Igbo have a highly structured reincarnation eschatology, it is not clear how much similar systemization is found in other groups in

West Africa. So is it with Melanesia, although early ethnographers such as Gregory Bateson did make stray references to reincarnation.[19] Like their African counterparts, ethnographers of Melanesia were not attuned to reporting, or attributing cultural significance to, a phenomenon alien to their own European experience and cultural heritage. I think I can show this in relation to the most thoroughgoing example of a reincarnation eschatology reported for Melanesia by the very paragon of fieldwork, Bronislaw Malinowski. Malinowski's material is especially interesting because it comes from a cultural and geographic area that is quite remote from all the others represented in this book, yet it shows striking family resemblances to them.

Malinowski wrote two major accounts of reincarnation. The first appears in his well-known paper "Baloma: The Spirits of the Dead in the Trobriand Islands," which he wrote during his first visit to Trobriand (his second expedition to New Guinea) in 1915–16. The other was published in 1927 as *The Father in Primitive Psychology,* after his second visit (1917–18), and was later incorporated into his well-known book *The Sexual Life of Savages* (1929).[20] The two accounts differ in important details, with Malinowski favoring the second owing to information supplied by several new informants, including a shaman named Tomwaya Lakwabulo, who visited the otherworld and supplied eschatological information to the ethnographer (and also to Lakwabulo's fellow citizens).

According to Trobriand rebirth eschatology a new life begins at the death of the individual, when the *baloma* (spirit or "soul," as Malinowski translates it elsewhere), moves to Tuma. On the one hand Tuma is an actual inhabited island ten miles northwest of Trobriand, and on the other it is a place where the invisible spirits live. The deceased's body is adorned with finery, and his or her possessions are placed beside the body so that their essences can accompany the baloma.

The baloma reaches Tuma by taking the same route that ordinary travelers do, but the baloma is invisible and travels in an invisible canoe. When the brief mourning ceremonies have ended, the baloma is on its own; kinfolk's wailings do not reach it. Malinowski is puzzled that the living do not seem to care about the dead person's departure in their funeral rituals and wake. Owing to Malinowski's lack of understanding of reincarnation eschatologies, he is quite unaware of the rationale behind this attitude. If the deceased's spirit is going to live with other departed kin in Tuma and will eventually return to earth, there is no reason to overdramatize the departure. A similar attitude to the dead is reflected in the mortuary practices of the Buddhist Gurungs of Nepal.[21]

By contrast, it is the baloma that misses its kinfolk: the baloma reaches the beach at Tuma and is met by dead friends and kin, who squat down with the spirit and join in its lamentations; some sing the funeral lament exactly as it was performed by living kinfolk for the deceased.[22]

Malinowski describes the various steps the baloma takes prior to its arrival in Tuma, among them its meeting with Topolita, the headman of the villages of the dead, who, in theory, can refuse admission; "*his decision does not, however, rest on moral considerations of any sort*" (B, 132, my italics). Topolita asks the newcomer the cause of death, of which there are three kinds in descending order of goodness and worth: death in war, death by suicide, and death by sorcery (the way that most people die, because all natural deaths are explained in terms of sorcery). The newcomer has to make a payment to Topolita, and the rare case of failure will result in the spirit's being confined to the sea or converted into a monstrous fish (which perhaps implies the denial of reincarnation). Having passed Topolita the spirit enters a village in Tuma, where it will thenceforth live.

Now we come to the description of Tuma and life therein, a description Malinowski partially recanted later. The male baloma lives with relatives until a house is built for him. The newly arrived spirit is sad for a while, but other baloma, particularly females, help him to forge new relationships and forget old ones. Female spirits also console him with sexual pleasures, although we are not told whether the reverse obtains for female entrants. Soon the spirit "settles down to a happy existence," where it spends another "lifetime," an indefinite concept that is not related specifically to the human life span. Eventually the baloma dies in Tuma and is reborn on earth.

While in Tuma the spirit continues to be in touch with the living. "And there was hardly anybody who had not had some experience of the *baloma*" (B, 136). In particular, those who visit Tuma (the physical place) have had experiences with dead souls in various shapes and forms. Those Trobrianders subject to possession states ("short fits") also talk to the baloma. Baloma might in turn communicate with the living through dreams to give them news of dead kinfolk or to inform of a pregnancy.

The most important context in which ancestral spirits appear is during the main Trobriand ceremonial cycle known as the *milamala,* performed after harvest, on the full moon in August or September. When the festival is announced, the baloma sail from Tuma and come to their home village, where food and valuables are placed for them on platforms in order to please them. On the first day food is cooked in each household for the baloma and, after about an hour, removed and given to a relative or friend who will reciprocate with a similar dish. Food and valuables are also offered on the last day during the ritual for sending the spirits back to Tuma; the spirits take with them the essence (or "baloma") of the offerings. In between these two events the baloma of the recent dead may appear in dreams asking for food, or they may have a message to impart. Malinowski records one such message in which angry baloma claimed they sent constant rain because they were not given food. Finally, the baloma, like some of their African counterparts, "keep strict watch over the maintenance of custom, and they punish with their displeasure any infraction of the traditional customary rules which ought to be observed during the *milamala*" (B, 159).

Malinowski says that the presence of the baloma in the village "is not a matter of great importance in the mind of the native" (B, 158). Once again the ethnographer does not seem to have understood the paradoxical relationship between the living and the dead in the Trobriands. It is rare that individually recognizable kin descend into the village during milamala; rather it is the collectivity of ancestors per se who are concerned as a group that the traditional norms prevail. There is rarely personal interaction with them as such; yet the baloma as a collectivity are recognized, honored, feasted, and given valuables whose essences they take back with them. Malinowski himself says that the baloma are "like visitors from another place" and are "left to a great extent to themselves" (B, 165). The baloma, for their own part, might resent this lack of personal recognition, for it must be remembered that each baloma was originally a unique member of the human society. In their earthly existence they had enjoyed love and fellowship with their friends and kin; now, after some initial difficulty, they have recouped similar relationships in Tuma. The living have had no such double experience, and they do not know the baloma as individuals. The neglected baloma therefore demand food, that primordial symbol of love and fellowship, and they may get angry when this is not given. Malinowski himself realized this but failed to see the cultural significance of this paradoxical condition. "Except in the cases of the people recently dead, there is little personal feeling about the spirits. There are no provisions for singling out individual *baloma* and preparing a special reception for them, except perhaps the gifts of food solicited by individual *baloma*" (B, 165).

How does a baloma look, and how does it pass time in Tuma? Malinowski pushed his informants to answer these questions. When informants replied that a baloma was like a reflection, Malinowski badgered them with practical questions about the shadowy balomas' capacity to eat, drink, shout, and have intercourse. The natives' reply that they were reflections *and* they were also like humans was no solace to the empiricist Malinowski, although he did come to the following conclusion: "There is not the slightest doubt that a *baloma* retains the semblance of the man he represents, so that if you see the *baloma,* you recognize the man that was. The *baloma* live the life of men; they get older; they eat, sleep, love both whilst in Tuma and on visits which they pay to their villages" (B, 143). And he admits that village views on baloma have "not crystallized into any orthodox and definite doctrine" (B, 145).

As for where the baloma live, Malinowski received different answers. The first is that baloma actually live invisibly and nonmaterially in villages on the island of Tuma, sharing its surface with human beings. The other version is that they descend underground and live in Tumaviaka, or Great Tuma. This fits with the Trobriand theory of autochthonous origins and the idea that Topolita sent men and women from Tuma to populate the earth while he himself remained underground. According to one set of opinions, this underworld is two tiered, and when a baloma dies it descends into the second tier and thence to the human world. Most Trobrianders, however, accept the theory of a single underworld, which, among all the theories about Tuma, remains the "most orthodox version" (B, 146).

In his description of Tuma Malinowski was fully aware of persons of both sexes claiming to "have visited Tuma and returned to the upper world" (B, 137). One woman continually visited Tuma, and a man brought "personal messages from various spirits [of the recent dead] to their families" (B, 138). Malinowski says that the information provided by these shamanic wanderers "was told by them to everybody and was thus public property" (B, 138). But the ethnographer seems to have accepted the criticism of two informants, one of them a boy, that these spirit journeyings are "down right lies" and that one well-known seer was a "humbug" (B, 138). This attitude prevented Malinowski from presenting a sympathetic account of shamanic spirit journeyings, which we know are also found in other rebirth eschatologies.

Malinowski's simplistic empiricism seems to have changed somewhat during his second visit as a result of his acquaintance with the shaman (spirit medium) Tomwaya Lakwabulo.[23] In *The Father in Primitive Psychology* the ethnographer gives a different version of life in Tuma. In the earlier account Tuma and the life lived therein were a kind of reflection of earthly society. But now we are told that although the individual leads a pleasant life analogous to the terrestrial life, his or her existence is much happier. Moreover, life in the otherworld is characterized by "perpetual youth preserved by the powers of [bodily] rejuvenation. . . . When the spirit *(baloma)* sees that bodily hair is covering his skin, that his skin is getting loose and wrinkled, and that his hair is turning grey, he simply sloughs his covering and appears with a new and young surface—black locks, smooth skin, and an absence of bodily hair" (*FPP,* 29–30). The power of rejuvenation was enjoyed by those ancestors who lived in Tuma in primordial times prior to their emergence on earth. After their arrival they retained this same power but soon lost it through "inadvertence and ill will." But those who die and return to Tuma continue to enjoy this privilege. Malinowski treats this new account as orthodox, not realizing that Tomwaya Lakwabulo's is *one* account that, like those of other shamans, became "public property" and that the multiple versions of the otherworld in fact come from shamanic visitations. Neither does Malinowski ask whether Tomwaya's creative vision was influenced by the Christianity recently introduced by the missions, at least in its notion of a "fall" owing to inadvertence.

To get back to this new vision of Tuma: when a spirit becomes tired of constant rejuvenation, it may want to return to life on earth. To do this, the spirit "leaps far back in age and becomes a small, unborn infant" (*FPP,* 31). Some of Malinowski's informants explained why spirits become tired of their heavenly abode. They said that in Tuma, as on earth, there are sorcerers. Evil sorcery is frequently practiced and can reach a spirit and make it weak, sick and tired of life. Then, guided by another baloma, the spirit will go back to the human world. However, one cannot ever kill a spirit with evil magic or accident as in the human world because "his end will always mean a new beginning" (*FPP,* 31). These rejuvenated spirits, or preincarnated infants or spirit children, are the only source from which humanity draws its very supplies of life. A spirit child finds itself back in the Trobriands in the womb of a woman of the same matrilineal clan and subclan. There are different versions explaining how this occurs but little controversy about its actual occurrence, says Malinowski. The main facts have always been that "all the spirits have ultimately to end their life in Tuma and turn into unborn infants; that every child born in this world has come into existence *(ibubuli)* in Tuma through the metamorphosis of a spirit: that the main reason and the real cause of every birth lies in nothing else but in the spiritual action" (*FPP,* 32).

Any rebirth eschatology, by definition, requires the spirit to eventually come down to earth; nevertheless, within this scheme there are disagreements, multiple views, and inevitable debates regarding the nature of otherworldly existence and reincarnation provoked by shamans like Tomwaya Lakwabulo who have had "frequent intercourse with the spirits." Here are several versions from Malinowski's *The Father in Primitive Psychology:*

1. The shamanic theoretician Tomwaya Lakwabulo says: "the *baloma* go to a spring called *sopiwina* (literally, 'washing water'); it lies on the beach" (33). Here baloma wash their skin and become "young men." But before they turn into infants prior to reincarnation, they go to the sea and bathe in salt water, which converts them into spirit babies floating on sea scum, driftwood, seaweed, and leaves that litter the sea surface (33). They do not go much beyond the island of Tuma; from here each spirit infant is escorted to the destined mother by another spirit, or baloma, for example, the spirit of the mother or father of the woman who is going to conceive the child. This guiding baloma puts the infant spirit on the head or hair of the woman; the child descends into the belly, and the woman becomes pregnant. In the earlier account the spirit child is called the *waiwaia,* which is also the term for embryo and neonate, whereas the term *baloma* is reserved for its guiding spirit. However, when discoursing on reincarnation processes people do not explicitly refer to the waiwaia but always say that "*baloma* [the guiding spirit] is the real cause of childbirth" (36).

2. Frequently, the woman mentions the identity of the baloma who inserted the spirit child into her. Malinowski gives several examples from his informants, but generally "it is some maternal relative of the mother who bestows the gift" (37). Once the spirit child is laid on the head of the woman, blood from her body rushes there, and this blood tide pushes the baby into the womb, the woman becomes pregnant, and her menstruation ceases. Others say that the spirit child is inserted into the vagina by the baloma.

3. A version found in Malinowski's two accounts emphasizes the motivation or will of the preincarnated spirit, or waiwaia. It floats on its own accord and enters the body of the woman as she bathes. Hence, in one village girls will not enter the water

when there is much debris caused by the wind or tide lest they get pregnant. By contrast, women who wish to get pregnant might ask a brother or a mother's brother to scoop some water when they feel that the spirit child is around, for example, through the wailing sounds it makes. Then the waiwaia may enter the vagina of the woman. Most often the woman does not initiate the process on her own but acts on some prognostication supplied in a dream (37–40).

4. Such dream prognoses were given greater prominence in Malinowski's earlier account, where he mentions several fascinating instances. A female baloma, or occasionally a male, of the same matrilineal clan appears in a dream, and the woman might say: "I dreamed that my mother (or maternal aunt, or my elder sister or grandmother) inserted a child into me; my breasts are swelling" (B, 193). Several of Malinowski's key informants knew the identity of the baloma who brought them to their mother, but most did not. In all of these cases rebirth occurs unmediated by sexual intercourse.

When we compare the reincarnation beliefs of Trobrianders with others in small-scale societies, we see that Trobriand beliefs are unique in one respect at least: the identity of the neonate (waiwaia) cannot be determined. It is the identity of the baloma, not the impregnating spirit child, that is known. The baloma directs the unknown spirit child from the ancestral pool into the head or vagina of a woman of the matrilineage; or the unknown spirit child, or waiwaia, directs itself into a maternal womb. Whatever the process, the spirit child is not identifiable. According to Trobriand cultural logic, the reincarnating spirit, in the process of regressing into an infant, cannot remember its past life on earth or its life in Tuma. Malinowski did not recognize the logic of the system although he correctly identified the practical end result: "no one knows whose incarnation the infant is—who he was in his previous existence" (*FPP*, 44). Precisely because the identity of the neonate is unknown, the newly born person can be a unique individual rather than a replication of a known matrilineal ancestor.

Further, extrapolating from Trobriand cosmography, one can say that there were originally a number of men and women who emerged autochthonously from the underworld. These died and got reborn, and the cycle continues. Thus there is a fixed ancestral pool from which souls circulate endlessly from Tuma to earth and back again. Trobrianders are not unique in believing this. The Druze believe in a fixed number of souls "and instant rebirth after death, which means that the number of the living Druze is believed to remain always the same."[24] The fixity of souls among Druze and Trobrianders and the almost inexorable nature of the rebirth cycle seem to echo the "continuous incarnation" and the lack of population growth that Lee Guemple formulated for the Inuit of Belcher Island in southeastern Hudson Bay.[25]

When there is the notion of a fixed pool of souls, as with Trobrianders, the Igbo, and the Druze, one might expect a concomitant problem of explaining population increase or decline, a fact that some people would surely have noticed consequent to wars, famines, and other natural disasters. Thus Raphael Patai says that the Druze cannot explain population change owing to the fixed number of souls who at death are immediately reborn.[26] I doubt that this situation exists elsewhere. Trobriander ancestors are not required to reincarnate at the will of humans; they can go on living in Tuma for long periods. Consequently population decline (and subsequent increase) could easily be related to the willingness or unwillingness of the ancestors to return to earth. Theories of multiple souls (as with the Igbo) or of split souls or of a deity that can control the flow of souls (as with the Qiqiqtamiut Inuit of Belcher Island) can serve a similar function, and it may well be that even the Druze have a way out of this dilemma, as, for example, with their idea that although the number of souls is fixed, no one knows the exact number or that some Druze can be reborn in distant China, a mythic land for them.[27]

Let me conclude this discussion with reference to Malinowski's extraordinary attitude to reincarnation. Having discussed Trobriand reincarnation belief in rich detail, Malinowski confidently asserts that "it does not play an important role in social life" (B, 194). Characteristically, he ignores what it might have meant in the *personal* life of Trobrianders: the idea of personal continuity in Tuma, the mystical idea that one is a matrilineal ancestor returned and that the milamala is conducted under watchful ancestral eyes. One might wonder why so many Trobriand shamans went to Tuma and came back to relay information that the public accepted if such beliefs were not socially important.

Malinowski, like his African successors, defined *reincarnation* narrowly and specifically as the return of the ancestor into the womb of a woman, the dictionary definition of the term. But reincarnation in this narrow sense scarcely exists in reality because it is always constituted within a larger cosmological and eschatological frame. The ethnography of the spirits of the dead, or baloma, is what interests him, and reincarnation is only a small part of it, so that in *The Father in Primitive Psychology* he has a chapter titled "Reincarnation and the Way to Life from the Spirit World," which describes the baloma cult in terms of the African ethnographers' "ancestor worship." It is doubtful that Tomwaya Lakwabulo saw reincarnation in quite that fashion. Thus, although it is true that Christianity eventually eroded belief in reincarnation, ethnographers still had a chance to record it, but they were not attuned to seeing its presence or its larger cultural significance as part of a complex of beliefs about the afterworld and about life in general.

## ANIMAL AND HUMAN REINCARNATION: NORTHWEST COAST INDIANS AND INUIT (ESKIMO)

In a recent collection of essays that reevaluate Amerindian and Inuit reincarnation, scholars produce convincing evidence that such beliefs were prevalent to some degree among virtually all North American Indian groups, although their centrality in the overall cosmology of each group is difficult to ascertain.[28] These ideas were probably part of an ancient, wider circumpolar cultural complex represented strongly by Northwest Coast Indians, Inuit, and Siberian peoples and perhaps stretching into all of central Asia.

It is no longer possible to depict with any certainty the forms and features of reincarnation beliefs as they existed prior to Western contact and the introduction of Christianity. In his discussion of the Kutchin of the Canadian Northwest Territories and the Yukon, Richard Slobodin shows that although there are only a few reports of reincarnation *memories* nowadays, this was not the case in precolonial times. Slobodin's own vivid case histories suggest the power of these beliefs even in the face of intense missionary activity for over a century. He thinks that virtually everyone among the Kutchin believes in reincarnation, including the horrendously un-Christian idea that animals have souls! Among those Kutchin who gave the anthropologist information on the reality of reincarnation were three ordained Anglican priests; two Anglican catechists; a Pentecostal lay reader; a dozen of the most devout Roman Catholic and Anglican laity, and two notorious "free thinkers."[29]

The situation is no different among Northwest Coast and Inuit groups, where there is a strong cultural belief that both humans and animals reincarnate. In her study of the distribution of these beliefs, Mills says that virtually every American Indian group believes in animal reincarnation. It is likely that missionary influence undermined the idea of human reincarnation among some of them, but it did not shake their beliefs in animal reincarnation. Mills also shows that for many present-day Amerindian groups reincarnation is *one* of the eschatological possibilities after death.[30] For others, especially Inuit and Northwest Coast Indians, the centrality of reincarnation can no longer be disputed. Everywhere, however, ideas of reincarnation are themselves embedded in complex and larger cosmological schemas, described in detail for the Northwest Coast by such ethnographers as Boas, Goldman, Walens, Mills, de Laguna, and others.

First let me deal with the work of Antonia Mills, who studied in great detail the rebirth beliefs of three contiguous Amerindian groups in British Columbia: the Athapaskan-speaking Wet'suwet'en, who live on the Morice Lake and Bulkley River drainage and whose rhythm of social existence is attuned to the migration of salmon up the rivers and to trout from the lakes; the Beaver, also a group of Athapaskan speakers, living on the eastern side of the Rocky Mountain trench, who have no salmon; and the Gitksan, closer in culture to the main Northwest Coast Indians like the Kwakiutl and Tsimshian, speaking a Tsimshian language and living in an economic environment geared to salmon and steelhead trout. The economic plenitude in which the Gitksan lived permitted them to found five villages made up of cedar longhouses. "Each longhouse was presided over by a hereditary chief who controlled access to the territory and fishing sites associated with the founding and history of the house. This history was cryptically portrayed in the totem pole erected before the house by successive househead chiefs."[31] Both Wet'suwet'en and Gitksan have matrilineal lineages, whereas the Beaver "do not have lineages, clans or houses, totem poles or associated chiefly titles. They reckon kinship bilaterally, making distinctions between cross and parallel relatives. . . . The Beaver preserve the typical Athapaskan reticence about revealing names or powers acquired in highly personal vision quests" (CWC, 388). It is difficult to imagine a group of societies more remote from the Indic ones that developed around the sixth century, yet they show striking similarity in their eschatological beliefs pertaining to rebirth. Like Indic cultures, these three groups and others in this vast region have a conception of both human and animal reincarnation, each having its own rebirth cycles. "Like the Tlingit and Haida, the Wet'suwet'en, Gitksan, and Beaver Indians expect humans to reincarnate as humans and fish, game, and fowl each to be reborn into their own species" (CWC, 388). Their theories have an underlying ideological resemblance to South Asian religions, especially Jainism, in the view that animals and even plants are endowed with consciousness and belong with humans to a larger order of sentient existence—an issue I will develop later.

All three groups seek contact with the spirit homes of other species in their vision quests. Animals are often perceived as material embodiments of spirit animals who act as helpers and guardian spirits of those who seek them. These groups "believe that humans after death travel to the land of the dead, analogous to the spirit homes of the animal species, from which they may appear to the living as ghosts. In the Gitksan and Wet'suwet'en oral traditions the spirit village must be entered through a mountain and across a river over which one must be ferried. The prophets of the Beaver Indians "make maps of the intricate trails to the complex series of spirit realms one can attain after leaving the body" (CWC, 389). In all three groups the other world is based on the human world but without food scarcity or other forms of want. This is not surprising because the world we live in is an incontestable experienced reality that conditions any serious attempt by humans to construct an architecture of an alternative society, heavenly or earthly.

I noted that the logic of rebirth requires the sojourn to be temporary, whether in this world or in another. However, the length of stay in the otherworld varies with the three groups, such that the median interval between the death of the previous personality and the birth of the new is 12 months for Beaver, 16 for Gitksan, and 180 for the Wet'suwet'en. There is no clear-cut correlation between the length of one's stay in the otherworld and the recollection of "past birth memory" after he or she is born on earth, although some interesting interconnections can be discerned.

Virtually every society that believes in rebirth (except the Druze) believes firmly that only a fraction of those reborn can remember their previous earthly life persona. A Wet'suwet'en chief told Mills: "When we die we go to other realms and experience many things and learn many things. But [during] the experience of birth, from the first breath we take, we lose the memory of what we experienced in those other realms" (CWC, 391). For most people the intervening period in another realm obliterates the memory of experiences in the preceding human life. Yet two conditions might affect the retention of memory, at least for some groups: if the length of time spent in the other world was short, or if the other world has been bypassed entirely and the soul is directly reincarnated in another human body. "The cases in which a person's past life is discernable, the Beaver believe, are those cases in which the deceased person did not receive a resting place in an afterworld. Those who attain such an afterlife abode are expected to eventually reincarnate, but they are not expected to remember their past life nor have it revealed by others" (CWC, 398). It is not likely, however, that this cultural theory is strictly realized in practical reality. It also does not hold for the Wet'suwet'en, whose median stay in the otherworld is the longest for the three groups (180 months). Yet they expect to be recognized after they are reborn, largely because they have seers, diviners or prophets who specialize in diagnosing a person's past-life identity.

All three societies believe in the universality of rebirth, although it is not possible, for the most part, to identify the previous-life persona. Many simply assume that each infant is in fact the reincarnation of a dead kinsperson. Yet in spite of the small size of these communities, Mills collected a significant number of cases of persons whose previous life could be identified: twenty-eight cases in Wet'suwet'en (with a population of three thousand), twenty-three for Beaver (with a population of more than five hundred) and thirty-five for Gitksan (with a population of six thousand).[32] This is quite unusual from the perspective of Buddhist societies, where it is rare that the past-life persona can be identified. Thus, in Sri Lanka, with a population of more than eighteen million people, mostly Hindu and Buddhist, only a very few claim to remember their past births.

The techniques for identifying the past life of the newly born in these Amerindian groups are similar to those prevalent in Buddhist societies (whenever they occur) in West Africa and in many other parts of the world:[33]

1. In many instances birthmarks are signs of wounds that have been inflicted on the deceased in a previous existence. "The most striking example is a girl who was born with a birthmark on her back located where the presumed previous personality was stabbed by scissors" (CWC, 391). Stevenson reports for the Tlingit that many warriors traditionally preferred to die on the field of battle and achieve immediate rebirth, without incurring the misery of old age.[34]

2. Similarities in behavior are a common means of identifying the past persona in Buddhist and Amerindian cases also. Generally the child behaves, talks, or looks like a previously known person; that person is the being now reincarnated.

3. Diagnosis by seers or native doctors is quite common among the Wet'suwet'en and Gitksan but almost unheard of in Buddhist societies because according to Buddhism only the Buddha and *arahants* (those who have realized nirvana) have this power, and they are no longer around.[35] "In seven Wet'suwet'en cases, 'Indian doctors' or *kaluhim,* members of a secret healing society, discerned the past life identity of a person. Most involved newborn babies or small children, but the previous personalities of two people were not identified until they were adults" (CWC, 393).

4. An announcing dream: Mills mentions seven out of a sample of eighteen cases among the Wet'suwet'en. "In one of these cases, the coming baby's maternal grandmother dreamed about the person who was reincarnating in the baby to be born," and in two cases the dreams occurred after the birth of the child. In one interesting case Amelia dreamed that her dead mother's sister, Eliza, came to her, and Amelia asked her, "Is there eternal life?" The aunt responded, "No." When Amelia asked her whether there is reincarnation, Eliza said, "Yes there is, there are fourteen planes" (CWC, 391). These fourteen planes of existence are apparently a cosmological innovation of Eliza's, having no parallel in traditional eschatology. Reports from other areas in this region indicate the extreme importance of dreams in the prognostication of reincarnation.[36]

5. In rare cases relatives have had visions of the deceased person roaming about in public places or entering private homes where conception would occur, occasionally even entering the woman's body. Consider this Dene Tha utterance from a woman whose daughter was her father's brother reincarnated:

   My daughter, she is my uncle [father's brother]
   There is always somebody who knows who it is going to be.
   They see the spirit going into you.
   My dad saw me standing in a field
   and my (deceased) uncle was walking towards me.
   When he got to me, he disappeared.
   Then he [my father] knew it was going to be reincarnation.[37]

There is almost universal agreement that those who are reborn are close kinfolk. The Gitksan and Wet'suwet'en are matrilineal peoples and about 92 percent in each group are born in the same matriline or house and inherit the names and titles they had in their previous life. The Beaver practice bilateral kinship and marriage between cross relatives; they also expect to be reborn among close kin (CWC, 401). Some groups are much more specific: among the matrilineal Tlingit and with the bilateral Beaver "cross-cousin marriage preserves marriageable/unmarriageable categories, reincarnation after reincarnation," and the Tagish, as reported by McClellan, "remain related to one another in the same kind of way in successive lives."[38]

Mills also records important differences among the three groups she studied. The Gitksan and Beaver expressed rebirth wishes (Buddhists call these *prārthanā*) regarding the place of rebirth, the character traits they would like to possess, and preference for their future parents (CWC, 399). Mills however adds that all three groups expect to possess the traits they exhibited in their previous life, an expectation found even in forms of Greek rebirth. Another difference is that cross-sex births are possible in contemporary Beaver but not in Gitksan or in Wet'suwet'en, although earlier investigators recorded this belief. According to Mills there is a good sociological reason that inhibits cross-sex incarnations, namely, the sex-specific nature of name and title inheritance central to the prestige system of these societies (CWC, 403).

These Northwest Coast reincarnation theories are complicated by the fact that in most Amerindian societies (such as the Coast Tsimshian, Kwakiutl, Tlingit, Haida, Gitksan, Coast Salish, and especially the Inuit), a soul can achieve multiple reincarnations. The same person can in effect be reborn in different communities or as different persons. This is especially so when the dead person is a high chief; therefore, many would like to have him reincarnated among them.[39] Guemple found this puzzling from his strict Euro-rationalist viewpoint, but it is no more irrational than the idea that a South Asian deity, or the holy spirit in charismatic churches, can possess several people at the same time. These multiple reincarnations are perhaps related to the view that the soul can split into several entities that in turn can animate a new body.[40] Also related to this notion is the idea that the souls of different ancestors can be reincarnated in the single body of a descendant.

A further complication arises from the complex naming and title system in many Northwest Coast and Inuit societies. There are different forms of naming, some virtually synonymous with reincarnation, such that a baby is given the name of a person who is the reincarnated ancestor. On other occasions a name provides "a kind of guardian spirit protection for a child from a deceased and not yet incarnated relative."[41] In most cases, however, a person gets a variety of names and titles, and even with a theory of split souls and multiple reincarnations, it is impossible to entirely equate the naming system with the reincarnation belief.

According to Marie Mauze, the Kwakiutl have a naming system quite distinct from its reincarnation belief. A name, she says, is a spiritual entity separable from the body and located above the soul; she adds that all elements—body, soul, and name—are necessary in the naming of a person. "It is in acquiring, achieving and upholding names related to positions in the *numayn* [people of the same kind] that a person becomes a 'social' person and a 'moral' person aware of its self and destiny" (RKI, 184). Thus, names give a person a sense of individual identity and differentiate him or her from the reincarnated ancestor that the person also embodies. For example, let us say that the soul of my grandfather reincarnates in me; consequently, I am my grandfather to a greater or lesser degree. When this idea is carried to an extreme, a replicated ancestor might become a kind of characterless cipher. Empirical reality however disproves this simplistic equation, for no two persons are strictly alike. First, the returning ancestor is a complex being who has garnered many experiences from his previous interlinked existences. Second, names add a new dimension to one's identity, for the individual is now constituted, and continues to be constituted throughout his whole-life trajectory, by the characteristics embodied in the names he has inherited. Among the Kwakiutl these names are varied: nicknames, kin names, and title names for nobles. "Real names are endowed with power and correspond to spiritual qualities that men who carry them are expected to live up to" (RKI, 185). Like souls "names are autonomous entities which have eternal existence. The bearer may live or die, but their names will go on forever" (RKI, 186). If in post-Upanishadic Indic religions it is karma that brings a spiritual individuality to a person, in the Northwest Coast and among the Inuit (as in some of the African cases discussed earlier) it is the naming system. To sum up: the naming system, among other things, accounts for the fact that although I may be my ancestor reincarnated, I am not his clone but someone different from him because I am also constituted from the living and dead members of my social group.

## HUMAN AND ANIMAL TRANSFORMATIONS

I will use the label *species sentience* to designate the powerful ethical conception underlying Inuit and Amerindian rebirth beliefs, the idea that all living creatures belong to a larger, interconnected spirit-permeated order. This order comprises humans and animals and to a lesser degree plants. A common theme in Amerindian myth is that of human-into-animal transformations and vice versa. Some societies, such as the Kwakiutl, explicitly recognize in their myths that humans were originally animals. Thus Amerindian mythic thought often postulates a homology of a physical and spiritual nature between humans and animals, and this is manifest in the constant transformations, the boundary crossings, and the blurring of categorical distinctions between the two. The basis for this homology is the ethical notion of *species sentience:* nature is bound together through common sentience.

Let me now relate the Amerindian notion of the homology between human and animal to their conceptions of reincarnation. Antonia Mills and James Matlock rightly distinguish three forms of reincarnation: human-to-human rebirth, human-to-animal rebirth, and a human-to-animal-to-human cycle.[42] But given the homology between animals and humans these categories are constantly blurred. For my purposes I want to distinguish between two types of rebirth: first, that in which animals and humans have their own separate rebirth cycles and, second, that in which humans become animals and then move back into the rebirth cycle as humans once again. The latter form is very rare, found only among the Kwakiutl described by Boas, the Inuit described by Rasmussen, and a few other groups.[43] Its historic presence, I will show later, has been noted for the Tlingit, and it must surely have existed for other groups. I will label the first type "parallel-species reincarnation" and the second "cross-species reincarnation" (which I will sometimes shorten to "parallel-reincarnation" and "cross-reincarnation"). In both cases the animal-human homology is very much present, but in cross-species reincarnation the homology is a literal one because humans can be reincarnated as animals (or special classes of them) and vice versa. In parallel-species reincarnation, the more common form, animals and humans live in separate abodes in the otherworld, and because they share the same cosmic space, there is constant interrelation between the two worlds. This is clearly seen in the vision quest, where animals become spirit helpers and there is a spiritual partnership between humans and animal spirits such that the latter will help the former in all the trials of life, including the quest for game.

Ann Fienup-Riordan, in her discussion of "cosmological cycling" among the Nelson Island Eskimo (Yup'ik), refers to many tales in which "animals can be transformed into humans to meet men on their own grounds."[44] Human-to-animal transformation tales deal with women and children who seek "freedom, safety, or defense in their helpless condition" (*NIE*, 203) through animal transformations. Equally important are stories of men who see animals as humans; this permits humans to "see the world in a new way, from the animal's point of view" (*NIE*, 207). In one story "the shaman gives voice to the seals' opinions on their treatment during the past year when he returns at the end of his spiritual hunting" (*NIE*, 207). In other words, because of constant transformations people are animals, and animals are people. Thus "the mosquito people are depicted as skinny humans who bring home arms and legs from hunting, the counterparts to the bites they give. The people with no mouths (the worm people) eat food by smelling it, after which it becomes rotten" (*NIE*, 206). Boundaries get blurred in virtually all of Yup'ik eschatological notions. Thus *tarneq* (spirit or shade) is a component of a person's being that can, according to some accounts, be reincarnated five times, sometimes as an animal or as a *tuunraq* (shaman's helping spirit).

The constant blurring of human-animal categories and the empathy that humans are expected to have toward animals are based on the important eschatological assumption of "an originally undifferentiated universe in which the boundaries between the human and nonhuman, the spiritual and material, were shifting and permeable," quite unlike the Christian assumption that animals have no souls.[45] In Yup'ik conception animals have *yua*, the spiritual entity that is contained in the bladder; in the elaborate Bladder Festival the hunters put the bladders of the seals they have killed back into the water to ensure the seals' reincarnation. In addition, both animals and humans possess *ella* (awareness) resulting from experience and giving them a sense of control over their destiny.[46] They also believe, as do many Inuit and Amerindian peoples, that animals are direct descendants of mythic ancestors (*BP*, 62). And most important, "all living things participated in an endless cycle of birth and rebirth, contingent on right thought and action by others as well as self" (*BP*, 51).

Species sentience, then, is the idea that animate existence constitutes a single order held together by common sentience, both physical and spiritual. Several scholars have highlighted the important ethical implications of species sentience among Northwest Coast Indians and Inuit. Stanley Walens says of the Kwakiutl: "A human being kills because it is his responsibility to eat, his responsibility to be the vehicle of rebirth for those beings, human and otherwise, with whom he has a covenant."[47] This is also evident in Menovschikov's account of the Siberian Yup'iks (Eskimos): "According to the ideas of the Eskimoes, the game was not killed, it came spontaneously to the man as a guest. This guest, however, had to be brought down with the help of a harpoon or spear. The killed game was highly praised and persuaded not to be offended but to return again to the hunters."[48]

These Siberian Yup'ik cut the nose off the animal and throw it to the sea and plea for its return. Edith Turner describes a parallel Inuit case of a whale hunt in which "the head with its inner spirit was painstakingly returned to the sea, to grow its new parka, to reincarnate, 'reflesh' itself; people can actually perceive the spirit of the whale flashing upon the participants at the moment of its departure."[49] And Ann Fienup-Riordan says: "Men and seals are continually being taken apart and put back together again in the process of transformation from powerless flesh to spiritual efficacy and being, in an unending cycle of generation and regeneration, both spiritual and physical" (*NIE*, 207–8). Walens makes a similar point for the Kwakiutl Indians:

> The prayer signifies to the fish that humans will perform those actions that will ensure the reincarnation of the fish. Thus, certain motions must be made—for example, the fish must be hit on the head with the correct fish club once, but never twice. The woman who butchers the fish her husband has caught must repeat her husband's prayer (not exactly, but in the same form) so that the sacred state is continued; and thus the woman's butchering acts become sacred acts, again in this case, related to the release of the fish's soul, for the husband's prayer is in effect only while the fish is in the canoe and before it is put down on the beach.[50]

## KINSHIP, REBIRTH, AND DESIRE

In the societies discussed earlier the reborn child is an ancestor who has returned and will eventually die, only to be reborn again in an eternal recurrence that we can arbitrarily represent as a cycle. As an ancestor returned, the child is often subject to special treatment. When the identity of the neonate is known, the relation between the child and the rest of its living kinfolk becomes complicated. Many years ago I met a Balinese aristocrat who told me that he was his grandfather returned. "Whenever my father scolded me I told him to shut up because I was his father." The Northwest Coast Indians and the Inuit might rearrange their kinship terms and concomitant relationships if the returning soul can be identified.[51] I will demonstrate later that the karma theory tends to inhibit rebirth in the same family or kin group except in rare circumstances, such as the fulfillment of vows made by pious virtuosos. The only individual blessed by being born among some, but by no means all, members of his family in successive rebirths is the Buddha himself. Yet in spite of the doctrine, the power of *wanting* to be reborn in the bosom of one's own family is so strong that many in Buddhist societies will make a rebirth wish *(prārthanā)* to be reborn as the same wife, husband, or child in the next and in more distant reincarnations. By contrast, a deadly hatred is expressed in the curse that says, "May I never see you (in any one of my future births)," a curse as deadly as the Igbo curse quoted earlier.

Let me now consider the extraordinarily complex cases of the "third sex" discussed by Saladin d'Anglure for the Inuit group that he studied.[52] On one level their belief system produces complex sexual identities and transformations, from male to female and vice versa, and even a third composite gender that is in turn linked to the institution of shamanism. Yet underlying these transformations is the wish or the desire of the living, often the female who will incarnate and nurture the spirit in her womb. The preincarnate wish of a person can have no psychological consequence unless it corresponds to, or is in harmony with, the desire of the living. For example, a woman's father may wish to be reborn as her child, but that conception, in both senses of the term, may not take place unless the father's wish corresponds to the daughter's desire. In some cases the woman's desire can determine whether the person about to be born is going to be a boy or a girl. Let us consider the following situation. Say that the father wanted to be born as his daughter's daughter and that the woman acceded to his wish but the child was born biologically male. If her desire to fulfill her father's wish is strong, she might well bring up her son as a female, who might then end up becoming a shaman, a phenomenon well recognized in this vast circumpolar region. So it is with naming in general; the names of dead ancestors given to a person cannot by themselves create a "cultural identity." It is the desires of living kinfolk and the socialization of the child under the governance of these desires, combined with the desires of the person concerned as he or she grows up to and beyond adulthood, that bring about the culminating identity, which then is both personal and cultural at the same time. Sometimes it may superficially seem that a "cultural identity" is created when a ritual specialist or similar person external to the family identifies the neonate as a former kin. But once this identification is made, it influences the attitude of parents and kin, tapping imagination and desire and molding the child accordingly.

I will illustrate this process by Mills's account of the Wet'suwet'en case of Jeffery, which I quote verbatim:

> No one had an announcing dream before Jeffery was born in 1965. According to Louise Walters, Jeffery's maternal grandmother, an "Indian doctor" named Steven John held Jeffery when he was a baby and said that he was Will Walters reborn. Will was Jeffery's mother's brother. He had died some six years before Jeffery's birth when a horse he was harnessing kicked him in the stomach and the head. Will was thirty-one at the time of his death and was thought to be the reincarnation of another son named Will whom Louise and Allen Walters had lost before the second Will's birth. The first Will had died when he was four years old from hemorrhaging of the head. Louise had subsequently dreamed that the first Will was returning to them. The second Will was a favorite of his parents and already held a high chief's name, Maxlimlox, at the time of his death. His parents were so distraught at his sudden death that they left the site of the accident, a place they had camped for many years, abandoning power saws and other equipment, and did not return for eleven years.
>
> Jeffery's aunt Marilyn reported that she came to know that Jeffery was Will reborn when Jeffery was a baby. She said that she would sometimes take him from her sister to sleep with her in her bed. One night she woke up and could not find the baby in the bed beside her. She looked up and saw her late brother Will sitting on the bed facing her. She reached out for him, and her hand went through him; she couldn't feel him. "It was Will for sure. I got up and turned on the light and he went away and there was Jeffery laying there as a baby. . . ."
>
> When Jeffery was about five years old, he accompanied his grandparents and some other family members on their first return trip to the pole camp, the site of the accident that took Will's life. When they arrived at the spot, Jeffery entered a cabin that belonged to the section gang on the railway. His Aunt Patsy overheard him talking to himself, saying that he was Will come back, not Jeffery. Jeffery came out and said to Louise, "I'm not your grandson, I'm your son returned to you." Louise related how Jeffery recognized the site, described how they had skidded poles out of the bush, and identified the area where he, as Will, and Alex Martin had shot a moose. From that time Jeffery didn't call Louise "Grandma" any more, but "Mother," and he went to live with Allen and Louise as their son. Louise said, "That's why we love him so much and always give him money. We raised Jeffery ourselves. We raised him like our son."
>
> I went to see Jeffery, then twenty-two, to ask him if he remembered any of these "previous life memories." He said he no longer remembered what he said at the pole camp. He said he had heard that his Aunt Marilyn had dreamed of him as Will. However, he said that in his dreams he seems to know things that he could not know if he were not Will returned. He gave

> the example of recently dreaming that he (as Will) was pounding nails into the house that Louise and Allen had once lived in by Allen's totem pole. I asked if that was the house that burned down some time ago. He said, "No, it was the old house before that one." He said he was sure he was reborn because that house ceased to exist before he was born. He said that he used to see glimpses of the past in his dreams, but now his dreams are mostly of the future. . . .
>
> When I went back to ask Marilyn and Louise about the house at the totem pole, Marilyn confirmed that Will had built that house for his parents. It had later been superseded by a new house, the one which I had heard had burned down. Marilyn translated to Louise about Jeffery's dream of building the house, which was the first time that Louise or Marilyn had learned of this particular and recent dream.
>
> Louise said she continues to give Jeffery money and is trying to arrange a correct marriage for him as he was previously misallied with a girl from the same clan as himself. A year later I learned that Jeffery had formed a correct marriage and had moved his wife and grandmother-cum-mother into a new house built on the site of the one Will had made for his parents many years before, beside his grandfather-cum-father's totem pole. (CWC, 393–95)

Jeffery's rebirth path and his crosscutting kin relationships are illustrated in figure 2.

Jeffery cannot be converted psychologically into Will simply on the basis of the doctor's diagnosis. This diagnosis is itself probably conditioned by the fact that Will is a reincarnation of his brother, who died at age four; and neither reincarnation makes sense outside of the wish or desire of Mr. and Mrs. Allen, Jeffery's grandparents (his parents from the perspective of his previous persona) and in all likelihood of his mother (previously sister), who, along with his two aunts, Marilyn and Patsy (previously sisters), are also involved in this circuit of desire. Central to this coalition of forces is Jeffery himself; it is his motivation, reinforced by the unconscious conspiracy of those who love him, rather than divination or prophecy, that impels him to live with his grandparents and to call them mother and father. Unfortunately this kind of rich detail is not always available in the ethnographic record. In most instances ethnographers are so influenced by the powerful anthropological paradigm of kinship analysis that they ignore the networks of desire and focus instead on the networks of kinship and marriage in spirit incarnation itself, forgetting that there need not be a conflict between kinship and desire and that the exclusivist, deterministic, and totalizing nature of kinship is the paradigm of the analyst and not of the people themselves.

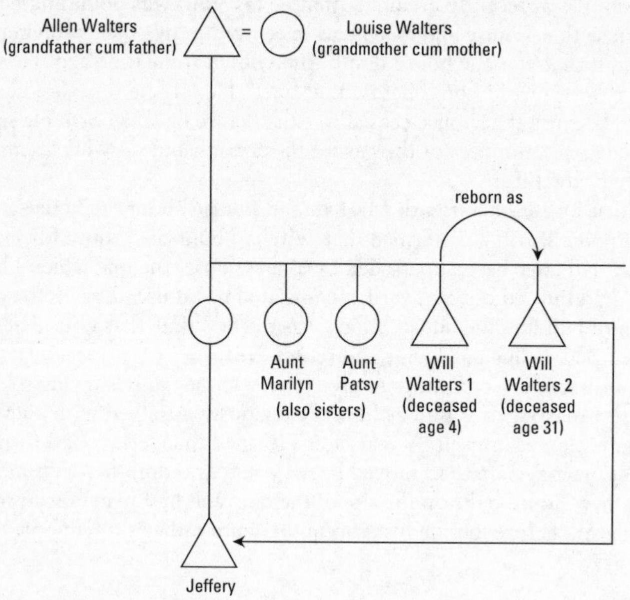


Figure 2. Genealogical chart of Jeffery's reincarnation.

## TLINGIT ESCHATOLOGY: REBIRTH, DESIRE, AND THE RETURN OF THE DEAD

In the preceding discussions I relied primarily on the recent collection edited by Antonia Mills and Richard Slobodin. For methodological reasons it seems desirable to move away from the concerns of that particular work and to consider a group that occupies the same region but that is not tied in any way to the Amerindian rebirth book. I choose the Tlingit of southeastern Alaska, particularly the coastal Tlingit, owing to the magnificent ethnographic documentation in the 1950s by Frederica de Laguna, along with the more recent work of Sergei Kan and that of nineteenth-century ethnographers, particularly George Emmons and Fr. Anatolii Kamenskii.[53] As always, I focus on Tlingit rebirth eschatology and refer the reader to the texts mentioned above for details of their ethnography.

The Tlingit are a conglomerate of tribes divided into matrilineal clans and lineages that are in turn grouped into two large exogamous moieties, the Raven and the Wolf (or sometimes Eagle). Territorial and land rights are exercised by the clan; the chiefs, or "big men," of the clan are the trustees and managers of the group property. As in many other Northwest Coast Indian groups, rank is important, the nobility being the headmen of clans and lineages, whereas the commoners are, at least in theory, their distant relatives. Below the commoners are the slaves, generally foreigners captured in war and occasionally killed at some important event like the death of a chief. The clans comprise lineages that, as in most unilinear societies, consist of matrilineal kinfolk who can trace precise genealogical connections with one another. Each lineage has its own crest, which represents its totems, that is, "certain animals, birds, fish, and invertebrates, heavenly bodies, prominent landmarks, and even ancestral heroes and certain supernatural beings associated with them."[54]

The Tlingit environment is a bountiful one, full of fish and sea mammals, as well as a variety of land mammals and birds that are used for consumption. Yet, as with the other groups in this cultural and geographic area, animal and human lives are interwoven in an intricate web of species sentience. Both humans and animals possess souls, and there is no fine line between the two because animals in their spirit homes look like people and live like them; they can even hear what people say (in Tlingit). Kindness to an animal may be miraculously rewarded by the ancestral spirits. "It is not clear whether plants and inanimate things . . . also have souls comparable to those of men and animals, although they are often said to have an in-dwelling spirit of some kind. . . . Man in his spiritual aspect is not fundamentally different from any other part of nature."[55] Owing to their belief that all life is interwoven (species sentience), there is a strong Tlingit reluctance to destroy nature, and the Tlingit hunter is averse to "killing creatures with souls akin to his own." No animal or bird should be needlessly hunted; nor, once hunted and killed, should the body be wasted. "Rather, the hunter would pray to the dead animal and to his own 'spirit above,' explaining his need and asking his forgiveness. The dead creature was thanked in song, perhaps honored with eagle down (like a noble guest); certain essential parts (head, bones, or vital organs, depending on the species) were interred, returned to the water, or cremated, to ensure reincarnation of the animal."[56]

Although de Laguna's informants do not entertain the notion of cross-species reincarnation, Fr. Kamenskii of the Russian Orthodox Church, who did missionary work among the group in the late nineteenth century, said the Tlingit do. "The Tlingit Indian strongly believes in the transmigration of the souls of the dead, assuming that the soul can come back to earth after being reborn in another human or animal form. . . . There are also cases of souls being reborn through animals—bear, hair seal, dog, deer, etc."[57] It is likely that at least some Tlingit groups did believe in cross-species reincarnation, whereas others did not; yet others believed in the possibility of gender changes at birth.[58]

Until recent times every Tlingit believed in the reality of reincarnation, "a key element of Tlingit ethnopsychology and eschatology."[59] Every baby, says de Laguna, was believed to be a reincarnation of a deceased matrilineal relative. A person speaking of the time before birth might say: "Then ashes I was; not yet was I born," a reference to the period of the cremation that released the spirit of the dead to the other world and eventually to this. At the death of a person, there are eight days of mourning; for most people cremation is on the fourth day. These ceremonies are discussed at great length by de Laguna.[60]

In de Laguna's ethnography the souls of those who die of disease or old age journey through tangled woods to the banks of a river that has bad weather; hence the Tlingit need to cover the corpse with heavy clothes, boots, mittens, and so forth. The dead person must cross this river to reach the land of the dead, "arranged in exactly the same manner as in the village of the living . . . [such that] the life of the spirits did not differ significantly from that of the living, except that they did not have to work but depended on their living matrikin for their survival."[61] Those who die by violence at their own hands or in battle go to much more desirable bourn, the land above, or *k'iwa'a.*[62] By contrast those slain by their fellows for misdeeds are sent to a "dog heaven," "an undefined abode now equated with hell." "Those who remain in Heaven *(k'iwa'a)* enjoy a happy existence, playing shinny on the open grass. They become the northern lights and [are] called *k'iwa q'awu,* 'people above.' They may appear after the funeral to greet their friends; on other occasions they prophesy war or that a relative will die by violence."[63] As one informant told de Laguna: "When we see lots of Northern Lights, we always say, 'that's the people of K'iwa'a playing ball.'"[64]

In Tlingit thought all the dead will eventually be reincarnated, irrespective of the nature of their past lives and the manner of their dying.[65] Most often the dead person decides the place of birth and the person who is going to conceive him or her; a living kinswoman may also desire to give birth to a particularly loved relative. In the former case a person will inform a close matrilineal kinswoman that he will be coming back and to name the child after him. If a person has a double soul (as is possible here), he or she could come back to two different women, and each woman will give the child the name of one of the deceased. In such cases the original spirit is said to divide in two. A dead person can also appear in a dream to a woman and promise to return, or the pregnant woman may know from a dream which person is about to be reincarnated in her. In some instances "the mother in childbed sees the spirit of the dead person waiting near her, apparently to forestall another soul that is also trying to claim the child,"[66] whereas in others the relatives try to identify the neonate through bodily markings, as with Northwest Coast Indians in general.

A common Tlingit strategy is for a would-be-mother to actively seek the reincarnation of a loved relative in her own womb, often by placing the hand of the dead person against her own breast.

> When the corpse has been buried (formerly cremated), she is led eight times around the grave (or pyre), and walks away, calling the name of the deceased, but not looking back lest the soul be driven away. On the ground she marks a short trail from the grave and urinates at the end of it (opening her womb?) and calling the spirit to return. She wears a lock of hair from the right side of the deceased's head or a nail paring from his right hand sewn to the waistband of her petticoat; and during pregnancy she keeps beside her bed a tiny basket filled with the food that babies like, to hasten the return of a beloved soul.[67]

De Laguna calls these motivations of mothers-to-be "planned reincarnations." In reality de Laguna's case studies suggest complex motivations at work, often in harmony but sometimes not. For example, consider the case of a man who before his death told one of his nieces: "You . . . think I'm coming back to you. You're crazy. I don't like you. If you are going to have a baby boy, don't name the baby after me!" Instead he chose another "niece," and sure enough, soon after his death the chosen niece performed the correct rituals and soon became pregnant.[68]

Whether planned or otherwise, the birth of the reincarnated ancestor can change the quality of kinship relations centering on the newborn. Thus, a man can call his son "father" because the baby bears the name of its father's father, and the former wife calls her husband's namesake "husband" and gives gifts to her "mother-in-law" (the baby's mother) and provides care for the baby.[69]

The types of reincarnation motivations mentioned above are only the dominant forms and do not exclude others. For example, several spirits, on their own volition, might fight among themselves for a chance to be born in the womb of an especially desirable woman, and this struggle either can lead to an exclusion of all except one or might bring about multiple births.[70]

The preceding discussion brings us once again to the Inuit and Northwest Coast preoccupation with naming and its relationship to reincarnation. The word for name in Tlingit is related to the word *breathe;* it suggests that names carry a kind of life force, but the exact significance of naming is not clear from any of the accounts of the Tlingit that I have read. Here is de Laguna: "For the possession of a name, or names, when several of the deceased's are given to a living namesake, makes reincarnation 'effective.' A child is given 'as many names as you can get ahold of,' and yet somehow each name embodies the essence of its previous holders."[71] It is the "yet somehow" that is difficult for me to grasp in de Laguna's account. As I see it, the Tlingit infant is given a name at birth; this name is that of a deceased ancestor who is incarnated in the child. I find this nonproblematic; so do the Tlingit, because they call this initial name a "real" or "ordinary" one.[72] At the other extreme are potlatch names given to chiefs; these are like titles that seem to pass from older to younger brother, from mother's brother to sister's son, or from grandfather to his son's son. De Laguna says that these names do not imply rebirth at all but are largely honorific. It is likely that nicknames too do not have rebirth connotations. Yet in between is a further category of "real" names of dead relatives; de Laguna seems unsure of the precise significance of these later names, and this is evident in her phrasing: "presumably thus embodying as many reincarnations."[73]

It seems to me that there are two reasonable interpretations of Tlingit naming. One is the idea that the ancestor is reborn in a descendant, and later the souls of other ancestors also descend into him so that he becomes the embodiment of multiple ancestral souls. In this case there is a primary ancestor and several secondary ones constituting the persona of the descendant. The interpretation I favor is that the initial name is of a specific deceased ancestor who wishes to be reborn in the matrilineage; or, initial naming occurs when a woman of the matrilineage plans to have a recently deceased and loved relative reborn in her womb. The later names given are those of dead ancestors whose spirits or souls live in the otherworld and have the capacity to infuse a person with their essences, through their "breaths" as it were, without actually leaving the otherworld. Either way the Tlingit material confirms, I think, my previous thesis that naming provides a cultural rationale for human individuality: it creates a person who is not the simple embodiment of a dead relative but rather an individual who is constituted out of the character traits of other dead ancestors also. Nicknames and potlatch names further this sense of individuality. Moreover, as a person grows up and experiences the world in his or her own unique way, the person becomes more and more a separate individual. Sergei Kan's material, however, suggests that naming is only one rationale for individuality: although spiritual qualities are inherited from one's matrilineal kin, some spiritual and behavioral characteristics could be inherited from one's paternal kin also. Once again this means that a person is not simply a clone of a matrilineal kinsperson but an individual in his or her own right.[74]

This shift to individuality is assisted by another characteristic process in Tlingit eschatology: although many Tlingit children have (or traditionally had) the capacity to remember their preceding birth, it is significant that few could remember it after around age nine or sometimes even earlier. This is also true of rebirth memories in other groups in this general area. The conclusion is irresistible: as a person grows older and his or her web of experiences expands, the person progressively ceases to be the reincarnated ancestor as far as characterological features are concerned, even though the person knows he or she is a reincarnation of a deceased ancestor and this knowledge of one's ancestorhood is reinforced by the attitude of the circle of kin. The forgetting of rebirth memories is concomitant with the emergence of individuality. Thus, it is only to outsider anthropologists that "primitive" people do not possess individuality; they do for the persons concerned, and this individuality, in the present sample, is compounded of a primary ancestor and later secondary ones (or their "breaths") combined with each person's own unique experiences through life's sojourn. The possession of "individuality," or "ego identity," does not necessarily correspond to Western "individualism"—a unique way of life associated with European (but not Japanese) capitalism that idealizes individual self-interest at the expense of the interests of the kin group (or larger entity) in the acquisition of capital, political power, and social status.[75]

De Laguna's study is especially important because she cites detailed cases of those who visited the otherworld and provided descriptions of it. Normally, this is the classic role of shamans; yet in de Laguna's cases ordinary individuals have these experiences, which are based on the *shamanic model* of spirit journeys. Both ordinary and shamanic journeys to the otherworld—analogous to the Greek *katabasis,* or underworld descent—imply that cultural eschatologies are constantly being constructed and reconstructed, interpreted and reinterpreted by Northwest Coast Indians, Inuit, and Yup'ik, as they are among Trobrianders. Hence, try as they might, the major Tlingit ethnographers cannot give us a uniform picture of Tlingit eschatology because such a task is impossible. What is striking in Tlingit spirit journeys is that ordinary people can go to the otherworld and back, but only shamans can go into the spirit worlds of animals.[76] Perhaps shamans offer more radical revisions of eschatologies, whereas the experiences of ordinary persons reinforce current eschatologies by bringing them vividly before our imaginations and the imaginations of the Tlingit.[77] For illustrative purposes I will summarize one case from de Laguna's repertoire.[78]

### *The Story of ʻAskadut*

This is a well-known story among the Tlingit, and de Laguna had several versions of it, as did a previous ethnographer, John Harrington. Here it is:

When ʻAskadut died, he did not know of it; he could however see his own body propped up, as was customary before cremation in order to help the soul to leave the body. ʻAskadut tried to get back into his body but to no avail. He saw his wife, parents, sister, and her husband grieving for him, and he tried to tell them that he was alive, but they couldn't hear him. He tried to put his arms around them, but he could only hear them sob. He got angry when he realized that he couldn't sleep with his wife as usual. His relations had summoned different clans for a feast, but although ʻAskadut knew that this feast was for him, he couldn't eat any of it. He became angry and asked his sister's husband: "Why didn't you give me anything to eat?" The brother-in-law seems to have responded: "Ha, my body twitches and at the same time the fire also makes a noise." Whenever ʻAskadut spoke, the fire sparked; he could not eat anything until people put some food that his wife was eating or drinking into a dish and placed this in the fire. (The references to the fire making noises or sparks are based on the belief that one can speak to the dead only in sighs and by making the fire spark. Whether the phenomenon is caused by ʻAskadut's own sighs or those of other dead ancestors is not clear. The Tlingit also believe that "the dead can eat only when food is put in the fire by the *gunetkanayi* [members of the opposite moiety] at the funeral feast, or later by the relatives and the deceased is called by name.")[79]

They took ʻAskadut's body to the cremation place, and he followed them there. He was afraid that the fire would hurt him, but it only felt warm; he watched them burn his corpse. When the cremation was over, his relations left, but ʻAskadut was unable to follow them. He stayed by the bushes; he then began to think of the place where the dead go and decided to walk there in the rain and the sleet, through devilclubs and thorny underbrush until his hands became sore. (The rain and sleet are, according to Tlingit ideas, a transformation of the tears of the bereaved;

the Tlingit also believe that the spirit is often dressed in mittens, gloves, and rough clothes to help ease the way through the thorny path to the world of the dead; the singing of the opposite moiety, or *gunetkanayi,* helps clear the spirit's path. This clearing of the way is done nowadays with the aid of Christian prayers.)

At last he came to the bank of a muddy river that he couldn't cross, but he knew that he must get to the other side. There he could see a village and people. He called out to them again and again, but they didn't hear; he tired of it and yawned. Immediately the people heard him and got excited and brought him over in a canoe. (The dead, says de Laguna, have "reversed characteristics." "To them a shout is inaudible, yet a yawn is a loud sound, and when they call to each other they do so in whispers. For this reason, perhaps, they are unable to communicate with the living except by inducing sighs and making the fire spark." The river or lake that the dead have to cross is called the "Lake of Dying" [*MSE,* 768–69].)

The land of the dead was a big town with many people. 'Askadut went into one of the houses, and according to one informant's rendering, he saw those long dead with moss all over their faces, with trees growing from their heads, and sunken eyes. The recently dead looked like ordinary human beings. (De Laguna thinks there is an implicit distinction here between the spirits who sit by the riverbank to be born again and those who cross to remain forever in the land of the dead. The latter are the mossy creatures (*MSE,* 769). This theory has to contend, however, with Tlingit beliefs in everyone's eventual reincarnation. Thus the above reference indicates either that there were widely differing Tlingit reincarnation beliefs or that the mossy creatures are those who will be reborn in an unforeseeable future, whereas the ancestors with human forms are those who will seek immediate rebirth.)

The text does not make clear, says de Laguna, why or how 'Askadut left the land of the dead. 'Askadut, however, has to come back; that is a structural requirement of the narrative. 'Askadut can remember his life in the otherworld so clearly because he has been there only for a short period. One informant posed the issue in terms of desire: 'Askadut wanted very badly to come back to his family. According to another informant, his aunt (probably his father's sister, who plays a similar role in other narratives) was among the recent dead and helped to ferry him back. In any case 'Askadut followed the river and got back. Tired, he sat at the foot of a tree near the riverbank. Because the tree began to drip, he moved to another and soon found a dry one with a branch sticking out and a nice mossy place under it. He sat down leaning against the tree and fell asleep.

> He remained there for nine days. Each day the riverbank caved in, a little bit at a time, and he heard the splash of the mud and sand falling into the water. Soon it came close to his foot, and he thought, "I'll wait till it comes closer, and then I'll move away." But he couldn't move anymore. And then it was caving away almost under him, and he thought, "Well, wait till I fall down that one, then I'll climb out of there." And then it caved underneath him, and he fell down the bank into the water. And he heard someone say, "He's born already!" (*MSE,* 767–68)

De Laguna exposes beautifully the underlying symbolism based on informant associations. The river of the dead that 'Askadut crosses is also connected with the symbolism of birth and the amniotic fluid. The dripping tree that 'Askadut avoids is a *gunetkanayi* woman to whom he must not be reborn, and the dry tree is his sister. What appears to him as nine days is in reality nine months, "and the caving down each day of the bank was the baby changing his position in the mother's womb each month . . . and it was also his mother's labor. He fell down at birth, because in the old days women gave birth 'sitting on top of a hole.' Perhaps the mossy spot under the tree also represented the moss in this hole" into which the baby fell (*MSE,* 769).[80]

To return to the story: The women took the baby up, and when 'Askadut looked around for his mother, he saw instead his own sister. But his former mother, who was there, exclaimed: "Oh, my son came back! That's 'Askadut's spirit!" And the baby replied: "Yes that's me. My name is 'Askadut. I came back. You cried so much, and I heard my wife weeping, so I came back." His former wife recognized him by the cut or scar on his foot. 'Askadut reached for his wife with a smile. "But he was ashamed of his sister that he wouldn't suck at her breast, and they had to get a woman of a different tribe (sib [clan], in the opposite moiety) to suckle him" (*MSE,* 768).[81]

## ANIMAL AND HUMAN REINCARNATION: AN ETHICAL DILEMMA AMONG THE KWAKIUTL

A structural feature that makes Amerindian reincarnation especially interesting from an Indic viewpoint is that along with the many societies that have parallel cycles of reincarnation, human and animal, there are also cases of boundary crossings from one species to another, what I have labeled cross-species reincarnation. I will now give a detailed description of human-to-animal reincarnation and of "species blurring" from the locus classicus of Northwest Coast ethnography, the Kwakiutl.

According to a recent reading of Kwakiutl ethnography by Marie Mauze, the soul *(bexwune)* lies in the head. "Being an autonomous entity, separable from the body even in life, the soul watches over people during the day, and travels about the world at night," often causing dreams (RKI, 180). It is conceptualized as an immaterial entity, "smoke" or "shadow" that can dilate and expand. Weakness, madness, or similar states are interpreted as loss of soul. As in many cultures, the soul at death leaves the body and the funeral ceremony "raises the dead to the status of an ancestor" (RKI, 180). In addition to the "soul" the Kwakiutl believe in another entity, the "ghost" *('lâ'lenoq),* which is perceived as a noncorporeal replica of the body although constituted of the bones of ancestors. Consequently, bones are also believed to be a permanent bodily element, and at death they have to be properly treated because they account for the regeneration of the body. Hence salmon bones, Mauze says, are thrown back into the sea to produce more salmon. The body of any human or animal must also have a soul in order to form a complete being, "which is constituted by the conjunction of two autonomous principles: that of regeneration [bones] and that of animation [soul]" (RKI, 181).

The soul of a dead person travels to the world of animals at death before coming back to the human world. Mauze, following Boas, says that the souls of sea hunters go to the home of killer whales, land hunters to wolves; common people become owls, and twins become salmon (RKI, 181). Specially designated animals are in a sense human spirits. Humans in turn are animals "who have removed their masks and costumes to return to their human state."[82] Given this powerful ethical conception of species sentience it is not surprising that "Kwakiutl believe that animals and spirits lead lives that are exactly equivalent to that of humans. They live in Winter villages, perform dances, wear masks, marry, and perform all other acts that humans perform."[83] Stanley Walens, in an influential interpretation of Kwakiutl culture, adds: "Thus we discover that Kwakiutl consider the animals and spirits to live in worlds structured exactly like those of humans, with villages, houses, tribes, marriages and so forth"; this is also the case with a related group, the Heiltsuk, studied by Michael Harkin.[84] Mauze sums up the Kwakiutl notion of cross-species reincarnation thus: "It appears that in the Kwakiutl system of belief the soul of a human has to reach an animal realm and inhabit an animal in order to be reborn in the body of another human" (RKI, 182). Not all souls are reincarnated eventually as humans. A person who dies at sea has his or her soul relegated to the world of the sea otters who capture it. "The soul is then lost. Since it has been released in a 'foreign' world, that of fish and sea mammals, it cannot be reborn in the human world" (RKI, 182).

The soul sojourns in the world of animal spirits until the body is fully decomposed. Then it is free to be reincarnated in the individual's grandchild, thus skipping one generation, although this rule is occasionally violated. Sometimes the interval between death and reincarnation is very short. "The Kwakiutl thought of babies as ancestors who had returned among the living, an event usually presaged by dreams" (RKI, 182). Mauze adds, "What is important is that souls return to the common stock of souls of the *numaym,* the *numaym* being the basic social unit in Kwakiutl organization; its name stands for the 'people of the same kind'" (RKI, 183). Yet the "people of the same kind" are not only humans but also animals, producing for the Kwakiutl a religious and ethical puzzle, an aporia that I will now explore.

First, Mauze's data are borrowed from Boas, and the evidence that all humans become animals, although congenial to the position taken in this book, is not altogether clear. Boas did claim that ordinary people become owls, but then when owls die their souls become extinguished. Yet Hunt, Boas's main informant, says in a later text, "For the owls of men are not the souls, for the owls of men are only one side."[85] Matlock, commenting on this text, says that "the human being is associated with the owl only partially; the death of an owl may lead to the death of a person with whom it is associated, but this does not imply the extinction of a person."[86] He adds: "This leaves open the possibility that there is another spiritual part of the human being that is free to go on to the land of the dead and reincarnate in due course."[87] Most ethnographers agree, however, that twins are salmon reborn. There is the fascinating case of an Oowekeeno Indian, a twin, who remembered his former existence when as a salmon he was "cooked, canned and shipped far away."[88] And Boas mentions a woman who possessed a birthmark that corresponded to a wound that had been inflicted on her when she was a salmon.[89] If twins are salmon reborn, then when twins die, they must become salmon once again. Although this is the general rule, Boas mentions three cases in which twins are reborn as humans without a prior salmon incarnation.[90]

Twins, like shamans, have special powers that are dreaded, including the capacity to remember previous lives. To get at the significance of the salmon-twin equation one must imaginatively get under the skin of Kwakiutl culture, so to speak. Although a salmon could be an ancestral twin reborn, there is no way whereby one could identify any of the salmon that abound in the rivers as instances of previous twins. Within the Amerindian scheme of things this indeterminism is analogous to the Calvinist assertion that only the elect will be saved although there is no way to identify the elect, thereby posing problems of meaning that demand attempts at resolution. The Kwakiutl problem of meaning pertaining to salmon can be posed as follows: salmon is the most desired food, and Kwakiutl society could not exist without this food source. Yet a salmon could be a twin from one's own group; hence, there is no way one can know whether in eating a salmon one is eating an ancestor or not, and a specially dreaded one at that, in effect committing endoanthropophagy.

Salmon are not the only creatures being reincarnated. Sea hunters become killer whales, and land hunters, wolves, but again the processes of reincarnation are unclear in Boas's account. Perhaps Matlock has the correct answer: "Kwakiutl twins return to the salmon and hunters become the animals they pursue, while other persons become ghosts."[91] Additionally, on occasion a person could be born as his totem animal: "the title holder is always an avatar of a mythical ancestor, who was often other-than-human."[92] More significant is the ability of everyone in principle to engage in shamanic "transpeciation," that is, the capacity to take the form of animals. According to Harkin there are many stories of people in this region encountering animals and *becoming* those animals. "One basic understanding is that animals are 'really human' under the skin. These stories apply mostly, though not exclusively, to food species."[93] It therefore seems that the Kwakiutl form of cross-reincarnation coexists with the consistent blurring of species distinctions. Thus the animal-human homology among the Kwakiutl is a near literal one because an animal could once have been a human being and an ancestor, which means that in eating an animal one might in effect be eating an ancestor. The clearest example is that of salmon, a desired and desirable food. Let me deal with the manner in which this dilemma of endoanthropophagy is expressed, if not resolved, by the Kwakiutl in their famous "cannibal dance" performed during the Winter Ceremonial.

Franz Boas demonstrated the power of the animal-human homology in several places in his great work *The Social Organization and Secret Societies of the Kwakiutl Indians* and in his posthumous *Kwakiutl Ethnography*.[94] Thus, says Boas, animals existed before humans, and it was animals that were differentiated later into humans. Kwakiutl secret societies are for the most part named after animals, and like other Amerindians Kwakiutl represent animals in their ceremonial dances.[95] The Winter Ceremonial itself "was instituted when men had still the form of animals. . . . [T]he present ceremonial is a repetition of the ceremonial performed by the man animals."[96] The officers participating in it as well as their names derive from that origin myth.[97] In the Winter Ceremonial that primordial identity is affirmed: the distinction between humans and animals is consistently blurred, particularly in ritual enactments of transpeciation. For example, in one of the myths associated with the *hamatsa* dance to be described below, the protagonist gets the names of all four major animals—the loon, sea lion, seal, and whale—which in turn illustrates his affinity with the larger sentient order.[98] In this dance the human actor is often naked, that is, he is divested of human attributes in order to wear the mask and adopt the persona of the ancestral being whom he impersonates. Sometimes he dances in a squatting position to imitate carnivorous animals and then moves without much of a break into an upright posture like that of human beings or of ancestral or mythic beings, once again blurring species distinctions throughout the dance.

The hamatsa was based on an earlier ritual complex known as the *hamṡhamtses*, now disparaged as a women's dance. In this earlier ritual the protectors of the hamṡhamtses are all animals, and Boas, somewhat puzzled, asks "why . . . so many different animals may become protectors of the *hamṡhamtses*."[99] Thus the fundamental principle of species sentience affirmed in Kwakiutl ritual and belief can be expressed in the circular logic of transpeciation: animal = human = animal = human. It is impossible for cosmologies associated with species sentience to produce the categorical distinction between nature and culture, that universalized obsession of European thought.

Now to the ethical paradox: the killing of the animal is a necessity for physical survival for groups inhabiting a vast and sometimes inhospitable circumpolar region. The animal killed has to be reborn to replenish the food supply; and this is done through respectful behavior toward the animal and through the kinds of ritual acts mentioned earlier. But given the animal-human homology, one is eating a being that shares a physical and spiritual affinity with oneself. This means that meat has been transvalued, and eating it is a reverential act. But I think there is another component to the act of eating, and that pertains to guilt. Consider the rite in which the hunter throws a piece of the animal and asks its forgiveness. I interpret this act as motivated by the hunter's unconscious desire to perform an act of expiation for eating a closely related being. "Animals are willing to die for one reason: without death there can be no rebirth in the eternal cycle of life. Without death, animals and humans grow old, feeble, senile and powerless. They must die so that they can be reborn. Thus, an animal is willing to die; but it will let itself be killed only by those hunters or fishermen who, by promising to perform the correct rituals, ensure that the animals' process of reincarnation will not be disrupted."[100] The ethical paradox involved here is compounded for the Kwakiutl. Although not consciously recognized, consuming an animal is not only eating a being related species-wise to oneself. In some instances, especially in the case of salmon, one might be eating an ancestor, a member of one's own social group, the numaym, which in a fundamental sense is a circulating pool of souls.

How is this ethical dilemma of endoanthropophagy dealt with in Kwakiutl religious life? Early ethnographers from Boas on did recognize the existence of rebirth ideas among the Kwakiutl but did not give those ideas any priority, conditioned as these ethnographers were by their own cultural presuppositions. This criticism applies also to Irwin Goldman, who in his important work on Kwakiutl religion, *The Mouth of Heaven,* paid little attention to doctrines of rebirth.[101] Walens, by contrast, placed considerable emphasis on Kwakiutl rebirth eschatology, but he makes no reference to the ethical dilemma of eating one's ancestor associated with societies subscribing to cross-species reincarnation. My own prejudice is to examine this dilemma as it is expressed in the famed "cannibal dances" of the Kwakiutl performed during their Winter Ceremonial for Man Eater, whose major form is Baxbakualanuxsiwae, "Man Eater at the Mouth of the River."

In examining this ceremonial complex I employ primarily Boas's material, supplemented by Goldman's summaries. The analytical work of Goldman and Walens, although containing superb symbolic interpretations of Kwakiutl religion and cosmology, slants the ethnography away from my own interest in the ethical dilemma of endoanthropophagy.[102] I am also aware that the Winter Ceremonial, like other ceremonies of its class, is overdetermined and multivalent and cannot be straitjacketed into a single interpretation.[103] I am therefore not attempting to interpret the "cannibal dances" as a totality but to underscore a major symbolic strand enshrined therein in terms of my hypothesis regarding the Kwakiutl ethical dilemma of consuming animals that are in a fundamental sense one's own kin.

The Winter Ceremonial implores the ancestral spirits who lived in mythic times to bestow their power on present-day descendants. The myths deal with these spirits, and the ceremony recreates these myths in dramatic enactments. According to the ceremonial rules the nobility alone are permitted to participate; they drop their summer names and take on their winter names. With this ritual, says Boas, the whole social structure gets realigned: clan organization is temporarily suspended, and in its stead the actors are regrouped according to the spirits who have initiated them.[104] These actors form two principal divisions: the Sparrows *(quequtsa)* and the Seals *(meemqat)*.[105] I refer the reader to Boas and Goldman for the details of the organization of these two divisions; suffice it here to state that both "agree in giving highest rank to the class of man-eating spirits and their human dance impersonators."[106] There is a lot of creative improvisation in this society, with new songs and dances being constantly invented and replacing older ones.

The Winter Ceremonial involves the initiation of a novice into the realm of spirit ancestors in order for him to partake of the ancestors' power by being possessed by them. This power can be dangerous if not controlled; therefore, the task of those who have gone into the house of Man Eater, have been fully initiated, and have learned his secrets is to tame the novice and control the fearful power he has just acquired and to make the novice one of them (the *laxla*). The *laxla* themselves can renew their power by being possessed by Man Eater; they run into the woods, the domain of Man Eater; they have to be "captured" and tamed and brought into the orbit of the civil order. In contrast to them are the *wixsa,* those who have merely tasted of the power or who have only "leaned against the walls" of the house of Man Eater.[107]

Man Eater, according to myth, lives with his wife and children in the mountainous regions outside of normal human habitations. His house is located at the headwaters of the rivers at the North End of the World. Goldman neatly summarizes Boas:

> Man Eater moves restlessly about the earth driven by his insatiable appetite for human flesh. An entourage that includes three categories of women assists him. Qominoqa is usually his wife. Kinqalatlala is a slave. A woman who is actually human is deeply rooted in the floor of his house. The women [except the Rooted Woman] are his provisioners, bringing him victims and corpses. Others in his entourage are Grizzly Bear, a vicious and fearless killer of men; Raven who feasts on men's eyes; Hoxhoq the Great Crane, who devours men's brains; and a humanoid male called Haialikilatl (Benefactor), all but the last in the general category of devourers. The chief devourer is Baxbakualanuxsiwae, whose insatiable appetite is depicted by the image of mouths all over his body.[108]

Whether it be the hamatsa or the earlier hamšhamtses, the myth of origin of the dance is similar.[109] According to this myth the chief, Nanwaqawe, warns his sons out hunting mountain goats to be careful of Grizzly Bear and Man Eater because Nakwaxdax tribesmen are disappearing mysteriously, presumably eaten by these devourers. The sons meet Grizzly Bear, fight and kill him, and then reach the house of Man Eater, which they recognize from the red smoke emanating from it. They go into the house, and there, rooted on the floor and unable to move, is a woman. She agrees to help them kill Man Eater by digging a trap-pit, covering it with boards, and filling it with hot coals. Man Eater, with his multiple mouths, arrives in a state of excitement, uttering his cry of eating, *hap*. He then retires into his secret room. Great Raven and Giant Crane, his attendants, come out and dance, and when they have finished, Man Eater comes out with his female attendants and dances. The dancing Man Eater steps on the fire pit, and one of the young men pulls out the boards. Man Eater falls in and dies. The women also die with him but not Crane and Raven, who only faint. "The youths seize the ritual ornaments and paraphernalia, the masks, the whistles, and the cannibal pole" and return home.[110]

The youths come back, bringing their father, Nanwaqawe, with them. The Rooted Woman teaches him the Man Eater ritual, the names and songs of Man Eater and his associates, and then reveals herself as Nanwaqawe's own daughter. The father wants to rescue the daughter but cannot cut deep into her roots for fear of killing her. The daughter advises the father to return home and institute the hamatsa dance.[111]

Goldman says that the killing of the Man Eater is depicted only in the myth; it is never enacted in the rituals of the hamatsa.

> Since the *hamatsa* [dancer] is a human being, he is literally a cannibal. His state of being is, nevertheless, ambiguous. He is human, but he is also mad, and possessed by the Man Eater spirit; and it is the spirit that is the devourer of men. To sustain this conception of *hamatsa* dancer as a spirit being, he is made to vomit every trace of the human flesh he has swallowed. In one sense the vomiting signifies, ritually, the miracle of resurrection. At the same time, the human being must be free of the taint of cannibalism.[112]

Goldman's interpretation is based mostly on Boas's description of the final sequence of the hamatsa, where a novice is being initiated:

> After biting persons, and particularly after eating slaves or bodies, the *hamatsa* must observe a great many rules. Immediately after they have eaten a corpse, the *heliga* ["healers," the servants of the *hamatsa*] brings them salt water, of which they drink great quantities in order to produce

> vomiting. If they do not vomit as many pieces as they have swallowed, their excrements are examined in order to ascertain if all the pieces of human flesh have passed the body. The bones of the body that they have eaten are kept for four months. They are kept alternatively for four days in their bedrooms on the north side of the house where the sun does not strike them, and four days under rocks in the sea. Finally they are thrown into the sea.[113]

Boas also describes the elaborate taboos and restrictions the hamatsa dancer has to observe, including abstinence from regular work and sexual intercourse. These abstinences can go on for about a year or even up to four years among some groups. The reason, says Boas, is that during the ceremonial season the hamatsa seems to have forgotten the ordinary ways of living, and these have to be learned anew. Like any other initiate he is isolated from the social world until such time as the spirit of the hamatsa has been fully civil-ized.

Let me now cite a few ritual texts that Boas collected. These will give the reader a vivid sense of the hamatsa's craving for flesh. Even though Boas's description of the hamatsa dances is based on informant statements and references in myth to older times, it gives a sense of the depth of Kwakiutl involvement in anthropophagy and its almost literal purgation. In his description of the very first hamatsa dance, with its formalized and elaborate seating arrangements, Boas says that the novice-initiate is possessed by Baxbakualanuxsiwae and is obsessed with the "violent desire of eating men." Here is a typical sequence: the cannibal "attacks every one upon whom he can lay hands. He bites pieces of flesh out of the arms and chests of people." And Boas adds: "In olden times, when the *hamatsa* was in a state of ecstasy, slaves were killed for him, whom he devoured."[114] Boas exaggerates here because he cites only two cases of informant recollections of anthropophagy from the past. In one case a slave was killed and the flesh distributed among the hamatsa and other dancers representing man-eating beings; in the other a woman slave was killed and eaten by the hamatsa himself.[115] Boas also says that in ancient times pieces of dried human flesh were "devoured" from corpses that were draped around trees (the traditional funeral procedure). Once again these seem, from his own description, highly ritualized procedures, quite unlike the Eurocentric perception of these as acts of "devouring." It is true that Man Eater himself is a devourer; but "devouring," when it is expressed in formalized ritual dances, is controlled from the very start. In the very first dance described by Boas the hamatsa is "looking for human flesh to eat," and this hunger is expressed in the act of actually biting those around or, more likely, in imitating the act of biting.[116] Many of the songs express the anthropophagous nature of Man Eater now possessing the hamatsa dancer, as for example the following, recorded by Boas:

1. HAMATSA SONG COMPOSED RECENTLY
I am going around the world eating everywhere with Baxbakualanuxsiwae.
I give you no time to escape from me when I go with Baxbakualanuxsiwae.
I am at the center of the world; for me Baxbakualanuxsiwae is crying
*hap.* . . .[117]

2. HAMATSA SONG OF THE LAUITSIS
I went all around the world to find food.
I went all around the world to find human flesh.
I went all around the world to find human heads.
I went all around the world to find corpses.

3. SECRET SONG OF THE HAMATSA WHO CARRIES A CORPSE
Now I am going to eat.
My face is ghastly pale.
I shall eat what is given to me by Baxbakualanuxsiwae.

4. FEAST SONG IN HONOR OF HAMATSA
I came to your dancing house to eat my fill.
It does not matter if your fire hurts me, and if I vomit all kinds of food that you set before us in your dancing house—you to whom everybody goes to get food.[118]

Boas shows that the same preoccupations are present in the songs of the hamŝhamtses that the hamatsa ritual displaced. In the ideal typical hamŝhamtses dance that Boas reconstructs the Man Eater has a large uvula, which the Kwakiutl thinks represents his voracity.

As Walens says, the metaphors and symbolic representations of eating and vomiting are endemic to Kwakiutl ritual life. Unfortunately, Walens, in his influential interpretation of Kwakiutl religious symbolism, sees vomiting as an expression and symbolic elaboration of the Kwakiutl concern with food scarcity and the vomit itself as a symbol of fertility that has pleasant connotations for them, even though he cannot get any informant statements to substantiate the latter assertion.[119] I am much more sympathetic to Goldman's interpretation of these symbols as depicting both a purgation and a "resurrection," a symbolic representation of devouring death and resurgent life, even though I think that Goldman's interpretation is slanted in a Christological direction and that he does not give a satisfactory explanation of what he calls "the taint of cannibalism," the powerful mimesis of eating human flesh. Boas's account shows dramatically that the anthropophagous act is inextricably related to the act of vomiting. A noxious substance that has been mimetically ingested has to be thrown out and the dancer "healed" by the *heliga.* Other contexts also suggest that vomiting is primarily an act of purgation, not an expression of an uncertain food supply. For example, in one dance of the Winter Ceremonial, the *mamaqa,* or "thrower," has within him a disease-giving object represented in a worm. "[The mamaqa] almost collapses, and tries to rid himself of the disease bringing object by vomiting. . . . [A]fter prolonged efforts he vomits the worm. At once he is hale and well and proceeds in the dance."[120] And when we move north to the Yup'ik (Eskimo) of Nelson Island, vomit clearly represents the antithesis of communal sharing, "the ultimate antisocial food experience," exactly as it is with the Kwakiutl.[121] The cannibal dances and the symbols of insatiable hunger, the distorted faces of dancers in anguished orality that Walens describes in great detail, act out or otherwise represent the irresolvable aporia of consuming one's own kind that lies at the heart of Kwakiutl unconscious ideation.[122] The cannibal dance that precedes the purgation is, in my reading, a mimetic enactment that has its psychic roots in the "repetition compulsion" and "the return of the repressed"—in this case the unconscious dread that one might have eaten an animal ancestor, one's own kin, a member of one's numaym.

In this eschatology three doctrines converge: those of cross-reincarnation, of transpeciation, and of humans as originary animals. Human beings kill animals, and humans must replenish those they have killed because these animals could be one's own ancestors or transformed humans. Man Eater, with his multiple mouths and his insatiable appetite for human flesh, is a mythic representation of the idea that humans are in fact anthropophagous and that this is a "normal" condition. Man Eater himself has a universal presence in Kwakiutl texts; they depict him as being in every area of the world, sometimes connecting the upper world with the human one through his "cannibal pole." Possessed by the spirit of Man Eater, the hamatsa dancer acts out and abreacts on behalf of the group the dilemma of eating one's own kind and the guilt that it entails, in the manner of Lévi-Strauss's sorcerer.[123]

The group as a whole is conspicuously present at the conclusion of the Winter Ceremonial. After he has been "tamed," that is, after his anthropophagous desires have been brought under control, the hamatsa and his associates are fed by the people, by which Boas means, I think, the community as a whole. By this act the group participates vicariously in the taming of the hamatsa and reincorporates him into the civil order by feeding him as if he were a child. Then the tribe reassembles at the house of the *yewixila,* "those who lean against [the cannibal]," that is, those charged with taming men possessed by the cannibal spirit. Then the house of ceremonies is ritually closed to all until the next winter—except for the hamatsa himself, who must remain in the house observing the taboos mentioned earlier and ritually cleanse himself of the pollution of eating human flesh, gradually preparing to join the human community outside.[124]

Where in my analysis is the space for what Goldman calls "devouring death" and "resurgent life"? I have shown that Man Eater is more than a representation of death; he is the dark side of Kwakiutl Man. I have already noted that replenishment of what humans have destroyed is done through the formal ritual procedures following a hunt; but the collective Winter Ceremonial, as Goldman shows, repeats this in more elaborate fashion. Man Eater is tamed in order to be made the giver of life and the one who replenishes what has been depleted during the year. It must be remembered that Man Eater is a male, and the hamatsa dance is a male dance. This is because hunting and salmon fishing are basically male activities; that which Man Eater destroys he must restore. In the myth Man Eater has women associates; this parallels the real-life scenario where women butcher the salmon that the men have caught.

How in the hamatsa ritual does Man restore the lives he has taken or undo his act of necessary destruction? Adopting a psychoanalytic perspective on symbolism might help here. Man must create new life to replenish that which he has destroyed, although in the actual human society it is Woman who physically creates new life through her womb. But this normal procedure is possible only if Man does his part in restoring the lives he has taken. Yet Man lacks the rebirth orifice to create new life. He must therefore achieve this through what I, in the spirit of Freud, would call the "displacement of orifices," as for example, when in mythic thought males sometimes give birth through an orifice such as the anus. Such displacements are based on the processes of symbol formation that one associates with the dream-work. In this case the orifice that the hamatsa uses for replenishment is the one that he uses to vomit the flesh he has eaten. Thus the mouth has a double symbolic function: it is the orifice that purges the guilt of eating a fellow being; it is also the orifice that replenishes what was lost.

Man then is the guilty figure; it is he who is the real killer. It is in the context of the male-centered nature of the hamatsa that Rooted Woman of the Man Eater myth makes sense. The Rooted Woman is central to the myth and may be, as Goldman suggests, indicative of the "mythological setting to marriage." But to me this is not self-evident. It is true that at marriage a woman stays rooted in her own matrilineal line, whereas the husband comes from the outside and marries into it. However, the Kwakiutl are not rigidly matrilineal. The rootedness of the woman in the house of Man Eater gives expression to an ideal ethical scenario. The ideal woman in this conception is rooted to the house, to a life that does not entail the destruction of one's own kind. Man Eater's wife and female assistants are those who violate the ideal scheme of things and assist him in fishing and hunting. In other words *some* women participate in killing, but for men it is a key vocation. In my interpretation the conversion of the earlier male hamšhamtses dance into a female one indicates a shift that occurred in Kwakiutl society when women, who ideally should have abstained from killing, began more fully to participate in it. Rooted Woman is the woman who does not kill; yet paradoxically she is the one who must help kill Man Eater, the consumer of life, because the killing of the killer is a precondition for replenishment, which in everyday life is the role of the woman. Man Eater must die that women can reproduce those killed by him. In conformity to the spirit of matrilineal kinship, the actual killing is done by the woman's brothers, who steal his paraphernalia and thus become the heirs of Man Eater. Yet Man Eater's death cannot be final either, according to the Kwakiutl scheme of things, where death must be followed by a rebirth. The killing of Man Eater releases his spirit, which now lives and possesses the men. It is therefore not Man Eater himself but his spirit that is invoked at the commencement of the Winter Ceremonial. Man Eater is then reborn in all of us during the Winter Ceremonial, and this destructive spirit must be tamed and domesticated so that those ancestor-animals who were killed, owing to human necessity, might be reborn.[125]

## CONCLUDING REMARKS

Beginning with West African examples I have selectively presented descriptions of rebirth beliefs from small-scale societies found in different parts of the world to give the reader a feeling for the richness, range, and spread of these eschatologies. I strongly doubt whether these eschatologies were "influenced" by Indian religions, although it is certainly possible for Amerindians at least to have been connected with Siberian religions that in turn might have developed in the vast Eurasian region, if not a specifically Indian one. In the next chapter of this book I will bring some order to this material by constructing a topographical model of a rebirth eschatology that deliberately reduces the complexity of the empirical cases presented earlier. I will manipulate this model, or experiment with it, in order to produce the structural transformations that lead to the Buddhist and Greek models of rebirth. Further, the use of a model will permit me to speak of a "rebirth eschatology" in general without always referring to specific examples. The varieties of rebirth eschatologies presented earlier are not equally relevant for comparison with the Greek and Indic material. As the title of this book suggests, it is Amerindian rebirth of the Inuit and Northwest Coast Indians that is directly relevant because these groups believed, as did the Greeks and the Buddhists, in the animal-human connection, including the idea that animals could be reborn as humans and vice versa, that is, the doctrine of cross-reincarnation, which is almost always associated with the powerful ethical belief in "species sentience." Nevertheless, the African and Melanesian reincarnation theories will often appear in our discussions even though they are not central to the experimental operations performed in this work.

# 3 THE IMAGINARY EXPERIMENT AND THE BUDDHIST IMPLICATIONS

Hands, do what you're bid:
  Bring the balloon of the mind
That bellies and drags in the wind
    Into its narrow shed.
      —W. B. Yeats,
      "The Balloon of the Mind"

## THE TRANSFORMATION OF THE REBIRTH ESCHATOLOGY

The idea of scale is useful because historians agree that religions such as Buddhism, with their "karmic eschatologies," emerged during India's "second urbanization"(the first of course associated with the Indus valley civilizations). During this period small communities were linked to each other by trade networks and the imperialist designs of emergent empires. Similar, although not identical, social changes were occurring in the small Greek city-states, although the scale of change was not as great as in India. Avoiding terms like *high* and *low, primitive* and *civilized, great* and *little, literate* and *preliterate, class* and *classless,* and other such dichotomies, I will construct transformational models to deliberately reduce the rich complexity of the empirical world and to narrow down and then highlight the critical differences among the various rebirth theories presented in this book.

Initially I will flesh out the model sketched at the beginning of this study (see fig. 1). Figure 3 will also ignore for the moment the differences among the Igbo, Trobriander, and Amerindian examples and focus instead on some of the common features of rebirth eschatologies in all of the societies presented above.

Let me outline a life trajectory of a hypothetical person in this scheme. Birth transfers the individual from some otherworld to the visible human world. Rites of passage at birth assist this transition, helping one to over-

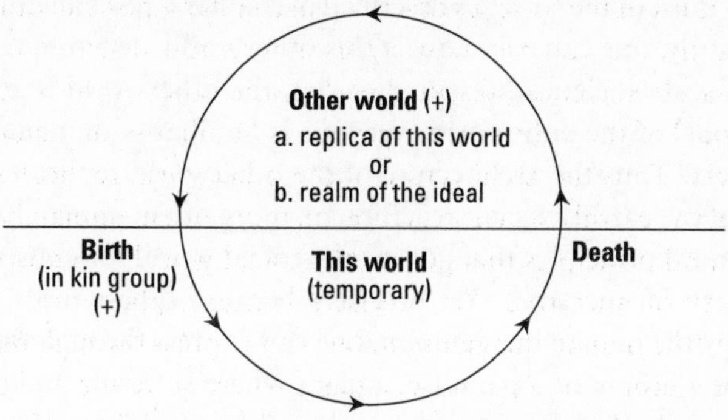


Figure 3. Some common topographical features of rebirth eschatologies wherein there is no ethicization. According to this scheme, there are standard techniques for identifying a neonate. In addition, rebirth memories are possible for ordinary folk.

come the perils of the soul (wherever such an idea exists) and of conception and fostering the nurture and protection of the fetus and the mother. The neonate is born into a family and a kin group for whom he or she is an ancestor returned. During the course of the individual's life, rites of passage assist transitions into critically important roles—for example at puberty and marriage. Each of these transitions, as ethnographers have consistently pointed out, can be viewed as a symbolic death and rebirth or, in Robert Hertz's words, as an "exclusion" followed by an "inclusion."[1] When real death occurs, funeral rites serve to transfer the individual once again into the invisible world of the ancestors. We can now posit an important feature of this otherworld, namely, its essential temporality, because a person must eventually leave this otherworld for the human one, and this must go on and on. In fact the only enduring thing is the rebirth cycle itself, which in principle at least can go on forever. There is little ethnographic data to indicate whether the temporal character of the otherworld and the perpetual recurrence of rebirth cycles are given existential meaning and significance in the eschatologies presented earlier, as they are in the Indic idea of samsara or in the Greek ideas of the processes of rebirth, variously conceptualized as *metacosmesis, metensomatosis,* or *metempsychosis.*

The otherworld may not exist, however, in a few of the eschatologies examined in this work, among some Greek Pythagoreans and the Druze;

and in some of the Amerindian ones it might on occasion be bypassed. However, most of the societies described in chapter 2 posit an otherworld. Consequently, one can ask: how is this otherworld structured? In all of the small-scale societies presented earlier, the otherworld is structured on the model of the only world everyone is familiar with, namely, one's own society. Thus the architecture of the otherworld replicates the key features of the earthly social structure, or, more often, human beings utilize structural principles that govern the social world for constructing a new society of ancestors. Yet precisely because otherworlds are constructed by the human imagination, one can express through them one's wishes for a utopia or a paradise, a place where suffering and privation are eliminated. "It is or can be the realm of the ideal," says Hertz.[2] The Trobriand eschatology defined by Tomwaya Lakwabulo is a good empirical approximation of this paradisiacal ideal; a few of the Northwest Coast societies come close to it in their idea of a land with abundant food.

Although the idea of a world of ancestors (paradisiacal or otherwise) is omnipresent, this is not so with the idea of a hell or a similar place of punishment. Occasionally there is a place where violators of taboos and those guilty of heinous acts such as incest and sorcery are confined, but there is no hell to which the bad are condemned. Most often, as with the Igbo, such persons are punished by being denied a human reincarnation. Entry into the otherworld rarely depends on the ethical nature of one's this-worldly behavior. With the exceptions already noted, entry into that otherworld is a privilege available to all, and this entry is achieved by the correct performance of the funeral rites.

I do not want to imply that small-scale societies have no ethics. On the contrary, their social morality might be complex, even stringent, but except in a very few cases this morality does not affect the fate of the soul after death. Malinowski put it rather bluntly in respect to Trobriand reincarnation: "There are no moral ideals of recompense or punishment embodied in their reincarnation theory" (*FPP*, 44). It is certainly the case that were I found guilty of offenses such as adultery or theft, I would be punished by a variety of punitive or restitutive sanctions meted out by some duly constituted legal authority in my group; but it is rare that I would expect to be punished *again,* in the otherworld, for these offenses against public morality. This does not imply that some lack a religious evaluation of moral action. The Northwest Coast Amerindians and the Igbo, as well as other West African groups, for example, have agencies such as ancestors or deities who will punish (and reward) in the here and now those who have violated (and conformed to) certain moral rules.

Here the ancestors punish transgressors in a manner that parallels decision making in secular courts. As with secular courts there is an immediacy of punishment, but this does not affect the person's entry into the world of the ancestors after death. Further, insofar as these ancestors afflict malefactors with illness and other misfortunes, they act, as Simon Ottenberg says, very much like the individual's conscience, punishing a person for the violation of the patriarchal values of the group.[3] In religions such as Buddhism and Christianity one can have all of this; yet there is in addition the critical feature of *delayed* punishments or rewards that are meted out only after death. In the rebirth eschatologies that I have discussed, the absence of such consequences means that the otherworld into which one enters after death is valued positively, and so is the ensuing rebirth on earth. This positive attitude is expressed in our topographical models in terms of plus signs.

By contrast, in religions like Buddhism and Christianity violation of a moral precept of virtually any sort implies ipso facto a violation of a religious precept for which I will surely be punished in the next world. Similarly, I will be rewarded for the good I do. I use the term *ethicization* to conceptualize the processes whereby a morally right or wrong action becomes a religiously right or wrong action that in turn affects a person's destiny after death. Ethicization deals with a thoroughgoing religious evaluation of morality that entails delayed punishments and rewards quite unlike the immediate or this-worldly compensations meted out by deities or ancestors.

I have already shown that Amerindian religions reflect profound ethical concerns in such beliefs as the interdependence of all species' existence, the value of the physical environment, and so forth. Yet these religions do not hold that their social morality is anything but social. By contrast, in the so-called historical religions or, as Jaspers puts it, those religions that developed with the "Axial Age" during the sixth century B.C.E. and after, this secular social morality is redefined as an intrinsic religious morality that has profound implications for society, culture, and the conscience.[4] Christians and Buddhists generally think that the morality expressed in the Ten Commandants or the Five Precepts is of a truly unique nature. Quite the contrary: the moral rules enshrined in them are very conventional for the most part and found virtually everywhere in small-scale societies because such rules are required for the minimal operation of an orderly society. Their unconventionality lies not in their substance but in their ethicization. It is ethicization that produced an important break or turn in the history of religion.

Because ethicization in my definition entails the conversion of a moral code into a religious code that in turn affects a person's after-death destiny, one must now ask whether such a process is reflected in the ethnographic material presented in chapter 2. The answer is that although some religious evaluation of moral action exists, it is not systematically carried through into life after death. On the other hand, in Buddhism and the great monotheisms virtually all morality is by definition religious and implicated in otherworldly recompense.

Nevertheless, a few societies in my sample exhibit what I would call "occasional ethicization" in respect to the rewards and punishments meted out in the otherworld if not in respect to the human world into which individuals will eventually be reborn. Perhaps the clearest example of ethicization in any rebirth eschatology comes from the Tlingit recorded by Frederica de Laguna, which I have already discussed in some detail. We noted that the afterworld of these Tlingit consists of three "layers": *k'iwa'a,* the heavenly abode of those who have died in war; the abode of those who die normally, located in a space near earth itself; and a "dog heaven" (actually a kind of "hell") located beneath the earth for those who have done wrongs. (According to some Tlingit groups "Raven's home" takes the place of the dog heaven [*MSE,* 772].) It is in relation to the dog heaven that compensatory ethics seem to surface. One informant told de Laguna that the dog heaven is the abode of those who commit suicide, whereas another claimed, "The people who get killed in war or in accident go to the real khiiwwaa'âa, way up above and the spirits are seen in the Northern Lights playing shinny. . . . Then between them and the earth, right on the clouds, the clouds going all around with them—this is where the dog spirits go, and they live among the dogs, suicides, and witch doctors [(witches?); the witch doctors] who are killed go to kheetl-khii-waa'âa," where they will live among the dogs (*MSE,* 771).[5] Others said that those who wasted food by killing what they did not need, especially small animals and little birds, went to dog heaven (*MSE,* 771). Some also believed that those who went to dog heaven could not be reborn on earth. Another remarked, "It's almost like the Bible, what they used to teach the young child when he was just learning to talk. They would say that bad people who kill a man, or who steal, will go to Dog Heaven . . . Just the bad people. That's why people are afraid to do anything wrong. . . . I'm surprised when I start to read the Bible. It's just what my grandma taught me" (*MSE,* 777).

In most of these cases only special instances of wrongs are listed, except for the last informant, who tended to include in the dog heaven all violators of social morality. As far as the good heaven is concerned, most informants thought it was a place for warriors who died in battle. Yet this good heaven of the warriors has also been influenced by Christianity, according to de Laguna.

> Since K'iwai'a is sometimes confused with the Christian Heaven, we might note that one of my informants did dream of her dead daughter in Heaven. This occurred on Easter Sunday, about a year after the girl's death. In her dream, Heaven appeared as a beautiful garden where the daughter reported that each good person has his or her own flower garden, the success of which depends upon the moral conduct of living relatives. . . . Every day they open a big book in which writing appears of itself to record all the bad things done by the living. (*MSE,* 777)

The Christian influence on Tlingit beliefs lends some support to my hypothesis that systematic ethicization is associated with "universalizing religions." Although the *otherworlds* of the societies I have discussed tend to be occasionally ethicized, it is rare that ethicization extends to rebirth in the *human world.* The Qiqiqtamiut Inuit of Belcher Island tend to exclude in a kind of negative reaction the immoral from rebirth in the human world, very much like the Tlingit and the Igbo. "Those who have led exemplary lives are thought to be assured that their name spirits will be conferred on new societal members. Those who have led opprobrious lives or who have died by violence are thought not to be recycled—for the reason that any bearer of the name will live a life of misfortune."[6]

In this case what constitutes an "exemplary" or "opprobrious" life is not spelled out, nor is there any specification of the moral rules involved. By contrast, Rasmussen's inland Inuit of eastern Canada seem to have a concept of punishment and reward that echoes the Indic notion of karma, at least as far as rebirth in the human world is concerned: "They are very little concerned about the idea of death; they believe that all men are born again, the soul passing on continually from one form of life to another. Good men return to earth as men, but evil doers are reborn as beasts, and in this way the earth is replenished, for no life once given can ever be destroyed."[7] In my view if these Inuit pushed their ideas of ethical recompense further, they would have invented their own version of a karma theory. But there is not enough ethnographic evidence to show that they did. Instead there is evidence that surrounding groups did not think animals were a lower form of existence; therefore, it could well have been that Rasmussen's Inuit were influenced by the ethics of the missionaries in their midst. Whether or not these Inuit were influenced by the missions, the example does illustrate the rare instance in which a rebirth eschatology develops into something like a karmic one.

Sometimes it is an individual rather than the group who gives a strong ethical slant to rebirth. Thus John, one of Mills's Gitksan informants, appears to reinvent some Greek and Indic notions of purification through the rebirth process. "Have you ever asked *why* there is reincarnation? It is a purification process. You bring back with you the good and the bad. It is like forging gold. In each life the other metals get burned off until there is pure gold" (CWC, 400). But John's theory of purification remains an idiosyncratic one: there is no conception of otherworldly rewards and punishments in his scheme.

## EMERGENCE OF THE KARMIC ESCHATOLOGY

When ethicization is systematically introduced into any rebirth eschatology, that rebirth eschatology must logically transform itself into a karmic eschatology. To put it differently: when ethicization occurs, the topographical model sketched in figure 3 must change into the model in figure 4. I will deal later with the historical conditions that brought about ethicization. For now I spell out in some detail the *logically expectable* changes or transformations that emerge with the introduction of ethicization into the ideal type or topographical model of the rebirth eschatology.

1. With ethicization morally good or bad actions are systematically converted into religiously good or bad actions. Inasmuch as any social morality must punish those who commit wrong and reward those who conform, so must a religious morality. Implicit in these notions of reward and punishment are such ideas as religious merit (the Buddhist *punya karma*) and "sin" (or the Buddhist *papa karma*). That is, the consequences of the rights and wrongs for which I am being rewarded or punished can be conceptualized for present purposes as "merit" and "sin."
2. A purely social morality is concerned with the earthly existence of human beings, but that must change drastically with ethicization. I might well be punished here and now for the wrongs I commit, or I might suffer the pangs of conscience; but beyond this, *religious rewards and punishments must extend to the whole eschatological sphere through the operation of what*

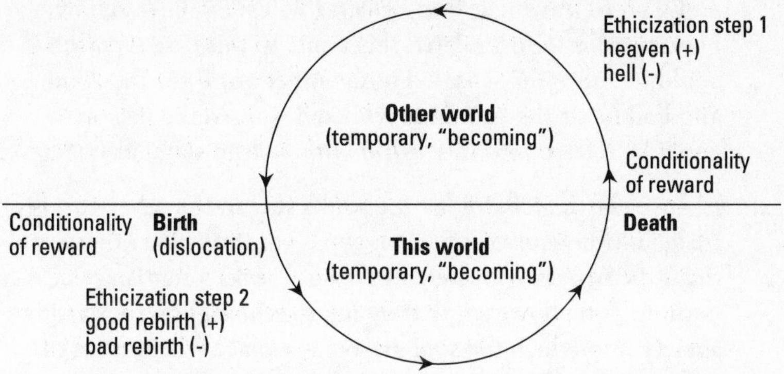


Figure 4. Karmic eschatology (ethicized rebirth eschatology). In this scheme, no salvation is possible, and nirvana and mokṣa occur outside the rebirth cycle. There are no standard techniques for identifying a neonate, nor are rebirth memories possible except for extraordinary individuals.

*I call the principle of the conditionality or contingency of reward.* Let me explain what I mean by this. In the rebirth topography (fig. 3) the transfer to the otherworld depends on the proper performance of the funeral rites. But when there is ethicization, entry to the otherworld must be *conditional,* depending on the ethical nature of one's this-worldly actions. When ethicization occurs, one cannot say that a person who has committed wrong can unconditionally enter the otherworld.

3. What then is the logical effect of the principle of the conditionality of reward on the structure of that otherworld? The otherworld must also be transformed into a world of retribution and reward. There can no longer be a single place for those who have done good and those who have done bad. The otherworld must minimally split into two, a world of retribution ("hell") and a world of reward ("heaven"). Heavens and hells have to be invented in any ethicized eschatology, and we see them in religions such as Buddhism, Christianity, and Islam. This crucial topographical transformation is *step 1* in the ethicization process; the "occasional ethicization" mentioned earlier stops for the most part at this point. Step 1 of ethicization can be represented in plus and minus signs, as I have done in figure 4. It is therefore possible to have a system of rewards and punishments in the otherworld

and then to leave it at that, which I will show later is how Platonic rebirth formulated this issue. In this case a person could be fully compensated in the otherworld for the good and bad he or she had done while alive; then the person could be reborn into this world with a clean slate, as it were.

4. In any rebirth eschatology the soul's stay in the otherworld is by definition temporary, or on some occasions the otherworld might be bypassed entirely as the soul seeks a human reincarnation. Note, however, that owing to ethicization the earthly society into which the soul arrives is a place where ideas of sin, merit, and the contingency of reward have already been developed. Therefore when ethicization is systematically pursued, there is a critical step 2, which requires that the next rebirth also be ethically conditioned. This conditioning inevitably takes into account one's actions in the *preceding* life. In other words the same principle of the contingency of reward that operated in respect to the otherworld must, in the context of systematic ethicization, also operate in respect to a person's rebirth in this world. This means that the human world into which one is born must also split into a good rebirth and a bad one, which can, once again, be topographically represented in plus and minus signs as in figure 4. Thus the human world into which the individual is reborn also becomes—in a kind of "protokarma" theory—a world of retribution and reward as a result of the second movement of ethicization. In principle and in practice step 2 of ethicization could exist independently of step 1. I will refer later to eschatologies in which the soul at death simply bypasses the otherworld and is immediately reborn in this world and is punished and rewarded for ethically relevant actions committed in the previous life.

5. To continue with our argument regarding step 2 of ethicization: If the person is assigned a good or bad rebirth that depends on the quality of his or her moral actions in a previous existence, then any prediction of the person's reincarnated status is rendered doubtful. One can no longer guarantee that a person will be reborn into his or her own lineage or family or kin group; there is a *dis-location* consequent to the person's rebirth that, rather than being based on kinship affiliations, is determined by and commensurate with his or her load of sin or

merit. Further, the continuation of group identity so significant in small-scale societies is ruptured; so is it with gender identity. Rebirth into the same group, gender, or location is possible but *not expectable* in general. Associated with this break in expectations is another transformational feature: the individual now reborn cannot be the same person he or she was in previous existence. The new persona is based on the load of sin and merit acquired in the individual's previous incarnation. This is easily illustrated from Buddhist societies where people claim that they could be born anywhere in their known world, depending on their good or bad karma. Let me give an example from a Pali text from the sixth century (translated, or transcreated, into Sinhala in the fourteenth century and available to monks and laypeople right down to our own times).

The story is about a female ascetic who, having achieved nirvana in around the second century B.C.E. in Sri Lanka, recollects some of her past existences:

> In former times I fell from human estate and was reborn as a hen. In this state of existence my head was cut off by a hawk. I was reborn at Rajagaha [Ganges valley], retired from the world, and became a wandering nun, and was reborn in the stage of the First Trance. Passing from that state of existence, I was reborn in the household of a treasurer. In but a short time I passed from that state of existence and was reborn as a young sow. Passing from that state of existence, I was reborn at Suvannabhumi [Burma, in a royal household]; passing from that state of existence, I was reborn at Benares; passing from that state of existence, I was reborn at Kavira Port [South India, in the household of a mariner]; passing from that state of existence, I was reborn at Anuradhapura [Sri Lanka, in the household of a nobleman]; passing from that state of existence, I was reborn in Bhokkanta village [in south Sri Lanka].[8]

6. In some rebirth eschatologies several ancestral spirits can be incarnated in the body of the neonate, particularly if the neonate belongs to an influential group. Alternatively, there could be double or multiple "souls," as with the Amerindian groups discussed earlier. With ethicization and the development of individual moral responsibility these features must necessarily drop out of the eschatology. The reincarnated person is a single individual who is responsible for his or her own ethically meaningful actions, but these actions in turn have the effect of changing the very character and life trajectory of that reincar-

nated individual. Thus the compensatory ethics associated with ethicization state that I am morally responsible for what I did in my past existence, yet that very responsibility means that I am also a different person. Buddhism carries this expectable logic to its extreme: here individuality is created without the need for naming and other devices.

7. Once reborn into a world where an ethicized morality already exists, individuals must continue in their life trajectory, doing good or bad, acquiring sin and merit. Then at death they are pushed once again into the otherworld and the cycle keeps going. Thus, ethicization of a rebirth eschatology, pushed to its logical extreme, connects one lifetime with another in a continuing series of ethical links. When this happens, a concomitant epistemological shift takes place: *it appears to those who live in these societies that rebirth is not a thing in itself but a product of the ethical nature of one's actions.* Rebirth cannot be divorced from ethics; it looks as if it is generated *from* ethics. Translated into Buddhist terms this means that the karma theory has fully developed, and it is karma that fuels the rebirth cycle known as samsara. In other words, if ethicization is carried out to embrace the whole eschatological sphere constituting the otherworld (or -worlds), as well as the human world into which one is reborn, and if this is followed through into finite or infinite rebirth cycles, then one will have created a theory like that of karma. Furthermore, this theory of impersonal and lawlike ethical compensations and rewards (or karma) cannot give primary consideration to *immediate* punishment. That is, I cannot be punished for the wrong I do now in this very same existence without converting the karmic eschatology back into a rebirth eschatology. The logical effect of any impersonal ethical law that punishes or rewards me straightaway for what I have done empties heavens and hells and good and bad rebirths of any ethical significance. For that reason immediate karmic punishment is rare in Indic religions except for especially heinous sins, and even these must be expiated *again* in the life after death.

This then is the "imaginary experiment." I have constructed a topographical model (figure 3) based on existent rebirth eschatologies, and I say that when ethicization is introduced into that model in two movements (steps 1 and 2), it gets transformed into another topographical model, which I have called the "karmic eschatology" (figure 4). Thus the karmic eschatology is derived from the experimental manipulation of the rebirth eschatology. The success of this operation depends on whether the rebirth topography I have constructed is, to use Weber's phrase, "objectively possible," that is, whether the conditions stipulated in the model violate or contradict empirical features of existent rebirth eschatologies. For the model to be "nomologically adequate" (another of Weber's terms), it must possess logical consistency and persuasiveness and must not contain features that are against the grain of empirical possibility. Now let me address this issue of objective possibility and nomological adequacy in some depth.

1. The rebirth topography sketched in figure 3 fits most of the Amerindian cases in my sample but with one important qualification. Almost all existent eschatologies from the Northwest Coast and Inuit recognize the existence of parallel rebirth cycles for humans and animals; in some it is possible for a human to be born as an animal and vice versa. I have omitted animal rebirth from the topographical model at this point because Trobriander and Igbo rebirth also can be fitted into this scheme without too much violation of the empirical record. Other reasons for the omission will be discussed later in this chapter.

2. In most cases a dead person's "soul" goes round and round in endless cycles of existence and reexistence. It is an automatic process, one might say, and only in exceptional cases is there any deity or other force to prevent it. The soul does not die; it might change form at the very most, but otherwise it goes on being reincarnated. This ineluctability or automatism, if one could formulate the soul's progress in this manner, is recognized in the rebirth topography of figure 3. When this topography is ethicized, the system of rewards and punishments also takes on this automatic or axiomatic character.

3. Is there any force or agency that can put a brake or roadblock on this ineluctability of the soul's continual, if not continuous, reincarnation? I have already noted ethicized instances in which the souls of the wicked are not permitted to reincarnate (as with the Igbo). It is not clear, however, whether this happens axiomat-

ically, where the bad *by virtue of their actions* are denied reincarnation, or whether there is an intercessory deity that prevents the bad from reincarnating. In parts of West Africa, and at least among the Qiqiqtamiut Inuit, there is a Creator God or a powerful intercessory deity who might have a role in preventing the bad from being reborn or in other ways block the inevitability of the rebirth process. One ought to deal with this possibility by imagining a model in which the automatism of the rebirth process is compounded by the active agency of a superordinate deity. Perhaps the early Christian heresies, influenced by Platonism, had to reconcile the notion of rebirth with the reality of an omnipotent God. So did the Druze and other Ismā'īlī-influenced sects, which we will examine in chapter 6.

## UPANISHADIC ETHICIZATION: THE EARLIEST INDIC MODEL

Let me now deal with the beginnings of ethicization in Indian history by reflecting once again on the *Bṛhadāraṇyaka* and *Chāndogya* Upanishads, texts that effected an important epistemic break in the dominant Vedic tradition. In chapter 1 I noted that there were two figures that introduce rebirth into the Upanishads, the Brahmin sage Yājñavalkya and the Kṣatriya Pravāhaṇa Jaivali. Let me come back to the more developed version of the "fire-water doctrine" by the Kṣatriya sage.

In this version the king discusses three paths available to souls at death. First, there is the path to Brahman for those who have true knowledge; they are fully saved, and they know no return or rebirth. This path is, however, called the *devayāna,* the path of the gods; the soul goes to the world of the gods and stays there for an indeterminate period and then goes into Brahman. Second, there is the path of the Fathers, or ancestors, the classic Vedic *pitṛyāna*. This is for those who have offered sacrifices in the old Vedic sense; they are reborn in the human world and keep going round and round in a cycle. Not all are continually reborn though, or in the same manner, according to the second Jaivali text, which affirms the fire-water doctrine but adds that those who live good and bad lives realize a good and bad rebirth, either as one of the twice-born *varṇa* categories or in a "foul womb." I noted that ethics have entered into the picture, even if they are the ethics of *varṇa*. The Upanishadic ethics mentioned on page 12 can now be better understood. They do not negate the ethics of karma based on the *varṇa* scheme but simply affirm the most deadly of the "sins" from the point of view of the priestly class: the one who steals gold, drinks liquor, kills a Brahmin, fornicates with his teacher's wife, and all who associate with the above.[9] Finally, there is the enigmatic category of insects that will never achieve a human rebirth. This category resists easy interpretation; it might refer to the Śūdra or, more likely, to those outside the pale of the *varṇa* scheme, the so-called Untouchables.

There is not much difference between these two Upanishadic thinkers: both believe in knowledge leading to Brahman; both believe in a lesser path, where one can be reborn according to one's karma, even if karma refers to *varṇa* ethics; both accept the fire-water doctrine of rebirth for unliberated souls; both articulate karma and rebirth with the major soteriological ideal of the Upanishadic tradition, the merging of atman with Brahman. Yājñavalkya presents "joyless" conditions at death for those who have violated *varṇa* ethics; Pravāhaṇa Jaivali does not mention this. Yājñavalkya is a Brahmin sage who takes his pupil *aside* as he enunciates the idea of karma and rebirth that he does not want to talk about "in public." "In public" surely does not mean in front of the general populace because no Upanishadic text talks to the public in that sense. The "public" in this context must refer to other Upanishadic seekers of salvation—teachers and their pupils. In this text Yājñavalkya imparts this knowledge to Arthabhaga privately. Implicit is the idea that knowledge of karma and rebirth is something new in the broader Vedic tradition—as if this is the first time these ideas have appeared. By contrast King Pravāhaṇa Jaivali assumes a different discursive posture. He clearly states that these doctrines are *not* new but that they were unknown to Brahmins; they are the prerogative of the Kṣatriyas, and that is why "government has belonged exclusively to royalty [kṣatriya]." The dialogues dramatize an important theme: that the rebirth theory is something new or ignored in the Brahmanic tradition but that it was well known to the Kṣatriyas.

If this is so, there is a historical question that must be answered even as informed guesswork. From where did the Kṣatriyas gain this knowledge? The only reasonable conclusion one can make is that these doctrines have come from some source outside the Vedic tradition and have been creatively incorporated into the Upanishadic tradition, although not into its mainstream. The scholarly opinion in general is that these early Upanishads were composed in the upper and middle reaches of the Ganges, where Brahmins were relative newcomers. I suggest that the Kṣatriya sage as a dramatis persona was voicing popular beliefs about rebirth that were known to many persons in this region and recasting them in a frame that might seem acceptable to Vedic thought. Brahmins either were indifferent to these ideas, which violated early Vedic eschatology, or did not know them. The early heartland of Brahmanic power was further west, in what was known as the Āryavartha, the region of the Āryas (noble ones). Hence the enigmatic statement of the king: that because the Brahmins were ignorant of these ideas, "government has belonged exclusively to royalty." This statement, I think, implies that knowledge of the rebirth ideas of large masses of people was necessary for dominion over them. Knowledge *is* power.

It should be remembered that the great religious innovators of the Ganges valley, such as the Buddha and Mahavira, were also Kṣatriya sages. Jaina traditions in particular emphasized that Mahavira belonged to a line of sages, and his teachings were partly based on those of a previous sage, or Jina, named Pārśvanātha, who, according to some scholars, lived around 850 B.C.E.[10] If so, the Jainism of Mahavira's time was the culmination of a longer process of religious exploration. Pursuing this line of guesswork, one might argue that there was a tradition of Kṣatriya sages in the region of the Ganges valley and that Pravāhaṇa Jaivali of the Upanishads was an early representative of that tradition.

In Pravāhaṇa Jaivali's scheme the way of the gods leading to union with Brahman is fully within the innovative soteriology of the early Upanishads, breaking away from the primacy of the sacrifice of the *Brāhmaṇa*s and the soul's journey into the realm of the Fathers (ancestors). In the Upanishadic transcendental state of the union of atman with Brahman there can be no further rebirth. The way of the Fathers, which was the goal of early Vedic thought, is now downgraded. It is no longer a paradisiacal realm where the souls of the dead comport with their ancestors but a temporary way station in the rebirth cycle. Figure 5 illustrates this latter rebirth topography.

The left side of the figure illustrates the trajectory for all those who have performed sacrifices, have given gifts to Brahmins, and have led good lives. They go to the realm of the Fathers, although they are not equal in ritual and moral status. Following the logic of rebirth theory the stay in the world of the Fathers is temporary; the caterpillar-like soul must move on. The relative good and bad done by people are recognized in the next human rebirth as they achieve reincarnation as one of the twice-born castes (Brahmin, Kṣatriya, or Vaiśya) via the complicated processes described in the texts (the fire-water doctrine). But what about those whose karma was bad, that is, those who did not follow the proper ritual and moral injunctions? The right side of the figure illustrates their

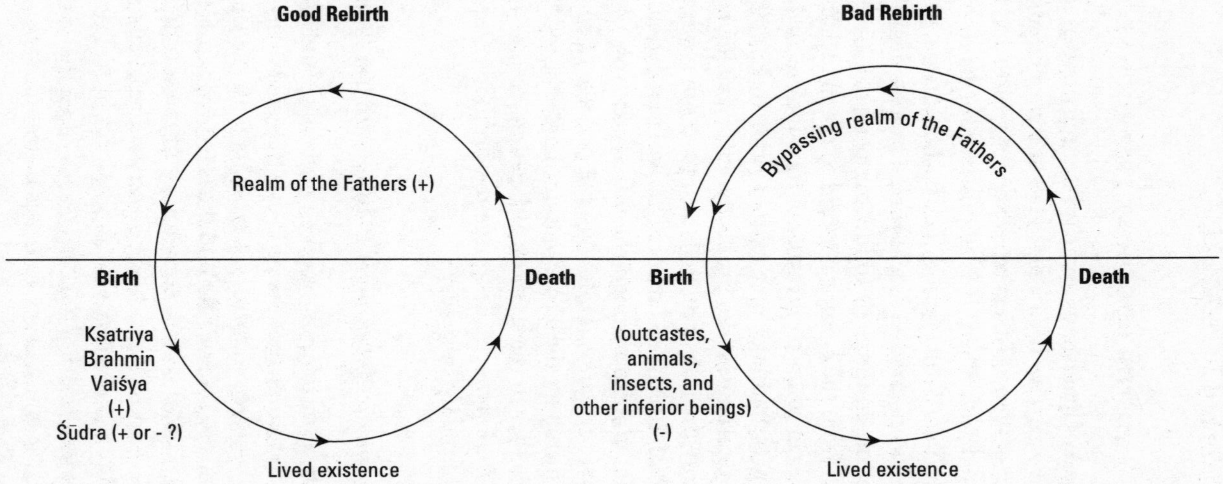


Figure 5. Upanishadic rebirth. Salvation, or mokṣa, is outside the rebirth cycle: atman equals Brahman.

fate: they bypass the desired world of the Fathers and achieve a low human or animal reincarnation. Fundamental Brahmanic values have been creatively transformed and ethicized.

## THE MODEL AND THE BUDDHIST INTERCONNECTIONS

Between the early Upanishads and the later religions of the Ganges valley there might well have been a period of at least a hundred years. If the former contain only the briefest references to rebirth and karma, the latter are saturated with them. It is impossible for us to figure out what happened in the intervening period. The Buddhist texts, perhaps, can give us clues as to how ethicization as a historical process might have occurred.

To begin let me continue to follow my perverse strategy and shuttle back and forth from the empirical world to the model, using Buddhism as my example, in order to investigate four interrelated problems: the kind of rebirth eschatology that existed prior to Buddhism; the problematics of vegetarianism; the problematics pertaining to sentient existence; and finally the role of animals and plants in rebirth eschatologies in contrast to Buddhism (and other religions of that period). The last three elements are interlinked through the differential role of animals in rebirth and karmic religions. Following the practice of some Indological scholars I will introduce the term *samanic* to describe the "new religions" of the Ganges valley in the sixth or fifth century B.C.E. and the already familiar term *Brahmanic* to designate the orthodox Vedic tradition up to the period of the Upanishads.[11]

### *The First Problematic: Inventing a Pre-Buddhist Tradition*

In following the principles of objective possibility and nomological adequacy I have to assume that the processes depicted in my imaginary experiment also occurred in history, beginning with the Upanishadic dialogues. I continue to assume that Buddhists following a similar trajectory ethicized a preexistent rebirth eschatology of the sort depicted in figure 3. It is virtually impossible to bring *direct* evidential support for the argument that this transformational process did in fact occur in history. When direct evidence is not available, as is often the case with the historical sciences, it is necessary to bring forth *indirect* evidence to substantiate the hypotheses formulated.

I will initially develop further the notion posited in chapter 2 of an affinity between Indic religions and the rebirth eschatologies to ask the following question: Which among the various rebirth eschatologies presented in chapter 2 comes closest to the Buddhist? An important feature of Buddhist and samanic eschatologies in general is that humans can be reborn as animals as a consequence of their karma. Jainism, following more closely on the two Upanishadic cases, goes even further than Buddhism in postulating that plants might also possess sentience, even though one cannot be reborn as a plant. It is certainly possible that the Buddhists and Jainas invented these ideas, as some Indologists claim; on the other hand the ideas might have been inherited from preceding eschatologies. As I have already shown, the only empirical cases similar to the Buddhist among small-scale societies outside the Indic area are those of the Northwest Coast Indians and the Inuit, because the Igbo and other West African groups and the Trobriand islanders have no notion of animal rebirths, parallel or cross. Amerindians and Inuit also occasionally recognize that plants too are forms of sentient existence, even though they are outside the rebirth scheme. Hence my conclusion: if it is indeed the case that Upanishadic theorists, Buddhists, Jainas, and other non-Brahmanic religions of the time did not invent the idea of animal reincarnation and the sentience of plants but inherited it from a preexisting tradition, then it is likely that that inherited tradition was similar to the eschatologies of the Northwest Coast Indians and Inuit. One cannot therefore entirely discount the idea that the circumpolar distribution of these rebirth eschatologies might well have extended from Siberia down into central Asia and then to the Indian subcontinent, although diffusion of ideas and the impact of "influences" are not directly relevant to my project.

The conclusion that the Indic religions show the closest structural similarity to the Amerindian-Inuit necessitates that we add the feature of animal rebirth to our topographical model and include this feature, as in figures 6 and 7. When this model is ethicized, it produces not just any theory of karma but specifically the Indic one. Consequently, for the most part I confine the term *rebirth eschatology* to the Northwest Coast Indians and Inuit depicted in figures 6 and 7; I will refer to the others by name when necessary, as for example, Igbo or Trobriander.

### *The Second Problematic: The Logic of Vegetarianism*

Having narrowed the focus of our inquiry to the rebirth eschatologies of the circumpolar regions and the karmic ones of the samanic religions, let me now deal with issues that arise from the idea shared by both—that

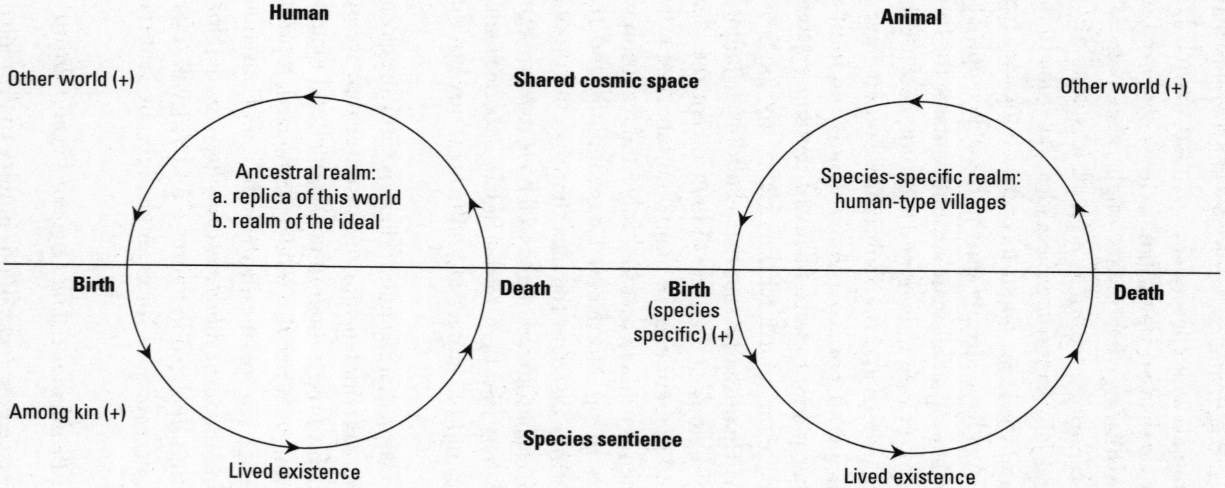


Figure 6. Parallel reincarnation: Northwest Coast Indians and Inuit. Among these groups, there is no salvation and no ethicization. There are standard techniques for identifying a neonate, and ordinary folk have rebirth memories. There are constant animal/human transformations.

humans and animals (and occasionally plants) give expression to a universal "species sentience." In the examples of rebirth eschatologies from the Inuit and the Northwest Coast I noted the omnipresence of animal-to-human transformations and vice versa. To eat animals, however, was both necessary and desirable, and eating was prefaced by a double act, first of killing the animal and then of ensuring its reincarnation. Animal consumption, then, is a reverential act, yet at least on an unconscious level there is guilt in recognizing the possibility that one may be eating an ancestor or someone closely related. In those rare cases of cross-species reincarnation it is not possible to escape the guilt pertaining to endoanthropophagy. Such a dilemma can be better dealt with in the Ganges valley of the sixth and fifth centuries B.C.E., where forests had been cleared and rice cultivation had been established. There was no need to eat one's ancestor; hence the samanic religions (and perhaps the rebirth eschatologies that preceded them) either had a vegetarian diet or expressly forbade the killing of animals.

The attitude toward animals depended on the paths of ethicization taken by the different samanic religions. It should be remembered that only selected animals incarnate as humans in the rebirth eschatologies. Perhaps the samanic religions universalized this idea to include all animals. One thing is clear though: in Buddhist ethicization, with its strong emphasis on motivation, it is the intentional killing of the animal rather than eating it that is at issue, whereas Jainism forbids not only killing but also eating animals, as well as selected sentient plants and vegetables. By contrast the Brahmanic religions right up to the period of the Upanishads permitted the killing and eating of animals. We also know that goats, sheep, and cattle were eaten in the religion of the Vedas, and huge numbers of cattle and horses were sacrificed in Brahmanic rituals for kings. Henk Bodewitz shows that the early Dharmasūtra texts, particularly Gautama (not to be confused with the Buddha, also called Gautama), probably compiled soon after the period of the Buddha, posit the doctrine of *ahiṃsā,* or noninjury to living things, although the word itself appears only once. He thinks that these texts have been influenced by the ideologies of the samanic religions.[12] Further, even Gautama permits Brahmins as well as renouncers to eat the "the flesh of animals killed by carnivorous beasts."[13] Āpastamba, another early Dharmasūtra authority, lists specific animal foods that Brahmins might eat;[14] Vāsiṣṭha is even more liberal, permitting "food given by a hunter" and such delicacies as porcupine, hedgehog, hare, tortoise, iguana, and some unspecified domestic animals except camels.[15] These facts force us to draw an im-

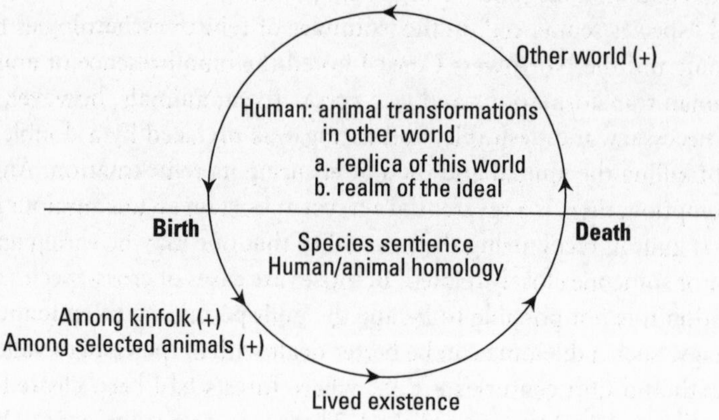


Figure 7. Cross-reincarnation: Kwakiutl.

portant conclusion: insofar as the karmic eschatology represented in figure 4 posits universal species sentience and respect for animal life, one can conclude that the early Brahmanic religion, with its killing of animals for the sacrifice, could not possibly have had any inner affinity with that model. This adds substance to our assertion that rebirth ideas came into Indic religions from a source outside the main Brahmanic tradition.

Some might reasonably argue that as far as the Indic traditions are concerned, vegetarianism is a direct effect of the *ahiṃsā* doctrine rather than the *ahiṃsā* doctrine itself being based on the doctrine of species sentience and the dread of endoanthropophagy expectable from my model.[16] But the relationship between vegetarianism and *ahiṃsā* is not straightforward. The Jainas have the strongest convictions regarding vegetarianism, which directly ties in with their theories of nonviolence, but some plants were taboo as food because they contained a life-essence. The Buddha permitted the eating of animals that were accidentally killed or that died of natural causes, much like the other Gautama of the Dharmasūtras. And the Brahmanic texts that came later incorporated vegetarianism rather than *ahiṃsā* per se into their encompassing conceptions of purity and impurity. Thus, although the equation expectable from my model suggesting "endoanthropophagy:vegetarianism:*ahiṃsā*," might be problematic, equally problematic is the direct tie-in between vegetarianism and the *ahiṃsā* doctrine of noninjury or nonviolence.

Now let me turn to a more complicated illustration of the relationship between rebirth and endoanthropophagy by examining once again the developed version of the fire-water doctrine of the *Chāndogya Upaniṣad*. We noted earlier that the souls that take the lesser path pass into the smoke, and after various other transformations they reach the world of the Fathers and then the moon, where they become the food of the gods. Then they follow a downward trajectory that takes them into a human rebirth: passing into the wind and to the sky and into rain and from the rain to earth, where they become food, that is, plants and cereals. Man repeats what the gods did previously; he consumes these foods, and they are converted into semen, which he injects into a woman's womb to beget children.

Consider the implications of this fascinating theory. In Presocratic Greek theory, which I will present later, a soul could be reborn in plant form; but insofar as the plant is an incarnated human soul, one cannot eat that particular species. I think similar ideas underlie Jaina theories of the sentience of plants. But the Upanishads have a complicated solution to this problem of endoanthropophagy: the soul gets embodied and transformed many times over until it becomes a plant or a cereal, not any kind of plant or cereal but those that humans eat. Consumption is a creative act that reproduces the previous archetypal act of the gods: eating human souls that have been transformed as divine food. These human souls are reborn and continue to do good or bad. Those who do good are reborn to replenish the human species of the first three orders, or *varṇas*. However, those who were bad ("of foul behavior") could be reborn in a "foul womb" as animals such as pigs or dogs, or as an outcaste, or, according to some unclear statements, as insects or creepy-crawlies.

Let me now develop the hidden implications of this theory in terms of our models. First, it seems that eating vegetarian foods is a form of endoanthropophagy but also a reverential act like that of the Amerindians, entailing a *transvaluation* but not a transubstantiation of ordinary food substances. Hence, as with Amerindian eating of animals, I would hesitate to call it a sacrament analogous to the Eucharist. The Upanishadic theory transvalues the doctrine of species sentience in a specific direction by postulating that plants and cereals, at least those we eat, are permeated with a mystical sentience. Wild plants that do not possess this form of sentience could presumably be eaten anyhow. Second, following this originary condition is the next incarnation, when those who did wrong are reincarnated directly after death in foul wombs as pigs, dogs, insects, and such. They are in effect the souls of recently dead humans;

they are also those that Brahmins (and the three *varṇa* classes) would not eat, or ought not to eat. Eating them would be tantamount to endoanthropophagy. But what about well-known domestic animals such as goats, sheep, cattle, and horses? The texts do not mention them. But silence is a symbolic language that demands interpretation. Although all sorts of sacrificial animals are mentioned in Vedic texts, the most regularly sacrificed were goats, sheep, cattle, and horses. It would not do for human souls to be reincarnated in the "foul wombs" of these creatures without raising for the higher classes the deadly possibility of endoanthropophagy unmediated by the complicated changes that vegetables and cereals undergo. Hence the texts make no reference to human beings reborn as domestic/sacrificial animals.

Finally, take the case of wild animals. One must presume that the Kṣatriyas hunted some of them and ate others; so did the Vaiśya classes; and some wild animals were permitted as food for Brahmins. These creatures are also not mentioned as carriers of souls in the texts discussed earlier. The presumption is that they are good to eat. But one text hints that such eating may not be entirely acceptable. This is the third Upanishad that deals with rebirth—the *Kauṣītaki*—which clearly indicates that rebirth as animals was a much wider phenomenon than reported in the *Bṛhadāraṇyaka* and *Chāndogya* Upanishads. This text says that the rain brings down to earth the souls of those who do not know the true knowledge, and, following the dictates of karma, they are incarnated "as a worm, an insect, a fish, a bird, a lion, a boar, a rhinoceros, a tiger, a man, *or some other creature*."[17] Thus the unliberated ones can be reborn as *any* kind of being, including wild animals, but the text leaves open whether these other creatures include the domestic animals ignored in the other two Upanishads. If this text reveals the hidden or silent message in the other two Upanishads, then it means that eating certain specified and unspecified animals, including wild animals, is in effect eating a former human being, a direct and vile anthropophagous act quite unlike the creative act of eating cereals and vegetables.[18] I think that the later Brahmanic taboo on meat eating and the high valuation of a vegetarian diet develop from this model, not from one based directly on the doctrine of noninjury, or *ahiṃsā*.

### *The Third Problematic: Ethicization and Species Sentience*

In my thinking the rebirth eschatologies of small-scale societies postulate a universal species sentience that can lead to the recognition of a spiritual equivalence between humans and animals. With ethicization, however, animals get "demoted." A person who does bad or commits "sin" *(pāpa karma)* might be punished by being reborn as an animal or some other lowly creature. Thus, in the samanic religions, there is a peculiar aporia whose poignancy appears only when we compare those religions to the simpler rebirth eschatologies: *although humans and animals belong to a common order of sentient existence, the latter are relegated to an inferior existence in ethicized samanic religions, and they lose the elevated status they had before.* This "fall" is nicely expressed in folk versions of the *Vessantara Jātaka,* the birth story that deals with the penultimate birth of the Buddha, where, as Prince Vessantara, he epitomized the perfect generosity of the seeker for Buddhahood who gave away as slaves to a greedy Brahmin what he most loved and valued—his two children and later his wife. In this story the wife goes in search of the missing children and asks the animals their whereabouts (in beautifully poignant poetry in the texts of the popular tradition). The animals, sympathetic to her plight, tell her what they know; but in doing so they inadvertently hinder the salvation quest of the Buddha, so they lose their capacity for speech!

The *Vessantara Jātaka* itself is one of the most popular tales from the compendium of 550 "birth stories" known as the *Jātaka* tales, which deal with the past lives of the Buddha. These tales in turn come from a miscellaneous collection of texts called the *Khuddaka Nikāya* (Minor collection), thus named to distinguish it from the major collections of the discourses of the Buddha. Scholars agree that the *Jātakas* were originally folktales circulating within a larger Indo-European orbit. Precisely because the *Jātakas* come from the folk repertoire, they do, I think, contain ideas from traditions that predated the samanic religions. One of the striking features of the *Jātakas*, prior to the penultimate *Vessantara Jātaka,* is that in many of them the Buddha himself appears as an animal, for example, as an elephant, a lion, a monkey, a lizard, a parrot, a pigeon, a hawk, a swallow, a cock bird, a peacock, a dog, a hare, a fish, a deer, a water buffalo, a bull, a horse, a goose *(haṃsa),* an antelope, a mallard, a frog, a garuda, an iguana, a snake, a sea sprite, a partridge, a vulture, a woodpecker, a quail, a rat—almost always to express the nobility of the creature.[19] There is little in these texts to indicate that animals were a degraded species or that the Buddha was an animal owing to his bad karma.[20] Animals have the capacity for speech, live in the same kinds of societies as humans, and are represented by a range of good and bad characters. These conceptions are similar to those of the Amerindian eschatologies in my sample and suggest that the samanic religions ethicized an eschatology that had either parallel- or cross-rebirth cycles for animals and that this idea is reflected in the texts of the folk traditions embodied in the *Jātakas*.[21]

### *The Fourth Problematic: Buddhism and the Sentience of Plants*

It is well known that Buddhism, unlike Jainism, does not teach the sentience of plants. Plants do not have centers of consciousness as animals do; therefore, taking the life of a plant is totally different from taking the life of an animal. However, in an important essay Lambert Schmithausen has shown that early Buddhists might well have believed in the sentience of plants.[22] Whether Schmithausen is correct is not as germane as his demonstration that such an idea was part of the popular culture and that Buddhism and Jainism dealt with it in different ways.

Schmithausen starts with a passage from the *Pātimokkha,* the Buddhist "confessional" for monks, which says: "If [a monk or a nun] is ruthless with regard to plants, this is an offence to be atoned" (*PSP,* 5). In a detailed exposition of this passage Schmithausen admits that it is not clear whether the text refers to plant sentience. The discourses *(suttas)* themselves contain several statements to the effect that monks should abstain from injuring seeds or plants, although these have sometimes been taken to mean a prohibition on agriculture. The *Pātimokkha* rule, however, is clear that injury to plants is equivalent to injury to animals. The commentary of the *Pātimokkha* gives two reasons for this rule: the first is that by cutting the tree the monk injured the child of the deity inhabiting the tree; the second, more germane to our argument, is that "this action was disapproved by the people as an act of injuring because they regard trees as living beings *(jīvasaññino . . . rukkhasmiṃ)*" (*PSP,* 14). The monks themselves did not accept this view, but they observed the rule out of respect to the public, a feature of ascetic decorum adopted by Buddhists.

Similar prohibitions are found elsewhere. In the *Khandhaka* section of the *Vinaya Piṭaka* (Book of the discipline) the Buddha blames monks for cutting young palmyra and bamboo leaves to make sandals. "Here, too, the reason adduced is that people consider trees to be living beings, more precisely: living beings with one sense-faculty *(ekindriya jīva),* and hence object to the monks cutting off shoots . . . as an act of injuring a living being. Here, too, the implication seems to be that the Buddhist monks themselves do not believe in the sentience of the plants concerned"

(*PSP,* 23). These kinds of plants are not normally the habitat of deities, and it is not likely that "living beings with one sense-faculty" refers to deities. Not all plants possess sentience; however, the prohibition on bamboo and palmyra suggests that plants producing shoots and, in other instances, grains capable of germination were viewed as especially sentient, although only possessing "one sense-faculty" (*PSP,* 41). Therefore, although it may be wrong to destroy certain plants, it is not possible to be reborn as a plant. Similar ideas are found in Jainism: perhaps following some enigmatic Upanishadic precedents, monks and nuns are not allowed to consume bulbs, bulbous roots, or other plants, such as sugarcane, that are capable of sprouting.[23] In later Jaina thought they are even said to possess souls.[24]

To sum up: there are at least three forms of plant sentience recorded in the Indic literature. First, there are those plants, already mentioned, that possess a single center of consciousness; because they are living beings, they must not be destroyed. It is not clear how these plants achieved sentience in the first place. Second, there is the Upanishadic form in which the spirit of an ancestor gets into certain plants that are creatively consumed by humans. Third, there are the well-known Indic cases in which a spirit can reside in especially large trees (such as a banyan) as the deity of the tree. Injuring these trees is a sin as far as orthodox Buddhist doctrine and popular beliefs are concerned.

## ETHICIZATION IN ITS HISTORICAL CONTEXT: THE SAMANIC RELIGIONS

I will now bring in detailed evidence of a slightly more direct sort to show that the historical process subsumed under the term *ethicization* did in fact occur in the samanic religions of the sixth (or fifth) century B.C.E. Initially I adopt a negative strategy and show the *lack* of ethicization in several areas of Indic religious life. Thus contemporary "tribal" religions in India exhibit little or no ethicization. My intention is not to argue that the presamanic religions of India were tribal; rather, I want to make the point that if small-scale societies in India are not concerned with ethicization now, it is unlikely that they would have been concerned with it then. I will also show that the Brahmanic traditions that preceded Buddhism were relatively unethicized. Thereafter I present evidence to suggest the existence of relatively unethicized yet complex rebirth doctrines prevalent among the contemporaries of the Buddha. Against this backdrop I examine the positive evidence for ethicization in the historical development of Buddhism at the time of its founding and conclude with a more sweeping view of ethicization in Buddhism and the Axial Age monotheisms.

## CONTEMPORARY TRIBAL RELIGIONS

The word *tribe* is in disfavor now. A convenient alternative is *ādivāsi,* "the ancient residents," the Indian government's official definition of *tribe,* even though this is a literal translation of the English *aboriginal,* a concept that, as far as I know, never existed in South Asia. Negative connotations unfortunately do not wither away through a change of terms, but the term *ādivāsi* does contain a historical truth in that it refers to people in small-scale societies in India who have often resisted incorporation into larger socioeconomic and cultural structures.

Christoph von Furer Haimendorf, the foremost ethnologist of Indian ādivāsi society, says that those groups least influenced by Hindu thought have "amoral" religions.[25] Regarding the Chenchus, Haimendorf says: "Supernatural sanctions, though not easily evaluated, came to play a comparatively small part in promoting conformity to the accepted moral standards. . . . There is little to suggest that moral lapses are subject to supernatural sanction" (*MM,* 23). The Reddis: "deities demand from man the observations of certain taboos . . . but the relation between man and man are to them a matter of indifference; there is no divine retribution of crime or reward for virtuous behavior" (*MM,* 43). "The Kamars' attitude to adultery is much the same as that of the Reddis" (*MM,* 45). The Daflas: "While an appeal to supernatural powers is used to strengthen a peace-pact, there is otherwise no suggestion that gods and spirits are concerned with the moral conduct of human beings" (*MM,* 69). "The Apa Tanis are sensitive to social approval or disapproval, and the fear of being 'shamed' is a powerful incentive to conformity. There is, on the other hand, no sense of 'sin' and no corresponding desire to acquire 'merit' in a system of supernatural rewards. . . . [Daflar and Apa Tanis] do not ascribe to their gods a general interest in the moral conduct of man" (*MM,* 79). Although some ādivāsis, such as the Gonds, do have notions of "sin," Haimendorf speculates that these are newly introduced notions. Haimendorf's material is extremely interesting because he wrote without any reference to the logic of ethicization that I have presented. In fact, my idea of ethicization is much narrower than his views of ādivāsi morals and merit. Haimendorf speaks of supernatural sanctions in general, including punishment by deities for wrong or immoral behavior, whereas I confine myself to the narrower sphere where moral ideas are converted into religious ideas that ipso facto are related to a system of otherworldly rewards and punishments. Yet it is clear from his account that ethicization, or rather its lack, is not simply a structural feature of my topographical models but is also a feature of at least some ādivāsi religions of India.[26]

## ETHICIZATION, AXIOLOGY, AND THE BRAHMANIC TRADITION

I will now demonstrate that ethicization is also alien to the Indic religious traditions prior to the samanic religions of the Ganges valley, as the studies by Arthur Berriedale Keith, Paul Deussen, and others indicate. The scholarly work of "colonialist" writers is under critical scrutiny nowadays, and one might wonder whether Keith's attribution of a lack of ethicization in Brahmanic religion is influenced by his orientalist presuppositions.[27] It is indeed true that Keith, E. W. Hopkins, and Deussen think that there is something morally dubious in the Indic tradition of constructing amoral religions. But this is not a feature of orientalism per se because even emancipated contemporary scholars have similar views and assume that the lack of ethicization is symptomatic of a moral lack. Most of us have been raised in traditions that make a virtue of ethicization. In this work I do not want to provoke arguments on the nature of ethics or whether the Brahmanic tradition was "ethical." I propose only that the latter did not possess ethicized religions in the sense in which I have used the term. The question of what morality *is* will lead us into a methodological bind from which it will be impossible to extricate ourselves. I am not condemning the *Brāhmaṇa*s for being indifferent to good and evil, as Keith does, nor praising them for possessing a "narrow" morality that can, in the context of ritual, dispense with general moral norms pertaining to such things as adultery and incest.[28] My question is a simple one: did the *Brāhmaṇa*s possess an ethicized religion or not? I think Keith is correct in saying that they did not.

Consider the *Ṛg Veda,* the oldest stratum of Brahmanic religion. The soul at death, driven by a chariot or on wings, takes the route of the Fathers and reaches a place of eternal rest. The *Ṛg Vedic* notion of heaven is a paradisiacal one: "there is light, the sun for the highest waters, every form of happiness, the Svadha, which is at once the food of the spirits and the power which they win by it, their self-determination" (*RP,* 2:407). As is well known, the major deity of the *Ṛg Veda* is Indra, who, along with other divinities, enjoys material luxury, intoxicants *(sura),* milk, ghee, honey, and *soma* (the drink of immortality), as well as the delights of love. There is also music and singing and a celestial fig tree where Yama drinks with the gods.

This eschatology is a paradisiacal, not a retributive, one. Keith notes that even Yama and Varuṇa, who sometimes might appear as ethical deities, do not "punish the dead or judge them for their sins" but grant a kind of unconditional pardon. Consequently, "the idea of a judgement of any kind is as foreign to the Rg Veda as to early Iran." He then adds that the notion of hell "was present in germ" in the *Ṛg Veda* (*RP,* 2:409). It is a place under the earth into which Indra and Soma are to hurl evildoers, these being the enemy, robbers, or demons. The *Atharva Veda* (c. 800 B.C.E.), which succeeded the *Ṛg Veda,* has the word *narakaloka* (bad place), which was later identified with ethicized hells known as *niraya* or *apāya.* This was a blind, black place where female goblins, sorceresses, and murderers were confined; here persons who injure Brahmins sit in streams of blood eating their hair. This bad world is similar to Igbo conceptions; those committed there have been guilty of specific offenses rather than the general categorical ones of ethicized religions. The *Atharva Veda* depicts at best a minimally or occasionally ethicized eschatology. Here also the otherworld is for all and is contingent on the performance of the correct rituals rather than on the moral nature of one's this-worldly actions.

I have already mentioned the *Brāhmaṇas,* so let me quote Keith's brief summary of their ethical stance: "The most convincing evidence of all regarding the almost ritual character of goodness in the view of the Brāhmaṇas is that their concept of torment is inextricably bound up with the correct practice . . . of the ritual" (*RP,* 2:473). It is true that at death a person is weighed in a balance to test the good and the bad, but this judgment is based primarily on violations of taboos and ritual interdictions. This comes out clearly in the vision of Bhṛgu in the *Śatapatha* and *Jaiminiya Brāhmaṇas,* where the persons confined to hell are those who cut wood without offering the *agnihotra* and those who kill and eat animals and even herbs without performing the correct rituals. In the *Kauṣītaki Brāhmaṇa* the animals will take revenge on a person in the next world unless he or she performs the correct ritual.[29] In the *Brāhmaṇa*s also there is occasional ethicization, but for the most part these texts are concerned with the violation of taboos and ritual interdictions.

The Upanishads, although belonging to the Vedic tradition, prove that a sophisticated speculative religion need not concern itself with otherworldly ethics, except for the few instances discussed earlier. This fact has dismayed scholars who are conditioned to think that a speculative soteriology must also entail an ethical soteriology. Thus Paul Deussen, in his exhaustive discussion, points out the absence of a moral concern in the Upanishads except for specific scattered injunctions. His own explanation is rather naive: "Lack of generalization, as well as the rarity of such warnings in Upanishad literature, proves that offenses of this character were not common."[30] He also argues that ethics have no objective or external work to do in the Upanishads, misjudging their ethical nature, because European religious traditions emphasize external, nonsubjective ethics, that is, ethics that seem to exist outside the individual. But he forgets that both Buddhism and Jainism had an external (or a social) morality very different from the subjective, internal ethics of the Upanishads. The fact is that the Upanishadic seeker of salvation can in some instances go beyond everyday morality. In the *Kauṣītaki Upaniṣad* the man who attains Brahman after passing by the river of immortality casts away his good and bad deeds; he is above all morality, even above such heinous deeds as the slaying of an embryo and the murder of a father or a mother, a position unthinkable in religions like Buddhism and Jainism.[31]

This kind of thinking goes back to such texts as the *Jaiminiya Brāhmaṇa* referred to earlier and anticipates the late Upanishadic texts of renunciation, such as the *Bhikṣuka Upaniṣad* and the *Bṛhat-Saṃnyāsa Upaniṣad*. In these later texts the renouncer is no longer part of the social world and is indifferent to its mores; hence he makes "no distinction between right and wrong."[32] Or, as the injunction in the *Bṛhat-Saṃnyāsa Upaniṣad* states: "Abandon right and wrong; abandon truth and untruth. Having abandoned both truth and untruth, abandon that by which you abandon."[33]

The renouncer, we know from the work of Patrick Olivelle, gives up the everyday life in a series of powerful symbolic actions, and in doing so he gives up everyday morality, the very morality that religions like Buddhism ethicized. The only place in Buddhism where a parallel situation seems to obtain is in the story of Vessantara, who gives away his wife and children to the greedy Brahmin Jūtaka, ignoring the norms of everyday morality. In this text, however, the reader or listener knows that the gods are going to rescue the Bodhisattva's wife and children, much as the Christian knows that Isaac is not going to die.[34] But there is no such escape clause in the texts on renunciation. Consequently one can accept Keith's characterization of the Upanishadic tradition in general without accepting his value judgment that "there is no attempt to make the theoretical philosophy a ground of morality of any sort" (*RP,* 2:584).

## NONETHICIZED SAMANIC RELIGIONS: THE DOCTRINES OF THE ĀJĪVIKAS

My experimental transformation of the rebirth eschatology into the karmic one only stipulates that good and bad actions have religious effects known in Indic thought as karma; it cannot specify whether these actions have to be intentional or otherwise. Interestingly enough, Buddhist reform has given karma intentionality *(cetana)* such that if I do something unintentionally I do not reap a karmic consequence (*karma phala,* "the fruit of karma"). Jainism took yet another route; it stipulated that karma produced irreversible effects, whether intentionally motivated or not. Now, if my assumption that this was a period of great intellectual ferment is correct, one would expect speculative thinkers to have produced not only ideas that transformed preexisting rebirth eschatologies into rationalized karmic ones (Buddhists and Jainas) but also rationalized doctrines that were nonkarmic or nonethicized. There is some evidence from Buddhist and Jaina texts for the existence of rebirth eschatologies of the latter sort. Indologists have rightly seen these as contemporary religions opposed to Buddhism and Jainism and as carrying on an argument with them. But given my set of assumptions I think there is something more to be considered here: they also seem to have a close affinity to the kind of rebirth topographies that I have sketched earlier (see figs. 3, 6, and 7).

In one of the most important texts of Buddhism, the "Sāmaññaphala Sutta" (The fruits of the life of a recluse), the parricide King Ajātasattu seeks healing for his troubled conscience by visiting the Buddha.[35] The Buddha questions him about the other teachers he has consulted, and Ajātasattu delivers a synopsis of their teachings. Ajātasattu refers to six teachers belonging to the samanic schools; most of them seem to take the doctrine of rebirth for granted but not the doctrine of karma as the Buddhists or Jainas understood it. There is no doubt that their doctrines have been oversimplified and distorted by the Buddhists, but for our purposes the outlines of their theories will suffice. Thus, according to Ajātasattu, the first teacher he visited, known as Pūraṇa Kassapa, taught that the practice of good or bad deeds has no karmic consequences whatever. The Buddhist disapproval is forcibly expressed in that part of the text that is supposed to represent Pūraṇa Kassapa's views:

> To him who acts . . . or causes another to act, to him who mutilates or causes another to mutilate, to him who punishes or causes others to punish . . . to him who kills a living creature, who takes what is not given . . . who commits dacoity, or robbery, or adultery, who speaks lies; to him thus acting there is no guilt [that is, no bad karma]. If a discus with a sharp edge like a razor should make all the living creatures on the earth one heap, one mass, of flesh, there would be no guilt thence resulting, no increase of guilt would ensue. Were he to go along the north bank of the Ganges giving alms, and ordering gifts to be given, offering sacrifices or causing them to be offered, there would be no merit there resulting, no increase of merit.[36]

No wonder Pūraṇa Kassapa gets a bad press in a religion that extols ethical causality! Ajātasattu tells the Buddha that this theory is one of nonaction, or *akiriyaṃ vyākāsi,* the belief that there are no karmic consequences. Pūraṇa Kassapa, however, is also hitting at religions like Buddhism, not only by denying the karmic effects of the Five Precepts, as is evident in the earlier quotation, but also by speaking against some of its higher ethics insofar as they produce karmic effects. "In generosity, in self-mastery, in control of the senses, in speaking truth there is neither merit nor increase of merit."[37]

Pūraṇa Kassapa is simply one among many teachers arguing *against* a view of ethical causality based on karma. Buddhists are wrong in assuming that Kassapa was an immoralist; he is simply saying there is no such thing as an ethical notion of karma. It is quite likely that he subscribed to an older view that the good or bad a person does has nothing to do with his or her fate in the afterlife. He surely knew that it could matter in *this* life because anyone who has committed the horrendous crimes he lists will certainly be punished by the secular authority.

Kassapa's teaching makes sense only if we consider the context in which it is made. He does not deny rebirth, unlike some other teachers of the period. Instead he is saying that although rebirth is a reality, there is no otherworldly retribution for immoral acts of a most deplorable kind. It seems to me that his teachings are a defense of an unethicized rebirth eschatology, one that must have existed as a "background religion" of the time. He was probably arguing against thinkers who insisted, as did the Buddha and Mahavira, that the violation of a social morality constitutes a "sin." He is also in effect telling Ajātasattu that his actions will have no bad karmic consequences. Finally, one must not forget that the Buddhists also had some interest in representing a rival teacher as a total immoralist rather than as someone subscribing to a secular code of ethics instead of a karmic one.

A. L. Basham, in his influential book *History and Doctrines of the Ājīvikas,* says that the most important thinker subscribing to the theory of rebirth but denying ethical causality is Makkhali Gosāla (Makkhali of the cowshed), whose teachings survived up to about the sixth or the eighth century C.E. in parts of southern India.[38] Basham shows that Pūraṇa Kassapa was also an Ājīvika, although not necessarily a follower of Makkhali Gosāla. Because both Pūraṇa Kassapa and Makkhali Gosāla believed in rebirth, it is not likely that a third "heretic," Ajita Kesakambili (Ajita of the hair blanket), was also an Ājīvika, as Basham thinks, because Ajita, an uncompromising materialist and "annihilationist," clearly did not subscribe to such a theory.[39]

In my view the Ājīvikas rationalized a preexisting rebirth eschatology without bringing in karmic causality. Makkhali Gosāla fully recognized the impersonal nature of the rebirth cycle and then gave it philosophical elaboration and conceptual formulation. He seems to have asked, What keeps the universe going in this manner? He suggested that an impersonal cosmic principle, or *niyati,* determines continuity. This doctrine denies an ethical theory of karma but does not deny an orderliness to the universe—what the Greeks called *cosmos.*[40] But Makkhali Gosāla added another element in his own rationalization of the rebirth eschatology, stating that the rebirth cycle cannot go on forever but will simply run out after many eons, at the end of which the soul will have attained bliss or salvation. I will argue later that this journey of the soul is not a fortuitous element in his teachings but is related to the double vision of salvation that Makkhali Gosāla, along with other thinkers of the time, formulated: one mode of salvation for the world-involved laity and another for the virtuoso.

Let me now present his teachings as depicted by Ajātasattu in the "Sāmaññaphala Sutta" of the *Majjhima Nikāya:*

> There is neither cause nor basis for the sins of living beings; they become sinful without cause or basis. Neither is there cause or basis for the purity of living beings; they become pure without cause or basis. There is no deed performed either by oneself or by others (which can affect one's future births), no human action, no strength, no courage, no human endurance or human prowess (which can affect one's destiny in this life). All beings, all that have breath, all that are born, all that have life, are without power, strength, or virtue, but are developed by destiny, chance, and nature, and experience joy and sorrow in the six classes (of existence).

The text then lists, in a very schematic manner, the multitudinous rebirths the soul undergoes during its long journey.

> There are 1,400,000 chief uterine births, 6,000 and 600; 500 *karmas*, 5 *karmas*, 3 *karmas*, a *karma*, and half a *karma;* 62 paths; 62 lesser *kalpas;* 6 classes (of human existence); 8 stages of man; 4,900 means of livelihood (?); 4,900 ascetics; 4,900 dwellings of *nāgas;* 2,000 faculties; 3,000 purgatories; 36 places covered with dust (?); 7 sentient births; 7 insentient births; 7 births from knots (?); 7 gods; 7 men; 7 *pisāca* (births?); 7 lakes; 7 knots (?), and 700; 7 dreams, and 700; and 8,400,000 great *kalpas* through which fool and wise alike will take their course, and make an end of sorrow. There is no question of bringing unripe *karma* to fruition, nor of exhausting *karma* already ripened, by virtuous conduct, by vows, by penance, or by chastity. That cannot be done. *Saṃsāra* is measured as with a bushel, with its joy and sorrow and its appointed end. It can neither be lessened nor increased, nor is there any excess or deficiency of it. Just as a ball of thread will, when thrown, unwind to its full length, so fool and wise alike will take their course, and make an end of sorrow. (*HD,* 13–14)[41]

This is the earliest and most detailed statement of Ājīvika thought by a contemporary, and although it is meant to be pejorative, even satiric, it does contain the elements of Gosāla's thought, in Basham's opinion.

The force that propels the rebirth cycle or samsara is *niyati* (Destiny or Fate), which is similar to karma in its impersonal and lawlike quality. Associated with niyati is *saṅgati* (chance) and *bhāva* (nature). Later Ājīvika thinkers identified *svabhāva,* or bhāva, with niyati itself. Here are two Jaina commentators on the importance of bhāva. Jñānavimala: "Some believe that the universe was produced by *Svabhāva,* and that everything comes about by *Svabhāva* only." Gunaratna: "What makes the sharpness of thorns and the varied nature of beasts and birds? All this comes about by *Svabhāva.* There is nothing which acts at will. What is the use of effort?" (*HD,* 226). This means that "nature," very broadly defined, incorporates everything in the sentient world, including all forms of human action. From a Buddhist point of view these kinds of thinkers are *ahetukavādins* (believers in causelessness) and *akriyāvādins* (disbelievers in the efficacy of works).

What is striking about the Ājīvika theory is that it does recognize "karma." Makkhali uses this word and describes the various kinds of karmas in almost casuistic fashion. Basham thinks that the Ājīvikas recognized karma on the nominal level but rejected it at a deeper essential level, a distinction well known in Indian thought. I do not think this is correct; Ājīvikas used the term but not in its Buddhist and Jaina sense. They were having an argument with their opponents in order to show that their "karma" was different from that of the others. It is highly unlikely that Makkhali would have given the term Jaina and Buddhist meanings because that would radically have undermined the theory of niyati and (sva)bhāva. He used the term *karma* to deconstruct it or to deny that karma was ethical and purposive.[42] Any purposive theory of action, be it karma or God, is anathema to the Ājīvikas (*HD,* 233). Instead, each person goes through a variety of rebirths in fantastic time cycles, and these rebirths include those of humans, animals, supernatural beings, even plants. It seems that the Ājīvika doctrine, more than any other known religion of the time, possessed a systematic notion of species sentience. Thus all beings must pass through all known forms of sentient existence. Ultimately this cycle stops "like a ball of thread that has unwound itself." Concomitantly, all persons will eventually achieve salvation, defined as the purity of the soul, irrespective of the quality of their this-worldly actions.

A man might think he is a free agent, but this is an illusion because even the belief in free will is determined by Destiny, Fate, or niyati and constitutes part of a natural process (bhāva or svabhāva). The stages of human life are controlled by Destiny, and so is life after death because "a new body is not obtained by anything else such as *karma*. . . . Under the compulsion of Destiny they experience various repulsive conditions, such as being humped-backed, one-eyed . . . a dwarf, . . . death, disease, and sorrow" (*HD,* 234). By formulating his own version of "karma" Makkhali Gosāla can carry on debates with his opponents who believe in another kind of karma. Nevertheless, irrespective of what he means by *karma,* Makkhali Gosāla is not denying that those who violate moral norms will be punished or rewarded *in their present existence*. It is difficult to imagine a sophisticated thinker being so ignorant of the realities of the world we live in. What *is* denied is a system of rewards and punishments that affect rebirth; instead, the rebirth cycle goes on according to natural principles, or bhāva, until it too, like time, must stop.[43]

There is another crucial issue pertaining to Ājīvika religion that scholars and commentators have not satisfactorily explained. Is the system totally and irrevocably deterministic? If everything must work itself out, according to principles of niyati, what is the significance of the extreme asceticism assiduously practiced by the Ājīvikas? The logically expectable answer that asceticism, like everything else, is determined by Destiny is not satisfactory. According to Buddhist sources the Ājīvikas divided humanity into six classes, and each class was given a particular psychic color. For example, black is the color of those who live by slaughter and cruelty, such as hunters, fishermen, thieves, and jailers; and white is the class that contains Ājīvika ascetics of both sexes. The purest color is "supremely white," but this class contains only three persons: Makkhali Gosāla and two other Ājīvika leaders, Nanda Vaccha and Kisa Saṇkicca. Basham rightly thinks that this class also contains the arahants and Tirthankaras of Ājīvika soteriology.[44] Nevertheless, if it is the case that *all* persons go through the same scheme of reincarnation and eventual salvation, why are there two special classes of highly advanced spiritual virtuosos? Why the preferential treatment? The answer, it seems to me, is that the Ājīvikas probably believed that the only thing that could hasten the salvation of the individual is asceticism. Asceticism cleanses the soul and permits the achievement of salvation even in this life. The idea of the *jīvan mukta,* the person who has achieved salvation in this very life, is common to the soteriologies of other samanic groups like the Jainas and Buddhists.

This reinterpretation of Ājīvikaism permits us to postulate two key features of its soteriology: a belief in niyati, or Destiny, that irrevocably and with unrelenting slowness brings about an eventual purification of the soul and with it an automatic end of the samsaric cycle; and a belief that this slow salvific process can be dramatically shortened by the purifying processes of extreme asceticism. My reformulation renders intelligible the similarities that scholars have noted between Ājīvikaism and Jainism. The difference is that Jainism has an ethical theory of karma, as in Buddhism. Yet in a unique departure from Buddhism, Jainism postulates that karmic actions produce a material component that taints the soul and weighs it down in both a physical and spiritual sense. Cleansing of the soul is through extreme asceticism. Here then is Jainism's resemblance to Ājīvikaism: even though Ājīvikaism did not subscribe to the ethical theory of karma as in Jainism, it probably believed with Jainism that "karmas" have a material component and hence can be classified casuistically. More important, it believed in the power of ascetic practices to purify the soul and thus achieve "nirvana" even in this life, as Jainas do, but through a form of nonmoral effort. Thus the Ājīvika ascetic, like those of other samanic religions, abolishes the rebirth cycle after the achievement of nirvana. Ordinary people will also eventually achieve nirvana but only through the long-term operation of niyati, or Destiny. Because Ājīvikaism did not subscribe to the karma theory, it in effect permitted everyone to achieve eventual salvation. This is probably why it became popular in India and at one time was a contender with Buddhism and Jainism. Although Ājīvikaism is closer to the rebirth eschatologies of small-scale societies in its rejection of karmic ethics and its conception of an impersonal cosmic process, it has inner affinity to the samanic religions in postulating a notion of salvation or nirvana outside of samsara, that is, by stopping the cycle of rebirth.

The idea that even a nonethicized and antikarmic religion like Ājīvikaism had a soteriology that brought it in line with the rationalizing spirit of other samanic religions of the time tempts me to reexamine the significance of "purification" and its relation to asceticism in Ājīvika thought, particularly because similar conceptions prevailed not only in India but also in Greece. Buddhist *Jātaka* texts refer to Ājīvika soteriology as *saṃsāra suddhi,* which can be translated as "samsaric purification," because the soul will eventually become purified and achieve salvation. "There is no short cut (lit. door) to bliss, Bijaka. Wait on Destiny. Whether (a man has) joy or sorrow, it is obtained through Destiny. All beings are purified through transmigration [rebirth], (so) do not be eager for that which is to come."[45] This quotation, in my view, refers to the ordinary road to salvation and is typical of the advice given to laypersons even by such thinkers as the Buddha to remind them that their time of salvation will eventually come and to encourage them to be patient. In my interpretation purification by asceticism in Ājīvikaism takes the place of the ethical notion of karma, whereas in Jainism, the religion closest to it, there is a coexistence of karma and purificatory asceticism.

One Ājīvika purifying practice is especially significant for my examination of Ājīvika ascesis. According to the Jaina text *Aupapātika Sutra,* the noblest Ājīvika ascetic, the *uṭṭiyāsamaṇa,* entered a large earthen pot in order to do "penance."[46] *Aupapātika* is the Sanskrit form of the Pali-Buddhist *opapātika,* that is, birth outside of normal bodily processes. In the context of this Jaina text I would interpret the action of the *uṭṭiyāsamaṇa* not as a literal nonbodily rebirth, as the term *aupapātika* implies, but a symbolic one. If the large earthenware pot symbolizes the womb, then the Ājīvika virtuoso practicing asceticism in such a vessel is reborn into a higher salvific state through a form of purificatory asceticism, subverting Destiny and abolishing the normal process of slow salvation available to all.

## EEL-WRIGGLERS AND HAIR-SPLITTERS: CONTENTIOUS DISCOURSES IN BUDDHIST THOUGHT

Recent scholarship has shown that the institution of world renunciation conjoined with asceticism had low priority in Brahmanic thought until the Upanishads. The Brahmin priests themselves were rarely given to renunciation; their later sympathy for renunciatory practices resulted from the influence of the Upanishads and the religions that I have labeled samanic. There is some evidence that yogic practices were known in the Indus valley civilizations from seals that depict ascetics in poses similar to those practiced by the later Jainas. It is certainly possible that with the abandonment of this civilization, renouncers (who by virtue of their vocation were relatively free of the sociopolitical order) might have moved along river routes into the Ganges valley, perhaps joining other population migrations.

The Vedic tradition essentially extolled the household life—marriage, earning, and the begetting of children—whereas the renouncer has rejected those very values to become a homeless one or an *anagārika,* to use a Buddhist term. The well-known division of Hindu society into four stages of life, or *āśramas*—student, householder, hermit, and renouncer—was formalized by the time of the Dharmasūtras (c. fourth century B.C.E.).[47] But Brahmanic thought produced contentious debates regarding the "legitimacy of the renouncer's *āśrama*" and the value of the householder's life traditionally praised in the Vedic literature. These debates continued "even during the medieval period."[48] One text says: "As all rivers, both great and small, find a resting-place in the ocean, even so men of all orders find protection with householders"; and Baudhāyana, who thinks that the demon Kapila invented the fourfold division of the life cycle, adds: "there is one *āśrama* only, because the others do not beget offspring."[49] The renouncer came to be fully incorporated into the Hindu worldview only after the institution of world renunciation had been established in the samanic traditions and had begun to be accepted by large segments of the population.[50]

The general term for ascetic renouncers was *paribbājaka* (Pali) or *parivrājaka* (Sanskrit), which means "those given to wandering," a term appropriated by the samanic traditions. Other terms, like *samaṇa (śramaṇa)* and *yati,* emphasize "effort," namely, an ascetic mode of existence, whereas *bhikkhu* (or *bhikṣu*) refers to a mode of living through "begging." The term *saṃnyāsin* (someone who has "thrown away" all possessions) was used more or less exclusively in the Brahmanic tradition. To quote Olivelle: "A *parivrājaka* was a person who had left home and family, had no fixed abode and lived on alms. His life had a basic religious dimension, since its final aim was the discovery of his individuality and his personal liberation."[51] Sukumar Dutt, who did the pioneering work on these wandering ascetics, says that the begging bowl was the symbol of their vocation; *brahmacariya* (a difficult term with many meanings that here could be glossed as "salvation quest") was their spiritual aim and *dharma* their religious doctrine.[52] The Buddhists sometimes make a distinction between samaṇas, to which they belong, and the general category of ascetic wanderers, the parivrājakas, whom they despise, although at other times these distinctions are blurred.

The Buddhist texts provide descriptions of the public life of these recluses. The *Majjhima Nikāya* (Middle length sayings) has an entire section titled "The Division of the Wanderers," which gives us valuable information on the various schools of wanderers. For example, in one text the wanderer named Sandaka is reputed to be staying "in the fig tree cave with a great company of wanderers, with at least 500 wanderers."[53] A wanderer named Uggahaman had a following of three hundred. The Buddhists despised these particular wanderers and felt no need to exaggerate their importance, although the rounded numbers are not to be taken literally. The texts clearly show that several schools of wanderers—like the Buddhist, Jaina, and other samaṇas—had large numbers of followers, and many other wanderers lived alone. All of them were a familiar feature of the social landscape of the Ganges valley and were generally highly regarded and patronized by the great, including kings and the newly emerging merchant classes.

There were special areas of the cities reserved for them. The "Mahā-Sakuludāyisutta" states that celebrated wanderers such as Anugāra, Varadhara, and Sakuludāyin stayed in the wanderers' park at the peacock feeding place near Rājagaha.[54] They also congregated in other places for debates: thus the Buddha debated Vacchagotta the wanderer in a special park, *ekapuṇḍarīka* (single white mango tree park), near Vesāli.[55] In the city of Sāvatthi was Queen Mallika's park, within which was a specially demarcated place "set around with a row of *tinduka* trees" and known as "One Hall."[56] The greeting with which Upaka, the naked ascetic, addressed the Buddha soon after his Awakening (Enlightenment) suggests a convention quite unlike the Brahmin one of inquiring about one's caste and lineage upon meeting a stranger: "On account of whom have you, your reverence, gone forth, or who is your teacher, or whose *dhamma* do you profess?"[57]

The kinds of places listed above were not only resting places but also arenas where rival groups debated each other or expounded their own doctrines, or *dhamma*. The wanderer Sakuludāyin gives a vivid account of the diverse schools of the time locked in debates with each other during the rain retreat.

> Sometime ago, revered sir, when divers members of other sects, recluses and brahmans, were gathered together and were sitting down in the debating hall, this chance conversation arose: "Indeed it is profitable for the people of Aṅga-Magadha . . . that these leaders in religious life, heads of companies, heads of groups, teachers of groups, well known, famous founders of sects, held in high repute by the many-folk, have come to Rājagaha for the rains-residence. This Pūraṇa Kassapa is a head of a company. . . . This Makkhali Gosāla too . . . This Ajita of the hair-blanket too . . . This Pakudha Kaccāyana too . . . This Sañjaya Belaṭṭhi's son too . . . This Nātaputta the Jain too . . . This recluse Gotama too is the head of a company, head of a group, the teacher of a group, he is well known, the famous founder of a sect, held in high repute by the many-folk; he too has come to Rājagaha for the rains-residence.[58]

In another very interesting account Kuṅḍaliya the wanderer tells the Buddha that after Kuṅḍaliya has his morning meal, "I roam from park to park, from garden to garden . . . [and] there I behold certain recluses and brahmins debating on the profit of freedom from controversy and the profit of wrangling."[59] It seems therefore that this period was bustling with intellectual activity, the spirit of which extended even to some householders. The latter also listen to sermons and engage in conversations with religious leaders such as the Buddha and Mahavira, and apparently there were debating assemblies set aside for the laity also. The Buddha himself idealized "full and frequent assemblies" of the sort he was used to in his own home "republic" of Kapilavastu. The public debates practiced by religious virtuosos were called *vāda-vivāda* (arguments and counterarguments) and were often very acrimonious. One gets a feel for the rhetorical strategies employed by contestants from the disparaging remarks made by Buddhists on the casuistry of "eel-wrigglers" and "hair-splitters" and other dialecticians.

It is out of this intense intellectual activity that the great speculative religions of the sixth and fifth centuries B.C.E. emerged, particularly the Upanishads, Buddhism, Jainism, and many lesser-known intellectual and religious movements described in Buddhist and Jaina texts. The period was conducive to philosophical and soteriological probing and the systematization of thought (what Max Weber called the "rationalization" of the religious life).[60] Nevertheless, speculative and systematic thinking need not produce ethicization. The Upanishads produced a great speculative soteriology that was not concerned with ethicization. What then is the critical feature of religions like Buddhism and Jainism that was conducive to systematically converting a social morality into a religious one?

The answer is that these religions were not simply those of the "homeless" interested in their personal salvation, as with the Upanishadic virtuosos; they were also concerned about the welfare of the ordinary person tied to a home. Buddhists extolled the renunciatory ideal that leads to salvation, but, in the spirit of Vedic thought, they also believed that the household life was necessary and desirable for those not driven by soteriological aspirations. Thus Buddhists and Jainas established connections with the lay community in a systematic manner and developed stable congregations of lay supporters. I am *not* suggesting that the Buddhists and Jainas introduced these connections for the first time in Indian history. Quite the contrary. These connections were probably created or imagined by others also. Just as an experiment has to be imagined before it can be created in a laboratory, so it is with ethicization. Thinkers must *imagine* a lay congregation before they actually create one, but even imagining such a community is impossible or meaningless if knowledge is secret or esoteric or if the salvific goal is for an exclusive elite. Buddhist texts give us insights regarding the processes whereby religious innovators established connections with the lay population.

Many groups of wanderers had the general support of the laypeople in their midst but were, like the Upanishadic ascetics, not interested in lay conversion. I suggest that it is in relation to a lay community that ethicization of the moral life occurs. This should not surprise us because ethicization is the conversion of the morality that governs the life of ordinary people into a religious one. Religions like Buddhism and Jainism simply continued this concern with ordinary or everyday ethics, but they projected these ethics onto a religious or eschatological plane. Let me spell these ideas out in respect to the contrasting ethical orientations in Buddhism and the main body of the Upanishads.

Whether etymologically justified or not, Indian writers usually define *upaniṣad* as "rahasyam" (secret). The term *rahasyam* captures the idea of an esoteric doctrine that the guru imparts to his pupil questing for salvation, similar to what the Greeks called *paradosis,* a transmission of esoteric knowledge, often on a one-to-one basis. Upanishadic paradosis often took place in an *āraṇya* (forest); hence the term *āraṇyaka* was also used. Certain physical gestures also indicate this esotericism, as, for example, when Yājñavalkya of the *Bṛhadāraṇyaka Upaniṣad* takes his questioner aside to discuss the nature of his doctrine. The seeker of salvation goes to a guru and learns the "secret" knowledge—rahasyam—which is also true of many of the wanderer schools of that time. But the term *rahasyam* must not be taken literally; knowledge *is* communicated, although in a special way. Rahasyam is the way of "paradosis," of which Deussen gives many examples:

> Chāndogya 3.11.5: "Therefore only to his eldest son shall the father as Brahman communicate it (this doctrine), but to no one else, whoever it may be."
>
> Śvetāśvatara 6.22: "Give it (this supreme secret) to none who is not tranquil, who is not a son, or at least a pupil."
>
> Bṛhadāraṇyaka 6.3.12: "This (the mixed drink, *mantha,* and its ritual) shall be communicated to no one except the son or the pupil.
>
> Nṛisiṃarvatāpanīya 1.3: "But if a woman or a Śūdra learns the Savitṛi formula, the Lakshmī formula, the Praṇava, one and all go downward after death. Therefore, let these never be communicated to such. If anyone communicates these to them, they and their teacher go downwards to death."
>
> Rāmapūrvatāpanīya 84: "Give it not (the diagram) to common men."[61]

What one finds in the Upanishads (and similar doctrines among both Indian and Pythagorean Greeks) is a preoccupation with the individual's personal salvation; the values of the society are irrelevant to the issue, and in extreme cases of renunciatory asceticism, they can be openly rejected. By contrast, in the samanic religions, such as Buddhism and Jainism, there was an additional interest in the soteriological-cum-ethical welfare of common men, women, and Śūdras, that is, of the larger lay community.

The theoretical significance of these divergent ethical orientations was neatly stated by Durkheim in his classic essay "The Determination of Moral Facts": individuals, he argued, cannot be moral objects unto themselves because the ground of morality is established in a social network.[62] One must qualify Durkheim somewhat and reaffirm that by *morality* we mean the kind of values necessary for the orderly conduct of social life—such things as respect for elders and injunctions on theft, adultery, lying, violence, among others. It is possible for someone to reject a social morality for a "higher" ethic, hence my reluctance to enter into axiological judgments. If social morality of the sort I have described is established only in our relationships with others, then one cannot expect it to have salience for any individualistic salvation quest. In such quests social morality is at best irrelevant, even a hindrance, insofar as social morality links a person to his or her group, whereas salvation entails removal from it.

Weber was therefore clearly wrong when he said that Buddhism emphasized the personal *certitudo salutis* rather than the welfare of the neighbor.[63] Although the doctrine of homelessness and ascetic withdrawal from the world was central to it, Buddhism was additionally concerned with conversion and the constitution of a lay community. This linkage was so powerful that the Buddhist salvation seeker could *not* be indifferent to morality; failure to adhere to conventional moral standards as stipulated in the Five Precepts will hinder the achievement of nirvana. The ascetic withdrawal from the world with its goal of personal salvation must be reconciled with the establishment of communication between layperson and monk.

Buddhism insisted that the monk should live "lonely as the single horn of the rhinoceros"; but he should also be concerned about the "welfare of the many."[64] Although there have been problems reconciling the goal of ascetic renunciation with the demands of the laity, there is not the slightest doubt that Buddhism was never Max Weber's exclusive "monks' religion." In a major Buddhist text Gautama, the Buddha of our era, was faced precisely with this dilemma. Here he recognized that the doctrine is difficult and meant for the few, and he was reluctant to preach it to the world. By not preaching it he would have opted for the goal of personal salvation.[65] This model does exist in Buddhism in the person of the *pacceka*-Buddha, a Buddha who has achieved true knowledge but is not interested in proclaiming his message. Such Buddhas have existed before and will appear again; they have realized nirvana, but they make no dent on the world. Gautama wondered, according to this text, whether he should adopt this path but then made his decision clear when Brahma himself interceded and urged him to proclaim the doctrine for the "welfare and the happiness of the many."[66] It is no accident that the Buddha's decision to save the world was a later thought. Although the Buddha discovered the main doctrinal tenets of Buddhism during his first tremendous meditative experience, or Awakening (Enlightenment), the Five Precepts pertaining to lay ethics were not one of them. They were invented when the early Buddhists, like the Jainas, decided to convert the laity.

The Buddhist discourses (suttas) are replete with statements that the doctrine is for both monk and layperson. Let us take a crucial text, the "Mahā Parinibbāna Sutta," which deals with the death of the Buddha. Here Māra, the personification of the world's ills, tells the Buddha that he should die straightaway, but the Buddha replies: "I shall not come to my final passing away, Malignant One, until my bhikkhus and bhikkhunis [monks and nuns], laymen and laywomen, have come to be true disciples—wise, well-disciplined, apt and learned, preservers of the Dhamma, living according to the Dhamma, abiding by the appropriate conduct, and having learned the Master's word, are able to expound it . . . and preach this liberating Dhamma."[67] The Buddha then says that this statement was uttered by him to Māra soon after the Buddha's Awakening at the foot of the goatherds' banyan tree, creating an impression that this has been a consistent position from the very beginning of the Buddha's career: "I shall not come to my final passing away, Malignant One, until this holy life taught by me shall become successful, prosperous, far-renowned, popular and widespread, until it is well proclaimed among gods and men."[68]

It therefore seems incontrovertible that early Buddhism and Jainism involved preaching to the world and establishing communication with the lay community, not only as a means of finding recruits for the order but also to create congregations. Communication with the laity was facilitated by the development of monasticism. When the Buddha entered a city, the monks there gathered to meet him, an indication that monastic communities, great or small, were inextricably associated with the development of early Buddhism. With the establishment of the "rain retreat" *(vassa)* monks had to stay three months in one place, generally in small shelters erected by lay devotees or with friends and relations "but always close to a village or town."[69] These lay congregations assemble to hear the Buddha preach. Hence, a crucial feature of early Buddhism was the public sermon, which has remained to this day a vehicle for the communication of doctrinal tradition to laypeople. These public sermons were open to all, unlike the closed esoteric world of the Upanishadic guru and his pupil.

## ETHICAL TRANSFORMATION AND THE AXIAL AGE: ETHICAL PROPHECY AND ETHICAL ASCETICISM

I have said to corruption, Thou art my father; to the
worm, Thou art my mother, and my sister.

—Job 17:14

Q: How should one reflect on the nature of the body
through "worms"?

A: This body is gnawed by eighty thousand worms.
The worm that relies on the hair is called "hair-iron."
The worm that relies on the skull is called "swollen
ear." The worm that relies on the brain is called "mad-

> dener." In this class there are four kinds. The first is called *ukurimba*. The second is called *shibara*. The third is called *daraka*. The fourth is called *dakashira*. . . . The worms that rely on the heart are of two kinds. The first is called *sibita*. The second is called *ubadabita*. The worms that rely on the root of the heart are of two kinds. The first is called *manka*. The second is called *sira*. . . . There are three kinds of worms that rely on the two lower orifices. The first is called *kurukulayuyu*. The second is called *sarayu*. The third is called *kandupada*. Thus one should recall to mind the nature of the body through "worms" [while meditating].
>
> —Upatissa Thera, *The Path of Freedom* (Vimuttimagga)

If Weber was wrong in characterizing Buddhism exclusively as an apolitical status religion, "a religious 'technology' of wandering and intellectually schooled mendicant monks," he was equally wrong in his estimate of the Buddha as a "prophet."[70] "We shall understand by 'prophet' to mean a purely individual bearer of charisma, who by virtue of his mission proclaims a religious doctrine or divine commandment."[71] Weber includes as prophets those who renew an older religion and those who proclaim a new one, for they merge into each other. Yet he is interested in a more fundamental typological distinction between two kinds of prophets, "one represented most clearly by the Buddha, and the other with special clarity by Zoroaster and Muhammed" (*SR*, 46). The former is an "exemplary prophet" who by "his personal example demonstrates to others the way to personal salvation," whereas the latter is an "ethical prophet" who becomes "an instrument for the proclamation of a god and his will, be this a concrete command or an abstract norm. Preaching as one who has received a commission from god, he demands obedience as an ethical duty" (*SR*, 55).

Developing this idea further Weber wrote that "the prophet, in our special sense, is never to be found where the proclamation of a religious truth of salvation through personal revelation was lacking. In our view, this qualification must be regarded as the decisive hallmark of prophecy" (*SR*, 54). In a beautiful passage Weber described the prophet presenting to his followers "a unified view of the world, derived from a consciously integrated and meaningful attitude towards life. To the prophet, both the life of man and the world, both social and cosmic events, have a certain systematic and coherent meaning. To this meaning the conduct of mankind must be oriented . . . if it is to bring salvation" (*SR*, 59). The prophet attempts to "systematize all the manifestations of life, regardless of the form it may take in the individual case" (*SR*, 59); or, as Arthur Mitzman felicitously put it, he becomes a "tool of the divine will."[72]

Although Weber brilliantly described the nature of ethical prophecy, his understanding of Buddhist "exemplary prophecy" is not very helpful. As Weber realized, all prophecy, whether the ethical or the nonethical oracular prophecies found in many societies, entails "possession" by a deity and/or some notion of "divine revelation," whereas for Buddhists such ideas contradict their ideal of a self-reliant individual dependent on no external support for salvation. It is impossible for the Buddha to become a tool of the divine will because no such will exists in the religion. Further, prophecy entails proclaiming the future or prognosticating the past; although the Buddha practiced both features of prophecy, these were not as central to the religion as in the case of ethical prophecy. Although the Buddha was "exemplary" in showing the path to salvation for others, the Buddhist tradition upholds the idea that he was a special person, a *mahāpuruṣa,* or great being, impossible to emulate but one whose conduct helps ordinary persons to reflect on their own imperfections. Most important, by polarizing ethical prophecy and exemplary prophecy, Weber underplayed the intrinsically *ethical* nature of the latter. If I were to distinguish the Buddhist ethical reform from that of the biblical tradition I would characterize it as "ethical asceticism." Asceticism is not necessarily ethical nor even necessarily salvific; often it is to acquire spiritual powers through bodily mortification. Indeed the Buddha's criticism of extreme asceticism was often on ethical grounds.

I now want to briefly refer to the ethical reform taking place in an adjacent civilization, namely Iran, by the great reformer Zoroaster. The Zoroastrian reform was the southern furthest reach of what Weber calls ethical prophecy. We know there were broad similarities in the larger Indo-Iranian cultural area prior to the sixth century B.C.E. In both the Indic and the Iranian traditions there was a systematic rethinking ("rationalization") of the preexisting traditions, the Indian through the samanic reform of ethical asceticism and the Iranian through "ethical prophecy" (*SR*, 55). A beautiful example of this ethical orientation is found in a hymn describing Zoroaster's vision of God, which transported him back in time to the creation of the world: "Then, Mazdah, did I realize that thou wast holy when I saw thee at the beginning, at the birth of existence, when thou didst ordain a (just) requital for deeds and words, an evil lot for evil (done) and a good one for a good deed."[73]

At the risk of some oversimplification let me now deal with the contrasting orientations of ethical prophecy and ethical asceticism, focusing on ethics, not soteriology.

1. The crux of ethical prophecy is that the prophet is the vehicle of a transcendental and unitary deity whose soteriological and ethical message he communicates to the world. The ethical ascetic, by contrast, *discovers* the truth of the world and of salvation from his own inward contemplation but the ethics he formulates have no transcendental quality. They are not eternal truths but guidelines for right conduct.

2. The nature of the prophet's message flows from the character of the deity: because it comes from God, it is a proclamation of the divine will. The prophetic ethics that ensue constitute "commandments." By contrast, the ascetic's ethical message does not come from God; it is a *precept* to be followed because of its inherent rightness. For example, Corinthians 7:6 makes a similar distinction in respect to marital ethics: "I speak of this by permission, and not commandment." The distinction between commandment and precept was crucial to the respective religious traditions in which ethical prophecy and ethical asceticism were institutionalized.

3. Because the prophetic message is from God, the command brooks no compromise. Thus ethical prophecy contains within it an uncompromising attitude to the world. Zoroaster sees his opponents as evil incarnate; in the extreme case no mercy or quarter is shown to nonbelievers, as in forms of Islam or Zoroastrianism and in many sectarian traditions of evangelical Protestantism. The preexisting religion is viewed with intolerance, regarded as the worship of sticks and stones. Thus, Zoroaster denounces the *soma* drinkers, very much in the spirit of the angry Jehovah and his prophets: "Wilt thou strike down this filthy drunkenness with which the priests evilly delude the people?"[74] In ethical asceticism, by contrast, the ethical message, insofar as it is based on practical considerations, is vulnerable to compromise and revision. The rules of the monk order underwent constant revision until the formalization

of the canon around the second century C.E.; such revision is extremely difficult to do with God's commands. In ethical asceticism the attitude to lay religion is tolerant, skeptical, and seen as folly rather than as evil. Contrary to the opinion of some scholars Buddhism does not contain a theory of radical evil like that found in the monotheisms.[75] The basic contrast is that for the monotheisms the preexisting (or alien) religions are evil, whereas for the Buddhist they are folly.

4. The uncompromising attitude of the ethical prophet almost inevitably leads him into conflict with the secular order. The prophet ethicizes a preexistent religion, and this often brings him into conflict with the established priesthood and the secular authority that is legitimated by that priesthood and religion. This was true of Jesus and of Mohammed and Zoroaster, at least in the initial period of their reforms. By contrast, ethical asceticism, lacking an uncompromising posture, does not threaten the secular order. Religions like Buddhism and Jainism have compromised with the secular authority. Buddhism, for example, was strongly critical of caste *(varṇa)*, but it nowhere attempted to reform the social order based on it. However, it did not provide any kind of validation for the caste order either.

5. The respective attitudes that I have sketched above affect the tone of the religious message. The prophet's message is intense, emotionally charged, and conveys a sense of urgency. It is expressed in condensed poetic language and metaphor, whereas the Buddhist suttas are expressed in ironic, reflective, and dialogical discourses containing seemingly endless repetitions and long discursive similes. The repetitions are mnemonic devices, yet, as Walter Kaufmann says, if a person "does not want to take the time to listen slowly, the Buddha might say, it will take him a long time to achieve salvation."[76] If in the suttas the technical and conceptual language is framed within a dialogical setting, not so with the commentarial tradition, the *Abhidhamma*, the third part of the canon, which has elaborate classificatory schemes and technical terminologies that have influenced the texts on meditation, such as the famous *Visuddhimagga* (Path of purification) by Buddhaghosa and the lesser known text quoted at the beginning of this section.

## RATIONALIZATION AND THE TRANSFORMATION OF THOUGHT

Having discussed ethicization at great length I would now like to evaluate the epistemological status of this concept. It is tempting to see ethicization as a (causal) variable; consequently, the methodological significance of my imaginary experiment would be to show how one kind of model or structure changes into another owing to the operation of the variable "ethicization." Model *a* (the rebirth eschatology) is transformed into model *b* (the karmic eschatology) as a consequence of the operation of *x* (ethicization), the causal variable. All this can be expressed elegantly and parsimoniously in verbal or figural form, yet it seems to me this way of representing social facts is misleading precisely on account of its oversimplification or "parsimony." The social reality of ethicization is far too complex to be isolated as a "cause." It has to be re-presented in such a way that the complexity is maintained; this can be done through descriptions of historical or social process. At best one could represent ethicization initially as a causal variable, but then one must unscramble and "complexify" it because, as I see it, the goal of the human sciences is not only to simplify the world but also to understand its complexities and existential predicaments. The Buddhists rightly say that conditionality is everywhere; one cannot compress that pervasive conditionality into a single causal variable or into isolatable "factors."

In line with these methodological precepts let me then use these models to further illustrate the complexity of the historical process during this period of intense intellectual activity. I have already indicated the usefulness of Karl Jaspers's idea of the Axial Age transformation of the religious life, without attempting any rigid periodization. In Jaspers's and in Shmuel Eisenstadt's recent reformulation this transformation entailed a preoccupation with soteriology and an ethics that transcended the world of everyday reality and the preexisting forms of religious life localized in the small community.[77] The Axial religions of India, as elsewhere, tended to be "universal" in the sense that their soteriology was meant for all. Following the creative thought of mathematician turned Indologist D. D. Kosambi, one could relate that expansion of thought to the changes taking place in India's "second urbanization."[78] This period saw profound changes in political and economic life in India that I will now briefly describe.

First, two new emerging empires, Kosala and Magadha, violently swallowed the many small independent Kṣatriya "republics," like the Buddha's own place of birth, that had collective decision-making assemblies known as *sanghas* or *gaṇas.*[79] To deal with this threat some small republics banded together in a loose political alliance known as the Vajjian confederacy, but this too was short-lived. Other republics lasted much longer. The "full and frequent assemblies" of these sanghas and gaṇas were so idealized by the Buddha that he not only named the Buddhist order after them but also borrowed their organizational principles and transferred them to the monastic assembly, as did his rival Mahavira, the spiritual leader of the Jainas.

Second, there was the emergence of new cities and the development of trade and commerce and concomitantly a new class of wealthy traders, bankers, and entrepreneurs generally known as *seṭṭhis.* Many of these seṭṭhis supported the new salvation religions. Kosambi argues that the development of trade and the movement of caravans transcended local groups and traditional political boundaries. Two caravan routes were especially significant: the *uttarāpatha,* the northern route into the Indus region of Brahmanic culture, and the *dakṣiṇāpatha,* which went south into the modern Deccan, both routes providing access for Buddhist monks and other teachers to spread their faiths.[80] These trade routes needed policing, which the new empires provided; thus was forged, says Kosambi, an alliance between the merchant classes and the kings. He adds that the time was right for the emergence of universalizing and transcendent religions that paralleled the obsolescence of older political communities and the creation of wider ones.[81]

I think it reasonable to assume that the breakdown of traditional social forms and the rise of new empires gave concrete embodiment to the older notion of a "universal ruler," or *cakravartin.* These changes in turn paralleled the outward-looking and universalizing orientations of the new religions, the one probably influencing the other. But an "orientation" cannot account for the content of a doctrine; therefore a direct tie-in between economic and political change and the *thought* of the new religions of the Ganges valley is difficult to substantiate. Some scholars have suggested that the sense of pessimism and the emphasis on suffering that these religions formulated can be related to the social disruptions and dislocations of traditional life-forms of the sort that Durkheim conceptualized as *anomie.*[82] But one can as easily argue that such conditions could lead to a preoccupation with hedonism instead of postulating a world of impermanence and hopelessness. Indeed, it can be demonstrated that the Buddha's own life, as reflected in myth, represented a recognition that hedonism is no solution to the ills of the world.

What seems to have occurred at this time is the emergence of thinkers questioning preexisting values and proposing a variety of salvific and nonsalvific solutions to the problems of existence. The Buddhist texts describe nonreligious thinkers such as various kinds of materialists, sophists, and nihilists. Many practitioners of extreme asceticism aimed, through the mastery of the world, at the mastery of the body of the world; others aspired to realize some kind of transcendent reality beneath the flux of everyday existence; yet others combined any number of these forms of religious and nonreligious speculations. The social changes of the time provoked thinkers to deal with a variety of existential issues, almost all geared to general and universalized knowledge that transcended, although they did not necessarily replace, the values and ideals of the local community. For example, the Buddha borrowed the model of the sangha from the republican organization of the time; but his sangha was no longer tied to a specific political unit; it was the universal church, "the *sangha* of the four quarters." So it was with the religious doctrine, or dhamma: it was not localized in any specific community or groups either but contained a salvific message for all. The figure of the founder is also not exempt from this process. Once the Buddha decides to become a renouncer, he ceases to be a member of the local community; furthermore, as the Buddha he is the seventh, twenty-fourth, or twenty-eighth (depending on which texts you choose) of a long line of redeemers, previous Buddhas. Thus the three main axes of the religion—the Buddha, the Dhamma, and the Sangha—are all universalizing conceptions.

Here then lies a major difference between the Axial Age religions in general and the eschatologies of the small-scale or ādivāsi societies that I presented earlier. None of the latter is involved in the universalizing process. It is certainly the case that after European colonization their physical worlds and geographic horizons drastically expanded, but the missionary religions took over the universalizing function, leaving little space for native intellectuals to forge larger worldviews out of their own localized religious traditions. This historical process is by no means closed, and native intellectuals might yet create new universalizing religious forms.

Is there any concept that one can employ to designate the multiple strands of the Indic reform that I have highlighted thus far? These ideas, namely, ethicization, the universalizing (and transcendental) thrusts in soteriology, and "axiologization" (a concept I will develop later), are part of the systematization of thought and life-forms that one might, following Weber, label as "rationalization." Weber used the term *rationalization* in a bewildering variety of ways, but I think it fair to say that one important sense of rationalization is "systematization of thought." However, this meaning of *rationalization* is useful only for identifying the general or totalizing sweep of thought unless one can specify some of its components, as I have done. Weber did have a restricted and more useful definition of *rationalization* as the kind of intellectual action that "the systematic thinker performs on the image of the world: an increasing theoretical mastery of reality by means of increasingly precise and abstract concepts."[83] I will resurrect the term *conceptualism* from medieval European scholasticism as the intermediate position between realism and nominalism and give it a different meaning to designate the invention and use of abstract terms and formulations. Thus *conceptualism* is not synonymous with *rationalization* but is one component of it.

The mastery of the world through the systematic imposition of abstract concepts makes fuzzy the conventional distinction between philosophy, science, and religious thought that Western epistemology has enshrined and permits us to focus on ratiocinative operations that are common to all three of the aforesaid domains, namely, the impetus to understand the nature of the world or the world of nature through the mediation of abstract concepts. It is difficult to believe, however, that conceptualism cannot occur in a multiplicity of cultures, small-scale or large; its occurrence and importance have to be demonstrated in context.

Although conceptualism is intrinsically associated with the systematization of thought or rationalization, one can have the systematization of thought without conceptualism. The unifying worldview of the ethical prophet can be seen as a systematization of thought.[84] Yet, although the prophet had abstract ideals, he hardly used abstract *concepts* to understand the world; indeed, he shunned such concepts or found them irrelevant to his passionate and intense soteriological vision. *Conceptualism,* as I have used it, is rarely found in the Bible; it is only in the Platonic heritage of later Christian and Islamic thinkers that one encounters careful and deliberate conceptualism. To conclude: what is unique to Axial Age religions is a form of "rationalization" that includes the development of transcendental and universalizing soteriologies, and ethicization is a basic feature of that universal and transcendental vision. These soteriologies do require systematic probing into the nature of existence, but they need not necessarily involve "conceptualism"; the latter entails the supervention of abstract concepts for grasping the nature of the world, and it is religions such as Buddhism (and the tradition of Greek soteriological thought that I will delineate later) that exemplify it.[85] In the Buddhist doctrinal tradition the conceptual imperative is so strong that one could reasonably speak of a "Buddhist Enlightenment" that parallels the Greek and the European.

My argument can be restated thus: the unique feature of Axial Age development in Indic religions is that their thought took a direction that ethical prophecy did not. Like later European philosophies or Pythagoreanism the samanic religions of India developed a set of abstract terms to grasp the transcendentalizing vision of their soteriologies. Hence one encounters such things as the Four Noble Truths; the doctrine of the impermanence of things; the five atomic principles, or *skandhas*, that constitute the body; the doctrine of "no soul"; the theory of causality known as *paticca samuppāda,* or dependent origination; the idea of rebirth linking consciousness; complex theories of perception and consciousness; the classification and analysis of states of concentration or absorption *(jhānas);* and so on. These ideas are rarely presented as purely abstract discourse until we come to the later philosophical and psychological analyses known as the *Abhidhamma.*[86] Rather concepts are woven into the dialogues of the Buddha that deal essentially with the nature of existence and the transcendence of the everyday world. The Buddhist dialogues, like the Upanishadic ones, have dramatis personae whose roles must be unfolded before we can begin to appreciate their content. Yet, although Buddhist conceptualism is necessary for an intellectual understanding of the religion, it has to be abandoned at a certain point in the salvation quest, along with discursive thought in general.

One can get a feel for the kind of speculative thought characteristic of the period by getting back to the "eel-wrigglers" and "hair-splitters" mentioned earlier. The reference to these dialecticians comes from one of the most interesting texts in Buddhism, known as the "Brahmajāla Sutta" (The net of Brahma). In it the Buddha discusses eleven *vāda* (false theories; lit., "arguments") about the soul.[87] Among the dialecticians of these theories are the eel-wrigglers, who, when a question is put to them, "resort to equivocation":

> In the first place, brethren, some recluse or Brahman does not understand the good in its real nature, nor the evil [bad]. And he thinks: "I neither know the good, as it really is, nor the evil. That being so, were I to pronounce this to be good or that to be evil [bad], I might be influenced therein by my feelings or desires, by ill will or resentment. [The same with wrong]. . . . [H]e will neither declare anything to be good, nor to be bad; but on a question being put to him on this or that, he resorts to eel-wriggling, to equivocation, and says: "I don't take it thus. I don't take it the other way. But I advance no different opinion. And I don't deny your position. And I don't say it is neither the one, nor the other." (*Dial.,* 1:37–38)

Eel-wrigglers are familiar to those of us in academia; so are hair-splitters, a subclass of eel-wrigglers, who "go about, methinks, breaking to pieces by their wisdom the speculations of others" (*Dial.,* 1:38–39). In fact, the next example of the language of these casuists seems like a parody of the Buddha's own:

> There is not another-world. There both is, and is not, another-world. There neither is, nor is not, another-world. There are Chance Beings (so called because they spring into existence, either here or in another-world, without the intervention of parents, and seem therefore to come without a cause). There are no such beings. There both are and are not, such beings. There neither are or are not, such beings. There is fruit, result, of good and bad actions. There is not. There both is, and is not. There neither is, nor is not. (*Dial.,* 1:39)

These kinds of dialectics are used by the Buddha himself when he deals with ideas that cannot be expressed in ordinary discursive language. Paradox and equivocation are part of the language the mystic uses to describe ineffable states, or the unity of self with god, or of all existence as refractions of the deity.[88] It is "neither this nor that," in the language of Meister Eckhart, or the "not this–not this" of the Upanishadic formula. It is the language of T. S. Eliot's "Ash Wednesday." And it is the language of Parmenides in Plato's *Parmenides:*

> So if, in every way, something is one and other things are not one, then the One would neither be a piece of whatever is not one nor as a whole of pieces. Nor, in turn, could the things that are not one be pieces of the One, nor as wholes to the One, as a piece. . . .
>
> Let this be said, then, and also that, so it looks, whether one *is* or *is* not, both it and the different things, both in relation to themselves and in relation to each other, all, in all ways, both *are* and *are* not and both appear and do not appear.[89]

Although parodied by the Buddha because of the extremes to which they are carried, the dialectics of the eel-wrigglers and hair-splitters indicate a powerful rationalizing impulse in any society.

## THE LIMITS OF INNOVATIVE THOUGHT: TEMPORALITY, IMPERMANENCE, NIRVANA

In the previous discussion I might have given Buddhist *ratio* and intellectualism a certain autonomy; that has now to be qualified. Does thought have this kind of autonomy? Earlier I was critical of the sociology of knowledge of Kosambi and others in imposing a rigid determinism on Buddhist and samanic thought. I will now switch to a middle path in order to show the interplay between the individual's freedom in creating new knowledge and the constraints imposed by the preexisting structures of knowledge curbing that very freedom. In this exercise I assume two prior systems of knowledge, the unethicized and ethicized eschatologies of rebirth topographically represented in figures 3 through 7. Continuing my imaginary experiment, I want to demonstrate the limitations that any kind of rebirth theory imposes on the soteriological innovations of thinkers such as the Buddha and the more drastic visions of those who followed them.

1. Built into a rebirth eschatology is the idea that the soul goes through cycles of existence. It is obvious that one could impose a limit on the number of times one is reborn, as Makkhali Gosāla, some Inuit, the African Benin, and the Greek Pythagoreans did. In both Trobriand and Buddhist eschatology the cycle is theoretically illimitable. Any innovative thinking must be contained within this unalterable parameter that takes for granted the continual or continuous cyclical journey of the soul.

2. With ethicization there is a qualitative change in the structure of continuity such that the rebirth cycle is propelled by ethics that now begin to generate good or bad otherworldly consequences. That too is given a name: karma. Karma fuels existence and reexistence that consequently begins to take new meaning, and this is also given terminological recognition: samsara. The thinker does not invent these ideas; he has no choice but to invent them because, as we have already noted, when ethicization is introduced and systematically pursued through steps 1 and 2, the ideas of karma and samsara must necessarily follow. What the thinker does is to articulate ideas implicit in this scheme and give them terminological recognition (conceptualism). Once conceptualism occurs he can manipulate terms in new ways and invent related concepts, which in turn gives him greater freedom to gain mastery over life, existence, or the world.

3. Take the first of the two interrelated terms forced on the thinker, namely *karma,* and consider its implication for his freedom to invent new ideas. One of the most interesting

notions in Buddhism is *anicca,* or impermanence, and it is karma that provides the stimulus for that line of thinking. According to the karma theory every good and bad action I perform must have its fruit *(phala)* or consequence *(vipāka).* Insofar as I cannot exist without continually performing good and bad actions, my "being" or spiritual state is also continually conditioned by karma. For example, my present existence is the product of my karmic actions in my previous birth and innumerable ones before that; this means that my present condition must continually change owing to the operation of these karmic fruits. So is it with my next birth, which is conditioned by the good and bad I now do combined with karmic residues from previous existences. Karma then is the great destabilizer, and it introduces the ideas of change and flux as part of sentient existence. "Impermanent are all conditioned things," say Buddhist texts, precepts, and practices everywhere. It is on the basis of karma that Buddhists have erected their radical theory of impermanence.

4. However, a theory of impermanence need not entail the denial of a stable entity that resists change, namely, the soul. There could exist a still point in the changing world, and Buddhists could easily have retained this idea from a previous rebirth eschatology or from the prior Upanishadic tradition. Yet they did not; for them there is no permanent substrate in the person, and the "soul" itself is a product of constantly changing aggregates, or skandhas. This is a radical innovative break in the tradition of previous thought and is entailed neither by the instability that the karma theory produces nor by the idea of impermanence developed by thinkers on the basis of that karma theory. With this idea Buddhist thinkers have embarked on a daring and autonomous direction that in turn will produce new debates provoked by the angst that the idea of "no soul" must have on those religiously musical people who have invested emotionally in ("cathected") the soul's existence.

5. Let me now deal with a crucial feature of a "rebirth eschatology": it does not concern itself with "salvation." In other words innovative thinkers in the small-scale societies that I have discussed are not obsessed with the idea of an ultimate state of bliss, that paradoxical terminal state in which the world is

transcended. Steps 1 and 2 of my imaginary experiment that produces the karma theory make no change in this situation; one can in principle have a karma theory without the notion of "salvation," if by salvation one means "a state or condition in which suffering is eliminated." Weber rightly noted, "Not every rational religious ethic is necessarily an ethic of salvation. Thus, Confucianism is a religious ethic but it knows nothing at all of a need for salvation. On the other hand, Buddhism is exclusively a doctrine of salvation" (*SR,* 146). And one might add Jainism and forms of Hinduism. All these religions use a term like *nirvana* or *mokṣa* to designate salvation, but although the theologians of these three religions define *nirvana* differently, their definitions have one thing in common: *nirvana has to be sought outside the cycle of rebirths, or samsara; it must result in the cessation of rebirth.* Because salvation or nirvana is neither the concern of a rebirth eschatology nor entailed by the karmic eschatology of our model, it has to be invented by the thinker. However, it is easy to show that once the thinker becomes interested in the idea of salvation, the rebirth eschatology imposes a restriction regarding its nature such that *there is no other way to achieve salvation except outside the rebirth cycle; or, to put it differently, one cannot achieve nirvana except by abolishing rebirth, or samsara.* Let me elaborate.

In a rebirth eschatology there can be no elimination of suffering, which is the sine qua non for any doctrine of salvation, Buddhist or Christian or Pythagorean or Whatever. There can logically be no permanent state of bliss. Why so? First, in a rebirth eschatology the soul's sojourn in the otherworld must perforce be *temporary.* Second, one is eventually reborn in an earthly existence that by any definition must entail suffering. This sojourn is also temporary because after one is born on earth, one has to be reborn in another sphere of existence. If a rebirth eschatology had some notion of a blissful place (as in Trobriand), it is at best an alleviation of suffering, not its elimination, because rebirth in the human world clearly implies its presence. This means that within the rebirth cycle one cannot achieve salvation, defined as either a permanent state of bliss or an elimination of suffering or both. The karmic eschatology of my model makes no difference to the conditions listed above but only exacerbates them. Hence there is no way to define *nirvana* except in such terms as "the elimination of suffering" or "the cessation of rebirth" or "the abolishing of karma." To recapitulate: the seeker of salvation is a creature of the Axial Age; in the Indic context the truth seeker has no choice but to define salvation as something occurring outside the samsaric cycle. As Braudel put it: "mental frameworks too can form prisons of the *longue durée*."[90]

6. Once a new concept has been introduced—in this case nirvana—it must loop back to the earlier concepts and infuse them with further meaning and significance. Such looping back and forth is intrinsic to the propensity that I have called "conceptualism." Thus the introduction of nirvana adds new meaning and significance to the idea of karma. For example, karma ties one down to the cycle of rebirths, or samsara, whereas nirvana is the cessation or transcendence of samsara. The idea of impermanence also gets further existential power because there is now a new eschatological principle that is opposed to it, or transcends it, or is in a dialectical relationship to it. Finally, when nirvana is conjoined with karma, samsara itself gets a further load of undesirable connotations quite unlike those accorded it in small-scale societies in which rebirth is a good thing. This latter idea is partially retained in Buddhism, which recognizes that although samsara is undesirable, birth in a human world is necessary for salvation. Even the highest god must have had a human rebirth at some point in his or her moral career to achieve salvation.

## KARMA, CAUSALITY, AND THE APORIAS OF EXISTENCE

In our imagined karmic eschatology I proposed that good and bad moral actions will have consequences for the after-death fate of an individual. The model postulates that if this logic is carried through, the samanic notion of karma will emerge. Once one has a definition of existence based on ethical causality of this sort, there seems on the face of it little freedom to maneuver for individual religious teachers—according to the logic of the karmic eschatology illustrated in figure 4. Expressing it rather differently, one might say that a strict determinism of karmic rewards and punishments is an *expectable* inference from my model. Yet what is expectable from an ideal scheme of things is never going to be replicated in empirical reality; even so, empirical reality cannot ignore karmic determinism because karma makes no sense without such a notion. Thus the ideal model, as Max Weber recognized, can serve as a means for assessing deviations from it; or, more reasonably, the ideal or utopian conditions postulated by the model might help us understand those complicating existential conditions that always occur in empirical reality.

Only a limited number of ideas could be introduced into the karma doctrine without necessarily affecting its strict determinism. In doctrinal Jainism one cannot escape karma's consequences, which operate irrevocably and mechanically. However, Buddhists gave the karma theory a different emphasis: only intentional and ethically motivated actions have karmic effects. Buddhists also added another dimension to karma by postulating that human pain and suffering can arise from nonkarmic causes. For example, illness can be caused by karma, but it can also be caused through the sole action of the bodily humors. Thus, although karma is deterministic, it is not exclusively so as far as human existence is concerned. In practice one can reconcile the karmic with the humoral by saying that it is a person's karmic condition that permitted the humors to affect his or her health. These qualifications do not affect the claim that karma will eventually have its way, as the following statements from three different texts indicate:

1. Possessed of my own deeds [karma], I am the inheritor of deeds, kin to deeds, one who has deeds as a refuge. Whatever deed I shall do, whether good or evil, I shall become the heir of it. This is to be contemplated by woman, and by man; by householder, and by him who has been taken into the order.[91]
2. Todeyya's son Subha asks the Buddha: "Master Gotama, what is the cause and condition why human beings are seen to be inferior and superior? For people are seen to be short-lived and long-lived, sickly and healthy, ugly and beautiful, uninfluential and influential, poor and wealthy, low-born and high-born, stupid and wise. What is the cause and condition, Master Gotama, why human beings are seen to be inferior and superior?"...

   The Buddha replies: "Student, beings are owners of their actions [karma], heirs of their actions; they originate from their actions, are bound to their actions, have their actions as their refuge. It is action [karma] that distinguishes beings as inferior and superior."[92]
3. The King [Menander or Milinda] said: "Why is it, Nagasena, that all men are not alike, but some are short-lived, some sick and some healthy, some ugly and some beautiful, some without influence and some of great power, some poor and some wealthy, some low-born and some

> high-born, some stupid and some otherwise?" The Elder [Nagasena, the monk] replied: "Why is it that all vegetables are not alike, but some sour, and some salt, and some pungent and some acid, and some astringent and some sweet?" "I fancy, sir, it is because they come from different kinds of seeds." "And just so, great King, are the differences you have mentioned among men to be explained." For it has been said by the Blessed One: "Beings, O Brahman, have each their karma, are inheritors of karma, belong to the tribe of karma, have each their own karma as their protecting overlord. It is karma that divides them into low and high and the like divisions."[93]

The last example in this list, from *The Questions of King Milinda,* was composed in the Indo-Greek kingdom of Bactria several centuries later than the passage preceding it, but the basic position remained unchanged, even though some tinkering with the doctrine of karma had taken place. It seems that Nagasena uses the previous text (or a similar one) as his authority. In all of these texts it is clear that karma is a deterministic force; therefore, it is no wonder that nineteenth-century scholars, influenced by the science of that period, thought that karma appeared to Buddhists as a "natural law." And even though nineteenth-century scientific philosophy is outdated, Buddhist intellectuals, who rarely have moved out of that century, even nowadays refer to karma as a "natural law" in order to designate its determinate and impersonal quality.

There is no way that one can affirm karma yet deny determinism in its operation. Nevertheless, it seems to me that with this determinism arise several existential puzzles, or aporias, that demand resolution; but the resolution of one existential puzzle leads to others, such that aporias are within aporias![94] Structuralists might formulate these aporias in terms of contradictions and their mediation. But I agree with Paul Ricoeur that to frame the issue in this way is to bypass the "aporias of existence" around which mythic and religious thought gravitates.[95] Therefore let me frame for Buddhism some of the aporias that arise from the logic of karmic determinism.

### *The First Aporia: Karma and Punishment*

According to the karmic prescription, if I have done something ethically wrong I will be punished in the future. What it is that I have done ethically wrong, or whether I have done anything ethically wrong at all, is not clear from the punishment I incur during my present existence. Let me give an example: I am young, yet I get an illness and I am to die. I might think that this is because of my bad karma, but I can never be more specific than that. I have to face the fact that although my karmic actions were nonspecific (or nonspecifiable), the punishment happens to be specific. That this has been an issue from the very start in Buddhism is clear from many Buddhist texts in which the Buddha tries to reverse the situation by specifying that such and such a bad rebirth was caused by a specifically bad karmic act; so is it with the good. On the popular level it has led to handbooks that specify a particular type of punishment for a particular karmic misdeed.

More significant is the related issue of whether in fact I know from my punishment whether I have committed a bad karmic act at all. Let us now say that I am old, I have contracted a disease, and I am about to die. Does this mean that I have done something ethically wrong in the past? After all, everyone dies, and my disease may have nothing to do with my karma but simply be due to my inevitable old age and mortality. I think it is to resolve this aporia that early Buddhism postulated nonkarmic causes for misfortune that I have already mentioned, such as humoral and natural calamities and the effect of seasons and climates on people. Thus, although all karma must bear fruit *(phala),* not all "fruit" has been produced by karma. This is an escape clause formulated very early in Buddhism to meet this particular aporia produced by the karma theory.

### *The Second Aporia: The Psychological Indeterminacy of Karma*

The problem with the karma theory is that although it is causally determinate (karma will pay), it leaves the individual in a particularly vulnerable position psychologically. According to karma the past determines my present condition, and my present karmic actions will determine my future-life fate. But here's the rub: my present life situation is, I am told, mostly, if not entirely, owing to what I have done in a past birth or births, *but of this I know nothing*. If I know nothing regarding my karmic past, then I will never know what my present existence holds for me. Consequently, sudden peaks and drops of fortune could occur as results of things I have done in a previous existence (of which I know nothing). Today I am a pauper, tomorrow a prince; today I am young and healthy, tomorrow stricken by a fatal disease. In a religion like Christianity we are all born with a constant load of original sin; any sin or meritorious action I commit is something I am for the most part conscious of. The effect of sin is *psychologically determinate,* and I can do something about it through what the religion has made available to me: faith, sacraments, confessionals, and the like. Not so in karma theory; not only is the load of sin or merit that I am born with different from everyone else's, but I do not know what that load is. Karma produces a *psychological indeterminacy* regarding the life contours of one's present existence that adds to the instability regarding one's moral and spiritual condition that I mentioned earlier. The only way to meet this situation is to know what that past was; but only the Buddha or the Jina or the arahants have the power to "retrocognize" the past. The former two are no longer present, and arahants, even if they are around, rarely proclaim their presence. Thus this problem cannot be resolved within the frame of Buddhist doctrine itself. Buddhists must perforce be satisfied with this indeterminacy, or they must go outside Buddhist doctrine to resolve it.[96]

In my view this is where astrology comes in. Astrology charts the life trajectory of an individual, but although astrology is a deterministic theory (like karma), it is also psychologically determinate. The certainty of astrology compensates for the uncertainty of karma; the astrologer tells you that although you are a pauper today, you will be a prince tomorrow, or that fatal illness will strike you even though you now seem in perfect health. The need to resolve the aporia pertaining to karmic indeterminacy is so great that, in spite of the doctrinal condemnation of astrology as one of the "beastly arts," Buddhist monks have taken over the astrologer role without too much misgiving. What the astrologer does is chart one's karma, and professional Buddhist astrologers will explicitly state this. One of Sri Lanka's most distinguished monks, the late Balangoda Ananda Maitreye, who claimed to be an aspirant for future Buddhahood, put it thus: "The child is born into an environment of planetary influences. . . . Therefore according to each one's karma they fall into different environments. The gravitational pull of planets, their changes and one's own karmic force are interconnected. With a knowledge of astrology, one can understand the karmic force at birth. . . . Therefore, the planets influence a person in accordance with his karma."[97] This posture, however, leads to another problem: once one knows one's karmic condition through astrology, then it is only to be expected that one wants to do something about it. Consequently, something outside of doctrinal Buddhism must again come into the picture and subvert the karmic law, this being the popular rituals denigrated in the doctrinal tradition. There arises an aporia within an aporia owing to an attempt to subvert karma, which in principle cannot be subverted.

### *The Third Aporia: Gods and the Subversion of Karma*

The attempt to ward off karma produces some fundamental "contradictions" in Buddhism as it is practiced. The doctrinal tradition does not seem to have budged on this issue; the gods themselves are karma-bound creatures in need of salvation. Yet, on the other hand, the existence of gods is clearly recognized everywhere in Buddhism; it is their power to subvert karma that is denied. The historical problem is easy to grasp; once the presence of the gods is recognized, as it is in early Buddhism, it is difficult to deny them the power they have always had in the consciousnesses of people who need their help in everyday existence. Although the doctrinal texts affirm that one's present status is karma dependent, popular rituals everywhere give gods the capacity to bring weal or woe to individuals and the group. This simply means that the old life-forms that propitiated gods went on in spite of Buddhism—but only after the gods had been "Buddhicized." I have discussed these processes of Buddhicization elsewhere.[98] The basic idea is that the major gods in a Theravada-Buddhist nation like Sri Lanka are Bodhisattvas, or Buddhas-to-be, and guardians of the secular and spiritual realms. People propitiate the gods and the gods help them; as a gesture of gratitude people transfer merit to the gods, whose own salvation will thereby be short-circuited. Although this theory has no justification in any of the texts of the doctrinal tradition, it appeared as soon as Buddhism became the religion of specific nations in South and Southeast Asia.

### *The Fourth Aporia: Theodicy and the Problem of Suffering*

The previous aporia pertained to the problems of meaning that arise from competing notions of power. It deals with an issue in the ideological system of Buddhism itself. Translated into human terms it means that the gods ameliorate suffering, which everyone knows is overwhelmingly caused by karma. However much the doctrine says that "karma will pay," people are going to be much more ambivalent. Karma will pay, but. . . . In its contestation with Brahmanic thought, Buddhism had to directly confront this issue in its critique of a powerful god who could mitigate human suffering and pain. Consider this portrait of Brahma found in the

*Bhūridatta Jātaka,* from the *Jātaka Tales,* that popular compendium of life stories of the Buddha:

> He who has eyes can see the sickening sight;
> Why does not Brahma set his creatures right?
>
> If his wide power no limits can restrain,
> Why is his hand so rarely spread to bless?
> Why are his creatures all condemned to pain?
> Why does he not to all give happiness?
>
> Why do fraud, lies, and ignorance prevail?
> Why triumphs falsehood,—truth and justice fail?
>
> I count your Brahma one th' unjust among,
> Who made a world in which to shelter wrong.[99]

It seems that even those Buddhist texts like the *Bhūridatta Jātaka* that arose from the popular tradition and fed into it deliberately raised the problem of theodicy: the inability of Brahma, the all-powerful god, to account for the imperfections of the world. In their debate with the Vedic tradition Buddhists scorned Brahma and reaffirmed the universality of karma. By contrast, in later Hinduism it became orthodox for someone to subscribe to the doctrine of karma and simultaneously to the belief in a powerful god (Brahma, Viṣṇu, Śiva, or any of their manifestations), who has the power to subvert it. The result is that in practice many Hindu movements, especially those influenced by *bhakti* devotionalism, are virtually (mono)theistic, so that karma becomes relatively unimportant and could be overcome by a single-minded devotion to god. But in Buddhism there is no such way out, and this entails a logical contradiction in the explanation of suffering: if the gods are powerful enough to ameliorate human suffering, then karma is not the deterministic doctrine it is claimed to be; if karma governs human suffering, then the gods cannot be powerful or capable of subverting it. It seems to me that these types of contradictions cannot be ironed out by scholarly dialectical devices that often impel us to reconcile and systematize them in relation to the rationalizing imperatives of our own disciplines. These "contradictions" are a consequence of the aporias that arise from within an ideology and in many instances *cannot* be resolved. In Theravada Buddhist practice they are expressed and debated in multiple, open-ended discourses, some "authorizing" karma, some de-authorizing it—for example, in popular Buddhist stories, in monk sermons and lay responses, in everyday conversations, as well as on special occasions such as funerals, in discussions about natural and human catastrophes, endlessly.[100] These kinds of aporetic issues and the debates they provoke are not unique to Buddhism but are inherent in any systematizing soteriology.

### *The Fifth Aporia: Doctrinal Responses to Popular Religiosity*

It now would seem apparent that aporias generate aporias; the "aporetic chain" is ultimately traceable to the problems that the doctrine of karmic causality unleashes on the world. It was fashionable in early Indological studies to see inherent contradictions in the belief system as a contamination of the "pure doctrine." But the pure doctrine has been "contaminated" from the very start in many ways. One must not imagine that the aporetic questions arose "later" and were incorporated into later texts or exclusively into the popular religion. If these aporias are not always reflected in the earliest texts, one must not assume that these issues were absent in the controversies of the day. Rather, there was a strong *resistance* on the part of the orthodox tradition to deal with them (resistance being as much a weapon of the strong as it is of the weak). We know that some of these issues were dealt with in the earliest texts, but others were not. Obviously, there cannot be a radical subversion of the karma doctrine that would undermine its totalizing embrace. Hence, little concession is made in the texts that would grant the deities power, and even late texts like the *Bhūridatta Jātaka* affirm the doctrinal position.

Nevertheless, the monks who composed texts dealt with this aporia of karma by rejecting the power of the gods and employing instead the recital of texts from their own tradition modeled on the Vedic practice of mantras, which gives power to the Word. For Buddhism, however, the Word contains the truth of the doctrine, and it is the power of the truth that was operative in the development of its apotropaic verses, some of which come from the oldest stratum of the canon. These are known as *parittas* (protections), and they are recited by monks to bring blessings on people suffering from such things as illnesses, demonic incursions, and other misfortunes. If the intention was to provide a substitute for the propitiation of gods from the preexisting or popular traditions, it certainly failed because now people had one more way to overcome the inexorability of karma!

### *The Sixth Aporia: Karma and Merit Making*

The inevitability of karmic causality is rarely contested in the main body of the doctrine. However, texts such as the "Mahākammavibhaṅga Sutta"

(The greater exposition of action) of the *Middle Length Discourses* could be used to justify the popular idea of counterkarma, the notion that good deeds could cancel the effect of the bad. In this text the Buddha muses on why those who do good might be reborn in good circumstances yet might also be reborn in hell:

> Either earlier he did an evil action to be felt as painful, or at the time of death he acquired and undertook [the] wrong view. Because of that, on the dissolution of the body, after death, he has reappeared in a state of deprivation . . . even in hell. But since he has here [also] abstained from killing living beings . . . and held [the] right view, he will experience the result of that either here or now, or in his next rebirth, or in some subsequent existence."

And for the same reasons (in reverse), those who do bad might be punished in hell, yet they might instead be rewarded in heaven. And the Buddha concludes: "Thus, Ananda, there is action that is incapable [of good result] and appears incapable; there is action that is incapable [of good result] and appears capable; there is action that is capable [of good result] and appears capable; and there is action that is capable [of good result] and appears incapable."[101] Additionally, a strong deed *(bālavakamma)* can on occasion overcome a weak deed *(dubbalakamma)* and produce what is known in the doctrinal tradition as *ahosi karma,* that is, karma that has "lapsed" as a result of its inability to produce "results" *(vipāka),* generally owing to the operation of a strong counteractive karma.[102] From here it is a short way for the popular tradition to reify the idea that a strong deed will cancel out the effect of the weak one and clear the path for merit making and for introducing an ethic of works that will coexist with an ethic of intention.

An important epistemic break occurs with those texts stipulating the three virtues conducive to the accumulation of good deeds or merit *(puñña),* these being, in conventional order, *dāna* (munificence), *sīla* (morality), and *bhāvanā* (meditation). It would seem that these qualities are formulated in terms of the interests of laypersons because meditation, the great Buddhist value, comes last.[103] For the moment let us consider *dāna,* or liberality, the most highly valued quality. *Dāna* has the best effect when it is "sown" in the proper field. A well-known text says that just as seed sown in a "field that is undulating, rocky and pebbly, saltish, without depth of tilth, without (water) outlet . . . is not very fruitful," so gifts [*dāna*] given to monks and men of bad character are barren of result. Similarly, in a "field perfected, when the seed that's sown is perfect and the deva rains perfecting it," one will have perfect grain; so too "perfect alms in perfect precept given lead to perfection—for one's deed is perfect."[104] And of course the best "field of merit" is the monk order!

The idea of the field of merit, with its symbolism of fertility, is obviously to keep the monastic order fed and looked after, but it seems that the doctrine has already tempered its ethic of intentions and opened the way for a Buddhist ethic of "works" whereby the acts of giving to hierarchically ordered fields of merit will have good effects. Thus, parallel with the theory of karma is merit accumulation through good works, a fundamental feature of popular religiosity in Buddhist societies everywhere.

The idea of merit making divorced from the ethic of intention was the major break that led to the mitigation of the harsh karma doctrine. Yet it is always possible to link merit making to intention and affirm that merit making has no real effect unless it is linked with intention. But the field is also clear for separating them and then for linking them up when expedient. Without the idea of merit making, and its relative independence of the ethic of intention, there could not have developed the notion of "merit transfer," a key feature of the popular tradition.

Merit transfer is very popular in everyday life. It postulates that the merit one has made can be transferred to a dead relative in need or to a deity. Regarding the latter there is the case of Nanda's mother, who promised the deity Vessavaṇa (Vaiśravaṇa, the god of the northern quarter) to comply with his wish that when she fed monks the next day she should transfer to him the merit accruing from that act. Consequently, she offered alms to Sāriputta, a senior disciple of the Buddha, and to other monks and then informed Sāriputta:

> "Reverend sir, let all the merit *(puñña)* in this giving be to the happiness of the Royal deva Vessavaṇa!"[105]

And in that most important text dealing with the death of the Buddha, the "Mahā Parinibbāna Sutta," a similar sentiment is expressed in respect to food given to monks:

> In whatever place the wise man makes his home,
> He should feed the virtuous leaders of the holy life.
> Whatever devas there are who report this offering,
> They will pay him respect and honour for this.[106]

Neither text supports the popular idea of merit transfer to dead kin, but the popular idea can derive support from such texts. However, the idea is clearly present in late canonical texts formulated around the second century B.C.E., particularly the *Petavattu,* that dealt with ancestors reborn as miserable spirits, or *pretas* (Pali, *peta*). In these texts the benefactor gives a gift to the monks "and declares the act of charity to be the peta's."[107] It should be added that the pretas need human help. Persons who are dispatched to hell can expiate their bad karma and get reborn on earth, whereas the pretas and demons have no such luck. Once in this miserable state they are in a bind: they have little or no opportunity to do good on their own, and they continue to do bad by causing hurt to humans; therefore, they cannot get out of their miserable state. The laity have little reason to transfer merit to the demons, but they have an obligation to help an ancestor reborn as a miserable preta. It is the case, however, that in Buddhist texts, early or late, merit transfer occurs only in respect to deities, good or bad, whereas ordinary Buddhists transfer merit to any dead kinsperson, enhancing that person's store of merit.

Does this mean that the Buddhists took over the idea of merit transfer from the texts and then extended it to include any dead kinsperson? I doubt this was the case; texts such as those I have quoted probably reflected monk responses to the demands of laypeople; and they tell us how the representatives of the doctrinal tradition were willing to meet those demands. Underlying these texts as we have them today are debates between monks and laypersons regarding the aporias that the karma theory has generated. Yet, as Richard Gombrich shows, the presence of a doctrinal position in turn has significance for lay religiosity also because sophisticated lay folk can refer to that position.[108]

In conclusion, let me consider an idea that appears in both doctrinal and popular levels as the "death wish." Again the older texts unequivocally assert that deeds done or thoughts developed at the point of death may affect the next birth, based on the doctrinal postulate that the last thought conditions the next and that death is simply a thought moment. Texts like the "Mahākammavibhaṅga Sutta" would say that such "thoughts" have to be related to the karmic ethic of intentions. But again is it not likely that the doctrine itself was developed under the influence of the popular thought that took the same idea (that between dying and rebirth is only a thought moment) and tried to condition that moment by apotropaic or magical means, such as the recital of paritta texts? The practices pertaining to merit are ubiquitous in Buddhist societies; but they are nothing new and must, I think, have made their advent in the early years of the founding of the religion.

## ETHICIZATION, KARMA, AND EVERYDAY LIFE

The sage who is accustomed to living in distant places, the egoless and well-conducted one and the householder who supports a family—they are not equal. For the householder is unrestrained and destroys living beings; the sage is self-restrained and protects living beings.

The blue necked peacock which flies through the air, never approaches the speed of the wild goose. Similarly, the householder can never resemble the monk who is endowed with the qualities of a sage who meditates, aloof, in the jungle.

—"Muni Sutta"[109]

The ethicized moral injunctions that govern life are known in Buddhism as *sīla*s, generally translated as "precepts." Of these, five are specially designated as the *panca sīla* (five precepts). If there is anything that marks a Buddhist as such, it is the recital of the Five Precepts. Every Buddhist ceremony or sermon starts with their recital, and it is rare to come across a Buddhist who cannot recite them and gloss their meanings, even though the precepts are formulated in Pali. In Western translations they are sometimes expressed as categorical prohibitions of the "thou shalt not" variety found in Exodus 20:13–16. But precepts, it should be clear from our previous discussions, are not commandments. In Christianity the violation of commandments, insofar as they are God's own imperatives, leads to alienation from God and, in principle at least, to a denial of salvation. This is not the case with the Buddhist precepts, which have little direct relevance to the soteriology.

The Five Precepts have been translated by Saddhatissa as follows:[110]

1. "I undertake the precept to abstain from the taking of life." This precept incorporates the Buddhist ethic of nonviolence, or *ahiṃsā* ("nonhurt"), which applies to all sentient existence.
2. "I undertake the precept not to take that which is not freely given." This precept covers much more than "theft" and includes all sorts of social responsibilities, as both Saddhatissa and Tachibana point out.[111] Marxist monks use this precept to indict capitalism.
3. "I undertake the precept to abstain from sexual misconduct." This precept includes adultery, but it could mean much more than that, although nowhere in the doctrinal texts is this precept explicitly spelled out.[112]

4. "I undertake the precept to abstain from false speech." This includes gossip, slander, and all forms of ill-mannered utterances.
5. "I undertake the precept to abstain from liquor that causes intoxication and sloth." It is interesting that the objection to alcohol is pragmatic; it causes mental sloth and should be avoided. No wonder this same precept could be used by both temperance workers and their opponents! This same pragmatic attitude to alcohol is found in the "Sigālovāda Sutta," where the Buddha advises Sigāla to adhere to precepts one to four (abstention from the four vices of conduct) but refers to alcohol only in the pragmatic context of the "six channels for dissipating wealth."[113]

It would seem that the Five Precepts do not have the specificity that characterizes the biblical commandments or, closer to home, the Jaina injunctions. The latter, no longer called *sīlas* (precepts) but *vratas* (vows), have an extraordinary specificity as befits a religion that enjoins asceticism for the laity.[114] But the seemingly vague Buddhist precepts, like the seemingly precise Jaina ones or the Christian commandments, are nevertheless carefully thought out and constructed, and they possess two significant features. First, there is the absence of a categorical imperative or specificity in formulation; second, it would be impossible to fulfill any of the precepts to the letter. These two features meant that the moral codes of the local community could be incorporated within the precepts and given Buddhist meaning. Therefore, the fact that people recite the Five Precepts surely implies an important affirmation of their belonging to a moral community of Buddhists; it is not necessarily an affirmation of ethical consensus, ideally or otherwise. For example, no one would disagree that adultery is a "sin," but it would be hard to find consensus among Buddhists in different societies on what constitutes "sexual misdemeanor." Historically viewed, the Five Precepts showed a Buddhist tolerance for the values of the local community, which could, without too much conflict, be incorporated into the precepts. This in turn led to the spread of Buddhism among people with differing moral codes, such that one found Buddhism existing in easy harmony with, for example, polygyny and polyandry. In some key texts a courtesan like Aṁbapālī is accepted without negative moral criticism or judgment. The tone of the texts that deal with lay morality is ironic, pragmatic, and lacking severity. Ethicization, in Buddhist societies, occurred without much social disruption or denigration of local values. This did not mean that Buddhist values had no impact. The injunction on ahiṃsā, or nonviolence, was particularly effective in the near elimination of animal sacrifices, helping in the long run to absorb hunting communities into pastoralism and agriculture.[115]

Laypersons are those who are caught in the rebirth cycle, now defined as samsara; they are not expected to renounce the world, so the rewards of salvation are available to them only in the long samsaric run. Thus, as Weber put it, the Five Precepts are "an insufficiency ethic of the weak."[116] One no longer can agree however with Weber's judgment that village Buddhism had no doctrinal sanction; the Five Precepts themselves are part of the doctrine, although invented with the laity in mind. What the doctrine in effect denies to the laity is the practical possibility of nirvana through the Noble Eightfold Path. Thus the laity are given a moral code commensurate with their religious goals, and instead of the primary compensations of nirvana they are given the secondary compensations of a heaven and a happy rebirth. The Five Precepts constitute an ethical framework for right action and are designed for the orderly conduct of social life and the control of drives and passions. A layperson ought to lead a life that avoids bad karmic effects and produces good ones. The Buddha himself put it thus:

> And, householders, there are these five advantages to one of good morality and of success in morality. What are they? In the first place, through careful attention to his affairs he gains much wealth. In the second place, he gets a good reputation for morality and good conduct. In the third place, whatever assembly he approaches, whether of Khattiyas, Brahmins, householders or ascetics, he does so with confidence and assurance. In the fourth place, he dies unconfused. In the fifth place, after death, at the breaking-up of the body, he arises in a good place, a heavenly world. These are the five advantages to one of good morality, and of success in morality.[117]

It is clear that Buddhism does not prescribe asceticism or withdrawal from the world for the laity. Texts such as the "Sigālovāda Sutta" and the "Cakkavatti Sīhanāda Sutta" contain explicit injunctions on how the good life may be led in the world; a virtuous, rather than a virtuoso, life was expected of the laity. A layperson is *expected* to form attachments; he or she need not renounce the world. A beautiful case of the soteriological gap between the layperson and the monk comes out in the conversation between Anāthapiṇḍika, the great physician and friend of the Buddha, as he lay dying, and Sāriputta, a senior disciple of the Buddha who consoled him with a sermon befitting the time of the "death wish." When Anāthapiṇḍika shed tears because he hadn't heard a sermon of that nature before, even though he had been closely associated with the monk order, Sāriputta replied that laypeople cannot understand such things; only monks can. According to Walpola Rahula the commentary on this text states that "lay people have a strong craving and attachment to their lands and fields, gold and wealth, wives and children and servants and that they neither understand nor like to hear a talk that advocates the renunciation of these possessions."[118] It is not surprising, Rahula adds, that one of the six duties of the monk is to show the way to heaven *(saggassa maggam)*, but the way to heaven is not the way to emancipation *(mokkhassa maggam)*.[119]

The many heavens in Buddhism are drawn in graphic detail in such late texts as the *Vimānavattu* (Stories of heavenly mansions) and in the popular imagination.[120] They are entirely sensuous, with women and music, dancing, and wish-fulfilling trees. Nevertheless, everyone in the lay community knows that these pleasures are characterized by impermanence. So are Buddhist hells, although a sinner can roast in them for eons before getting out. Although heaven titillates the senses and hells are nasty places that the virtuous should avoid, the truly serious lay preoccupation is with an imagined rebirth on earth. Most people attach a *prārthanā* (formal rebirth wish) when they perform a merit-producing act and ask for material rewards—health, wealth, sensuous delights, power, prestige, high caste status—and, if the devotee is a woman, sometimes the wish to be born as a male. By contrast a bad rebirth is literally a hell on earth. People generally know that no one leads a life of unmitigated earthly bliss; everyone, rich and poor, suffers the vicissitudes of fortune. Part of this inevitability of suffering in any human rebirth results from the fact that the precepts are impossible to wholly fulfill; there is no way that one can *not* be a sinner some of the time. Hence human life as seen and experienced on earth excites the Buddhist imagination as a powerful moral scenario. The beggar, the cripple, the destitute, the sick, and the ghostly spirits who haunt human habitations are all embodiments of suffering, symbolic representations of those who have sinned. So are animals, especially bulls (and, at one time, pack oxen), which, like the very poor, are destined to bear burdens; and those creatures, such as cobras, that creep into your house because of previous life attachments; they all affect the imagination in similar ways although not as powerfully as human sufferers. Thus the whole environment of humans and animals is an ethicized world—an ethicization that, we have already seen, is inevitable when the notions of "sin" and "merit" and the accompanying principle of the conditionality of reward is imposed on a rebirth eschatology.

## ASCETIC RELIGIOSITY AND THE ESCAPE FROM THE WORLD

Laypersons may be incapable of achieving salvation in this life, but they can achieve it in some future one. Thus the wish to eventually escape from the wheel of rebirth is part of the long-term soteriological motivations of most people. The renunciatory ideal itself is represented in the great ascetics of the Buddha's time, the "elders," or *theras,* after whom the religion Theravada is named. These monks have achieved nirvana and are therefore called arahants. The "arahant ideal" is a powerful conception in the imagination of the Buddhist laity, a measure by which ordinary people evaluate the virtue of monks. Although unreachable for the many, renunciation is the ideal for all. Yet as an ideal it is represented in different ways and at different levels in those persons who have, temporarily or permanently, renounced the world.

Let me begin with the situation on the village level in Sri Lanka; in virtually every village, nowadays, there are a few elderly laypersons known as *upāsakas* who have moved out of the daily routine of existence to adopt a special kind of asceticism. In the classical doctrine the term *upāsaka* simply meant "lay follower." But in the practical religion the upāsaka is a lay devotee who, in middle or old age, has made a partial withdrawal from the world, generally after his or her children have grown up and married. The renunciatory thrust of the upāsaka is expressed in the recital of the Eight or Ten Precepts (an artificial distinction because the Ten Precepts are only a reclassification of the Eight). The Ten Precepts are the more popular classification and include the Five Precepts plus five more:

6. Abstinence from eating at unseasonable times (that is, after 12 noon)
7. Abstinence from witnessing displays of dancing, singing, music
8. Abstinence from the use of garlands, unguents, scents
9. Abstinence from the use of a high or big bed
10. Abstinence from receiving gold and silver

The Ten are observed on the *uposatha* day, which occurs four times a month, corresponding to the four phases of the waxing and waning moon, the most important being the full-moon day. Popularly known as *poya* in Sri Lanka, the uposatha was a Buddhist adaptation of the Vedic *upavasatha,* in which the householder and his wife fasted one day every half lunar month while preparing for the sacrifice the next day. On poya the pious layperson is expected to devote the whole day to religious meditation and reading. Although this form of piety is theoretically open to all, irrespective of age and sex, its actual practice, until very recently, has been almost exclusively with the elderly.

The term *gṛhastha upāsaka* is sometimes reserved for those who regularly observe the Ten Precepts. *Gṛhastha* is the householder stage in the Brahmanic fourfold scheme of life, but it refers here to those who have temporarily renounced the world while still being householders. A few of these people may decide to practice the precepts not only on poya days but consistently as a way of life and therefore are designated "the *upāsakas* of the Ten Precepts." Because the Ten Precepts are also the code for the Buddhist novice, or *sāmaṇera,* an "*upāsaka* of the Ten Precepts" leads the life of a novice monk although technically a layperson. Sri Lanka does not have the institution that is omnipresent in Buddhist Southeast Asia, where young men get initiated as novices for a few months and actually live in monasteries. These temporary ordinations are again based on the ideology of renunciation and in turn, like that of the upāsaka lifestyle, reinforce that ideology.

There are important differences between the Five and the Ten Precepts: with the latter the upāsaka has moved into a form of life different from that of the ordinary layperson. First, precepts six to ten provide a specificity that the original five precepts lack. Second, the latter precepts require a partial suspension of lay living, a necessary requirement for the higher spiritual life. Thus the injunction on "gold and silver" requires one to withdraw from the economic life of the village. Further, the third precept of the Five Precepts is categorically redefined; the "sexual misdemeanor" of the original is reformulated as total sexual abstinence. Third, insofar as the Ten Precepts prescribe shunning worldly pleasures, total abstention from sexuality, and withdrawal from the economic life of society, there is no way that these ethics could ever operate as general societal norms. Or, to put it differently, you cannot have a social order constituted on the basis of the Ten Precepts. They constitute not an ethicization of a preexistent social morality but an invention of a new renunciatory ethic modeled on it.

It must be emphasized that the rules themselves merely set the stage for the devout life; they help the upāsaka to lead a life of piety and meditation away from the distractions of the world. It is generally the upāsakas who can afford to ignore the gods and resolve that particular aporia because, having renounced the lay life, they rarely need the gods for help in worldly matters. The demons, however, are not easy to refute because, at least in village life, their powers are being vindicated by the direct evidence of those who get possessed by them. In such instances upāsakas can at least affirm that they are personally safe from harm owing to their belief in the dhamma or because only sinners can be harmed by demons. Some upāsakas can even deny the efficacy of counterkarma, although rarely that of merit transfer owing to the doctrinal support given to the latter. For others counterkarma can be important because it can support the whole institution of upāsaka-hood, for according to counterkarma one can compensate for the indiscretions of one's youth by ascetic moral behavior in old age.

If the upāsaka and the novice have only to practice the Ten Precepts, the fully ordained *(upasampadā)* monk must adhere to the 220 rules laid down in the *Pātimokkha* section of the Vinaya (the books of the discipline).[121] All these rules are characterized by extreme specificity and are designed to move the monk away from the lay world and into the life of monastic asceticism. These special rules express the great soteriological gap that separates the monk from both the lay upāsaka (and novice) and the layperson and set the stage for a further and more drastic move toward renunciation and salvation. Not by themselves sufficient, they help frame acts of renunciatory behavior that take the actor away from the world.

We now encounter one of the great paradoxes of Buddhist monasticism: the rules are designed to take the monk away from the secular society, but they cannot be effective for two reasons. First, the monk has certain parish roles to fulfill, such as preaching to the laity and officiating at death and commemoration ceremonies and paritta recitals (but never at puberty rites and marriage, at least until very recent times). Second, although the monk has escaped from lay society, he is caught up in the social structure of the monastic community, which in turn takes its bearing from the lay social order outside. In the Buddhist world, as everywhere else, monks are involved in political conflicts and conflicts over power and position that operate within the order itself or between the order and the secular authorities. For example, monks are generally extremely inclined toward status and are addicted to titles and honorifics, which they love to display. Again: monks are expected to renounce caste, but in Sri Lanka, at least from the eighteenth century onward, the Siamese fraternity exclusively recruited its members from the high farmer *(goyigama)* caste, and especially wealthy temples tolerated chief monks from only the aristocratic segment of that caste. The colonial period gave impetus for the aspiring lower castes in the maritime areas to assert their dignity, and soon they went to Burma and inaugurated two new fraternities, the Amarapura and the Ramañña. Although these fraternities were more open in their recruitment patterns, each temple or monastery tended to favor its own caste members. In all three fraternities small groups of very low castes, such as *kinnaras* (mat weavers) and *roḍiyas* (professional beggars), are not represented at all and in rare instances are not even permitted to enter the temples. Monks from the traditional Siamese fraternity in the Kandyan areas often refuse to accept alms from them. Ironically, caste, status, and power distinctions within the order are important for the monks alone; for the laity in general anyone who wears a yellow robe is a "son of the Buddha" and worthy of respect. In fact, some high-caste groups may prefer to give alms to the Ramañña and Amarapura fraternities because they believe that they are more pious and less worldly than the monks of the dominant Siamese fraternity.

It therefore seems that the monk has escaped from one social structure only to get caught up in another. Moreover, that other society is also involved in the lay community, although in some historical periods more conspicuously involved than in others. If renunciation aims to remove the fetters that bind one to worldly affairs, the monk has not succeeded. It follows that although he represents a doctrine whose goal is salvation, he himself cannot achieve this salvation except in a later, even remote, rebirth. He, like his lay parishioner, is caught up in a social system that inhibits the Noble Eightfold Path, which alone can guide him to his idealized goal. In the time of the Buddha the textual tradition asserts the goal of nirvana was realized by many arahants; not so with the routinization of monasticism. The arahant goal has become remote for monk, upāsaka, and layperson alike. Yet nirvana remains the ideal still. How then can one reach the seemingly unreachable?

In later nondoctrinal religiosity it is said that one can achieve nirvana by being born in the dispensation of the next Buddha, Maitreye, and obtain release by listening to his sermons. It is not surprising that this doctrine of a future redeeming messiah should have developed. Many laypeople include this aspiration in their rebirth wishes, or *prārthanā.* But the interpretation of this doctrine is not uniform. For some laypeople listening to the sacred words of the messianic Maitreye alone might provide sudden illumination that leads them to the nirvanic path without renunciatory effort. But how is this possible? The Greek Bactrian king Milinda (Menander) asked the monk Nagasena how and why thousands of lay devotees in the Buddha's own time achieved nirvana without really trying! Milinda's dilemma could be summed up: If people can achieve nirvana without effort by being householders or gods (gods being a species of laypersons), what is the use of ascetic renunciation?[122]

Nagasena, the monk, replies that those laypersons who achieved nirvana did not do so without effort. In previous births they had performed the prerequisite ascetic renunciations, but the fruits of their efforts were realized only in the present rebirth. Hence ascetic renunciation at some point in one's samsaric career is absolutely necessary for salvation, but instead of being concentrated in one lifetime, it is scattered through many.

What then happens to the monk who wants to engage in the meditative effort that will hasten his salvation? The logical answer is simple enough: he must escape from his home in the monastery in a further flight into homelessness. This solution has in fact been institutionalized in the history of Theravada Buddhism in its two monastic orientations: the *grāmavāsin* (village dwellers), monks who live in temples and monasteries and perform parish roles, and the *vanavāsin* (forest dwellers), who pursue their own salvation with diligence away from it all. The main task of the former is *grantha dhura,* the way of learning and parish activity, whereas that of the latter is *vipassanā dhura,* or meditative work.[123] There is no question whatever that it is the vanavāsins who represent in the public imagination the approximation of the arahant ideal.

The modern resurgence of the forest-dwelling (vanavāsin) movement has been beautifully recorded by Michael Carrithers for Sri Lanka and by Stanley Tambiah for Thailand.[124] In contemporary Buddhist nations these monks are found living in isolation in forest hermitages. But even for the most assiduous of them final escape from the world is not easy. Soon their fame as "good monks" and as true "fields of merit" spread. There is no way that they can escape the relentless piety of devotees who seek them out in their forest fastnesses, invade their solitude, and thus help destroy the very saintliness that they so much admire.

I knew one such place in the late 1950s, named Salgala. Originally it was a place where a number of forest dwellers lived in caves and meditated. But soon their fame spread. Laypersons from all over the country wanted to come to Salgala to give alms (dāna) to these virtuous monks. The pressures were so great that a local committee had to be formed to coordinate the alms-giving arrangements. Soon the caves and cloisters were floored with cement and a *vihāra* (temple) was built in the forest. This pattern is not at all unusual and can be seen in several ancient archaeological sites.[125] Today this development can be bypassed altogether. Philanthropic donors build comfortable meditation chambers *(kuṭis)* in somewhat isolated places where monks, and nowadays pious laypeople and salvation-seeking foreign tourists, can meditate for short or long periods. Some monks, still dissatisfied with these bourgeois arrangements, take refuge in other caves in less-known places. But their respite is temporary. Even the most isolated hermit must from time to time wander into outlying villages in search of alms. But then, as his reputation for holiness spreads, he finds it ever more difficult to escape the curiosity and zeal of the pious; and the historic cycle keeps repeating itself.

# 4 THE BUDDHIST ASCESIS

## THE IMAGINED BUDDHA

In chapter 3 I showed how religious innovations are constrained within the limits of prior structures of thought. At the same time I also wanted to give agency and creative capacity to religious innovators, but I was constrained by the imprisoning frames imposed by prior scholarship and my own preconceptions. Although poorly documented, creativity and cultural innovativeness are found in small-scale societies—we know this from the early work of Paul Radin, the lives of prophets like Handsome Lake and, of course, the famed Ogotommeli.[1] When we move to Greece in chapter 5, we will find scholarly constructions of the "real Pythagoras" from a mass of mythic data considered empirically unreliable. So is it with Empedocles; but in him we can sense a passionately religious and creative mind actively inventing or reconstituting cosmological systems. The situation is no different in respect to the "historical" Buddha. The Theravada texts give us virtually no information on the actual life of the Buddha prior to his "Enlightenment." Undeterred by this limitation scholars have constructed the real Buddha from mostly mythic material in the texts. And almost any text on Buddhism can give a good account of his life and death. I am not against this procedure; there are good reasons for understanding the historical Buddha, if that is in any way possible. Nevertheless, I want to adopt another strategy and take seriously the *myths* about the Buddha's birth, renunciation, and Awakening (Enlightenment) for what they can tell us about his quest for salvation through specific forms of ascesis.

In my thinking the Buddha could be a historical figure without being a figure of the empirical historiography of the scholar. That is, Buddhists right down the ages thought that the Buddha was a historical being, *and* they believed literally in what we would call his mythos. Buddhism is also a historical religion in another sense: it traces its chronology from the death of the founder. It was immaterial from the subjective viewpoint of Buddhists whether different Buddhist traditions had different chronologies. In looking at mythic texts sympathetically I am arguing against a very powerful opinion among European scholars that Buddhism was a "rational religion" without a savior and a cult. This orientation of orientalists sympathetic to Buddhism had a double thrust. First, "rational Buddhism" was a way of holding up Christianity to critical reflection, especially its central mystery of the death and resurrection of Christ and, after Darwin, its creation myth. Second, Buddhism was a religion that went counter to the "irrationality" of Hinduism and of popular religions in both India and South Asia in general, and this included societies that were "officially" Buddhist. In this sense Buddhist rationality has to be understood against the backdrop of the larger discourse of orientalism in South Asia. Idealistically motivated orientalists arrested the negative images of South Asia fostered by orientalism and in its stead invented a rational religion, consonant with Europe's own Enlightenment. In India's general darkness Buddhism was the "light." This idea was given poetic expression and symbolic recognition in Sir Edwin Arnold's popular (and boring) Victorian poem "The Light of Asia." It is no wonder that native intellectuals have begun to accept this Western scholarly definition of Buddhism as the "pure Buddhism" of the Pali Canon. Scholars and educated laypersons are aware of the seemingly miraculous elements in the Buddha mythos but only as accretions to a pristine Buddhism that can be elicited by a critical reading of the Pali Canon.[2]

Certainly Buddhism encourages a modern rationalist interpretation. On one hand, there seems to be no central mystery in doctrinal Buddhism such as the resurrection; it has no creator god, no theodicy. Yet, on the other hand, the Buddha appears as a mythic persona even in the earliest body of texts, and although this belief is not necessary for salvation, practically every Buddhist thinker believed that the Buddha was a supernormal, if not a supernatural, being, that he possessed the thirty-two marks of the Great Man (Mahāpuruṣa), and that he was born in a miraculous manner, outside of normal bodily processes. Until modern times Buddhist thinkers never made the distinction between the rational and the miraculous elements in their religion. They did emphasize the historicity of the Buddha, but their notion of historicity was not the literal or empirical historicity of the scholarly imagination.

References to the miraculous birth of the Buddha occur in several ancient texts of the Pali Canon. In the "Acchariyabbhutadhammasutta" (Discourse on wonderful and marvellous qualities) the Buddha asks Ānanda, his personal attendant, cousin, and favorite disciple, to relate to the assembled monks the miracle of the Buddha's birth.[3] According to Ānanda the Buddha-to-be was born in the Tusita heaven, and, after his life span there was over, he decided to be reborn in the human world, "mindful and clearly conscious." He entered the mother's womb, mindful and clearly conscious, and when this happened the "ten-thousand-world system quaked, trembled and shook, and there appeared the illimitable glorious radiance surpassing even the divine majesty of the gods."[4] As he enters the womb, four gods guard the four quarters to prevent any human or nonhuman from annoying the Buddha-to-be or his mother. As for the mother, the text continues: "When, Ānanda, the Bodhisatta is entering his mother's womb, no desire connected with the strands of sensual pleasures rises in the Bodhisatta's mother towards men, and the Bodhisatta's mother is not to be transgressed against by any man of infatuated thoughts" (*MLS,* 3:166). There is another miracle: the mother sees the Buddha-to-be in her womb as an emerald jewel, and the child is "complete in all his limbs, his sense organs perfect" (*MLS,* 3:167). She gives birth to him exactly at ten months, and she does so while in an upright position. Moreover, as the Buddha is born, "he issues quite stainless, undefiled by watery matter, undefiled by mucus, undefiled by blood, undefiled by any impurity." He is "pure and stainless" (*MLS,* 3:168). The reason for his condition is also given in the text: it is because of the purity of both mother and son. The text lists other miracles also and mentions the fact that the mother of the Bodhisattva (the Buddha-to-be) dies seven days after he is born, and this is true of all Buddhas because they possess an identical life history.

Clearly then conception did not occur through sexual intercourse; moreover, although Māyā, the mother of the Buddha, could not be converted into a virgin in the historical traditions of Buddhism, she does avoid sexual relations at the time of conception. She observes the Five Precepts of Buddhism from her very birth, and she conceives the Buddha when she is observing celibacy (that is, the Ten Precepts, one of which enjoins celibacy). Yet what about the necessity for the mother to die in seven days? Some Theravada commentators say that this is to preserve the purity of the mother "because no other child is fit to be conceived in the same womb as a Buddha."[5] The most interesting answer is given in the *Mahāvastu,* the famous text of the Lokottaravadins (Transcendentalists), which postulates sexual rather than childbirth pollution. "I will descend," says the Bodhisattva, "into the womb of a woman who has only seven nights and ten months of her life remaining." And why so? "Because," says he, "it is not fitting that she who bears a Peerless One like me should afterwards indulge in love."[6] It therefore seems that the death of Māyā seven days after the Buddha's birth cannot be taken literally or even to mean that "she died soon after," as most assume. Rather, Māyā's death is a structural requirement of the myth: the pure womb from which the Buddha was born could not thereafter be contaminated by childbirth or sexual pollution.

And where was the Bodhisattva born? Most popular and doctrinal texts agree that he was born in a grove of *sāla* trees in Lumbini. Let me present one well-known version. The queen, Mahāmāya, informs Suddhodana, her husband, of her desire to visit her parents' home at Devadaha to give birth to her child (a perfectly normal custom in both India and other patrilineal societies for ensuring the psychological welfare of the woman at a critical phase in her life). Suddhodana consents, decorates the road between Kapilavastu, his capital, and Devadaha with plantain trees, pots full of water, and banners and streamers. "Now between the two towns there is a pleasure grove of Sāla-Trees, called the Lumbini Park, belonging to the citizens of both towns. At that time all the trees were one mass of blossoming flowers from the root to the topmost branches. In between the branches and the flowers swarms of bees of five varieties and flocks of birds of many species moved about warbling in sweet tones."[7] The Bodhisattva is born in a liminal space, in the home of neither the mother nor the father but in between, in a space that belonged to the citizens of both towns. This means that the hero does not belong to his father or mother but to the people or the world in general. The sāla trees under which he is born are not the trees found in Indian forests but a mythic sāla blooming from the root to the topmost branches. As he is born, he takes seven steps, and from each step a lotus flower blooms, presumably to prevent dust from touching his feet. I suspect that this mytheme derives from the seven steps of the Soma cow named Dakṣinā; ritual substances are put on each step, and the symbolism of the seventh step, on which gold and ghee are put according to J. C. Heesterman, is "the head of the earth" or "the sacrificial spot of the earth."[8] In similar fashion the Buddha also *surveys the four quarters of the world,* the locus of his transcendental and universal teaching. This miracle of the child-Buddha is, on another level, deliberately constructed to surpass that of the god Viṣṇu's crossing the earth in three strides and thereby symbolically acquiring dominion over the earth.

When the Buddha was born, the sage Asita predicted that he would be either a world-conquering monarch or a world-renouncing Buddha. Both are models of heroes or great men *(mahāpuruṣa),* but of radically different orientations, one totally involved in the world of wealth and power and the other totally removed from it. Their births and deaths are heralded with miraculous events. Both have the thirty-two marks of a Great Man, and these are spelled out in great detail in Theravada texts like the "Mahāpadāna Sutta."[9] Modern scholars who tell us that the Bodhisattva's father was a *rāja* (minor chief) are not only missing the point; they are guilty of extrapolating an empirical reality from a mythic or symbolic set of events. For all we know the *empirical* Buddha might not have had a father at all, or, more likely, he had ordinary parents. The *real* Buddha of the Buddhist imagination was born apposite to a world conqueror: the texts make this clear by the mythicization of his father, who is presented as a great king, living in wealth, splendor, and power. The father also wanted the Bodhisattva to be a world conqueror, as befits his heritage, and kept him confined to the walls of the palace. The mansion of the prince has everything to satisfy the senses: women, music and dancing, luxury. Given this context, the birth of the Buddha makes sense: he is cast in the heroic mold of the world-conqueror *(jina),* the conqueror over the very things that embodied his other and more profound birthright—that of Buddhahood.

The confrontation of the two ideal models—royalty and renunciation—occurs in the famous myth of the four signs. The great Buddhist scholar Aśvaghoṣa says that the four signs were created by the gods, and the popular *Jātaka Nidāna* says that the deities thought thus: "Prince Siddhārtha's time for Enlightenment is drawing near; let us show him the Omens [signs]."[10] As I read this myth, the prince was a prisoner of hedonism prevented from knowing the outside world by his well-intentioned father. One day the prince goes for a drive into the city with his charioteer, Channa. There he meets with the spectacle of a feeble old man, a sight that he has never seen before. In other visits to the city he sees the spectacle of sickness, then death, and then the transcendence of all of these in the serene calm of the yellow-robed renouncer. The hero is confronted with the skull beneath the skin, the true nature of the world from which he had been insulated, the world of transience and decay, and he is also presented a model for overcoming them all in that of the renouncer. Note the setting: the hero goes in his chariot in splendor into the city; what confronts him there is the very opposite of what exists within the walls of the palace. When he comes back from his last trip to the city and witnesses the final sign of the homeless renouncer, he is told that a son is born to him, reminding him that he is trapped in a life of domesticity, that of the home. The child is named Rāhula, etymologically the diminutive of *Rāhu,* the demon who swallows the moon and causes the world to darken. Perhaps this signifies that the birth of the heir is a threat to the aspirations of the Buddha, the moon. Theravada Buddhists, however, have ignored this etymology and invented their own: Rāhula is the "fetter," the chain that binds the Bodhisattva to the home. But he decides to break this fetter, and silently bidding his wife and son farewell, he prepares to leave the palace. Oldenberg summarizes this part of the myth as follows:

> In his palace the prince was surrounded by beautiful, gaily attired handmaids, who sought to dissipate his thoughts with music and dance: but he neither looks upon nor listens to them, and soon falls into sleep. He wakes up at night and sees by the light of the lamps those dancing girls wrapt in slumber, some talking in their sleep, some with running mouths, and of others again the clothes have become disarranged and exposed repulsive deformities of the body. At this sight it was to him as if he were in a burial place full of disfigured corpses, as if the house around was in flames.[11]

This powerful myth is known to practically every Buddhist; it is also a "myth model" for other stories and other lives in the Buddhist tradition—that of someone who is a prisoner of hedonism seeing its unsatisfactory nature and deciding to renounce the world. Historically viewed, the Buddha myth with its ideal of homelessness and the rejection of family life must be seen in an ironic relation to Brahmanic ideals that extol their very opposites, that is, the importance of domestic life and ritual and especially the birth of the son, who is necessary for the salvation of the father.

Satiated with hedonism, the Bodhisattva leaves his palace, accompanied by Channa, his charioteer, and his horse, Kanthaka. The horse is also portrayed in heroic dimensions: he "was eighteen cubits in length starting from his neck, and was of proportionate height; he was strong and fleet of foot, all-white as a cleansed chank (shell)."[12] The Bodhisattva rides the horse while Channa clings to his tail. The horse clears the ramparts of the city, eighteen cubits high, in one bound; he then leaps over the river Anomā. Here the Bodhisattva cuts his hair and beard, sheds his royal clothes, and dons the mendicant garb. The gods carry his hair to the Tāvatiṃsa heaven, where it is enshrined. This part of the text constitutes a myth-charter for the enshrinement of the Buddha's relics in later times.

Crossing the river in this and in similar cases is also a symbolic act: a movement from one form of life to another, from the world of the world-conqueror to that of the world-renouncer. The cutting off of worldly ties is complete, but the hero has still not achieved his goal. It should be remembered that the Buddha's personal name is Siddhārtha, meaning "he whose aim is accomplished." But the Bodhisattva is not yet a Buddha; he still remains a liminal persona. He has given up his royal status, but he has not yet accomplished his aim. Like neophytes in initiation rites and like other heroes of myth, the Bodhisattva has many obstacles to overcome before he reaches his goal. These are not physical obstacles, however, but ones that are moral and spiritual. Let me mention two such obstacles well known in both the popular and doctrinal traditions.

After he renounces the world the Bodhisattva seeks the help of gurus, as is customary in the Indic traditions. Following their advice he courts forms of extreme physical penance and deprivation, also common at the time, for six years. The pain, endurance, and suffering of the Bodhisattva are described in the first person in several texts, and his physical emaciation is vividly represented in memorable Buddhist sculptures. One of the most powerful texts dealing with this topic is the "Mahāsīhanāda-sutta" (Greater discourse on the lion's roar). Here the Buddha tells Sāriputta, his major disciple, that he lived on virtually nothing, "unclothed, flouting life's decencies, licking my hands (after meals)."[13] The Buddha then describes taboos pertaining to the acceptance of food. Such taboos were common among ascetic sects of the time and totally against the highly decorous practices initiated by the Buddha after the monk order was established. So was it with the kinds of clothes he wore: "I wore rags taken from the dust heap, and I wore tree-bark fibre. . . . I wore a blanket of human hair, and I wore a blanket of animal hair, and I wore owl's feathers. I was one who plucked out the hair of his head and beard. . . . I made my bed on covered thorns. . . . Thus in many a way did I live intent on the practice of mortifying and tormenting my body" (*MLS,* 1:104–5). And the effect of these practices?

> Because I ate so little, all my limbs became like the knotted joints of withered creepers; because I ate so little, my buttocks became like a bullock's hoof; because I ate so little my protruding backbone became like a string of balls; because I ate so little my gaunt ribs became like the crazy rafters of a tumble-down shed; because I ate so little, the pupils of my eyes appeared lying low and deep in their sockets as sparkles of water in a deep well appear lying low and deep; because I ate so little, my scalp became shrivelled and shrunk as a bitter white gourd cut before it is ripe becomes shrivelled and shrunk by a hot wind. If I, Sāriputta, thought: "I will touch the skin of my belly," it was my backbone that I took hold of. For because I ate so little, the skin

> on my belly, Sariputta, came to be cleaving to my backbone. If I, Sāriputta, thought: "I will obey the calls of nature" I fell down on my face then and there, because I ate so little. (*MLS,* 1:107)

What then is happening here? The Bodhisattva is now the prisoner of asceticism! Let me now reflect on the earlier part of the Buddha myth: the Buddha's father, the great Suddhodana, has a palace for each of the three seasons; he provides hedonistic pleasures for his son, including music and dancing women. In practicing asceticism the Bodhisattva has moved from the indulgence of sensual pleasures to its very opposite—the mortification of the body. On another level one might attribute unconscious personal meaning to his asceticism: by punishing himself he is trying to expiate the guilt he feels for violating powerful family values and ideals of filial and domestic piety by forsaking his wife, son, and parents. He must overcome this obstacle to achieve the "middle path."

According to some texts, the night he gave up asceticism he dreamed five dreams prognosticating that he would be a Buddha. The Buddha decides to eat food; his first meal consists appropriately of a food consumed on auspicious occasions, namely, milk rice. It is given to him by a woman from the merchant class who had vowed to offer food to the deity of the banyan tree under which the Buddha was seated. Some accounts say that she was the first human witness to the new birth, or Awakening; hence she is Sujātā (happy birth). Aśvaghoṣa, attuned to the larger symbolic tradition of Indian myth, has the milk rice given to the Buddha by Nandabālā, daughter of a chief of cowherds—nurturant, milk-producing folk.

After the Buddha consumes this meal, he wants to know whether he is going to achieve true knowledge. He vows that if his begging bowl goes upstream when placed in the river Nerañjarā, he will accept this as a sign that he has achieved the true knowledge. This happens, and the bowl is carried by the river's vortex into the realm of the *nāga*s (mythic cobra beings), always devotees of the Buddha, and there it meets the bowls of three previous Buddhas. The symbolism here I think is clear: in practicing austerities the Buddha has experienced a kind of death; he is reborn by the food offered by a woman from the merchant class, the very class that supported Buddhism later on. But this physical rebirth or awakening is not the crucial one; it is followed by a psychological and spiritual reawakening. The bowl that goes "against the current" symbolizes a teaching that goes counter to people's normal drives.

The Buddha now moves from the banyan tree to the Bodhi tree *(ficus religiosa)* nearby, the tree under which he will achieve an Awakening.

Facing the East, again symbolizing a rising, he decides not to move until he has found out the truth of existence. The next great mythic episode occurs when, meditating under the Bodhi tree, he is assailed by Māra, Death himself, who is also Ananga, the Indian Cupid waging war against the Buddha. This episode is described in graphic detail in the popular traditions, and I will not deal with it here except to say that Māra attacks the Buddha with multiple weapons, but the imperturbable sage remains untouched, such being the power of the perfections *(pāramitā)* practiced in past births.

In the first watch of the night the Buddha enters into the four states of meditative trance leading to complete equanimity. In this state he has a "divine vision" through which details of his former existences—hundreds and thousands of them—appear before his consciousness. During the second watch he sees in his vision the passing and rising of human beings through the universal action of karma and rebirth; and in the last watch he sees the nature of error, the Four Noble Truths of Buddhism, and, according to some sources, the difficult theory of causality known as *paticcasamuppāda* (dependent origination).[14] After his Awakening he spends seven weeks in meditation, during which he meets with further spiritual adventures. In the most famous of these, Māra appears before him, enticing him with the sensual passions represented by Māra's voluptuous daughters. After seven weeks the hero is reborn again, or in Buddhist terminology, he is the "*Fully* Awakened One," a term European scholars, influenced by their own Enlightenment, have generously sanctified as "the Enlightenment." The Buddha's Awakening *is* the *mysterium tremendum et fascinans* of Buddhism idealized by others who follow the path of meditative ascesis. The double entendre of *awakened* is significant: first, the Buddha has passed the liminal stage and emerged into a new life-form and into the founding of a new order; second, his is a spiritual awareness, a discovery of a way of salvific knowledge, an Awakening, not an "Enlightenment."[15] The latter, I will show in chapter 6, would come later.

## THE RENUNCIATORY IDEAL IN THE BUDDHIST IMAGINATION

The Buddhist ideal, mirrored in the Buddha myth, is a renunciatory one in which deep meditative asceses open the way to salvation. This salvation is theoretically available to all but effectively for those who have opted for the homeless life. The great virtuosos who have adopted the Buddha's own example and training are the elders of old, the arahants, men and women who, like the master himself, have realized nirvana. The question I will now pose is one I cannot fully answer myself: why the powerful hold of the "arahant ideal" in the consciousness and imagination of ordinary Buddhists?

The place to begin is today, when politically involved monks have deliberately renounced the detached stance of the classic ideal, actively participating in political and social events, sometimes encouraging violence, even practicing it on occasion. The public have a very ambivalent attitude to such monks, and they often rationalize the honor they pay them by saying "we worship the yellow robe and not the person"; that is, they honor what the vestment represents, not the person wearing it. When the monk wears the yellow robe and has the bearing of the "true monk" with his slow walk, bowed head, and air of indifference to the world outside, people imagine him to represent the old ideal. I have known white robed lay virtuosos, or upāsakas, who are highly regarded by villagers, more so than their own monks, because of their detached bearing and decorous demeanor. In the popular imagination these embodiments of the arahant ideal represent what we, as laypersons, are not. We are caught up in social networks, in deep attachments, in the world of striving and want and in the samsaric struggle of living in general. Or, as the Buddha himself put it, laypersons are "bound to others by their obligations," whereas the arahant ideal represents the transcendence of all of these.[16] The arahant mirrors the calm that we also seek but can never hope to achieve.

Emile Durkheim understood well the historic role of the ascetic but not its meaning in the imagination of the believer. To him the ascetic ideal exemplifies in exaggerated form the inhibition of drives that is a prerequisite for the conduct of orderly social life:

> [It] is a necessary school where men form and transform themselves, and acquire the qualities of disinterestedness and endurance without which there would be no religion. If this result is to be obtained, it is even a good thing that the ascetic ideal be incarnated in certain persons whose speciality so to speak is to represent almost with excess this aspect of the ritual life; *for they are like so many living models inciting to effort.* Such is the historic role of the great ascetics. When their deeds and acts are analysed in detail, one asks what useful end they can have. He is struck by the fact that there is something excessive in the disdain they profess for all that ordinarily impassions men. But these exaggerations are necessary to sustain among the believers a sufficient disgust for an easy life and common pleasure. It

> is necessary that an elite put the end too high, if the crowd is not to put it too low. It is necessary that some exaggerate if the average is to remain at a fitting level.[17]

The Buddha himself made a similar point over two millennia before Durkheim and, with greater insight, indicated why we project onto the arahant those ideals we have failed to realize, trammeled as we are in the coils of social existence.

> Then the Aryan disciple thus ponders: As long as they live, the Arahants, by abandoning the slaying of creatures, are abstemious from the slaying of creatures, have laid aside the rod; they are modest, show kindness, they abide friendly and compassionate to all creatures and all beings. So also do I abide this night and day . . . abstaining from such actions . . . showing kindness to all beings. By this observance I too imitate the Arahants and I shall have kept the Sabbath [i.e., the *uposatha* or *poya*].[18]

The same formula is repeated for stealing and taking that which is not freely given; for sexual chastity; for alcohol, which causes sloth; for abstention from afternoon meals; and for singing and dancing. These injunctions conclude: "As long as they do live, the Arahants, by abandoning the use of high wide couches, abstain therefrom: they make their bed lowly, on a pallet or on a spread of rushes, I also this night and day do likewise. By this observance, I too imitate the Arahants . . . and I shall have kept my sabbath."[19]

I have referred to the power of the arahant ideal in Buddhist life. This is what the Buddhists "imitate" at various levels, just as Christians imitate Christ's love and humility. For, in spite of Thomas à Kempis, one wonders how Jesus' experience of the "royal road of the Cross," the *mysterium tremendum et fascinans* of the crucifixion, resurrection, and ascension can ever be imitated by the devotee.

## THE BUDDHA AS SEER: THE LIFE FATE OF THE BUDDHIST DEAD

> The starting point of his [Pythagoras's] system of education was recall of the lives which souls had lived before entering the bodies they now happen to inhabit.
>
> —Iamblichus, *De vita Pythagorica*

In chapter 3 I showed that although Buddhists can, like the Northwest Coast Indians, make a rebirth wish to be born into the same family, there is no guarantee that this wish will be realized. Thus Buddhists rarely bother with their former life (or lives) because there is simply no way of knowing it.[20] Moreover, the Buddhist tradition is firm in the belief that only the Buddha or arahants can retrocognize past lives, and because there is no living Buddha nowadays and no publicly acclaimed arahants, it is impossible for anyone to know his or her past lives. Any such past life recollection is purely fortuitous; these claims are rare and often viewed with skepticism. Thus, although both Northwest Coast Indians and Buddhists believe in rebirth, only on rare occasions do the latter show interest in the diagnostic procedures employed for identifying the previous-life persona of an individual.

This was not, however, what the ancient Buddhist texts reveal. The problem of figuring out past lives was a hot topic of discussion by monks, as is evident in texts like the "Mahāpadāna Sutta": "Now among many bhikkhus who had returned from their alms tour and were assembled, sitting together after their meal, in the pavilion of the Kareri grounds, a religious conversation bearing on previous births arose, to the effect that thus and thus were previous births."[21] The Buddha overheard this conversation and asked the monks whether they would be interested "to hear some religious talk on the subject of former lives." The monks naturally agreed, and the Buddha himself gave a list of six former Buddhas, the seventh (the auspicious number) being himself. How does the Buddha possess this power of discernment? First: "It is through his clear discernment of the truth, brethren, that the Tathagatha [Buddha] is able to remember [the lives of past Buddhas]." Second: "And gods also revealed these matters to him, enabling him to remember [all those things]."[22]

A detailed account of the Seer's remembrance of things past is found in an old, little-known discourse, the "Janavasabha Sutta," meant mostly for laypersons. This interesting text is treated rather offhandedly by Rhys Davids as a "fairy tale," although well told and edifying, presumably because it does not fit the scholarly version of Theravada as a "Euro-rational" religion. In this text the Buddha is staying in Magadha in the village of Nādikā at the "Brick House," and the laity want to know from the Buddha, as a wise seer, what happened to their friends and kinfolk after death: "Now at that time the Exalted One was wont to make declarations as to the rebirth of such followers (of the doctrine) as had passed away in death among the tribes round about on every side—among the Kāsis and Kosalans, the Vajjians and Mallas . . . saying: Such a one has been reborn there, and such and such a one there."[23]

This text considers it perfectly normal for people living in large communities and kingdoms like the Kāsis, Vajjians, Kosalans, and Mallas to ask the Seer about the postmortem destiny of their loved ones. Because such questions were rarely asked in the later history of Buddhism, it looks as if they reflected a publicly known tradition of rebirth divination of the sort found in the rebirth eschatologies discussed earlier. Here is the Buddha's response:

> From Nādikā upwards of fifty adherents, who passed away in death after having completely destroyed the Five Bonds that bind people to this world, have become inheritors of the highest heavens, there to pass utterly away, thence never to return. Full ninety adherents in Nādikā, who have passed away in death after having completely destroyed the Three Bonds, and reduced to a minimum lust, ill-will and delusion, have become Once-returners, and on their first return to this world shall make an end of pain. Over five hundred adherents of Nādikā, who have passed away in death after having completely destroyed the Three Bonds, and become converted, cannot be reborn in any state of woe, but are assured of attaining to the Insight (of the higher stages of the Path). (*Dial.,* 2:237)

These were responses to questions that were troubling people; therefore, "when they heard these revelations, [people] were pleased, gladdened and filled with joy and happiness at these *solutions by the Exalted One of the problems that had been put to him.*"[24]

In the "Janavasabha Sutta" the Buddha's role is analogous to that of the diviner among the Amerindians or the Igbo, except that the Buddha is more interested in the fate of a person after death than in the identity of the neonate at birth. Unlike the *Jātaka* and popular tales, the after-death inquiry fits the ethical and soteriological thrust of the main doctrinal texts with their emphases on ethical actions and consequences. In spite of his reluctance the Buddha continues to respond to the wishes of people, this time those of Magadha, because Ānanda, expressing the will of the people, asks him: "How should there be no declaration from the Exalted One concerning adherents in Magadha who have passed away in death?" (*Dial.,* 2:238). Magadhans, he adds, are especially concerned about the fate of Bimbisāra, their king (who was a friend and patron of the Buddha). "If the Exalted One declares nothing concerning them, they (the people) will be hurt. And since they will be hurt, how can the Exalted One keep silent?" (*Dial.,* 2:238). And then Ānanda adds a further incentive for the Buddha: when people realize that adherents of the Buddha are reborn in happy planes of existence, others also will want to follow their example and become good Buddhists. Perhaps Ānanda articulates an important reason for the popularity of Buddhism at that time.

The text now has a fascinating account of how the Buddha set about this task. The Buddha, still in Nādikā at the Brick House, "sat down on a seat made ready, thinking over and cogitating upon and concentrating his whole mind on the Magadhese adherents, saying to himself: 'I will find out their future, their fate after this life, whither these good men are bound, what their destiny is'" (*Dial.,* 2:239). While the Buddha is in this state of intense meditation, a spirit, invisible to all except the Buddha, appears before him, saying, "I am Janavasabha, O Exalted One, I am Janavasabha, O Welcome One!" (*Dial.,* 2:240). Then Janavasabha reveals to the Buddha his own identity: he is none other than his friend King Bimbisāra of Magadha, now born in the company of Vessavana (Vaiśravaṇa), the great god of the Northern Quarter. "Deceased as a human king, I am in heaven become a non-human king" (*Dial.,* 2:240). He is a Once-Returner *(sakadāgāmin);* that is, he will be born only once more on earth, and then he will achieve nirvana.

How did Janavasabha appear in the Buddha's meditative vision? Janavasabha says that he was carrying a message from Vessavana to Virulhaka (Virūḍha, the god of the Southern Quarter) when he saw the Buddha meditating in the Brick House, resolving to find out the destinies of the Magadhan devotees. Therefore he decided to help the Buddha. How so? Janavasabha had heard about the Buddha's cogitations "only the moment before" at the assembly of the god Vessavana "face to face from his [Vessavana's] own mouth" (*Dial.,* 2:241).

Consider what is going on here: the Buddha's former friend Bimbisāra, now a divinity in the assembly of Vessavana (Vaiśravaṇa), hears from the god himself what happened to various people of Magadha; he therefore appears before the Buddha and gives him this information. But this is not all that Janavasabha does; he gives the Buddha a graphic description of the whole divine assembly in the heaven of the thirty-three gods (thirty-three being the standard number of the Vedic pantheon). Indeed, he describes the complex status hierarchy in heaven headed by the Brahma Sanaṃkumāra (one of seven Brahmas), who, with his divine power, knew of the Buddha's cogitations and relayed the information to Vessavana (*Dial.,* 2:241–44). In helping the Buddha to solve the problem of the Magadhan dead, Janavasabha acts very much like the helping spirit, although not a guardian deity, associated with forms of shamanism. Underlying Janavasabha's action is Buddhist reciprocity: the Buddha helped the earthly Janavasabha (Bimbisāra) to achieve his high divine status by preaching the dhamma to him; now Janavasabha repays that favor. The text ends thus:

> This was the matter whereof Brahma Sanaṃkumāra spoke to the Thirty Three Gods. And this matter the Great King Vessavana, when he had, in his own person heard it and assented to it, reported to his own following. And this matter the spirit Janavasabha, when he had in his own person heard it so reported by Vessavana, reported to the Exalted One. And this matter the Exalted One, when he had in his own person heard it and assented to it, *and had also intuitively discerned it,* reported it to Ānanda. And this matter the Venerable Ānanda, when he had in his own person heard it from the Exalted One and assented to it, reported to the brethren and the sisterhood, to believing laymen and laywomen. And the System waxed influential and prosperous and expanded and broadened with the numbers that joined, so well was it spread abroad among men." (*Dial.,* 2:252, my italics)

Thus the knowledge-information circuit oscillates between ordinary people and the gods in heaven. The crucial figure is Janavasabha, a spirit medium, supplying the Buddha with information. This, however, poses a problem: does the Buddha need this intermediary, given that he has the capacity for retrocognition through his own meditative concentration? What is the relationship between meditation and spirit mediumship?

## SAMANISM AND SHAMANISM: ECSTASIS, ENSTASIS, AND SPIRIT POSSESSION

Mircea Eliade, in his famous study of shamanism, made an important distinction between enstasis and ecstasis. "Any ecstatic cannot be considered a shaman; the shaman specializes in a trance during which his soul is believed to leave his body and ascend to the sky and descend to the underworld."[25] Eliade deliberately restricts his definition to the classic shamanism of Siberia (the home of the term), which is also the way of Inuit and Northwest Coast Indians. In anthropology the definition of shamanism is broader and includes those religious healers who are possessed by an intruding spirit. Such spirit possession trances, as I. M. Lewis says, could also be classed as "ecstatic religion."[26] For present purposes I want to make three distinctions: first, ecstasis, in which the soul leaves the body, as in Eliade's idealized vision of shamanism; second, enstasis (or enstasy), in which one engages in inward contemplation of the "soul"; and third, spirit possession, in which the body is possessed by an outside agency or spirit. Both ecstasis and spirit possession are found in Siberia and among Inuit and Northwest Coast Indians although the primary mode of shamanic trance is achieved through ecstasis. Spirit possession is also well known in ancient and contemporary cultures, including India, where it is described in such technical terms as *āveśa* and *āruḍha* (lighted upon or mounted upon [by a spirit]). By contrast "yoga," says Eliade, "pursues enstasis, final concentration of the spirit and 'escape' from the cosmos."[27]

Buddhism also favors enstasis because, among other things, it provides access to knowledge and power without recourse to an external spirit, thus maintaining the Buddhist posture of the self-reliant individual pursuing salvation unaided by any external help. Buddhism also cannot subscribe to the idea of the soul leaving the body because it denies the very existence of such an entity. Hence shamanic trances that eject the soul from the body are antipathetic to Buddhist enstasis. We now can come back to the problem in the "Janavasabha Sutta": if Janavasabha did give information on the fate of the Magadhans to the Buddha, what then is the significance of the Buddha's own power to obtain the same knowledge through contemplative trance or enstasis or *samādhi?* The solution in this text is not very satisfactory; it tells us that Janavasabha gave the Buddha what the Buddha had already "intuitively discerned." The divinely revealed knowledge is only a confirmation of the intuitively discerned knowledge. But behind this attempt at reconciliation is the recognition of two modes of knowing, and the "Mahāpadāna Sutta" as much as admits it in the statement that not only is the truth directly discerned by the Buddha himself, but the "gods also revealed these matters to him, enabling him to remember [all those things]."[28]

The Buddha gets information from the gods but not by being possessed by them. Janavasabha appeared on his own volition before the Buddha; it was the time when the Buddha was in *samādhi,* an enstatic state, a point well put by Marasinghe in his study of the gods in early Buddhism. "In the majority of the instances recorded of the visits by the different *devas* [deities] to the Buddha, these visits take place either towards the latter part of the night . . . or when the Buddha was spending his siesta in meditation. . . . In both cases, it seems positively clear that the gods visit him whilst in *samādhi.*"[29] Thus in the "Ariyapariyesanasutta" the Buddha tells his monks: "Then, monks, devatas [deities] having approached me, spoke thus: 'Lord Uddaka . . . passed away last night.' So knowledge and vision arose in me that Uddaka, Rāma's son, had passed away last night."[30] In another discourse the king of the gods, Śakra (Pali, Sakka, the Vedic Indra), tells his musician Pañcasikha that he (Śakra) cannot approach the Buddha when he (and arahants in general) are "enjoying the bliss of meditation, and therefore withdrawn." However, Śakra adds, Pañcasikha might succeed.[31] Pañcasikha then plays on his lute and praises the Buddha in song, which the latter hears through his trance-like state, or samādhi (presumably because certain kinds of music can penetrate the mind of the virtuoso engaged in contemplation, as I think it does in Pythagorean ascesis also). That this kind of knowledge often comes through samādhi is explicitly indicated when a monk in the fourth stage of meditative absorption "falls into conversation with these *devatās*."[32]

Knowledge engendered through enstasis is beautifully described in such texts as the "Bhayabherava Sutta" (Discourse on fear and dread); and in the "Sāmaññaphala Sutta" (Fruits of the life of a recluse), from which I quote:

> With his heart thus serene, he directs and bends down his mind to the knowledge of the memory of his previous temporary states. He recalls to mind his various temporary states in days gone by—one birth, or two or three or four or five births, or ten or twenty or thirty or forty or fifty or a hundred or a thousand or a hundred thousand births, through many an aeon of dissolution and evolution. "In such a place such was my name, such my family, such my caste, such my food, such my experience of discomfort or of ease, and such the limits of my life. When I passed away from that state, I took form again in such a place. There I had such and such a name and family and caste and food and experience of discomfort or of ease, such was the limit of my life. When I passed away from that state I took form again here"—thus does he call to mind his temporary state in days gone by in all their details, and in all their modes.[33]

In these states of trance the meditator acquires certain supernormal powers known as *iddhi.* For example, in the "Kevaddha Sutta" a young householder named Kevaddha asks the Buddha to make a monk perform wonders so that the laypeople of Nalanda might be converted to the religion. The Buddha refuses to adopt such measures but gently tells Kevaddha that if a monk were to perform such "miracles," there would be unbelievers who would say that they were products not of iddhi but of charms. "It is because I perceive danger in the practice of mystic wonders, that I loathe, and abhor, and am ashamed thereof."[34] Nevertheless, the Buddha does say that he himself has "understood and realized them, have made [them] known to others."[35] One such "wonder" is reminiscent of shamanic powers.

> From being one he becomes multiform, from being multiform he becomes one: from being visible he becomes invisible: he passes without hindrance to the further side of a wall or a battlement or a mountain, as if through air: he penetrates up and down through solid ground, as if through water: he walks on water without dividing it, as if on solid ground: he travels cross-legged through the sky, like the birds on wing: he touches and feels

> with the hand even the Moon and the Sun, beings of mystic power and potency though they be: he reaches, even in the body, up to the heaven of Brahma.[36]

This is not the gods giving the Buddha information; it is the seer himself reaching into heavenly realms, making himself permeable through his powers of iddhi. This kind of description could as easily have come from accounts of ecstatic spirit journeys in which the soul of the shaman leaves the body, wanders into different realms, and then comes back to earth and reports to humans what it has seen. I have already shown how new cosmological knowledge is invented by the shaman through these experiences in other realms. In the Buddha's visionary trance Janavasabha appears before him and gives him a description of heaven that is then communicated to laypersons—and also to us scholars—in texts like the "Janavasabha Sutta." These powers are also not unlike those religious specialists, pejoratively described in a later *Ṛg Veda* (10:136) as *munis,* or the "silent ones," who "wear the wind as their girdle, and who, drunk with their own silence, rise in the wind, and fly in the paths of the demigods and birds."[37] But the Buddha, also known as Muni, achieves this state through enstasy, not ecstasy, quite unlike the munis of the *Ṛg Veda,* who are "drunk with the magic of the cup of Rudra [Śiva], which is poison to ordinary mortals."[38]

Yet it seems to me that at some level these distinctions get blurred. Although the Buddha says that he goes into the realm of Brahma, "even in the body," he must surely mean that it is his spiritual body that achieves these cosmic travels. On one level the Buddhist meditator lets his mind penetrate *inwardly* as he recollects his own past lives (through enstasis). But if he is to get at the past lives of others or witness the dissolution and coming into being of past and present universes, either he must seek the help of a god like Janavasabha, or he must let his mind penetrate *outwardly* into other cosmic realms (through something like ecstasis). But this surely means being able to reach out of the body and, as with other Indic virtuosos, on occasion being able to project a mind-image of the physical Buddha. If my line of speculation is correct, what seems to have happened here is that ecstasy has been absorbed into enstasy; the samaṇa has incorporated into his very being some of the attributes of the shaman. In being thus transformed the Buddha of the "Janavasabha Sutta," it seems to me, joins the class of heroes who appear in this work—Tomwaya Lakwabulo, 'Askadut, Er, Pythagoras, and Empedocles.

If shamanism gets absorbed into samanism, spirit possession exists in a relation of dialectical opposition to Buddhism. One form of spirit possession takes place when an intruding spirit enters the unsuspecting body of an afflicted person. In the other, a spirit medium or a similar religious specialist voluntarily invites a spirit to inhabit his or her person in order to effect cures. The two forms of possession we know are often related, such that the sick person who is controlled by spirits may end up as a controller of spirits.[39] We have seen that in the Buddhist scheme of things the act of being possessed by a spirit, voluntarily or involuntarily, constitutes an abdication of the idea of the self-reliant individual who rejects external support and only depends on the dhamma. This ideal has persisted throughout the history of Buddhism in spite of its many vicissitudes and is exemplified in the lifestyle of forest-dwelling monks.

Spirit possession also pertains to illness and its cure, whereas the monk's quest is the overcoming of the ills of *existence*. The one is world involved; the other is world rejecting. The monk's rational alternative to spirit possession is meditation. The calm and serene expression of the meditator contrasts with the violence of the person possessed by spirits. The one involves silence; the other involves noise. It is very likely that spirit possession is the older form in South Asia. The contemplative trance of the monk exists in a schismogenetic relationship with the possession trance of the spirit medium, the practice of the one form heightening the sense of contrast with the other. Could it be that the meditative response was a soteriological reaction by a speculative priesthood against the seeming "irrationality" of possession trance? It must be remembered that meditation, in its fully developed form in Indian religions, meets the challenge of possession trance by producing its own forms of trance, in which visions, states of contemplative bliss, or mystical union with the godhead is achieved. Unlike possession trances, which imply shaking and violent body movements, meditation attempts to achieve control and awareness, serenity and calm, all passion spent. Contemplation is the meditator's enstatic answer to spirit possession.[40]

## ETHICIZATION AND THE CREATION OF A GOD-MAKING MACHINE

In his *Two Sources of Morality and Religion* Henri Bergson discusses the "god-making fantasy" in the history of religions.[41] He might well have qualified this profound tautology had he known that in Buddhism karma is the fantastic machine that churns out the gods and continuously populates the heavens with an overload of new denizens. To illustrate this propensity of the karma theory, let me get back to the now not-so-neglected "Janavasabha Sutta." In this text Janavasabha describes the Hall of Good Counsel, where the gods assemble in the following order of precedence: the god of the Eastern Quarter, seated facing west and presiding over his hosts; the gods of the South, West, and North, all facing the opposite direction (as Indian convention demands) and accompanied by their retinues; and the well-known category of Thirty-Three Gods and their hosts. But, Janavasabha tells the Buddha, there is now a new set of beings in heaven, those who lead the "higher life" enjoined by the new religion.[42] The same sentiment is soon expressed in verse form by Śakra, the ruler of the gods, and is repeated by Brahma Sanaṃkumāra:

> The Three and Thirty, verily, both gods and lord, rejoice,
> Tathagata [Buddha] they honour and the cosmic law sublime
> Whereas they see the gods new-risen, beautiful and bright,
> Who erst the holy life had lived, under the Happy One,
> The Mighty Sage's hearers, who had won the higher truths,
> Come hither; and in glory all the other gods outshine. (*Dial.*, 2:242–43)

These new arrivals were originally laypersons, like Janavasabha, who, having missed the nirvanic path, are now born in heaven. It should not surprise us if the heavens soon get crowded. Thus Brahma Sanaṃkumāra tells the Thirty-Three Gods that there are already one million (ten lakhs) of "Magadha disciples dead and gone" lodged there. Although thirty-three is the classic Vedic number of major gods, the Sri Lankan popular religious imagination of later times multiplies this number into thirty three *koṭi*s of gods, each koṭi being ten million![43] But this text is significant in another way: it seems that the Buddha is, implicitly, having an argument with the Upanishadic tradition represented by another Kṣatriya sage, Pravāhaṇa Jaivali. A central question for the latter was why the other-worlds are *not* getting filled up. I noted that this is because of the peculiar rebirth theory sketched by Jaivali, in which the Buddhist form of karma does not operate. The Buddhist response is that the otherworlds get overcrowded owing to the practice of Buddhism and the operation of the ethical law of karma.

The Brahma Sanaṃkumāra, being a good Buddhist, affirms the classic position that those who have been born in the various heavens are there by virtue of the good they have done, some in the higher heavens, others in lower ones. Those who have taken the upper road, such as the Thirty-Three Gods and some of the good folk of Magadha, have hope of eventual salvation. They must, like any other salvation seeker, practice the Noble Eightfold Path. They are the fortunate ones for whom, says Brahma Sanaṃkumāra, "wide open are the portals of Nirvana." In his address to the gods Sanaṃkumāra preaches a Buddhist sermon and then adds that the newcomers, as well as the older occupants, are either nonreturners (*anāgāmin,* those who will soon attain nirvana right there in heaven itself) or once-returners (*sakadāgāmin*, those who will be reborn once on earth and then achieve nirvana).[44] No strait gate here: instead, wide open are the portals of nirvana!

If the heavens are crowded with pious laypersons (in Buddhism gods are a part of the lay community), so are the other realms of rebirth. The " Devadūtasutta" (Discourse on the divine messengers) has the conventional list of these realms. In this text also the Buddha claims that he can, through his "*deva*-vision surpassing that of men," actually *see* people being reborn according to their good and bad actions in the following spheres of existence:

1. Those who have led exceptionally good lives "at the breaking up of the body after dying are arising in a good bourn, a heaven world."
2. Similar worthy beings at the breaking up of the body after dying are arising among human beings.
3. Those worthy beings guilty of wrong conduct are arising in an animal womb.
4. And finally those worthy beings endowed with wrong conduct "are arising in the sorrowful ways, the bad bourn, the Downfall, Niraya Hell."[45]

This list is repeated in the "Mahāsīhanādasutta" (Greater discourse on the lion's roar), which has an added category of the "departed," namely, the pretas, although no description of this realm is given.[46] The pretas are graphically described in later texts and in the popular imagination as ancestors reborn in the proximity of their previous families and possessing needle-like throats and huge bellies owing to their greed or attachment to the living. I think pretas deliberately caricature a pre-Buddhist idea of rebirth in the same family and lineage extolled by "rebirth eschatologies" everywhere.

Overcrowding of heavens and hells, then, is a further consequence of the ethicization in all Axial Age religions. In the samanic religions not only are the afterlife realms of Vedic religion ethicized, but their numbers are increased and entry into them karmically regulated. Thus, Buddhism has multiple heavenly abodes. Particularly important are Tāvatimsa, whose ruler is Śakra (Indra), and the Tusita heaven, where Buddhas-to-be are reborn before they come down to earth in their final incarnation as Buddhas.[47] Additionally, there are four continents where humans are born, the best known being Jambudīpa, the Rose-Apple Continent, which constituted the known world of that time, and Uttarakuru, the northern continent, a blessed isle where the people do not own property because things grow on their own, where all wants are supplied, and where the inhabitants ride on cows and on men and women, maids and youths—a reified heaven on earth.[48] There are at least ten types of hells, or *niraya,* the most deadly being the Mahāniraya (the "great hell," also known as *avīci*), whose overlord is the Vedic deity Yama. Priestly casuistry certainly operates in these kinds of classifications, which are found in all ethicized religions, but this ubiquity is by no means all there is to it.

Let me highlight a further feature of these abodes that pertains to Buddhism, namely, that both hedonism and excessive asceticism banned from the spiritual life of ethical asceticism reappear in the sensual and sensuous life enjoyed by the devotee in heaven and in the torture chambers of the hells. The features of these otherworldly abodes are overdetermined in another way also; nowhere has monastic life managed to completely sublimate or otherwise modify human desire. Hence, the deprived sexuality of monks is given free rein in the gloriously sensual and sometimes sexual pleasures of the various heavens, whereas the dark underside of their sexual lives is expressed in their sadistic inventions of hell. The latter is evident in texts such as the " Devadūtasutta" (Discourse on the divine messengers) and the " Bālapaṇḍitasutta" (Discourse on the foolish and the wise), which, until recently, were modified and enacted in popular dramas in Buddhist temples in Sri Lanka as "The Judgement of King Yama" *(Yama rajjuruvangē naḍu tīnduva).*

In the "Devadūtasutta" the lord of the underworld, Yama, asks the sinner in a very dry and detached manner why he had not paid heed to the five divine *(deva)* signs that had appeared before him, warning him of the nature of samsara. The "divine signs" are in fact very ordinary ones, such as a young child lying helpless in its own excrement or an aged person "bent, leaning on a stick, going along palsied, miserable, youth gone, teeth broken, hair thinned, skin wrinkled, stumbling along, the limbs discoloured."[49] They are "divine" because they take their existential meaning from the four signs created by the gods that lead to the Buddha's own renunciation. With the insight gained thereby, one should be able to lead a good life. These sinners, however, have not done so, and Yama tells them that "this evil deed was done by you; it is you that will experience its ripening." He then confines them to suffer terrifying torment, graphically described in passages such as the following:

> But, monks, adjacent to this Great Niraya Hell is the Great Filth Hell. He falls into it. And, monks, in that Filth Hell needle-mouth creatures cut away his skin; having cut away his skin they cut away his hide; having cut away his hide they cut away his flesh; having cut away his flesh they cut away his tendons; having cut away his tendons they cut away his bones; having cut away his bones they devour the marrow of his bones. Thereat he feels feelings that are painful, sharp, severe. But he does not do his time until he makes an end of that evil deed. . . .
>
> Monks, the guardians of Niraya Hell haul him out with a fish-hook [out of the River of Caustic Water, where he has been previously immersed] set him on dry land and speak thus to him: "My good man, what do you want?" He speaks thus: "I am hungry, revered sirs." Monks, the guardians of Niraya Hell, opening his mouth with a glowing iron spike, burning, aflame, ablaze, then push into his mouth a glowing copper pellet, burning, aflame, ablaze. It burns his lips and it burns his mouth and it burns his throat and it burns his intestines. (*MLS,* 3:228–29)

It is now impossible to shirk an unpleasant conclusion. In all Axial Age religions ethicization has a dark side that is psychically connected to the deep motivations of sexually repressed religious specialists. In Buddhism it converts animals into miserable sinful beings and creates sadistic and violent worlds in which sinners are confined. In the samanic religions these ideas are further translated into the sphere of earthly existence in the lives of those who are miserable—the poor, the maimed, the subaltern—who also become products of karma and are therefore being punished in a hell right here on earth. But beyond that one can argue that hells have been models in both Buddhism and Christianity for other arenas of torment. This is neatly exemplified in a Buddhist Sanskrit text, known as the Aśokāvadāna, about the model Buddhist king Aśoka, when he was known as Caṇḍāśoka, "Aśoka, the Cruel," prior to his conversion to Buddhism.[50]

In this text there is reference to Caṇḍagirika (Girika, the Cruel), who was chosen by Aśoka's men for the role of the king's executioner. When his parents refused to allow him to take this role, he killed them both and joined Aśoka. Girika's first task was to build a torture chamber. "Aśoka had one built immediately; it was lovely from the outside as far as the gate, but inside it was actually a very frightful place, and people called it the 'beautiful gaol'" (*LKA,* 212), a state-of-the-art prison that death penalty supporters might appreciate. The king granted Girika his one request: "that whosoever should enter this place should not come out alive" (*LKA,* 212). Soon after, Girika heard a Buddhist monk recite the "Bālapaṇḍitasutta," with its gruesome descriptions of the five tortures of hell, the fifth of which is quoted below:

> Finally, there are beings who are reborn in hell whom the hell-guardians grab, and stretch out on their backs on a fiery floor of red-hot iron that is but a mass of flames. Then they carry out the torture of the five-fold tether; they drive two iron stakes through their hands; they drive two iron stakes though their feet; and they drive one iron stake through their heart. Truly, O monks, hell is a place of great suffering.
>
> "Such are the five great agonies," Girika reflected, and he began to inflict these same tortures on people in his prison. (*LKA,* 213)[51]

It is likely that Girika got his idea of prison torture from the "Bālapaṇḍitasutta" itself, where the parallelism is drawn between the king's punishment and the tortures of hell. In it the Buddha has a graphic description of the various kinds of tortures inflicted by the king on a thief, and he says that the sufferings of a thief (for example, when he is stabbed by three hundred spears) is nothing in comparison to the tortures of hell.[52] It is likely that earthly sovereigns were in fact influenced by such texts as the "Bālapaṇḍitasutta" and by the example of Yama, the sadistic ruler of the Great Hell, in the penal institutions they created or imagined—in such things as mutilation, torture, impaling a person through the anus with a sharp stake, and trial by ordeal. But it is also likely that the gruesome rules of these penal institutions were rarely put into practice and that their effect was similar to that of the hells in respect to sin—to create fear and dread in the population as to what might occur if heinous crimes are committed. Their very horror led Buddhist kings on occasion to abolish torture and capital punishment. And, in fairness to Buddhist history, it did not transfer these schemas of hell into religious institutions such as the various Inquisitions.

## ETHICIZATION AND AXIOLOGIZATION

If Buddhism joined the ranks of other ethicized religions in inventing hedonistic heavens and sadistic hells, the very logic of karma theory prevents such otherworldly existences from being anything but temporary. Even the worst sinner, like Devadatta, the Buddha's arch enemy from many previous existences, will be reborn on earth after expiating his sins in a variety of sadistic hells and at last become a Buddha himself. It is impossible to have radical good and evil in this system because all good and bad karma is eventually expiated, and one continues to be reborn in some sphere or other. Consequently, in Buddhist theory there can never be eternal damnation or eternal bliss within samsara. Yet, although the temporal logic of a karmic eschatology cannot confine a Devadatta to eternal damnation, there is nothing in that logic that should grant him eventual salvation and nirvana. The latter is something that Buddhist ethics has invented. Buddhism grants the person who has committed the worst crime (according to its own ethics) the capacity to become a Buddha. The constraints imposed by the model have been overcome, giving the thinker (or a tradition of thought) a considerable degree of autonomy. Once again we are dealing with the interplay between the logic of a belief system and the capacity for creative improvisation and the invention of new ideas by speculative thinkers operating within a specific tradition.

The particular set of innovations that I will now describe expands our discussion of the Buddhist ethical reform subsumed under the somewhat restrictive term *ethicization*. Buddhist ethical reform is much broader in scope and embraces the prior religious traditions that Buddhism had to contend with. I will call the powerful ethical impetus underlying such transformations *axiologization,* the deliberate and self-conscious transfiguring of local, preexisting, or contending values that gives them deeper ethical and symbolic significance, often universal, even cosmic, in scope. This again is part of the powerful rationalization thrust of Axial Age religions. This is not to deny that small-scale societies did not produce speculative traditions with a high degree of ethical sophistication. Thus the Amerindian and Inuit religions that I presented earlier have, in my view, a more sensitive notion of "species sentience" than the Axial Age religions, a notion that respected animal life in general, not only those confined to the territory in which the group lived. The impetus to axiologization is latent in small-scale societies, but their thinkers have not been impelled to self-consciously proclaim a universal message, perhaps because their social worlds have not been opened up by the kinds of upheavals that Buddhist and other Axial societies experienced. No society has been isolated in reality; nevertheless, the self-conscious wish of many small-scale societies to think of themselves as separate from others has often led to an exclusivist labeling of their own group as "the world" or "human beings." Here lies an irony that I want to highlight: if Amerindian religions practiced a doctrine of species sentience that respected animals in the larger realms in which they lived, not so with their relationship to human outsiders. As much as Buddhism demoted animals by virtue of its doctrine of karma, Amerindians demoted those outside their group as not fully "human" and consequently justified them as fit objects for conquest or extermination. By contrast, a universal proclamatory thrust is very characteristic of the soteriology of Axial religions and is intrinsically connected to the expanding consciousnesses of people concomitant with their expanding physical and social worlds. To put it differently: scholars may see that the Amerindian notion of species sentience can have universal significance, but I doubt that Amerindians have proclaimed that message as a universal one (except perhaps until very recently, when challenged by other axiologizing religions). Indeed, there are serious sociological blocks inhibiting the expansion of such an ethical vision because one group is often endemically at war with another. It is now impossible to shirk another unpleasant conclusion, this time in respect to small-scale societies: *The principle of species sentience applies to one's own social group and to animals everywhere; it does not and could not be extended to embrace Others, including neighbors, who, occasionally, could be killed with impunity.*

Let me now develop the distinction between everyday social morality, whether ethicized or not, and axiologization as I have defined it. When everyday morality is ethicized, it continues to operate in that everyday sphere. Even if I violate an ethicized Buddhist norm, I will know the consequences of this violation as much as an Australian ādivāsi knows what to expect from his group if he is found guilty of adultery. These norms are locked into social control and the socialization of the conscience. The difference is that a Buddhist would know that such violations will produce bad karmic fruit *(karma phala)* and might do something about it, for example, practicing merit-making actions. By contrast, axiological values need not have that kind of social significance, nor have they always permeated social life and consciousness in any depth. Thus a typical anthropological problem: there are some axiologized values that do not necessarily impinge on the public consciousness or conscience.

A clear example of this pertains to the maxim that one should love one's enemy or to the kind of radical nonviolence envisaged in Buddhist texts that can hardly be implemented in the everyday existence of either monks or laypersons. Such maxims are part of the debate that Axial thinkers had to have with others and themselves. To give an extreme example from the Buddha's sayings: "Bhikkhus, even if bandits were to sever you savagely limb by limb with a two-handled saw, he who gave rise to a mind of hate towards them would not be carrying out my teaching."[53] Buddhist texts are full of similar unrealistic, and sometimes even unreasonable, ethical injunctions to both monks and laity. However, even extreme axiological values are not closed; only the conduits between them and the everyday world are by no means clear and must be elucidated through ethnographic and historical analysis.[54]

## BUDDHISM, AXIOLOGIZATION, AND THE VEDIC TRADITION

Early Buddhism, much more than any other Indic religion, possessed a relentless axiologizing imperative aimed at transforming every aspect of species existence. This feature of Buddhism is so well known to Indologists that it is not necessary to deal with it at any length except to give some examples for anthropologists unfamiliar with the religion. Let me pick up once again the theme of species sentience. Such a doctrine was present in Pythagorean eschatology; in Buddhism it led to a demotion of animals; in small-scale societies it stopped at the door of one's own group as far as panhuman sentience was concerned. In Buddhism the ethical denigration of animals is mitigated, however, by its own unique axiologization of species sentience in a very radical direction as nonhurt, or ahiṃsā, the central tenet of Buddhist ethics. Thus the ethic of species sentience is given a universalizing thrust through the doctrine of ahiṃsā. If the killing of an animal is a kind of endoanthropophagy in Kwakiutl thought and in some forms of Pythagoreanism, this is now superseded in Buddhist doctrine, although not in its practical ethics, by the idea of nonviolence that extends to every living creature, including one's enemies. Nonviolence is linked in turn to an ethic of intention, the specifically Buddhist ingredient in the karma doctrine. Hence vegetarianism per se is never enjoined in Buddhism because one could eat an animal that was not intentionally killed for the consumer. To sum up: in my view the development of the Buddhist doctrine of ahiṃsā, or nonviolence, is ultimately traceable to an axiologization of species sentience associated with rebirth eschatologies, possibly one that had cross-species reincarnation. It gave new ethical meaning to the original idea of killing an animal ancestor and extended it to include all beings belonging to a single sentient order of existence; it then gave that idea universal significance.

Let me now briefly deal with another axiological aspect of early Buddhism through its continuing dialectic with Vedic or Brahmanic values. In the doctrinal texts virtually every ritual or soteriological feature of the Brahmanic tradition is rejected and redefined axiologically. This is done in a variety of ways. The gods of the Vedic pantheon are demoted and converted into a species of Buddhist laypersons, karma-bound beings themselves in need of salvation. Thus the powerful god Indra of the *Ṛg Veda* is converted into Śakra (Sakka, "Truth"), a kind of protector of the Buddhist church, or *sāsana,* a benevolent being who often descends to earth when his seat becomes "hot" and sets aright injustice. The great Vedic god Brahma is also demoted, initially by deconstructing his origin myth. In the "Brahmajāla Sutta" the Buddha says, somewhat ironically, that when a new cosmic cycle comes into existence, the world system begins to evolve once again and the first being arises. As the first created being he thinks: "I am Brahma, the Great Brahma, the Supreme One, the Mighty, the All-seeing, the Ruler, the Lord of all, the Maker, the Creator, the Chief of all, appointing to each his place . . . the Father of all." People who come later agree; because he was here before, "we must have been created by him" (*Dial.,* 1:31–32). And so the self-delusion goes on.

Concomitantly, Buddhism employs the familiar strategy of the karma machine to multiply the number of Brahmas. Thus there are seven major Brahmas, or Mahā Brahmas, and one of them, Sahampati, actually tells the Buddha soon after his Awakening that he (the Buddha) should not be satisfied with his personal salvation but should teach the doctrine for the welfare of the many. We have already met another in the Brahma Sanaṃkumāra, a pious Buddhist devotee who preaches Buddhism to his fellow denizens in heaven.[55] Not satisfied with this, early Buddhists, building on the Upanishadic tradition, created a Brahma world consisting of twenty rarified heavens where truly pious laypersons could expect to be born as passionless male Brahmas subsisting on trance alone.[56] All the converted Vedic gods, if they are truly good Buddhists, can even become arahants, some in heaven itself and some after being reborn on earth.

Scholars now know that the Buddha was familiar with both Vedic and Upanishadic thought. How therefore does the Buddha relate to Brahman, the neuter of Upanishadic soteriology? In the Upanishadic tradition Brahman is the impersonal entity manifested on the personal level as Brahma, the creator. The Buddhists, by attacking Brahma, simultaneously attack Brahman and then axiologize the latter in such texts as the "Tevijja Sutta." And in the "Ambaṭṭha Sutta" the Buddha ridicules the pretensions of Brahmin teachers of the Three Vedas who claim to be descended from Brahma's head and others who want to identify with Brahma/Brahman. To give the reader a feel for these dialogues, I will deal with the former text at some length.[57]

The Buddha, journeying through the kingdom of Kosala with a company of about five hundred brethren, came upon a Brahmin village and decided to rest there in a mango grove on the banks of a river. At that time a group of wealthy and distinguished Brahmins, some named in the text, were also in that village. Two Brahmins, Vāseṭṭha (Sanskrit, Vasiṣṭha) and Bhāradvaja, were walking up and down in thoughtful mood (exercising after their bath) and discoursing on the "straight path . . . which makes for salvation, and leads him, who acts according to it, into a state of union with Brahma[n]" (*Dial.,* 1:301). The debate between the two was this: whether the way to Brahma[n] announced by the Brahmin Pokkharasāti (favored by Vāseṭṭha) or that of Tārukkha (favored by Bhāradvaja) was correct. But because Vāseṭṭha and Bhāradvaja could not agree, they decided to go see the Buddha to resolve this issue, following the already established Upanishadic convention of Brahmins consulting Kṣatriya sages. Vāseṭṭha asks whether the multiple paths leading to salvation according to various Brahmins are equally valid, and if they all lead to a fellowship (or "union") with Brahma.[58] The Buddha poses a series of questions that progressively build up the idea that Brahmin teachers who have not seen the Brahma cannot possibly have knowledge of Brahma, and the Buddha ridicules the Upanishadic idea of union with Brahma (even though similar pragmatic criticisms could apply to the Buddhist idea of nirvana!).

Consider this very typical Buddhist dialogue:

> "But then Vāseṭṭha, is there a single one of the Brahmans versed in the Three Vedas who has ever seen Brahma face to face?"
>
> "No, indeed, Gotama!"
>
> "But is there then, Vāseṭṭha, a single one of the teachers of the Brahmans versed in the Three Vedas who has seen Brahma face to face?"
>
> "No indeed, Gotama!"
>
> "But is there then, Vāseṭṭha, a single one of the Brahmans up to the seventh generation who has seen Brahma face to face?"
>
> "No, indeed, Gotama!"
>
> "Well then, Vāseṭṭha, those ancient Rishis of the Brahmans versed in the Three Vedas, the authors of the verses, the utterers of the verses, whose ancient form of words so chaunted, uttered, or composed, the Brahmans of today chaunt over again or repeat; intoning or reciting exactly as has been intoned or recited . . . did even they speak thus, saying: 'We know it, we have seen it, where Brahma is, whence Brahma is, whither Brahma is?'"
>
> "Not so, Gotama!" . . .
>
> "Verily, Vāseṭṭha, that Brahmans versed in the Three Vedas should be able to show the way to a union with that which they do not know, neither have seen—such a condition of things has no existence!

"Just, Vāseṭṭha, as when a string of blind men are clinging one to the other, neither can the foremost see, nor can the middle one see, nor can the hindmost see—just even so, methinks Vāseṭṭha, is the talk of the Brahmans versed in the Three Vedas but blind talk: the first sees not, the middle one sees not, nor can the latest see. The talk then of these Brahmans versed in the Three Vedas turns out to be ridiculous, mere words, a vain and empty thing!"[59]

The text ends with the affirmation of Buddhist ethics for monks and axiologizes the Brahma[n] in Buddhist fashion as "compassion":

And he [the meditator] lets his mind pervade one quarter of the world with thoughts of Love [*mettā,* "loving-kindness"], and so the second, and so the third, and so the fourth. And thus the whole wide world, above, around, and everywhere, does he continue to pervade with heart of Love [mettā] far-reaching, grown great, and beyond measure. . . . Verily this, Vāseṭṭha, is the way to a state of union [fellowship] with Brahma[n].

And he lets his mind pervade one quarter of the world with thoughts of pity, sympathy, and equanimity, and so the second, and so the third, and so the fourth. And thus the whole wide world . . . does he continue to pervade with heart of pity [*karuṇā,* "compassion"], sympathy [*muditā,* "sympathetic joy" or "tenderness"], and equanimity [*upekkhā*], far-reaching, grown great, and beyond measure. (*Dial.,* 1:317–18)

Thus, identification with Brahma[n] is retranslated in terms of the four *brahma-vihāras* of Buddhism—*mettā, karuṇā, muditā, upekkhā*—themselves powerful axiologizing concepts.[60] The term *brahma-vihāra* itself axiologizes the idea of Brahman in a Buddhist direction.

The whole idea of the Brahmanical sacrifice, already given ethical meaning in the Upanishads, is ironically rejected in numerous places. Let me deal with a story within a story from the "Kūṭadanta Sutta" (Discourse on the Brahmin Pointed Tooth) that transvalues the idea of the sacrifice.[61] In this text a Brahmin named Kūṭadanta wants to perform a spectacular sacrifice with a hundred steers, bulls, rams, goats, and heifers, but he has second thoughts about this and decides to consult the Buddha. The Buddha tells him a story of a powerful king, Wide-realm, of times long ago, who also wanted to perform a sacrifice for his own personal "weal and welfare." Wide-realm sought the advice of his Brahmin chaplain *(purohita)* (who we later learn is none other than the Buddha in a previous birth). The chaplain tells the king that this is not right: to perform a sacrifice when the country is being harassed by robbers would be in effect levying a new tax on the people. The king's immediate reaction is the law-and-order one; the robbers should be apprehended and given condign punishment. The chaplain replies that this will not solve the problem because as long as there is want and poverty, there will be thieves.

> Now there is one method to adopt to put a thorough end to this disorder. Whosoever there be in the king's realm who devote themselves to keeping cattle and the farm, to them let his majesty give food and seed-corn. Whosoever there be in the king's realm who devote themselves to trade, to them let his majesty the king give capital. Whosoever there be in the king's realm who devote themselves to government service, to them let his majesty the king give wages and food. Then these men, following each his own business, will no longer harass the realm; the king's revenue will go up; the country will be quiet and at peace; and the populace, pleased one with another and happy, dancing their children in their arms, will dwell with open doors. (*Dial.,* 1:176)

And, surely as the chaplain predicted, the king's realm prospered, and the king himself renounced the sacrifice of animals and the wasteful cutting of trees for sacrificial posts. Slaves and workmen did their jobs without compulsion, and instead of animals, ghee and oil and butter and milk and honey were offered as sacrifices to the gods, as if Empedocles' ideal age was being realized in a Buddhist story! No wonder the Brahmin Kūṭadanta was converted: "And myself, O Gotama, will have the seven hundred [each of bulls, rams, steers, goats, heifers] set free. To them I grant their life. Let them eat green grass and drink fresh water, and may cool breezes waft around them" (*Dial.,* 1:185).

This text and related ones such as the "Cakkavatti Sīhanāda Sutta"—which deals with the righteous monarch who rules according to the "ten principles of kingly virtue"—have been taken by modern-day Buddhist activists as justification for the equitable distribution of wealth in socialist fashion. To me these Buddhist stories are primarily ethical in significance; they are not of much use for practical economics or polity, then or now, although their ethical message might well have influenced the economic thinking of Buddhist kings. The Buddha was not a social reformer; what is impressive is the axiologizing imperative of his discourses.

In even more down-to-earth terms several texts give symbolic meaning to the crucial Vedic household fire ritual for Agni, known as the *agnihotra,* and to Brahmanic purificatory rites and other forms of ritualism that are seen as purely external and nonethical markers.[62] There are also cases of "negative axiologization," where Brahmanic eschatological ideas are given universal value but in a negative sense. The most dramatic example is the idea of *preta,* the departed: in Vedic thought when a person dies his or her preta, or disembodied soul, is released. This spirit is in a dangerous, liminal state until the rites of death known as *sapiṇḍīkaraṇa* (offering of food rolled into a ball) converts the preta into a *pitr* (father). This pitr eventually goes to the realm of the ancestors or Fathers *(pitaraḥ),* a paradisiacal abode.[63] In Buddhism pretas are those dead kinfolk who, owing to their excessive greed and attachment to the world, live out miserable existences hovering about the abodes of the living. They personify the Buddhist idea of desire, *taṇhā.*

One of the most famous Buddhist texts is called the "Sigālovāda Sutta" (The Sigāla homily), sometimes known as "the code for the laity" because it gives pragmatic injunctions on how to lead a good life and obtain the rewards of heaven, making no reference whatever to soteriology.[64] In it, in typical ironic style, the Buddha mildly chastises a Brahmin youth, Sigāla, for profitlessly worshiping the [gods of the] Six Quarters. Instead: "The following should be looked upon as the six quarters: parents as the east, teachers as the south, wife and children as the west, friends and companions as the north, servants and work people as the nadir, and religious teachers and Brahmins as the zenith" (*Dial.,* 3:180).[65] Then he gives the appropriate conduct for those who now symbolically occupy these places. For example: "In five ways should a wife as western quarter be ministered to by her husband: by respect, by courtesy, by faithfulness, by handing over authority to her, by providing her with adornment." And for the husband a wife should see that "her duties are well performed, by hospitality to the kin of both, by faithfulness, by watching over the goods he brings, and by skill and industry in discharging all her business" (*Dial.,* 3:181–82). Very bourgeois values, one might say.

The preceding myths imply that the axiologizing imperative operates in two ways. First, there is a universalizing of values in a purely abstract sense; and, parallel with this, pre-Buddhist or non-Buddhist religious practices are given ethical and symbolic significance, often in terms of these very universalizing values. Thus nonviolence (ahiṃsā) is a universal abstract value; in the story of King Wide-realm this value is given specificity in relation to the concrete case of the sacrifice. The sacrifice now is what the king himself must make for the welfare of the people; the king recognizes this by changing the sacrificial substances and Kūṭadanta, impressed by that story, releases his own sacrificial animals. The "Sigālovāda Sutta" is much more pragmatic: it gives symbolic meaning to the act of worshiping the Six Quarters in terms of very practical values suitable for lay life.[66]

## AXIOLOGIZATION CONTINUED: HOMO HIERARCHICUS AND HOMO AEQUALIS IN INDIA

> For the polity of the Indians being distributed into many parts, there is one tribe among them of men divinely wise, whom the Greeks are accustomed to call Gymnosophists. But of these there are two sects, one over which the Bramins preside, but over the other the Samanaeans. The race of Bramins, however, receive divine wisdom of this kind by succession, in the same manner as the priesthood. But the Samanaeans are elected and consist of those who wish to possess divine knowledge. . . . All the Bramins originate from one stock; for all of them are derived from one father and one mother. But the Samanaeans are not the offspring of one family, being, as we have said, collected from every nation of Indians.
>
> —Porphyry, *De Abstinentia*

From an anthropological viewpoint the most interesting feature of the Buddhist axiological thrust lies in its attempt to symbolically redefine Brahmin status superiority, justified in the Vedic tradition and given legal, moral, and spiritual meaning in the early Dharmasūtras. In conformity with the spirit of ethical asceticism this is done with irony and good humor, never in the wrathful language one encounters in ethical prophecy. Let me illustrate this with the Buddhist critique of the Brahmanic division of the society into four *varṇas* (lit., "colors" and often translated by early Indologists as "caste").[67] In this scheme, as is well known, the multiplicity of different hierarchically graded groups scattered in India and generally known as *jāti* are subsumed under the following four orders in descending status: the Brahmins, or priestly groups; the Kṣatriya, or ruling classes; the Vaiśya, or groups involved in trade, commerce, and banking (known as *vessa* in Buddhist texts); and the Śūdras, mostly peasants and artisans. Buddhists rarely mention specific jāti, only specific *varṇas*. In particular, they argue against the classic Brahmanic myth that postulates a homology between the body of god and the body politic: the Brahmin class emerged from the head of Brahma, the Kṣatriya from his breast, the Vaiśya from his belly and the Śūdra from his feet. Later texts describe a motley group of the lowest of the low, labeled "untouchables" in recent times, beyond the pale of the *varṇas* and of orthodox society in general.[68] In Buddhist texts the fourfold *varṇa* scheme is given symbolic and ethical meaning, and the Brahmanic claim to superiority is deflated.

There are at least four major texts that deal with this issue and many verses affirming human equality in late canonical texts like the *Dhammapada* and *Udāna* that probably reached audiences of ordinary people. Let me briefly present the dialogue between the Brahmin youth Vāseṭṭha and the Buddha in the "Vāseṭṭha Sutta" of the late collection known as the *Sutta-Nipāta,* which is similar to an earlier text with the same title in the *Majjhima Nikāya* (Middle length sayings).

In this text the two Brahmin youths we met earlier, Vāseṭṭha and Bhāradvaja, "both students of the orthodox teachings and . . . experts in the study of the Vedas" and "qualified to teach the subjects of metre, grammar and chanting," come to the Buddha to clarify the relation between ancestral purity and social status. Vāseṭṭha thinks that ancestral purity is not significant, whereas his friend, Bhāradvaja, asserts that "if one's family background is pure, and there has been no intermarriage with other castes for seven generations back, on either one's mother's or one's father's side, then one is a Brahmin."[69] The Buddha's axiologizing answer is that animals, plants, insects, fish, and birds are differentiated into species, but the distinctions among human beings are purely nominal or convention bound:

> "Vāseṭṭha," said the Lord, "I will expound
> To you in gradual and very truth
> Division in the kinds of living things;
> For kinds divide. Behold the grass and trees!
> They reason not, yet they possess the mark
> After their kind, for kinds indeed divide.
> Consider then the beetles, moths and ants:
> They after their kind too possess the mark . . .
> And so four-footed creatures, great and small . . .
> The reptiles, snakes, the long-backed animals . . .
> Fish and pond-feeders, water denizens . . .
> They after their own kind possess the mark;
> For kinds divide. Each after his kind bears
> His mark; in man there is not manifold.
> Not in the hair or head or ears or eyes,
> Not in the mouth or nose or lips or brows,
> Not in the throat, hips, belly or the back,
> Not in the rump, sex-organs or the breast,
> Not in the hands or feet, fingers or nails,
> Not in the legs or thighs, colour or voice,

Is mark that forms his kind as in all else.
Nothing unique is in men's bodies found:
The difference in men is nominal." (*MLS,* 2:381–82)

To fully appreciate this extraordinarily modern-sounding statement, we must remember that Plato, writing more than a hundred years later, could not visualize his ideal community without slaves. In denying the significance of physiological markers the Buddha was probably arguing against the Vedic notion of *dasyus* (slaves), who were, according to many scholars, the dark-skinned indigenous folk displaced by the Indo-European speakers. Following the Buddha's nominalistic view of human differences is a discussion of the four *varṇas* that the anthropologist Edmund Leach would surely have appreciated: it is all a matter of the division of labor! Then in twenty-seven stanzas the Buddha describes the moral qualities of righteous persons culminating in the renouncer. Each stanza ends with the refrain: "brahman him I call," giving ethical and symbolic significance to the word *Brahmin,* an axiologization of the Brahmin *varṇa* that repeatedly occurs in this and many other texts.

The "Vāseṭṭha Sutta" affirms that one is not a Brahmin by birth or social status but by the operation of karma, which applies to all equally:

What the world holds as "name" and "lineage"
Is indeed nominal, terms risen here
And there by popular opinion,
Adhered to long, views of the ignorant!
The ignorant declare: "A brahman is
By birth." None is by birth a brahman; none
By birth no brahmana; by deeds [karma] is one
A brahmana, by deeds [karma] no brahmana!
By deeds one is a farmer and by deeds
An artisan, by deeds a trader too. . . . (*MLS,* 2:384–85)

Karmic deeds themselves cannot be understood except by "way of cause," that is, through the Buddhist notion of conditioned genesis, in which everything in the world is causally interconnected.

The critique of *varṇa* and the discussion of Brahmin claims lead to a conception of *human* species equality, a radical rejection of Otherness (whose complicated historical vicissitudes cannot be discussed here). Nevertheless, the exceptions are extremely significant and indicative of the socially grounded debates going on in the society. The "Madhurāsutta" deals with caste in a completely pragmatic manner, and the dramatis personae fit the tone of the text.[70] Avantiputta, the king of Madhurā, engages in a dialogue with a Buddhist monk, Kaccāna, in order to clarify

Brahmin pretensions that "only brahmans form the best caste, all other castes are low; only brahmans form the fair caste, all other castes are dark; only brahmans are own sons of Brahma, born of his mouth, born of Brahma, formed by Brahma, heirs to Brahma. What does the revered Kaccāna say to this?" (*MLS* 2: 273). The monk responds by giving the king examples from everyday living showing that non-Brahmin *varṇas* are equal to the others in law; and in economic terms any *varṇa* could as easily rise in the social scale owing to wealth, industry, and so forth and even employ higher castes, including Brahmins, as servants. The king is made to agree with the Buddhist idea that *varṇa* makes no difference as far as ethical rewards and punishments are concerned either. Finally, Buddhist values are reaffirmed: these conventional designations disappear when one becomes a "recluse." The king utters in agreement the refrain that peppers this text: "Indeed, good Kaccāna, this being so, these four castes [*varṇas*] are exactly the same; I do not see any difference between them in this regard" (*MLS,* 2:277).

I think that local arguments such as the above get universalized in texts like the "Vāseṭṭha Sutta." For example, the Brahmin claim to a fair skin and purity of lineage (and perhaps other physical signs of superiority) might have led to the Buddhist universalist discourse that physical differences are purely external markers. Other debates, however, are much more parochial, such as the ones reflected in the "Ambaṭṭha Sutta," where the Buddha claims his *varṇa* is superior to the Brahmin and that "even when a Kṣatriya has fallen into the deepest degradation, still it holds good that the Kṣatriyas are higher, and the Brahmins are inferior."[71] Then, in a piece of casuistry that is not too far removed from his opponents', the Buddha justifies the purity of his own *varṇa* and even relates a myth to show the origin of its superior status![72] But even here there is no notion of "intrinsic inequality," such as the Brahmanic one ordained by divine decree. The Buddhist position implies that although people are *intrinsically* equal, there is nevertheless an omnipresence of inequality. The karma theory in Indic thought is consistent with, and can be used to justify, either intrinsic equality or inequality.

Nevertheless one can ask why the kind of parochialism reflected in the "Ambaṭṭha Sutta" should have been enshrined in the Buddhist doctrinal tradition. Here we confront once again the problem of "contradictions" in these Buddhist texts, even in the earliest ones. I noted that, in general, Indological scholars and modern Buddhist intellectuals have dealt with these contradictions by suggesting they result from "interpolations" that crept in later or from popular religiosity that has distorted the original purity of Buddhism. I see the problem otherwise. These contradictions are there from the very start because the "Buddha" and the "Dhamma" of these texts are constructions that represent the many voices of the times. Some of these texts have to resolve certain existential or intellectual dilemmas (or theodicies, paradoxes, or aporias) that Buddhists have had to face. The particular aporia pertaining to the Buddha's caste is well illustrated in later texts: the Buddhas generally belong to the Brahmin or Kṣatriya *varṇa,* never to the Vaiśyas or Śūdras although in the *Jātaka,* or birth stories, the Buddha-to-be can be born in any caste, including the lowest of the low. The *varṇa* debates pertain to the fact that the Buddha of our epoch was born a Kṣatriya. Naturally he cannot be made inferior to the Brahmins, whose very ideology he was contesting. Hence, the *varṇa* of the Buddha has to be superior to that of the Brahmins. The "Ambaṭṭha Sutta" simply turns the Brahmin's claim to ancestral purity on its head by saying that the Buddha's own Sākya lineage practiced sibling marriages in order to maintain its purity!

The common sociological explanation of this text (and others that call into question the superiority of Brahmins) is that the caste order was not formalized in this period in the Ganges valley; consequently, the Buddhist texts show the contestation of power between Brahmins and Kṣatriyas. I think this is correct only up to a point: historical research teaches us that the Buddha came from the independent "republics" of the period, and in them the Brahmins had no real standing. Indeed, the region in which Buddhism arose was considered an unhealthy and unsuitable place for Brahmins. One of the most important Brahmanic texts, the "Dharmasūtra of Baudhāyana," probably composed not too long after the period of the Buddha, mentions the areas of the Magadhas as consisting of low *varṇas* and mixed ones.[73] Yet the same period shows the emergence of empires and the role of Brahmins as palace officials and ritual specialists performing sacrifices and calendrical rituals necessary for the welfare of the state, which is pretty much what they did in the Brahmanic heartland known as the Āryavartha. Thus, the Buddhist texts in which the king says that Brahmins are equal with others in law and that economic opportunity erases differences and so forth may reflect a reality of the "republics" of the time. They do not reflect the emergent reality of empire, nor do they reflect the Dharmasūtra texts, which constantly emphasize the differential legal treatment of the four *varṇas.*

Even when the Buddhists ridicule Brahmanic ideas of purification, as they sometimes do, there is a hint that these values are part of the social reality of the time. In the late canonical text *Therigāthā* (Elders' verses) the elder Puṇṇikā meets a Brahmin who believes that the ill effects of karma can be wiped out by purifying oneself with water, and the nun responds satirically:

> Who indeed told you this, ignorant to the ignorant: Truly, he is released from his evil action by ablution in the water?
>
> Now (if this is so) all frogs and turtles will go to heaven, and alligators and crocodiles and the other water-dwellers.
>
> Sheep-butchers, pork-butchers, fishermen, animal-trappers, thieves and executioners, and other evil-doers, even they will be released from their evil action by ablution in water.
>
> If these streams carried away for you the evil previously done, they would carry away your merit too; thereby you would be outside (devoid of both). (vv. 240–43)

The Brahmin converts to Buddhism by uttering the formula that other Brahmin converts also make in the *Therigāthā:* "Formerly, I was a kinsman of Brahma; today I am truly a brahman. I possess the triple knowledge, I am endowed with knowledge, and I am versed in sacred lore; (and) I am washed clean."[74]

In all of these texts purity is axiologized as an internal condition, or *visuddhi,* achieved through Buddhist meditational ascesis. The "triple knowledge" of this text puns on the triple Veda and then implicitly refers to the three parts of the Buddhist canon. Yet the very stridency of the Buddhist contestation of Brahmanical claims might well indicate that Brahmins were already a force to reckon with in the Ganges valley of the Buddha's time. Remember that the samanic religious virtuosos were probably much more critical of Brahmanic claims than were ordinary people, and it is this samanic viewpoint that is expressed in the texts. Buddhist texts everywhere recognize, but do not accept, the Brahmin as the superior *varṇa* in both the worldly and the spiritual sense; and the standard phrase "Brāhmaṇas and samaṇas (recluses)" that the Buddha uses gives implicit recognition to this fact. So does the idea that some Buddhas of the past were Brahmins. Moreover, the Buddha's own lineage name, Gautama or Gotama, is a well-known Brahmanic one; and whether it was adopted or not, it does legitimize the religion's founder and his contesting of the ethical thought attributed to the other Gautama, an important Brahmin sage of both the Upanishads and the Dharmasūtras. The very fact that the Buddha had to contest Brahmanic claims and give axiological meaning to *Brahmin* further suggests the critical importance of the Brahmanic status. It seems that the Brahmins' claim to be the "highest *varṇa*" was being reinforced by their role in the new empires and, at the same time, was being contested by those nurtured in the social formations of the Ganges valley. The power of the Buddha's critique of *varṇa* lies primarily in its axiological thrust, its affirmation of the nominalistic nature of social divisions, that right conduct is the guarantor of virtue and that all humans are biologically equal in spite of external bodily markers. The deaxiologizing thrust that extols the Buddha's caste as superior must be seen in relation to much more parochial debates going on at the same time between Buddhists and Brahmins and their supporters, on the ground, as it were.

These oppositional dialectics are not only verbal; they are, as I have already pointed out, manifest in the oppositional lifestyles of the two groups, "Brāhmaṇas and samaṇas." If purifying practices express the lifestyle of the Brahmins, the repudiation of ritual purification and the adoption of a deliberate lifestyle of impurity through the alms-round represent the samanic affirmation of equality. Additionally, Buddhist monks wore patched garments or "rags," sometimes gathered from a dustheap and then cleaned and stitched together, a practice perhaps borrowed from the antecedent tradition of renouncers described in the early Upanishadic literature. Embedded here is the notion that although physical purity is important (the rules of the order emphasize cleanliness and decorum), ritual impurity can be deliberately flaunted. Conspicuous dress codes and overt lifestyles among "samaṇas and Brāhmaṇas" must have had considerable visual impact on ordinary people in this region.

One can put the Brahmanic-Buddhist opposition in the following way. The Brahmanic concern with *varṇa* is clearly seen in the Dharmasūtra texts already mentioned. Buddhists are constantly arguing against the hierarchy of the *varṇas,* if not the hierarchy of purity-impurity central to Louis Dumont's argument.[75] The latter, as Olivelle points out in an important paper, is *not* a concern in the Dharmasūtra texts.[76] Instead, these texts deal with the multiple ways of purifying oneself when one comes into contact with sources of impurity, which as far as human beings are concerned almost always refers to bodily effusions, bringing Brahmanic ideas of pollution-purification in line with similar obsessions in other cultures. Although Olivelle is right in saying that the Dharmasūtra references to purification read as if they were injunctions to all classes *(varṇas),* one cannot miss the Brahmanic-centeredness of these texts. I think it almost certain that in actual practice it was the Brahmin *varṇa,* then as well as now, that was primarily preoccupied with implementing the Dharmasūtra injunctions of purification; many of these norms seem alien to the lifestyles of the other classes. Given Brahmanic practices it would not be surprising if there were popular conceptions that did in fact treat the Brahmin class as "intrinsically pure" in Dumont's sense, as, for example, the Brahmin affirmation in the "Vāseṭṭha Sutta" that Brahmin purity can be maintained only if there has been lineage purity for seven generations on both the mother's and father's sides. So is it with the Buddhist nun: When she scoffs at a particular Brahmin individual's practice of ritual cleansing, she is also scoffing at Brahmins as a class, and this exemplifies the Buddhist position in general. However, although it is the case that "ritual purification" and any claims to intrinsic purity are denied in Buddhism, its main ethical critique of the Brahmin class is in respect to Brahmin claims to high status, as vindicated in the founding myth of the four *varṇas*.[77]

Dumont is, however, correct in another area of ancient Indian life, namely the powerful coalition between Brahmin and king. During most of Indian history the Brahmins were spiritual advisers and chaplains, or *purohitas,* of the kings; and kings, we know, gave extensive gifts to Brahmins. There is no question that this combination of Brahmin and king was a hegemonic one; what is not clear is the nature of that hegemony, its historical vicissitudes over time and place and in varying political conditions. Although Dumont is correct in stipulating the importance of the Brahmin-Kṣatriya coalition, he underrates its shifting and variable hegemony, including the tensions in the coalition itself. The Ganges valley in the time of the Buddha was outside the main orbit of Brahmanic influence. But with the emergence of empires the Brahmin-king coalition would soon become established and routinized in different ways in this region also. But this is not a working out of Brahmanic texts; those texts too had to be adapted to political and social realities. The Buddhists were one of the earliest groups to openly contest Brahmanic claims because the small "republics" from which the Buddha came did not recognize their status superiority, even though these claims were being publicly propagated. In my thinking the samanic, and specifically the Buddhist, opposition to Brahmanic claims of superiority created an important precedent in the Indian tradition for similar contestations right through history.[78]

# 5 ESCHATOLOGY AND SOTERIOLOGY IN GREEK REBIRTH

## METHODOLOGICAL REMARKS

I will now bring to bear on my imaginary experiment the traditions of thought in ancient Greece, conveniently labeled "Pythagorean," that also contained multiple theories of rebirth. Most of the doctrines of rebirth discussed earlier have both historical and contemporary relevance, but for Greece one has no choice but to deal exclusively with the historical traditions, beginning with the figure most associated with rebirth doctrines, Pythagoras. Pythagoras, like similar figures in religious history, is simultaneously a historical and mythic persona such that it makes little sense to differentiate the two. Myth *is* history for those who believe in it. To complicate matters, there is no information on Pythagoras from contemporary or near-contemporary records. All early records are very fragmentary, at least until we reach the third and fourth centuries C.E., when two detailed Neoplatonic texts on the life of Pythagoras became available, one by Porphyry and the other, a more interesting account, by his student, the Neoplatonist Iamblichus. This lack of contemporary data poses a huge methodological problem: how does one use this interesting yet patently late information for the study of early (or for that matter late) Pythagoreanism? Virtually every classical scholar, even those skeptical of the Neoplatonic writers, does in fact use this data, but it is not clear on what bases. From my point of view there is a justification to use later texts because information about

Pythagoras, whether mythic or no, went down into later Greek tradition. Porphyry and Iamblichus did not self-consciously fabricate these accounts but simply put down in writing existing information about Pythagoras and Pythagoreanism. One can therefore say that Pythagoras, as he appears in later texts, is a construction of Pythagoreanism, that is, the tradition of thought built on the work of a mythic founder. Although we know that traditions are being constantly invented, it is also the case that some ideational forms, or epistemes, show remarkable consistency over time, good examples being Buddhist ideas of karma, samsara, nirvana, and so forth. Otherwise no idea of enduring structures makes sense. Even a radical thinker such as Michel Foucault dealt with the remarkable persistence of epistemes in Western civilization through time, effectively showing that the great poststructuralist remains a structuralist after all! Further, when traditions or epistemic forms are being invented, they are rarely invented de novo. Thus, there is justification for using later works as part of an ongoing tradition of Pythagoreanism or as a depository of that tradition. Iamblichus's Pythagoras may not be the real Pythagoras (if ever there was such a being), but his is a legitimate version of Pythagoras that some persons, including Iamblichus, believed in. He is a figure of the Greek imagination as the Buddha is of the Indian.

Let me justify my approach by sketching those elements of the Pythagorean tradition that constituted, according to earlier fragments and late accounts, epistemes of the long run in the imagination of the Greeks. I will spell them out schematically and then deal with them at length; this will enable others to disagree with me. As one goes down the following list one moves from the fairly certain to the fairly speculative.

1. There does not seem to be the slightest doubt that Pythagoras (hereafter meaning the figure of the Greek imagination) believed in reincarnation, and I will demonstrate that the Pythagoreans had several models of it.

2. Early as well as late references indicate that this rebirth eschatology entailed animal rebirths, which therefore explains the strong injunction against consuming flesh. Associated with this is also a doctrine of species sentience.

3. The tradition of a vegetarian diet was also pronounced although some accommodations were made to the popular Greek cuisine of the sacrifice.

4. Pythagoras was sometimes depicted as a ridiculous figure by mainline Greek thinkers and as a divine, semidivine, or superhuman being by believers, followers, and intellectual admirers.
5. Among his miraculous powers was the power of retrocognition, such that he could recollect past lives, although up to a limited period only.
6. On the other hand, Pythagoras was considered the founder of Greek mathematics and a "philosopher." I think it wrong to extrapolate Pythagoras's philosophical thought and label it as "real" to contrast with the mythic elements; both are inextricably part of the imagined Pythagoras.
7. There were almost certainly early Pythagorean communities that espoused secret doctrines and adopted formulas of a highly symbolic sort. The details of the lifeways of these communities are in later accounts such as Iamblichus's; many accounts, early and late, portray them as given to "silence."
8. Although the outlines of Pythagorean eschatologies are easy to figure out, the details are difficult. Hence, formulations of such phenomena as ethicization must be speculative although they are derived from and reinforced by the models constructed earlier and by the comparative material.
9. The same is true of the Pythagorean soteriologies, although it is virtually certain that Pythagoras himself was concerned with the emancipation from the rebirth cycle.
10. This is because there is considerable evidence that Pythagoreans shared with some Orphic communities an understanding of the body as a prison of the soul; hence the need for the soul's release.

What then is the task of the historian or ethnographer? All he or she can do is weave a narrative, or "story," incorporating these hypothesized features of Pythagoreanism. Plato, that great storyteller, honestly recognized this function of narrative whenever he or his Socrates spoke of a "probable mythos" or when he asserted that the facts need not be "exactly as I have described them" but that "something very like it is a true account."[1] Even the most erudite of classical scholars must adopt this kind of strategy in respect to fragmentary material scattered through a long historical period, although few would be willing to admit it. The historian or ethnographer is a special type of storyteller, the history teller (or *histor*), who weaves "facts" into the fabric of a narrative. Therefore, historical accounts have to be justified by evidence or admitted as speculative and, in the latter instance, defended with good reasoning. This concern with evidence and the logical justification of speculation is what gives "truth-value" to historical and ethnographic descriptions as against fiction and other purely invented genres. Hence the paradox: verisimilitude is simply impossible in history or ethnography, but it is entirely possible in fictional narratives, where the messiness of "truth" is no impediment to storytelling.[2]

## PYTHAGORAS AND PYTHAGOREANISM: A PROBABLE MYTHOS

Pythagoras apparently was born on the island of Samos and lived there during the time of the tyrant Polycrates, who came into power c. 540 B.C.E. According to most accounts Pythagoras left Samos, perhaps because of political opposition to Polycrates, and went west after traveling in foreign lands. According to some sources he sojourned in Egypt and even visited Zoroaster. Ultimately he settled in Croton, in southern Italy, around age forty and there formulated his doctrines of salvation, perhaps influenced by the prevailing mystery religions and varieties of Orphic soteriology that had taken root in this region.[3]

Pythagoras is thought to have been the great founder of Greek mathematics and of a religious-cum-philosophical creed that had reincarnation as the central tenet along with strict dietary prohibitions pertaining to the consumption of meat and some select vegetable substances. Some think that the reincarnation eschatology was formulated before Pythagoras by an older contemporary, Pherekydes, Pythagoras's teacher, but for our purposes it is convenient to start with Pythagoras himself.[4] We know that the Pythagoreans had schools, sodalities, or orders whose origins were not in Greece proper but in Magna Graecia, that is, outside of the Greek mainland, in what is now southern Italy and Sicily. This region was also the home of the most famous of the later Pythagoreans, Empedocles, who lived around the middle of the fifth century B.C.E.

Let me begin with Herodotus, who, writing in the mid-fifth century, clearly refers to rebirth doctrines among Greeks:

> The Egyptians are the first to have told the story also, that the soul of man is immortal and that, when the body dies, the soul creeps into some other living thing then coming to birth; and when it has gone through all things,

> of land and sea and air, it creeps again into a human body at its birth. The cycle for the soul is, they say, three thousand years. There are some Greeks who have used this story, some earlier and some later, as though it were something of their own. I know their names but will not write them down.[5]

H. S. Long suggests that because Herodotus's account did not fit the rebirth eschatologies of Pindar, Empedocles, and Plato, he must have referred to the only other leading contender, Pythagoras.[6] But this assumes that in Herodotus's time there were no rebirth theories other than Pythagoras's, which is most unlikely, particularly given that Herodotus suggests in a discussion of burial customs that other groups believed in rebirth:

> [The Egyptians] wear linen tunics, with fringes about their legs which they call "calasiris," and they wear white woolen mantles on top of these again. But they never bring into the temple anything of wool, nor may they be buried in such. That contravenes their religion. In this they agree with those rites that are called Orphic and Bacchic but are in fact Egyptian and Pythagorean. For in the case of these rites, too, whoever has a share in them may not be buried in woolen garments. There is a holy tale about this.[7]

Herodotus's reference to the taboo on wool makes sense in terms of what we know to be a common practice among virtually all Greek believers in rebirth, namely, a symbolic affirmation of purity. Wool, after all, comes from animals that will be killed (for the sacrifice). The taboo is therefore analogous to the orthodox Brahmin's refusal to wear leather shoes.

Herodotus seems to refer to a specific doctrine of rebirth with which he was familiar, one that had a fixed cycle of three thousand years during which the soul gets reincarnated in land, sea, and air creatures, a set of predetermined births that end up in a human reincarnation, thus completing the full cycle. There is no mention of a doctrine of salvation, and it is unlikely to be Pythagoras's own doctrine, unless the missing reference is simply an omission. The length of the cycle itself is based on formal key numbers: ten (the perfect number for Pythagoreans) and three (representing for Pythagoreans the idea of beginning, middle, and end). These numbers were subsequently used by all Greek rebirth theorists, including Plato. Regarding the taboo on wool Herodotus's statement hints at Pythagorean *acusmata* (oral instruction) or at special ritual and other injunctions that members of the order had to observe.

Because those in Greece proper had little patience with either reincarnation or strict asceticism, the Pythagoreans were ridiculed by Greek satirists. Thus Xenophanes (a near contemporary) laughs at Pythagoras who, seeing a dog being maltreated, cried out in pity:

> And once he passed a puppy that was being whipped
> They say he took pity on it and made this remark:
> "Stop, do not beat it; for it is a soul of a dear friend—
> I recognized it when I heard the voice."[8]

But as Peris and others have shown, the satire does indicate evidence for the form of rebirth I have called cross-reincarnation.[9] Xenophanes' sarcasm aside, there is also an implicit notion linking the idea of species sentience with that of reincarnation: one must have sympathy for animals because a former known human spirit might have been resident in it.[10]

A less mechanical notion of the rebirth cycle and of memory emerges from Heraclides, a student of Plato and a member of the academy who speaks of Pythagoras's previous lives, ostensibly on the authority of the master himself:

> He was once Aethalides, who, when his father Hermes offered him any gift except immortality, chose to retain both in life and in death the memory of what happened to him. Later he became the Homeric hero Euphorbus, wounded in battle by Menelaus, who was wont to recount the wanderings of his soul in animals and *plants as well as human bodies,* and tell of the fate of souls in Hades. Next his soul entered Hermotimus, who authenticated the story of his previous life by identifying the rotting shield of Menelaus in the temple of Apollo at Branchidae. It them became a Delian fisherman named Pyrrhus, and finally Pythagoras, carrying with it still the memory of its previous phases of existence.[11]

In this eschatology one can be reborn as an animal without having to go through a complete cycle, as in Herodotus's account. It also contains the idea, missing in Herodotus, that one can be incarnated in a plant. The reference to Pythagoras's recollection of past lives is not through a special ascesis but by a boon given by Hermes in an early incarnation. There is also the vindication of past memory by reference to "proofs," such as the rotting shield of Menelaus. In addition to Pythagorean vegetarianism, Heraclides also refers to the strong taboo on beans. "Heraclides explains the Pythagorean ban on beans by the curious superstition that if a bean is laid in a new tomb and covered with dung for forty days, it takes on the appearance of a man."[12] This may not make sense to us, but it was surely embedded in a larger text, part of the secret acusmata of the sect and its esoteric symbology, communicated to its selected membership as *paradosis,* as *rahasyam.*

Now for the final set of references: Porphyry, in his *Life of Pythagoras,* attributes to Empedocles a saying that, in all likelihood, referred to Pythagoras himself. "There was among them a man of surpassing knowledge, who possessed vast wealth of understanding, capable of all kinds of cunning acts; for when he exerted himself with all his understanding, easily did he see every one of all the things that are, in ten and twenty human lives."[13] And Iamblichus refers to this superman, who "knew his own previous lives, and began his training of others by awakening their memory of an earlier existence."[14] Memory is a key feature in rebirth eschatologies, so it is not surprising that Iamblichus can say that in Pythagorean training disciples were expected to "set great store by memory" because "nothing has more effect on knowledge, experience and understanding than the ability to remember."[15] The tradition was strong that Pythagoras possessed the facility of retrocognition based on some unspecified forms of spiritual ascesis. But unlike the Buddha's retrocognition, Pythagoras's was for ten or twenty human lives, once again based on the number ten. Porphyry also has a neat and cautious account of Pythagoras's rebirth doctrine imagined at this late date. After mentioning that many men and women joined Pythagoras, and the silence he observed, he adds this key passage:

> But especially well known among all were first that they said that the soul was immortal, next, that it went across to other kinds of animals, and in addition to these, that what had once taken place takes place again according to certain cycles [*periodous*], but that nothing is altogether [*(h)aplos*] new and that it is necessary to consider all existing living things [*empsycha*] to be kin [*homogene*]. For it appears that the first to bring this teaching to Greece was Pythagoras.[16]

It seems to me that the preceding accounts of Greek rebirth suggest two models, the first by Herodotus and Porphyry and the second by Heraclides. Both may be seen as variations of the rebirth topography sketched in figure 3. Consider the model mentioned by Herodotus; in it the soul wanders through a fixed cycle, automatically going through a round of all the land, sea, and air creatures and then coming back to the human body in a cycle that takes three thousand years. One would have hesitated to take Herodotus seriously but for the fact that his model is both logically and empirically feasible, and it also shows a similarity to the *Ājīvika* rebirth schema. That virtually the same scheme was attested by Porphyry indicates that the Herodotus model continued into later times as an episteme of the long run. Further, it is also of the sort that Lee Guemple has labeled "continuous incarnation," in which the soul keeps incarnating in different human or other forms, as in the case of the Qiqiqtamiut Inuit and the Trobrianders. Because the same soul incarnates in different kinds of bodies, it is not likely that the same *person* is being continuously reincarnated. It is hard to believe that the Greeks thought that there was no *person* difference between, let us say, a human incarnation and a fish incarnation! The absence of reference to rebirth as a plant need not be seen as an oversight because we do know that such rebirth is rarely mentioned in the cross-cultural record. Nevertheless, there is a difference between the Herodotus and Porphyry models: the latter assumes periodic cycles with events repeating themselves, something that is structurally difficult if not impossible in Buddhism, where, in general, events are conditioned by karma. Yet even in Buddhism all Buddhas follow an identical life pattern—but then they are karma-free beings. That the Greek idea of an eternal return is an episteme of the long run is evident from the more forceful (and more simplistic) statement attributed to Eudemus (c. mid-fourth century B.C.E.), a student of Aristotle's: "If anyone were to believe the Pythagoreans that things will repeat themselves individually, and I shall be talking to you holding my stick as you sit here, and everything will be as it is now, it is reasonable to say that time repeats itself."[17]

I think it reasonable to say that there were multiple models of rebirth circulating in Greece, especially in Magna Graecia, and the fragmentary record outlines a few of them. As in the Amerindian cases, the rebirth doctrine is closely associated with the kinship of all living beings. And this, rather than an abstract idea like the Buddhist ahiṃsā, accounts for the vegetarian diet. These ethics of species sentience go right down to Plato, who says in *Meno* that "the whole of nature is akin."[18] As already noted, this doctrine, when associated with cross-reincarnation, could produce the idea that eating an animal is in effect eating an ancestor and tantamount to endoanthropophagy. I came to this conclusion via the Kwakiutl data and before I had access to the Greek. Because the Greek evidence is unequivocal in this regard, it provides indirect substantiation of our interpretation of the Kwakiutl cannibal dance as a catharsis or purification of the taint of endoanthropophagy; and the Kwakiutl data in turn throw light on both the Greek phobia of endoanthropophagy and the peculiar Upanishadic "water doctrine" in a circular hermeneutical logic of validation. The difference between the Kwakiutl and the Greek is that in the former a vegetarian solution to the aporia of eating one's ancestor is impossible to envision, given Kwakiutl dependence on, and high cultural valuation of, meat eating. In Greece, owing to the agrar-

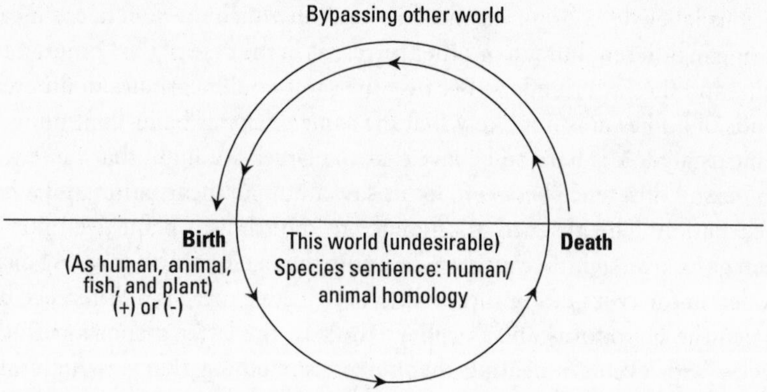


Figure 8. Pythagorean rebirth (after Herodotus, Porphyry, Heraclides). In this system, the process of rebirth is metacosmesis. The duration of rebirth cycles is 3,000 years. Salvation is outside the rebirth cycle. Rebirth memories are possible only for extraordinary individuals. The ideal food is vegetarian.

ian economy in which they operated, Pythagoreans (like Buddhists, Jainas, and Hindus) could and often did practice vegetarianism. If, however, the soul gets incarnated in a plant, then that plant also cannot be eaten or destroyed.

What might account for the absence of ethicization in the early Pythagorean eschatology? It seems that although Pythagoras and his followers were clearly involved in the world, they were not involved in the conversion of ordinary citizens into their sodalities. And because of the strict, exclusive nature of the order, the Pythagoreans would find it impossible to be so. Their numbers were small, and they were interested only in their own personal salvation, very much like the Upanishadic virtuosos.

This was not the situation in the religions of the Ganges valley of a slightly later period, when doctrines of salvation were publicly aired and monks were actively involved in converting lay folk into larger religious congregations. Like Pythagoreans, Buddhist monks and nuns belonged to an order whose goal was nirvana. But Buddhism did provide for the laity the secondary compensations of a happy afterlife, punishment for the wicked, and the possibility of a distant achievement of nirvana. Rulers in India, as well as large sectors of the population such as the merchant orders and ordinary folk, subscribed to the new doctrines. But no such inclusion took place in early Pythagoreanism. Hence the paradoxical nature of their life situation: on the one hand they followed tradition by being involved in the political life (perhaps necessary for their survival as a sodality); on the other hand they had to isolate themselves from the world outside, engaged in their own salvation quest. Little reference to ethicization exists in later Pythagoreanism either, if we take Iamblichus's *De Vita Pythagorica* as a test case. Iamblichus extensively documents Pythagoras's concern with everyday social morality for his followers but nowhere does Iamblichus's Pythagoras indicate that conformity to or violation of this morality will lead to rewards or punishments in the afterworld or in another rebirth.[19]

In the preceding account I considered two Pythagorean models: the Herodotus-Porphyry model, in which the soul goes through a predetermined cycle, and the Heraclides model, in which it does not, although one has to be reborn as an animal or plant at some time or other. One could include as a third Aristotle's snide comment that according to "Pythagorean stories" it was possible "for any soul to be clothed in any body."[20] None of these models can be dismissed because all are nomologically adequate and objectively possible, which means, to restate, they possess a coherent internal logic, and they present features that do not contradict norms found in clearly documented examples from the empirical record. Moreover, even if one assumes for the moment that these models were not those of early Pythagoreans but were invented by Herodotus, Porphyry, and Aristotle, they illustrate the proposition that invention does not take place de novo but in relation to existing ideas; and these existing ideas must surely derive from traditions of Pythagoreanism; further, all three rebirth models must logically and reductively circulate around the elementary model of rebirth sketched earlier (see fig. 1).

It is also virtually certain that all Pythagorean theories entail rebirth into nonhuman forms of sentient existence. In this context one can, I think, reinterpret the well-known statements attributed to the Pythagoreans and "Orphics" that the "body is the prison or the tomb of the soul." Contrary to modern interpretations influenced by Christian "prejudices," reference here to the body as the soul's prison does not refer to the human body in one's present existence but to the body's incarceration of the soul in the total rebirth cycle. It implies an eschatology in which the preexistent soul gets "continuously incarnated" in the bodies of four-legged animals, birds, fish, and some plants. Therefore, from a logical point of view the soul is imprisoned in various bodies. But the soul's imprisonment cannot be separated from a doctrine that deals with its release from that prison. Thus, from a soteriological point of view the question posed by all Pythagorean eschatologies is this: how can the soul be released from the prison of the body? And this question implies the release from the rebirth cycle itself given that continuous embodiment is intrinsically associated with that cycle. That release, it seems, could only be obtained in a human birth, as the examples of both Pythagoras and Empedocles illustrate (see fig. 8).

## HISTORY TELLING CONTINUED: PYTHAGOREAN BEGINNINGS AND LIFEWAYS

Classical scholars, like their Indian counterparts, have raised the issue of the origins of their rebirth eschatologies. Consider the obvious presuppositions: that rebirth was invented by the Greeks de novo or that it was diffused from India or vice versa. The diffusion hypothesis is certainly possible, although no one has convincingly argued how this could have occurred either way. This hypothesis depends not only on rebirth theories but also on the striking similarity between the mathematical ideas of Pythagoras and the thought of Sāṃkhya and other philosophies in India.[21] Yet it is not clear whether the Indian mathematics antedated or postdated Pythagoras. As for rebirth doctrines it is certain that Pythagoras antedated the Buddha, although we know from the Upanishadic references that these ideas were probably prevalent in India on the popular level much earlier. I am sympathetic to that hypothesis for the Greeks also, although the evidence is lacking.

E. R. Dodds made a case for a different kind of diffusion in his influential work *The Greeks and the Irrational.* He is rightly critical of M. P. Nilsson and others who thought that "the doctrine of rebirth is a product of 'pure logic,' and that the Greeks invented it because they were 'pure logicians.'"[22] Alternatively, he proposes a popular shamanic source for Greek rebirth: the shaman, as psychopomp, can recollect his past births through ecstatic journeyings of the soul. Interestingly, Dodds argues that shamanism was the model that the Greeks developed "for a deliberate *askesis,* a conscious training of the psychic powers through abstinence and spiritual exercises." The shaman uses his experience of past births to enhance his power, but unfortunately this "original Greek point of view" took a beating "when rebirth was attributed to *all* human souls. . . . [I]t became a burden instead of a privilege, and was used to explain the inequalities of our earthly portion and to show that, in the words of a Pythagorean poet, man's sufferings are self-incurred."[23] Thus, in Dodds's conception shamanic rebirth became generalized later as a popular eschatological one, and although some contemporary scholars subscribe to this theory, it seems to me quite untenable on the basis of our current knowledge.

Shamanism is associated with ascetic practices and with rebirth theories in the Trobriander, Inuit, and Amerindian cases but less so in West Africa, and the evidence is not clear for some of the Siberian societies themselves. One can have shamanism in societies without rebirth doctrines; in the rare instances where shamans recollect their former lives, as with the brilliant Winnebago shaman Thunder Cloud, it is because they live in a society dominated by these ideas and not because they have invented them.[24] Dodds's knowledge of rebirth comes from James Frazer, whereas we are fortunate to have more clearly documented cases of rebirth eschatologies existing independently of the contemporary or historical practice of shamanism. Although Dodds was wrong in assuming that Pythagoras was a Siberian kind of shaman and that shamanism was at the root of Greek rebirth, he was, I think, correct to postulate the prevalence in Greece of multiple forms of popular religion that showed a wide distribution in Eurasia. This has been amply confirmed in recent research.[25]

The background of the Greek states in Magna Graecia has been discussed in detail by such scholars as T. J. Dunbabin and Edwin Minar, and I refer the reader to their work.[26] In brief the social and economic conditions of the Western Greeks were quite different from those of small-scale societies such as the Amerindians and also those of the Ganges valley in the time of the Buddha. There were a multitude of small independent republican states modeled on mainland Greek city-states, many of them warring with each other and competing for control of the maritime trade in the Mediterranean and North Africa. As a result of increasing wealth there was considerable internal stratification and the rise of wealthy classes. In other words Western Greeks were living in a world rapidly expanding culturally and economically through trade networks that in turn facilitated the diffusion of ideas from North and West Africa into southern Italy. However, unlike the situation in India of the same period, none of the city-states of Magna Graecia showed the beginnings of grand empires like that of Kosala and Magadha, which were swallowing up the small independent republics of the time. I think social change helps to expand the intellectual horizons of both ordinary citizens and thinkers, but, as with the Indic material, I resist formulating a direct causal tie-in between social change and eschatological and soteriological beliefs.

Many ancient authors mention the political control that early Pythagoreans exercised in Croton and other cities. It is impossible to know the exact nature of Pythagorean political influence. It is almost certain that, like the Orphics, Pythagoreans had exclusive religious communities in various parts of Magna Graecia, probably held together as translocal communities by the founder or by his teachings.[27] And although Pythagoreans could, and probably did, exert political influence, they were also politically vulnerable for precisely the same reason. Several early accounts mention Pythagoras's activities in Croton in Italy, where he apparently emigrated; there, with his three hundred pupils constituting a "secret band of conspirators," he was able to control and administer the affairs of state.[28] It should not surprise us, therefore, that according to some accounts Crotonites rose in revolt against him and he withdrew to the neighboring city of Metapontum, where he died.[29] However, other accounts propose that although Pythagoreans were politically influential, there was nothing like a "Pythagorean rule" in southern Italy, although everywhere Pythagorean influence was moral and exemplary.[30]

The numbers that formed these Pythagorean sodalities cannot be easily determined because, as in India, they have been fused into formal numerology. Thus the tradition coming from the fourth-century B.C.E. Sicilian thinker Timaeus and preserved by Iamblichus simply multiplies the earlier number by two. Although the number is doubtful, the account does say that Pythagoras won disciples through "preaching," that people accepted his "philosophy," and that his followers lived as "philosophers" in "what is called the common life, according to his command."[31] Forms of such "common life" were known throughout the Greek world at that time and later as *thiasoi, koina,* and *hetaireiai* and during Roman times as *collegia* or *sodalitates.*[32] What is unusual is the Pythagorean form of such associations: those who belonged to a Pythagorean sodality maintained an extraordinary silence (for long periods according to some accounts) and a secretiveness regarding their "philosophical" beliefs, which were generally expressed through an esoteric symbology, the acusmata, some of which Iamblichus has preserved in his *Protrepticus.*[33] Pythagorean silence must not be conflated with the penitentiary vows of silence taken by some Christian orders; silence probably indicated an attitude to the world in respect to Pythagorean teaching like the *rahasyam* (secret knowledge) of the Upanishads. Perhaps the silence was also associated with the practice of religious concentration or meditative ascesis.

Edwin Minar has summarized some of the features of Pythagorean sodalities from Iamblichus's account. Members apparently applied to join and were put through a series of rigid tests. For example, the opinions of parents and others regarding a candidate's character were solicited. According to Pythagorean beliefs external appearance indicated internal character; hence they observed the "candidate's features, his manner of walking, and other purely external traits," perhaps implying that, like the Buddhists, they stressed decorum and personal demeanor. If candidates passed the preliminary examination, they entered into a three-year apprenticeship in which "they were tested for firmness of spirit, love of wisdom and contempt for worldly honor."[34] Women were included, but their exact status in the overall organization is not clear. If Iamblichus's account of Pythagoras's followers has any relevance to the past, there were 218 men but only 17 women—still a very significant amount considering the fact that women in ancient Greece were not generally included in the philosophic life:[35]

> During the next five years they became active members, giving their goods over to the common stock and entering into a regimen of silence. They underwent various purificatory rites and were initiated into certain of the mysteries of the society. This tested their fitness to be entrusted with the deepest secrets of the society. The fortunate ones . . . were admitted "behind the veil," and from thenceforth they not only heard but saw the divine Pythagoras as he performed the mystic rites.[36]

We do not know the nature of these "mystic rites." If they existed they must surely have been influenced by the mystery religions of the time. Those who failed the Pythagorean tests were considered "dead."[37]

Let me now consider the fantastic powers of Pythagoras. Greek scholars find it convenient to dismiss the "miracles" attributed to Pythagoras by later doxographers and commentators. For Burkert, following Dodds, all this indicates the power of the "shamanistic" tradition.[38] It is the case that some of the miracles attributed to Pythagoras much later were modeled on the shamanic retrieval of the soul exemplified in Orpheus's *Descent to Hades.* Although I do not deny the importance of shamanism on forms of Greek religion, I doubt that it can explain the fantastic powers of the legendary Pythagoras. By that token Jesus would also be a shaman; so would Moses and virtually every religious virtuoso in Buddhism. "Miracles" are not unique to shamanism, nor could they be simplistically subsumed under the dubious label of "magic." Here our comparison with Buddhism is instructive: Buddhist ascesis is essentially contemplative, analogous to the Greek *theoria,* and although it displaced shamanism (and spirit possession), it was also influenced by it. Further, Burkert compiles two lists of the miracles attributed to Pythagoras, one containing thirteen and the other four.[39] None involves shamanic or any other form of ecstasy. Most of them are predictions and although shamans also prophesy, this propensity is not their exclusive preserve. Jesus and the Buddha made similar predictions; so do today's palm readers and newspaper astrologers. In one "miracle" Pythagoras was present at "Metapontum in Italy, and Tauromenium in Sicily, and discoursed in common with his disciples in both places," which is again a capacity that Buddhist arahants claimed by virtue of their contemplative powers.[40] Iamblichus mentions Pythagoras showing his "golden thigh to the Hyporean Abaris," but this is no more than the Buddha presenting to an interlocutor the thirty-two marks of the Great Man (including showing the wondrous organ encased in a sheath, with a wonderful irony missed by uptight translators).[41] Finally, if Pythagoras was called the "Hyperborean Apollo" by the people of Croton, this means he was what Nietzsche would have termed an Apollonian rather than a shamanic Dionysian figure, if one were to recognize that Apollonian thought does not necessarily exclude emotion, although it does eschew "excess."[42]

I noted that early accounts emphasize the Pythagorean vegetarian diet. Let us now see how this episteme is woven into later ones. Iamblichus says that Pythagoras "taught his disciples abstinence from all animal flesh and also from certain foods, which are a hindrance to alert and pure reasoning," along with abstinence from wine and moderation in eating.[43] Nevertheless, after his discussion of ordinary (or later) Pythagoreans, he refers to Pythagoras's followers and their nonvegetarian regimen. Having bathed in the evening and walked in groups of two or three, they assembled not more than ten at a time for supper, which they finished before the setting of the sun. They were permitted wine and barley and vegetables and the "flesh of sacrificial animals," although eating fish was discouraged. Animals that were "harmless by nature to the human race" should not be harmed or destroyed. As expected, hunting was not approved of. Again, Iamblichus continued, Pythagoras forbade "the most contemplative group of philosophers, especially those at the highest level, the use of superfluous and ill-gotten foods, by instructing them never to eat anything animate and never to drink wine; neither to sacrifice living beings to the gods nor to harm them in any way." These injunctions were relaxed for those whose life "was not entirely purified, holy and philosophic." The latter were expected to observe periods of abstinence, but they were not permitted to eat the heart or the brain on both practical and religious grounds.[44] So it was with mallows and, of course, beans. Iamblichus also gives clear expression to species sentience in the idea found in virtually every form of Pythagorean-influenced thought that "animals are akin to us."[45] Greeks of this period employed the term *empsychon* to designate the idea of nature permeated with *psyche,* or soul, bringing Greek thought in line with that of the small-scale societies discussed in the previous chapter.[46]

Iamblichus permits two reasonable interpretations. First, it seems that there were different classes of ordinary followers, as well as specialists or philosophers, following appropriate life-forms in accordance with their spiritual accomplishments. Second, the strict rules of early Pythagoreanism were modified later on, as was the case with similar groups, including Buddhists, and these modifications were noted in early and late accounts. Thus Aristotle refers to a Pythagorean belief that "purity is achieved by cleansing rites and . . . abstaining from meat and flesh of animals that have died, mullet, blacktail, eggs and oviparous animals, [and] beans."[47] Now consider a crucial qualification in the injunction against meat eating: several sources say that the Pythagoreans permitted the eating of sacrificed animals, which, according to our previous analysis, was confined either to ordinary followers of Pythagoras or to later Pythagoreans or both. Porphyry: "Of sacrificed animals he bade them not to eat the loin, testicles and privy parts, marrow, feet or head." Porphyry adds that these parts were given symbolic interpretation by Pythagoras; they were the parts that signified the foundation, genesis, growth, beginning, and end of the body.[48] A similar symbolic meaning was perhaps attached, according to Aristotle, to white cocks because they are sacred to the lunar god and further because white represents good and black evil. Iamblichus not only reiterates these but also says that "the soul of man alone does not enter into these animals. Hence it is proper to eat those animals alone which it is fit to slay, but no other animal whatever."[49] By contrast fish seems to have been taboo even for lay followers of Pythagoras, perhaps because the soul of a human being can enter fish.

Iamblichus himself mentions three groups of Pythagoreans: the highly accomplished contemplative thinkers known as the *Mathematici,* who sacrificed to the gods with millet, cakes, honeycombs, and incense and abstained from animal sacrifices; the lesser *Acusmatici;* and the *Politici.* The latter two groups were permitted to sacrifice select animals "such as a cock, or a lamb, or some other animal recently born, but not frequently."[50] But these distinctions of grade, as Iamblichus himself seemed to have realized, developed much later.

The Pythagorean injunction against eating the meat of sacrificed animals meant in effect abstention from meat eating in general because for Greeks, according to Marcel Detienne and his colleagues, every act of meat eating was a sacrifice, and every sacrifice entailed meat eating.[51]

The rationale for abstention from meat eating was cogently argued by Porphyry in his treatise *De Abstinentia.* Porphyry's argument, based on species sentience, is that all animals have souls, reason, and sense and that, consequently, they share the same spiritual nature as humans. Hence "brutes are rational animals"; they possess *dianoia,* "the discursive energy of reason."[52] This is not to say that all animals have these virtues in the same proportion or quality because there are spiritual differences among different kinds of animals, as there are between humans and animals and humans and gods.[53] But because all animal life shares the same spiritual essence, it is rational to abstain from eating flesh.

*De Abstinentia* is written as an epistle to a friend who had given up vegetarianism and adopted Christianity; it is also addressed to those who believed neither in vegetarianism nor in reincarnation. The style is sober, detached, and unemotional. Yet the text indirectly implies that Pythagoreans had strong views on this subject. For example, "the plebians and the vulgar" condemn vegetarians by using the argument of endoanthropophagy (*PA,* 30). Porphyry's plebeians say that Pythagoras thought it "was an equal crime [for humans] to devour each other, and to eat the flesh of oxen and swine." They sarcastically add that Pythagoras and his followers were "anthropophagites" (*PA,* 30, 35).[54] There is little discussion in Porphyry or Iamblichus regarding the relation between rebirth theory and vegetarianism. However, Porphyry mentions his opponents, the Stoics and the Peripatetics, who mention it. "For indeed, what greater injury does he do, who cuts the throat of an ox or a sheep, than he who cuts down a fir tree or an oak? Since, from the doctrine of transmigration, a soul is also implanted in these" (*PA,* 24). The plebeians, not to be outdone, further argued: "But, if as they [the Pythagoreans] say, plants also have a soul, what will become of our life if we neither destroy animals or plants? If, therefore, he is impious who cuts off plants, neither will he be who kills animals" (*PA,* 33). Thus Porphyry's own reference to men and animals having "kindred natures" might have a deeper significance when seen through the arguments of his opponents. One might reasonably conclude that even in Porphyry's time (the mid-third century C.E.) the tradition was strong regarding the following Pythagorean rebirth beliefs: all animate nature (including some plants) were kin; they possessed souls that reincarnated; therefore, destroying them was tantamount to endoanthropophagy.

To sum up: in these several injunctions the basic principle underlying the prohibition against killing animals and an ideal vegetarian diet is affirmed; namely, humans have a soul, and because this soul could easily enter an animal as a result of reincarnation, one cannot kill it. But killing an animal is permitted when it does not have a soul. These qualifications must surely have been an accommodation to popular Greek religiosity. In some instances there might well have been ritual techniques for the elimination of the soul from the body of the sacrificial animal, permitting the slaying of the creature.

Now we can return to an important issue that arises from species sentience, namely, the major injunction of the Pythagoreans against the eating of beans. The examples from Buddhism and Jainism may give us a clue to the reasons underlying this prohibition; certain kinds of seeds capable of germination and plants with bulbous roots are believed to possess sentience and, for early Upanishadic thinkers and later Jainas, even souls. The idea that beans contain a life principle is again implicit in an injunction reported by Porphyry that Pythagoreans must abstain from eating beans as they do from eating human flesh. And there was a Pythagorean saying attributed to Orpheus that eating beans is like eating the heads of one's parents, perhaps a reference to an ancestral life force contained in the head.[55]

This overvaluation of beans is based on a stronger version of species sentience than that found in any of our rebirth eschatologies and much stronger than the Buddhist view that some plants have a single center of consciousness, or *ekindriya.* One can dismiss Guthrie's naive idea that species sentience is based on sympathetic magic alien to the "civilized mind" and accept his more reasoned view that there is "a connexion between beans and life, death or the soul."[56] To conclude: the root belief pertaining to beans is related to species sentience, as in Amerindian rebirth eschatologies, but elaborated in Pythagorean thought and symbology to an extreme degree.

## PYTHAGOREAN SOTERIOLOGY

Most recent interpreters of Pythagoreanism would agree that "religion and science were, to Pythagoras, not two separate departments between which there was not contact, but rather the two inseparable factors in a single way of life."[57] Because the distinction between science and philosophy did not exist at that time, it would seem that what one nowadays understands by science, philosophy, and religion did not make sense to early Pythagoreans either. Yet even those who wish to blur these distinctions continue to compartmentalize these three domains separately. What we lack is an accounting of the unified worldview of these thinkers for whom science and philosophy are in the service of their soteriology. However, these thinkers have their own take on the three key notions that Greeks of this period and later strongly believed in: *kosmos,* or the orderliness in the arrangement of the universe; *theoria,* or contemplation; and *katharsis,* or purification.[58]

For my argument it is necessary to stress the conceptual imperative that guides Pythagorean thought, just as in the case of Buddhism and Greek thinking in general. This conceptual imperative emerges from Aristotle's view of Pythagoreanism, and some scholars think that it partially reflects the thought of Philolaus, an early Pythagorean (born c. 474 B.C.E.).[59] This worldview is rooted in a fundamental dualism that governs the universe, namely that of the limited *(peras)* and the unlimited *(apeiron)*. These cosmological first principles, or *archai,* are themselves apparently made on the basis of the discovery (some think by the founder himself) of musical harmony, namely, "that the chief musical intervals are expressible in simple numerical ratios between the first four integers."[60] As Aristotle put it: "since, then, all other things seemed in the whole of nature to be modelled after numbers, and numbers seemed to be the first things in the whole of nature, they supposed the elements of numbers to be the elements of all things, and the whole heaven to be an attunement and a number."[61] To put it simply: in the musical scale a mathematical pattern lies hidden, and this hidden pattern can be found everywhere, including the very constitution of the universe. Moreover, because the first four integers add up to ten, that number is perfection itself. The numbers were arranged visually with pebbles or dots in the shape of an equilateral triangle and venerated as the Tetractys of the Decad, thus:

```
   *
  * *
 * * *
* * * *
```

Much as the geometrical *yantra*s and *mandala*s were for the Indians, the *tetractys* was the primary sacred symbol for the Greeks and was used for the swearing of oaths in which the founder himself was recognized: "By him who handed down to us the tetractys, source and root of everlasting nature."[62]

Once again it is Aristotle on whom we have to depend for the further elaboration of the theory of numbers. "The elements of number are the even and the odd, and of these the latter is limited and the former unlimited. The One is composed of both of these (for it is both even and odd) and number springs from the One; and numbers, as I have said, constitute the whole universe."[63] The starting point of the whole scheme is the unit (that is, the One) because the zero was unknown at this time and the first true odd number is three, which, as I have noted, had considerable significance for the Pythagoreans, representing for them things that have a beginning, middle, and end.[64] When odd numbers are graphically represented in dots in the form of *gnomons* (right-angle forms), the resulting figure is a square; but when even numbers are represented in the same way, the result is infinitely variable, as figures 9 and 10 illustrate. Figures 9 and 10 can be extended *ad infinitum*. However, figure 9 has the gnomon placed under the One (unit); when this is extended by placing more gnomons, the figure still remains a square (nonvariable), whereas when gnomons are arranged under the two (as in figure 10), the result is infinitely variable.[65] It is therefore to be expected that the perfection of the square will be associated with the limited and the imperfection of the oblong with the unlimited.[66] What does not emerge from Aristotle is the manner in which the number theory is implicated in ethics and soteriology.

The derivation of the cosmogony from numbers is not clear, and I refer the reader to the work of Francis Cornford and others.[67] Fortunately for us the Pythagorean cosmology is more relevant for soteriology than is the cosmogony, although one should bear in mind that this kind of abstract cosmology is not generally associated with forms of passionate or Dionysian religiosity or with mystery religions in general, Greek or otherwise. Again the information comes from Aristotle, who shows that the Pythagorean (read Philolaic) reification of the number ten was extended to include the number of planets. But because only nine planets (including the sun) were observable, Philolaus apparently introduced the critical notion of the "counter earth." "Most people say that the earth lies at the center of the Universe . . . but the Italian philosophers known as Pythagoreans take a contrary view. At the centre, they say, is fire, and the earth is one of the stars, creating night and day by its circular motion about the centre. They further construct another earth in opposition to ours to which they give the name counter-earth."[68] Although this is a bold and imaginative theory, it is not a heliocentric one, as some imagine it. The fire at the center, also known as the "Guard-house of Zeus," is invisible because we live on a side of the earth that is turned away from it. In a further leap of the imagination, some thought, says Aëtius, that

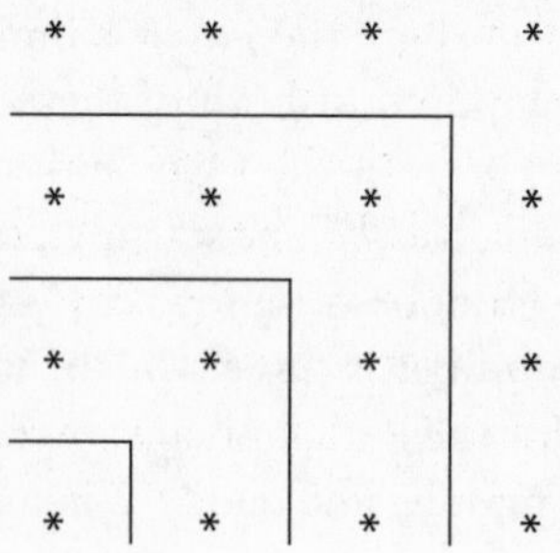

Figure 9. Odd numbers: The limited.

the moon is a world "inhabited like our own, with living creatures and plants that are bigger and fairer than ours. Indeed the animals on it are fifteen times as powerful and do not excrete, and the day is correspondingly long."[69] Parallel with the Philolaic speculations others held a geocentric model with a fire at the earth's center.[70]

Now we can get to that part of the Pythagorean cosmology that is directly relevant for soteriology, namely, the doctrine of the harmony of the spheres, as Aristotle neatly formulates it, and which Kahn thinks could be reasonably viewed as "an invention of the superhuman prophet of archaic times," that is, the imagined Pythagoras.[71]

> From all this it is clear that the theory that the movement of the stars produces a harmony, because the sounds they make are concordant. . . . Some thinkers suppose that the motion of bodies of that size must produce a noise, since on our earth the motion of bodies far inferior in size and in speed of movement has that effect. Also, when the sun and the moon, they say, and all the stars, so great in number and in size, are moving with so rapid a motion, how should they not produce a sound immensely great? Starting from this argument and from the hypothesis that their speeds, as measured by their distances, are in the same ratios as musical concordances, they assert that the sound given forth by the circular movement of the stars is a harmony. Since, however, it appears unaccountable that we should not hear this music, they explain this by saying that the sound is in our ears from the very moment of birth and is thus indistinguishable from its contrary silence, since sound and silence are discriminated by mutual contrast. What happens to men, then, is just what happens to coppersmiths, who are so accustomed to the noise of the smithy that it makes no difference to them.[72]

In an admittedly speculative manner I will now pin down the soteriology in terms of its intrinsic connection with Pythagorean conceptual thought or "science," that is, with number and harmony culminating in the doctrine of the "harmony of the spheres." The idea that seemingly

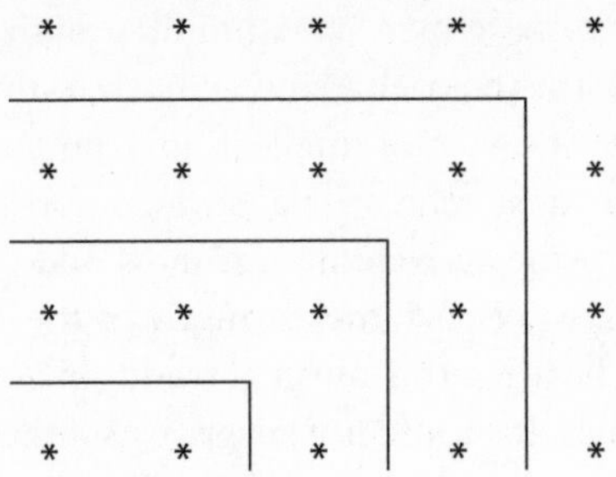

Figure 10. Even numbers: The unlimited.

abstract conceptions such as the limited and unlimited have spatial form and magnitude should not blind us to the "conceptualist imperative" that underlies their formulation. Number and harmony are mathematical notions, even if they are neither technically fully abstract nor located outside space.

Let me begin my examination of the soteriology with an account from later Graeco-Roman times, when Cicero, in his *Dream of Scipio,* has his protagonist, Scipio Aemilianus, fall into a deep sleep and meet Scipio Africanus, his adoptive grandfather, who, among other things, speaks of the movement of the planets. Scipio Aemilianus then experiences the music of the spheres in his dream vision:

> I looked at these things in amazement; then I collected myself and said, "What is this loud and sweet sound that now fills my ears?" "That," he said, "is the sound that is made by these very spheres, as they move and are driven onwards, producing varied harmonies smoothly by mixing high and low notes; it is composed of a series of unequal intervals which are nevertheless marked off from each other in strict proportion. For it is not possible for such great movements to be produced in silence; and it is ordained by nature that the furthest parts at one extreme should sound at a high pitch, while the other extreme sounds at a low pitch. Thus the highest orbit, that of Heaven, carrying the stars, since its revolution is faster, moves with a high and lively note; the lunar sphere, the lowest, sounds the lowest note; for the earth, the ninth in order, remains immovable and is held constantly in one position, containing within itself the central point of the universe."[73]

In Scipio's case the experience occurred in a dream, that is, when there had been a suspension of discursive thought. Although the music is an experienced reality, "this sound, caused by the extremely rapid circular motion of the whole universe, is so great that the ears of men cannot perceive it." Yet Cicero adds that Scipio's is not the only way of apprehending that reality: "All this, wise men have imitated with strings and voices, and have opened up for themselves a way back to this place, along with those who with great powers of intellect have pursued divine studies in human life."[74] Thus music of a special sort also presumably produces a similar suspension of the active consciousness and permits one to enter into this region and experience the harmony of the spheres through the harmony of music. Further, this musical tradition comes from those engaged in divine studies. It should not surprise us if the imagined Pythagoras could himself hear that divine music, as Porphyry claims: "He himself heard and understood the harmony of the universe, the universal harmony of the spheres and the stars that move them, which we do not hear because of our puny natures."[75] Or as Iamblichus puts it: "It seemed as if he alone could hear and understand the universal harmony and music of the spheres and of the stars which move within them, uttering a song more complete and satisfying than any human melody, composed of subtly varied sounds of motion and speeds and sizes and positions, organized in a logical and harmonious relation to each other, and achieving a melodious circuit of subtle and exceptional beauty."[76] According to Iamblichus, however, Pythagoras experienced this state not through musical instruments but through mental concentration, focusing his mind on hearing it.[77]

Now I can present another feature of Pythagoreanism that aligns itself with Indic religions, assuming that hearing the music of the spheres is at least a primary goal (if not the only goal) of the soteriological experience. As with Indic soteriologies, this supreme experience can be apprehended *while one is living in the world* of becoming; consequently the reality to be experienced is associated with the world of being because the Pythagorean cosmic harmony is a transcendental and unchanging condition. It is the soul that permits the resting consciousness to grasp this transcendental reality while living in the mundane world of becoming.

The form of Pythagorean soteriology I have isolated above poses two problems. First, under certain conditions the soul can apprehend the music of the spheres. This capacity could be cultivated by Pythagorean virtuosos in special circumstances in their closed communities. But Pythagoreans were also active in the world of politics; it is therefore not likely that access to this "region" was available to them most of the time. Second, what happens to the soul at death? Clearly it continues to be reborn in various human and animal existences. However, I have shown that, according to the inexorable logic of any rebirth eschatology, there can be no salvation or state of transcendental bliss within the rebirth cycle. Consequently, one might expect to achieve automatic salvation at the end of a finite cycle, or salvation simply will not be available to anyone in this scheme.

The latter seems an extremely plausible scenario for Pythagoreans. Many of them lived among people whose orthodox beliefs for the most part did not tolerate rebirth doctrines. But Pythagoreans surely did not think that only believers were reborn; rebirth was a natural process that applied to all sentient existence, and this included nonbelievers. Thus a doctrine of nonsalvation within the rebirth cycle for the many would be consonant with the realities the Pythagoreans had to face. It therefore would make sense for them to ensure their own salvation by living in sodalities. Isolated from the unsympathetic world around them, they could engage in spiritual exercises that permitted them to purify their souls and experience the music of the spheres. This could be experienced at various levels depending on the purity or soteriological status of the aspirant, for example, through suspension of discursive thought or through music or, in the ideal represented by Pythagoras himself, through intense concentration. In this conception music, which provided the original theory of harmony, becomes significant in everyday life. Thus, Iamblichus again tells us that Pythagoreans used songs and music to "enchant" themselves to sleep and dream good dreams; and sometimes "they healed emotions and certain sicknesses" by singing and incantation.[78]

But then the question remains: What happens after death? The *expectable* soteriological answer is that the transcendental experience of the music of the spheres cannot be something temporary. At death the soul must *permanently* experience it. If so, the spiritual goal of Pythagoreanism (or an important component of it) is twofold: to occasionally, and sometimes imperfectly, experience the harmony of the spheres while living in the world and to permanently experience it at death, when the soul, material or not, is released from the body and the harmony of the soul and the harmony of the spheres are in perfect concordance. In this scheme there is no attempt to convert the generality of nonbelievers; it is a soteriological ideal for a small intellectual elite.

What then are the soteriological solutions that are *not* expectable in early Pythagoreanism? There is not the slightest evidence that salvation entailed a mystical identity of the soul with the Divine. It is true that, according to Aristotle, the Pythagoreans thought the unit to be a divinity, but mystical identity with the number one seems improbable for a variety of reasons. The unit itself is not the ultimate reality; unity is generated from the limited and unlimited, two conceptual principles that are not subsumed under a larger unitary order. And although the world is a conflict (and sometimes an interchange) between these two entities, there is nothing to suggest that one can identify with the limited, however divine it may be, because the times (in which the Pythagoreans lived) are characterized by conflict between the two principles, hardly a situation that makes identification appealing. It is true that the universe is a living thing according to some Pythagoreans, and as such it possesses a soul. If so, one's own soul at death can merge with the universal soul, which is how Guthrie formulates the issue.[79] But this virtually identifies Pythagoreanism with the Brahman of Upanishadic soteriology. It cannot bring into the soteriological picture what we have asserted about Pythagoreanism, namely, the doctrine of the harmony of the spheres. The spheres themselves are part of the universe; identifying with the soul of the universe would be in effect to identify with the spheres rather than to engage in experiencing the harmony of the spheres. To make sense of this harmony as a soteriological condition, the soul must exist separately, not in union with some form of the "divine."

What about the idea, clearly formulated in Platonic soteriology, that the purified soul becomes a god at death? There is little evidence for this in early Pythagoreanism although it is an entirely plausible interpretation. But this line of reasoning is not to be confused with the details of Plato's theory, which states that the soul at death becomes a star (a god in Greek thought). This notion of "astral immortality" has been criticized by Burkert, who shows that although the idea was well known in Ionian thought, it was uncharacteristic of early Pythagoreanism. Yet these astral ideas, he says, have been at some time or other ascribed to Pythagoras. "But in Pindar's exposition of metempsychosis there is no more trace of astral motifs than in Empedocles' theory of the fallen *daimon* exiled to earth. . . . In the monuments of southern Italian eschatology, there is no reliable, early evidence for belief in astral immortality."[80] Burkert may be right, but one cannot ignore the fact that astral ideas have been ascribed to the imagined Pythagoras. Moreover, the harmony of the spheres is itself a kind of "astral immortality." Thus, once again it is important to recognize not only multiple forms of rebirth but perhaps also several soteriological forms showing family resemblances *within* the Greek Pythagorean tradition.

## ETHICIZATION AND SOTERIOLOGY IN EMPEDOCLES

It is impossible to consider Greek rebirth without reference to Empedocles because there is more extant information about the man and his works than for virtually any other Presocratic Greek thinker. Most accounts say that he was born into an aristocratic family c. 492 B.C.E. in Acragas, Sicily, during the reign of the tyrant Theron. His father, Meton, apparently took an important role in his opposition to tyranny in the turmoil that followed Theron's death, and Empedocles himself has been credited with the breakup of an oligarchical organization known as the Thousand. According to Aristotle he was offered the kingship of Acragas, which he refused, and he emerges as the great champion of democracy in political myths constructed 150 years after his death. Apparently, during his absence abroad his enemies opposed his return, and he died in exile in the Peloponnese.[81]

Empedocles' thought is expressed in two great poems, *On Nature* (Physics) and *Purifications* (Katharmoi), originally containing two thousand and three thousand verses respectively. Only about a fifth of the first poem is extant, and the crucial soteriological poem is even more fragmentary, rendering impossible any definitive statement of Empedocles' religious thought.[82] The splitting of Empedocles' thought into the rational and mystical has bedeviled Greek scholarship, as classicists such as John Burnet have noted.[83] But as Guthrie says, it is the "union of rational thought with mystical exaltation, that Empedocles sums up and personifies the spirit of his age and race."[84] Unfortunately, Guthrie follows others in treating the politics of Empedocles as if they were empirically true and the "miracles" that were associated with him as having no basis in reality, a position that does not make ethnographic sense, as we have already seen.[85] Like the Buddha and Pythagoras Empedocles appears as a mythic persona. Further, because Empedocles was a charismatic healer and prophet drawing large crowds, he was the kind of person easily subject to multiple mythicizations. It also seems likely that his democratic politics and political popularity rested on his popular public persona as a healer and miracle worker. This public popularity might have resulted in his unpopularity with the political establishment, as was the case with Pythagoras.

The assumption that the two poems are unrelated, with *On Nature* dealing with the scientific or philosophical and *Purifications* with the mystical, has forced scholars to assign the available fragments to one or the other poem, thus in effect helping to reinvent these lost poems.[86] Assuming for the moment that there are two, one notices a critical distinction between the beginning and end of the two poems that seems to violate our contemporary commonsense assumptions regarding the public nature of science and the private, inner-oriented nature of mysticism.

Let me therefore begin with this issue, which in turn should take us to the heart of Empedocles' thought.

The "scientific" poem *On Nature* is addressed to Empedocles' favorite pupil, Pausanias, whom he enjoins to secrecy, urging him "to keep within thy dumb heart [the contents of the poem]." By contrast *Purifications* is "almost shouted from the rooftops":[87] "My friends who live in the tawny town of Akragas, on the city's citadel, who care for good deeds (haven of kindness for strangers, men ignorant of misfortune), greetings!"[88] It seems to me that it is the "scientific" or "mathematical" aspects of Empedocles' thought, rather than his doctrine of rebirth, that are jealously guarded, as was probably the case with Pythagoras.[89] In early Pythagoreanism itself there was probably no soteriological distinction between the *mathematici* and the *acusmatici* because both branches of knowledge were geared to the goal of self-discovery and salvation. So is it with Buddhist logic: the abstract doctrine of "dependent origination" (or "dependent co-arising"), which showed that the world is enmeshed in causality, was formulated in a soteriological context dealing with the nature of existence itself. For Empedocles natural science is in the service of his religious thought, including its doctrine of salvation. As with Pythagoras, it was necessary for him to understand the nature and constitution of the cosmos for soteriological reasons rather than for purely "philosophical" ones. Galen thought that Empedocles was the founder of Greek medical science based on the doctrine of the four elements. But unlike Galen Empedocles was not only interested in curing ordinary bodily afflictions; he also dealt with the most unusual of medical practices. Hence we have the fascinating and poetic conclusion of the "scientific" treatise (which some think should properly be at the beginning):[90]

> You [Pausanias] will learn remedies for ills against old age, since for you alone shall I accomplish all these things. You will check the force of tireless winds, which sweep over land and destroy fields with their blasts; and again, if you wish, you will restore compensating breezes. After black rain you will bring dry weather in season for men, and too after summer dryness you will bring tree-nourishing showers (which live in air), and you will lead from Hades the life-force of a dead man.[91]

Not only is science at the service of soteriology, but also the soteriology is not part of publicly available knowledge. Consequently, one should expect "science" to share soteriology's private character. Empedocles himself never made *On Nature* available to the public. Whoever made it public (some speculate it was Pausanias himself) refused to divulge the esoteric doctrine. For example, there is nothing in the extant scientific text that tells people how to control the winds or make rain or bring back the life essence of a dead person even though the conclusion of the text indicates that is what Pausanias will eventually know. What the text gives is the scientific or philosophical or "mathematical" basis for that knowledge in, among other things, the doctrine of the four elements and the two grand dualisms, Love and Strife. *On Nature* was probably that part of the esoteric knowledge that could be eventually divulged to the public after the death of the master without violating the core of esoteric or acousmatic knowledge.

How does one reconcile the previous argument with Empedocles' public declamation at the commencement of the *Purifications* after he greeted the people of Acragas? "I tell you I travel up and down as an immortal god, mortal no longer, honored by all as it seems, crowned with ribbons and fresh garlands. Whenever I enter prospering towns I am revered by both men and women. They follow me in countless numbers, to ask where their advantage lies, some seeking prophecies, others, long pierced by harsh pains, ask to hear the word of healing for all kinds of illnesses."[92] In this crucial statement Empedocles makes a public proclamation, but it is *not* the proclamation of a soteriological message. Let me deliberately skew my perspective and look at him from an Indological perspective. Once a mortal, Empedocles claims he is no longer one; like his contemporaries in India he claims to be a *jīvan mukta,* one who has achieved salvation while living in the world. Possession by deities was familiar to Greeks from their popular religion (as it was to Buddhists), and the specialists of the mystery cults believed that one can become a god *after* death. Empedocles' case is different: he *is* a deity incarnate. This is implied in other fragments also, for example, in 105 (113): "But why do I lay stress on this, as if it were some great achievement of mine, if I am superior to many-times-dying mortal men?" Empedocles is a god among men, one who has achieved salvation or a god status while living in the world, whereas ordinary people are "many-times-dying," that is, born and reborn. No wonder this charismatic person attracts throngs of people as he goes from place to place lending power and authenticity to his public role as a healer and prophet. In his healing role Empedocles is an *iatromantis,* a combination of physician and seer, a title given to Apollo and Asclepius.

Later in this poem Empedocles refers to both rebirth and the sin of eating meat. But neither rebirth nor vegetarianism is part of the *esoteric* doctrine of Empedocles or Pythagoras or the Orphics. It was information that could scarcely be hidden from public scrutiny. Further, there is nothing unusual in talking about rebirth in Sicily (Acragas), and Magna

Graecia generally, because such doctrines were apparently well known there and accepted by at least some of the populace. Even in Athens and the mainland Pythagorean rebirth was known, although lampooned as un-Greek. What was unique about Empedocles and the early Pythagoreans was not their rebirth theories but their doctrines of salvation, which taught followers to break the rebirth cycle and achieve release from it through esoteric knowledge, including "mathematical" knowledge, a difficult symbology, or acusmata, and forms of spiritual ascesis. This knowledge and ascesis were never publicly proclaimed. In this sense Empedoclean thought and Pythagoreanism share an affinity with the Orphic mysteries without being one of them.

Charles H. Kahn has demonstrated that the very foundational principles of Empedoclean science illustrate its mystical and revelatory nature and that "the physical poem is also a religious work."[93] Empedocles' thought has raised a considerable controversy recently, and it would be foolhardy for me to formulate a definitive position. Instead, let me present his thought for the nonspecialist readers of this book, focusing for the most part on his rebirth theory and its implications for the problem of structural transformations.

For Empedocles the material basis of all things consists of the four elements—fire, air, earth, and water—and in the history of Greek thought he was first to systematize them. Here I rather suspect Indian "influence" because such systematization had already occurred in India in Buddhist monasteries even though classical scholars think that these were Empedocles' reformulations of prior Greek ideas.[94] If in the Pythagorean oath the tetractys "contains the springs and root of everlasting nature," so did the four elements for Empedocles. They are the "four roots of all things," personified and identified with "bright Zeus and life-bringing Hera and Aidoneus and Nestis whose tears are the source of mortal streams."[95] As "roots" the elements nourish and bring forth physical and sentient life. The elements cannot be divorced from the two great Empedoclean dualisms, Love and Strife, which give life and movement to them, starting the process of continuous world formation, continuity, and destruction and leading to the creation of living forms and their inevitable destruction. To put it differently: the four elements, the building blocks of the universe, are made pregnant with the sentience brought about by Love and Strife:

> But come, if the form of my preceding argument was in any way incomplete, take note of the witnesses of these to what I have said before: sun

> with its radiant appearance and pervading warmth, heavenly bodies bathed in heat and shining light, rain everywhere dark and chill, and from earth issue firmly rooted solids. Under Strife they have different forms and are all separate, but they come together in Love and are desired by one another. From them comes all that was and is and will be hereafter—trees have sprung from them, and men and women, and animals and birds and water-nourished fish, and long-lived gods too, highest in honor. For these are the only real things, and as they run through each other they assume different shapes, for the mixing interchanges them.[96]

Thus Love is the life-affirming principle that brings about a creative and harmonious unity among the elements, whereas Strife tears them apart and thus brings about disintegration of the Sphere, Empedocles' somewhat unclear vision of the cosmos.[97] The interaction of the two dualisms in relation to the elements sets in motion the formation of life and the Sphere. For purposes of convenience one can formulate the issue thus: the interplay between Love and Strife, their "mixing," brings about the varieties of sentient existence, including the gods. But this interaction or mixing is regulated: Love is the creative principle and is personified by Aphrodite, whereas "mad Strife" brings about the scattering of the elements and the process of world dissolution. If either Love or Strife were to exist on its own (which one can envisage only theoretically), no form of sentient life would be possible.

What is the relationship between the dualisms as they create life and the world? British classicists following John Burnet have formulated Empedocles' thought as four cosmic cycles, which according to some are related to parallel stages of evolution. Such a formal schema can be presented as follows:

| COSMIC PERIODS (OR FLOWS) | ASSOCIATED EVOLUTIONARY MOVEMENTS OR "STAGES" |
|---|---|
| Period One: Love alone, Strife dormant | No sentient life-forms |
| Period Two: Love and Strife | "Stages" 3 and 4: whole-natured forms (extinct) and current life-forms |
| Period Three: Strife alone, Love dormant | No sentient life-forms |
| Period Four: Strife and Love | "Stages" 1 and 2: disjointed limbs and monstrous forms |

Because this schema, as well as similar ones, has been subjected to recent criticism as not being Empedocles' own but an imposition from the outside, I will use it only advisedly, although no one can avoid imposing his or her own vision on the fragmentary material available to us.[98]

There are many tropes in the literature that describe the movements of the dualisms, but the one I favor is the waxing and waning of Love and Strife in a single circular movement on a horizontal plane (as in a potter's wheel), which could be contrasted to the rebirth cycle, which moves on a vertical plane (as in a spinning wheel). The logic of the system is such that when the two dualisms are farthest apart, they do not produce creativity, an idea that makes good psychological sense. This insight is common to both Empedocles and Freud. Love cannot create life by itself;[99] it can do so only in conjunction with Strife, and the forms of creation depend on the closeness or distance of the relationship as these forces wax and wane. And Strife without Love, or with a minimum of it, will only produce a Hobbesian state of chaos. Fragment 50 illustrates the situation when Strife is the dominant force and when Love is on the wane: "Here [on earth] many heads sprang up without necks, bare arms were wandering without shoulders, and eyes needing foreheads strayed singly."[100] The disjointed body parts, incapable of reproducing themselves, are created by Strife without the active participation of Love. The composite creatures that emerge as Strife begins to interact more closely with Love are described in fragment 52 (61): "Many creatures with a face and breasts on both sides were produced, man-faced bulls arose and again bull-headed men, (others) with male and female nature combined, and the bodies they had were dark ("shadowed," according to some translations)."[101] As is expectable in a situation where Strife is the dominant force, heterosexual reproduction cannot occur at this time either; some monsters are probably neuters, whereas others possess male and female natures that possibly make them capable of "autoreproduction," as with trees, although no details are available.

Although conceptions of free-floating limbs may have seemed crazy to Aristotle, they ought to be more intelligible to those of us familiar with Balinese fantasy and myth and their formulations in the contemporary art of that nation. In this art body parts and limbs are sometimes represented as if existing on their own, in limbo as it were. Similar conceptions of hell and torture chambers, in which limbs are severed from whole bodies, are found in the world's historical religions, as are popular fantasies of the body being cut up in cannibalism or the practices of quartering the body in premodern Europe. The ways in which these images are represented seem to tap what Lacan (following Melanie Klein) has with great insight called the "imagos of the fragmented body," a product of the infant's perception of its imperfect body and absence of "ego" (moi) in the pre–mirror stage of psychosexual development and before linguistic capacity develops.[102] "This fragmented body . . . usually manifests itself in dreams . . . [and] then appears in the form of disjointed limbs, or of those organs represented in exoscopy" and immortalized by the visionary Hieronymus Bosch and the elder Breughel; in later life they continue to give the ego its phantasmal and unstable character.[103] They are then put together, says Lacan, into a totality that he calls "orthopaedic," which fits nicely with Empedocles' composite creatures—found in virtually all mythological traditions in their representations of monsters. Both stages are preoedipal; hence there is no notion yet of heterosexual procreation.

A form of sexual autoreproduction reappears but in a completely different guise when Love emerges as the dominant force, initially producing "whole-natured forms," of which we know very little. Fragment 53.62 describes them arising from the earth as a result of the primary elements, fire and water.[104] Aëtius, a later doxographer, puts it thus:

> Empedocles says that trees were the first living things to grow out of the earth, before the sun was spread around and day and night were distinguished. Owing to the matching of the elements in their mixture, they combined the formula for male and female. They grow by being pushed up by the heat in the earth, so that they are parts of the earth just as embryos in the belly are parts of the womb.[105]

Whole-natured forms produced under the domination of Love are near-perfect acts of creation. These forms resulted initially from the actions of the elements (in conjunction with Love and Strife), but it is not clear how they reproduced. If trees were the first instance of "whole-natured forms," then one could say that they were also capable of sexual "autoreproduction" rather than heterosexual reproduction, for in fragment 65 (79) Empedocles says that "tall trees produce olive eggs first," implying, according to Aristotle, that the fruit is analogous to an egg and that therefore plants are bisexual in nature, that is, given to autoreproduction. In my interpretation "whole-natured" refers to those life-forms (from trees to mushrooms) that are capable of reproducing themselves unmediated by conventional heterosexual intercourse. It thus seems reasonable for Empedocles to say that whole-natured forms "did not yet display the desirable form of limbs nor voice, which is the part proper to men."[106]

The situation changes when Love and Strife have moved closer to each other to produce fishes, birds, and land animals that depend on heterosexual reproduction. When Love is dominant in its partnership with Strife, a critical break in the evolution of life has occurred: under the aegis of Love life can now reproduce itself without direct assistance from the four elements.[107] This must be true of whole-natured ones also, but, says Aëtius, those life-forms as we know them were capable of sexual reproduction animated by libidinal urges. Finally, when biological reproduction emerges, human life recycles or re-creates itself through the processes of reincarnation. It is the case that a human being (or, rather, his or her *daimon*) may be reincarnated in an animal or plant, but it is not clear whether an animal can achieve reincarnation on its own, as in the case of Buddhism. If it cannot, then it would mean that Empedocles also had a theory similar to that of "continuous incarnation" discussed earlier.

Now let me pose a difficult and probably insoluble problem regarding the identity of the entity that gets reincarnated. If in other Greek thinkers the word for soul is *psyche,* not so for Empedocles, who uses that word only once, more or less as "mind."[108] The critical word is *daimon;* little is known about the Empedoclean daimon, although it seems that Empedocles is using the older Greek term in a very specific technical sense. Let me present two Empedoclean views of daimon and then see whether they are reconcilable.

Many later commentators, particularly Plutarch and Plotinus, have associated *daimon* with the old idea of the soul.[109] Following this tradition Charles Kahn has defined *daimon* as the "deified human soul," although he tries to divest the specific Neoplatonist notion of soul from that of Empedocles' more fluid concept.[110] However, for Empedocles the "soul" reincarnates in a variety of sentient forms; hence *daimon* can be glossed more like the fluid Buddhist concept of "the rebirth-seeking entity." One might ask why Empedocles chose the word *daimon*, with its conventional Greek notions of being "alive." Here again the comparative material might help because we know that the "rebirth-seeking entity" in Buddhism and the soul in some Amerindian societies (Inuit, for example) are endowed with some of the characteristics they possessed while on earth, indeed sometimes more refined than earthly characteristics. Empedocles' daimon fuses the traditional Greek idea of psyche with that of daimon; not so much a "deified human soul" but a "soul" possessing certain features of vision, consciousness, and will.

Now consider a more technical meaning of the term *daimon,* found in one of the most important fragments:

> There is a decree of necessity, ratified long ago by gods, eternal and sealed by broad oaths, that whenever one in error, from fear, (defiles) his own limbs, having by his error made false the oath he swore—daimons to whom life long-lasting is apportioned—he wanders from the blessed ones for three times countless [most readings, "ten thousand"] years, being born throughout the time as all sorts of mortal forms, exchanging one hard way of life for another. For the force of the air pursues him into sea, and sea spits him out onto earth's surface, earth casts him into the rays of blazing sun, and sun into the eddies of the air; one takes him from another, and all abhor him. I too am now one of these, an exile from the gods and a wanderer, having put my trust in raving [mad] Strife.[111]

This fragment has troubled later Greek commentators because for many of them the soul is a pure and immortal entity and could not be "sinful" or "polluted" in Empedocles' sense. Yet in interpreting this fragment we must recognize that Empedocles' usage makes sense in the context of his rebirth eschatology. We are in the world as we now know it, that is, where Love is waxing in the cosmic scheme and where Ananke, or Necessity, reigns along with Chance. In this situation where do human beings stand? It seems that in Empedocles, as in Plato, there is the idea of choice; one must choose between Love and Strife, which exist both in the world outside and within us. Choice is hard because, as Plato recognized, it is easy to make the wrong choice in the world of Necessity, where power and scarcity reign. That Empedocles himself once made the wrong choice and paid for it is clear from the fragment quoted above.

What kind of choice must one make though? The ancient decree of the gods enjoins the daimon, the spiritual agency within oneself, to refrain from two heinous acts: shedding blood and uttering a false oath. It seems from the subsequent fragments that the first was the more serious sin, whereas the second was a very common preoccupation in Greece and the ancient world in general. It is of course possible that "false oath" ought to be related to the first injunction itself, namely, the violation of a primordial oath against bloodshed. The universality of the latter emerges from fragment 121 (135): "the law for all extends throughout the wide-ruling air and measureless sunlight." This inherent law sealed by an ancient compact is violated when a person chooses Strife rather than Love, for although Love and Strife are both necessary for the world's continuity, it is Strife that is associated with violence and bloodshed. The consequence of choosing "mad Strife," as Empedocles once did, also emerges in the text: one continues to be born and reborn in various mortal forms up to "thrice ten thousand seasons," and one is punished by the elements. Although some think that "there is no evidence to substantiate the conjecture" that this refers to the rebirth cycle, the evidence of Plato's *Phaedrus* suggests that it is the case.[112] Punishment occurs for the most part during the processes of rebirth, or metacosmesis, rather than through anything like a karmic agency. For example, when one is being reborn, one gets buffeted by the elements of ocean (water), air, earth, and fire.

There are further problems with the above fragment. The term *daimon,* which commentators have glossed as "soul," is plural. It is not clear from the text whether *daimon* refers to Love and Strife or to the "soul" seeking reincarnation or to two daimons within the person, a refraction of the cosmic dualisms, for it does make psychological sense.[113] If *daimon* is "soul" and a single entity, then it would seem that *the daimon is constituted of both Love and Strife, and the struggle in the cosmos is reflected in the individual's daimon, in the homology between macrocosm and microcosm.*[114]

This in turn leads us to a critical question of motivation or intent: who is it that makes the choice, the individual person or the daimon within? Following our previous argument one might say that the daimon is the entity that achieves "continuous incarnation," and insofar as it is a complex entity that exists in conjunction with the psyche (mind), it can, once lodged in the consciousness of a person, make intentional decisions, such as seeking mad strife or shedding blood. Wrongful intentional action means that the daimon remains imprisoned in the fleshy garment of the body through various rebirths and cannot achieve salvation. The path to salvation must unfold when a person chooses Love and abjures the original guilt of killing. In the context of mainline Greek thought this is an extraordinarily difficult task because killing and eating an animal always occur with the sacrifice, the central feature of Greek religion.

The question remains: Why is Empedocles an exile from the gods if he is himself a "god immortal"? I think the several references to his own "guilt" might help elucidate the issue. "Alas, that the pitiless day did not destroy me first, before I devised for my lips the cruel deed of eating flesh."[115]

It should now be apparent that this crucial issue of endoanthropophagy is central to my thesis. Here is Empedocles' violation of the oath, in all likelihood in a previous existence. The oath itself pertains to the fundamental feature of species sentience and beyond that, in the logic of cross-species reincarnation, to eating one's own ancestor or kinsperson or fellow citizen. "The father will lift up his dear son in a changed form, and, blind fool, as he prays he will slay him, and those who take part in the sacrifice ?bring (the victim) as he pleads. But the father, deaf to his cries, slays him in his house and prepares an evil feast. In the same way son seizes father, and children their mother, and having bereaved them of life devour the flesh of those they love."[116] The sacrificial animal, like other sentient beings, must surely possess a daimon of a previous human being, which is why it can pathetically ask for mercy. Unlike some Pythagoreans, Empedocles makes no concession to the popular religiosity of the sacrifice.[117]

He rails against the killers who violate the universal law pertaining to the taking of animal life. "Will you not cease from this ill-sounding slaughter? See ye not that ye are devouring one another in the thoughtlessness of your hearts?"[118] The emotional reaction associated with eating meat is sometimes displaced to a species of bean or laurel when a daimon enters it.[119] Yet Empedocles' moral law is not an *abstract* ethical ideal, like Buddhism's ahiṃsā, but one directly grounded in a theory of cross-reincarnation and eventual rebirth in one's own group. This ideal poses the dilemma of "endoanthropophagy" that we examined in previous cases also. In the Greek case older kin groups and lineages were probably being eroded by the expanding commerce of the city-states. Hence eating meat is eating a fellow *citizen;* but Empedocles also resurrects powerful familial values, perhaps tapping an older tradition to underscore the general idea that eating an animal is effectively eating one's own close familial kin. Yet Empedoclean ethics is not karmic ethics; the latter disrupts the idea that one could be reborn into the same kin or communal group (including one's own city) and converts the primordial idea of endoanthropophagy into the abstract ethics of ahiṃsā.

To get back to Empedocles' own guilt and suffering for the crime of eating flesh: Empedocles has been born and reborn in different forms, and there is no escape from this cycle, which in its relentless inevitability reminds one of the Ājīvika eschatology. "For before now I have been at some time boy and girl, bush [laurel], bird and a mute fish in the sea."[120] He describes what must surely be the entrance to the earth, the rebirth orifice, as in the myth of 'Askadut and also, we shall soon see, according to Plato's myth of Er. "We have come under this roofed cave."[121] Then, as some commentators have noted, comes the actual birth as an infant in a particular rebirth followed by a very pessimistic view of metacosmesis and human existence. "I wept and wailed on seeing an unfamiliar place [or land]."[122] This trauma of birth is apparently the condition of all humans. "Alas, poor unhappy race of mortal creatures, from what strifes and lamentations were you born."[123] This is followed by what seems like another rebirth in a very specific and unpleasant place: "(a joyless place) where (there are) slaughter and hatred and hordes of other violent deaths (and parching fevers and consumptions and ?dropsy) . . . they wander in darkness over the fields of Ate [Doom]."[124] And then a more realistic and complex assessment of the human world governed by Necessity, where, under the aegis of Love and Strife, both good and bad prevail, personified as nymphs who, according to Burnet, are based on a catalog of Nymphs in the *Iliad.*[125] Empedocles creates in the dualisms and their movement a nonteleological and discontinuous world of becoming over which the goddess Ananke, or Necessity, reigns.

Now we can return to fragment 115, which finds Empedocles in exile, a wanderer from the gods. How can we reconcile this condition with the exalted beginning of the *Purifications,* where he claims he is a god incarnate? In the absence of a fuller context one can only make an informed guess. It is very likely, although by no means self-evident, that Empedocles, like Pythagoras, remembers his former lives. Fragment 115 must therefore refer to a past existence of his when, as a punishment for shedding blood and endoanthropophagy, he is buffeted by the elements as he continues to be reborn in the world of suffering and want. This interpretation seems vindicated in the conventional numbering of the fragments that follow, all of which refer to past existences. It might therefore seem that the "now" in the text refers to a past state that he retrocognizes and, not unnaturally, describes in presentist terms. Empedocles seems to have been alienated from the gods as a consequence of primal guilt, but at the point of writing *Purifications* this alienation is abolished because he is a god, a mortal no more. Somehow he has escaped from the cycle of existence defined by him (in the same fragment) as the constant change from "one toilsome path to another."

Although several ancient and contemporary interpreters of Empedocles have argued for a scale of rebirths with forms of human existence on top and a bush at the lowest, there is little in the extant fragments that suggests a clear-cut status hierarchy. For example, in fragment 108 (117) Empedocles' birth as a bush comes immediately after his birth as a girl and before his birth as a bird and a dumb fish of the sea. In another fragment there is a suggestion that some animal and tree incarnations might even be desirable. "Among animals they are born as lions that make their lairs in the hills and bed on the ground; and among fair-leafed trees as laurels."[126] Perhaps one can agree with Aelian that "the best move is into a man, but if his lot transfer him to a beast, then a lion, or if a plant, a bay [laurel]."[127] Empedocles nowhere rails against particular forms of rebirth in a way that even vaguely parallels the intensity of his reaction to killing. As far as the rebirth cycle is concerned, his emotional reaction pertains to the "toil" and misery associated with the *processes* of being reborn, or metacosmesis, and the dreariness of the rebirth cycle itself, which imprisons the daimon.

There is, however, one preferred form of rebirth: human. This is perhaps obvious insofar as one can only become a god if one is a human being. Thus, there is a gradation of human reincarnations, culminating in the final and most desirable rebirth "among men on earth as prophets, minstrels, physicians and leaders; and from these they arise as gods highest in honour." And the next fragment: "With other immortals they share hearth and table, having no part in human sorrows, unwearied."[128] Although not explicitly stated, it is very likely that this culminating rebirth must apply to those who chose Love, abjuring bloodshed. Yet, surely, Empedocles must know that there are false prophets, bad doctors and bards, and evil princes. If so, he must refer to those who, at some point in the rebirth cycle, had made the right ethical choice. Or he must refer to those with a spiritual inclination to join followers of Empedocles who, engaging in forms of spiritual exercises or asceses, will be purified of the guilt of bloodshed. When they die they become gods and comport with other immortal beings like them, sharing their hearth and table, a powerful idea in traditional Greek eschatology that I will examine in Pindar's second Olympian Ode. It therefore seems that the Empedoclean soteriology entails a person's eventually becoming a god and living and sharing food and fellowship with other gods.

There is, however, one striking exception: the introductory verses of *Purifications* make clear that Empedocles himself has become a god while actually living in the world. There is nothing unusual in this. The entity being reborn is a daimon enveloped in an external fleshy vestment, as with the Pythagoreans in general and some Orphic groups. Thus: "(The goddess) clothing them with a strange garment of flesh," refers, according to Porphyry, to a goddess Heimarmene (Fate), who is in charge of metacosmesis.[129] It does make logical sense that special individuals can have access to powerful modes of ascesis that can fully purify the daimon of primal guilt and either restore its godly nature or effect a conversion of daimon into god. If so, someone such as Empedocles (or Pythagoras) could become a god while still being swathed in a garment of flesh. The famed apotheoses of these two redoubtable persons make logical sense within their own scheme of things, which I have argued is also consonant with the Indic.

My discussion of the Empedoclean rebirth eschatology is not complete without considering those fragments that deal with an idealized age prior to what some have called a "fall." Virtually every scholar has noted its affinity with Hesiod's "golden age of mortal men" who "lived in the reign of Kronos, king of heaven."[130] But for Empedocles the ideal age existed *before* Kronos, when Aphrodite, a female deity, reigned:

> They did not have Ares as god or Kydoimos, not king Zeus nor Kronos nor Poseidon, but queen Kypris [Aphrodite]. Her they propitiated with holy images and painted animal figures, with perfumes of subtle fragrance and offerings of distilled myrrh and sweet-smelling frankincense, and pouring on the earth libations of golden honey. Their altar was not drenched by the (?unspeakable) slaughter of bulls, but this was the greatest defilement among men—to bereave of life and eat noble limbs.[131]

It seems to me that this fragment is not simply based on Hesiod's myth *Works and Days* but is a deliberate reversal of it. As Detienne and his colleagues have shown, the "cuisine of sacrifice" central to Greek religion is given a detailed cosmological grounding in Hesiod's *Theogony.*[132] For Empedocles the golden age is not the Hesiodic one but a prior time, when the cuisine of sacrifice did not exist. With this audacious restatement of the golden age Empedocles introduces another unorthodox Greek idea, vegetarianism, the inferior cuisine (one that is on occasion associated with the women of Demeter).[133] This inferior food is reified as the superior one and a female deity (Kypris or Aphrodite or Love) presides over the ideal age. The older idea that the bull (the sacrificial animal) is "pure" because his meat is blessed by the gods and consumed by men is given different ethical and symbolic meaning, as with the Buddhist myth of Kūṭadanta (see pp. 179–80). The sacrificial animal is also a sacred creature in the Empedoclean scheme simply because it is, or could be, an ancestor reborn, perhaps producing qualms of conscience among actual or potential followers and even creating anxiety among ordinary Greeks who revered their ancestors.[134]

The idea of a golden age has further significance at two levels: as a charter, in Malinowski's sense, for Empedocles' present-day followers and as an actual condition of primal innocence in the past. As charter the ideal age contrasts with the present degenerate one and becomes a model for followers to emulate. The reference to bulls and men indicates that, as an actual occurrence, the ideal age emerges when Love holds unquestioned dominion. The fact that the age of peace, innocence, and harmony, as well as the arising of sentient life as we know it and the commencement of the rebirth cycle, occurred during this cosmic flow suggests the enormity of the duration of these movements for Empedocles, as it does for his Indian counterparts. To sum up: for Empedocles there was a period when people lived in harmony, worshiping Kypris, Love apotheosized, and avoiding the shedding of the blood of sacrificial bulls. "For all creatures, both animals and birds, were tame and gentle to men, and bright was the flame of their friendship."[135] What is implied here is that this innocence was lost in Hesiodic times with the "cuisine of sacrifice." Meat eating, which is eating one's own kind, has occurred: if so, Empedocles' own guilt in eating flesh is the guilt of Everyman.

In this context fragment 111 (119) bears reinterpretation: "From what honor and from what great extent of happiness [have I fallen]."[136] The conventional reading coming from Plutarch suggests that Empedocles has fallen among mortals from a prior unspecified state of bliss.[137] But what state of bliss? For me a reasonable interpretation would be a fall from the ideal age under Aphrodite, and the fall must surely result from the eating of flesh, the sin of anthropophagy.

Where do the gods come into the picture? This is more problematic. Fragment 14 (21) puts it thus:

> Under Strife they have different forms and are all separate, but they come together in Love and are desired by one another. From them [Love and Strife] comes all that was or is and will be hereafter—trees that have sprung from them, and men and women, and animals and birds and water nourished fish, and long-lived gods too, highest in honor. For these are the only real things, and as they run through each other they assume different shapes, for the mixing interchanges them.[138]

The very next fragment uses the analogy of mixing paints to describe the same interplay of dualisms and says that not only trees, animals, and humans but also gods were created in that manner. Because there is no question that the gods were also created through the intermixing of Love and Strife, the question one must ask is When were the gods created? The existing fragments do not provide an answer, but one might infer an answer from Empedocles' thought.

It is obvious that gods existed before human beings, animals, or fish, and unlike fish, flesh, and fowl they are perfect acts of creation and in this respect similar to whole-natured forms. Therefore one might infer that they came forth either before or after the creation of whole-natured forms and prior to the creation of human and other animate life. Whole-natured forms, including the gods, occur when Strife's influence on Love is minimal. A further problematic arises now: what happened to the gods after they were created? One of two things must have occurred: either they evolved through further mixing of the dualisms into human beings or their prototypes; or, more likely, they continued to exist in the realms of the blessed, later sharing a hearth and home with those human beings who have escaped from the rebirth cycle.

In conclusion let me sum up features of Empedoclean eschatology that can be tied to the general argument of this book. Empedoclean rebirth confirms the logic of expectations arising from the rebirth eschatology: where there is species sentience and kinship with nature in conjunction with animal reincarnation, one would expect the eating of an animal to be associated with a strong affect based on the idea that the animal was once a human being. Although this association is also characteristic of Pythagorean thought in general, Empedoclean rebirth is the most powerful example of it in the ethnographic record anywhere. Empedocles' passionate rejection of meat eating and the cuisine of the sacrifice also has significance for his conscience, as is evident from his feelings of guilt, repentance, and punishment. Punishment is through the actual processes of rebirth, or metacosmesis, and further through being born and reborn in the rebirth cycle. Remorse of conscience for the primal crime is also linked to the two dualisms such that one must (through the agency of one's daimon) at a certain point in one's rebirth career opt for Love rather than "mad Strife," which is associated with violence and killing, also endemic in our species' existence. In this sense, for Empedocles as well as for the later Freud, these dualisms are both cosmic and ethical principles evident in the smallest particles of life.[139] It should now be clear that the "philosophy" of *On Nature* cannot be divorced from the eschatology of *Purifications*.

However, the idea that rebirth itself is propelled by the ethics of flesh eating and anthropophagy defies our logic of expectations, although it makes sense within the frame of Empedoclean thought. This idea has its corollary in the extremely pessimistic view of species life in the rebirth cycle—what Buddhists call samsara. It seems there is no give or hope in Empedoclean samsara; consequently, it is unlikely that Empedocles' religious thought could possibly have become popular, quite unlike the Orphic mysteries or the kind of religion represented in Pindar's poems. As a matter of fact one might say that Empedoclean eschatology is not simply a continuation of the Pythagorean traditions. Its uniqueness comes from a double reaction: against the popular sacrifice in mainline Greek religion and against a popular and humane rebirth eschatology in Acragas itself and represented in Pindar (to be dealt with presently). In this harsh scheme of things the one hope for human beings is to make the correct choice: refrain from the eating of flesh and the wanton slaughter of the sacrifice. Only then can one be born as minstrel, physician, and so forth and eventually comport with the gods. The only other way out is the example of Empedocles himself, that is, to become a god while living in the world very much like the Indian *jīvan mukta.* Ordinary folk must continue to live without hope and, as that wonderful phrase puts it, continuing forever as "many-times-dying mortal men."

Now let me address the crucial issue of ethicization. It seems to me that Empedocles' passionate message could appeal to only a very few, perhaps those of a small group of followers inspired by his message and personal charisma. His is primarily an intense personal vision of life and salvation rather than a communal one. At best it might contain a soteriology for an elite, and there is little indication that Empedocles was interested in converting the general Greek population, even those living anywhere in Magna Graecia. There is no evidence for enduring Empedoclean spiritual communities either. If, as I have argued, ethicization occurs in relation to the soteriological welfare of the group, then one cannot expect Empedoclean rebirth to be concerned with ethicization. Ethics does operate in soteriology, in its doctrine of ethical choice, but it does not produce ethicized heavens and hells, as one expects from our model. There is a limited ethicization, though, in respect to the generality of human beings. The many who have committed the sin of eating flesh (and those who continue to do so) will be punished in endless rebirths in entirely undesirable forms of animate existence; only those who have made the right ethical choice will be redeemed at death. There is no indication of rebirth rewards and punishments in "hells." Indeed such arenas of ethical compensation cannot exist in Empedoclean thought because rebirth *rewards* would contradict the ethical stance that life on earth is an arena of punishment; and rebirth punishment in Tartarus or in a similar hell is similarly redundant because ordinary folk who are punished in being reborn need not be punished again in hell. It is therefore an eschatology in which the soul, or daimon, is at death immediately reborn into the human world without a temporary stay in some other world, which is the case with Pythagorean rebirth in general.

The Empedoclean rebirth theory is in itself an interesting variation of "continuous incarnation." One might more appropriately call it *discontinuous* incarnation because although the soul continues to be reborn in various forms of animate life, there does not seem to be a systematic and regular form of reincarnation. For example, in the *Ājīvika* scheme of things the soul undergoes reincarnation in every form of species until it achieves final release. Not so with Empedocles, who at some time was born as a boy, a girl, a bush, a bird, and a mute fish of the sea, whereas those who are to be saved are born finally as minstrels, physicians, prophets, and leaders. Although the latter category makes soteriological sense, the former seem to indicate purely fortuitous rebirths. This is not surprising given that the two cosmic dualisms themselves bring about discontinuous and disjunctive movements: hence, rebirth itself, which is part of that larger process, must reflect such disjunctions.

Finally, let me briefly note that one of the expectations from either the rebirth or the karmic eschatology is that logically there is no way to achieve salvation except outside the rebirth cycle. Is our logic of expectations disconfirmed because there is no indication whatever in *Purifications* that salvation (comporting with the gods) is in effect the cessation of rebirth? No Greek scholar or commentator in the long history of Greek thought has mentioned it either. But this is precisely the strength of the model; it helps us to fill lacunae in these texts. Thus the souls of those who have made the right ethical choice are reborn as good people, and after death they will share board and lodging with the deities. As Empedocles himself says, that divine abode is a place without "sorrows," whereas the human world is an utterly awful and sorrowful place. It is impossible for the Empedoclean daimon to be reborn on earth after a sojourn in the divine world. Were that to happen, the realm of the gods to which the good soul ascends must be temporary; and ephemeral bliss is not salvation. If it were, the world of the gods would simply become a way station for the good, and Empedoclean eschatology could not possess a doctrine of salvation. But surely that is not the case?

## ETHICIZATION STEP I: POPULAR RELIGIOSITY IN PINDAR

Early Pythagoreans, I have suggested, constituted small sodalities that contained individuals interested in personal salvation rather than in the conversion of the Greek populace. This, as Burkert suggests, is true even of the mystery religions; people who were attracted to them were selectively initiated. None produced "congregations" in the manner of Buddhists or Christians (and perhaps some Bacchic communities).[140] Moreover, I think the eschatologies attributed to Pythagoras by near contemporaries as well as later writers seem to have two salient features that mark out what one could for convenience' sake label "Pythagoreanism." First, Pythagoreanism postulates a cyclical theory of continuity in which the individual is reborn on earth without an intermediate sojourn in a heaven or a hell. Second, this meant that it did not incorporate much of mainline Greek ideas of Hades, Tartarus, or the Abodes of the Blessed (or at best only nominally incorporated them), lending plausibility to the view that their rebirth theories came from the "outside" and were given special eschatological development and meaning by Pythagoreans. The exceptions are few: for example, the statement attributed to Heraclides that Pythagoras could "tell of the fate of souls in Hades," although this could be a way of saying that he could tell what happened to people after their deaths. Empedocles tried to incorporate mainline Greek ideas more systematically, but in this he was perhaps influenced by the mystery religions and the tradition represented by Pindar. Hence he tells Pausanias that if Pausanias learns about Empedocles' knowledge of drugs, he will have the capacity to bring back the dead or recover their spiritual essences from Hades. This could mean, as Kingsley suggests, the claimed capacity to actually go to Hades and bring the dead back; or, in my thinking, it promises Pausanias the capacity to bring back a dead person or that person's life essence through spiritual techniques and drugs. The drugs need not be part of physical medicine as in the Galenic or Indian Ayurvedic systems. Any ethnographer who has worked with South Asian virtuosos, or with shamans anywhere, knows that such medicines are given by the gods or obtained through a variety of spiritual techniques. And we already know, from Inuit and Northwest Coast Indians, that a shaman has the capacity to send his own soul to retrieve a person's soul lost in the underworld or one that has escaped from a sick person's body owing to illness. This does not convert Empedocles into a shamanic figure; as with the Buddha the case of Empedocles only illustrates the influence of shamanism on his ascesis.

Yet it is in Acragas itself that one can find evidence for the incorporation of mainline Greek ideas into the rebirth eschatology and with clear reference to the first step of ethicization. In *Meno* Plato gives a succinct account of a rebirth theory attributed to Pindar and other poets:

> They say that the human soul is immortal; at times it comes to an end, which they call dying, at times it is reborn, but it is never destroyed, and one must live one's life piously as possible:
>
> *Persephone will return to the sun above in the ninth year*
> *the souls of those for whom*
> *she will extract punishment for old miseries,*
> *and from these will come noble kings,*
> *mighty in strength and greatest in wisdom,*
> *and for the rest of time men will call them sacred heroes.*

> As the soul is immortal, has been born often and has seen all things here and in the underworld, there is nothing which it has not learned; so it is in no way surprising that it can recollect the things it knew before, both about virtue and other things. (81b–d)

A section of a poem by Pindar (518–438 B.C.E.), no longer extant, is wedged between Plato's own comments where he outlines a rebirth eschatology but adds the importance of ethical (pious) living. Further, Plato thinks that no new knowledge arises and the soul can recollect what it had known in previous rebirths. I deal with Plato's theory of memory later; however, the capacity for the soul to retrocognize the past in this manner is neither Pythagorean nor Empedoclean. For the latter, retrocognition is the gift of those who practice special forms of ascesis. Both would be astonished to know that Meno's slave could passively recollect the past, as Plato describes in *Meno* 82–85. The sandwiched quotation is even more interesting. Although the details are obscure, the general meaning is reasonably clear, as Long suggests in his commentary: "After a life upon earth, some souls continue in the realm of Persephone for eight years atoning for sins they committed while in this world. In the ninth year, Persephone sends them up to the region of sunlight and they assume various of the more desirable forms of human existence. After they "die" the second time, they become heroes for evermore."[141] There is a clear and unequivocal indication of punishment for immorality but with a promise of eventual salvation.

There is no evidence that Pindar belonged to a sodality. Plato seems to think that he personally believed in reincarnation, but whether he did or not is irrelevant to the significance of the poem. Pindar's poems celebrate public occasions, and the ode that contains a more detailed account of reincarnation, *Olympian* 2, was dedicated to the tyrant Theron of Acragas (the home of Empedocles) on his victory in the four-horse chariot race in the Olympic games of 476 B.C.E. Here are the relevant lines from Frank Nisetich's translation:

> And wealth, uplifted by nobility,
> gives scope for actions of every kind,
> kindling the heart with zeal for achievement,
> a star far-seen, a man's truest beacon-light.
> And if, possessing it, one knows what must befall—
> that of those who die here, the arrogant
> are punished without delay,
> for someone under the earth

weighs transgressions in this realm of Zeus,
and there is iron compulsion in his word.

But with equal nights
and equal days,
possessing the sun forever,
the noble enjoy an easy existence, troubling
neither earth nor the sea's waters
in might of hand
for an empty living,
but with the gods they honored, all
who delighted in oath-keeping
abide free of affliction, while the others
go through pain not to be looked at.

And those who have endured
three times in either realm
to keep their souls untainted
by any injustice, travel
Zeus' road to the tower of Kronos,
where ocean-born breezes blow around
the island of the blest
and sprays of gold flower
from the earth and from the sea—
with these they wreathe their hands
and crown their heads,
obeying the high decrees of Rhadamanthys,
who sits a ready companion, beside
the great Father, consort of Rhea throned on high.
Among them dwell the heroes of Peleus and Kadmos.[142]

Once again, although the details are unclear, there is not the slightest doubt that we are dealing with an ethicized eschatology of a specific sort: the wicked, and this includes not only humans but gods who have perjured themselves, straightaway pay the penalty imposed by some judge in the underworld.[143] Apparently, having been judged by the lawgiver Rhadamanthys, the redeemed soul of both gods and humans sits with Zeus, the "great Father" himself, along with the heroes of the past.[144] The text, like others of its class discussed previously, does not make reference to a karma-like system of rewards and punishments in the next rebirth.

This Pindaric ode has further implications that I must now explore with my characteristic imprudence. Because this poem praises the person who is honored therein, it could not possibly have expressed religious sentiments offensive to Theron. And because Pindar is not a soteriological innovator, his poem suggests that, in addition to Theron, there were ordinary people in this city who believed in rebirth theories containing a system of afterlife rewards and punishments and, most impressively, a realistic goal of salvation rather than one exclusively reserved for an elite. A popularization of a rebirth eschatology seems to have taken place in Acragas, probably fostered by the incorporation of older Greek eschatological concepts into the theory of the rebirth cycle. To put it differently: *there seems to have been an open congregation of believers in rebirth and, parallel with this, step 1 of ethicization.* However, there is no evidence that ethicization extended to the human rebirth.

Let me reiterate the rationality of this model. In every society with or without a theory of rebirth people are punished here on earth (by secular authorities or by deities) for wrongs. But with ethicization step 1 they continue to be punished or rewarded in some hell or heaven. If they have been punished and rewarded then there is no reason for them to suffer or be rewarded in the next reincarnation (step 2). This is everywhere the Greek model. But it does produce an aporia specific to that model. What happens when a person is reincarnated once again on earth? Consider the Pindaric scheme: those who have led bad lives, and especially those who have violated oaths (and this might even include some of the gods), are punished in an underworld; those who have led good lives go to a happy place free of labor and, for those who have honored their oaths, to a pleasant existence with the gods. Presumably, they are reborn and the cycle continues. But those who have led good lives keeping their souls pure for three rebirths enter the Isles of the Blessed, where they live forever. It is implied that in this salvific state they cease to be reborn. Ethicization step 2 hardly occurs here, and one might add that given this Greek model it is impossible to produce systematic ethicization of the human rebirth. The thinker, and the larger tradition of Greek thought, cannot escape from the cultural episteme created with the rational termination of ethicization at step 1.

Yet Pindar reflects a clear epistemic break in the tradition of Greek rebirth eschatologies discussed earlier. Pythagorean forms of reincarnation, including Empedocles', had no reference to an intermediate stay in heaven. What Pindar has inherited is a doctrine wherein older Greek ideas of Tartarus and the realm of the Blessed have been ethicized.

## ORPHIC REINCARNATION: A BRIEF ASIDE

Several authors have suggested that the Pindaric form of reincarnation could be related to a much wider movement of popular religion reflected in the eschatology of the Orphic poems and that of the famed gold leaf inscriptions found in southern Italy, both perhaps traceable in their earliest forms to at least the fifth century B.C.E. M.L. West's persuasive analysis of the genealogy of the Orphic poems gives me a chance to deal with what seems a form of reincarnation theory associated with initiation into Bacchic mystery religions and, for present purposes, with a form of ethicization that shows structural affinity, but not identity, with the Pindaric one. This affinity suggests that multiple forms of reincarnation with ethicized heavens and hells and doctrines of salvation were circulating in Greece during the fifth century B.C.E. and that the Pindaric and "Orphic" forms were simply representatives of a larger class. The doctrines of release or salvation are fundamentally different in the Pindaric and the Orphic. To me it is methodologically fallacious to fuse them into a single coherent "tradition," as scholars such as Keith Guthrie and Gunter Zuntz do in their opposed ways.

West's main thrust is to debunk the idea of a unitary Orphic religion and theology associated with a doctrine of salvation through initiation into the mysteries. This thesis has been the subject of older scholarship, exemplified in Guthrie's *Orpheus and Greek Religion.* Rather, echoing I.M. Linforth's *Arts of Orpheus* and Zuntz's *Persephone,* West makes the case that Orpheus was a mythic founder of a variety of poetic, mythic, and ritual traditions that need not have any substantive connections with each other.[145] Nevertheless, West examines a series of Orphic theogonies that show an identifiable genealogy going back to a prototype poem, the Protogonos Theogony, which he constructs primarily from the extant fragments of the oldest theogony, the Derveni Theogony, and from the most complex and detailed of the Orphic theogonies composed in the late Hellenistic period, the Rhapsodic Theogony.[146] Although these theogonies exhibit a single "genealogy," they do not constitute a single "tradition"—using my terms rather than West's. That is, although they all share family resemblances, they do not constitute a coherent religion or theology, even though most of them are associated with the cult of Dionysus. Thus, not all share a doctrine of reincarnation: the cases that do are the Rhapsodic, the Derveni, and the original (reconstructed) Protogonos Theogony, although the absence of reference to reincarnation in the extant fragments of the others does not necessarily imply the absence of reincarnation.

Because the Protogonos Theogony is West's hypothetical construction, it makes sense to start with the Derveni Theogony, which West has neatly summarized:

> In a brief proem Orpheus announced that he would sing, for those with insight, of the wondrous works of Zeus and the gods born from him. His narrative began at the moment where Zeus was due to assume power and took advice from Night. Zeus swallowed Protogonos ["first born"]; at this point the poet worked in a mention of the outstanding events of earlier ages, Protogonos' first appearance, the genealogy of Protogonos/Night—Uranos—Kronos, the castration of Uranos, the kingship succession Uranos—Kronos—Zeus. With the swallowing of Protogonos everything became one in Zeus, whose universality was celebrated in a hymn-like section.
>
> Then Zeus began to bring the gods forth again from his mouth; ejaculated seed which became Aphrodite; and created anew earth, heaven, rivers, and luminaries, among which the moon claimed the poet's particular interest. Once the world was restored Zeus conceived a desire for his mother, Rhea who was also Demeter. They mated as snakes, and Rhea gave birth to Kore. Still (or again) in the form of a snake Zeus impregnated Kore, and she gave birth to Dionysus, whom the nurse Hipa carried away in a winnowing-basket with a snake wound round it.
>
> Kore and Dionysus both perhaps received instruction about their future destinies, Kore from her mother, Dionysus from Night. Kore was to bear the Eumenides in union with Apollo (and, no doubt, to reign in the lower world, supervising the treatment administered there to souls). Dionysus was to rule in the upper world, receiving sacrifices from initiates and rewarding them with salvation.
>
> This is the third race of men, this one that lives under Zeus' dispensation. There was a golden race under Protogonos, and a silver one under Kronos. The soul is immortal, and passes through different human and animal bodies. After a human incarnation it stands trial, and the good and the wicked go separate ways. Tartarus, where the wicked go, also accommodates gods who have sworn falsely on the water of Styx [echoing the Pindaric]. After 300 years the souls are reincarnated. Such are the hardships from which Dionysus is able to deliver men. (And perhaps all this was set out in the revelation he received from Night.) (*OP*, 100–101)

It is the doctrine of reincarnation that is relevant to my argument. There is not the slightest doubt that ethicization step 1 has occurred in the Derveni, the Rhapsodic and the Protogonos theogonies according to the information supplied by West. Further, there is the doctrine of reincarnation through "animal bodies"; how this occurs is not clear from the text, and there is little to suggest whether animals were degraded. Again one can reasonably assume that ethicization step 2 did not take place here; there is no hint of it in any of the theogonies (or in the later gold leaf tablets), and its absence certainly fits the general Greek pattern sketched earlier. However, ideas of punishments and rewards in another world (ethicization step 1) would mean, according to my analysis, that the Orphic priestly thinkers, unlike Pythagoras (or the early Pythagorean thinkers), were interested not only in the salvation of the individual but also in the common welfare of Bacchic or Dionysian communities that met as "congregations."

These Bacchic communities were around in many parts of Greece, although West thinks they originated in Ionia around 500 B.C.E. They had a "gospel of salvation by Dionysus," but like other Bacchic cults they were probably given to forms of ecstatic or passionate religiosity and most certainly to initiation rituals that guaranteed them salvation from the "wheel" of existence. According to the Rhapsodic Theogony (which develops the previous theogonies) Zeus mates with Kore in Crete in the guise of a snake; Kore gives birth to Dionysus, who is killed and dismembered by the Titans (who are painted with gypsum); he is restored to life and becomes Kore's own partner, "helping men to escape from the cycle of reincarnation" (*OP*, 95). Not only is Dionysus cut up and eaten, but the "story of the gypsum-painted Titans with their mirror, bull-roarer, and so forth, is likely enough, a frightening charade enacted round a candidate for initiation and signifying his mock death" (*OP*, 160).

Although some of these Bacchic cults practiced vegetarianism, the internal evidence of the Orphic theogonies suggests that many celebrated the dismemberment of Dionysus and his resurrection in public festivities and, more important, in the sacrifice of animals, which were cut up and eaten, sometimes cooked and sometimes raw (omophagia). The animal might have been a stand-in for a human at the moment he or she was about to be killed. "This sort of arrangement perhaps lies behind certain Greek myths which account for animal victims, particularly in cults of Dionysus, as surrogates for original human victims. More than one author says that the Bacchic practice of tearing a live animal limb from limb commemorates what was done to Dionysus himself" (*OP*, 160). In some rituals a special place was given to the heart of the victim; this commemorates Athena, who saved Dionysus's living heart, from which he was later reconstituted. Athena herself was probably represented in some initiation sequences; the animal's heart was removed and placed in a casket. In other sequences, West speculates, the heart was put back into a human effigy; this ritual action could only refer to the "reanimation of the candidate [for initiation] who was supposedly dead" (*OP*, 162–63).[147]

These Bacchic mysteries associated with the Orphic theogonies pose problems for the obsessive position taken by some scholars (including West) that "Orpheus" was a shamanic figure. Shamanism can only account for the incorporation of such elements into a cult that transcended its origins; in this sense it is no different from the Buddhist tradition. I noted earlier that shamanic rituals primarily pertain to healing and divination; I know not a single instance of their association with a doctrine of salvation. The ritual ingestion of the body of Dionysus is closer to the Christian mystery of transubstantiation than to anything in shamanism, however uncomfortable the latter idea might be to many classical scholars repelled by the "bizarre" Dionysian myth of origins and Dionysian ritual "excess." Likewise is the scholarly use of Asia as a scapegoat for all sorts of "irrational" practices, such as that of animal reincarnation, omophagia, and other nasty elements in Bacchic initiation and myth. "Influences," whether shamanic or Asiatic, are obviously important for historical reconstruction but not as *explanations* of Bacchic practice. What is important is West's showing us how these diverse influences have been incorporated into a system of beliefs and practices, a cult, associated with initiatory rituals and a powerful ethic, theology, and doctrine of salvation with its own inner logic and integrity—and "Greekness."

## BRIDGING MULTIPLE WORLDS: PLATO AND THE MYTH OF ER

In chapter 6 I will present Plato's speculative soteriology based on Reason and the implications thereof, but here I am going to take liberties with textual chronology and discuss his narration of Er's experiences, which connects nicely with the preceding arguments. The myth of Er concludes the tenth and final chapter of the *Republic.* Although Plato's individualistic soteriology comes from a variety of sources, the evidence of *Meno,* already presented, suggests that one such source was the tradition represented in Pindar.

Long argues that a critical break occurs between the *Gorgias,* which does not contain references to reincarnation, and *Meno,* which does. This, he says, is because of Plato's temporary exile in Sicily, where he picked up Pythagorean ideas. This is possible, although the *Gorgias* itself has a somewhat sympathetic view of Pythagoreanism and Orphism: "Our body is the tomb in which we are buried, and the part of the soul in which our appetites reside is liable by reason of its gullibility to be carried in the most contrary directions."[148] If Plato was already sympathetic to rebirth ideas, his visits to Italy could have been, among other things, spiritual journeys to the home of Pythagorean and Orphic thought.[149]

One can identify the immediate sources of Plato's ideas. First, Plato was influenced both by Pythagorean and by mainline Greek cosmological and eschatological conceptions. Second, his texts on rebirth also deal with step 1 of ethicization. Both suggest that Plato developed a popular tradition of the sort that existed in Acragas, according to my analysis of the Pindaric fragments. Nevertheless, the Sicilian influence was but one component in his complex and innovative soteriology. Further, Plato himself did not belong to, or create, any sodality or soteriological school.[150] Rather reincarnation seemed almost a personal belief that became more and more important in later texts like *Timaeus*.

The Er narrative, in my reading, is based on the shamanic model of the soul's journey to the otherworld well known in Greece and structurally similar to the Tlingit narrative of 'Askadut. In both, the soul of the dead person goes to the otherworld in order to come back and describe the nature of that world to the denizens living on earth. Plato imposes his own (or Socrates') ideas on this familiar narrative. The story itself, if not its ethics, owing to its striking resemblance to shamanic journeyings, need not have been Plato's invention as most scholars surmise. At the very least it was one that Plato or Socrates picked up from a prior shamanic or Orphic tradition. Yet unlike shamanic narratives the Platonic one, like the Pindaric, is strongly permeated with ethics.

Plato's own concern with ethicization is explicit in Er's story, which illustrates "the things that await the just man and unjust man after death" (*Rep.*, 10.614a).[151] The story is told to Socrates by Er himself, and we have no reason to doubt the veracity, if not the empirical truth, of the core narrative any more than 'Askadut's story. I think it wrong to inject our contemporary standards of rationality into this account and treat it simply as allegory of the sort depicted in *Phaedrus*. It is close to the ethical spirit of *Gorgias,* where Socrates literally believes, as Pindar does, that the good will go to the Isles of the Blessed and the wicked to a place of retribution. There he tells Callicles "a story that proves this" and adds: "Give ear then as they say, to a very fine story, which will, I suppose, seem fiction to you but is fact to me; what I am going to tell you I tell you as the truth."[152] So is it with Er: in fact Socrates says that his story is quite unlike Odysseus's recital of his adventures to Alcinous, king of Phaecia. The latter is an overlong account dealing with, among other things, Odysseus's journey to the realms of the dead; it would have been rejected by Plato, says Cornford, as a "misleading picture of the after-life."[153]

Let me begin with Socrates' narration of Er's own narrative. "He was killed in battle, and when the dead were taken up on the tenth day the rest were already decomposing, but he was still quite sound; he was taken home and was to be buried on the twelfth day, and was lying on the funeral pyre, when he came to life again and told the story of what he had seen in the other-world."[154] Like 'Askadut and Pythagoras himself in a previous birth, Er dies on the field of battle, which implies that this is a privileged way of dying. I do not know the significance of some interesting ethnographic facts in this myth, such as why those who died in battle are taken up on the tenth day or Er's own cremation on the twelfth, although both are standard numbers. There is, however, a structural reason for the preservation of Er's corpse. Unlike 'Askadut, who is reborn in a human womb soon after he leaves the otherworld, Er has to come back to his own corpse, which must therefore be in a state of preservation:

> He said that when his soul left his body it travelled in company with many others till they came to a wonderfully strange place, where there were, close to each other, two gaping chasms in the earth, and opposite and above them two other chasms in the sky. Between the chasms sat Judges, who having delivered judgment, ordered the just to take the right-hand road that led up through the sky, and fastened the evidence for the judgment in front of them, while they ordered the unjust, who also carried the evidence of all that they had done behind them, to take the left-hand road that led downwards. When Er came before them, they said that he was to be a messenger to men about the other-world, and ordered him to listen to and watch all that went on in that place. He then saw the souls, when judgment had been passed on them, departing some by one of the heavenly and some by one of the earthly chasms; while by the other chasms some souls rose out of the earth, stained with the dust of travel, and others descended from heaven, pure and clean. (*Rep.*, 10.614b–e)[155]

Thus, there are two sets of travelers here. The first set comprises the arrivals from earth; the judges will decide who will take the road to heaven and who will take the underground road of suffering and punishment. The other set depicts what the first will eventually achieve: having received the rewards of heaven or the punishments of the world under the earth, they now await reincarnation in the human world.

The idea of judgment implies a strong ethical component, already noted for the Pindaric and Orphic eschatologies. For example, as far as the new arrivals are concerned, the good souls take the rightful right path, the bad the devalued left path. Plato's Socrates describes an eschatology derived from his "informant," Er, in which step 1 of the ethicization process has already taken place.

Socrates goes on to describe Er's experiences, this time focusing exclusively on those souls who have already been rewarded or punished. Those coming from the under-earth meet the souls coming from heaven in a meadow, where they greet each other in festive mood and recount each other's experiences. "And those from [under the] earth told theirs with sorrow and tears, as they recalled all they had suffered and seen on their underground journey, which lasted a thousand years, while the others told of the delights of heaven and of the wonderful beauty of what they had seen" (*Rep.*, 10.614e–15a). Then Socrates goes on to describe otherworldly punishments and rewards entailed by ethicization.

> For every wrong he has done to anyone a man must pay the penalty in turn, ten times for each, that is to say, once every hundred years, this being reckoned as the span of a man's life. He pays, therefore tenfold retribution for each crime, and so for instance those who have been responsible for many deaths, by betraying state or army, or have cast others into slavery, or had a hand in any other crime, must pay tenfold in suffering for each offence. And correspondingly those who have done good and been just and god-fearing are rewarded in the same proportion." (*Rep.*, 10.615a–b)

Yet because wrongdoers have been punished and the good rewarded, they are all free souls now and can meet in the meadow and talk and socialize among themselves as moral equals. The only exceptions are especially cruel tyrants, who cannot ascend the chasm or enter the orifice that leads to rebirth. Er overhears one soul tell another the punishments meted out to tyrants and the very wicked.

> For this is one of the terrible things we saw. We were near the mouth of the chasm and about to go up through it after all our sufferings when we suddenly saw him [Ardiaeus, the tyrant] and others, most of them tyrants, though there were a few who had behaved very wickedly in private life, whom the mouth [of the chasm] would not receive when they thought they were going to pass through. . . . There were some fierce and fiery-looking men standing by, who . . . seized some and led them away, while others like Ardiaeus they bound hand and foot and neck, flung them down and flayed them, and then impaled them on thorns by the roadside; and they told the passers-by the reason why this was done and said they were to be flung into Tartarus. (*Rep.*, 10.615e–16a)

Socrates concludes this part of the narrative: "These, then, are the punishments and penalties and the corresponding rewards of the other world" (*Rep.*, 10.616e).

The souls awaiting reentry into the human world have gathered in the meadow, where they spend seven days. They catch sight of a pillar of light that connects the heavens and the earth—an *axis mundi* familiar again in the shamanic traditions. Er has a beautiful description of this axis mundi, describing it as huge whorls of a spindle nesting on each other like bowls and supporting the planets and the stars. The whorls are under the control of Ananke, or Necessity. Ananke's daughters are the three

Fates, each one singing of things past, present, and future and turning the spindles that whirl the whorls, causing the movement of the heavenly spheres. I will skip the details and get to the judgment made by one of the Fates, the goddess Lachesis, assisted by an Interpreter.

The souls awaiting reincarnation assemble in groups before her and take numbered lots and also a multiplicity of life-forms of the sort found in our imperfect human world. The goddess tells them that they "must begin another round of mortal life whose end is death" (*Rep.*, 10.617d). No guardian spirit *(daimon)* is to be allotted to them; instead, they must choose their own. Each soul picks the lot that falls nearest it and then, on the basis of the numbered lots, begins to choose its next earthly life-form. "Then the Interpreter set before them on the ground the different patterns of life, far more in number than the souls who were to choose them. They were of every conceivable kind, animal and human. For there were tyrannies among them, some life-long, some falling in mid-career and ending in poverty, exile and beggary" (*Rep.*, 10.618a). There also were many good lives and bad both for men and for women to choose from. "There was no choice of quality of character since of necessity each soul must assume a character appropriate to its choice; but wealth and poverty, health and disease were all mixed in varying degrees in the lives to be chosen" (*Rep.*, 10.618b). Now Socrates, rather than Er, interrupts and exhorts us to choose wisely because the decision is a free one; we should be unmoved by the temptation of wealth and other evils and choose a middle course, specially avoiding "falling into the life of a tyrant or other evil doer and perpetrating unbearable evil" (*Rep.*, 10.619a).

The Interpreter then exhorts everyone to choose wisely because even the person with the last number has some choices left. In fact, the person who picked the first lot chose to be a tyrant owing to his "folly and greed" and lack of reflection. He did not realize that "it was his fate to eat his children and suffer other horrors; when he examined it at leisure, he beat his breast and bewailed his choice . . . and forgot that his misfortunes were his own fault" (*Rep.*, 10.619c).

What is striking about these rebirth choices is that souls who make the *wrong* choices came from heaven because they lacked "the discipline of suffering, while those who came from earth had suffered themselves and seen others suffer and were not so hasty with their choice" (*Rep.*, 10.619d). Here again Socrates intervenes and reveals the paradox in this situation: those who go back to earth and lead good lives will at death avoid the stony ground of the underworld (the region of punishment) and move instead along the smooth road of heaven. Yet those very people in heaven, because of their lack of acquaintance with suffering, will end up by making bad rebirth choices. Ethicization step 2 associated with the karmic eschatology seems to be missing here.

The other rebirth choices that people make provoke pity, wonder, and laughter, says Er.

> For the most part they followed the habits of their former life. And so he saw the soul that once had been Orpheus choose the life of a swan; it was unwilling to be born of a woman because it hated all women after its death at their hands . . . and he saw a swan and other singing birds choose the life of a man. . . . Agammemnon who also because of his sufferings hated humanity chose to be an eagle. . . . And there were many other changes from beast to man and beast to beast, the unjust changing into wild animals and the just into tame in every kind of interchange. (*Rep.*, 10.620a–d).

It seems there is an eschatological feature that is not explicitly spelled out in the text: in addition to the humans there are animals and birds assembled here, but it is not clear whether they all had free choice.

Once the souls have made their choices, they come back to Lachesis, who allocates each its chosen guardian spirit to guide it through life according to the choices the souls have made; Clotho ratifies the decision, and Atropos makes it irreversible. Then all the souls come to the throne of Ananke, or Necessity. The world into which they are about to be reborn is governed by scarcity, want, and lack of order, and it is appropriate that Ananke should be the one to see them off. From there to the barren plain of Lethe "through a terrible and stifling heat; for the land was without trees or any vegetation" (*Rep.*, 10.621a).

The climax of the story takes place when Er gets back into his own undecomposed corpse.

> In the evening they encamped by the Forgetful River [Lethe] whose water no pitcher can hold. And all were compelled to drink a certain measure of its water; and those who had no wisdom to save them drank more than the measure. And as each man drank he forgot everything. They then went to sleep and when midnight came there was an earthquake and thunder, and like shooting stars they were all swept suddenly up and away, this way and that, to their birth. (*Rep.*, 10.621a–b).

Er alone is not required to drink from the river. According to the logic of the story, he cannot be permitted to drink the waters of forgetfulness because he must get back to his own body and report his experiences. He did not have 'Askadut's choice of being reborn in his sister's womb and retrocognizing his recent sojourn in the otherworld. "Er himself was forbidden to drink, and could not tell by what manner of means he returned to his body; but suddenly he opened his eyes and it was dawn and he was lying on the pyre" (*Rep.*, 10.621b).

Let me now compare the eschatology underlying the myth of Er with the rebirth and karmic eschatologies and the preceding Greek ones. Insofar as animal rebirths are intrinsic to the Platonic eschatology of the myth of Er, it is, on the one hand, close to the Amerindian ones. Nevertheless, as in Buddhism, there is a strong development of judgmental ethics, although exclusively in respect to the otherworld (heaven and hell). We are back to the aporetic dilemma highlighted in respect to the Pindaric eschatology; namely, *if people are punished and rewarded in the other world for what they have done on earth, then each person's slate has been wiped clean so that there is no need for rewards and punishments in the next human rebirth.* A similar dilemma is recognized by the Indian sage Vasiṣṭha when he says that "men who have committed offences and have received from kings the punishment (due to them), go pure to heaven, and (become) as holy as the virtuous."[156] This dilemma is one that Buddhism ignores.

Let me consider how Plato tackles this problem. Those who have been good have gone to heaven and now are assembled at the meadow, where they meet those who have traveled underground for a thousand years undergoing suffering in the process. The latter have been immoral while on earth and have had to expiate their sins. Now they have a chance to be reborn once again on earth but without experiencing the joys of heaven; that prospect is available if they lead moral lives during their next rebirth. For now virtually everyone has reaped rewards or paid penalties, except for those whose sins have been so great that they are denied reentry into the human world. These extreme sinners suffer terribly in underworld hells like Tartarus. This issue is developed at length in Plato's earlier text *Phaedo*. Aside from these doomed ones, there is now a logical problem of how to dispose of the rest assembled at the rebirth orifice or, to put it less facetiously, how to put them back into the human world. Plato thus confronts the same problem that any rebirth eschatology must resolve.

Let me examine Plato's solution, beginning with what he does *not* do. He does not, and cannot, adopt the Amerindian solution in which the dead person is circled back into the same kin group. Plato lived in a society where such kinship ties made little sense. Moreover, having adopted a stern social morality at step 1 of the ethicization process, he cannot drop ethics in respect to the human rebirth. Instead Plato postulates a different kind of ethics: *because those who are seeking rebirth have fully expended their load of sin and merit, they now are given the freedom to choose what they want to be in their next incarnation.* This freedom of choice is extended to the selection of a guardian spirit, or daimon. This is a logically impeccable solution and, given Athenian (democratic) values, a very reasonable one. However, "free choice" can produce its own dilemmas, which Plato does not mention: what if most people decide to be born as kings or as rich folk or as handsome ones? Indeed such choices would be motivationally expectable, yet most of us know that only a few kings or rich or handsome people live among us. This is apparently because Ananke and her daughters reign over the world of suffering and want. Hence Plato's unique solution: it is only the very few with a philosophical bent who can retain "an iron grip" at this critical juncture when "everything is at stake" and make truly reasoned choices. Most do not make reasoned choices because they are greedy or, more frequently, "because they followed the habits of their former life."[157] Moreover, once the choice has been made, there is no way it can be reversed, and the soul's fate on earth is sealed by Atropos.

However unique Plato's vision, the core of the Er eschatology then seems to be another logical way in which the rebirth eschatology is transformed. Considered in terms of that model, the entry to the otherworld is *conditioned* by the moral quality of one's life in this world. In the otherworld sin and merit are given appropriate punishments and rewards but with a finality that permits no carryover into the next human incarnation. A karma theory cannot emerge here because the conditionality of reward stops at step 1 of ethicization. Although this eschatology does not permit rebirth in the same kin group as in the Amerindian, its idea of species sentience is closer to the latter because it does not downgrade all animal rebirths as karmic eschatologies do. It does say, however, that those with evil dispositions will be born as wild animals and those with good dispositions as tame ones and yet others as befits their previous-life persona—but more of this in other Platonic myths. The myth of Er also ignores plants in its scheme of sentience, although this theme is picked up in the *Timaeus*. Finally, the Er eschatology, unlike the karma theory, is not a logic-tight system of ethical causality. Unlike Pindar's more humane and perhaps more representative popular vision, the myth of Er has a cynical view of human motivation. Free choice does not do much good for ordinary humanity because people will do what they have always done.

Although Plato's thesis might be true of much of human behavior, its motivational system of free choice cannot explain soteriologically why people are born maimed, blind, or crippled; why the just suffer and evil flourishes like the green bay tree; or why infants die prematurely. In fact Er himself is much more sensitive to the last issue than Socrates. Er "told me too about infants who died as soon as they were born or who lived only a short time, but what he said is not worth recalling" (*Rep.*, 10.615c). In my view there is an ethical lack here: Plato's Socrates is not primarily interested in the fate of those ordinary persons trapped in the prison of the body. He is more concerned with the philosopher, who, as the true embodiment of wisdom and virtue, cultivates the soul and disregards the body. This aspect of Plato's thought is well known, and I will deal briefly with it in the next part of this book.

# 6 REBIRTH AND REASON

## METACOSMESIS IN THE *PHAEDO*

Where does Plato come into our scheme of things? With him we are dealing with a thinker who carefully worked out a cosmology and eschatology of rebirth. I doubt that he would have done so had he not personally believed in its truth, and, for me, it is senseless to convert figures like the Buddha and Plato into figures of the European Enlightenment or, as some do, into modern and postmodern thinkers. Plato was not interested in conversion, but he addressed his message to those willing to listen, which for the most part meant the members of his academy. Nevertheless, like us he had to persuade his listeners and interlocutors to agree with him, and, like the Buddha, he did it through a form of dialogical discourse with dramatis personae who acted as strategic interlocutors. But unlike those of any other thinker that we have dealt with, Plato's doctrines of rebirth derived their force through the human faculty of Reason. I want to contrast this apotheosized Reason of the Greek Enlightenment with the "Buddhist Enlightenment," in which reason is only given secondary place. All forms of Buddhism subscribe to the distinction between conventional and ultimate truths (Pali, *sammuti sacca* and *paramattha sacca*); ultimate truths are apprehended through penetration *(pativedha)*, that is, through meditational ascesis and not through reason.

Socrates' retelling of Er's death and return is prefaced by a discussion of the evidences for the immortality of the soul, a well-known Platonic theme. Briefly stated, Plato insists that the soul may seem to us to be weighted with corporeality and contaminated by injustice, indiscipline, cowardice, and ignorance, but in its origin it possesses "a kinship with the divine" (*Rep.*, 10.611e), that is, a shared affinity with the gods. Further, the number of souls is finite and can never be increased or decreased; this brings Plato's theory in line with other Greek theories (and those of several small-scale societies) in which souls are "continuously incarnated" in various forms of sentient existence.

If the soul was originally divine, then its contamination results from immoral behavior in its incarnation in human (and other forms of) existence. But good and bad cannot remain unrewarded or unpunished. Because neither the just nor the unjust person's character is hidden from the gods, whomever the gods love will be blessed by heaven, and for the bad there is necessary punishment for offenses committed in a former life (*Rep.*, 10.612–13). The myth of Er deals with these afterlife rewards and punishments. However, in terms of my argument, Plato also says that the good and the bad will receive compensation and reward in this very life itself. As if echoing the Buddha, Plato says that the just man will get "the rewards and the good name among his fellows." More problematically, the unjust person, even if he gets away with it while young, will in his old age be miserable, held in contempt by all and punished by the secular authorities with such things as torture and branding.

This whole argument is anticipated in Plato's earlier work, the *Phaedo,* written c. 390 B.C.E. and belonging to the middle period of his life, along with the *Phaedrus* and the *Republic,* although perhaps antedating both. The context is highly appropriate for talking about salvation because it deals with the last hours of Socrates as he calmly awaits death. Socrates is fearless and confident because, as a philosopher, his very lifestyle is given to "practising death."[1] This training for death is in reality the cultivation of the soul, rendering it pure and recognizing its immortality. It means leading a pure life untrammeled by the body so that the soul will at last be released from the body's bondage. In response to a question by Cebes, Socrates makes it clear that the soul is "tainted and impure" in those who have been beguiled by bodily pleasures (*Phd.,* 81b). For Socrates also the body imprisons the soul and awaits the wise man to set it free. "Every seeker after wisdom knows that up to the time when philosophy takes it over his soul is a helpless prisoner, chained hand and foot in the body, compelled to view reality not directly but only through its prison bars, and wallowing in utter ignorance" (*Phd.,* 82e).

*Phaedo* resembles Buddhist texts in emphasizing craving as the cause of continuity in the rebirth cycle. For Plato's Socrates, however, it is "craving for the corporeal which unceasingly pursues them [until] they are imprisoned once more in a body" (*Phd.,* 81d–e). Once again we encounter the Pythagorean-Orphic theme: the soul is imprisoned in the body not just in one lifetime but throughout the whole rebirth cycle. In the thinking of *Phaedo* not only the bad things that people do but also ordinary goodness is ultimately rooted in corporeality. This "heavy, oppressive, earthly and visible" physical life keeps the processes of rebirth, or metacosmesis, going and therefore takes the place of the karma doctrine in Buddhism; indeed, "every pleasure or pain has a sort of rivet with which it fastens the soul to the body and pins it down and makes it corporeal." Saturated with corporeality the soul "soon falls back into another body, where it takes root and grows" (*Phd.,* 83d–e). Because corporeal craving and consequent metacosmesis affect those who have been bad as well as those who have been decent citizens, one might now ask, What is the manner of their respective rebirths?

Socrates gives examples of rebirth to illustrate the theme that people are "attached to the same sort of character or nature which they have developed during life." To begin with, "those who have cultivated gluttony or selfishness or drunkenness, instead of taking pains to avoid them, are likely to assume the form of donkeys and other perverse animals." Then "those who have deliberately preferred a life of irresponsible lawlessness and violence become wolves and hawks and kites." And finally, there are those who "have cultivated the goodness of an ordinary citizen—what is called self-control and integrity—which is acquired by habit and practice, *without the help of philosophy and reason.*" The last, Socrates says with a touch of irony, are the really happy ones who "will probably pass into some other kind of social and disciplined creature like bees, wasps, and ants; or even back into the human race again, becoming decent citizens" (*Phd.,* 81e–82b, my italics).

Thus far the *Phaedo* account is perfectly consonant with the eschatology of the Er myth. In *Phaedo* the various animals being reborn correspond to those of the Er myth who have assembled before Lachesis and chosen their next rebirth. As in the myth of Er, in *Phaedo* also Plato's human beings awaiting rebirth reproduce what they have been before, once again rendering free choice a kind of unfree reality. The details of the wanderings of the dead are given in much greater length, along with the punishments and rewards in the otherworld.

I will not deal with the cosmography of the otherworld except to say that human beings live in the hollow of the earth, oblivious to the pure and heaven-like nature of earth's true surface. There is also an underground, a cavity in the earth that leads to Tartarus. Of the many rivers that flow into Tartarus, four are eschatologically relevant, the most important being Acheron, "where the souls of the dead for the most part come, and after staying there for certain fixed periods, longer or shorter, are sent forth again to the births of living creatures" (*Phd.*, 112e–13a).[2] The dead, conducted by their guardian spirit, or daimon (chosen by them in the previous underworld sojourn according to the Er myth), are submitted to judgment in several ways. First, "those who are judged to have lived a neutral life set out for Acheron, and embarking in those vessels which await them, are conveyed in them to the lake where they dwell, and undergoing purification are both absolved by punishment for any sins that they have committed, and rewarded for their good deeds, according to each man's deserts." Second, reminiscent of the tyrants of the myth of Er are "those who on account of their sins are judged to be incurable, as having committed many gross acts of sacrilege or many wicked and lawless murders or any other such crimes—these are hurled by their appropriated destiny into Tartarus, from whence they emerge no more." Third are those "judged to have been guilty of sins which, though great are curable," for example, those who in a fit of passion have committed manslaughter or violence to a parent and have since lived in penitence. They too are cast into Tartarus but after a year the surge casts them out, with the manslayers going down the river Cocytus and those guilty of acts against parents down Pyriphlegethon, two of the four rivers mentioned earlier. They are then swept to the Acherusian Lake, where they call on those whom they have harmed. If they are forgiven by their victims, they are relieved from suffering; but if they are not, they too are permanently cast into Tartarus (*Phd.*, 113d–14a).

Let me now see whether the eschatological details in *Phaedo* are reconcilable with the myth of Er. The Tartarus account deals with the souls' immediate entry into the underworld long before their meeting with Lachesis, which occurs only after a thousand years. There are different kinds of souls punished in accordance with the nature of their this-worldly lives, but the really bad ones are confined forever in Tartarus. Repentance is important in the Platonic scheme, but it must be accompanied by the forgiveness of the victims. Neutral or ordinary citizens are punished for the wrongs they have done, after which they are rewarded. Who are the latter in terms of the Er myth? They are very likely those who have come down from "heaven," which probably refers to the pure or heavenly surface of the earth. A further clue is given in the Er myth in respect to one soul "who had come from heaven, having lived his previous life in a well-governed state, but *having owed his goodness to habit and custom and not to philosophy*" (*Rep.*, 619c–d, my italics). His type, Socrates adds, constitutes the majority. They clearly are the neutral or ordinary citizens of the *Phaedo*. In addition, the *Phaedo* refers to a group of people "deemed to have lived an extremely pious life" (*Phd.*, 114c) without actually being true philosophers.[3] They presumably do not suffer punishment at all but go straight to the pure regions of the earth's heavenly surface.

The list of those punished in the *Phaedo* is not meant to be exhaustive but consists of select examples of those who have committed horrendous evil. There ought to be plenty of persons who, having been punished, are not confined eternally to Tartarus. They and the repentant and forgiven ones walk the long road that ultimately brings them before Lachesis and then join their luckier friends and acquaintances coming down from "heaven," all of them awaiting "free choice" in their next rebirth. One need not, however, expect perfect consonance between the *Phaedo* and Er accounts because, as Socrates says, the facts need not be "exactly as I have described them," but "something very like it is a true account of our souls and their future habitations" (*Phd.*, 114d). Reason has its imperfections and limitations, a result of the uncertainty of factual evidence in the storyteller's craft.

I have not yet dealt with the fate of the crucial minority of philosophers who, unmoved by the passions and constraints of the body, nurture and cultivate the soul. The true philosopher's soul escapes the bondage of the body by following "reason and abiding in her company . . . contemplating the true and divine and unconjecturable, and drawing inspiration from it . . . [so] that after death it reaches a place which is kindred and similar to its own nature, and there is rid for ever of human ills" (*Phd.*, 84a–b). The "place" is not specified in the *Phaedo*, although it is developed in other accounts. What is clear though is that the philosopher's soul alone can be saved (after three human incarnations, according to other accounts), which, in Greek as in Buddhist soteriology, means the cessation of rebirth. The reason is that the philosopher's soul is free of bodily craving, which effects continuity of sentient bodies in the rebirth cycle and the souls' imprisonment in them. Unlike the neutral and the ordinary and even the especially good or holy who eventually get embodied, those who "have purified themselves sufficiently by philosophy live thereafter altogether without bodies, and reach habitations even more beautiful" (*Phd.*, 114c). No wonder Socrates, that practitioner of death, can calmly drink the poison provided by the Athenian jury.

## THE SOTERIOLOGY AND ESCHATOLOGY OF THE *PHAEDRUS*

Some features of the Platonic eschatology that are undeveloped or unclear in the myth of Er and in *Phaedo* are spelled out in the *Phaedrus,* probably written not long after *Phaedo*. *Phaedrus* commences with its protagonist quoting at length a rhetorical discourse on love by the celebrated orator Lysias. Lysias's speech is written for a man who tries to persuade a boy to yield to him, even though he is not consumed by the passionate madness of the true lover but would instead have the boy to satisfy his desires. Socrates dislikes this speech and comes out, reluctantly, with his own refutation of Lysias. He thinks that Lysias's lover is only pretending not to be in love; thus he can defend one kind of nonlover, the man who loves the boy, but at a distance as it were. This detached, or "Platonic," love is much better than the irrationality of the mad lover, who in this scheme of things is an older man infatuated by a young boy. Having made this point Socrates then recants it by affirming the divine nature of passionate love. The irrationality or madness of the lover is not wrong (as he had previously indicated) because there are parallel states of inspired madness or possession that can set us on the "right track about the future."[4] This is, of course, divination or prophecy, which Socrates says was originally called the *manic* art and later became the *mantic* art. Then there is possession, which can through prayer and purification wipe out the sins coming from the past (the ancestors). He adds that, according to their Greek ancestors, possession was noble because "madness comes from God, whereas sober sense is merely human." Socrates then deals with madness from possession by the Muses, another instance of "heaven sent madness," which is "the greatest benefit that heaven can confer on us" (*Phdr.,* 245). The madness of the pederastic lover is the fourth kind of divine madness.

Socrates says that to fully understand divine madness, one must begin to understand the nature of the soul. With it we come to the familiar Platonic idea that "everything that is generated must be generated from a beginning, but the beginning is not generated from anything. . . . And since it is ungenerated it must be also indestructible" (*Phdr.,* 245d).[5] One has no hesitation in identifying it with "the essence and definition of the soul," which is "ungenerated and immortal" (*Phdr.,* 246d). The soul permeates the whole universe and traverses through it taking different forms at different times in the process. "When it is perfect and winged it moves on high and governs all creation, but the soul that has shed its wings falls until it encounters solid matter." There it puts on an earthly body, and this combination of soul and body is what constitutes a "mortal" being. In contrast to the mortal, the immortal can be neither seen nor described; nevertheless one can imagine it being similar to ourselves but with "a combination of soul and body indissolubly joined for ever" (*Phdr.,* 246). Although the soul itself is an enigma known only to the gods, it is possible for us to describe how a soul loses its wings and becomes human and mortal.

Socrates plans to demonstrate this through a special allegorical method, namely, by comparing the soul to a winged charioteer and his team acting together. "Now the horses and charioteers of the gods are all good and of good descent, but those of other races are mixed" (*Phdr.,* 246a–b, Fowler's trans.). By contrast, in men (the gender use is not merely nominal) the "ruling power" drives a pair of horses, one fine and of good stock and the other the very opposite. The function of the soul's wing is to take what is heavy and raise it to the heavens, where the gods dwell. "Behold, first in the procession, driving his winged team, goes Zeus the mighty leader of the heavenly array, whose providence orders and watches over all things," followed by a host of gods and spirits marshaled in eleven bands (except Hestia, the earth goddess, who stays behind) (*Phdr.,* 246–47).[6] "Now the souls that are termed immortal [the gods], when they reach the summit of the arch [supporting the outer heaven] go outside the vault [of heaven] and stand upon the back of the universe; standing there they are carried round by its revolution while they contemplate what lies outside the heavens." What then is being contemplated? It is a vision of reality, without doubt the realm of the Platonic Ideal Forms, "a reality without colour or shape, intangible but utterly real, apprehensible only by intellect which is the pilot of the soul." The mind of an immortal god can apprehend this "vision of reality," which is "nourished and made happy by the contemplation of truth, until the circular revolution brings it back to its starting point." When the heavenly circuit is completed, "the charioteer sets his horses at their manger and puts ambrosia before them and with it a draught of nectar to drink" (*Phdr.,* 247). Note that Plato, who is primarily an ethical and political thinker, never uses the terms *soteriology* or *salvation.* Instead he uses *nous* or *noesis,* and sometimes *episteme,* to designate one's knowledge of this realm of being, which is opposed to the world of coming-into-being or becoming, where one is enmeshed in taken-for-granted beliefs, or *doxa.*[7] Nevertheless, the sense of happiness or bliss inextricably associated with the *contemplation* of that reality can reasonably be translated as "salvific."

In my view the foregoing account is central to understanding Plato's theory of rebirth and the doctrine of salvation implicit in it. Plato does postulate an apprehension of a transcendental reality, but this remains the privilege of the immortal gods.[8] Let us now continue the narrative to see what lies in store for lesser beings and us ordinary mortals.

Those spirits closest to the gods also manage to make the full circuit, but they are not able to enjoy the full apprehension of the true reality because the unruly behavior of their horses impairs their vision. Others sometimes sink and sometimes rise in their winged chariots and, owing to the restiveness of the horses, have only a partial glimpse of that reality. The rest try to reach the upper world but fail in spite of their struggles; their wings get broken, their souls become lame, and "they depart without achieving initiation into the vision of reality." They fall to earth and into the world of becoming and are reborn there. And this, says Socrates, is the "law":

> In its first incarnation no soul is born in the likeness of a beast; the soul that has seen the most [of the true reality] enters into a human infant who is destined to become a follower of the Muses and a lover; the next most perceptive is born as a law-abiding monarch or as a warrior and commander; the third as a man of affairs or the manager of a household or financier; the fourth is to be a lover of physical activity or a trainer or physician; the fifth is given the life of a soothsayer or an official of the mysteries; the sixth will make a poet or a practitioner of some other imaginative art; the seventh an artisan or a farmer; the eighth a popular teacher or a demagogue; the ninth a tyrant. (*Phdr.,* 248)

On the face of it this might seem a skewed account of rebirth in the human world, but the list is limited to those who have had a partial vision of the true reality in descending degrees of apprehension. What is striking is that these are all male human beings; beasts are excluded because "it is impossible for a soul that has never seen the truth to enter into our human shape" (*Phdr.,* 249). But *human,* we know from the later *Timaeus,* means "male."

What then happens after the first human incarnation mentioned above? This depends on "the goodness or badness of his previous life." The cycle of rebirths ends after ten thousand years; it takes that long for the soul to grow its wings once again and go back to where it originally came from. In Plato's reckoning a person is brought to judgment *after the first incarnation:* "some go to expiate their sins in places of punishment beneath the earth, while others are borne aloft by justice to a certain region of the heavens to enjoy the reward which their previous life in human form has earned" (*Phdr.,* 249). We are now fully into the eschatology of Er in the *Republic.* In the *Phaedrus* account each person enjoys heavenly bliss or suffers pain in the underworld for a thousand years, after which one must draw lots and then be reborn on earth for the second incarnation. There are ten such thousand-year incarnations, at the end of which the whole process of becoming comes to an end.

Let me now consider what happens at the end of the first incarnation that we have already described and when lots have been drawn. "At this moment a human soul may take upon itself the life of a beast, *or a soul that was originally human may change from beast back to man*" (*Phdr.,* 249, my italics). It is not explicitly stated how someone could change from beast to man, if what we have here are those who come together before Lachesis after their first incarnation. The implicit answer is clear though: there are beings here from *previous incarnations* who have *not* obtained final release, and these leftovers are primarily animals. Others are those like the ones debarred by Lachesis from entry into the rebirth chasm of the Er myth.

Is there any way to short-circuit the ten incarnations adding up to a cycle of ten thousand years? Those who wisely pick their lots (presumably before Lachesis of the myth of Er) and choose to be reborn three times consecutively as a philosopher will regain their wings at the end of the third incarnation "and in the three-thousandth year win their release." This gift is given to the philosopher who has sought wisdom without guile or, better still, has combined that search with a love for a boy (presumably love of the "Platonic" sort). He alone has the capacity to recollect his original prefallen state of soul through "the right use of such aids to recollection, which form a continual initiation into the perfect mystic vision that a man can become perfect in the true sense of the word" (*Phdr.,* 249). Because of this propensity, the philosopher stands outside ordinary human desire and the life of the world; therefore, people think him mad. But his is the final and most noble form of divine madness; he too is possessed by a god.

In the context of the *Phaedrus* possession refers to the philosopher's recollection of his original god-like state before he lost his wings and fell to earth. However the *glimpse* of the mystic vision, like the Pythagorean apprehension of the music of the spheres, is not its full and final realization. Putting the evidence of *Phaedo* and *Phaedrus* together, it seems that the gods have the mystical apprehension of Reality, the world of Forms. This means that the metaphysics of Forms has been converted into a soteriology. The philosopher's soul at death will be separated from the body and, living in fellowship with the gods, will apprehend the mystic vision, the privilege of the gods (stars). Plato's severed soul is itself a kind of god, enjoying the mystical vision that the gods possessed. In terms of the metaphors of the *Phaedrus,* the soul of the philosopher attempts to reach the salvific condition that existed before the fall. The implicit doctrine here is that of the soul, now a god and living with other gods, enjoying a transcendental vision rather than merging with a god or God as in the Upanishadic identification of atman with Brahman. Like Empedocles before him, Plato transfigures into an entirely idealistic and spiritual plane the older Greek idea of fellowship with the gods associated with commensality and carousing, all bodily pleasures. Also implicit is the idea that the soul is now in the world of Being, and it can never get caught in the coils of the rebirth cycle, the world of becoming and corporeality.

## THE COSMOLOGY OF THE *TIMAEUS*

The *Phaedrus* left several important questions unanswered. The myth of the winged charioteers does not tell us how the souls of the gods and their followers got there in the first place. This is primarily a question of eschatology and cosmology rather than of soteriology, although these distinctions are blurred in Platonic texts. In *Phaedrus* Socrates is the reluctant soteriologist, more at home in the polis than in the cosmos. He is forced into salvific matters by his interlocutor, Phaedrus. In the *Timaeus* Plato dumps Socrates, as it were, and makes Timaeus—a native of southern Italy, the home of rebirth eschatologies—the appropriate dramatis persona for relating "a likely story" or "a probable mythos" to depict the origin of the cosmos.[9] The *Timaeus* and the incomplete *Critias* are considered two of Plato's latest works, and they are enormously significant for understanding Plato's mature metaphysics. If the *Republic* dealt with the form and content of the ideal polity, the *Timaeus* is the other side of the coin, the cosmos on which the polis itself ultimately rests. Hence, although *Timaeus* was written long after the *Republic,* it is set on the day after Socrates depicts the ideal republic in the latter text. In the *Phaedrus* Plato is self-consciously a philosopher, but he is not a philosopher trying to understand nature and the civil world systematically, as Aristotle did. He was, like the Buddha, a philosopher and a religious thinker at the same time; and it is likely that he followed the model of his intellectual precursors, Empedocles and Pythagoras, in this regard, constructing in the *Timaeus* a cosmology that supplements the soteriology of the *Phaedrus* and the idealized polity of the *Republic.* The text, as many classicists recognize, is obscure and open to conflicting interpretations. I have adopted a reading relevant to my own intellectual concerns in this book. I refer the reader to A. E. Taylor's and Francis Cornford's commentaries and exegeses for the details of Plato's cosmology and doctrine of creation.[10] I will focus on those details of the cosmology that help recenter Plato's rebirth eschatology and soteriology.

The *Timaeus* adds a powerful cosmological and eschatological dimension to the theory of Forms, which inherently lacks such a provision. As we know, the world we live in is for Plato a fluctuating, illusory, and impermanent realm of becoming, whereas the realm of Being is that of the Forms. To put it in terms of another well-known distinction: there is the material, or "sensible," world, easily grasped with our sense faculties, and the immaterial, or "intelligible," world of Forms, which can be known only through the faculty of Reason. Thus the objects of the material world are but shadows of the world of Forms. "The one is apprehensible by intelligence with the aid of reasoning, being eternally the same, the other is the object of opinion and irrational sensation, coming to be and ceasing to be, but never fully real" (*Ti.,* 3.28). As Cornford says about the latter, "there can never be a final statement of exact truth about this changing object."[11] A more non-Buddhist truth could scarcely be invented!

The doctrine of Forms has no God or creation myth, but the *Timaeus* supplies both without in any way supplanting the Forms themselves. The latter exist independent of the Demiurge *[demiourgos],* said to be the Father and a Craftsman or Maker molding the world according to a rational design. With the introduction of the Demiurge the Greek rebirth theory gets a teleological component that is possible neither in the doctrine of Forms per se nor in doctrines like the Buddhist karma. The Demiurge is Reason itself, and the cosmos, its creation, exhibits that attribute. If the philosopher Plato imagined a world of Being that he could rationally infer from the experienced reality of the world of becoming, so his Craftsman creates a world of Becoming on the model of the world of Being. How then is this world created?

Plato's God is not an omnipotent being. Although perfect and good, embodying Reason itself, this God has to create the universe with whatever materials are available, even though the model for creating the world is the ideal one of Forms. Moreover, the Maker, although perfect, must of necessity create an imperfect world. Yet there is a problem here that reappears later in God's creation of the other gods (stars): the Demiurge is perfection itself, and whatever he makes must approximate his own being in spite of the limitations imposed by the materials at hand. Thus, in section 5, there is an elaborate description of the creation of the form of the universe out of the four constituent atomic principles: earth, air, fire, and water. The body of the world, itself a god, must have "a suitable shape for a living being that was to contain within itself all living beings" or "all possible figures within itself." As with Empedocles the ideal shape would be a sphere with a "perfectly smooth external finish all round" (*Ti.*, 5.33). What is striking about the body of the world is that, although it contains within itself all the possibilities of living beings or their paradigmatic forms, it has none of the attributes that living beings possess, that is, sight, hearing, ingestion or digestion, and locomotion (feet or legs). I think the reason is clear enough and is related to the Demiurge's own nature: he cannot make anything that is imperfect, whereas living beings, excluding the gods, epitomize imperfection. They belong to the world of becoming, over which the Demiurge has no responsibility, as we will see.

At this point Plato's Timaeus reminds us that although he has given temporal priority in his account to the creation of the body of the world, this is not how it in fact happened. "God created the soul before the body [of the world] and gave it precedence both in time and value, and made it the dominating and controlling partner" (*Ti.*, 6.34). God, the craftsman, cuts and weaves the soul together very much in the manner of a tailor. If the body of the world is visible, its soul suffuses the whole body and is "invisible and endowed with reason and harmony, being the best creation of the best of intelligible and eternal things" and compounded in harmonious fashion of Sameness, Difference, and Existence, or Being (*Ti.*, 6.37).[12] Then comes the constitution of Time through the creation of the sun, the moon, and the five planets, which, like the world's body, are gods. As Cornford says, "[T]here is a tradition running throughout the whole of Greek thought, which always associated Time with a circular movement." And life itself, he adds, "moves in a cycle of Time, the wheel of becoming—birth, growth, maturity, decay, death, and rebirth."[13] Proclus, commenting on Plato's own idea of time revolving according to number, emphasizes its circularity and further notes: "The notion of Time joins the end to the beginning, and this an infinite number of times."[14] Here also, as with the Buddhist, cosmic cycles are wheels within wheels!

Following the creation of Time and the harmonious circularity of the planets come the four classes of living creatures, these being the gods (stars), birds, water animals, and land animals. The Demiurge only creates the heavenly race of the gods, the fixed stars, who are primarily composed of the element of fire and thereby possess the quality of luminosity. The traditional gods of the Greek pantheon are only formally recognized in this text; their role has already been depicted in the *Phaedrus* and the *Republic.* At this point the Demiurge addresses the gods and tells them that although they are not "entirely immortal," they still share the qualities of their Maker and will therefore "never be dissolved nor taste death." The Demiurge then tells the lesser gods that there are three other classes of beings yet to be created to complete the world picture. "But if these were created and given life by me, they would be equal to gods," which of course will not do. Thus, the making of the other living creatures is assigned by the Demiurge to the gods (stars) but with an important proviso:

> And in so far as there ought to be something in them that can be named immortal, something called divine, to guide those of them who are ready to follow you and the right, I will begin by sowing the seed of it and then hand it on to you; it remains for you to weave mortal and immortal together and create living creatures. Bring them to birth, give them food and growth, and when they perish receive them again. (*Ti.,* 9.41)

The seed that the Demiurge sows is the soul, the immortal part of human beings. How does he do it though? "So speaking, he turned again to the same bowl in which he had mixed the soul of the universe and poured into it what was left of its former ingredients, mixing them in much the same fashion as before, only not quite so pure, but in a second and third degree" (*Ti.,* 10.41–42). This is new information because there was no reference to a mixing bowl in the section dealing with the world soul.[15] Nevertheless, the idea of the mixing bowl is appropriate for the Sicilian Timaeus because it comes from Orphism, as does the image of weaving, and might well have served "for an act of cosmic mixing (or a mixing of constituents of man); or perhaps souls drank from it during initiation."[16]

The previous episode elicits a comment on the construction of Platonic dialogues. As in the Buddhist ones, the dramatis personae have two functions: the dialogues must fit the speaker's character or mentality, and they must help express the thoughts of the author (Plato), generally through some protagonist, such as Socrates or Timaeus. I have already shown the need to make Timaeus Plato's mouthpiece. And Timaeus, unlike Socrates, is given to mixing his metaphors, moving without warning from tailoring to sowing to cooking or medicine making. Timaeus does what Socrates would not: he ignores chronological sequence in his narrative when he deals with the creation of the body of the universe before the soul was created. He is full of "contradictions."[17] This is not Plato speaking directly to us; it is Timaeus speaking, and his narration is in character.

Timaeus continues: God then divided this concoction into as many souls as there are stars

> and allotted each soul to a star. And mounting them on their stars, as if on chariots, he showed them the nature of the universe and told them the laws of their destiny. To ensure fair treatment for each at his hands, the first incarnation would be one and the same for all and each would be sown in its appropriate instrument of time and be born as the most god-fearing of living things; and human-kind being of two sexes, the better of the two was that which in future would be called man. (*Ti.*, 10.42)

With the creation of Man we are thrust into the world of becoming. Human beings, says the creator, are subject to physical gain and loss and are endowed with senses such as those of pain and pleasure, fear and anger. Those who master the senses will lead a good life, whereas those who are subject to them will be wicked:

> And anyone who lived well for his appointed time would return home to his native star and live an appropriately happy life; but anyone who failed to do so would be changed into a woman at his second birth. And if he did not refrain from wrong, he would be changed into some animal suitable to his particular kind of wrongdoing, and would have no respite from change and suffering until he allowed the motion of the Same and uniform in himself to subdue all that multitude of riotous and irrational feelings which have clung to it since its association with fire, water, air and earth, and with reason thus in control returned once more to his first and best form. (*Ti.*, 10.42)

Having sowed the soul and proclaimed his ordinances for the future and for the welfare of humans, the Demiurge now moves from the scene of his creation, leaving the lesser gods (stars) to finish the task of making the human body and encasing the soul within it. God has become otiose for good reason: the world's imperfections cannot be attributed to a perfect being.

The star-gods are much more constrained than their Father because they have to create sense-bound beings. But they do the best they can, combining the dictates of Reason with the constraints imposed by Necessity, or Ananke, the principle that operates in the world of becoming. This lesser task of the gods is described in minute detail in the main body of the *Timaeus* (sections 11–37), but it is not relevant to our analysis. It is in respect to the human soul that we pick up the thread of the narrative once again.

The work of the gods is to implant the soul in the mortal body, but this task poses several problems. The soul is tripartite and contained in the body's marrow, which is the life substance. The divine element of Reason is in the marrow of the brain; the neck acts as an "isthmus" to connect head (container of the brain) with the mortal elements of the soul, located in "the breast and the trunk" (*Ti.*, 38.69–70). Timaeus then describes at length the physiology of the body in relation to the functioning of the mortal parts of the soul, as for example when he locates courage, passion, and ambition between the midriff and the neck so "it could be well-placed to listen to the commands of reason [in the head] and combine with it in forcibly restraining the appetites when they refused to obey the word of command from the citadel" (*Ti.*, 38.70–71)—beautifully confusing metaphors once again.

Some of the irrational parts of the soul can be made to act beneficially; witness the power of prophecy, which Plato apparently firmly believes in. This power appears in dreaming, when our capacity for understanding is down, or in abnormal conditions such as those associated with disease or divine inspiration. But the dreamer or the prophet cannot interpret his own utterances; that has to be done by special spokespersons. Plato is fully aware of the diseases of the mind or soul (both psychosomatic and somatopsychic), which he elaborately discusses following his equally elaborate description of bodily diseases based on the lack of balance between the four elements of earth, fire, air, and water, further compounded by those secondary formations caused by bile, wind, and phlegm—very much in the tradition of earlier Greek medicine (and Ayurvedic medicine in India during the same period).[18]

Thus far the *Timaeus* deals with the making of human beings, specifically Man. Unlike in Plato's previous accounts, plants are mentioned here but not given much significance except as a source of food for mortal creatures. But because "everything that has life has a right to be called a living thing," plants too are part of a larger order to which I have attributed "species sentience." They therefore possess souls but of a "third sort," analogous to the lower part of the soul of humans, "located between midriff and navel and which is without belief or reason or understanding but has appetite and a sense of pleasure and pain." Like the Buddhist and Jaina idea of *ekindriya,* a single center of consciousness, it is passive and without the capacity for reflection. Hence I suspect this is why one cannot be reborn as a plant, quite unlike in the Empedoclean (and Plotinian) eschatology, although more in tune with the Buddhist. Further, a plant is "fixed and rooted because it has no self-motion" (*Ti.*, 41.77), unlike the divine part of the human soul, which can move in and around itself and reflect on itself, presumably because it shares the essence of the Demiurge himself.

The creation of the "other animals," he says, warrants only a brief account, beginning with women and then birds, animals, reptiles, and fish. "The men of the first generation who lived cowardly or immoral lives were, it is reasonable to suppose, reborn in the second generation as women; and it was therefore at that point of time that the gods produced sexual love, constructing in us and in women a living creature itself instinct with life" (*Ti.*, 49.91). Plato then describes how the sexual organs of both male and female were created. It is clear that sexuality itself results from the creation of women, who were originally fallen men.

Note another fascinating feature of this myth. In the first place there is a doctrine of the emergence of human and animal kind necessary for any creation myth but framed within a rebirth doctrine. Second, it reverses a Greek creation myth of "autochthonous origins" highlighted by Lévi-Strauss; autochthonous origins eliminate the structural problem found in creation myths, like the biblical one, which says that humankind was produced from the intercourse of an original man (Adam) and woman (Eve).[19] This kind of myth must produce brother-sister incest in the second generation if there is going to be progeny, or parent-child incest in the first, or a combination of the two, as in the hermaphroditic creation expounded in the Rhapsodic Theogony.[20] Thus a peculiar aporia of such creation myths: the human race arose out of an action that human beings everywhere consider reprehensible. By contrast when humans appear full blown in the Greek myth of autochthonous origins (or the Trobriander one), there is no need for incestuous unions to propagate the human race. The Platonic reincarnation myth provides another way to bypass the incest issue: men and women can copulate and replenish the earth in their second incarnation without recourse to incest.

So much for women and men, but what about other forms of sentient life? "Birds were produced by a process of transformation, growing feathers instead of hair, from harmless empty-headed men, who were interested in the heavens but were silly enough to think that visible evidence was all the foundation that astronomy needs" (*Ti.*, 49.91)—a neat attack on empiricists like Plato's own student Aristotle. Land animals were reincarnations of those men who had no use for philosophy and who had ceased to use the higher divine part of the soul, relying on the soul-substance lower down in the breast. Because of their downward-looking nature they were literally grounded, supported on earth by forelimbs, and their skulls were formed into various shapes by their lack of use of the divine faculty located in the head. The more stupid sort had four or more feet because they needed supports

> to tie them more closely to the earth. And the stupidest of the land animals, whose whole bodies lay stretched on the earth, the gods turned into reptiles, giving them no feet, because they had no further need for them. But the most unintelligent and ignorant of all turned into the fourth kind of creature that lives in water. Their souls were hopelessly steeped in every kind of error, and so their makers thought them unfit to breathe pure clean air, and made them inhale water. . . . That is the origin of fish, shell-fish and everything else that lives in water; they live in the depths as a punishment for the depth of their stupidity. *These are the principles on which living creatures change and have always changed into each other, the transformation depending on the loss or gain of understanding or folly.* (*Ti.*, 49.92, my italics)[21]

These principles that entail entry of souls into bodies is given a label: *metensomatosis,* the soul's embodiment or a body's "ensoulment," a theme taken up in further detail by Plato's later disciple Plotinus.

This might be an appropriate place to consider an important aspect of Plato's thought, represented well by A. E. Taylor. Taylor thinks that Plato's "is the foundation of all subsequent 'natural' theology, the first attempt in all the literature of the world to demonstrate God's existence and moral government of the world from the known facts of the visible order."[22] Although the first part of the statement is true, namely that Plato's work is the foundation of Neoplatonist natural theology, including Christian Neoplatonism, the second is extremely dubious in light of the preceding discussion. The Demiurge is not God in any theistic or monotheistic sense: he creates the world only to move out of its historical unfolding by leaving the creation of imperfect humanity to the lesser gods, who, after the first humans are created, also become otiose. Thereafter, it is metensomatosis, or ensoulment, and metacosmesis, or the processes of reincarnation, that drive human and other kinds of sentient existence in the world of becoming, and in this scheme God as a moral arbiter simply has no place. In spite of radical differences regarding the nature of the soul, Plato is closer to thinkers like the Buddha than he is to those who invented a Neoplatonist tradition of natural theology to vindicate God's existence and omnipresence.[23]

## COSMOLOGICAL HOMOEROTICISM, HETEROPHOBIA, AND FEMALE NATURE IN PLATONIC REBIRTH

The *Timaeus* has been a troubling discourse for those who find it difficult to reconcile its negative view of women with the positive one in the *Republic.* In my thinking one must deal with the male heterophobia of the academy before one can confront the ideal polity sketched in the *Republic,* which gives women similar, if not identical, capabilities to males. The peculiar cosmology of the *Timaeus* makes sense in relation to the male homoeroticism of the academy and its denizens; but it is a heterophobic homoeroticism that we rarely associate nowadays with homosexuality, although it is fairly common among Catholic and Buddhist monk orders, where comradeship with men and antipathy for women are widespread, as is pederasty (at least among Buddhist monastics).

Take the myth of creation: the gods originally create Men. These men are free of sexual feelings, which emerge only with the creation of women in the second incarnation. Yet, structurally speaking, a myth of creation must contain a myth of procreation in order to account for the existence of the human race. Unhappily the original community of the *Timaeus* was an ideal community of males without sexual organs; the love that bonds them cannot be sexual (homoerotic), only asexual, or "Platonic." Plato's Timaeus says that some men have fallen from their high state as a result of immorality or cowardice and "it becomes reasonable to suppose" that they become women or other kinds of creatures. Sexual love was created by the gods at that time only. Plato describes in some detail how man's body was changed to create the desire for procreation and the organs to ensure it. In this new situation "man's genitals are naturally disobedient and self-willed, like a creature that will not listen to reason, and will do anything in their mad lust for possession." By contrast a woman has a different form of unreason: her lust is to bear children in the matrix, or womb. "If it is left unfertilized long beyond the normal time, it causes extreme unrest . . . [and] this goes on until the woman's longing and the man's desire meet" (*Ti.,* 49.91). Plato does not tell us what happens when women's passion for procreation is not fulfilled through men's desire. I assume that women's "unrest" causes their wombs to wander, and they become "hysterics."

Thus a peculiar situation: the original love was between men, and it was devoid of passion; when women arose, men were given sexual passion and women a drive for offspring, or "womb-passion," if I may use that phrase. This must inevitably result in a change in the relations between males; now that men have been given wayward genitals and sexual passion, it is they who can properly exercise *mutual sexual love*. Procreation and sexual passion have been split in the relations between men and women on the one hand and between men and men on the other. Thus, in male-to-male relationships there are two types of homoeroticism: first, the sublimated variety that recapitulates the original nonerotic love between males; second, a passionate sexual love between two males, preferably pederasty (of the sort celebrated in the *Phaedrus* and elsewhere).[24] It is logical, although by no means empirically clear, that the true philosopher questing for salvation must develop a transcendental love reflective of the original situation rather than the physical passion of the second incarnation, which is locked into bodily dross. In light of the preceding interpretation it is likely that the construction of Plato's cosmology is overdetermined on the unconscious level by a form of heterophobia (rather than misogyny) that has entailed a *denial,* in the psychoanalytic sense, of female sexuality.[25] This denial then is rationalized and woven into the myth of origin.

How far does the *Timaeus* account accord with the much earlier beautiful paean praising love in the *Symposium?* In the *Symposium* (meaning "the drinking party") there is a greater recognition by some of the dramatis personae of the complexity of love as a lived experience. Let me illustrate: Pausanias, for example, recognizes the love between men and women and between men and men (but ignores lesbians, consonant with the thought of *Timaeus* on this subject). This is however a "base love," the province of the "Common Aphrodite," who was born of heterosexual intercourse. Noble love, however, is love of the spiritual in the physical under the aegis of the "Heavenly Aphrodite," who "has no female strain in her but springs entirely from the male."[26] Thus Pausanias can elevate male homoeroticism that combines the physical and the spiritual in opposition to the lower heterosexual form. By contrast Aristophanes in his speech recognizes the reality of the existent world in his myth of hermaphrodite origins that I have already referred to. Thus, when male and female, male and male, and female and female cohabit, they are uniting with parts of their original whole-natured being severed by Zeus. I think it reasonable to suppose that Plato recognized the validity of Aristophanes' view of the real world but then qualified it in Socrates' famous concluding speech.

However, Plato does not make Socrates speak directly: for the first time a woman's voice enters the dialogue. Socrates says that he learned the wisdom of love from Diotima. Diotima recognizes the reality of love in procreation, but procreation is in turn nothing but a manifestation of the yearning for immortality by replenishing society with new members.[27] It is an avenue through which ordinary mortals can achieve immortality. This applies to the world of birds and beasts also. When they desire progeny, they are "plagued by the disease of Love" and "sick for intercourse."[28] Thus it is the desire for progeny (what I have called "womb-passion") that produces the lovesickness, not the other way around. But this desire is a veiled recognition of the desire for immortality, albeit through an inferior vehicle. "So don't be surprised if everything naturally values its own offspring, because it is for the sake of immortality that everything shows this zeal, which is Love."[29] However, if the love for immortality is the real underlying (unconscious) reason, then it means there are other and nobler ways of seeking immortality. "Now some people are pregnant in body, and for this reason turn more to women and pursue love in that way, providing themselves through childbirth with immortality and remembrance and happiness, as they think, for all time to come."[30] But for the nobler ones this is unsatisfactory; they "are pregnant in soul" or "long to beget spiritually, not physically."[31]

To better achieve spiritual ends one must move away from the progenial impulse, a movement from heterosexuality to male homoeroticism. Thus, a noble person when young will fall in love with another beautiful male and "beget beautiful ideas" through that partnership. But then he realizes that a single beautiful person is only a manifestation of a more general beauty found in other males, and with this realization "he must become a lover of all beautiful bodies, and he must think that this wild gaping *[agape]* after one body is a small thing and despise it." Then, says Diotima, he will soon recognize that it is beauty of soul that matters and beyond that Beauty in its unalloyed essence. "But how would it be, in our view, if someone got to see the Beautiful itself, absolute, pure, unmixed, not polluted by human flesh or colors or any other great nonsense of mortality, but if he could see the divine Beauty itself in its one form?" That person is one who possesses true virtue, and "the love of the gods belongs to anyone who has given birth to true virtue and nourished it, and if any human being could be immortal, it would be he."[32]

The nature of that immortality is left unsaid in Diotima's speech, but we know what it is from *Phaedrus* and *Timaeus*. It is the final emancipation from the rebirth cycle and the apprehension of the transcendental reality of the Forms. This position links with Plato's denigration of passion; ordinary people caught in the procreative net cannot achieve salvation; they are expressing their urge for immortality but through a futile vehicle that only promotes progeny and thereby the continuity of the rebirth cycle. Even the nobler copulating males who can conjoin physical and spiritual love must graduate from that point to the "Platonic" form of love before they can achieve the great salvific vision.

Let me phrase the situation differently: Diotima is a response to Aristophanes' view of multiple, if not polymorphously perverse, eroticism and to Pausanias's ignoring of lesbians. As a wise woman she starts by admitting the possibility of a noble heterosexual love and soon downgrades it; then she admits to a nobler male homoerotic one, which is in turn downgraded to a passion for immortality, not its realization. The process is one of progressive sublimation, about which Plato has more to say than Freud. Diotima's discourse on love's hierarchy illustrates partially the homoerotic career of Plato's Socrates. In the *Gorgias* one is not sure whether Socrates' love for Alcibiades is physical; in the *Symposium* it clearly is not. There, like Gandhi experimenting with sexuality by sleeping with young girls but abstaining from physical relations, Socrates too can sleep with Alcibiades. But, says Alcibiades, "my night with Socrates went no further than if I had spent it with my own father or older brother!"[33] By the time *Timaeus* was written, in Plato's old age, he must have lost his passion anyway, and Diotima could be dispensed with and along with her any recognition of erotic love between men and women.

The idealized version of Plato's utopian women having capabilities equal to those of men does not alter this picture. In the *Republic* women have a role consonant with the way they have been created in the *Timaeus* myth. They simply act out the role for which they were originally designed. They are breeders of good stock for the ideal state, and in bearing children they can satisfy their "womb-passion," as defined in the *Timaeus*. When Plato talks about love in the *Republic,* it is once again idealistically homoerotic.[34] But Plato is not self-consciously misogynist: women's lack of sexual passion is part of their nature (*Timaeus*) or secondary to their progenial impulse *(Symposium)* and does not inhibit them from having capabilities similar to those of men. In performing men's tasks women might sometimes look ludicrous (when, for example, as convention dictates, they have to exercise without their clothes in the gymnasium). Here also Plato ignores nude women's capacity to arouse sexual impulses in men; he is concerned with their awkwardness and enjoins people not to laugh at them.[35] There is no emancipatory message for women in the *Republic.*

## ETHICIZATION AND SOTERIOLOGY IN THE PLATONIC DIALOGUES

Plato's soteriology has an abstract quality that is rooted in the mathematics and physics of early Pythagoreanism rather than in the passion, drama, and initiatory ecstasy that one associates with Orphism and the mystery religions in general.[36] In addition, as far as his rebirth eschatology was concerned, he was probably "influenced" by the popular tradition represented by Pindar, as I suggested earlier. This is not surprising given his several sojourns in Sicily. Plato, in contrast to Pindar, was a soteriological innovator. He was also not a founder of a religious brotherhood, quite unlike Pythagoras. His academy, although elitist, was not a seminary either; originally a garden, it contained a limited public space, not an open arena for the conversion of the masses. However, it was possible for Plato, unlike the Upanishadic guru or the Pythagorean virtuoso, to *imagine* a larger congregation. Although Plato was a political and ethical thinker, there is little to suggest that he wanted to convert and save the *ordinary* public—a futile task in terms of his own elitist thinking. His social and political ideologies, as well as his religious beliefs, were publicly available to be debated, even though they were effectively restricted to male intellectuals.

Plato, then, was interested in everyday morality and public ethics even in early works such as the *Gorgias*. In this work Socrates plainly says that the orator (one who addresses a public) "must be upright and understand right and wrong" and ought to persuade listeners to be good citizens. An important theme running through the text argues for just punishment and proclaims, further, that "wrong doing is the worst harm that can befall a wrong doer" (*Grg.*, 509). The ideal therefore is to live without "sin" because "to enter the next world with one's soul loaded with sins is the supreme misfortune" (*Grg.*, 522). But although he could and did imagine a lay audience, his vision was limited by his elitist thinking. Basically, it seems to me that he is simply reaffirming the kind of prior ethicization of the otherworld represented in the Acragas of Pindar, even though Pindar's extant verses do not mention Tartarus per se, as Plato's do. Perhaps Plato takes his ideas self-consciously from Homer: but whereas Tartarus was for Homer a place where the Titans were imprisoned, for Plato, following Hesiod and more particularly the Pythagorean Philolaus, it is a place for the "wicked and godless."[37] It seems, then, that Plato inherited the ethicization of the otherworld from prior traditions but developed it further in his own way. Yet it is soteriology, not otherworldly ethics, that is important for Plato. Let me therefore cross-examine Platonic ethicization and soteriology of rebirth.

In the myth of Er and in the *Phaedo* there is step 1 of ethicization in a scheme of otherworldly rewards and punishments; this step is followed by "free choice" (in practice unfree habit), which obviates rebirth in terms of ethics (step 2 of ethicization). Salvation is available to the true philosopher, who after the third rebirth (note the Pindaric and Empedoclean connection) can achieve a mode of being that permits spiritual fellowship with the gods and contemplation of the transcendental vision of Reality. The philosopher ceases to be reborn in the world of becoming, whereas other human beings continue in it until the tenth rebirth, when the cycle of rebirth lasting ten thousand years ends and a new one begins. Unfortunately, we are not told what happens to ordinary humans at the end of the cycle, leaving unresolved the crucial question of the soteriological destiny of ordinary folk that the Pindaric ode mentioned. We do know that some are left over, and these would be, at the very least, evil people and innumerable animals confined to Tartarus and other unpleasant realms.

At a first reading the absence of step 2 in ethicization appears to be contradicted in the *Timaeus* account. Here we are told that those given to immorality, cowardice, and folly in the original community of men were reborn as women, birds, insects, animals, reptiles, and fish (and some men). However, one must remember that Plato is dealing here with the original creation of the various beings living in the world. The *Timaeus* is the charter-myth that accounts for the *origin* of women and other creatures owing to the immorality and cowardice of men in the first incarnation. Women and other animals belonged to the second incarnation (the first *re*incarnation). Once the full complement of mortal beings has been created, the rebirth cycle goes on in the manner of the myth of Er, *Phaedo,* and *Phaedrus. Timaeus* also repeats the explanation in Er and *Phaedo* in respect to humans born as donkeys and such: it simply repeats the kind of life one led after that first incarnation and subsequent reincarnations. Once one is in the flow of the rebirth cycle at the first reincarnation (second incarnation), punishment for right and wrong automatically follows, after which the task of the allocation of one's rebirth status is by a different set of deities—Lachesis, Ananke, Atropos, and others. The gods who originally created mortal forms are not involved in what happens to their creation after the first reincarnation; they too, like the Demiurge himself, and for similar reasons, have become otiose and uninvolved in the world of becoming. A new ethical dynamic takes over mortal existence, but it temporarily ends in step 1 of the ethicization process, when rewards and punishments are meted out after death. As in the karmic eschatology this seems to be an inevitable process: the good go to "heaven" (wherever it is located) and the bad are punished in Tartarus and other places (the details of which we are not told) and then for a thousand years must travel a dusty road. According to Plato these rewards and punishments replicate in the eschatological realm the kinds of rewards and punishments that people experience in their life on earth as a consequence of virtuous or immoral living. It is after this that people appear before Lachesis and are given the illusory "free choice." When rebirth occurs, morality takes over once again in the human world, and this process continues until the tenth rebirth, when the cycle ends, as depicted in figure 11.

What would be the result, however, if one were to *imagine* that Plato continued the rebirth dynamic postulated after the first reincarnation such that the scheme of rewards and punishments was carried a further step into subsequent rebirths? In this hypothetical situation Platonism would inevitably have developed a karmic eschatology. Moreover, in such an imaginary experiment, one cannot cut off the karmic flow at the tenth incarnation unless there is a mechanism that guarantees universal salvation of the sort formulated by some Indian thinkers, such as the Ājīvikas.

Some classicists have attributed to Plato step 2 of ethicization, but I have argued against this hypothesis. I have suggested that Plato inherited an ethicized rebirth cosmology, such as the one represented in Pindar, and that he reformulated it in his own unique speculative manner. Thus ethicization step 1 is not Plato's own invention but one element in his ethical thought. His "higher" ethical thought, as I have already indicated, is founded on a key principle: it is the body that keeps the human soul from understanding its true nature, and this is expressed in the asceticism of the *Phaedo* and in the myth of the charioteers in the *Phaedrus*. The violation of conventional morality, stupidity, and folly adds to the contamination of the soul, but other things also do, as, for example, all human passions. The true philosopher "has abandoned bodily pleasures and adornments, as foreign to his purpose and likely to do more harm than good."[38] This harsh asceticism gets modified somewhat in the nonsoteriological texts such as the *Republic* and *Philebus*, but it remained a cardinal part of the doctrine.

Important differences aside, Plato's philosophy shares key components with early Buddhism, which has a much more complex soteriology but not as complex a cosmology. First, Plato says that one must be emancipated

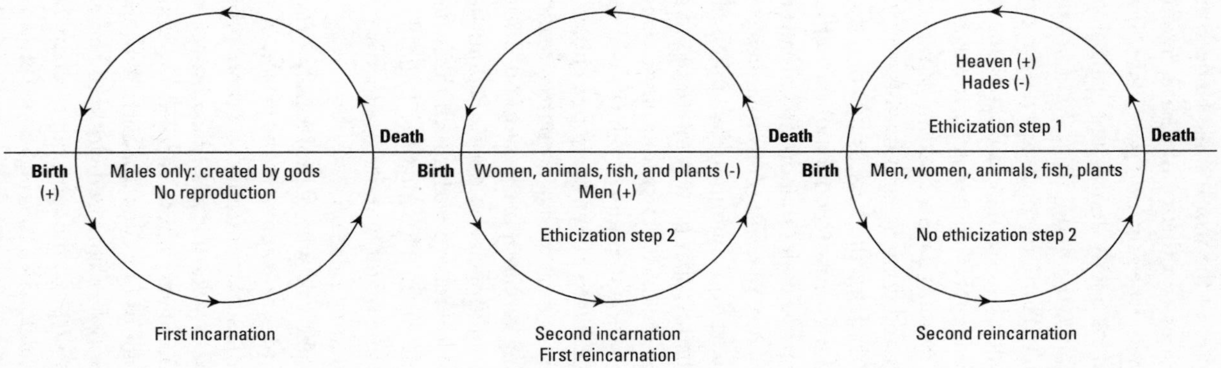


Figure 11. Platonic rebirth cycle. Reincarnation is based on “free choice” and/or replication of the previous lifestyle. According to the theory of memory/recollection, rebirth memories occur only under special conditions. Each rebirth cycle lasts one thousand years; there are ten such cycles to be completed, short-circuited only by the sage.

from the body, which is, in a sense, to be emancipated from the world, although he does not systematically follow through with this idea, as do the Buddhist analyses of the world's ills. Underlying Plato's conception of the body's passions is a theory of desire, again spelled out like the Buddhist one. Second, true salvation is available only to the philosopher who has controlled his bodily desires and leads an ascetic existence. The true philosopher is like the Buddhist arahant, a practitioner of death in order to transcend it. Third, the ordinary person cannot hope to achieve salvation easily, much less so than in Buddhism, where salvation is the ideal goal for all and laypersons can achieve it, albeit in some distant future. Fourth, both systems have a doctrine of free choice, but each gives different emphases and content; and both have constraints that hinder free choice. Plato, like Jaina thinkers, argues that the body, via sinful acts, stains the soul and prevents freedom and the achievement of salvation; in Buddhism it is karmic ethics that directly affects the path to salvation.

Let me now spell out, in terms of my imaginary experiment, why this second step of ethicization could not have taken place in Plato's soteriology, in spite of the fact that he was interested in ordinary morality as well as the "higher ethics."[39] First, one must remember that Plato inherited a perfectly rational model of rebirth wherein ethicization effectively stops at step 1. Plato's doctrine of free choice is not altogether satisfactory because it is in actuality an unfree reality. Do ethics operate when a human being is reborn in this world of scarcity and want, riches and glory, with its multiplicity of ills, its hedonistic desires? Plato's answer is that people are reborn with much the same character that they had in previous existences. This might be logically satisfactory, appealing to reason, but one might wonder whether it is a psychologically or existentially satisfactory solution.

Second, one might ask why a profoundly original and speculative thinker such as Plato was trapped in the prison of the preexisting tradition. Why could he not have introduced a more profound idea of rebirth ethics (not necessarily a karmic one) into his scheme of things? I have said that ethicization everywhere entailed the conversion of ordinary morality into a religious one concomitantly with the creation of congregations. Plato inherited an ethicized world of hell and heaven from Pindaric (and possibly Orphic) thought, but to create a rebirth ethic would have required the creation of a congregation. This was impossible in Plato's academy, which was confined to a very small elite that excluded women. Plato might well have imagined an *audience;* but he could not possibly have created a *congregation.* His was an exclusive soteriology for the philosopher. In his idealized republic the people of the polis are simply incapable of ever apprehending the true reality, the world of Forms.[40] The philosopher is the only kind of being who can transcend bodily desires and worldly wants, who can glimpse the original pure condition from whence he sprang. It is he who can ultimately experience the vision of the Realm of Forms. Like the Upanishadic guru, Plato was not interested in the salvation of common men, women, or Śūdras.

## REGROUPING: REBIRTH, MEMORY, AND RETROCOGNITION

No theory of rebirth can avoid confrontation with problems of memory and retrocognition. If I have lived before, then shouldn't I be able to remember my past? The past is a reservoir of memory that is available for tapping. Yet everyone knows that this memory is not available for most people; hence, rebirth theories have an inbuilt assumption that in the process of being born, one's past memory becomes obliterated. And the deeper one gets into past lives, the more difficult it is to retrieve memory, hence the Amerindian belief that for the most part only the immediately preceding existence can be recollected by a few ordinary persons. Further, these memories are rarely deliberately cultivated by the actively reasoning consciousness. Thoughts *appear* before the person, seemingly spontaneously, or are provoked by standardized cues, for example, when someone whose rebirth identity is already known by birthmarks or other indices may dream about his or her previous-life persona. As I have stated, past-life recollections provide validation of the truth of rebirth.

In addition to ordinary folk there are extraordinary people who can cultivate the art of recollecting the past, not only of themselves but of others. We have already met them in shamans and other seers, in "awakened" ones like the Buddha and Mahavira and the arahants of South Asian religions, and in virtuosos like Pythagoras. For example, it might be possible for a shaman to send his soul to capture the soul of a person about to be born, find out its life history and then inform those who are awaiting its arrival in the human world. By contrast, the virtuoso arahants of Buddhist texts recover their pasts and the pasts of others through a mental act of deep concentration.

The mythic Pythagoras is closer to the mythic Buddha in this regard. In the probable mythos that I have invented Pythagoras did practice concentration, but whether he used this for retrocognition of the past is not clear. We do not know whether his retrocognitive gifts were shamanic or given by a god such as Apollo or Hermes, as some believed. We know that Porphyry reporting Empedocles' view of Pythagoras's retrocognitive powers claimed that the latter could easily see things that happened in "ten and even twenty human lives."[41] Iamblichus noted that the recollection of past lives was part of Pythagorean education. And in Heraclides' beautiful account Pythagoras could remember the wanderings of his own soul in animals and plants, the fate of souls in Hades, and his last rebirth, owing to a gift given by Hermes.[42] Such a gift could coexist with meditative ascesis.

According to Heraclides the soul retains the knowledge acquired in previous existences, and this knowledge is available to a person like Pythagoras.[43] Recovery of the past is also a recovery of knowledge not just about persons who lived before but about cosmological matters, such as the knowledge provided by shamans in their out-of-the-body journeys. It is from such retrieved knowledge that rebirth eschatologies are invented, and they in turn affect the personal cosmic experiences of the virtuosos and help to structure the narratives of their individual experiences. But what happens if a religious thinker has not developed the capacity for retrocognition? Such a thinker will have to rely on those within his or her own religious or soteriological tradition who do have such a capacity.

Plato represents Socrates as someone who believed in rebirth but lacked special retrocognitive powers. To convince the youthful intellectuals in fourth-century B.C.E. Athens of the truth of the rebirth cosmology, Socrates recounts the experience of Er, who did visit the otherworld and gave him a firsthand account of it. Although Er's cosmological knowledge is detailed, he does not offer a doctrine of salvation in his discourse. Plato thus had to provide a soteriology based on previous traditions—Pythagorean, Orphic, and "Pindaric"—reinforced by his own reified Reason. Although Plato's Reason has inner affinity with Pythagoreanism in its intellectualism, it has little to do with the spiritual asceses that defined the Orphic tradition or the mystery religions in general.

It is through Reason that Plato justifies the key notion of the soul on which his soteriology rests. Although Reason is fallible, Plato is convinced that his soteriology is true even if one cannot be sure about the details. Thus he says in *Phaedo:* "Of course, no reasonable man ought to insist that the facts are exactly as I have described them. But that either this or something very like it is a true account of our souls and their future habitations—since we have clear evidence that the soul is immortal—this, I think, is both a reasonable contention and a belief worth risking; for the risk is a noble one" (*Phd.,* 114d). No such risk exists as far as the truth-value of Er's testimony is concerned. The *Phaedo* reference does not imply that Plato was constructing an elaborate metaphor or a demystified allegory, as some think. It simply indicated the fallibility of Reason, which cannot guarantee truth.

Reason also permits Plato to recover the past retrocognitively, but he implies that this can occur only passively—at least in his initial formulation in *Meno* in a well-known experiment. Here Socrates tells the young Thessalian Meno that the soul is immortal and that although one thinks it ceases to exist at death, it is reborn many times over. Consequently, the soul can remember what occurred before; therefore, what one calls learning and knowledge is nothing but recollection. To finally clinch the issue, Socrates poses a geometrical puzzle to Meno's slave to solve, which he does. Meno knows that his slave is not an educated person and could not have solved the problem on his own. The solution must therefore have retrocognitively emerged from previous memory, thus proving Socrates' thesis on memory, which in turn rests on the reality of rebirth. Nowhere in *Meno* does Socrates show how the soul communicated this knowledge to Meno's slave, who seems to have been a kind of passive receptacle. Socrates' proof is so manifestly poor that one can only assume that Plato himself implicitly and uncritically ("doxologically") believed in both rebirth and the soul's passive cognition of the past at this period in his life.

Such ideas must derive from the broader Pythagorean heritage, especially the kind of popular sources that Pindar used. For example, both Porphyry and Eudemus attribute to Pythagoras the view that events repeat themselves in a cyclic process and that nothing is altogether new. These kinds of beliefs can be inferred from any rebirth eschatology: if I am an ancestor reborn, then it is certainly possible for me, in principle at least, to tap past memory and recollect the events of my past life and with it the knowledges and skills I once possessed. Given the commitment to these beliefs, it might even be reasonable to extend the argument and say that the past contains a reservoir of knowledge and that the religious virtuoso can tap that reservoir through divergent forms of ascesis. But to say that no *new* knowledge is possible is not entailed or warranted by any rebirth eschatology or its implicit doctrine of memory.

Let me now examine Plato's important theory of memory in the *Phaedo*, which qualifies the account in *Meno:*

1. Initially Plato's Socrates states that "coming to life again [rebirth] is a fact"; related to it is the fact "that the living come

from the dead," and this is because "the souls of the dead exist." Cebes, his interlocutor, then speaks of a theory "often described to us—that what we call learning is just recollection." If that is the case, then recollection is impossible "unless our souls existed somewhere before they entered this human shape." For Cebes this suggests that the "soul is immortal" (*Phd.*, 72d–73a). Perhaps because of his poor logic, Simmias, the other person associated with this dialogue, wants proof. Thus Cebes now brings out what he should have mentioned earlier, namely, the kind of experiment in *Meno* as proof of recollections from previous births.

2. At this point Socrates intervenes with his lucid logical discourse on memory. To be reminded of anything, one must have first known it sometime or other. Knowledge is recollection, but it comes "in a particular way." I might see my beloved's musical instrument, which has no resemblance to her, but this object helps me to conjure up a picture of my beloved. I see my youthful friend Cebes, and I conjure up Simmias, another youthful friend. Or I see a portrait of Simmias, and I conjure up Simmias. Thus the trigger itself may be similar or dissimilar to the object recollected. Even when one is reminded of something on the basis of similarity, one is conscious whether the resemblance is perfect or only partial (73d–e). This is what is called recollection; but recollection is especially significant in relation to things long forgotten.

3. "Here is a further step," says Socrates. We will all admit that there is something like perfect equality—not the equality of stick to stick or stone to stone but beyond all that and distinct from it to an idea of absolute equality (73d). Where then did we get that knowledge? It was from those particular examples mentioned earlier. "Was it not from equal sticks and stones and other equal objects that we get the notion of equality, although it is quite distinct from them . . . [for] equal sticks and stones sometimes, without changing themselves, appear equal to one person and unequal to another?" Thus, although we get the ideal of equality from seeing equal objects, the notion of equality itself is distinct from those objects. Further, those material objects that I perceive as equal may not be perceived as equal

by another person. And no one would confuse these seemingly equal objects with "absolute equality." Yet the fact is that these very material objects gave us the knowledge of absolute equality, although they (such things as equal sticks and stones) are distinct from it (74a–d).

4. Now suppose someone were to see some object and say that it resembles something but is a "poor imitation" of it. It follows that that person must have had a prior knowledge of it (that is, a knowledge of that which the material object imitates).

5. This, says Socrates, is his position with equal things and absolute equality. To render it differently: equal objects are poor imitations of absolute equality; they can at best imitate an absolute equality. Although I measure the material object in absolute terms, I myself have had no contact with absolute equality in the way I have with equal sticks and stones. Therefore "we must have had some previous knowledge of [absolute] equality before the time when we first saw equal things and realized that they were striving after [absolute] equality, but fell short of it" (74e).

6. Now there is a subtle but important shift in the argument. I must apprehend the material object (equal sticks and stones) with my senses, but I could not possibly apprehend that which the material object imitates (absolute equality) with my senses. If this is true, we must have gotten the notion of absolute equality *before* we began to see or hear or tap our other senses. "Otherwise we would never have realized by using it as a standard for comparison, that all equal objects of sense are desirous of being like it, but are only imperfect copies" (75a). But note: we obtained our senses only at birth, yet we obtained our knowledge of equality before we obtained our senses. Therefore, it follows that we must have obtained the notion of perfect equality before birth.

7. Plato then comes to the crux of his argument: "Then if we obtained it before our birth, and possessed it before we were born, we had knowledge, both before and at the time of our birth, not only of equality and relative magnitudes, but of all absolute standards. Our present argument applies no more

> to equality than it does to absolute beauty, goodness, uprightness, holiness, and, as I maintain, all those characteristics which we designate in discussions by the term 'absolute'" (75e). The knowledge is there but we have forgotten it, in which case forgetting is simply "the loss of knowledge." Learning is the recovery of that knowledge "by the exercise of our senses upon sensible objects" in the same rational manner when we figured out the idea of absolute equality by sensing equal objects like sticks and stones. But this knowledge comes from before birth; if this is so, there must be some entity that is the repository of that knowledge, and that entity must be the soul. "Then our souls had a previous existence, Simmias, before they took on this human shape; they were independent of our bodies; and they were possessed of intelligence" (76a–e). Plato's Socrates not only has adduced rational proof for the existence of the soul and of Ideal Forms, as most scholars have read this text; he has also simultaneously proved the reality of rebirth and the special form of retrocognition based on it. Further, he has radically reformulated the thesis on memory formulated in *Meno*. We are dealing now with a theory of memory that says that absolute truths are not new, unlike those "truths" associated with the world of becoming.[44]

Let me now summarize the rest of the argument. It seems that the route just taken brings Plato to his theory of Ideal Forms, although he does not name them as such in this text. These Forms were there before us, and they can be validated by our sense perception of the external world, by inferring the universal from the particular. If this is accurate, all "absolute realities" such as Beauty and Goodness exist before us and will continue to exist afterward, and the ordinary sense perceptions exist nominally as copies of those Forms. Plato now can link this with a previous argument that the soul existed before the body. The soul too has had a previous existence, and if the Ideal Forms exist, so must souls; and if souls exist, so must Ideal Forms. These share the same characteristics: they are noncomposite, invariable, and invisible, whereas their opposites, namely, the body and the objects of the physical world, are composite, variable, and visible. It therefore follows that if the body and world of phenomena perish, the soul and the absolute realities do not. The latter share the qualities of the divine, having originated in it; therefore, one should not be afraid of "practicing death." "A soul in this state makes its way to the invisible, which is like itself, the divine and immortal and wise, and arriving there it can be happy, having rid itself of confusion, ignorance, fear, violent desires and the other human ills and, as it is said of the initiates [of the Orphic rites], truly spend the rest of time with the gods."[45] The reference to the mysteries indicates that for Socrates the soul's residence with gods (who, we know from the *Timaeus*, are stars) is a doctrine of salvation that parallels the Orphic, but it is one that can be realized only by a reflective philosophical elite.

Let us now see whether the examination of related eschatologies will cast some light on Plato's own. From previous discussions we know that the "soul" is the one entity that flows through life in any rebirth eschatology. In some eschatologies, such as those of the Trobrianders, the Dene Tha, and the Druze, there is a body of souls that move through rebirth cycles, incarnating in the physical bodies of humans, very much like the souls of Plato's cosmology. Even when this notion of a soul is rejected, as in the Buddhist doctrine of *anatta*, or "no-soul," something has to take its place to demonstrate continuity from one existence to another, even if it is not strictly "rebirth" but "rebecoming" *(punarbhava)*.

It is fascinating to find in the Buddha's own time soul doctrines similar to Plato's and others like his. The "Brahmajāla Sutta" mentions a theory labeled by the Buddha as "eternalism," or *sassata-vāda*. The Buddha says that some samanas and Brahmins proclaim that the soul and the world are eternal and that these samaṇas and Brahmins have come to that conclusion on the basis of their retrocognitive knowledge of past births, up to several hundreds of thousands. Because such a person has been born and reborn continuously, he or she thinks: "Eternal is the soul; and the world, giving birth to nothing new, is steadfast as a mountain peak, as a pillar firmly fixed; and though these living creatures transmigrate and pass away, fall from one state of existence and spring up in another, yet they are for ever and ever."[46] The Buddha condemns the eternalists as "addicted to logic and reasoning" and lacking deep intuitive judgments that permit them to see the transitoriness of the soul. The eternalists certainly represent one logical way a rebirth eschatology can be transformed into another form or structure. These ideas are *expectable* philosophical speculations on rebirth arising from a logic that thinkers from disparate cultures were compelled to recognize.

Yet was the Buddha himself wholly exempt from a theory of memory implicit in the doctrine that there is nothing new in an *absolute* sense? The Buddhist karmic eschatology postulated the lack of all essences, including that invisible but Platonically or Upanishadically knowable entity, the soul. The soul too shares the features of temporality and impermanence that are true of the phenomenal world. Hence there is no soul that spills over from incarnation to incarnation, only a continual "rebecoming" propelled by karmic forces. Yet in this eternally ceaseless flow there is something enduring, a still point, nirvana. No wonder Buddhists found it difficult to describe it; and some, such as that radical Buddhist deconstructionist Nagarjuna, went so far as to say that nirvana itself shares with samsara features of conditionality and impermanence.

If only for argument's sake let us agree with Nagarjuna that nirvana is samsara. Nevertheless, that idea was based on the Four Noble Truths discovered by Gautama Buddha: that life is suffering (unsatisfactoriness) and characterized by impermanence; that the cause of suffering is craving or attachment; that there is a way of overcoming craving through the "Noble Eightfold Path"; and that the cessation of craving through meditative regimes will result in that ineffable state, or nonstate, nirvana, achievable in this very existence. This truth has always been there, and the Buddha, following the example of previous Buddhas, discovered, not invented, it. As one late canonical text put it: "[T]he words of the Buddhas are eternal and sure."[47] The truth emerged through the Buddha's inward meditative contemplation, leading to a deep penetrative understanding quite different from the formal Reason of the Platonic variety mediated by the active agency of the thinking ego.

Scholars as well as laymen have been puzzled that the Buddha's teaching has been described in texts as *sanātana dhamma,* the perpetual or all-abiding teaching, even though the Buddha condemned eternalism and insisted on the impermanence of all conditioned things, including the doctrine itself. Nevertheless, the doctrine is "eternal" in the very unconventional sense that it is always there waiting to be discovered. If the Buddha discovered the truth of existence, then there are others who could do the same when the memory of that truth has faded. Thus there have been named Buddhas who have known the truth—seven, twenty-four, twenty-eight Buddhas—not to mention innumerable and unknown minor Buddhas who have discovered the truth but have not proclaimed it to the world. And all named Buddhas are born, live, and die in almost identical ways in an ongoing myth of an eternal return that Buddhists have formulated in later texts. It is true that the truth the Buddhas discover is not the truth of the soul of the Pythagorean, Platonic, or Amerindian variety or that of the Eternalists with whom the Buddha was conducting an argument about the existence of absolute truth. The Buddha deconstructs that truth to put in its place a truth about that deconstruction. Unpalatable absolute truths have been displaced for a more palatable one. By this I mean that one might find it easier to climb the edge of the razor than to escape the "paradox of thought"—the idea that although one can state that others' views are false, or that there is no possibility of discovering truths, or that truths can be deconstructed, it is much more difficult, if not impossible, to deny the truth-value of one's own stance, even if that stance proclaims the truth of deconstruction.

## REASON, CONVICTION, AND ESCHATOLOGY IN PLATONIC, BUDDHIST, AND AMERINDIAN THOUGHT

It is in relation to soteriology rather than political theory that one can properly appreciate the complicated role that Reason plays in Platonic thought. Reason is the objective faculty that permits one to understand the nature of the world, both the external and the internal. Plato is one of the earliest proponents of "methodological objectivism," namely that the subject we study is methodologically separate and unaffected by the studying subject. The faculty that one utilizes to understand the world and what it contains is Reason, the reflective-cum-ratiocinative element of human consciousness that is available for cultivation by anyone but in reality is the special prerogative of the philosopher. Because the philosopher is a person of virtue, one who has cultivated the soul and recognized its immortal nature and essential difference from the body, Reason itself cannot be divorced from virtue but is intrinsic to it. However, whereas Reason is inextricably tied to soteriology, soteriology is not tied to Reason in the same intrinsic sense. Why do I say this?

It seems to me that the *Phaedo* provides the answer. This is the dialogue in which Socrates awaits his death the next morning. Socrates is filled with a passionate conviction of the soul's immortality and, in his case at least, of its imminent release from the rebirth cycle. For Plato's Socrates there is no personal doubt regarding the soteriology that I sketched earlier. Yet looking at this text from another viewpoint, one may think that Socrates' personal conviction is not simply an inference made from Reason. Reason provides a rationale or a defense of a prior soteriological conviction and is epistemologically locked into that conviction. The various cosmological and cosmogonic discourses ground that personal conviction in an acceptable framework in Reason; or, to put it in more radical fashion, Logos itself is the mythos that frames the core conviction. Further, Reason is not infallible. Hence, the myths of cosmogenesis in *Timaeus* and of the soul's descent in *Phaedrus* are probable stories about which sensible persons may disagree, but their broad outlines are expected to produce an eventual intersubjective consensus in reasonable people—among Plato's followers at least. I think that for Plato the cosmological and cosmogonic myths are not intrinsic to conviction; they are what Reason has created as a support for the soteriology.

In light of the preceding argument let me come back to the epistemological status of the myth of Er. It seems to me that for Plato's Socrates this myth is something that is accepted at face value, for myths are fictions carrying allegorical or symbolic import only for those who have demythologized them. Although Plato, like the Buddha, uses myths allegorically, he can no more than any of us escape mythic convictions. Unlike the cosmogonic ones, the myth of Er is also a piece of *evidence,* although not the kind of evidence that the protagonists of the European Enlightenment (or Plato's pupil Aristotle) would generally approve of. Hence it would be wrong to extrapolate Plato's enlightened Reason from that of the European thinkers of later times. Many thinkers of the European Enlightenment could easily believe in forms of rationalized Deism but not the equation of mythos with logos. This did not present a problem during the period of the Greek Enlightenment, when the products of what later Europeans would consider nonreason were perfectly acceptable. Thus Plato himself believed in the Delphic oracle, as did the intellectuals of the time; the evidence of the *Phaedrus* indicates that he believed in such things as possession by spirits and other forms of mantic madness; and the Socrates of the *Apology* believed unashamedly in oracles and mantic dreams and divine signs sent by his "god." Such lifeforms were not validated by Reason, either, but were accepted on what one can legitimately call empirical evidence, a form of evidentiary truth that reinforces faith and is characteristic of the Northwest Coast Indians, the Inuit, Buddhists, and laypeople everywhere.

Many "reasonable people" sharing common values might believe in the validity of such things as spirit healing on the basis that it works and that its efficacy can be empirically demonstrated. Whether its empirical efficacy results from a self-fulfilling prophecy, or whatever, is immaterial to the public consciousness of its truth-value. Similarly, I think that the truth of the myth of Er rests on a comparable assumption; Er tells Socrates of his own firsthand experience of an "out-of-body experience" but one framed in the cultural context of shamanic-type beliefs adapted to a Greek rebirth eschatology. There must surely have been persons like 'Askadut-Er in Greece of that time and especially among those who were influenced by the mysteries and forms of Bacchic or Dionysiac Orphism. The Socrates-

Plato who believed in the Delphic oracle could easily have believed in the descent and return from the underworld, particularly as evidentiary support of his personal convictions. It is no accident that the Greeks in general had a term for the underworld descent, *katabasis,* and both ordinary people and intellectuals accepted it as a reality.

Nevertheless Reason is apotheosized as the key ratiocinative principle in Plato's thought, whether as a rationalization of personally held convictions (*Phaedo, Phaedrus, Timaeus*) or as the fount for the discovery of new knowledge of the world (the Ideal Forms, for example) or for thinking out the polities of the ideal republic. Nothing in Plato indicates a personal commitment to a mystical or passionate *(enthousiasmos)* way of seeking knowledge. The Reason that animates Plato's Socrates is inimical to a *mysterium tremendum et fascinans* of the sort found in the mystery religions. Further, some Bacchic rites pertaining to public possession and processional display of emotional religiosity and to private initiation rites have as their soteriological goal emancipation from the rebirth cycle itself. The soteriological journey enacted in such mysteries is a kind of experience that is at once inner and outer. There is no attempt to rationalize the experience in terms of Reason. Probably Reason is hostile to salvation in Orphic mysteries.

The Buddhist Awakening is different, it seems to me. The Buddha initially engages in all forms of bodily mortification in order to find the Truth. These exercises do not succeed, and his Awakening is the discovery of a special form of ascesis conjoined to soteriological knowledge. That ascesis is meditation; that knowledge is that of the Four Noble Truths and what follows from them. Reason comes afterward as a discursive strategy for proclaiming the truth. Although important, it is not the way of discovering truth but of "rationalizing" it, giving it conceptual form and a logical and argumentative rigor. Such a situation creates no problem for a religious virtuoso like the Buddha to conjoin a conceptual imperative with such things as "miracles" and shamanic-type soul journeyings. The question of the latter's being irrational only emerges if Reason or Rationality has already been reified, as was the case with European Enlightenment thinkers or to a lesser degree with Plato or his Socrates.

What do the foregoing reflections on the three Enlightenments tell us about the truth ways of the Northwest Coast Indians and Inuit? I have already stated that in the latter there is no concern with salvation or the transcendence of the rebirth cycle; neither is there any concern with the Platonic idea of Reason or any variation thereof that states that the world could be understood systematically in terms of the active ratiocinative consciousness. However, whether we are talking of the Greeks, the Buddhists, or the Amerindians, the central validating principle of religious experience is a form of "empiricism." Without getting into the hopelessly vexed question of "rationality" one can say that here is a domain where it is possible to effect consensus among reasonable people. Empirical validation manifests itself in the multiple techniques of discovering the identity of the neonate; it also occurs in the intersubjective consensus regarding the spiritual powers of shamans and the efficacy of shamanic healing. Needless to say, the kind of "everyday empiricism" that I have highlighted is not to be conflated with the reification and conceptual elaboration of that empiricism into the philosophical system or scientific ideology that one nowadays associates with English thought.

What then is the empirical significance of 'Askadut's *katabasis?* This case does not produce evidence in the ordinary sense; it is a taken-for-granted story or myth, something handed down from generation to generation. Unlike Er, 'Askadut does not narrate his experiences to a known person directly; therefore, although few would question the truth-value of his story, it is one that cannot be empirically validated as a truth. On the other hand, the various "tests" of neonatal identity contain empirical validations, as do shamanic cures.[48] But whereas the 'Askadut story is a myth for us, it is not an *improbable mythos* for Tlingit Indians. Why so? Because empirically acceptable accounts of similar phenomena would be related to Tlingit by their shamans, occasionally now, but more commonly during the heyday of their culture. Similarly, in shamanic healing rituals ordinary Tlingit would hear, if not see, the shaman fly to cosmological realms to retrieve the lost soul of a sick person.

It is the shaman or a similar figure who represents an extraordinary or ecstatic form of religious experience that parallels what Nietzsche, in *The Birth of Tragedy,* labeled "Dionysian." Similar models are available for ordinary persons—in such things as the vision quest for a spirit guardian or in the rituals of the Kwakiutl Winter Ceremonial. None of this is articulated as a soteriological quest, as in Buddhism or in some of the Orphic mysteries. And although the shamanic myth is an empirically acceptable reality for Socrates, it is not something that he would himself engage in, for such an experience is inimical to Reason. He could believe in the reality of mantic possession, but he simply would not (and could not) get possessed.

Buddhism once again presents an intermediate situation in its meditational ascesis. It is true that one can understand the world conceptually within the frame espoused by the Buddha, but anything like Platonic

Reason, along with all forms of discursive thought, must eventually be dethroned in the quest for salvation. Thus, in the final sense Reason itself is an obstacle to the apprehension or realization of some transcendental realities such as nirvana or mokṣa, quite unthinkable in the Platonic vision of salvation. There are no spiritual techniques as such in Platonism, no meditational techniques such as those of Buddhism or even the multiple asceses that in all likelihood characterized Pythagorean and Empedoclean quests for salvation.

Nevertheless, there is an irony or a paradox in the Platonic quest. If it is the case that Plato's own personal conviction was epistemologically prior to Reason, then how can a soteriology of Reason ever have a popular emotional appeal or convince ordinary people or even specially selected virtuosos? For Plato the truth is realizable through Reason that is inextricably tied to virtue. It is available to a person who has led a virtuous life during three incarnations such that at the end of the third the soul becomes so purified that it can reside in the realm of the gods, comporting with them, and experiencing the world of Forms, that ultimate world of Being. But how can the philosopher know in the first place the truth of the doctrine of salvation, that is, at his own *first* incarnation before he has had a chance to practice virtue under the aegis of Reason? It surely must be by conviction outside of Reason, such as the experience of Meno's slave. Reason can *explain* the slave's experience, but that experience itself is not a product of the slave's Reason. Finally, it seems to me, without a powerful message of salvation articulated to spiritual techniques with emotional power, the Platonic soteriology of Reason can only become a way of salvation for Plato himself. It is therefore not surprising that "Hellenistic and post-Hellenistic Orphic poetry showed a considerable lack of interest in Plato's writing"[49] and that his persona resisted popular mythicization, quite unlike the cases of Pythagoras, Empedocles, the Buddha, Mahavira, Zoroaster, and Jesus.

## "KARMA" IN GREEK THOUGHT: PLOTINIAN ESCHATOLOGY AND SOTERIOLOGY

"Now Socrates, now a horse."

—Plotinus, *Enneads*

I speculated that Plato inherited an already ethicized religion of the sort represented in Pindar and that from that base he wove his speculations on otherworldly rewards and punishments (ethicization step 1). Although we do not know how the Pindaric form came to be invented, we do know that ethicization as a rationalizing process had already occurred in the south and east of the Greek world in the reforms of Zoroaster and those of the samanic religions of the Ganges valley; and nearer home it perhaps appeared in the Orphic theogonies. Whether or not these movements "influenced" the Pindaric rebirth in any significant way, we can at least draw an important conclusion regarding ethicization. Once ethicization is "naturalized," or becomes part of the publicly accepted culture, philosophers, like any one of us, simply inherit it as the accepted reality. They can reject it, but this is not likely because ethicization is easily perceived as an advance in the history of ethics. The thinkers might at best modify it and bring it within the frame of their own speculative thinking.

There is a further complication with Greek ethicization that I will now explore. In my imaginary experiment I suggested that all that is required for the karma theory and the idea of samsara to emerge is ethicization steps 1 and 2, which are systematically carried out through a finite or infinite series of rebirths. I have also shown that the Pythagorean tradition prior to Pindar did not produce systematic ethicization for the good reason that the thinkers of this tradition were not interested in the soteriological welfare of the ordinary person. Perhaps this was not true of the Orphics; certainly it was not so in the tradition represented in Pindar, where a larger community of believers was involved. But the Pindaric stopped as far as we know at step 1 of ethicization; it did not ethicize rebirth in the human world and therefore did not produce an eschatology that was isomorphic with the Indian theory of karma. It is Plotinus who comes close to developing such a theory, although it was hinted at by Plato himself when he began to think seriously about ordinary citizens in his posthumous and incomplete work, the *Laws*.

The *Laws,* we know, deal with Plato's practical utopia, named Magnesia, in Crete, quite unlike the impractical ideal represented in the *Republic.* In his imagined utopia Plato is primarily thinking of the laws that make for a viable community of ordinary Greek citizens, properly selected of course, not the elite toward whose consumption the earlier philosophical discourses were formulated. In the *Laws* Plato addresses an *imaginary* audience; consequently, one might expect him to deal with punishments and rewards in the otherworld, as he did in *Timaeus*. However, these topics are never spelled out in any detail. In the new state people are expected to honor the Olympian gods, then the gods of the underworld, followed by the worship of spirits, and then heroes.[50] In the section that deals with religion in book 10 there is not the remotest reference to reincarnation. Only very general normative practices of mainline Greek religion are mentioned as central to the welfare of Magnesia: the priority of the soul and the existence of the gods, their justice, and that they cannot be "bought" by sacrifices. There is a very brief mention that souls who have "sinned" will be confined to Hades, whereas the good go to a pleasant abode.[51] A very ordinary Greek eschatology indeed! Predictably, then, the details of the punishments and rewards expressed in the *Timaeus* as part of its rebirth theory are simply ignored in the *Laws*. It is therefore somewhat surprising to find ideas of rebirth in the human world and the punishments enacted therein in two places in the *Laws*, not in the sections on religion but on the law of homicide, when Plato discourses on one of the most horrendous acts that a person can commit against Magnesia, namely, premeditated murder. Plato lists the many this-worldly punishments that should be meted out to those who commit this type of crime; then there appear two references to afterlife punishments, not in Hades, as one would have expected, but in a human reincarnation:

> Vengeance is exacted for these crimes in the after-life, and when a man returns to this world again he is ineluctably obliged to pay the penalty prescribed by the law of nature—to undergo the same treatment as he himself meted out to his victim, and to conclude his earthly existence by encountering a similar fate at the hands of someone else. (*Laws* 9.870)

Later in the same text Plato speaks of "the law we have just mentioned" in relation to those who have spilled the blood of kinfolk:

> If ever a man has murdered his father, in the course of time he must suffer the same fate from violent treatment at the hands of his children. A matricide, before being reborn, must adopt the female sex, and after being born a woman and bearing children, be dispatched subsequently by them. No other purification is available when common blood has been polluted; the pollution resists cleansing until, murder for murder, the guilty soul has paid the penalty and by this appeasement has soothed the anger of the deceased's entire line. (*Laws* 9.872–73)

This harsh doctrine does not entail "systematic ethicization" of the human rebirth because only especially horrendous crime has been singled out, not morally wrong acts in general. Nor does Plato deal with compensatory rebirth rewards for the good. Plato's highly emotional reaction seems hugely overdetermined. It is as if a personal belief has erupted into a context where it does not belong or as if Plato is forced to deal with the peculiar aporia associated with Greek rebirth, namely, the difficulty of really ignoring rebirth punishments for those who have committed appallingly heinous crimes. Plato is not satisfied with the punishment accorded these persons in Tartarus; he wants to see them punished again in the human world. His is an "occasional ethicization," like that formulated by individual Amerindians in respect to the otherworld.

These brief references to rebirth punishments were taken up by Plato's later disciple Plotinus (204–70 C.E.) and spelled out in systematic detail by inventing a moral scheme that shows, at least on the surface, an affinity with the karma doctrine. Yet it must be remembered that Plotinus was also a thinker who did not actively engage in creating a congregation. Hence, although his theory of rebirth punishments is more systematically dealt with than in Plato, he also does not develop the idea of rebirth rewards for the good (for reasons that will soon be apparent). Further, he seems to follow a pre-Pindaric Pythagorean tradition that was not seriously concerned with rewards and punishments in a hell or a heaven, reversing Platonic priorities in this regard. Nevertheless, it is striking that not only does Plotinus develop the eschatology and soteriology of the *Timaeus,* a favorite Middle and Neoplatonic text, but his morality of compensatory ethics moves Greek rebirth away from both Pindaric eschatology and the Platonic rebirth prior to the *Laws.*

Plotinus's thinking is important for other reasons also. As with Plato and many Pythagoreans he took for granted rebirth in the world of humans and animals literally, even though he took considerable liberties with Platonic cosmology and soteriology. Although Plotinus thought of himself as Plato's heir, there is as much an epistemic break between Plato and Plotinus as between the Upanishads and early Buddhism, at least as far as Plato's soteriology and doctrine of rebirth are concerned. Because Plotinus's philosophical thought has been dealt with at length in recent research, I will briefly present it insofar as it relates to his lesser-known rebirth eschatology and soteriology. I want to draw attention to his karma-like doctrine of ethical compensation and his doctrine of salvation, which even more provocatively than Empedocles' incorporation of the four elements, shows striking resemblance to the Indian. Let me first present his rebirth theory and then deal with the problems it raises.

References to rebirth are scattered in Plotinus's masterwork, the *Enneads,* almost always in discussions of the soul and as part of an ineluctable cosmic law. These concepts of the soul in turn make sense only in relation to Plotinus's highly innovative cosmology, which he developed not only in relation to Plato's thought but also in debates with Aristotle, with the Stoics, with contemporary Gnostic doctrines, and perhaps even with the Christians.[52]

Briefly stated, Plotinus believed that all reality is united in the One that is beyond all knowing. The One, also known as the Good, is derived (historically at least) from Plato's brief references to such an entity in the *Republic* and the more detailed discussion in *Parmenides,* along with the work of middle Platonists, such as Plotinus's precursor Numenius of Apamea.[53] In the Plotinian conception the One is beyond Being; however, it emanates other forms of Being, which Plotinus labels as the first principles, or hypostases. Although the One is unknowable, the derivative hypostases are knowable forms of Being, spelled out in some detail in the fifth and sixth *Enneads.*

In this conception the One radiates the other realms of Being, beginning with the second hypostasis, the Nous, or the Intellect (variously translated as Divine Intellect, Intelligence, Intellectual Principle, or the Divine Mind). The problematic relation between the first hypostasis, the One, or the Good, and the second derivative hypostasis can be put thus: if the One is immobile and cannot produce anything, how can one say that the second hypostasis derives from the first? Plotinus illustrates this problem with a well-known trope. "It must be a circumradiation—produced from the Supreme but from the Supreme unaltering—and may be compared to a brilliant light encircling the sun and ceaselessly generated from that unchanging substance."[54] All "existences" have this character: they are emanations of a superior principle and share the nature of that principle, whereas the superior does not share the features of the lower principle.

Nous (Intellect or Intellectual Principle) will perhaps make more sense to contemporary readers if it is viewed as "Divine Mind," as Stephen MacKenna suggests (although not, I think, as "Spirit").[55] Nous contains the intelligible universe, and in it are Plato's Ideal Forms, those universals that in turn generate the particularities and the multiplicities of our known world. Thus the multiple realities of lived existence are reflections of the archetypes of Forms that radiate from the Intellect and ultimately unite in it. The relation between Intellect and Forms has been a controversial one in Neoplatonism. Dominic O'Meara makes the reasonable proposition that for Plotinus "the Forms are the thoughts, the thinking activity, of the divine intellect."[56]

The Intellectual Principle, or Nous, in turn irradiates the Soul such that the whole world is "ensouled." Soul "envelops the heavenly system and guides all to its purposes: for it has bestowed itself upon all that huge expanse so that every interval, small and great alike, all has been ensouled. . . . By the power of the Soul the manifold and diverse heavenly system is a unit: through soul this universe is a God: and the sun is a God, because it is ensouled; so too the stars: and whatsoever we ourselves may be" (*Enn.*, 5.1.2). Here Plotinus follows the Greek tradition of *empsychon,* the world permeated with soul, although the immediate precursor of his view is the Stoic conception of the universe filled with spirit. Yet beyond this the Plotinian conception has its cross-cultural and historical parallels in the doctrine of species sentience that we have associated with rebirth eschatologies, including Plato's notion that all nature is kin. Plotinus transforms the older Greek idea of ensoulment in his own highly idealistic way.[57]

As with Plato, the beings who inhabit our world are not ensouled in the same degree: animals are not ensouled in the same manner as human beings, and plants are even worse off because, unlike animals, they have no capacity for feeling. The universal soul is therefore compounded into diversity or subject to "engroupment," as was the case with the Nous:

> Thus we have in the *Enneads* a verbal partition of the All-Soul; we hear of the Leading-Principle of the Soul or the Celestial Soul, concentrated in contemplation of its superior, and the Lower Soul, called also the Nature-Looking and Generative Soul, whose operation is to generate or fashion the lower, the material Universe upon the model of the Divine Thoughts, the "Ideas" laid up within the Divine Mind [Nous]: this lower principle in the Soul is sometimes called the Logos of the Universe, or the "Reason-Principle" of the Universe.[58]

If the Reasoning-Soul (or the rational soul of other translators) is what makes us human as we aspire to reach Being and beyond Being into the originary One, the unreasoning aspect of Soul is characteristic of animal life.

Plotinus has a knack of formulating each issue in different ways. Thus in a complicated discussion he shows how Soul further diversifies into another engroupment, Sense and Nature. For present purposes let me focus on the latter:

> In the case of a soul entering some vegetal form, what is there is one phase, the more rebellious and less intellectual, outgone to that extreme; in a soul entering an animal, the faculty of sensation has been dominant and brought it there; in soul entering man, the movement outward has either been wholly of its reasoning part or has come from the Intellectual Principle [Nous] in

> the sense that the soul, possessing that principle as immanent to its being, has an inborn desire for intellectual activity and of movement in general. (*Enn.*, 5.2.2)

One can put it differently: there is no radical gap between the divine intellect and "our habitual and discursive form of thought," for "since divine intellect constitutes soul, it is always present to soul and thus to our souls; we always remain in contact with it and we can reach it through the deepening of our insight."[59]

Thus, although the Soul emanates from the Intellect, its particular reflections in the phenomenal world will be diverse. "The depth of the descent [of the soul], also, will differ—sometimes lower, sometimes less low—and this even in its entry into any given Kind: all that is fixed is that each several soul descends into a recipient indicated by affinity of condition; it moves towards the thing which it There resembled, and enters, accordingly, into the body of man or animal" (*Enn.*, 4.3.12).

This Plotinian reformulation of Platonic rebirth is spelled out in detail in Ennead 3.4 in a discussion of the guardian spirit. According to this conception humans share the characteristics of other living beings, including plants, insofar as their lives are governed by sense perception. But humans do not live by sense perception alone because of the rational soul that characterizes our very being. Nevertheless, humans do have sense organs, and "in many ways we live like plants, for we have a body which grows and reproduces." Consequently one's soul must not be tied down by our senses in such things as reproductive sexuality and gluttony. Instead a human being must "escape" from such activities and "rise to the intelligible and intellect and God [Good]," which is the natural inclination of the soul.[60] Human beings then have a choice: to follow the daimon, or guardian spirit, in this upward movement of the soul or to let the soul be dragged down by the dross of wrong and materiality. At death those possessed of the purified higher soul (the celestial soul) will follow the upward movement toward Intellect and beyond that to the Good, whereas ordinary humans, possessors of the lower, or rational, soul, will be caught in the rebirth process, or *metensomatosis* (changing from body to body). Plotinus says about the latter:

> Those, then, that guarded the man in them, become men again. Those who lived by sense alone become animals; but if their sense-perceptions have been accompanied by passionate temper they become wild animals. . . . But if they did not even live by sense along with their desires but coupled them with dullness of perception, they even turn to plants. . . . Those who loved music but were in other ways respectable turn into song-birds; kings who

> ruled stupidly into eagles, if they had no other vices; astronomers who were always raising themselves to the sky without philosophical reflection turn into birds which fly high. The man who practiced community virtue becomes a man again; but one who has a lesser share of it a creature that lives in community, a bee or something of the sort.[61]

As in Plato this account emphasizes the correspondence of the present life with the former one and the importance of "choice." Plato's souls, it should be remembered, have free choice because they have already been rewarded and punished in the otherworld. Plotinus, however, only formally recognizes this aspect of the Platonic myth. Instead, his focus is on the rebirth punishments. Hence, in the above passage all animal rebirths imply punishment for wrong choice, although some births, such as those of eagles and bees, are less degraded than others, and songbirds perhaps are not so badly off. In this account Plotinus is still rooted in the Platonic idea of the correspondence between the past and present, and he does not wholly deal with ethics. Soon, however, he moves in the direction of *ethical* choice in his discussion of the guardian spirit as the spiritual principle in oneself, thus axiologizing the Platonic notion of daimon.[62] We must *choose* the rational principle in our present life; otherwise, when we die the soul weighted by the dross of unethical behavior must pay the penalty in another rebirth. Hence Plotinus qualifies the previous account: "The wicked man, since the principle which worked in him during his life has pressed him down to the worse, towards what is like himself, enters into the life of a beast."[63] Then, in a further ethical development, the guardian spirit, or daimon, as the spiritual agency within us will punish us for our wrongdoings, very much like the Freudian conscience.[64] This comes out in Ennead 4.8.5: "For the faults committed here, the lesser penalty is to enter body after body—and soon to return—by judgement according to desert, the word *judgement* indicating a divine ordinance; but any outrageous form of ill-doing incurs a proportionately greater punishment administered under the *surveillance of chastising daimons*" (MacKenna trans., my italics).

These ideas are given a different ethical turn in the third Ennead, "On Providence: First Treatise," in relation to problems of theodicy. The basic argument is that everything in the universe flows according to a rational plan centering on the One, or the Good. As far as ensoulment is concerned this rational plan implies that "in the heavens of our universe, while the whole has life eternally, the souls pass from body to body entering into varied forms." In some cases "a soul will arise outside of the realm of birth and dwell with the one Soul of all" (*Enn.*, 3.2.4)—in effect abolishing metensomatosis. Plotinus seems to say that the Soul—the world soul—is eternal, but when a soul gets embodied in the rebirth process it lacks that eternality unless it returns to the world soul and from there back to Nous and then to the One. Thus, if there is an ineluctable law of descent from the One, there is also one of *ascent* in the reverse direction from the third principle to the first. Yet if everything emanates from the Good and flows backward toward the Good, why is there wrongdoing and bad in the world?

We are back in the Platonic world of the soul dragged down by the body's dross, an idea that is further developed in the Plotinian doctrine of Matter, according to which the body is the "container of soul and of nature" (*Enn.,* 4.4.18). The wrongdoing of human beings does not invalidate the notion that persons aspire to the Good, but "foiled, in their weakness, of their true desire, they turn against each other: still, when they do wrong they pay the penalty—that of having hurt their souls by their evil conduct and of degradation to a lower place—for nothing can ever escape what stands decreed in the law of the Universe." Thus punishment and reward are automatic processes, part of that "law of the Universe." "Punishment naturally follows: there is no injustice in a man suffering what belongs to the condition in which he is; nor can we ask to be happy when our actions have not earned us happiness; the good, only, are happy; divine beings are happy only because they are good" (*Enn.,* 3.2.4).

It seems that for Plotinus the nagging problem remains: how can the horrendous things that human beings do be reconciled with Providence, the Good? Fortunately, Plotinus does not have to deal with the idea of an omnipotent deity with whom theodicy becomes a problem. The One is not a living God in any theistic sense; like Plato's Demiurge it cannot be held accountable for the world's ills. Evildoers, however, "will not get off by death" (*Enn.,* 3.2.8) but will be punished in another life. This is the "ordinance of the cosmos and in keeping with the Intellectual Principle [Nous]" (*Enn.,* 3.2.13). This ordinance is a karma-like automatic process:

> Thus a man, once a ruler, will be made a slave because he abused his power and because the fall is to his future good. Those that have misused money will be made poor—and to the good poverty is no hindrance. Those that have unjustly killed, are killed in turn, unjustly as regards the murderer but justly as regards the victim, and those that are to suffer are thrown into the path of those that administer the merited treatment.
>
> It is not an accident that makes a man a slave; no one is prisoner by

> chance; every bodily outrage has its due cause. The man once did what he now suffers. A man that murders his mother will become a woman and be murdered by a son; a man that wrongs a woman will become a woman, to be wronged.[65]

Hence that "awesome word Adrasteia (the Inevadable Retribution)"—similar to what the Indian samanic religions conceptualized as *karma vipāka,* the fruits of karma.

I have already noted that in Plotinian thought, as with Buddhism, the automatism of punishment results in the degradation and demotion of animals. Hence one could be Plotinus now, now a horse; or an "ox-soul which was once a man." However, it is not clear how the horse can re-become Plotinus or an ox can reemerge as a man (unlike in Buddhism, where this can happen when one's bad karma is over). Neither do we know whether plants are part of the same process, simply because they lack feeling. As far as animals are concerned "the degradation," says Plotinus, "is just" (*Enn.,* 3.3.4). Yet in Plotinus's unique conception of species sentience as the permeation of the universe by soul, animals, although degraded, ought to be able to achieve eventual happiness by the mere fact that they possess souls. The awesome way in which the world is *enlinked* (Plotinus's term) in a scheme of cosmic harmony is stated in a magnificent passage:

> No one can ever escape the suffering entailed by ill deeds done: the divine law is ineluctable, carrying bound up, as one with it, the fore-ordained execution of its doom. The sufferer, all unaware, is swept onward towards his due, hurried always by the restless driving of his errors, until at last wearied out by that against which he struggled, he falls into his fit place and, by self-chosen movement, is brought to *the lot he never chose.* And the law decrees, also, the intensity and duration of the suffering while it carries with it, too, the lifting of chastisement and the faculty of rising from those places of pain—all by the power of the harmony that maintains the universal scheme. (*Enn.,* 4.3.24, my italics)

"The lot he never chose": it is now clear that Plotinus does not subscribe to the voluntarism of the myth of Er. Certainly there is choice, but ethical choice leads to a karmic kind of determinism. Adrasteia is not the Greek goddess of the mystery religions exacting punishment but a metaphor for the automatism of punishment for wrongs done. Yet on the formal level this strand of compensatory ethics in Plotinus is quite unlike that of Plato and the Buddha. Although Plotinus pays lip service to Plato's ideas of heaven and hell when he is commenting on Platonic texts, in reality he ignores these realms. They are effectively bypassed as the soul gets reincarnated as man, woman, and animal (also as plant), depending on the ethical actions of the motivating individual. Plotinus in effect *reverses* Plato's scheme of rewards and punishments administered in a heaven and a hell; this also means that the role of Plato's guardian spirit becomes restricted because it has no role in accompanying the dead person in its underworld journey. Hence it is not surprising that the daimon is axiologized in Plotinus's thought.

What is the way of escape from the continual ensoulment in human and beast as part of the cosmic scheme of reincarnation? The answer is also found in Plotinus's doctrine of the irradiation process in reverse, the law of sympathy that ties the universe together: the soul's ascent to the World Soul and then to Nous and then beyond all Being into the One. Plotinus discusses this in involuted detail, but I will give the gist of his thesis, beginning with what happens to the soul after leaving the body at death.

The soul cannot remain in the mundane world of becoming, which is an element alien to it, but must seek upward movement toward the sphere to which it naturally belongs, "wayfaring towards the Intellectual Realm" (*Enn.*, 4.8.1). Those souls that are "body-bound" (tied to the senses) by ill deeds are subject to "body punishment" through metensomatosis, whereas "clear souls" (celestial or higher souls), possessing no vestige of body, move upward, drawn to where there is Essence and Being. Thus, as I noted earlier, in human beings there are two kinds of soul: the rational soul, which at death seeks another body but might give that body a divine quality by its mere presence, and the higher, or clear, soul freed of body and of ill deeds and moving upward. Following Platonic tradition, the latter ideal is typically the soul of the sage or philosopher.

What memory of the past do these respective souls retain? Basically the Plotinian thesis is that memory belongs to soul, not body, which by its materiality cannot be the vehicle for the Nous, the sphere to which the soul is naturally drawn. Soul uses the body and its organs, but body, owing to its shifting and fleeting nature, can only be an impediment to memory. Both kinds of souls have memories. After death, as time passes, the higher soul will remember past lives, and dismissing some of the events of the immediately left life as trivial, it will revive things forgotten in the corporeal state owing to embodiment; it will begin to remember its originary condition. But what of the lower soul, which seeks one body after another in the rebirth process? "It will tell over the events of the discarded life, it will treat as present that which it has just left, and it will remember much from the former existence" (*Enn.*, 4.3.27).

This is an important statement because I think Plotinus is trying to incorporate into his theory of memory a popular idea—ultimately grounded in rebirth eschatologies—that the newly born person might be able to recollect former life memories. Plotinus tries to give that theory a psychological and philosophical grounding in his doctrine of the soul with its "imaging faculty," the seat of memory.

If the lower (rational) soul in humanity seeks continual embodiment, the higher soul moves in the direction of the Supreme and into Nous, the sphere immediately above it, and as it does, it forgets the past. In that sense "the good soul is the forgetful." But what is most important is that "even in this world the soul which has the desire of the other is putting away, amid its actual life, all that is foreign to that order" (*Enn.*, 4.3.32). That is, even the soul that is embodied tries to put away dross and move upward, quite unlike the unreasoning animal soul. This is the natural movement for both kinds of souls in us humans, but the embodied soul cannot ascend easily, weighted as it is by "sin," which is ultimately translatable as materiality and dross.

The soul that is freed of body—the clear soul—moving upward to its source in the Nous, the Intellectual Realm, will eventually find its way to that Essence. It will have no memory whatever because the Essence, or Being, has no memory, even of the profoundest thoughts or experiences. In this realm of Nous there is "no discursive thought, no passing from one point to another," and "all is presence" (*Enn.*, 4.4.1).

Plotinus attempts the difficult task of describing the mystical reach of the soul to the Nous:

> Once pure in the Intellectual, it [the Soul] too possesses the same unchangeableness: for it possesses identity of essence; when it is in that region it must of necessity enter into oneness with the Intellectual Principle [Nous] by the sheer fact of its self-orientation, for by that intention all interval disappears; the Soul advances and is taken into unison, and in that association becomes one with the Intellectual Principle—but not to its own destruction: the two are one, and two. In such a state there is no question of stage and change: the Soul, without motion (but by right of its essential being) would be intent upon its intellectual act, and in possession, simultaneously, of its self-awareness; for it has become one simultaneous existence with the Supreme. (*Enn.*, 4.4.2)

To better understand this stage of the Plotinian soteriology as "the simultaneous existence with the Supreme," let me deal with Plotinus's own experience, when, in a state of contemplative ecstasy, he had entered into a transcendental condition:

> Many times this has happened: lifted out of the body into myself: becoming external to all other things and self-encentered; beholding a marvellous beauty; then, more than ever, assured of community with the loftiest order; enacting the noblest life, acquiring identity with the divine; stationing within It by having attained that activity; poised above whatsoever within the Intellectual is less than the Supreme: yet, there comes the moment of descent from intellection to reasoning, and after that sojourn in the divine, I ask myself how it happens that I can now be descending, and how did the Soul ever enter into my body, the Soul which, even within the body, is the high thing it has shown itself to be. (*Enn.*, 4.8.1)

What is fascinating about Plotinus's oft-repeated experience of his own soul's ascent and descent is that it provides us with a glimpse of the salvific condition, even though his experience of it was temporary. The soul, released from the body during a state of "concentration," experiences the ecstasy of a sojourn with the divine. The resting soul of the Plotinian sage has taken over the qualities of the *jīvan mukta* of the Indic tradition.

Although Wallis says that Plotinus "experienced union with God or Ultimate Reality,"[66] it is not clear whether this condition is identity with the One or an experience that describes the soul going into its own proper sphere of the Nous, or Intellect, the world of Forms. In my opinion Plotinian logic requires the latter as the likely one. Nous is "intellection," not reasoning; reasoning is the operation of soul, itself an emanation from Nous. Hence, contrary to that of some commentators, for whom Plotinus combined rationality with religious passion, my reading suggests that for Plotinus, as for the Buddha and for all mystical virtuosos, Reason has to be downgraded at a critical point in the soteriological quest. Yet identity with Nous means a duality still: the two are one and two, but duality is not the ultimate goal of the soteriological vision. The soul must ascend still further, beyond Nous and beyond Being, into the One. If the intellectual realm contains the world of Forms, perhaps Plotinus's own ascent into it is still rooted in the Platonic experience of the soul engaged in the contemplation of the world of Forms. The further movement beyond Nous into the One by the human soul bereft of dross is beautifully described in the mystical language of "On the Good, or the One" (*Enn.*, 6.9).

Here Plotinus makes a philosophical case for the One as Unity, but, more important, he raises the issue of how we, our souls, can "reach toward the Supreme" (*Enn.*, 6.9.8). To achieve this state, one must withdraw from external stimuli and, immersing inward, engage in the contemplation of the Supreme. Plotinus says that one might even be able to report to others about that communion. But how is this possible, one might ask, if in the next breath he can say that communion with the One is beyond reason, that it is reason's Prior?[67] Plotinus recognizes the problem; one cannot speak of the Other authoritatively; one can only infer it. This must necessarily be through our developed rational faculties or through a further rational understanding of Plotinus's own mystical experience in the realm of the Nous. Plotinus can describe identity with Nous because in Nous his soul is still in Reason's sway; he is both one and two, whereas the ineffable condition of mystical identity with the One cannot be described in the discursive language of reason. Here all dualities are abolished, and the soul of the sage fully merges with the One, very much like that of atman with the Brahman of the Upanishadic sage. Yet the problem faced by the Neoplatonic mystic remains: how can he describe that which is indescribable, and how does he even know for certain what the salvific condition is, given the fact that he is only a human being (even though a sage) engaged in forms of discursive reasoning, however superior or soul-endowed that reasoning might be? Because union with the One cannot be a description of an experienced reality, it must be a rationally inferred reality from Plotinus's own experienced mystical state of the soul reaching Nous in a state of deep concentration.

There is further evidence that Plotinus's personal mystical experience concerns his soul's reach into Intellect, or Nous, rather than its union with the One, in terms of his own epistemological stance. Plotinus believed, along with many other Greek thinkers, that complex or compounded phenomena must ultimately rest on simpler phenomena. In this particular instance he held that, contrary to Aristotle and much of middle-Platonic thought, Intellect is not the ultimate simple but is itself composed of a dual status; both Soul and Intellect are part of the world and above the world. For example, the very fact that Intellect "thinks out" the Forms indicates its dual role; there is both an activity and emanation, which he conceptualizes as analogous to thinking, and there is an object of thinking involved. In terms of this logic Soul and Intellect are both compound and composite, although obviously simple in relation to the multiplex phenomenal world they generate. As O'Meara puts it, Plotinus believed that not only does the composite devolve ultimately in the simple, which is prior to it, but also the simple and prior must of necessity be the more perfect and the more powerful. This is an epistemic break from both "Platonists and Aristotelians who held that the unity of divine intellect and its objects of thought is such that it is absolutely simple and therefore ultimate."[68] Plotinus's idea that compounded entities nest in progressively simpler forms constitutes an epistemological rationale for his doctrine of emanation and his "radical monism" pertaining to the ultimate One.

In terms of our prior argument, this means that the soul of the person seeking salvation must move from Intellect into the One, and Plotinus is bold enough to imagine what that entails in Ennead 6.9 ("On the Good or the One"). He states with rare clarity the reach of the soul toward the One among those who can free themselves from the deceptions of the world of becoming and realize the soul's true nature, which comes from the One and begins to love the One. In a fine simile he describes the relationship of the purified soul to the Good as a kind of choral dance: "We truly dance our god-inspired dance around him [the One]."[69] It seems that during this part of the ascent Plotinus still thinks of the soul as separate from the One, standing outside, as it were, in mystical contemplation of it. This is what he meant earlier when he referred to the soul in Nous as being in a "simultaneous existence with the Supreme" rather than an identity with it. "There one can see both him and oneself and oneself as it is right to see: the self glorified, full of intelligible light—but rather itself pure light—weightless, floating free, having become—but rather being—a god; set on fire then, but the fire seems to go out if one is weighed down again."[70] This is perhaps a further move toward the One than Plotinus's own mystical ascent; one is away from Nous and closer to the One although still not merged with the One. Hence the question: "How is it, then, that one does not remain there?" And the answer: "It is because one has not yet totally come out of this world."[71] But that time will come for those whose souls are ready, for example, the initiates in the mysteries, who can only experience the mystical state but cannot and must not speak of it. Hence Plotinus borrows a dictum from the mysteries: "Whoever has seen, knows what I am saying."[72] Nevertheless, unlike in the mysteries Plotinus does attempt to express in discursive language that final reach of the soul with the One, as the following translation by MacKenna beautifully captures:

> In this seeing, we neither hold an object nor trace distinction; there is no two. The man is changed, no longer himself nor self-belonging; he is merged with the Supreme, sunken into it, one with it: centre coincides with centre, for centres of circles, even here below, are one when they unite, and two when they separate; and it is in this sense that we now (after the vision) speak of the Supreme as separate. This is why the *vision baffles telling;* we cannot detach the Supreme to state it; if we have seen something thus detached we have failed of the Supreme which is known only as one with ourselves. (*Enn.,* 6.9.10, my italics)

This text is very much in the Indian style. Once filled with the One a person has even passed the "choir of the virtues"; that is, he is beyond good and evil. And what is most impressive is that Reason itself, that great Platonic virtue, is in abeyance: "no movement now, no passion, no outlooking desire, once this ascent is achieved . . . utterly resting he has become the very rest" (*Enn.*, 6.9.11). This final rest in the One is the privilege of the gods or of those who are godlike among mortals. It is a "liberation from the alien that besets us here, a life taking no pleasure in the things of earth, the passing of solitary to solitary" (*Enn.*, 6.9.11). It is clear that this liberation can be achieved by human beings in this very existence, although there is no indication that Plotinus himself achieved it. In his earlier mystical experience he uses the phrase "many times it has happened," but this is surely not true of the union with the One because once a person has had that ultimate experience, it stays with that person; he or she is "sunken" in it, as in Upanishadic or Buddhist salvation. Plotinian thought requires that salvation can also be reached by the virtuoso at death, as with the sages in Plato's soteriology of rebirth.

I am now tempted to posit Indian influence on both eschatological and soteriological levels. I was reluctant to do so in my discussion of Pythagorean eschatology (but not for the Empedoclean), although interconnections between the Greek and Indian worlds were entirely possible and likely. With Plotinus there is greater indication of Indian thought in respect to the salvation quest itself that, epistemically speaking, broke the Platonic apotheosis of Reason and the goal of salvation as contemplation of the sublime beauty of Ideal Forms. Indian ideas were floating in the first centuries of the Christian era in Gnostic thought, especially that of Basilides; or there might have been a more direct influence from his predecessor, Numenius, and his teacher, Ammonius Saccas, who apparently were receptive to Indian ideas.

According to his biographer Porphyry, Plotinus "became eager to investigate the Persian methods and the system adopted among the Indians."[73] But what is striking about Plotinus is his rare attempt to describe the indescribable—the numinous, mokṣa, or nirvana—in a philosophical discourse, something that the Buddha refused to do. But Plotinus does not give up the task of describing the indescribable: he realizes that the soteriological vision "baffles telling" because active ratiocination and egoistic thinking cannot prevail there. Perhaps the "not this, not that" of the mystic is only a baffled attempt to express the inexpressible, as it was with Plotinus's own "negative theology," where, for the most part, the Good is portrayed in negative terms.[74]

In engaging in this very Greek enterprise of philosophical exegesis and discursive reasoning Plotinus occasionally verges on the unintelligible.[75] He is a compulsive conceptualist: reading his philosophical exposition of difficult salvific concepts one wonders how anyone, except its author and those whom he labels "sages," could ever understand the salvific condition. The philosophical quest seems an exclusivist and elitist one. Plotinus refused to compromise with popular religiosity; thus for him astrology and other popular beliefs were true in a limited sense only.[76] Like the Buddha, who castigated them as "base arts," Plotinus thought that they had little to do with the upward-moving higher soul of human beings and gods.[77] When one of his disciples "grew ritualistic" and asked "if he could take Plotinus along" to the temples and the feasts of the gods, the philosopher-sage made a very Buddhist reply: "They ought to come to me, not I to them."[78] He describes the soteriological goal, but, unlike the Buddha, he describes neither the path for achieving that goal nor the spiritual technology or ascesis for realizing it, reversing Indic priorities. It is therefore not surprising that when Christians such as St. Augustine absorbed Plotinus's abstract soteriology, they gave it greater personal immediacy and meaning by converting identity with the One into a mystical identity with a living God, however unknowable that God might be.[79] So with the Ismā'īlī philosopher al-Nasafi, who introduced Neoplatonic thought, particularly the Plotinian hypostases that "became basic to much of Ismā'īlī esoteric doctrine throughout the Fatimid age."[80] Those heretical Ismā'īlīs, the Druze, gave a further concreteness to Plotinianism by embodying the hypostases in historical individuals, such that when Ḥamza became Imām, he came to embody the Nous, or Intellect, and identified some of his assistants as manifestations of the Universal Soul, whereas the Caliph al-Ḥākim and his predecessors were manifestations of the transcendent Godhead [One].[81] Yet although Plotinus's thought is abstract and sometimes unintelligible, his personal mystical experience, although maddeningly incomplete, is well known to us from the cross-cultural record. The ego of the rational consciousness is suspended in Plotinus's dreamlike state of ecstasy. In a state of intense concentration (achievable in multiple ways in different historical traditions) the soul, or self, escapes from the body and traverses into divine realms, experiences a "vision" of the truth and finally "identifies" with the divine. The philosophical exposition is different in the different systems of thought known to us, but the psychic experience sounds extremely familiar.[82]

I now want to address some difficult problems regarding Plotinus's doctrine of rebirth and salvation. Let me start with a question often posed by critics and commentators: how is that soul, which is in essence pure, sharing the character of Nous, able to produce impurity or imperfection in the phenomenal world, particularly in the absence of creator gods, those willfully otiose like Plato's Demiurge, or those who bear responsibility for the imperfections of the lived world? One answer found in Plotinus himself is that as the soul makes its descent or downward emanation, there comes a point where good itself terminates, that point being Matter, which is "evil" in a purely abstract sense: "It is also possible to grasp the necessity of evil in this way. For since there is not only the Good, there must be, in the going out beyond it, or, if one wishes to say it in this way, in the descent and departure, the end beyond which nothing more emerges, and this is evil. There must be something after the first and also the last, but this is matter, having nothing of the first."[83] The point is well put; it is the case that Plotinus's doctrine of Matter is discussed at abstruse lengths in such texts as Ennead 2.4, "On Matter." Yet his late text Ennead 1.8 suggests to me that Plotinus's notion of matter as ipso-facto evil and pure negativity does not derive from his philosophy as such but is a product of his confrontation with lived existence, specifically with the theodicy. Consider the phrase "necessity of evil" in the above quotation: Plotinus's reification of evil is necessitated by his recognition of the world's imperfections because one might argue that the downward emanation of soul cannot produce a totally "evil" Matter because, definitionally, soul must also permeate Matter. Thus, although Plotinus talks of matter as "evil," he cannot surely be dealing with "radical evil" in the Christian sense (although this is what he claims) because such a position is incompatible with his doctrine of ensoulment. One way of reconciling the existence of radical Evil with the Good, or the One, is to adopt the Stoic position, taken by later Christians also in their response to the theodicy; namely, Evil is ultimately good because it moulds one and makes one morally strong. But Plotinus refuses to take this easy way out.

In my view one has to read Plotinus through a different set of methodological lenses to better understand his doctrine of matter and the form that the soul takes in its encounter with matter. One has to drop the idea of Plotinus as a "philosopher" in the sense of someone probing the nature of the world purely for the purposes of understanding it and bringing that understanding within the frame of conceptual thought. There are perhaps only a very few who have speculated philosophically in a vacuum, divorced from our existential or religious convictions about life in general. Wittgenstein, we now know, could no more escape this than those who, following Descartes, heralded Enlightenment thought. This is not to say that philosophers were also religious teachers; many were not. I am only suggesting that their thinking was not insulated from life and the world and their taken-for-granted religious or sociopolitical or ethical convictions. Few scholars would of course deny this: but such cultural or personal presuppositions or prejudices rarely appear in the scholarly exposition of philosophical thought unless the philosopher possessed convictions that outraged our contemporary values, as, for example, the Nazism of Heidegger or Paul de Man. It is only in such instances that the philosopher's philosophy becomes suspect unless a philosopher believed in such acceptable verities as God, Soul, Mind, and so forth. But what if a philosopher believed in such things as species sentience or doctrines of reincarnation? These ideas are outside the dominant discourse of Western philosophical thought. These embarrassments in the midst of riches have been dealt with in many ways: by eliding them from the thinker's philosophy, by treating them as survivals of "primitive" thinking, by seeing them as "allegories" or "illustrative stories" that serious philosophers like Plato could simply not have believed in. Or, as O'Meara says: "it [reincarnation] was far more convincing to Plotinus's contemporaries than it would be to us"—which to me would be a good reason to take it seriously rather than to dismiss it perfunctorily, as he does ("be that as it may").[84]

Plotinus poses another problem for philosophy. All Greek thinkers were dealing with foundational ideas that were at once philosophical and religious, for example, that of Divine Intellect, the Soul, the One, and so forth. Philosophical speculations were rooted in these foundational ideas. Yet it is hard to believe that Aristotle was a "religious thinker," that is, someone interested primarily in soteriology and eschatology. In contrast to Aristotle, Plotinus followed the broad tradition of Greek reincarnation theories (and this includes Plato) in being a philosopher and a religious thinker at the same time. The "age of anxiety" in which Plotinus lived had enough soteriological challenges—from Gnosticism, from Christianity, and of course from the mystery religions that operated as the background religions for Pythagoreans and served similar functions in Plotinus's time. Plotinus does not practice philosophy for philosophy's sake; he was practicing philosophy for the sake of salvation, not salvation of the world but for those sages and philosophers who would be interested in his message. Like Pythagoras and Plato he has blended his mystical and soteriological vision into a system of abstract thought (a "philosophy"), such that it becomes meaningless to separate the two.

Such a blending was not characteristic of "ethical prophecy," as I mentioned earlier; it did, however, occur in the Christianity of St. Augustine, St. Thomas Aquinas, and other early church fathers.

Now one can deal with the matter of Matter. As a great religious and mystical virtuoso Plotinus had to relate his soteriological-cum-philosophical thought to the realities of the lived-in world. A doctrine that specifically dealt with the Good—the One—could hardly ignore the fact of the world's imperfections. In some mystical philosophies such a confrontation did not always entail a theodicy but, as with Plato and the Buddha, might even bypass the theodicy. In Plotinus's case there is a form of theodicy unique to his scheme: If the soul permeating the sensible world emanates from Nous, which in turn is an emanation of the Good (the One), how can it produce anti-Being or Matter, the negation of Good? Plotinus's view of abstract evil is, I think, a philosophical attempt to justify the existence of "evils" in the imperfect, experienced world we live in, posing an opposition between Soul as Being derived from the One and Matter as anti-Being, thereby introducing an inevitable contradiction into his basic epistemological-cum-soteriological postulates. Thus an attempt to explain evil or evils (the world's imperfections) leads to a paradox, a theodicy implicit in Plotinus's religious philosophy. This paradox exists only if there is a radical opposition between Soul (Being) and Matter (anti-Being), and there is no doubt that at times Plotinus thought of the issue in these terms. At other times, however, Matter eludes the theodicy. Back to my earlier example: if Soul is the principle that permeates everything, it must also permeate Matter, albeit in attenuated form, during its downward emanation. Matter, therefore, cannot be defined as abstract, metaphysical, or radical evil: the world's imperfections are caused by Soul being dragged down by Matter, bringing Plotinus's thought more in line with that of his master, Plato. Here any issue of theodicy simply cannot arise.

The problem of the world's imperfections is dealt with in yet another way in Plotinus's thought, not in terms of the foundational concepts of his philosophy but once more in relation to life and the world. Plotinus knew, as we all do, that "evils" (in the plural) and good and ill deeds are a part of everyday life. "Living beings which have a self-willed movement incline sometimes to the better things, sometimes to the worse. It is perhaps not worth enquiring about the turning of oneself to the worse. And if attention is not paid to the first step and what happens suddenly and it is not rectified at once, a commitment is generated to that to which one fell."[85] Everyday morality can obviously be justified in terms of either the first or second version of Matter discussed above; they are expressions of evil, *kakon,* whether radical or not. But this doctrine cannot explain human *motivations* for practicing "evil" except to assert, as in the preceding quotation, that such is what humans do. Nevertheless, neither the theory of Matter nor the commonsense recognition of quotidian morality can help bring that morality within the frame of everyday human existence governed by justice or righteousness. It is in relation to this last issue that another powerful background belief of Plotinus is relevant—rebirth and its karma-like doctrine that, unlike the Buddhist, emphasized primarily the punishment of the wicked, not a happy rebirth for the plurality of ordinary decent citizens. One can agree with both Gerson and O'Meara that Plotinus, like many Neopythagoreans and Neoplatonists, personally believed in the reality of rebirth. But what does this doctrine do in respect to everyday morality? It disposes of the question of the plural "evils" that we all know exist: there is just retribution for those who do wrong, and there is no unjust suffering in the world. There can arise no theodicy as far as everyday morality in the world is concerned. Even if "evil" exists on the abstract level, it is resolved on the concrete level of everyday life in Plotinus's positing of a just social order geared to an ethicized doctrine of rebirth.

But what about the other side of the coin, the compensations for those who do good in everyday living? This is not explicit in Plotinus's thought. Although the system of punishments and degradations reads very much like Buddhist karma, Plotinus has little to say about a system of rewards. In Buddhism and Indic religions in general rebirth rewards often relate to status; now a prince, now a pauper. Such a position may be implicit in Plotinus, but it is obviously not significant enough for elaboration. Why so? We are back to Plotinus's philosophical soteriology. The punishment of the bad can be related to his doctrine of Matter and to the vexed problem of theodicy, but the reward of the good is not directly related to it. Those who do good cultivate their souls; they are actually or potentially in the upward move to the realm of Nous and beyond. Plotinus is silent about the details of this move as far as his eschatology of rebirth is concerned, and there is no way one can fill this lacuna in his texts. But what about the majority, who do ordinary good and continue to be reborn? Plotinus does mention cases of persons reborn in good circumstances, but he is generally silent about this silent majority. Do they gradually shed material dross and evil and, at some point in the rebirth process, make an upward ascent? This logically ought to be the case; nevertheless, his concern is with the sage who can achieve this upward ascent in this very life. As in Plato, this can also occur at death, although this idea is also not fully developed in the Plotinian texts. Plotinian preoccupation with what seems like karmic ethics is, strictly speaking, not "ethicization" in our sense of the term; it is geared to an elitist soteriology and not toward the soteriological welfare of ordinary folk, women, and Śūdras. No wonder it had little chance against a powerful and universally ethicizing religion such as Christianity.

Some of the problems raised in the preceding discussion bring us once again to the limitations imposed on the thinker by the very logic of the system he has created. Consider how some of the implications of Plotinus's originary One compare to Plato's Demiurge of the *Timaeus*. There is no active creator of the Universe in Plotinus, only a passive series of emanations or derivations. Plato has no problem with theodicy; the imperfections of the world make perfect sense within the parameters of his thought. Plato can also deal logically with the beginnings of reincarnation and its continuity in terms of the *Timaeus* cosmology. This Plotinus cannot do in his scheme. For this to occur there has to be a creation myth; but how can one have a creation myth without a Creator, a Maker, a Demiurge? Thus Plotinus must perforce adopt another schema, which has its parallels in Indic thought: the world and the universe have always existed; consequently, there is no need to explain the beginnings of the reincarnation cycle.[86] What must be explained is the *continuity* of that cycle in terms of a notion of moral order and the way in which that cycle can be short-circuited or terminated through a mode of gnosis available to the sage. Yet, whether one is dealing with Plato, the Buddha, or Plotinus, there is no way that salvation can otherwise be realized: it cannot logically occur within the rebirth cycle.

## REBIRTH AND THE IDEA OF GOD: THE DRUZE CASE

The Plotinian theory of rebirth (following a previous Pythagorean genealogy but not the Pindaric or Platonic model) bypasses the otherworld and effects a direct and immediate reincarnation in this world; this genealogy can be traced further to the several Ismā'īlī sects (vaguely classified as Shi'ites) influenced by Plotinus, the outstanding contemporary examples being the Druze (Durūz) of Syria, Lebanon, and Israel and lesser-known groups in Syria, as well as the Arabic speaking Shi'ite Alevis of southern Turkey. I will deal with the fascinating case of the Druze and only briefly refer to the others.[87] As always I will focus on problems of rebirth in relation to the presence or absence of ethicization using the scanty material available.[88]

The Druze faith arose in the eleventh century in Egypt during the last years of the Fatimid Caliphate of al-Ḥākim (996–1021 C.E.) and was the offshoot of the dissident Ismā'īlī communities that had already adopted a Neoplatonist cosmology. Al-Ḥākim later claimed to be a divine figure, and a cult formed around him. One of his followers, al-Darazī, a non-Arab, after whom the religion and people were named, gave theological meaning and a wider public acceptance to the cult. Al-Darazī saw the movement in terms of Ismā'īlī doctrine, which gave prominence to *ta'wil* (inner truth) and its representative the imām, with al-Ḥākim being the current imām, embodying the Cosmic Intellect (Nous). It rejected the orthodox Shi'ite tradition of outward revelation, or *tanzīl,* and its representative, the prophet.

The al-Daraziyya movement was soon supplanted by the Iranian Ḥamza ibn 'Ali in 1017 C.E., the year Druze history officially commences. With the death of al-Darazī, Ḥamza gave the Druze doctrine its present stamp, a significant variation of Ismā'īlīsm. "For Ḥamza, al-Ḥākim was no longer merely *imām,* however highly exalted. Ḥamza himself was the *imām,* the human guide, and therefore *al-'aḳl al-kullī,* the first cosmic principle; while al-Ḥākim was the embodiment of the ultimate One, the Godhead who created the Intellect itself and was accordingly Himself beyond name and office, beyond even good and evil."[89] This Godhead—a personification of the Plotinian One—was present in history in the person of al-Ḥākim, whereas Ḥamza now took over the position of imām. As a result Druze became an independent faith, no longer an offshoot of Ismā'īlīsm. Because of the prominence given to the One and to al-Ḥākim as its embodiment, the movement came to be seen as a kind of "Unitarianism" in the sense that the lower cosmic principles unite under the higher ones, and all get their bearing and significance from the One, which is beyond intellect and understanding. I refer the reader to Hodgson for the complex hierarchy of followers known as the *hudūd* and their opponents, the false *hudūd,* who were nonbelievers, and the eschatological drama being waged by these two groups.

In al-Ḥākim's own time the movement disappeared from Egypt but became "the ideology for a wave of peasant revolts in Syria," which, however, did not succeed.[90] At some point al-Ḥākim and Ḥamza themselves "retired," that is, went into concealment (awaiting the right moment for their reappearance). The leadership was taken over by al-Muḳtanā, who kept the authority of Ḥamza alive and initiated the final period of proselytization. He too retired in 1034 C.E., and, "according to tradition, no new converts have been accepted and the religion has remained secret."[91] The pastoral letters of al-Muḳtanā and the teachings of Ḥamza constituted the scriptures of the Druze. During this period of isolation the old religious hierarchy introduced by Ḥamza gradually atrophied, perhaps by the time of the great Druze moralist 'Abd Allāh al-Tanū<u>kh</u>ī (d. 1480 C.E.).

Although the older hierarchical system was modified into a much more egalitarian one, all Druze expect the return of Ḥamza and al-Ḥākim. In this newer scheme the Druze community was divided into *'ukkal* (sages, sing. *akil*), who have been initiated into the secret truths, and the uninitiated majority, or *d<u>j</u>uhhāl* (the ignorant, sing. *djahil*). Any Druze man or woman, however, can be initiated after being tested by a long trial. According to some accounts, about one-third of Druze *'ukkal* are women, although other sources say that it is much easier for women to become *'ukkal* than for men.[92] The more pious among the male sages are given special authority as *<u>sh</u>ay<u>kh</u>s,* and they alone can be expected to live on the alms and beneficence of the faithful. Each village has at least one *<u>sh</u>ay<u>kh</u>,* and the head of the Druze community (in Israel at least) is chosen from among them (IEC, 41). Many of the *<u>sh</u>ay<u>kh</u>s* spend much time copying religious texts or living in retreats or religious retirement homes located in secluded spots, and a few withdraw completely from lay life. All accounts agree that the *'ukkal,* or sages, alone are permitted to read the secret doctrine. Given this fact any historical or ethnographic account of Druze religion is nearly impossible. This difficulty is compounded by the fact that although the Druze must speak the truth among themselves, they are free to dissimulate when confronted with unbelievers, which includes non-Druze Christians, Jews, and Muslims, and this must surely include ethnographers and historians.

Thus although some Druze may publicly claim that their doctrines do not violate Islam, this claim cannot be taken at face value. The Druze are not expected to follow the Pillars of Islam but instead to practice the following, as formulated by Ḥamza:

1. truthfulness among Druze but dissimulation toward non-Druze when necessary
2. mutual aid and defense among Druze
3. repudiation of other religions
4. avoidance of association with nonbelievers

5. recognition of the unity of God in all ages
6. contentment with God's acts
7. submission to God's orders and ministers[93]

In addition, there are rules that prescribe chastity for both males and females and forbid divorce. Bodily decoration and show are discouraged, and religious meetings and weddings function without music or dance, and funerals are quiet and sedate affairs without much overt emotional display (IEC, 50–51). Circumcision is permitted, although it has no religious significance.[94]

Although the authoritative teachings of the Druze have been known to scholars since around the nineteenth century, outsiders are not taught the interpretation of texts. The esoteric doctrines and symbology are very much in the spirit of Pythagorean acusmata and the mystery cults in this regard. This tradition of esotericism "involves the deliberate disorganization of arguments, the use of vague metaphors, and the discussion of apparently trivial subjects while actually treating important issues. As a consequence, even when non-Druze have gained access to scripture it has not been of great concern to the Druze because only the initiates of the religion can understand the actual meaning of a text."[95] The doctrine of rebirth, however, is part of public knowledge, even though its deeper soteriological meanings may not be proclaimed to outsiders. This doctrine is neatly summarized by Hodgson:

> The number of souls in existence is fixed, all souls being reincarnated immediately upon death (unless having reached perfection they ascend the stars); those which believed in Ḥamza's time are always reincarnated as Druzes, either in Syria or in a supposed Druze community in China. The variety of incarnations each soul passes through gives a thorough moral testing. (Some of the *d̲juhhāl* believe in reincarnation of the wicked in lower animals.) In the end when al-Ḥākim and Ḥamza reappear to conquer and establish justice in the whole world, those Druzes who have shown up well will be the rulers of all mankind. The best will then dwell nearest to God—a notion which the *'ukkal* understand, like much else, in a spiritual sense.[96]

Let me spell out these ideas in more detail. The idea of "instantaneous rebirth" implies that many remember portions of their immediately preceding life. However, an aporia arises if I say that I was "X" in a preceding birth when everyone knows that "X" died a considerable time before I was born, thus precluding instantaneous reincarnation. In such a case the gap between the present birth and the previous one is attributed to an "intermediate life," generally of someone who died as a small child or infant and had nothing memorable to remember. Another puzzlement with instantaneous rebirth occurs during war and famine, where many die, and there are not enough babies being born to meet the reincarnation demand. It is then believed that the Druze soul gets incarnated in other countries, such as China, where Druze live, although they would not necessarily be called Druze. This happens until "ample embryos in the Near East make it feasible for them to return to their homelands again."[97] Finally, instantaneous rebirth can be affected by the last moments of the dying person. In the Druze case it is to ensure "the departing soul a comfortable departure and tranquil journey to its immediately reached next physical body" and to avoid "painful memories of mourning scenes." Yet the Druze also believe that any moral improvement or reform a person achieves at the moment of dying may influence "the character he or she will be in the next life" (*TC,* 7), an idea that Buddhists also seem to share.

Ian Stevenson makes the point that although the Druze actually believe in instantaneous rebirth and explain any delay in terms of an intermediate life, the empirical reality is somewhat different, with a Druze median interval of six months between dying and rebirth, the shortest of intervals except that of the Northwest Coast Haida, whose interval is four (*TC,* 10). Stevenson is interested in the empirical reality of reincarnation, but given our own comparative method, the Druze's actual belief in instantaneous reincarnation is what matters. Owing to the absence of a significant time gap between dying and rebirth, most Druze believe that one can recall events from the immediately preceding existence—something quite unusual in the ethnographic record. Druze parents encourage their children to actively re-cognize this past. Owing to the strength of this belief, some of the common features of rebirth eschatologies are rendered redundant. Hence, there are no phantasmal experiences of the dead person's appearing before the living prior to actual incarnation in a new body. Nor are there "announcing dreams," in which the dead person appears before a pregnant woman. Again no Druze claimed to remember his or her own funeral; it was thought that this was impossible given instantaneous reincarnation. However, some Druze claim to remember the events immediately preceding their death, which fits perfectly with Druze foundational beliefs (*TC,* 12).

Stevenson notes that the doctrine of reincarnation "is a major part of Druse religion" and people strongly adhere to it.[98] In this conception each Druze incarnates a soul of a Druze who had adopted the religion in

Ḥamza's time. This is a variation of the rebirth eschatology of small-scale societies, but instead of being born into the same kin group, one is born into an original community of believers. Yet one need not be, and often is not, born into the same family. For example, those who have been enemies now may be kinfolk later. However, there is no way a Druze can be reborn as non-Druze and all Druze are souls that circulate from the time the religion was created. In this conception the soul is permanent and is being "continuously incarnated," whereas the body is temporary, often described as "kamis, shirt, to indicate its temporary nature."[99] And "spirit" is God's immanence in the world. The soul leaves the body at death and enters the body of a neonate. Sex change is not possible, nor is it possible to become other than human.[100]

Thus, contrary to Hodgson, most contemporary Druze scholars make no reference to reincarnation as animals. Besterman cites older sources to justify the reality of animal reincarnation; such beliefs do exist in other Ismā'īlī sects and might well have existed historically among some Druze also. The eliding of such beliefs is probably the work of Islam and the other monotheisms in this region. Moreover, although some European writers have subsumed the Druze theory into a karma-like system, this does not seem to be the case in reality. Stevenson puts it well:

> The Druses believe that perfect justice requires man to undergo a succession of lives in different situations in order to perfect himself. . . . Everyone should know wealth and poverty, health and sickness . . . so that in each life he or she may strive a little more toward the perfection of character that God wishes each person to attain. At the Day of Judgement, a crisis far removed from our present lives but inevitable, the sums of conduct will be added up and, after reading the ledger of the virtuous and wicked actions, God will dispatch each soul to Heaven or Hell for eternity. (*TC*, 6)

It is not clear how this adaptation to the prevailing monotheisms can be reconciled with the Platonic notion of "astral immortality," which the Druze also believed in.

Let us see whether the seemingly contradictory elements in Druze soteriology can be reconciled at some level. Take the Druze belief that rebirth must lead to a purification of the soul. Those who have achieved such a condition will ascend to the stars, where they presumably will dwell with or near God. This doctrine of "astral immortality" is widespread among other Ismā'īlī-derived sects also. "Thus, a modern traveller spoke to an old Nusairi [Nuṣayrīyah] who was sitting one evening surrounded by his boys, saying,—'Speak: Where are the sons of your youth? these are the sons of your old age.' 'My son,' the old sheikh replied looking up, 'is there; nightly he smiles on me, and invites me to come.'"[101]

Alongside this doctrine of "astral immortality" is a messianic religious vision known to us only sparsely. "Those souls who have reached a sufficient stage of purification or merit are reborn into Chinese Druzes. It is not clear whether this can occur before the return of al-Ḥākim; but at any rate when he does return all faithful Druze will follow him in that triumphal march from China during which he will conquer the whole world and make the Druze religion to prevail over all others" (BR, 11). The messianic vision creates a universal Druze brotherhood, whereas the soteriological vision eventually abolishes the rebirth cycle. Perhaps the relation between the two visions can be formulated as follows: those whose souls have been purified through successive rebirths achieve "astral immortality" and become stars; others continue to roll round in this imperfect cycle of existence and reexistence, engaged in the task of purifying their souls for a finite period. At the end of this period all Druze, led by the returning messiahs al-Ḥākim and Ḥamza, will convert the world into a universal Druze faith with good Druze becoming rulers of humankind. These good beings also will become stars and live close to God in a spiritual, not literal, sense. At some indeterminate future time there will be a further reckoning on Judgment Day. The Platonic notion of astral immortality, the Plotinian doctrines of the Nous and the One and their manifestations in historical actors, the widespread idea in rebirth theories that the processes of reincarnation lead to the purification of the soul, and the doctrine of an omnipotent and compassionate God of the prevailing monotheisms are woven together in Druze rebirth.

Is there anything here that resembles the Indic or Plotinian karma-like notions? According to Stevenson ordinary Druze do not speculate about the processes of rebirth, which they claim are in the hands of God, whereas it is impossible for Buddhists to talk about rebirth without bringing in karma (*TC*, 7). For Druze what one does in this life has little or no bearing on the next. This does not mean the absence of ethics in Druze belief because God takes over the karmic functions. God can reward the virtuous; concomitantly he can presumably punish. Even basic problems of theodicy can be resolved through this dialectic. Thus in an apocryphal story a sage was asked by an Emir why he (the Emir) was blessed with fortune and wealth although he was thoroughly evil. The sage answered: "Perhaps in a previous life once having found someone sleeping in the sun, you were kind enough to wake him and ask him to move into the shade. That kindness alone is enough to have God bestow on you a life such as you are now living."[102]

The preceding story illustrates the persistence of a discourse of rebirth rewards and punishments that thrives in spite of orthodox denials. Even Stevenson admits that "one occasionally finds hints among the Druses of a belief in retribution in one life for wickedness in a preceding one"; for example, a "wealthy and boastful man [might] die in his mansion and be instantly reborn in a hut" (*TC*, 187, 7). But these instances indicate not the automatism of karma but the administration of otherworldly justice by God. Besterman reports: "A modern Druze . . . will point out that many are doomed to a life of suffering and misery, while others enjoy an opposite condition. Now, this cannot be consistent with the goodness and justice of God unless one supposes that their moral actions during their previous lives were such to necessitate the present dealings of God with them" (BR, 9–10). In this situation a karma theory can hardly be expected to surface, much less survive; nor is there any incentive to adopt Platonic or Plotinian forms of ethical retribution and reward.

The material from related Ismā'īlī sects is even more interesting because it does show that, contrary to orthodoxy, some did believe in animal reincarnation. This is true of sects such as the "Assassins" (a Nuṣayrīyah group disparagingly referred to as "consumers of hashish"), the Nuṣayrīyah of western Syria and other communities for whom historical information is available. Besterman mentions the case of Rashīd al-Dīn Sinān, who came to Syria from Persia around 1160 C.E. and became the leader of the Assassins. Here is an account of him from about 1335 C.E.: "One day a big serpent started up on the road along which Rashīd was travelling. His guards hurried to kill it, but Rashīd stopped them saying, 'This serpent is so-and-so: his metamorphosis is his purgatory, for he was heavy with sin. Do not deliver him from this condition'" (BR, 4). On another occasion he saw a monkey and gave it a coin. The monkey looked at it for a long time and suddenly died. Rashīd's interpretation was that the monkey was the king whose face appeared on the coin. God caused him to remember his past life, and the monkey, recollecting his past glory and present abasement, died in sorrow. Other stories recorded by Besterman indicate that in spite of orthodox beliefs there was at least an occasional or minor tradition of animal rebirths. Such stories are to be expected in a tradition influenced by Greek rebirth. This tradition is even stronger in the Shi'ite Nuṣayrīyah sect (c. eleventh century C.E.) of western Syria.

Like the Druze the Nuṣayrīyah view rebirth as a privation to be endured until the soul is ultimately purified. The soul of a wise or observant person passes through only seven incarnations, whereas the souls of ordinary folk go through eighty. Those who do not pray to 'Ali, the legitimate successor of the prophet, will be born as camels, mules, donkeys, and sheep—all domestic animals condemned to suffering. However not "all human incarnations [are] looked upon as equally fortunate: the worse fate is to be born as a Jew, a Sunnite, or a Christian." More clearly than the Druze, contemporary Nuṣayrīyah "justify their belief in rebirth by asking how one can explain a man being born blind if this fate is not an expiation for sins committed in a former state" (BR, 5–6). According to another nineteenth-century source, they point to living animals "seen with scars on their body corresponding to the wounds of which certain individuals have died in these places."[103] This is a neat inversion of the common belief in rebirth eschatologies that a scar or birthmark found on a *human* neonate is a sign of a wound inflicted during the previous existence. Many of these Ismā'īlī sects also have presaging dreams of the sort already discussed for Amerindians.

It seems that these Ismā'īlī rebirth theories share common eschatological features. They all bypass the world of ancestors entirely; instead of sojourning there a person is born after death in the human world (and occasionally as an animal). It is a world of just retribution and reward, but unlike the karmic eschatology it is a retribution effected by God.

Like the Nuṣayrīyah, the Alevis of south central Turkey interviewed by Stevenson and his colleagues have clearly defined notions of compensatory rewards and punishments. One can be reborn as an animal as a consequence of misbehavior in the previous existence. "If the record of an immediately previous life fails to indicate sinful conduct that could explain a congenital disease or other misfortune, they may surmise its origin in conduct during a wicked life farther removed in time" (*TC*, 186). Stevenson rightly says that these concepts are not well developed and do not share the automatism that karma entails. The general answer everywhere among these Ismā'īlī groups is the conventional one found among orthodox Muslims: "God willed it," or "Only God knows" (*TC*, 187). Nevertheless, the mere fact that ethicization step 2, however weakly developed, prevails among Nuṣayrīyah and Alevis means that some *dislocation* at birth is possible, quite unlike the Druze situation. Thus "an Alevi may be born as a person of another nation or religion, and persons of other groups may incarnate as Alevis" (*TC*, 186). All these groups believe that the good and bad one does in past lives will have a reckoning on the day of judgment.

Let me draw some of the implications of these varying forms of Ismā'īlī rebirth. There seems to be a widespread dispersal of the model of instantaneous rebirth among all these heterodox Ismā'īlī groups. This model of rebirth has had a wide dispersal, not only in the early Greek world but also throughout western Asia. It would not be too rash to suggest that it existed in this region prior to the advent of the monotheisms. Further, one can make two informed guesses to account for their wide distribution. First, the Ismā'īlī sects borrowed these ideas from the Neoplatonists; or, second, they merely imposed Neoplatonist thought on earlier models. If the latter, one can argue that the Ismā'īlī evidence indicates that the doctrine of "instantaneous rebirth" that we speculatively attributed to the Pythagoreans *enlinks* a larger geocultural region. I am sympathetic to the idea that the Greeks might have borrowed doctrines of reincarnation from the "Egyptians," as Herodotus says, because the Egyptians in the *History* occupied a large territory between Libya and Ethiopia containing different ethnic groups and a variety of religious practices that Herodotus describes at considerable length.[104] Thus one cannot exclude the possibility of reincarnation beliefs among ordinary "Egyptians" as a popular religious form, as was the case with the upper and middle Ganges valley during the time of the early Upanishads. Moreover, the Greeks also had another model of rebirth, in which the soul at death temporarily sojourns in some otherworld before reincarnating in this world. This model also exists to this day in the contemporary religions of West Africa, such as that of the Igbo, and surely had a much wider spread before the advent of modern missionary movements. Thus the two models—instantaneous rebirth and delayed rebirth—are found throughout western Africa and Asia in their various cultural and ethical transformations. One must assume that similar variations were scattered across large areas of ancient Europe and in other parts of Africa.

What then were the transformative elements that were introduced into the basic model of instantaneous reincarnation among the Druze? First, there was imposed on this model a Platonic and Plotinian frame systematically worked out through the conceptual imperative that guided early Druze thinkers. These thinkers might also have incorporated a Plotinian version of punishment in the next reincarnation (which is consonant with instant rebirth). Whether animal rebirth existed prior to or after the adoption of this frame is impossible to determine.[105]

Second, there is another frame, that of God, although we do not know which came first, the Neoplatonist or the monotheistic. When the idea of God and the day of judgment is introduced, it is difficult to sustain any form of ethicization on the karmic model because the consequences of good and bad actions can only be the work of God. Finally, the God of the Near Eastern monotheisms puts soul-possessing human beings at the center of creation, thereby eroding the idea of animal rebirth and subverting any prior doctrine of species sentience.[106]

# 7 IMPRISONING FRAMES AND OPEN DEBATES

## *Trobriander, Buddhist, and Balinese Rebirth Revisited*

### REINCARNATION, PROCREATION, AND THE EMBODIMENT OF THE SOUL

In this final chapter I want to further explore a theme that pervades much of this work, that even radical religious innovation must occur within the frame of preexisting structures of thought, which can on occasion act as "prisons of the *longue durée.*" As usual I will place that notion within ethnographic and historical contexts, returning to the "small-scale" societies discussed in chapter 2, especially Trobriand. Then, varying our theme somewhat, I deal with Bali, a "nation" consisting of villages that resemble the small-scale societies of our sample yet have historical connections with Buddhist and Hindu cultures.

Let me begin with an existential puzzle, or aporia, that is *expectable* in any rebirth eschatology and that is waiting to surface under suitable circumstances. The spirit or soul at death must eventually come back to earth, and for this to happen the spirit must find its way into the womb of a woman. Take the not-unusual case of the Kutchin, reported by Slobodin, in which the spirit, in the form of a small creature such as a mouse, creeps into the vagina of the woman just before parturition.[1] Or consider the invisible spirit child of the Trobrianders, who clings to driftwood or a similar object and waits to enter into a woman of the same matriclan. *If it is indeed the spirit that initially gets incarnated or reincarnated in the human womb, then what is the role of coitus and semi-*

*nal ejaculation in conception?* This is a key aporia of any rebirth eschatology, and it differs from the Christological idea of the Virgin birth, which is considered miraculous and pertains to none but Jesus' immaculate conception. One must not assume, however, that ordinary people are any more obsessed with solving aporias of existence simply because they are expectable from our model than ordinary Christians are with resolving their theodicy. Aporias of existence become relevant to ordinary people only when they are hit by untoward events or when they are forced to confront personal or familial crises.

Let me begin with Plato's idea of that wonderful original society of men without genitalia. Immoral men in this group are punished by being reincarnated as women, beasts, and plants, whereas good males reincarnate in their original form. Therefore, in this first reincarnation souls became embodied with no reference to sexual intercourse whatever, and metacosmesis as a process independent of procreation occurs. Afterward sexual intercourse becomes necessary for procreation, but women's womb-passion poses an issue that Plato never raised, namely, whether it was possible for them to conceive without coitus and seminal injection. Souls could also be embodied in plants during the first reincarnation and presumably later on as well; this at least is not a result of intercourse! So is it with Pythagoras's being reborn as a tree and Empedocles as a laurel, although the latter at least believed in autoreproduction among "whole-natured things."

To resolve this issue let me refer to a famous controversy that animated the anthropological imagination in the late 1960s. Provoked by Edmund Leach's well-known essay "Virgin Birth" and Melford E. Spiro's spirited response, numerous debates arose in *Man* on whether Trobrianders and the Australian ādivāsis (aborigines) were ignorant about physical paternity, specifically, the idea that "sexual connection is the cause of conception" or that coitus is at least a necessary condition for the formation of a fetus.[2] This argument, as David Schneider shrewdly put it, ignores the fact that even in sophisticated modern societies virtually everyone is in some sense ignorant of the "true" knowledge of physiological paternity, except in the simple sense of a correlation between coital insemination and conception as part of the process.[3] In the 1960s one could frame the issue in terms of necessary and sufficient conditions; in the new millennium this terminology is rendered dubious by the knowledge that conception can indeed be engineered without coitus. Thus, in hindsight a cynic may argue that anthropologists of the 1960s, who were postulating a causal connection between coitus and conception, were also ignorant of the nature of physical conception! Perhaps the cosmological ideas underlying rebirth eschatologies can help revitalize the old debate and simultaneously illustrate the epistemological issue of imprisoning frames.

Before I embark on this topic, I want to further clarify the distinction between incarnation and reincarnation. As Lee Guemple has pointed out the Qiqiqtamiut Inuit of the Belcher Islands believe in the continuous incarnation of ancestral spirits.[4] Similarly, the Trobrianders, like many others in this work, and this includes Plato, implicitly recognize a fixed spirit pool of ancestors who achieve continual or continuous incarnation. However, the Western term *incarnation* relates to the spirit's assumption of a bodily form, the spirit made flesh as it were, the archetypal case being Jesus. On the other hand, *reincarnation,* as the *Oxford English Dictionary* defines it, is to "incarnate anew" or "incarnate again," and as it permeates popular thought, it refers to successive generational incarnations in different bodies. I suspect that anthropologists such as Guemple want to make a different kind of distinction: reincarnation refers to the familiar idea of a person who after death is reborn in another human womb, whereas continuous incarnation is a preexistent spirit realizing bodily form in successive rebirths. The latter idea is present in some of the Greek traditions and in the non-Theravada traditions of Buddhism in respect to the founder: the Buddha is a transcendental essence that manifests itself in outer form in particular Buddhas.[5] To put it differently: Buddhas are continuous incarnations of a transcendent Buddha spirit. Such Buddhas are karma free and can be born and reborn without any real change of being.

One can argue that a theory of continuous incarnation is logically entailed by a rebirth eschatology (although not by a karmic one). If, let us say, the spirit or soul of my grandfather was incarnated in me, then my grandson will be my incarnation. However, insofar as my grandson embodies my spirit, and my spirit is my grandfather's, we are really talking about "incarnation anew," or the same spirit being repeatedly incarnated in different persons. If we follow this logic backward, there will be a spirit pool or a primordial collection of ancestral spirits who receive continuous incarnation. The cosmological theory that defines and describes this "spirit pool" can vary, or there might be no explicit cosmological theory at all. And often enough the distinction between continuous incarnation and reincarnation becomes so fuzzy that for most purposes it makes sense to simply use the term *reincarnation.*

To bring order to the aporia of the soul's conception in a female body, let me get back to the ethnographic data and examine the notions of physiological paternity in rebirth eschatologies, focusing initially on the Dene Tha, an Amerindian group, followed by the classic Trobriander case.

The Dene Tha are a Northern Athapaskan group in northwestern Alberta related to the Beaver and Wet'suwet'en. In spite of intense missionary activity since the early nineteenth century, they still maintain some of their indigenous religious beliefs, according to ethnographer Jean-Guy Goulet. Informants in the ethnographer's field site believed that humans lived in the *ndahdigeh,* or "our land," in contrast to the "other land" known as *ech'undigeh,* also referred to as *yake,* "god's land," perhaps influenced by Christian beliefs. Communication between these two planes of existence takes place through dreams and visions. In "our land" actual animals found in the bush are only material embodiments of spirit animals, and they can be used, as with other groups in this region, as one's spiritual helpers. Contact and appropriation of the animal helper or guardian spirit is through the vision quest during adolescence. It is the spirit helper that gives the "dreamer" or "prophet" *(ndatin)* the power to travel to and from these two planes of existence in a manner very much like that of Siberian shamans.[6]

After death the soul is released and often sighted around burial grounds or seen at night around people's houses. "The soul of an individual who dies may seek on its own to enter the womb of a woman and be born again in 'this land,' rather than journey to the 'other land'" (CDT, 161). Here is an eschatology that credits the soul with voluntarism and the capacity to bypass the otherworld entirely. However, says Goulet, "the soul of an individual who dies may also be born again in 'our land,' not out of his or her [voluntary] desire, but because of a decision made by the parents or relatives, who call on fellow Dene Tha to use their animal helpers and powers to bring someone's soul back to this land" (CDT, 161). To complicate matters, the soul can be here and there at the same time. "Time after time I met Dene Tha who prayed to a relative they thought of in heaven when in need of assistance in stressful and difficult situations, while maintaining that this same relative had already returned to them to 'be made again' and be raised by them as a child" (CDT, 157).

Having sketched this background, let us consider Dene Tha reproduction beliefs. According to Goulet's somewhat inapposite phrasing, sexual intercourse is a necessary but not sufficient condition for pregnancy and childbirth. "Conception often occurs after the wife or husband 'sees' a deceased relative coming back to them to be born again" (CDT, 164). The contemporary Dene Tha, like other societies with similar eschatologies, believe that spirit entry does occur and is indispensable for pregnancy and reproduction, as is coitus. They also believe that coitus is required, but neither its precise role nor the debates it might have fostered are available in Goulet's account. However, he neatly documents the introduction of sterilization (reportedly without the female's consent) and other birth control techniques among the Dene Tha. I think such sterilization would inevitably have given rise to troubled discourses regarding the soul's reincarnation when the wombs of mature women have become barren.

Consider the debate that birth control introduces: the cycle of reincarnation requires "fertile women," but many of the available women have been sterilized, and mostly younger women and adolescents are available for spirit conception. Because Dene Tha know that sterilized women cannot reproduce, it follows that these women cannot receive the spirit entity for conception. Hence teenage pregnancies are attributed to the lack of availability of fertile women. Goulet's cases are very instructive in highlighting the dilemma facing the Dene Tha.

Take the case of Luke, the son of Andrew's brother. Luke is going to be reborn in the womb of Andrew's daughter (that is, Luke's father's brother's daughter). The case is reported by Andrew's sister-in-law, Julie, who is the mother's mother's sister of the reincarnated baby:

> Andrew's brother, his boy died. Not long after I went to visit [my sister] Susan [Andrew's wife]. Andrew started to talk about this little boy [his deceased brother's son], and Andrew was crying like a baby. He said: "Why nowadays do these women have to use birth control. I've seen Luke [his brother's dead son] standing at a corner of the house. He had no place to go. He had no choice but to come to my house, that is how my daughter is pregnant."
>
> Beverly [Andrew's daughter; Julie's sister's daughter] had a boy [Luke reincarnated].[7]

Goulet reports another case of a man crying as he related the case of his pregnant teenage daughter. "The man stated that the deceased had no choice but to come to his daughter as too many other women of childbearing age were not available to come back to because they had been sterilized" (CDT, 165). The emotional pathos of these parents must be seen in the larger context of debates and troubled discourses that arose from the introduction of sterilization techniques into this society. One thing is clear though: if fertile married women are not around, the spirit will seek entry in the womb of fertile teenagers, but whether teenagers have to have sexual intercourse to bring this about is not clear.

In "Baloma: The Spirits of the Dead in the Trobriand Islands," Malinowski dealt with Trobriand ideas of conception, which in turn provoked the modern debate on the "virgin birth" in *Man*.[8] Among the matrilineal Trobrianders of Kiriwina the child traces descent through its mother, and its conception is attributed to the entry of a spirit child into a womb rather than to the sexual intercourse of the parents, approximating the model of "continuous reincarnation." Yet insofar as the spirit is never identified with a *known* matrilineal ancestor, there is no need for a person to be other than what he or she is, because unknown ancestors or those long dead can be molded in any way one wishes by the person in whom he or she is incarnated.

Malinowski's views remained virtually unchanged: pregnancy is solely caused by spirit incarnations of matrilineal ancestors. The father has nothing to do with physical paternity; however, the path to the womb has to be opened up for the spirit to enter, and this is done through sexual intercourse. No virgin can conceive because of the blocked pathway. But, says Malinowski, the pathways can be opened by artificial means also. After the spirit enters the womb there is no further need for coitus for the woman to conceive. In response to Malinowski's inquiries the Trobrianders made an important proviso in respect to pigs. An informant told him: "They copulate, copulate, presently the female will give birth." Malinowski tentatively concluded, therefore, that in this case "copulation appears to be the *u'ula* (cause) of pregnancy." But further questioning proved otherwise because the question of animal reincarnation was of no importance to the Trobrianders. "Thus, in the case of animals, the whole problem about reincarnation and about the formation of new life is simply ignored." After many interviews and debates with natives Malinowski concluded that a virgin cannot give birth to a child because her vagina was closed up; hence intercourse or some other form of vaginal dilation was necessary. "My informants dwelt on this subject with much relish, graphically and diagrammatically explaining to me all the details of this process. Their account did not leave the slightest doubt about their sincere belief in the possibility of women becoming pregnant without intercourse" (B, 201–4). Trobrianders added that animals die by natural causes, whereas human death is always a result of some supernatural agency.

In the anthropological debate both parties agree that Trobrianders and some Australians believe in spirit impregnation. However, Leach's point is that this does not entitle us to infer that either group is *ignorant* of physiological paternity, the position taken by Malinowski and his modern-day supporters Melford Spiro, Ashley Montague, Phyllis Kaberry, and others. Leach recognizes that it is possible, but not likely, for a group to be ignorant of physiological paternity because everywhere people have widespread practical knowledge of human and animal procreation. He thinks that such beliefs are no stranger than beliefs in the Virgin birth or the more general Christian belief that a person has a soul given to him or to her by God and that we are in a sense God's creatures. Many devout monotheists would in fact deny that physiological paternity is all that important in conception.

Leach's argument is coupled with a strong ethical concern that I share. "It seems evident that Western European scholars are strongly predisposed to believe that *other people* should believe in versions of the myth of the Virgin birth. If *we* believe in such things we are devout: if *others* do they are idiots."[9] Strongly put. But Leach's opponents respond that they are not implying an absence of rationality among natives, only an "ignorance" or lack of knowledge, or, as Ashley Montague put it, following nineteenth-century usage, a "nescience," which was also Malinowski's position.[10] But is "ignorance" simply a lack of knowledge? We do not tell our students that they are ignorant if they lack knowledge; nor is an ignoramus simply a person who lacks knowledge. And would one have the temerity to say that the anthropologists of the 1960s who thought that intercourse was a necessary but not sufficient condition for pregnancy were ignorant of the facts of physiological paternity? And what does it mean to say euphemistically that Trobrianders and Australian ādivāsis were "nescient" of the facts of physiological paternity? I could as easily say that the European ethnographers were nescient about Trobriander beliefs or that my students are nescient about Buddhism and go on talking about nescience in this nescient fashion.

It seems that the role of the Trobrianders and Australians is to provide *facts* that will permit either side to justify or validate its own point of view. It is impossible for these ethnographers to imagine that natives too might be carrying on their own debates on these very topics! To show that some such thing is indeed happening, let me move from Malinowski to Leo Austen, who in 1934 published an important study of Trobriander procreation.[11]

Austen was the assistant resident magistrate who interviewed fifty persons in Kiriwina village. Austen had formulated an open-ended set of questions that were to be combined with interviews initially conducted in English but later substantiated with statements taken down in Kiriwinian and translated by him at leisure. The whole strategy of research was to get specific information in order to confirm or disconfirm Malinowski and not to get involved in contentious discourses ("debates") among the Kiriwinians themselves on the subject of spirit conception. In fact Austen (like many others) probably discouraged native debates from erupting and fouling the hypothesis-specific nature of the interviews. It is not surprising, then, that the interviews confirmed Malinowski's hypotheses. Additionally, Austen provided detailed technical information on fetal development from the very entry of the spirit to the formation of a near-complete fetus (TI, 108–10). He also confirmed Malinowski's claim that Trobrianders believed the vagina of a virgin must be opened up by intercourse, but he denied that, except for mythical cases, it was permissible to dilate the vagina artificially. Again: "Until the menstrual flow has ceased, a female cannot conceive; and the monthly flow of menstrual blood is checked by sexual intercourse." Yet semen also has no role whatever in conception. And he adds that "the greater number of my informants laid down with no uncertainty that the *baloma,* or the reincarnating *waiwaia* (spirit child) was undoubtedly the cause of pregnancy" (TI, 103–7). When a woman is about three months pregnant she dreams that "a spirit child or reincarnating *waiwaia* is brought to her by some baloma or spirit of a dead relative" (TI, 110) and is placed on her head. Thereafter the spirit child waits, floating in drift logs, leaves, boughs, or weeds, ready to enter a woman, as Malinowski also asserted.

All this seems a near-perfect confirmation of Malinowski except for the jarring fact that some of Austen's informants had *another* view of pregnancy, also consonant with matrilineal kinship and, more important, affirming the agency of women:

> One of my best informants, who did not believe in the reincarnating *waiwaia* being the cause of conception, still accepted the belief that pregnancy did not take place until after the second month from the cessation of the menses. She was an old woman, married about forty years ago [a young woman when Malinowski was there], had had five children, and on no occasion had she dreamt of a *baloma* bringing her a spirit child. She was the strongest advocate of the belief that blood in the uterus brought the child into existence without the aid of a reincarnating *waiwaia* . . . [which] did not greatly interest her. (TI, 110)

Austen says that this woman's ideas on the development of the fetus were quite unorthodox; furthermore, she did not think the father had anything to do with it. "And this fact was brought out forcibly by some few other married women who were unorthodox to believe that children were brought into existence by the 'turning over' of the blood in the uterus"

(TI, 109–10). Here were some women, including one of Austen's "best informants," who, while supporting the unity of the lineage by affirming *their* exclusive role in procreation, were also affirming *physiological maternity,* minimizing, if not denying, the role of the father as genitor (which is easy to do in Trobriand) and seemingly denying the idea of spirit conception as well—a rather drastic heterodoxy erupting from the strait-jacket of Austen's prearranged questions.

For Austen this heterodoxy seemed more apparent than real: "when the point cropped up as to whether their children possessed a *baloma* or spirit, *they were ready to fall back upon the orthodox idea of a reincarnating waiwaia.*"[12] Austen believed that this statement indicated the relative lack of importance of dissident opinions. I look at it differently, as another manifestation of the aporia that any rebirth eschatology poses, namely, the reconciliation of the role of spirit conception with, in this case, physiological *maternity.* "Ready to fall back upon the orthodox idea" is surely the ethnographer's conclusion. Once these women affirmed their relative autonomy in procreation, they were posed with the problem of reconciling this with the rebirth theory that postulated that children are ancestors reborn. Consequently, they were saying that the ancestral spirit inhabited the child *after* it was born, a viewpoint that Malinowski also recorded from an informant in the coastal village of Kavataria.[13]

Austen's female informants thus preserved the idea that the actual physical procreation of the child was the mother's responsibility, although these informants did not express in their interviews what role, if any, the father might have had in that process. It is likely that these women, when they talked among themselves, unimpeded by the prearranged scenario with the white magistrate, would have had much more spirited arguments on spirit conception. To put it differently: an ethnographic inquiry such as Austen's is itself the narrow shed (or frame) that encapsulates the native discourse, not easily permitting contentious arguments to move out of its confines. When they threaten to do so, the ethnographer pulls them back into the shed because it must be remembered that many of the questions asked by the interlocutor (the ethnographer, the missionary, the traveler, the administrator) basically concern debates in his or her own circles about the nature of the other culture.

Malinowski was sensitive to the voices of his informants and recorded multiple opinions on various subjects. However, like other ethnographers of the time, he wanted to distinguish the "orthodox" views of specialists from popular views and individual speculations; at other times he was trying to formulate a "clear and final solution" out of the "contradictions which cropped up in the course of inquiries."[14] In his second Trobriand visit, however, Malinowski was much more receptive to local debates, as I have already pointed out in respect to his informant Tomwaya Lakwabulo. In his 1927 book *The Father in Primitive Psychology* he admits that natives have a "diversity of views *only partially merging into a consistent story*" (*FPP,* 41–42, my italics). During this second visit he engaged "definitively and aggressively" in open debates with natives on their procreation beliefs only to find that he "had been preceded in this attack by the missionary teachers" (*FPP,* 55, 57).

Confronted with these contentious debates Malinowski's informants reaffirmed even more vehemently their view of spirit conception, this time even denying that pigs procreate through sexual intercourse. Thus they produced many dogmatic answers regarding both humans and pigs. When Malinowski posed "an arrogantly framed affirmation that the missionaries are right" to one of his most intelligent informants, the latter retorted: "Not at all, the missionaries are mistaken; always unmarried girls continually have intercourse, and yet have no children." Another said: "They talk that seminal fluid makes a child. Lie! The spirits indeed bring [children] at night time" (*FPP,* 60, 62). Yet another informant stated that although there is no baloma involved in pig procreation, "the female pig breeds by itself," thus bringing into question the earlier view of pig procreation and proving that pigs, too, like Austen's female informant, can produce babies through internal processes, although lacking the later intervention of a baloma. Further proof of perverse porcine procreation was supplied by another informant, no doubt provoked by Malinowski's own dogma that testes alone contain the generative substance: "From all male pigs we cut off the testes. They copulate not. Yet females bring forth" (*FPP,* 64), conveniently ignoring, said Malinowski, the fact that actual copulation of the domestic female is the work of wandering feral pigs. What seems to have happened here is a powerful native reaction in the face of an "arrogant" assault on their views, initially by the missions and then by the ethnographer, resulting in a firm schismogenetic insistence of one view as the only view. Pestered by outsider Europeans, the native is the one who now retreats into a narrow shed, denying the multiplicity of indigenous opinions about rebirth.

Malinowski, for his own part, humbly admitted that his earlier view of pig copulation through heterosexual intercourse was wrong. But was it? His activity and that of the missions probably temporarily silenced the earlier debate: "They copulate, copulate, presently the female will give birth." This view of animals is not unique to Trobriand; some Australian ādivāsis have similar opinions. It therefore seems entirely likely that Malinowski did record an alternative view of procreation in his earlier visit. In order to record unusual cultural beliefs so opposed to the European ones, he simply ignored the voices that expressed similarity between pigs and humans. Thus there are multiple debates and multiple reactions among native populations as a consequence of the alien presence.

One such reaction is when the unwary informant is compelled by the presence of the outsider to answer a question to which he or she had not given much thought. The paradigmatic story is where a curious Western interlocutor begins to ask questions regarding the puzzles that puzzle *him*. Naturally, this fuels an already existing debate in the society; or if the topic is not a subject of internal debate, the new inquiry introduced by the outsider might spark contentious discourses (debates) on the subject. In some instances the ethnographic inquiry itself might well have created the contentious problem, although this is not the way anthropologists have seen it. Take a statement by a hypothetical informant who says, "In my group we think that in addition to the entry of a spirit, sexual relations are also important in the creation of a fetus." This might mean to my hypothetical interlocutor that group "X" does have notions of physiological paternity. Or take the opposite statement, of the sort that in fact did occur in Kiriwina: "Missions say that the fetus is the product of sexual relations between men and women but they are wrong; it is due to spirit impregnation." Once again, it might be an affirmation of an important spiritual principle to counter the equally important spiritual principle affirmed by the missions. Alternatively, these responses might well be a reflection of debates going on in the society itself, partly provoked by the new intrusive European presence, which raises doubts among informants themselves regarding the central rebirth aporia that I stated earlier. None of Austen's informants, for example, could confirm Malinowski's contention that Trobrianders thought that the artificial dilation of the vagina would do for spirit impregnation. It is likely that this answer was provoked by Malinowski's unrelenting inquiries on the subject and that natives, pushed to the wall, were compelled to invent this piece of native custom. Malinowski asserted that the natives dwelt on this topic with "relish" and illustrated this process "diagrammatically." To me the evidence of Malinowski's diary suggests that the ethnographer's own sexual frustrations prompted this line of inquiry and that the natives' relish and diagrams were initiated by Malinowski himself.[15]

We often think and act as if the dialogues that informants engage in with us contain evidence that validates our hypotheses about them. Surely this is only partially true, for in engaging in dialogue with us they might well be engaging in debates with us or giving us discursive information about debates that exist in their own society. The latter is especially true of issues that are controversial to them also. In this type of situation "information" given to ethnographers is central to our understanding contentious discourses in that society and is not simply data that validates a particular ethnographic hypothesis on such topics as the ignorance of physiological paternity. From such information one cannot infer the dominant form of procreation beliefs in a society; one can only infer the existence of debates regarding the aporia of rebirth that I have sketched and multiple notions regarding coitus, procreation, and rebirth. Yet these multiple responses do not occur willy-nilly: they hover around the central issue of any rebirth eschatology, the nature and role of the spirit being reborn in a woman's womb, which is also the receptacle for intercourse and semen ejaculation.

In such a case the ethnographer might simply be a convenient vehicle by which natives air the debates going on in their own society. The ethnographer is deluded into thinking that these informant discourses validate his hypothesis; in reality the discourses of both informant and ethnographer belong to the same class of statements, namely, those containing hypotheses regarding the nature of conception. This does not mean that one should not look for evidence to validate an ethnographic hypothesis, only that evidence is equivocal and its equivocal nature must be recognized, critically evaluated, and understood before it is used to validate any single interpretation. Hence, in the context of the preceding discussions, the statements of informants could be used for understanding the content and complexity of debates about physiological or spirit conception that occur in that society rather than as evidence to validate an ethnographic hypothesis regarding what Trobrianders or Australian ādivāsis knew about those very same phenomena. Malinowski, I think, correctly sketched an important view of Trobriander spirit conception, but it is unlikely that it was the only one. Yet he was trapped in his own imprisoning theoretical frame such that he had to convert that conception into a native "dogma," refusing to recognize alternative views. Moreover, virtually all of his informants were male, thereby silencing the powerful contradictory views of females, who, by his own thinking, were a strong force in this matrilineal society. These women were staking a position strongly opposed to Malinowski's, but it was not a "paradigm shift" because they were still concerned with the entry of the spirit child into the womb of a woman *after* conception has occurred through unique biological processes pertaining to "blood" within her own uterus. The *abandonment* of native beliefs regarding spirit conception will occur when Trobrianders have, for various reasons, forsaken them for Christian eschatology and soteriology.

## BUDDHISM, PROCREATION, AND REBIRTH

If indigenous debates about spirit entities and procreation are smothered in European representations of native beliefs, not so with Buddhism. Buddhist texts deal with four ways by which life arises: from an egg, from moisture (as with worms and other creatures), from a womb, and from spontaneous arising *(opapātika)*.[16] The normal way for humans to be born is through the womb, but spontaneous arising, normal for deities, sometimes occurs in humans. By the time the early Buddhist texts were compiled, there was no question that, for the most part, conception could not occur without intercourse and the injection of semen. This understanding probably co-occurred with the development of Ayurvedic medicine, which placed considerable emphasis on bodily processes and experimentation.[17] The Buddhist form of the rebirth aporia had to contend with increasing knowledge of the physiology of conception, development, and birth of the fetus. In general, Buddhists could not believe that the entity about to be reborn could achieve conception without coitus; nevertheless, an alternative explanation was available through the notion of spontaneous generation.

The aporia of rebirth in Buddhism's context is complicated by its theory of no-soul, or *anatta*. If there is no entity like a soul, then what brings about the linkage between one existence and another, or *paṭisandhi*? Because karma operates, the person who is reborn is neither the same nor different from the person in the previous birth. The rebirth-seeking entity that moves from one birth to another is the *gandhabba* (Sanskrit, *gandharva*), the "rebirth-linking consciousness," and not a discrete spirit entity. An early text says that three conditions are necessary for conception to take place: "there must be sexual intercourse between the parents, the mother must be in the proper phase of her menstrual cycle, and a *gandhabba* must be present."[18] The Buddhist controversy is not about the relevance of physiological conception in normal human rebirth but the more serious concern, unthinkable in most rebirth theories, of what gets reborn in the absence of a soul. Thus a variety of philosophical positions have been taken, mostly by non-Theravadins, about an "intermediate-state being," or *antara bhāva,* "existing" between death and rebirth.

Many controversies arose among the different schools of Buddhism regarding the intermediate-state being, but let me present the views of the fifth-century philosopher Vasubandhu. On the one hand Vasubandhu insists that the *antara bhāva* is not a Hindu-type soul but is constituted of the five changing aggregates, or *skandha*s; yet, on the other hand, he maintains that it does have sense perceptions, feelings, and unusual powers—features found among Inuit spirits (and also attributed by me to Empedocles' daimon). The spirit entity is also immaterial and incandescent and survives by feeding on odors. It arises at the place where death occurs and can, depending on its karma, be driven to a variety of rebirths. In human rebirth, the rebirth-linking consciousness operates thus:

> An intermediate being is produced with a view to going to the place of its realm of rebirth where it should go. It possesses, by virtue of its actions, the divine eye. Even though distant he sees the place of his rebirth. There he sees his father and mother united. His mind is troubled by the effects of sex and hostility. When the intermediate being is male, it is gripped by a male desire with regard to the mother; when it is female, it is gripped by a female desire with regard to the father; and inversely it hates either the father, or the mother, whom it regards as either a male or female rival. As it is said in the *Pragnapti,* "Then either a mind of lust, or a mind of hatred is produced in the Gandharva [Pali, gandhabba, the being about to be reborn]."[19]

The mind of the intermediate being, troubled by these erroneous thoughts, attaches itself to where the sexual organs unite, "imagining that it is he with whom they unite." Then in the midst of the impurities of blood and semen it finds a home. "Then the *skandha*s harden; the intermediate being perishes; and birth arises that is called 'reincarnation' *(pratisaṃdhi):* with the male on the right side of the womb and the female on the left."[20] This is followed by a detailed description of the formation of male, female, and neuter fetuses in the womb.

The conception, development, and gestation of the intermediate being and the fetus are intrinsically linked with *taṇhā* (desire). *Taṇhā* is the "second noble truth" in Buddhism and is the genesis of "suffering," the first noble truth. In Vasubandhu's version *taṇhā* is living according to "pleasure" and is epitomized by sexual desire, itself based on the very primordial oedipal experiences of the rebirth-seeking entity.[21]

According to this model there is a cluster of conditions necessary for conception to occur, including the karma of the rebirth-seeking entity and that of the parents. This, however, is only normal procreation; antedating it is the notion of spontaneous generation mentioned earlier, the form of arising that occurs totally outside of physiological processes and that is fully recognized in the popular traditions of Buddhism. In Buddhism divine beings always appear in this manner, but on occasion humans do also. The prime example is the Buddha himself, who descended from the Tusita heaven into his mother's womb at a time when she was abstaining from intercourse with her husband.

The references to such rebirths are scattered throughout Buddhist literature, early and late, and in the popular traditions affected by it. Consider the thirty-second chapter of the *Mahāvaṃsa,* the great Pali history of Sri Lanka written around the sixth century C.E., which describes the birth of the Buddhist hero, Duṭṭhagāmani, from the womb of his mother, Vihāra Mahā Devi. Vihāra Mahā Devi told a monk that even though she and her husband had performed meritorious actions, she had had no children. "Lo, our happiness is therefore barren!"[22] On the advice of a senior monk the queen went to a dying novice and pleaded with him to be reborn in her womb, promising him "great and beautiful offerings of flowers" along with gifts to the brotherhood of monks. "Then did he desire (rebirth for himself in) the king's family, and she caused the place to be richly adorned and taking her leave she mounted her car and went her way. Hereupon the novice passed away, and he returned to a new life in the womb of the queen while she was yet upon her journey; when she perceived this she halted. She sent that message to the king and returned with the king."[23] It is clear not only that the queen was barren when she approached the novice but also that the gandhabba entered her womb when the king was away, thus precluding any possibility that conventional conception had taken place. Thus the *Mahāvaṃsa* clearly implies that Duṭṭhagāmani's birth was a spontaneous (opapātika) one, unmediated by coitus, very much paralleling that of the Buddha himself. But precisely because of this, the *ṭīkā,* or commentary, on the *Mahāvaṃsa* has to explicitly deny it (the actual debates no longer survive), giving a "long account of the Buddhist concept of birth as a synchronism of three factors: the union of parents, mother's fertility and the presence of a being to be reborn."[24]

Another famous case from the early Buddhist literature is that of Aṁbapālī, the beautiful courtesan of Vesāli (Vaiśāli) and disciple of the Buddha who had "come spontaneously into being at Vesāli in the gardens of the king."[25] The texts mention her karmic past through innumerable previous existences, and it is clear that Aṁbapālī's birth, although "spontaneous," was karmically determined. It is therefore implied that although she appeared without parents, she did possess a rebirth connection (paṭisandhi) with her previous existences. Although her body form may have emerged in a spontaneous, or opapātika, manner, her spiritual form, or gandhabba, had to have been present. The *Jātaka,* or birth stories of the Buddha, have many cases of opapātika births, for example, the reference to the future Buddha conceived in the barren womb of Queen Candāvatī on the instructions of the god Śakra along with five hundred deities born in the same manner to the king's ministers.[26]

These kinds of births are quite common in the eschatologies discussed earlier. Sometimes spirit conception is implicit in informant accounts: when Tully River ādivāsi Australians say that a woman gets pregnant because she has been sitting on a fire on which she has roasted a particular species of black bream which must have been given by her prospective husband or by catching a species of bullfrog, we are not dealing with idiots.[27] Their statements contain implicit ideas of spirit conception that are impossible to articulate to an investigator unfamiliar with the local language. So it is with the miraculous births of the goddess Pattini—in a flower, in a mango, from the tear of a cobra, from lightning, from a shawl, and in many more forms.[28] They are miraculous because they flout the normal Buddhist idea of conception as defined in the texts and accepted by the people. Yet Pattini herself, like Aṁbapālī, is a karmically bound being, and she could not have been born in lightning or from a flower without the key component: the gandhabba, or karma-bound intermediate-state being. It is the spiritual element that permits a being to be incarnated in plants and natural phenomena. What one finds in these Buddhist cases is a *minor* tradition of conception that has a label—opapātika—and is recognized as a legitimate process. These opapātika births entail a form of spirit conception unmediated by coitus and insemination.

## BALINESE REBIRTH: CONTENTIOUS DISCOURSES ON REBIRTH AND KARMIC ESCHATOLOGIES

Bali provides an illustrative case of the resistance and then an accommodation by a rebirth eschatology of the more complex karmic eschatologies that also coexisted as an ideology or an ideal for both the "traditional" and recently educated elite of that nation. Following the theme of imprisoning frames I contend that resistance and accommodation are also precipitates of "debates," those contentious arguments that erupt in history and hover around these two competing models, making it difficult, if not impossible, to effect the sort of "paradigm changes" that Kuhn has depicted in respect to the seemingly "exact" sciences.

I have already noted that Bali has suffered the fate of other societies when it comes to ethnographic accounts of rebirth eschatologies. For example, a recent book on Balinese religion has not a single reference to reincarnation in its index.[29] The ethnographic stereotype of Bali is that of a society subscribing to "ancestor worship," a practice well documented among and associated with "primitive societies." But the few who have written on the subject clearly point out that Balinese "ancestor worship" exists not by itself but rather in a larger cosmological context.[30] The return of a dead kinsperson as a living relative is a taken-for-granted belief among Balinese of virtually every social strata, whether they subscribe to the karma theory in some form or not.

The problem of the karmic versus the rebirth eschatology has been stated by James Boon: "Balinese Hindu-Buddhism is incompatible with a full-fledged ethical karma-samsara doctrine because of the force of an Indonesia-style ancestor cult with its hierarchy of rites, vocabularies, social structures, and in particular marriage types. Balinese culture has long been exposed to karma theories but they have never become central."[31] Boon adds that ordinary villagers have been little affected by the karma doctrine, even though they use the word *karma* in a nonethical sense. Karma is "borrowed without being embraced," although elites with access to palm leaf manuscripts *(lontar)* and contact with Brahmin priests known as *pedanda* perhaps partially embraced and modified it. It is this "modification" that I want to deal with, followed by the work of recent middle-class intellectuals and religious reformers who have pushed hard to get the ethical theory of karma accepted by ordinary folk. They have had only limited success; ordinary villagers seem to believe in a form of ancestor worship combined with the idea of a reincarnating ancestor. This idea is indigenously Balinese (and Indonesian and stretching into parts of Melanesia), a belief structurally compatible with my topographical representation of the rebirth eschatology (see fig. 3). It seems that Balinese ancestors resist being chased away by the karma theory. This tension between karmic and rebirth eschatologies must surely have occurred, and perhaps still does, in actual practice in many parts of the Hindu and Buddhist world.

Let me begin with a brief case, that of an English-speaking, upper-caste, educated Balinese male whom I interviewed in 1995. I will then place this case in the larger context of Balinese debates on reincarnation. It will be evident that my informant, whom I call M, subscribes to a version of the karma theory that has accommodated itself reasonably well with that of reincarnating ancestors, even though M's karma theory is derived from the new reformist Hinduism.

Let me begin with death, which, M says, is the end of life in this world. He then qualifies this claim with his view of the afterlife, which ideally should be the achievement of mokṣa (salvation) or, more generally and realistically, reincarnation within the family. Few ordinary Balinese, he says, ask why some people simply never come back, although theoretically the question is important. One may not come back because of bad karma, when the ancestor gets reborn in an inferior rebirth or in hell, or because of the reverse if he or she has achieved salvation, or mokṣa. When ancestors do come back, you don't inquire whether they are bad persons or not, that is, whether they had accumulated bad karma; you simply accept them as ancestors returned. In other words if you subscribe to the ancestor cult, then karma theory is an embarrassment that has to be dealt with. Yet educated persons such as M cannot ignore the karma theory, which has come to be the ethic of Balinese intellectuals.

To continue with M's account: the immediate parent never returns to the family; he or she lives in the heaven-world of the ancestors. Rather it is a great-grandparent *(kumpi)* or sometimes an ancestor from the remote past who gets reincarnated. M mentioned the case of one of his sisters. When she was born, the family went to a spirit medium, known as a *balian* (or *dukun*), who contacted the recently reincarnated ancestor. The balian became possessed by that ancestral spirit and spoke in the voice of that ancestor (even though the ancestor was not personally known to the family). In his sister's case the balian spoke of "your ancestor behind the mountain," that is, the range of mountains north and east of Bali. This is important because M's family originated from that area, the Bulena region. Thus, the ancestor reincarnating in his sister is an unknown person from the area from which M's family originally came. This knowledge helps the family to reestablish contact and ensure continuity with their ancestral past. By contrast, M told us that his brother was his great-grandfather reincarnated and that the brother has the great-grandfather's name appended to his own. Generally, when a boy is born, one expects him to be a great-grandfather returned. (The unity between the two is expressed in the term *kumpi,* which applies to them both.)

The technical term for ancestral spirit is *leluhur* (something that comes from above), that is, the rebirth-seeking entity.[32] Generally people go to the balian three days after the birth. However, they do not take the infant out of the compound; rather it is the family that consults a balian who specializes in this task. The idea is to identify and greet the deceased ancestor incarnated in the neonate. As M put it: just as we greet a relative that visits us, so we greet the returned ancestor (which after all is the same thing). Thus the birth of a baby is a double joy: the arrival of the neonate, as well as the return of the ancestor who is reincarnated in it. M added that the verdict of the balian is not final, and this is true of the other services rendered by the balian, such that if one is not satisfied with the verdict of the balian, one can consult another. "We must be persuaded from the way the balian speaks in the trance that the voice is one of our ancestors." One knows this through empirical verification or practical proofs. For example, the ancestor must know some of the family secrets, such as family squabbles or land sales. This is evidence that the balian's verdict is correct. To be doubly sure, one might go to a balian who is outside the village and whom one did not know personally. There is nothing to prevent one from going to the same balian for another birth consultation; or one could go to another or consult several balians. We are once again into the everyday empirical validations discussed earlier.

M gave an example from another one of his three sisters. When he was only thirteen, he went with his mother to consult a balian regarding the rebirth identity of his infant sister. This balian worked in a Chinese temple *(kelentena)* in another village; during the balian's trance she "spoke" to M's mother initially in Chinese, or what seemed to them to be Chinese. Yet when she got possessed by the reincarnating ancestor during that same trance sequence, the medium spoke Balinese. M's mother conversed with the ancestor, who spoke through the balian with the conventional, "I came to ask for rice *(nāsi),*" which I interpret as meaning "love." And the mother responded, "Yes, we are glad, please accept what I have [a sign of humble respect]." When the balian came back to consciousness, she asked M's mother, "What did I utter?" and she then told the balian the details of the conversation.

The most common custom is to give the child a name after 105 days, when for the first time the infant is ritually placed on the floor of the compound. One does not have to give the child the name of the ancestor, even if the ancestor is known. Further, the child is not necessarily given special respect simply because it is a known returning ancestor, although this might in fact happen. In M's brother's case the ancestor was known. "When the child was in school and growing tall, my mother used to say he's just like his great-grandfather." In his sister's case the reincarnating ancestor was not known, but it is important to know that it *was* an ancestor.

Now let me place my informant's statements within the larger context of Balinese rebirth sketched by scholars of Bali. The spirit mediums, or balians, whom most Balinese consult, often act as midwives, bonesetters, and masseurs. They are "usually illiterate in classical texts," but they have spiritual power, or *sakti* (from the Sanskrit *śakti,* designating the creative power of the deity), which "equips them to intervene with supernatural forces on behalf of clients."[33] Linda Connor recorded seventy-nine séances with eleven mediums in the Bangli district of Bali and found that 6 percent of all cases had to do with identifying the reincarnating ancestor.[34] As with shamans, and other ecstatics elsewhere, the balian is someone who has become a vehicle for a spirit after having become its victim. Like shamans, the balian often resists the summons to adopt the profession and as a result suffers physically and spiritually in a dark-night-of-the-soul type of experience.[35]

If *sakti* is the Indic term used to describe the power of the balian, the creative energy given to her, there is an indigenous concept, *taksu,* that refers to the medium's own guiding spirit, which "facilitates the communication of verbal messages from the other world through consecrated spirit mediums."[36] In a more abstract sense *taksu* is "also a force which enhances successful and even inspired performances in all varieties of ritual dramatic arts" (DL, 204). It is therefore not surprising that my informant, M, identified *taksu* in the latter sense with the Indic idea of *sakti.* One balian told Connor that "*taksu* is like a deified guardian spirit inside me, which I have had since birth and which gives me the facility to be used as a spirit medium." The consecration of the balian further empowers the taksu to act on her behalf. There is a taksu shrine in every Balinese temple, and the balian herself is often referred to as *balian taksu* (DL, 203–4).

Linda Connor's work indicates the substantive differences in the rebirth ideologies within Bali. In the Bangli district where she worked Connor noted that the people consulted the balian twelve days after a birth (not three days after, as with my informant, M). Further, the reincarnating spirit affects the persona of the neonate such that prominent character traits of the latter are similar to those of the ancestor. Although the spirit is incarnated in the child at birth, it is not firmly anchored during the first few days. Then the parents have to "pay any debts the reincarnating spirit owes to the various deities of the world from whence it has just come" (DL, 207). This practice is apparently an extension of one performed at the kinsperson's death, according to M. "At this time we go to a balian to contact the soul [he uses the classic Sanskrit term *ātma*] to find out why he or she died and to be sure that while the person was alive there was no debt incurred, not just money but also such things as promises. The soul of the dead person will tell this through the balian. We must inform the Brahmin high priest who conducts the cremation rites that we will pay the debts incurred by the deceased."

The available information suggests the prevalence of two forms of karmic eschatology in Bali, that of the traditional intellectuals and that of the new proselytizing elite, but both models are compounded by multiple empirical variations. Connor's assertion (which is Boon's also) that the karmic theory is entirely something imposed on Bali recently or earlier by literate scholars and "not endorsed in popular religion" is to some degree contradicted by Jero Tapakan, her chief informant, as she described one of her visions during her dark night: "Those lakes [she saw in her visions] were there for the souls [ātma] of the dead. The souls of good, peaceful people will stay here in Bali. The sinful ones suffer there, with the rocks tied to their feet. There were three lakes. Those who were suffering were in one. Those who were righteous were in another. Those who were sinful or die unnatural deaths were in the third. Do you see how it was?" (DL, 46).

There is no doubt that Jero Tapakan presents an ethicized hell, and her vision does not make sense except in terms of prior debates on the karma theory consistently operating in Bali such that Jero Tapakan has had to make her own reconciliation with it, although the details of how that reconciliation was made are unavailable to us. Yet Connor and Boon are probably right that many ordinary villagers do not believe in the karma theory at all. But the very fact that they use the term *karma* (whatever meaning they impose on the term) implies the existence of conduits that connect the village tradition with that of Indic thought. There surely must be others like Jero Tapakan who had to deal with the debates that the karma theory has provoked, and they must have had to reconcile karma in differing ways with older ideas of the returning ancestor. This should not surprise us because that theory, along with other Indic concepts such as *sakti,* has already been indigenized in popular Balinese culture. So is it with M: he voices an educated person's view of karma, differing both from that of ordinary villagers and from the newer and more radical version stemming from reform Hinduism and Buddhism. "Our duty is to pray for the salvation of the ancestral spirit but whether it goes there or not is based on his *subha* or *asubhakarma* [propitious or unpropitious] karma." In other words there are those who achieve mokṣa, or final salvation, and are not reborn, whereas those with good or bad karma come back to the family. Yet he qualifies this again: "we don't ask whether a particular ancestor is loaded with bad karma. It is tabu to talk of the bad karma of a dead ancestor." This is not surprising. One cannot have the ancestor who has returned to live with his or her kinfolk saddled with "sin" because that would bring misfortune and discontent into the family. Hence, one simply does not talk about the bad karma of the returning ancestor, or one could relegate that ancestor to a heaven (the ancestral world from which he or she came) or to a hell. But if some do not talk about the bad karma of the returning ancestor, others surely do. Jero Tapakan's hell is the precipitate of such talk. More commonly, the bad karma of an ancestor might come up if the descendant has experienced a serious misfortune, in which case the balian might say that the person's present trouble is a punishment for sins in an earlier life. There is yet another expectable consequence from our discussion of ethicization step 1: after a soul has gone to heaven or hell and has been rewarded or punished, he or she can come back to the family with a clean slate. This structural expectation, I believe, was empirically realized in Balinese rebirth, although the meager data available do not confirm it.

In my thinking, debates about karma have had a long historical run in Bali, and there are further data in ordinary life that indicate their precipitates. For example, the cremation rituals performed by the Brahmin pedanda are crucial to Balinese death, whether one is a villager or one of the traditional elite. Through these rituals the corpse is purified and returned to the five constituent elements of the universe *(pañca mahā bhūta).* If the Brahmin can send the soul to its salvation through these ritual procedures, then obviously that ancestor will not return to the living. Alternatively, the Brahmin priest can only purge the bad karma of the dead person through the cremation rituals or reward the good in the ancestral world. The latter rituals permit the dead to return to the kin group on the model of ethicization step 1. Some such idea was expressed by M, combining as always elitist Sanskrit and Balinese technical terminology:

> Ancestors live in a higher place with the deities and are themselves deities. How does this happen? After the body is cremated the spirit becomes an *ātma-siddha devata.* When the body is burned it reverts back to the five elements or *pañca mahā bhūta.* Then there is another ceremony for the purification of the soul or *ātma* and known as *mukur* [cremation ceremony]. They [priests] make a distinction between the *sthula sarīra* "the coarse body" and the *sūkṣma sarīra,* "the fine body" and [are] influenced by three of the *bhūta*s—*vāyu* [air], *teja* [fire, heat], *ākāsa* [ether]. We have to free

> the *ātma* from these three elements because the *indriya* (senses) are still resident there. The spirit that is freed is known as the *ātma-indriya-devata*. This spirit is enshrined in the family compound in the shrine for dead ancestors and is worshipped there. We pray that the ancestor "goes to the right place," that is, eventually achieve[s] *mokṣa* by uniting with the Almighty God (*ida sanghyang widi wasa*). This is the phrase that is used without reference to any specific deity like Śiva.

This is elite discourse only partially influenced by the Vedantic discourse of neo-Hinduism. Yet M uses *ātma* very much like the balian Jero Tapakan to simply designate the soul that gets reincarnated without reference to the atman idea of Vedantic Hinduism, which equates the individual's soul with that of God viewed as neuter (Brahman). Such uses of *ātma* as the reincarnating entity are common on the popular level in Hindu and Buddhist societies elsewhere.

The idea that the bad karma of the dead person could be purified and converted into a *pitaraḥ* through the cremation ceremonies performed by the Brahmin priest is part of the older Balinese elite religion, and it does not displace the ancestors in any radical fashion.[37] That happens with the new karma theories that operate inexorably to produce steps 1 and 2 of ethicization. In that case dislocation must inevitably result, and there is no way that the ancestor could be reborn in the kin group, except in rare cases. In this schema God may judge the moral worth of action and allocate a person's rebirth destiny, but there is little God can do to change it.[38] According to Connor's account this stern religious doctrine has no appeal to villagers, but it did become accepted in the early 1920s by the rising indigenous bourgeoisie in the Dutch East Indies (DL, 265–67). This emerging middle class was influenced by Theosophy and then later by those who wanted to convert Balinese religion into a universal Hindu religion of the neo-Vedantic type represented by Indian reform movements such as that of Swami Vivekananda and the Ramakrishna Society.

The latter situation is described in some detail by F. L. Bakker in his fascinating account of Balinese intellectuals engaged in refashioning their religion in a Hindu modernist direction.[39] I think Bakker is wrong in saying that "traditional religious documents in Bali pay little attention to the subject" of karma, but he is surely right about the new intellectuals. Thus Anandakusuma, a reformer, believes that "*karmaphala* [the fruits of karma] determines the kind of life to which the spirit is reborn, which explains why it is possible for a good man to find himself in miserable circumstances; his present misery is the result of acts in a previous life, acts which Anandakusuma names *karma.*"[40] So it is with other thinkers such as Gusti Agung Gede Putra, who was director general of the Hinduism and Buddhism department of the ministry of religion in Jakarta and came under the influence of both contemporary Vedanta and Sai Baba, the well-known guru and god incarnation of contemporary Hinduism. Yet like other Hindu modernists in both Bali and India Gusti Agung Gede Putra has had to reconcile karma with the idea of God. "Through this law God ensures that *subha karma* has a good result and *asubha karma* a bad result. *Subha karma* purifies the *ātman* so that it is better equipped to reflect God in a perfect way, whereas *asubha karma* defiles it and binds it more strongly with the material. It is thought which determines the quantity of *karma,* so that the intention underlying the action is decisive."[41]

Rich and multiple theories of karma and rebirth are being formulated and reformulated as Balinese intellectuals confront their old beliefs with the new intellectual currents stemming from Buddhist and Hindu modernism. M's discourse is one such reaction, but although he firmly clings to the older notion of the returning ancestor, he also has an impressive array of terms from the new reformist Hinduism, as well as from traditional elites who were also reacting to karma doctrines in their own fashion.

I can now sum up the implications of Balinese rebirth. Quite unlike in the Indic societies I have discussed, there are two dominant and opposed rebirth ideologies: the rebirth and karmic eschatologies topographically represented in figures 3 and 4. Scholars of Bali are probably right that the Balinese rebirth eschatology is the older, indigenous one that resisted supplanting by the karma theories stemming from Indic Hinduism and Buddhism. But resistance ends neither in capitulation nor in victory. Ordinary villagers continue to believe in the circulation of souls into the world of the ancestors and then to the family, and for the most part they do not accept the ethical theory of karma. Nor do they explicitly deny it. There is also very little to indicate acceptance of cross-species reincarnation in Bali, except in rare instances. Much as one resists the idea that an ancestor reborn is saddled with bad karma, so is it hard to accept an animal reincarnation for an ancestor, given the fact that animals are an inferior form of existence in Balinese thought. That latter view is itself a precipitate of debates with the karma theory because it is that theory that degrades animals. And it is not surprising that although village Balinese accept the theory of animal reincarnation in principle, they resist its reality.

That principle was given public recognition in 1979 during the ceremony of Eka Dasa Rudra, a major Bali-wide exorcism ritual lasting for a year, when many animals were killed for offerings. The Brahmin high priests explained that these animals were sacrificing their lives and that in return they were going to be reborn as humans.[42] But the data available do not permit us to make any comments about the debates that that particular discourse might have unleashed on the Balinese world.

The reality of karma, however, is also complicated as far as the traditional elites are concerned. In Balinese Hinduism represented by its Brahmin high priests karma could be purified by ritual, which, I have shown, could easily be accommodated to village beliefs pertaining to the recycling of ancestors. These beliefs are not the exclusive privilege of nonliterate peasants; traditional elites also believed in them. This means that karma in Balinese elite conceptions stops at step 1 of ethicization, not because they believe that the karma theory is false but because it has been short-circuited through ritual techniques. This again is not unusual in many of the forms of Indic Hinduism, where ritual acts, as well as a single-minded devotion to God *(bhakti)*, can short-circuit the karmic cycle. Nevertheless, I believe it is probably rare in Hindu thought, popular or otherwise, to find cases matching the Balinese village idea of ancestral souls circling back into the kin group without any reference to the karma theory. However, in India, as in the Buddhist nations, the *individual wish* to have the ancestor back in the family might well result in the short-circuiting of the karma theory, although this would rarely occur on the group level as in Bali. And when it comes to modern Balinese intellectuals, with their more recent orthodoxies imported from Indian centers of learning, an important shift has occurred. Here karma is the inescapable law, like the awesome Adrasteia of Plotinus, and it operates at steps 1 and 2 of ethicization, such that it can no longer be reconciled with the village view of the returning ancestral spirit. In my view the new doctrines are bound to gain hegemonic ground as Balinese villagers become more and more educated and are gradually drawn into the larger polity of the Indonesian nation (or for that matter into an evolving consciousness of Balinese nationhood or ethnicity transcending village ties). This might erode the field of the balian; alternatively, it might only displace it because there will be enough educated members of the bourgeoisie curious to know who they were in their immediately past existence or even in earlier ones. Such influential diviners have already emerged in Sri Lanka (and perhaps in other parts of the Hindu and Buddhist world).

What is the cultural significance of the emergence of new diviners in places like Sri Lanka? Remember that although the karma theory produces dislocation and the dispersal of kin, it is unsuccessful in displacing the rebirth wish (prārthanā) that people often make—the desire to be reborn in the same kin group or, more commonly, a wish to be reborn as the same spouse or child or as the child or grandchild of a child or as some loved person. This means that an aporia has emerged related to the very first model I sketched in figure 1, the elementary form of a rebirth eschatology, with its powerful motivation to bring the dead ancestor back to the bosom of the family. It seems as if that primordial motivation cannot be extinguished in spite of the increasing power of the karma theory in contemporary Buddhist nations. Further, one could make a statement that defies our logic of expectations, namely, that with the greater hegemonizing of the karma theory in its intellectualist sense there would be an increasing dispersal of dead kin, which means that rebirth into the same family would be increasingly difficult. But the new hegemonizing karma might actually motivate people to *want* to do something about it. Either people want to be reborn as a close family member, or they want to know who they were in their past lives, in effect trying to give personal meaning and significance to counter the increasing impersonality of the intellectualist vision of karma that brooks little compromise with popular religion. In Sri Lanka the latter movement has been given a filip through the work of Ian Stevenson, who has tried to prove the reality of rebirth through intensive and serious research on recollected rebirth memories from societies all over the world. Stevenson's work, alongside more dubious studies, has been widely circulated in the media. Hence new diviners, although few in number, have arisen to meet the new demands. For Bali this might mean that the debates with the highly intellectualized karma doctrines from neo-Vedantic Hinduism and Buddhism might provide the old balians with a new kind of future.

## METHODOLOGICAL POSTSCRIPT

The methodological thrust of my argument was briefly stated in the preface, in the formal models constructed in chapters 1 and 3, and in the body of this work, where the implications of these models are spelled out. In this conclusion I want to restate these methodological arguments in a coherent concluding statement.

I start with the demonstrable assumption that rebirth eschatologies have an inescapable elementary structure, which is depicted in figure 1:

the soul at death is reborn in the human world, with or without an intermediate sojourn in another world. This structure or elementary form is my construction, and although it is nomologically adequate and objectively possible, it does not exist in the real world. As an infrastructure it underlies all the variety and multiplicity of existent forms of rebirth anywhere. Borrowing a trope from Lévi-Strauss I would say that it is the "atom of rebirth" from which larger cosmological and eschatological systems are constructed, much as the avunculate is the atom of kinship.[43] All existent forms of rebirth theories have to be built around this elementary form. What then are the existent rebirth theories, and how can they be studied in order to reveal their structural transformations?

Let me review my strategy, beginning with my ethnographic descriptions of existent rebirth eschatologies in small-scale societies. They too are multiple and diverse, but insofar as they are built around the elementary form, the seemingly substantive variations reveal structural consistencies that I have delineated at some length. These pertain to such things as the sojourn of the soul at death in another world, followed by rebirth in the same kin group, and, with the exception of Trobrianders, the presence of techniques for identifying the previous-life persona of the neonate. These structural features are present in rebirth eschatologies of the small-scale societies I have described irrespective of their location in larger geographic and culture areas. There are other structural features that are not shared by all rebirth eschatologies. Perhaps the most important dividing line between divergent eschatologies is marked by the belief in rebirth as subhuman creatures. The animal-human divide helps me to limit the major thrust of my argument to a comparison of the Northwest Coast Indians and Inuit, the Hindus and Buddhists, and the Greeks of the "Pythagorean" tradition, broadly defined. Once this distinction is made, one can perform further operations for achieving the goal of this project, which is to study those ethical transformations that lead to the Indic and Greek theories of otherworldly compensations and rewards.

The method also permits me to make structural comparisons *within* each cultural region now delimited. Thus, there are important structural variations in the rebirth eschatologies of small-scale societies themselves, in effect the societies of the large circumpolar region stretching from the Northwest Coast of the Americas to the Inuit and across to Eastern Siberia (although I do not have detailed enough empirical information to deal with the last region). An important difference pertains to the nature of animal rebirth such that one could have parallel-species reincarnation or cross-species reincarnation. Either way, these societies show a constant transformation between human and animal lives, a blurring of species distinctions, and the wide prevalence of transpeciation. However, and this is an admittedly controversial part of my argument, where cross-species reincarnation occurs, there is a further psychic-cum-structural dilemma of endoanthropophagy, exemplified in Kwakiutl eschatology (which in turn opens a window into the Greek and Indian forms of the same dilemma). Underlying these two forms of animal reincarnation is an ethical principle I have labeled "species sentience," a doctrine that abolishes the well-known European distinction between nature and culture. However, although species sentience is always associated with animal reincarnation, it probably coexists with other eschatologies also, and in this sense it is akin to the role of shamanism.

Shamanism exists in all the societies of the circumpolar belt that I have associated with animal reincarnation. But shamanism is also found in societies that do not have animal reincarnation, for example, among the Ibo. Moreover, shamanism can easily be shown to exist in societies that do not possess rebirth eschatologies. But insofar as it is associated with rebirth eschatologies, shamanism, like the doctrine of species sentience, becomes important for the themes of this book. I have demonstrated the role of shamanism in the more complex eschatologies of the Greeks and Indians through textual, ethnohistorical, and structural analyses without committing the mistake of claiming that the ritual specialists of these civilizations are shamans.

The main thrust of my argument is to depict the processes whereby rebirth eschatologies are transformed into the ethicized eschatologies of the Indians and the Greeks. These processes of transformation cannot be studied substantively in terms of diffusion or spread. One cannot say that the rebirth eschatologies I have presented have helped form the more complex ones associated with Greek and Indic civilizations or that the one form "influenced" the other in empirical reality, although such influences did occur, and I have discussed them wherever feasible. Unfortunately, there is little one can do analytically with "influences." Sometimes "influences" can even impede understanding, as when scholars of Hinduism see Vedic "influences" on Upanishadic reincarnation or when Greek scholars see the influence of Hesiod's rather simple idea of Strife or of the "god of oaths" on Empedocles' much more complex thought.

Hence we have the utility of structure and structural transformations, which can be studied with a certain intellectual rigor. I do this in chapter 3 of this book, where I sketch an ideal type of "rebirth eschatology" based on the existent forms already presented. This ideal type is crucial to my analysis and is topographically represented in figure 3. In it I have tried to deal with structural features common to all rebirth eschatologies, that is, those rebirth theories found in small-scale societies, whether or not they feature animal reincarnation.

Once again the model that I have constructed cannot be replicated in any existent reality, although, unlike the previous elementary form, it is closer to the empirical reality, and, like the previous elementary form, it does not flout that reality. Having constructed this topographical model I now perform a key operation on it (the "imaginary experiment") by posing the following question: how does the rebirth eschatology I have constructed get transformed into the karmic and Greek eschatologies? I have suggested that only one critical structural variable is necessary for this to occur, what I have called ethicization. But ethicization is more than a "structural variable." It is something I have abstracted from the flow of history, a complex process in which a secular morality is converted into a religious one. Once this process occurs, the entry into the otherworld is "conditional," that is, dependent on the good and bad one does in this world. Hence when ethicization is introduced into the model of the rebirth eschatology, that model gets transformed in two directions. First, owing to the principle of the conditionality of reward, the otherworld in which the spirit sojourns gets transformed minimally into a world of reward and of punishment, a heaven and a hell. Second, when ethicization is carried out in respect to the next rebirth, that rebirth also becomes minimally a good rebirth and a bad one. In my language these are steps 1 and 2 of ethicization.

These two steps can be combined in three basic ways in extant forms of rebirth. There might exist step 1 of ethicization alone; this is exemplified in the Platonic and Pindaric forms of rebirth. Step 2 could also exist by itself, as in the eschatology of Plotinus and its derivatives in forms of heterodox Ismā'īlī thought. When steps 1 and 2 are combined, the "karmic eschatology" of the Indic religions develops. Thus the operations I perform on the model of the rebirth topography can produce, through structural analysis, the Greek and Indic rebirth theories found in the empirical record. Nevertheless, the imaginary experiment per se is somewhat empty of significance unless it can be put back into what Wittgenstein called "the stream of life," which is the world of experience, existence, and the unfolding of empirical history.

Included in this stream of life are the motivational activities of religious virtuosos. In my usage "structure" is linked with "agency." Although I can only sporadically demonstrate the manner in which specialists such as shamans help create the world in "small-scale societies," I demonstrate in greater detail the ways that religious specialists in both Greece and India impose their vision on the world and help to change it. These visions of the world, that is, the life-forms and epistemes created by thinkers, are not to be confused with structure but rather are "parole" or "culture" in our usage. It is in this realm that ideational differences or cultural relativism prevails, either within a particular society or across societies and cultures—a theme I will develop further in a moment. For present purposes let me state that one invents structures out of these life-forms that then help abolish their very uniqueness. Yet contextual and agency analysis can at any time restore that uniqueness, and this implies that sameness and difference are inextricably woven into the analytical or methodological discourse of the ethnographer or historian.

Yet it must be remembered that those who invent the world are not fully autonomous beings. Whether their vision gets accepted by the world depends on complex political and socioeconomic conditions as I have demonstrated in the Indic cases—for example, the breakdown of small-scale societies and the emergence of empires, the cultural conditions favoring argument and debate, and above all the emergence of stable congregations of lay folk, the result of the work of religious virtuosos who are driven to "convert" others into their own ways of thought. These phenomena, along with such processes as conceptualism and axiologization, I derive from the Indic material. My knowledge of ancient Greek thought and history is limited; therefore, I can only tentatively develop for Greece some of the issues that I have extrapolated from Indian religions.

We have also seen that there are many thinkers in both Indic and Greek thought who are not interested in converting the world. In the time of the Buddha there were those who simply engaged others in "disputations," without demonstrating much concern for the welfare of the world. Within the Buddhist scheme of things there also were the "pacceka Buddhas," those Buddhas who have discovered the truth but have not been motivated to proclaim it. In the Greek world early Pythagoreans produced sodalities of elites, but like the Upanishadic thinkers they were not interested in conversion and the formation of congregations; this changed in southern Italy in the eschatology represented by Pindar. And then there were figures such as Plato and Plotinus, both profound speculative thinkers, who were concerned only with the soteriological welfare of specially worthy individuals, although their thought filtered into later religious communities such as the early Christian fathers and the later Druze and other Ismā'īlīs.

The structural models that I have presented have another function in my text: they provide a disciplinary focus for recalcitrant descriptive material on the various forms of rebirth enveloped in the larger Greek and Indic cultures. What is the nature of this disciplinary focus? Structures, models, ideal types provide stable points for comparative analysis; they are attempts to produce order from the flow of human existence. It is in this flow of existence that cultural relativism and historical specificity prevail, whereas it is through structures, themselves multifarious (social, economic, psychic, cultural), that one can bring order into time and history and thereby produce forms of analysis or interpretations that defy the conventional bounds of what constitutes "a culture." What do I mean by this?

It should now be obvious that a "unique" structure is a contradiction in terms. The very structuralization of phenomena abolishes uniqueness, which is a characteristic of the phenomenal world. That world in its flow is structureless, or so it seems. This leads me to a further critique of relativism. To put it differently: my structural models of rebirth defy cultural relativism because cultural relativism lies in the phenomenological flow of existence that these models arrest. Employing this form of analysis I have shown common forms of thinking across conventional cultural boundaries—Melanesia, West Africa, Northwest Coast, and Inuit—and then into further leaps of both imagination and history I progress into the more complex forms of Greek and Indian thinking. Although common thinking processes and constructions of similar life-forms occur across cultural and geographical boundaries, our models also permit the discussion of structural variation or transformation. That is the whole point of structural analysis, for without transformation any notion of structure becomes a static, descriptive piece of labeling. For example, if I had stopped at a description of the Trobrianders' rebirth eschatology, I would have accomplished very little, except what might be called, in Geertz's now fashionable terminology, a "thick description" of a particular life-form. But the very act of comparison of related structures, that is, of similar life-forms in other small-scale societies, shows common human thought processes at work, cutting across the phenomenological flow of relativism, or the world of "becoming," that the many thinkers in my text have bemoaned. Structural differences can exist, but difference in this scheme of things is not that which springs from the kind of uniqueness (parole) discussed earlier but rather that which springs from structural transformations. Hence, transformations also constitute a field of difference in any serious kind of comparative analysis. Thus Buddhist rebirth, structurally speaking, is different from the Greek and the Amerindian forms, sometimes radically so, but those differences could be topographically described and interpreted.

One can no longer avoid a discussion of the analytical status of the type of structural analysis that engages me here. It is obvious that anyone dealing with structural transformations is indebted to Claude Lévi-Strauss. In my particular case I am more attuned to his early work on the avunculate than to his later brand of structural analysis, which posits what I have already labeled as an epistemological view of structure—"epistemological" because it entails a theory of knowledge that I find unacceptable. Lévi-Strauss's structural epistemology contains four fundamental ideas. First, it is based on the distinction between langue and parole formulated by Jakobson, in which parole, the messiness of the ordinary world, is pushed aside in the quest for some infrastructure that underlies it. This to me is unacceptable because these infrastructures are formulated at such a level of abstraction that they hardly permit engagement with the lived world. Or alternatively, the structures that emerge are too commonplace to be interesting, for example, the opposition between nature and culture, good and evil, left and right, head and foot, and so forth in the manner already anticipated in the Pythagorean table of opposites (see note 66 of chapter 5). Second, structures have a binary character in general, although Lévi-Strauss himself is less given to binarism than are his followers. For me binarism cannot explain anything; it is a phenomenon to be explained. Third, Lévi-Strauss's brand of structuralism entails a universalist view of the human mind (and underlying that, of the human brain) such that structures must exist in the world by the very constitution of our minds and brains. Although I am sympathetic to a general view of human nature, including universal neurological structures, I also think we are in no position to force structuralism, or any other theory in the human sciences, into a definitive neurological schema. The reductive anchorage of structures to the brain is not a very useful way of looking at what human beings invent to resolve existential dilemmas, although without our complex brains those existential dilemmas could never have arisen, let alone be resolved. Fourth, Lévi-Strauss's view of structure is totalistic: the world, as we know it, has structure. Structures do not exist on the surface; hence the object of analysis is to rescue these unconscious infrastructures from their embodiment in the phenomenal world of becoming. I think we have come too perilously close to an essentialist definition of structure, an almost Platonic conception, and this is what I want to avoid.

I have pretty much stated in the body of this work that I favor an ad hoc view of structure in the spirit of Max Weber's ideal types or of Fernand Braudel's structures of the long run, both of which assume that structures or types or models are constructions of scholars, not universals waiting to be discovered. Now let me develop these ideas further. I want to seek structure not in langue but in parole, rejecting the language model coming down from de Saussure through Jakobson and Troubetskoy to Lévi-Strauss. By *parole* I refer not to the spoken word per se but to the worlds that exist out there in what ethnographers call "culture"—the worlds of meaning to which we as human beings orient ourselves. I start from the premise that the phenomenal world does not exist outside of meaning-frames imposed on it by human beings, which is what I would like to understand by that much misused word *culture*. These meanings are not totalistic or uniform in any society but exhibit breaks, discontinuities, and differences, and might vary by gender, class or rank, and religious status. For example, it goes without saying that a particular shaman's view of religion is different from the layperson's and that different shamans may have varying views in one and the same society. Consequently, cosmologies are always in the making in those societies in which shamanism predominates.

In spite of differences, the meanings constructed by human beings can and will often exhibit order and similarity within and across cultures. This fact was expressed by Wittgenstein in his notion of "forms of life" that exhibit "family resemblances." I can, as an ethnographer, point out forms of life that exhibit family resemblances on the phenomenological level, the level of parole. For example, such cross-culturally existent phenomena or representations as sorcery and witchcraft need not share identical characteristics. This is impossible. What they share are family resemblances, which then permit us to locate the "family" to which they belong.

Nevertheless the implementation of the Wittgensteinian idea, as far as the human sciences are concerned, poses serious problems pertaining to the *identification of resemblances,* of the sort that bedeviled the analysis of "traits" in early American ethnology and culture history. What is a trait to me is not a trait to you. In principle traits are identifiable if the analyst defines the relevant characteristics. But if this defining process is difficult, even more difficult is achieving intersubjective consensus regarding the operational features of traits, quite unlike the situation in respect to units such as phonemes, cells, atoms, and so forth. So it is with family resemblances. Although this term is used by many scholars, few have attempted to systematically develop the idea that Wittgenstein formulated in sections 66 and 67 of *Philosophical Investigations,* that is, to show family resemblances as polythetic classification, in the sense that Rodney Needham described them.[44] For example, following Wittgenstein, I can say that one form of life exhibits the features a, b, c, d, e, f . . . n; and the second features a, b, c, g, h, i . . . n; and the third a, b, h, i, p, q . . . n. The problem still remains that the identification of resemblances (features) is a somewhat arbitrary task. Thus I could say that Wet'suwet'en Indian rebirth contains the following features:

a. there is rebirth in an afterworld;
b. that afterworld is structured like this world;
c. after a sojourn in the afterworld the individual is born into the same kin group;
d. there are techniques for identification of the neonate; and so on until . . . n.

I can show that the Igbo beliefs share all these similarities, but they possess other features that the Wet'suwet'en Indians do not have:

e. there is a nasty world into which taboo violators are hurled;
f. there is transmigration and nonreturn into the human world; and so on.

I can show that Trobrianders do not imagine feature d of the Wet'suwet'en nor features e and f of the Igbo; instead they have other features that can be put down as g, h, and i . . . n.

Although this seems simple enough to do in principle, there are problems with the application of this strategy. Arbitrariness of trait or feature identification aside, there is a further logistical problem. One can show family resemblances (and nonresemblances) even *within* a single cluster of related societies, such as the Northwest Coast Amerindians, and go on in this manner ad infinitum. The principle of family resemblances among forms of life is invaluable; demonstrating them with any degree of economy or sophistication is difficult, if not impossible, in the human sciences.

Let me discuss how I deal with this problem, albeit in an un-Wittgensteinian manner. Family resemblances among forms of rebirth eschatologies are useful for pointing out phenomena amenable for comparison. Thus, without entering into impossibly detailed polythetic classifications I can point out some key features that occur and recur in the various eschatologies of small-scale societies described in chapter 2. In other words I can describe family resemblances in terms of the goals of my project. I then make the Wittgensteinian assumption that these family resemblances exist because of the existence of a *family,* which is for me, although not for Wittgenstein, an identifiable structure from which resemblances and differences fan out. This line of argument leads me to a structural idea of "family resemblances," formulated by the un-Wittgensteinian Nietzsche, that seems close to the spirit of my own argument: "The strange family resemblance of all Indian, Greek, and German philosophising is explained easily enough. Where there is affinity of languages, it cannot fail, owing to the common philosophy of grammar—I mean, owing to the unconscious domination and guidance by similar grammatical functions—that everything is prepared at the outset for a similar development and sequence of philosophical systems; just as the way seems barred against other possibilities of world-interpretation."[45]

The underlying Nietzschean idea that family resemblances imply a common structure permits me to sketch the models that I have presented in figures 1 and 3 and to move from there into the realm of structural transformations. There is then a method to the idea of family resemblances; resemblances exist because they are the demonstrably expectable consequences of a common form or structure (family); but that common form or structure would not have been known to us but for already available empirical information on family resemblances. Hence the logic is deliberately circular, with the one illuminating the other on the model of the hermeneutical circle.

The notion of structure formulated above has emancipatory implications for ethnography, if not for the other human sciences, freeing it from the stultifying preoccupation with cultural differences, the emphasis on the uniqueness of each culture, placing cultures in glass cases as it were, museologizing their relativity and in effect exoticizing them and treating them as alien, unrelated to what is often unrealistically dubbed "Western" civilization. This term, like its opposite, "non-Western," might be useful for ordinary discourse or for sorting things out in a preliminary fashion but not for serious methodological discourses. In the general ethnographic imagination, "Westerners are not like the others."

By contrast consider the strategies I have employed in the foregoing pages. Our ideal models cut across conventional ethnographic and cultural boundaries, showing similar life-forms in seemingly disparate cultures. The existence of shared features does not obviously imply cultural intercourse among different peoples, but it does imply such a possibility and sometimes the historical realization of that possibility. For me the mere fact that peoples from different parts of the world have invented rebirth eschatologies and ethicized versions based on them is enough to dispel the illusion that even Wittgenstein erroneously assumed—the idea that forms of life are incommensurable. Quite the contrary, commensurability of forms of life is possible although those life-forms are enclosed in larger life-worlds that are different, even incommensurable. This potential for commensurability has been known to us for some time, although ethnographers have not always dealt with its implications. For example, early kinship studies documented near-identical structures in vastly different cultural areas although, except for Lévi-Strauss, the epistemological implications of this finding were not pursued.

When I facetiously echoed Marcel Detienne—Westerners are not like the others—I did not mean to take sides in a "particularism" versus "universalism" debate. Resistance to relativism is not to deny the particularity of individual cultures but to open our minds to resemblances that exist across cultures and to construct models on the basis of such similarities. Greek and Buddhist cultures as totalities are different; and both are different from Amerindians in their historical unfolding, ethnographic settings, and socioeconomic systems. Yet underlying these great divisions and differences are segments of the world on which human beings impose meaning, for example, in such domains as sorcery, witchcraft, shamanism, spirit possession, astrology, divination, and humoral theories of medicine. To phrase the argument differently: one sees in the European past and present and in Greek history cultural beliefs and practices that show striking family resemblances to forms of life elsewhere, and because forms of life might indicate underlying structures, it is possible to engage in comparative structural interpretation. Structural analysis then brings different life-forms within the orbit of similarity.

Structural comparison also permits the elucidation of difference or disjuncture through transformational analysis. Thus, in this work ethicization produces an epistemic break that effects a gap between Amerindians on the one hand and Greek and Buddhists on the other; and the forms of ethicization adopted by Greeks and Buddhists make for epistemic breaks within each culture, as for example, between Pythagoreans and Plato, Plotinus and Pindar, and between the Upanishadic thinkers and the Buddha and Mahavira and Makkhali Gosala.

Through my particular form of structural analysis I can show how cultural differences develop on the ground although they are constrained within the frame of preexisting structures of thought. These eschatological structures—epistemes, forms of life—impose certain limits on the further development of thought and might even act as "prisons of the *longue durée,*" restricting the worldview of the believer. They are like scientific paradigms that both facilitate the work of the thinker and restrict his or her field of operations. At the worst they trap believers, forcing them to turn their backs on alternative forms of thought. This is true whether we are speaking of rebirth or of monotheistic structures or scientific paradigms.

A good instance of this comes from our discussion of the problem of salvation within the frame of a rebirth theory. I have shown that even the most innovative thinker has to work within this frame such that there is no way that one can achieve salvation without abolishing the rebirth cycle. Salvation has to be sought outside of it. Nevertheless, although the paradigm imposes limits on the development of thought, this does not mean that human creativity has been closed off. I have demonstrated the presence of considerable, occasionally even radical, innovativeness and creativity occurring within that frame. In that sense there is little difference in the creative activity of the religious thinker and the scientist operating within their respective paradigms. Yet I am not suggesting that religions and scientific paradigms are equivalent in respect to change. Quite the contrary: in the long history of Buddhism (or for that matter in the history of the monotheisms) there have been no real paradigm changes. The divide between Theravada and Mahayana is significant enough, but Mahayana has not dislodged the main concepts of early Buddhism that both share. Religions can produce all sorts of "epistemic shifts," some more radical than others, but paradigm changes are impossible when we think of religion. For example, there is no way that Buddhism can do away with the karma theory or rebirth without abandoning the religion. "Paradigm abandonment," rather than change, is characteristic of the fate of religions. One does not abandon an earlier paradigm as far as a major system of scientific thought is concerned; thus the Newtonian paradigm remains significant for understanding the Einsteinian. But this is not true when a Buddhist converts to Christianity. I can no longer claim that my former religion is part of the living tradition of the latter.

Yet the recognition of freedom permitted to a thinker within a paradigmatic frame makes me less of an "epistemic determinist" (my phrase) than is Foucault. I will admit that forms of rebirth are enclosed in larger universes of meaning or epistemes and that they operate within a field of power. But that must apply to Foucault's own thought also: his also must be a form of knowledge located within prestructuralist and poststructuralist epistemic frames. Yet such embeddedness in prior historically given and conditioned universes of meaning has not hindered Foucault's creativity and innovativeness or his formulation of new knowledge. So is it with many of us thinkers. My form of analysis imposes certain restrictions on my creative capacity, forcing me at times into my own narrow shed and at other times permitting me to soar ahead—yet I am held within the parameters imposed by the logic of my analysis. I am the shadow of the very thinkers whom I study.

I now want to give pretentious justification for the loose manner of inference that I have adopted right through this work and which I think is endemic to the human sciences. I call it the "logic of expectability" in contrast to the more deterministic inferential modes adopted by some of us who claim to be natural scientists. Let me illustrate this mode of thinking with examples from my text by going back to the "elementary form" of a rebirth eschatology that I depicted in figure 1. This figure in reality implies a very basic model in which death is followed by rebirth; it also implies a slightly more complex model containing an intermediate stay in the otherworld before one is reborn on earth. But the logically simpler model need not reflect a historically prior condition. One might argue that it is a simplification of a historically prior model of initial ascent into the world of the ancestors. I think the question of historical priority cannot be solved by us without independent ethnographic information. Either way one can posit an *expectable motivation* in the two variations I have synthesized as figure 1, namely, the wish to bring the dead kinsperson or ancestor back to the very kin group that he or she has left, back to the bosom of the family, as it were. When this occurs and recurs, the various empirical rebirth eschatologies discussed in chapter 2 begin to take shape. Although scattered in different geographic and cultural regions, these eschatologies show *expectable* similarities and differences. Thus where the unilinear principle is important we ought to *expect* the return of ancestors to the matrilineal or patrilineal kin group in which they lived. With looser bilateral structures the person has more leeway but still joins the larger familial kindred. That too is expectable for those familiar with bilateral kinship. But kinship structures do not exclusively determine rebirth affiliations; personal wishes and motivations often complicate the picture, fouling the logic of expectations or introducing another field of expectations.

The most rigid cycling back into the same unilinear kin group is in Trobriand; here the ancestor is not generally a known person but a spirit or soul who descends from the otherworld into the very matrilineal kin group in which she or he was born. I tried to show that when this happens, one does not *expect* a great deal of interest in identifying the neonate. However, in the other eschatologies discussed in chapter 2 there is the inevitable preoccupation with figuring out the identity of the recently returned being, an expectable motivational feature of those eschatologies where the sojourn in the otherworld is limited or bypassed altogether. The argument in chapter 2 could be methodologically reformulated as follows: given the basic or elementary forms of rebirth there are certain expectable features of rebirth eschatologies that are found in the empirical record irrespective of geographic distance and larger cultural difference. Although the "logic of determinism" can be used by scientists to perform operations in those arenas where things or beings do not talk back at them or balk at their activities, the "logic of expectability" is the nomological feature that we ought to look for, if ought we could, in the argumentative disciplines that constitute the human sciences, where those we study in the field are also studying us, and both they and we are engaged in dialogical exchanges, sometimes harmonious, sometimes not, sometimes conducive to understanding, sometimes conducive to misunderstanding. Given this situation it is no wonder that our expectations are simply not fulfilled and indeed might get deliberately subverted. But the logic of expectability at least provides us with a reasonably rigorous inferential method such that, when the *un*expected occurs, we can provide some sensible answer or rationale for its occurrence. For example, I could say that avoiding the eating of animals who could be one's ancestors is to be expected when rebirth eschatologies are associated with animal reincarnation, particularly of the cross-species variety; but often enough "abstinence from animal food" does *not* occur, forcing me to deal with the conditions that inhibit its realization in particular instances, such as in Buddhism and among the Kwakiutl. The logic of expectability is a situational logic: it is not a form of reasoning that exists totally removed from the stream of life, like the so-called laws of thought. One can have inferences from a rigorously sketched ethnographic account; or, more appositely, one makes inferences from such methodological devices as ideal types, models, or structures. Once anchored to structure, the logic of expectability achieves a rigor it would not otherwise possess, for one could make *expectability statements* of the following sort: given the ideal form of a rebirth eschatology, we could expect kinfolk to be recycled back to the lineage when one is dealing with a society organized in terms of unilineal descent groups. The logic of expectability is also the basis for my imaginary experiment, indeed for all imaginary experiments we construct. For example, the link connecting ethicization, conditionality of reward, and the structuralization of the otherworld and the next rebirth is not causal, for if it were, we could "predict" the otherworldly consequences of ethicization. But this we cannot do: we know that with ethicization the life after death is conditional, based on the good and bad one does in this existence, but there is no way that we can predict that steps 1 and 2 of ethicization will naturally follow in particular cases. That which is logically expectable need not be empirically realizable. On the other hand, once expectability is rigorously formulated, as in our imaginary experiment, then the expectable consequences or inferences can be "logic tight," and we can make expectability statements such as the following: with ethicization the soul after death will be reborn in a heaven or a hell (ethicization step 1), or it will achieve a bad or good rebirth (ethicization step 2), or it will combine both. Empirical cases must fall within the frame of these expectations; from there we could move into a description of the actual life-forms that give body to these logical inferences or "expectability statements" from an ideal model.

These empirically existent life-forms are diverse. Not only are there multiple forms of rebirth eschatologies in diverse kinds of small-scale societies, but they are also present in those social conditions such as the ones I have described for the period of the Buddha. But beyond that, even in small-scale societies, there can be "occasional ethicization," whereas the reverse is even more common. For example, although India may have had a whole historical tradition of ethicization, this does not exclude the coexistence of nonethicized forms of rebirth. Why is this the case? This might be due to the power of individual motivations or the power of prior structures of thought that are not easily dispelled by the hegemonic sway of ethicized religions, or both. Let me deal with these empirical situations separately.

As far as individual motivations are concerned, it is a commonplace in Buddhist societies to make a wish that the dead kinsperson be reborn in the same family, even though most people recognize that this will not happen. Although I do not have detailed case studies for Hinduism, there are some groups, such as the Smartha Brahmins, who believe that "children are incarnations of dead grandparents," thereby seeming to flout karma as a doctrine of ethical compensation and reward.[46] As James Boon says, once the idea of karma is "localized" one should expect multiple forms to exist on the ground.[47] Because ancestors have been crucial to Hindu eschatology from Vedic times, one should expect Hindus to devise ways of recycling the ancestor back into the group. There are perhaps many ways this could be done; equally there ought to be ways of justifying karma or subverting it in such cases. One of the most obvious ways to overcome karma in the Hindu context is *bhakti,* or devotion to God, who then provides direct soteriological access to the devotee, thereby subverting or abolishing or bypassing karma.[48] The Balinese case is especially interesting because, in spite of long contact with both Buddhism and Hinduism, ordinary Balinese villagers have resisted ethicization and have, with some qualifications, adhered to the view that at death the soul is reborn in the same kin group or community, generally with a temporary sojourn in the world of the ancestors. By contrast, Balinese Brahmin priests, some balians, and modern-day intellectuals have taken over an ethical notion of karma with all of its consequences for kinship and community, ethics, and existence in general.

Bali illustrates what happens when we construct a formal model of any eschatology. The empirical cases of karmic and rebirth eschatologies are multiple, whereas the models or structures that I have constructed are strictly limited. I noted that within the limits imposed by structural parameters, a largesse of empirical variations can exist on the ground. Bali is a good example, where, owing to the presence of two dominant models, there is considerable richness and variety to the way people, communities, and innovators formulate their rebirth doctrines. But this richness is illusory: Balinese thinkers have only a limited leeway for playing intellectual or philosophical games. Their thoughts are also expectable and fall within the frame permitted by several models—the models of the rebirth eschatology or the karmic eschatology or variations thereof, underlying all of which lies the atom of rebirth sketched in figure 1. To use our previous tropes, even the most productive innovators are constrained by the prison house of the long durée; by the parameters of topographical or structural models or ideal types; or by the narrow shed that draws the thinker into its fold, that is, by enshrouding epistemic presuppositions; or by some fundamental scheme or elementary structure that generates all sorts of expectable possibilities. But was Nietzsche right when he wrote the somewhat pessimistic conclusion for this book?

> That individual philosophical concepts are not anything capricious or autonomously evolving, but grow up in connection and relationship with each other; that, however suddenly and arbitrarily they seem to appear in

> the history of thought, they nevertheless belong just as much to a system as all the members of the fauna of a continent—is betrayed in the end also by the fact that the most diverse philosophers keep filling in a definite fundamental scheme of possible philosophies.[49]

Yet on a more hopeful note one might add that although my Nietzschean conclusion implies the impossibility of "free will" in human affairs, it is also the case that the human will is never fully "unfree" and that "systems" could be shattered or dissolved to let innovation and creativity spring forth from within the prison houses in which we live. This is what I suppose Zarathustra meant when he spoke thus: "I say unto you: one must still have chaos in oneself to be able to give birth to a dancing star."[50]

# NOTES

## PREFACE

1. Gananath Obeyesekere, "Theodicy, Sin, and Salvation in a Sociology of Buddhism," in *Dialectic in Practical Religion,* ed. Edmund R. Leach (Cambridge: Cambridge University Press, 1968), 7–49.

2. Gananath Obeyesekere, "The Rebirth Eschatology and Its Transformations: A Contribution to the Sociology of Early Buddhism," in *Karma and Rebirth in Classical Indian Traditions,* ed. Wendy Doniger O'Flaherty (Berkeley: University of California Press, 1980), 137–64.

3. Gananath Obeyesekere, "Reincarnation Eschatologies and the Comparative Study of Religions," foreword to *Amerindian Rebirth: Reincarnation Belief among North American Indians and Inuit,* ed. Antonia Mills and Richard Slobodin (Toronto: University of Toronto Press, 1994), xi–xxiv.

4. Herbert Strainge Long, *A Study of the Doctrine of Metempsychosis in Greece from Pythagoras to Plato* (Baltimore: J. H. Furst, 1948); Merlin Peris, "Greek Teachings of Reincarnation from Orpheus to Plato" (Ph.D. diss., University of London, Queen Mary College, 1963). It is a pity that Peris's comprehensive 759-page study has not yet been published. I found myself overwhelmed by the mass of data painstakingly garnered by Peris, and for the most part I have referred to his important work in endnotes.

5. Peter Kingsley, *Ancient Philosophy and Magic: Empedocles and the Pythagorean Tradition* (Oxford: Clarendon Press, 1995). Unfortunately, this imaginative study is devoid of theoretical understanding and is full of ad hoc interpretations. Not one modern thinker is mentioned in the bibliography, except Jung, who is cited for his work on alchemy.

6. Lloyd P. Gerson, *Plotinus* (London: Routledge, 1998), 209.

7. R. T. Wallis, *Neoplatonism,* 2d ed. (London: Gerald Duckworth, 1995), 32.

8. Walter Burkert, *Ancient Mystery Cults* (Cambridge: Harvard University Press, 1987), 87.

9. Walter Burkert, *Greek Religion* (Oxford: Blackwell, 1996), 298.

10. See chap. 1 in Marcel Detienne, *Dionysus Slain* (Baltimore: Johns Hopkins University Press, 1979).

11. Larry J. Alderink, *Creation and Salvation in Ancient Orphism* (Chico, Calif.: Scholars Press, 1981), 56.

12. See Robert Parker, "Early Orphism," in *The Greek World,* ed. A. Powell (London: Routledge, 1995), 483–510.

13. M. L. West, *The Orphic Poems* (Oxford: Clarendon Press, 1983).

14. W. D. Whitney, *Oriental and Linguistic Studies* (New York: Scribner, Armstrong, and Co., 1873), 61; for details see the important paper by Hendrik W. Bodewitz, "The Hindu Doctrine of Transmigration: Its Origin and Background," in *Professor Gregory M. Bongard-Levin Felicitation Volume,* in *Indologica Taurinensia* (Torino) 23–24 (1997): 583–605.

15. Maurice Walshe, *The Long Discourses of the Buddha* (Boston: Wisdom, 1995).

16. Bhikkhu Ñāṇamoli and Bhikkhu Bodhi, trans. and ed., *The Middle Length Discourses of the Buddha* (Boston: Wisdom, 1995).

17. Patrick Olivelle, *Upaniṣads* (New York: Oxford, 1996).

18. W. K. C. Guthrie, *The Earlier Presocratics and the Pythagoreans,* vol. 1 of *A History of Greek Philosophy* (1971; reprint, Cambridge: Cambridge University Press, 1992); W. K. C. Guthrie, *The Presocratic Tradition from Parmenides to Democritus,* vol. 2 of *A History of Greek Philosophy* (1971; reprint, Cambridge: Cambridge University Press, 1995).

19. M. R. Wright, *Empedocles: The Extant Fragments* (London: Bristol Classical Press, 1995); Brad Inwood, trans., *The Poem of Empedocles* (Toronto: University of Toronto Press, 1992).

20. G. S. Kirk and J. E. Raven, eds., *The Presocratic Philosophers* (Cambridge: Cambridge University Press, 1957); G. S. Kirk, J. E. Raven, and M. Schofield, eds., *The Presocratic Philosophers,* 2d ed. (Cambridge: Cambridge University Press, 1983).

21. Thomas Taylor, trans., *Iamblichus' "Life of Pythagoras"* (Rochester, Vt.: Inner Traditions International, 1986); Thomas Taylor, trans., *Porphyry on Abstinence from Animal Food* (London: Centaur Press, 1965).

22. Gillian Clark, trans., *Iamblichus: On the Pythagorean Life* (Cambridge: Liverpool University Press, 1982); John Dillon and Jackson Hershbell, trans., *Iamblichus: On the Pythagorean Way of Life* (Atlanta: Scholars Press, 1991).

23. MacKenna, Stephen, trans., *Plotinus: The Enneads,* abr. ed. (London: Penguin Classics, 1991); A. H. Armstrong, trans. and ed., *Plotinus,* 7 vols. (Cambridge: Harvard University Press, 1966–88).

## CHAPTER 1. KARMA AND REBIRTH IN INDIC RELIGIONS

1. For an excellent survey of this issue see Hendrik W. Bodewitz, "The Hindu Doctrine of Transmigration: Its Origin and Background," in *Professor*

*Gregory M. Bongard-Levin Felicitation Volume,* in *Indologica Taurinensia* (Torino) 23–24 (1997): 583–605."

2. These texts are available in several translations: Franklin Edgerton, *The Beginnings of Indian Philosophy* (Cambridge: Harvard University Press, 1970); S. Radhakrishnan, *The Principal Upanishads* (London: George Allen and Unwin, 1953); Max Müller, *The Upaniṣads,* 2 vols. (1879; reprint, New York: Dover, 1962); and Patrick Olivelle, trans., *Upaniṣads* (Oxford: Oxford University Press, 1996). Unless otherwise indicated, quoted passages are from Olivelle's translation.

3. T. W. Rhys Davids, an enormously erudite scholar, was the first to point out the widespread distribution of rebirth theories in so-called primitive societies. See "The Buddhist Theory of Karma," in his *Lectures on the Origin and Growth of Religion* (London: Williams and Norgate, 1881), 73–121.

4. A. L. Basham, *The Origins and Development of Classical Hinduism* (Boston: Beacon Press, 1989), 42–43.

5. Herman W. Tull, *The Vedic Origins of Karma* (New York: SUNY Press, 1989), 25.

6. Patrick Olivelle, trans., *Saṃnyāsa Upaniṣads: Hindu Scriptures on Asceticism and Renunciation* (New York: Oxford University Press, 1992).

7. Bodewitz, in "The Hindu Doctrine of Transmigration," says: "So the term *karman* has a Vedic previous history, but ritual *karman* (the Vedic ideal) hardly suits the doctrine of transmigration which disqualifies the sacrifices. Ethical *karman* is barely found in the Vedic texts before the Upaniṣads" (592).

8. J. C. Heesterman, *The Inner Conflict of Tradition* (Chicago: University of Chicago Press, 1985), 24. See also Steven Collins, *Selfless Persons: Imagery and Thought in Theravada Buddhism* (Cambridge: Cambridge University Press, 1982), 51.

9. Olivelle, *Upaniṣads.* When subsequent quotations from Olivelle's translation are cited in the text, they are referenced parenthetically by Upanishad title.

10. Hermann Oldenberg's extensive discussion of this problem is found in *The Doctrine of the Upaniṣads and the Early Buddhism,* trans. Shridhar B. Shrotri (Delhi: Motilal Banarsidass, 1991), 63–68; see also Surendranath Dasgupta, *A History of Indian Philosophy* (Delhi: Motilal Banarsidass, 1988), 1:53–57.

11. Tull, *Vedic Origins,* 31. The *Brāhmaṇas,* composed c. 900–700 B.C.E., were texts on the technology and practice of sacrifice. Sacrifices on which the order of the world depended could not be performed without the group of ritual specialists known also as *brāhmaṇa*s, that is, those whom nowadays we call "Brahmins." To avoid confusion I shall use the term *Brahmin* to designate the latter except when I cite someone else. I shall use the conventional term *Brahman* to designate the neuter of *Brahma,* the all-knowing god of the Vedic tradition. The *Brāhmaṇas* were an integral part of the Vedic tradition, beginning with the *Ṛg Veda,* the collection of hymns of the earliest Indo-European people who settled in the upper reaches of the Indus, close to the abandonment of the prior urban civilization of the Indus valley, c. 2300–1700 B.C.E. The *Ṛg Veda* was followed by a collection of magical chants and medical cures known as the *Atharvaveda,* c. 900 B.C.E. The early Upanishads must come from around 700 B.C.E. and antedated Buddhism by perhaps a hundred years. None of the above dates can be calculated with certainty.

12. Tull, *Vedic Origins,* 30–31.

13. Here is Edgerton's translation from the Madhyandina recension in *The Beginnings of Indian Philosophy:* "Just as an embroiderer takes off a part from an embroidered garment and weaves for himself another, newer and more beautiful, pattern, even so this Spirit, when it has rid itself of this body and cast off ignorance, weaves for itself another newer form—either of a departed spirit *(pitar)* or of a gandharva or of (an inhabitant of) Brahma('s world) or of (an inhabitant of) Prajāpati('s world) or of a god *or of a man* or from other creatures" (161, my italics).

14. In addition to Pravāhaṇa Jaivali of Pañcāla, the Upanishads mention other Kṣatriya sages, such as Aśvapati of Kekaya, Ajātaśatru of Kāsi, and Janaka of Videha.

15. Fire sacrifices are central to Vedic belief, especially in households. As Olivelle says in his *Upaniṣads:* "The central feature of all vedic sacrifices, from the simplest to the most complex, is the ritual fire" (42–44). The three ritual fires of the Vedic sacrifice are the householder's fire, the southern fire, and the offertorial fire. The Upanishads mention two other fires, the domestic fire "lit on the day of a man's marriage and continuously maintained and the so-called assembly fire, probably associated with a king's assembly hall." For a more detailed discussion see Paul Deussen, *The System of the Vedanta* (New York: Dover, 1973), 361–66.

16. Richard F. Gombrich, *How Buddhism Began: The Conditioned Genesis of the Early Teachings* (London: Athlone Press, 1996), 65–72.

17. This fascinating discussion starts with the world out there as a fire; it gradually moves to lesser things—to rain clouds, to the world down here, to man, to woman, and to the corpse. When we come down to the corpse, the fire is a literal one from which man's spirit emerges.

18. Olivelle, *Upaniṣads.* Max Müller's older translation makes more sense for a nonspecialist: "When they have thus reached the place of lightning a spirit comes near them, and leads them to the worlds of the (conditioned) Brahman. In these worlds of the Brahman they dwell exalted for ages. There is no returning for them" (Müller, *Upaniṣads,* 2:208).

19. See Tull, *Vedic Origins,* 32–34, for a fuller discussion of this issue.

20. The four categories in the *varṇa* scheme are the following (in order of status): Brahmins (priests), Kṣatriya (royalty), Vaiśya (middle range of craftsmen, artisans, merchants, etc.), and Śūdra (peasants, workers).

21. This question was not answered in the previous text, which deals with the intercourse between man and woman and the birth of a new being, who will eventually die and be cremated. The present text develops this further: "Therefore it is said: 'at the fifth offering the waters take on a human voice.' Covered by the placenta, the foetus lies inside the womb for nine months or ten months or thereabouts and is then born. Once born, he lives his allotted life span. When he has departed, when he has reached his appointed time—they take him to the very fire from which he came, from which he sprung" (*Chān. Upan.,* 5.9.1–2).

22. G. C. Pande, in *Studies in the Origins of Buddhism,* 4th rev. ed. (Delhi: Motilal Banarsidass, 1995), 313–14, makes a reasonable inference that this indicates "a philosophical tradition of the royal sages" and a Kṣatriya tradition of knowledge.

23. Eric Frauwallner, *History of Indian Philosophy,* vol. 1, trans. V. M. Be-

dekar (Delhi: Motilal Banarsidass, 1973), 36–41. Frauwallner's is a larger thesis in which he deals with the creative and regenerative power of water in Indian thought. I have appropriated his phrase "the water-doctrine" and converted it into "fire-water doctrine" to designate the specific Upanishadic example.

24. G. C. Pande, *Studies in the Origins of Buddhism,* 1st ed. (Allahabad: University of Allahabad, 1957), 265.

25. See D. D. Kosambi, *An Introduction to the Study of Indian History* (Bombay: Popular Book Depot, 1956), and *The Culture and Civilization of Ancient India in Historical Outline* (New Delhi: Vikas Publishing, 1976).

26. Max Weber, "Objectivity in Social Science and Social Policy," in *The Methodology of the Social Sciences,* ed. Edward A. Shils and Henry A. Finch (New York: Free Press, 1949), 89–98.

27. Max Weber, "The Logic of the Cultural Sciences," in *The Methodology of the Social Sciences,* ed. Edward A. Shils and Henry A. Finch (New York: Free Press, 1949), 174–75.

28. Fernand Braudel, "History and the Social Sciences: The *longue durée,*" in *On History,* trans. Sarah Matthews (Chicago: University of Chicago Press, 1980), 31 (Braudel's italics). In spite of his avowed idealization of Lévi-Strauss everywhere in his work, Braudel has a view of structure and of *longue durée* that is more in line with Max Weber's. His conception of structure seems to me to be an ad hoc, invented thing, geared toward a specific research problem rather than toward the "epistemological" notion of structure that I have criticized.

## CHAPTER 2. NON-INDIC THEORIES OF REBIRTH

1. See Antonia Mills and Richard Slobodin, eds., *Amerindian Rebirth: Reincarnation Belief among North American Indians and Inuit* (Toronto: University of Toronto Press, 1994).

2. For a critique of the term *ancestor worship* as an instance of "the ethnocentric categorization of anthropological data," see Igor Kopytoff, "Ancestors as Elders in Africa," in *Africa* 41 (April 1971): 137.

3. See, e.g., A. R. Radcliffe-Brown, "The Mother's Brother in South Africa," in *Structure and Function in Primitive Society* (New York: Free Press, 1965), 15–31, where Radcliffe-Brown says that reincarnation is in the male line among the matrilineal society of the Balla of Rhodesia and that a man is reincarnated generally as his son's son, not his daughter's son. M. J. Field says that the first-born son is a reincarnation of his "grandfather" and the younger sons their "grand uncles," whereas girls reincarnate their paternal grandfather's sisters. This is given legitimation in naming (see M. J. Field, *Religion and Medicine of the Ga People* [London: Oxford University Press, 1937], 174). The vagueness in the ethnography is seen clearly in the following account of the Krobo of West Africa, although, as in Field's account, the continuity of the ancestor's name is important:

> It appears to be a rather widely accepted opinion that sometimes old people, shortly after their death, are born again into this world. This belief may have contributed to the practice of giving a child the name of one of his "grandfathers." It is for the diviner to identify a particular ancestor in the person of a newly-born child. Often a reborn ancestor is recognized only later on when the infant falls sick and the diviner

> detects that the illness was caused by the child's grandfather who, returning in the babe, was not duly welcomed by his family. (Hugo Huber, *The Krobo: Traditional Social and Religious Life of a West African People* [St. Augustin near Bonn: Studia Instituti Anthropos, 1963], 16:160)

4. Melville J. Herskovits, *Dahomey: An Ancient West African Kingdom* (New York: J. J. Augustin, 1938), 233–37.

5. Flora *Edouwaye* S. Kaplan, "Some Thoughts on Ideology, Beliefs, and Sacred Kingship among the Edo [Benin] People of Nigeria," in *African Spirituality: Forms, Meanings, and Expressions,* ed. Jacob Olupona (New York: Crossroads Press, 2000), 119. The Benin were historically related to the Yoruba. James Lorand Matory has a brief discussion of Yoruba reincarnation in "Vessels of Power: The Dialectical Symbolism of Power in Yoruba Religion and Polity" (master's thesis, University of Chicago, 1986), esp. 80.

6. Richard N. Henderson, *The King in Every Man* (New Haven: Yale University Press, 1972); Victor Uchendu, *The Igbo of Southeast Nigeria* (New York: Holt, Rinehart, and Winston, 1965); and Simon Ottenberg, "Reincarnation and Masking: Two Aspects of the Self in Afikpo," unpublished paper, 1992 (manuscript in possession of the author). An earlier paper on Igbo reincarnation is probably too general but may be of limited use: John A. Noon, "A Preliminary Examination of the Death Concepts of the Igbo," *American Anthropologist* 44, no. 3. (1942): 638–54.

7. Henderson, *King in Every Man,* 107. Subsequent quotations from this work are cited in the text with the abbreviation *KEM*.

8. Ibid., 110. It is not clear to me what Henderson means by "other forms."

9. Uchendu, *Igbo of Southeast Nigeria,* 94–102. Subsequent quotations from this work are cited in the text with the abbreviation *ISN*.

10. Victor Uchendu, "The Status Implications of Igbo Religious Beliefs," *Nigerian Field* 29 (1964): 35. Subsequent quotations from this work are cited in the text with the abbreviation SI.

11. See ibid., 27–37; and Uchendu, *Igbo of Southeast Nigeria.*

12. According to James G. Matlock, 74 percent of Igbo are born in the same patrilineage. See "Alternate-Generation Equivalence and the Recycling of Souls: Amerindian Rebirth in Global Perspective," in Mills and Slobodin, *Amerindian Rebirth,* 264.

13. Ottenberg, "Reincarnation and Masking," 1. Subsequent quotations from this work are cited in the text with the abbreviation RM.

14. Simon Ottenberg, personal communication, July 11, 1998.

15. Ibid.

16. Ibid.

17. See Field, *Religion and Medicine,* and note 3 above.

18. G. T. Basden, *Among the Ibos of Nigeria* (Philadelphia: Lippincott, 1921), 60, my italics.

19. For example, Gregory Bateson mentions that the Iatmul have a "patrilineal theory of reincarnation" in which the "child is *concretely* stated to be a reincarnation of a father's father." Bateson adds that "reincarnation and succession are based on the naming system" and that conception is believed to oc-

cur when "the ghost of the dead is blown as mist by the East Wind up the river and into the womb of a deceased's son's wife" (Gregory Bateson, *Naven,* 2d ed. [Stanford: Stanford University Press, 1965], 43).

20. Bronislaw Malinowski, "Baloma: The Spirits of the Dead in the Trobriand Islands," in *Magic, Science, and Religion and Other Essays* (1916; reprint, Boston: Beacon Press, 1948), 125–227; *The Father in Primitive Psychology* (1927; reprint, New York: Norton, 1966); *The Sexual Life of Savages in North-Western Melanesia* (London: George Routledge, 1929). Quotations from these three works by Malinowski are cited in the text with the following abbreviations: B, *FPP,* and *SLS,* respectively.

21. See Ernestine McHugh, "Reconstituting the Self in Tibetan Tradition: Models of Death and the Practice of Mourning in the Himalayas," in *Tibetan Studies: Proceedings of the Seventh Seminar of the International Association for Tibetan Studies,* vol. 2, ed. Ernest Steinkeller, 633–39. Vienna: Austrian Academy of Sciences, 1997.

22. Malinowski, "Baloma," 131.

23. In *The Father in Primitive Psychology* Malinowski refers in a footnote to his earlier paper, "Baloma": "The material there contained was limited, and I was not in possession of some of the most important pieces of evidence here given. These I obtained from my acquaintance with Tomwaya Lakwabulo of Oburaku, a medium of very high standing" (29n1). I cannot account for Malinowski's change of attitude to these ritual specialists.

24. Raphael Patai, *Druze,* in *The Encyclopedia of Religion,* ed. Mircea Eliade (New York: Collier Macmillan, 1987), 4:504.

25. Lee Guemple, "Born-Again Pagans: The Inuit Cycle of Spirits," in Mills and Slobodin, *Amerindian Rebirth,* 120–21. Guemple also says that humans and animals have a limited supply of souls that move through rebirth cycles inexorably; hence, "population dynamics is a zero-sum game" (107).

26. Patai, *Druze,* 504.

27. See Guemple, "Born-Again Pagans," 107–22; for the Druze see chapter 6 of this volume.

28. Antonia Mills, introduction to Mills and Slobodin, *Amerindian Rebirth,* 3–14.

29. Richard Slobodin, "Kutchin Concepts of Reincarnation," in Mills and Slobodin, *Amerindian Rebirth,* 145–46.

30. Antonia Mills, "Reincarnation Belief among North American Indians and Inuit: Context, Distribution, and Variation," in Mills and Slobodin, *Amerindian Rebirth,* 20–21.

31. Antonia Mills, "A Comparison of the Wet'suwet'en Cases of the Reincarnation Type with Gitksan and Beaver," *Journal of Anthropological Research* 44 (1988): 388. Subsequent quotations from this work are cited in the text with the abbreviation CWC.

32. Antonia Mills, personal communication, c. 1995.

33. Ian Stevenson has done extensive research on remembered memories of reincarnation. His most important works are *Twenty Cases Suggestive of Reincarnation* (New York: Society for Psychical Research, 1966); and *Cases of the Reincarnation Type,* 4 vols. (Charlottesville: University Press of Virginia, 1975–83).

34. Ian Stevenson, "Cultural Patterns in Cases Suggestive of Reincarnation among the Tlingit Indians of Southeastern Alaska," in Mills and Slobodin, *Amerindian Rebirth,* 248. For a critical discussion of birthmarks among the Dene Tha see Jean-Guy Goulet, "Reincarnation as a Fact of Life among Contemporary Dene Tha," in the same volume, 166–68.

35. There has recently been an increase in interest among Buddhists and non-Buddhists in Sri Lanka regarding past births. I know of at least one astrologer who can tell you, in addition to your present- and future-life condition, your most recent previous existence and sometimes a few earlier ones also. I think there are many others who claim to be able to do likewise; public interest in this subject has been influenced by the scholarly work of Ian Stevenson and many local scientists of dubious scholarly repute, all of whom have been featured in the local media.

36. Ronald Olson, e.g., reports for the Haisla that prospective fathers dreamed of a dead person later identified with a newly born child, who would be given the deceased person's name. See Ronald Olson, "Field Notes Taken at Rivers Inlet and Bella Bella, British Columbia," unpublished ms., 1935, 1949, Bancroft Library, University of California, Berkeley. See also Michael Harkin's comment on the Oowekeeno:

> Among the Oowekeeno dead kinsmen appeared in two types of dreams. In one type the deceased beckoned the dreamer to follow him; if the dreamer did so, he would sicken and perhaps die. In a second type of dream, which appeared only to women, a dead kinsman held out an infant. If the woman accepted it, the kinsman would be reincarnated. The reincarnated child would be the same sex, and hold the same names, as the relative appearing in the dream. (Harkin, "Person, Time, and Being," in Mills and Slobodin, *Amerindian Rebirth,* 198)

37. Jean-Guy Goulet, "Contemporary Dene Tha," 162.

38. Quoted in Mills, "Reincarnation Belief," 30. See also Harkin, "Person, Time, and Being," 199.

39. Mills, "Reincarnation Belief," 32, citing Paula Rubel and Abraham Rosman, "The Evolution of Exchange Structures and Ranking: Some Northwest Coast and Athabaskan Examples," *Journal of Anthropological Research* 39, no. 1 (1983): 1–25. Mills proposes in the same essay that the idea of multiple reincarnations developed among the Kwakiutl consequent to serious population decline following European contact (29). This seems to me an extremely plausible interpretation. See also Marie Mauze, "The Concept of the Person and Reincarnation among the Kwakiutl Indians," in Mills and Slobodin, *Amerindian Rebirth,* esp. 186–87. Quotations from Mauze's essay will be cited in the text with the abbreviation RKI.

40. There is nothing unusual in multiple or split souls. They are recorded for West Africa, Thailand, and Burma and were recognized even by Robert Burton for European societies. See Robert Burton, *The Anatomy of Melancholy,* vol. 1 (1621; reprint, London: Dent, 1964), esp. subsecs. V, "Of the Soul and Her Faculties" (154–57), and IX, "Of the Rational Soul" (162–65). These ideas are not found, however, among the Wet'suwet'en and Beaver. See Mills, "A Comparison of Wet'suwet'en Cases," 396–97.

41. Mills, "Reincarnation Belief," 32.

42. James G. Matlock and Antonia Mills, "Appendix: A Trait Index to North American Indian and Inuit Reincarnation," in Mills and Slobodin, *Amerindian Rebirth,* 301.

43. Ibid, 307–9.

44. Ann Fienup-Riordan, *The Nelson Island Eskimo: Social Structure and Ritual Distribution* (Anchorage: Alaska Pacific University Press, 1983), 203. Subsequent quotations from this work are cited in the text with the abbreviation *NIE.*

45. Ann Fienup-Riordan, *Boundaries and Passages: Rule and Ritual in Yup'ik Eskimo Oral Tradition* (Norman: University of Oklahoma Press, 1994), 46. Subsequent quotations from this work are cited in the text with the abbreviation *BP.*

46. For an important discussion of the relationship between humans and animals see Fienup-Riordan's chapter "The Relationship between Humans and Animals," in *Boundaries and Passages,* 46–87.

47. Stanley Walens, *Feasting with Cannibals: An Essay on Kwakiutl Cosmology* (Princeton: Princeton University Press, 1981), 163.

48. G. A. Menovschikov, "Popular Conceptions, Religious Beliefs, and Rites of the Asiatic Eskimoes," in *Popular Beliefs and Folklore Tradition in Siberia,* ed. V. Dioszegi (The Hague: Mouton, 1968), 433–49; also cited in Edith Turner, "Behind Inupiaq Reincarnation," in Mills and Slobodin, *Amerindian Rebirth,* 72.

49. Turner, "Behind Inuit Reincarnation," 73.

50. Walens, *Feasting with Cannibals,* 28.

51. In his description of the West Greenland Inuit Mark Nuttal says that if a sibling dies, its name can be given to the next same-sex child born to the mother and that there will be a concomitant realignment of kin relationships. See Mark Nuttal, "The Name Never Dies," in Mills and Slobodin, *Amerindian Rebirth,* 131. See also the case of Jeffery, discussed later on in this section.

52. See Bernard Saladin d'Anglure, "From Foetus to Shaman," in Mills and Slobodin, *Amerindian Rebirth,* 82–106.

53. Frederica de Laguna, *Under Mount Saint Elias: The History and Culture of the Yakutat Tlingit* (Washington, D.C.: Smithsonian Institution Press, 1972); Sergei Kan, *Symbolic Immortality: The Tlingit Potlatch of the Nineteenth Century* (Washington, D.C.: Smithsonian Institution Press, 1989); George Thornton Emmons, *The Tlingit Indians,* ed. Frederica de Laguna (Seattle: University of Washington Press, 1991); Archimandrite Anatolii Kamenskii, *Tlingit Indians of Alaska,* trans. Sergei Kan (Fairbanks: University of Alaska Press, 1985).

54. Frederica de Laguna, "Tlingit," in *Handbook of North American Indians,* vol. 70, ed. Wayne Suttles (Washington, D.C.: Smithsonian Institution Press, 1990), 213.

55. Frederica de Laguna, "Tlingit Ideas about the Individual," *Southwestern Journal of Anthropology* 10, no. 2 (1954): 179–80. Emmons, in *The Tlingit Indians,* puts it thus: "All animals, in fact all nature, inanimate and animate, is possessed of a spirit" (373). This cosmography, he says, permits the shaman to accumulate as many spirits as possible.

56. de Laguna, "Tlingit," 209.

57. Kamenskii, *Tlingit Indians of Alaska,* 72. Kamenskii notes that the Tlingit have three afterlife abodes: *keewakáawu* (de Laguna's *k'iwa'a*), where the souls

of warriors live prosperously, waited on by those they have killed; *daganku,* which is also a comfortable place, but which one has to go through water and tundra to reach; and *s'igeekaawu,* an underworld where souls suffer cold and discomfort, but that is not as terrifying as the Christian hell (73). Those in the last place get reborn as animals. For a different interpretation of *s'igeekaawu* see Kan, *Symbolic Immortality,* 116. Kamenskii goes on to say that there was "definite evidence in ancient time of the belief in the possibility of transmigration of the human soul into the land otter, brown bear, sea otter, petrel, etc. . . . [T]hese animals have human souls and can understand human speech. . . . In former times, to kill them was considered a great shame" (73). Although Kamenskii might have been influenced by Christian ideas in his notion of *s'igeekaawu,* I think he is right in his view that human souls could be reincarnated as special animals whose killing is then taboo. As we will see later, this places the Tlingit closer to the Kwakiutl.

58. Sergei Kan (personal communication, c. 1997) tells me that

> at least in the Tlingit case . . . we have to differentiate between the "mythical era" and the "post-mythical era" (i.e., the era that follows the differentiation of the inhabitants of the universe into humans, terrestrial animals, fish, etc. . . .). During the latter, transformation and especially reincarnation of humans into animals was no longer possible (or very rare). Fr. Anatolii Kamenskii is the only ethnographer who makes the claim that such transformation was possible and common but his ethnography is not as reliable as the works of Emmons, Swanton, de Laguna.

I am not, however, willing to dismiss Kamenskii entirely because I believe that a particular group might well have had multiple conceptions of reincarnation.

59. Kan, *Symbolic Immortality,* 109.

60. Apparently, the funeral of a shaman reverses some of the customs associated with those of ordinary persons. Rather than being cremated, the body is put into a small house or cave, with some of the shaman's paraphernalia and an image of a spirit guardian (*Under Mount Saint Elias,* 673, 699). De Laguna does not explain why this is the case, but my guess is that the custom relates to the fact that a shaman gets his power through the help of an animal spirit familiar, who either possesses him or helps him to bring back a lost or sick soul from wherever it has strayed. The commonest of the shamanic spirit familiars is the land otter; this animal is also fearsome to ordinary people because those who die in water or disappear in the woods (the worst forms of death) are denied entry into the normal spirit world of the ordinary dead and wander on earth as land otters. One of the shamanic tasks is in fact to retrieve and redeem the souls of "land otter men," those lost souls who are transformed into land otter form. The idea of not burying the shaman is to keep his soul in the earth itself, the world of the land otter, the special shamanic spirit familiar that may even be made available to the shamans who succeed him. For an excellent account of the death and placement of a shaman in a "grave-house" see Emmons, *The Tlingit Indians,* 391–97. In many places Emmons mentions the importance of the land otter for shamanic séances.

61. Kan, *Symbolic Immortality,* 116.

62. See also Emmons, *The Tlingit Indians,* 289; Kamenskii, *Tlingit Indians of Alaska,* 71. The term *k'iwa'a* is de Laguna's; Emmons uses *kee-ea-kow-anne*

(above people's country), which was reached by means of the rainbow. This is rendered as *kiuakau* by Kamenskii and as *keewakáawu* by Sergei Kan. There are also differences in the interpretation of this place, but these I think are not because of ethnographic neglect but because of diverging views of the afterlife.

63. de Laguna, "Tlingit Ideas," 191.

64. de Laguna, *Under Mount St. Elias,* 771.

65. In *Under Mount St. Elias,* 777, de Laguna expresses some informant doubts whether those bad people born in dog heaven or the drowned born as land otter men can be reincarnated. She then refers to one exception in respect to the former; in respect to the latter she refers to an informant who said that a person born as a land otter can die there and get reborn on earth, or after about two years he may be released from this grim place.

66. de Laguna, "Tlingit Ideas about the Individual," in *Southwestern Journal of Anthropology* 10, no. 2 (1954): 121.

67. de Laguna, "Tlingit Ideas," 182–83; see also Kan, *Symbolic Immortality,* 109.

68. de Laguna, *Under Mount St. Elias,* 778.

69. Ibid., "Tlingit Ideas," 184.

70. Ibid., *Under Mount St. Elias,* 779; for further details read the section "Multiple Souls," 779–80. For other interesting cases from the late nineteenth century see Emmons, *The Tlingit Indians,* 287–88.

71. de Laguna, "Tlingit Ideas," 183.

72. In *Symbolic Immortality* Kan says: "If the identity of the spirit was in doubt, a name of a close matrilineal ancestor (often a grandparent) was given and the act of naming itself, in effect, achieved reincarnation" (71).

73. de Laguna, *Under Mount St. Elias,* 184.

74. Kan, *Symbolic Immortality,* 68.

75. Unfortunately, in his important book *Symbolic Immortality* Sergei Kan falls into the typical anthropological trap of equating individuality and individualism: "In this cyclical [rebirth] model, the living were the incarnations of their dead matrikin, whose life they were said to be imitating. This concept left little room for individuality and made a person's idiosyncratic biography and accomplishments relatively insignificant" (77). The first part of the last sentence deals with the issue of "individuality," which Tlingit, like others, possess; the second deals with "individualism," which they lack. Kan tells me that he himself is now critical of his "strong position" on Tlingit individuality; elsewhere he adopts a more flexible position (personal communication, c. 1997).

76. For vivid accounts of shamanic journeys see Tom Lowenstein, *The Things That Were Said of Them: Shaman Stories and Oral Histories of the Tikigaq People* (Berkeley: University of California Press, 1992).

77. Similar journeys have been recorded by Fienup-Riordan in *Boundaries and Passages* for the Nelson Island Eskimo. Such people "communicated to humankind an understanding of the underground land of the dead and the ceremonies that should attend them" (240).

78. For other interesting cases see Kan, *Symbolic Immortality,* 115–16.

79. de Laguna, *Under Mount Saint Elias,* 768. Subsequent quotations from this work are cited in the text with the abbreviation *MSE.*

80. For a related experience of rebirth through a "womb door" see the experiences of the Winnebago shaman Thunder Cloud in Paul Radin, "The Reincarnations of Thunder Cloud, a Winnebago Indian," in Mills and Slobodin, *Amerindian Rebirth*, 61.

81. See also the interesting case of Qawusa from de Laguna's ethnography (*Under Mount Saint Elias,* 774).

82. Walens, *Feasting with Cannibals,* 23.

83. Ibid.

84. Ibid., 42; Harkin, "Person, Time, and Being," 202.

85. Franz Boas, *The Religion of the Kwakiutl Indians* (New York: Columbia University Press, 1930), 2:257.

86. James Matlock, "Of Names and Signs: Reincarnation, Inheritance, and Social Structure on the Northwest Coast," *Anthropology of Consciousness* 1 (1990): 11.

87. James Matlock, personal communication, c. 1997. According to Matlock, Boas says in another paper that common people become ghosts. Matlock says that these two ideas—that common people become ghosts and that they become owls—are not irreconcilable. Each ordinary Kwakiutl has an owl or "owl mask" to which his soul goes at death, but his soul is at the same time transformed into a ghost. "This latter transformation, as also the transformation into wolves and killer-whales, is not permanent, and the transformed soul will later detach itself and become reincarnated in a new human body" ("Of Names and Signs," 11).

88. Harkin, "Person, Time, and Being," 200 (citing Ronald Olson's field notes for 1949 deposited at the Bancroft Library at the University of California, Berkeley).

89. Cited in Mills, "Reincarnation Belief," in Mills and Slobodin, *Amerindian Rebirth,* 33.

90. Matlock, "Of Names and Signs," 12.

91. Ibid., 11.

92. Michael Harkin, personal communication, c. 1997.

93. Michael Harkin, personal communication, c. 1997.

94. Franz Boas, *The Social Organization and the Secret Societies of the Kwakiutl Indians* (Washington, D.C.: Smithsonian Institution Press, 1897; reprint, New York: Johnson Reprint, 1970); *Kwakiutl Ethnography,* ed. Helen Cordere (Chicago: University of Chicago Press, 1966).

95. Boas, *Social Organization,* 418–20.

96. Ibid., 420–21.

97. Ibid., 501; for a description of the archetypal festival of bringing back the novice see 538–39.

98. Boas, *Secret Societies,* 449–52.

99. Ibid., 463.

100. Walens, *Feasting with Cannibals,* 72–73.

101. Irving Goldman, *The Mouth of Heaven: An Introduction to Kwakiutl Religious Thought* (New York: John Wiley, 1975).

102. I prefer the term *endoanthropophagy* to *cannibalism:* the latter term is I think tainted with popular mythologizing and ought to be reserved for the wide-

spread fantasy that the Other is going to devour us. However, I sometimes use the term *cannibalism* to highlight the use of this word by other scholars.

103. In "Person, Time, and Being" Michael Harkin formulates the overdetermined nature of similar ritual forms among the Heiltsuk: "The dances they performed represented death, destruction, cannibalism, and other forces antithetical to the social order. After the *caiqa* performances were complete, initiates were 'healed' and eventually reintegrated into the social order" (203).

104. Boas, *Secret Societies,* 418.

105. Here and elsewhere I use the simplified spelling of Kwakiutl names adopted by Irving Goldman rather than the phonetically accurate but difficult nomenclature of Boas. To achieve consistency I will substitute Goldman's terms even when I am quoting Boas. The descriptive part of the Winter Ceremonial is based on both Boas and Goldman.

106. Goldman, *The Mouth of Heaven,* 89; Boas, *Secret Societies,* 419. Goldman adds: "The top-ranking group includes (following Boas's list) the war spirit and a variety of man-eating spirits and their animal and humanoid helpers. A middle group includes Fool Dancers (warrior figures), Wolves, Thunderbirds, Whales, Killer Whales, Otters, Dogs, Ravens, Sea Monsters, Mink, Sunrise and Salmon. The low group include Eagle Shaman, Ghost, Wasp, Salmon, Property Distribution, and at the bottom, Eagle Down" (89).

107. Boas, *Secret Societies,* 420; Goldman, *The Mouth of Heaven,* 89.

108. Goldman, *The Mouth of Heaven,* 111; see also Boas, *Secret Societies,* 395–406.

109. A detailed account of the myth is found in Boas, *Secret Societies,* 396–400.

110. Goldman, *The Mouth of Heaven,* 95.

111. Ibid., 95–96.

112. Ibid., 96.

113. Boas, *Secret Societies,* 537.

114. Ibid., 439.

115. Ibid., 439–40.

116. Ibid., 443. These sequences of biting are described everywhere by Boas in his accounts of the Winter Ceremonial. However, in his actual eyewitness account of a ritual in 1895–96 at Fort Rupert, Boas says the possessed hamatsa only imitates the act of biting, particularly the arms of those around. Boas says that in the past the hamatsa dancer actually bit and ate pieces of human flesh. This is entirely possible although it cannot be taken as self-evidently true because the crux of the issue is not the actual consumption of flesh but the acting out of the Man Eater role in the ecstatic dance of the hamatsa. This can be depicted as easily by the imitating of eating human flesh as by its actual consumption. Thus, it might well be the case that the accounts of eating human flesh are based on informants' versions that are not entirely reliable and also, probably, filtered through the imagination of European reporters or ethnographers. The references to Man Eater eating human flesh, including the dried flesh of corpses, is certainly found in the songs of the Man Eater sung by the hamatsa dancer, but this is no proof that the myth was actually literalized in the ritual.

117. Ibid., 457.

118. Ibid., 460.

119. Walens, *Feasting with Cannibals,* 146–48. This important book is vitiated by symbolic overinterpretation without adequate empirical evidence or substantiation. Walens thinks that the perception of vomit as "disgusting" is a Western ethnocentric assumption. Yet there is no empirical evidence that the Kwakiutl thought that vomiting was pleasant and desirable or, even more outrageously, that it represented "the first stage of causality, the state of existence that precedes order and purpose." Walens is critical of Ruth Benedict, who sees "vomiting as a rejection, a renunciation of cannibalism." I think Benedict was right but for the wrong reasons. It is also hard for me to believe that the Kwakiutl preoccupation with orality and multiple mouths in their art indicates an anxiety with food scarcity: this seems too pragmatic an interpretation by someone in general given to symbolic overinterpretation. The Kwakiutl lived in a more bounteous environment than many other groups in the region, and there would have been little reason for them to be obsessed with hunger (12–13).

120. Boas, *Secret Societies,* 486. Boas goes on to say that the dancer throws up again, and only then the worm comes out.

121. Fienup-Riordan, *Nelson Island Eskimo,* 212.

122. I doubt that the ethnographers I have consulted will agree with my interpretation of the "cannibal dance." My interpretation takes into account the powerful emotional feel of the cannibal dances. Many ethnographers would also find my use of the term *guilt* to characterize some of the feelings of the Kwakiutl unsatisfactory, but I perversely continue to believe that "guilt" is a broad-based human emotion. For an exposition of this point of view see my *Medusa's Hair: An Essay on Personal Symbols and Religious Experience* (Chicago: University of Chicago Press, 1981), 76–83; see also Gananath Obeyesekere, *The Work of Culture: Symbolic Transformation in Psychoanalysis and Anthropology* (Chicago: University of Chicago Press, 1990).

123. Claude Lévi-Strauss, "The Sorcerer and His Magic," in *Structural Anthropology* (New York: Basic Books, 1963), 167–85.

124. Boas, *Secret Societies,* 536–37.

125. Any evidential support for my hypotheses pertaining to the "cannibal dance" must await a historical reexamination of Northwest Coast societies, emphasizing their "rebirth eschatologies," the prevalence of cross-reincarnation, or, at the very least, an examination of the prevalence and distribution of human-to-animal-to-human transformations in reincarnation processes, in foundation myths, and in other ways that depict the identity of human ancestors with animals. Regarding the "cannibal dance" itself, Michael Harkin was gracious enough to send me the following information:

> The cannibal dance complex *(hamatsa* or *tanis)* appears to have originated among the Heiltsuk, and diffused in three directions. The Tsimshian in the north have such a dance, which is restricted to chiefs. There are no really good accounts of the dance extant, but it seems to have the essential features you have outlined. This dance is closely related to the nulim or dogeaters dance, which also existed among the Heiltsuk. In this dance, as the name implies, the basic "cannibalistic" themes are recapitulated with respect to dogs. This dance was found widely among the northern groups, including the Tlingit and Haida, and apparently diffused to the south. It is also found among the Coast Salish and Chinook to the south. Pamela Amoss, in a chapter in *The Tsim-*

> *shian and Their Neighbors,* states that this wider diffusion suggests greater time depth. If this is the case, then the Cannibal Dance itself probably originated in the Nulim. This agrees with Boas' observation that the Cannibal Dance came to the Kwakiutl in the mid-19th century.
>
> To the east, the Bella Coola practiced a variant of the Cannibal Dance which can involve humans (dead or alive), dogs, or even raw salmon. . . . According to McIlwraith, the performance lacked the intensity of the Heiltsuk. Also, it was not restricted to chiefs, as it was generally elsewhere, but could be performed as well by commoners. McIlwraith states that poor men were the most feared Cannibals. . . .
>
> To the south, the Oowekeeno, closely related to the Heiltsuk, had a similar performance. It is quite clear that among them, as among all the North Wakasan speaking groups, the Cannibal was the resident of the Winter Ceremonial. (personal communication, 1995)

## CHAPTER 3. THE IMAGINARY EXPERIMENT AND THE BUDDHIST IMPLICATIONS

1. Robert Hertz, *Death and the Right Hand,* trans. R. Needham and C. Needham (Glencoe, Ill.: Free Press, 1960).

2. Ibid., 70.

3. See Ottenberg, "Reincarnation and Masking"; see also chap. 2, 27–28, in this volume.

4. Karl Jaspers, *Vom Ursprung und Ziel der Geschichte* (Zurich: Artemiss-Verlag, 1949); for a reformulation of "Axial Age" see Shmuel N. Eisenstadt, "The Axial Age: The Emergence of Transcendental Visions and the Rise of Clerics," *European Journal of Sociology* 23 (1982): 294–314; Shmuel N. Eisenstadt, "Fundamentalism, Phenomenology, and Comparative Dimensions," in *Fundamentalisms Comprehended,* ed. Martin S. Marty and R. Scott Appleby (Chicago: University of Chicago Press, 1995), 260–62. I am also more interested in the "transcendental visions" of the Axial Age than in its periodization or emergence at a certain juncture in history. I find this term an appropriate label to designate the "historical religions" of the ancient world that formulated a universalizing and transcendental vision. This vision might be the "axis" that unites religions such as Zoroastrianism, Buddhism, Christianity, and Islam.

5. Although this and other informants said that suicides went to the dog heaven, de Laguna says in an earlier article, "Tlingit Ideas about the Individual," that "those who die by violence at their own hands" (191) also go to the good heaven. Some of the ideas pertaining to suicide might have been influenced by Christianity.

6. Guemple, "Born-Again Pagans," 117.

7. Knud Rasmussen, *Across Arctic America: Narrative of the Fifth Thule Expedition* (New York: Putnam, 1932), quoted in Turner, "Behind Inupiaq Reincarnation," 68.

8. E. W. Burlingame, trans., *Buddhist Legends (Dhammapada Commentary)* (London: Pali Text Society, 1979), 3:221.

9. Olivelle, *Upaniṣads,* 142.

10. Padmanabh Jaini, *The Jaina Path of Purification* (Berkeley: University of California Press, 1979), 11.

11. I think it was Hermann Oldenberg who popularized this distinction. See Oldenberg, *Doctrine of the Upaniṣads,* 116–17.

12. Henk W. Bodewitz, "Hindu *Ahimsa* and Its Roots," in *Violence Denied: Violence, Non-violence and Rationalization of Violence in South Asian Cultural History*, ed. Jan E. M. Houben and Karel R. Van Kooij (Leiden: Brill, 1999), 17–44. Bodewitz argues against Indologists such as J. C. Heesterman, who sees the doctrine of ahiṃsā coming down uninterrupted from the Vedic tradition. Bodewitz argues convincingly that the term *ahiṃsā* in pre-Upanishadic texts means "security" and "safeness." For arguments to show a continuous tradition see H.-P. Schmidt, "The Origin of *ahiṃsā*," in *Mélanges d'Indianisme à la mémoire de Louis Renou* (Paris: E. de Boccard, 1968), 625–55; J. C. Heesterman, "Non-Violence and Sacrifice," *Indologica Taurinensia* 12 (1984): 119–27; Hermann Tull, "The Killing That Is Not Killing: Men, Cattle, and the Origin of Non-Violence (*ahiṃsa*) in the Vedic Sacrifice," *Indo-Iranian Journal* 39 (1996): 223–44; Unto Tahtinen, *Ahiṃsa: Non-Violence in Indian Tradition* (London: Rider, 1976); see also D. S. Ruegg, "Ahiṃsā and Vegetarianism in the History of Buddhism," in *Buddhist Studies in Honour of Walpola Rahula* (London: Gordon Frazer, 1980), 234–41. For an important essay that deals with the later justification for ritual killing and the tension between Vedic ritualism and ahiṃsā see Wilhelm Halbfass, "Vedic Apologetics, Ritual Killing, and the Foundation of Ethics," in *Tradition and Reflection: Explorations in Indian Thought* (New York: SUNY Press, 1991), 87–129.

13. Georg Buhler, *The Sacred Laws of the Āryas* (Oxford: Clarendon Press, 1879), 1:267; see also 1:193.

14. Ibid., 141. Āpastamba's injunctions permit the offerings of beef and buffalo meat and tame and wild animals as oblations for ancestors; foods good for Brahmins to eat include rhinoceros meat, special kinds of fish, and birds.

15. Georg Buhler, *Sacred Laws of the Āryas* (Oxford: Clarendon Press, 1882), 2:69–75.

16. This is the position taken by Bodewitz in "Hindu *Ahiṃsa*."

17. *Kauṣītaki Upaniṣad* 1.2, in Olivelle, *Upaniṣads*, 202 (my italics). The theory of rebirth very briefly spelled out here is an interesting variation of the "fire-water theory." After death people depart to the moon world; during the fortnight of the waning moon the souls are propelled to a new birth. Those who fail to answer the moon's questions are reborn in the human world, whereas those who answer correctly (know the truth) go to the world of the gods and then to Brahman. Karma in this scheme is not ethical; it is knowledge or lack of knowledge of the truth of Brahman, as in the Yājñavalkya text of the *Bṛhadāraṇyaka Upaniṣad*.

18. Indeed, some of the animals mentioned here are those hunted by royalty (lions, tigers, wild boar, rhinoceros) and those permitted in the Brahmanic diet up to the time of the early Dharmasūtras (fish, birds, rhinoceros).

19. There is a nice list of these animal rebirths of the Buddha in the thirteenth-century Sinhala text, *Pūjāvaliya* (Garland of offerings), ed. Pandit Kiriällē Gñānavimala (Colombo: Gunasena, 1986), 62–63. For details see E. B. Cowell, ed., *The Jātaka; or, Stories of the Buddha's Former Births*, 6 vols. (London: Pali Text Society, 1981), esp. 6–7 of the general index under "Bodhisatta."

20. One exception is the *Mūga-Pakkha Jātaka* (no. 538), where the logic of the story requires Temiya (the future Buddha) to experience hell, that is, for him to know that if he becomes a king, he will eventually be consigned to hell because kings are by definition sinners, having to execute people.

21. Although the Buddha is often born as an animal, nowhere in the *Jātakas* is he ever born as a woman. In my view this idea is only indirectly a matter of the inferiority status of women; it is primarily a structural feature of the *Jātaka* narrative. The Buddha is born as a male; and in many of these tales he has a wife and children. These beings must remain his family through the various existences; therefore, there is no way that the Buddha could change his gender identity.

22. Lambert Schmithausen, *The Problem of the Sentience of Plants in Earliest Buddhism,* Studia Philologica Buddhica Monograph Series 6 (Tokyo: International Institute for Buddhist Studies, 1991). Subsequent quotations from this work are cited parenthetically in the text with the abbreviation *PSP.*

23. These Upanishadic references are as follows: *Chāndogya* 6.3.1 mentions "three sources from which these creatures here originate; they are born from eggs, from living individuals, or from sprouts." The text does not develop the idea of sentient existence emerging from sprouts, nor does the other Upanishadic reference in *Aitareya* 3.3 clarify it, except perhaps in reference to the permeation of divinity, or Brahman, in nature. See Olivelle, *Upaniṣads,* 149, 198–99.

24. See Schmithausen, *Sentience of Plants,* 44. For a detailed and insightful analysis of contemporary practice of Jaina vegetarianism and its relation to ahiṃsā see James Laidlaw, *Riches and Renunciation: Religion, Economy, and Society among the Jains* (Oxford: Oxford University Press, 1995), esp. chap. 7, "The Ascetic Imperative," 151–89. I doubt that Laidlaw's data could be applicable to all contemporary Jaina groups.

25. Christoph von Furer-Haimendorf, *Morals and Merit: A Study of Values and Social Controls in South Asian Societies* (London: Weidenfeld and Nicholson, 1967). Subsequent quotations from this work are cited in the text with the abbreviation *MM.*

26. For further details on Indian tribal religions and reincarnation, see Robert Parkin, *The Munda of Central India: An Account of Their Social Organization* (Delhi: Oxford University Press, 1992), 203–27.

27. Arthur Berriedale Keith, *The Religion and Philosophy of the Veda and Upanishads,* 2 vols. (Cambridge: Harvard University Press, 1925). Subsequent quotations from this work are cited in the text with the abbreviation *RP.*

28. For discussion of this issue see Tull, *Vedic Origins of Karma,* 30.

29. See Keith, *Religion and Philosophy,* 2:474–75.

30. Paul Deussen, *Philosophy of the Upanishads* (1906; reprint, New York: Dover, 1966), 366.

31. *Kauṣītaki Upaniṣad,* 3.1, in Olivelle, *Upaniṣads,* 216.

32. Olivelle, *Saṃnyāsa Upaniṣads,* 237.

33. Quoted in ibid., 244.

34. See Margaret Cone and Richard F. Gombrich, trans., *The Perfect Generosity of Prince Vessantara: A Buddhist Epic* (Oxford: Clarendon Press, 1977); see also "Vessantara Jātaka," in Cowell, *Jātaka,* 6:247–305.

35. "Sāmaññaphala Sutta," in T. W. Rhys Davids, trans., *Dialogues of the Buddha* (London: Pali Text Society, 1977), 1:65–95. Subsequent citations of Rhys Davids's translation are referenced with the abbreviation *Dial.*

36. Ibid., 69–70.

37. Ibid., 70.

38. A.L. Basham, *History and Doctrines of the Ājīvikas* (London: Luzac, 1951). When subsequent quotations from this work are cited in the text, they are referenced parenthetically as *HD*. For the influence of the *Ājīvikas* on the merchant classes in South India c. 500–900 C.E. see Gananath Obeyesekere, *The Cult of the Goddess Pattini* (Chicago: University of Chicago Press, 1984), 65.

39. Ajita Kesakambili believed that a body is constituted of the four elements alone and that when a person dies, nothing remains. For Rhys Davids's views see "Sāmaññaphala Sutta," 73–74.

40. See Basham, *History and Doctrines,* 224–35.

41. The question marks are Basham's. See also Rhys Davids's translation in *Dial.,* 1:71–73.

42. See the exposition of Ājīvika views on karma by the Jaina commentator Sīlaṇka in Basham, *History and Doctrines,* 232.

43. With apologies to Hotspur.

44. A Tirthankara is for Jainism what the Buddha is for Buddhism.

45. Quoted in Basham, *History and Doctrines,* 227–28.

46. Ibid., 111. The idea of using a large earthenware pot might well have been influenced by prehistoric urn burials, which occurred throughout South Asia.

47. A clear statement of the four *āśrama*s is found in the Dharmasūtra of Apastamba. See Buhler, *Sacred Laws of the Āryas,* 1:151–53. For a detailed discussion of this issue see Patrick Olivelle, *Rules and Regulations of Brahmanical Asceticism* (New York: SUNY Press, 1995); and Patrick Olivelle, *The Origin and Early Development of Buddhist Monachism* (Colombo: Gunasena, 1974). For a different view, emphasizing later development, see Romila Thapar, "Renunciation: The Making of a Counter Culture?" in *Ancient Indian Social History* (Delhi: Orient Longmans, 1978), 63–104; and Pande, *Origins of Buddhism.*

48. Olivelle, *Rules and Regulations,* 7.

49. Olivelle, *Buddhist Monachism,* 5; see also Patrick Olivelle, *The Āśrama System* (New York: Oxford, 1993), 73. Bodewitz, in "Hindu *Ahiṃsa*" sums up this point of view: "It is doubtful whether renouncement had its roots in the orthodox Vedic tradition characterized by rituals. The so-called *āśrama* system formed a rather late development. Originally renouncement was not the period of life but an alternative to, for example, the way of life of the householder and in the oldest Dharmasūtras this institution was not favourably judged," 27.

50. For a good overview of this issue see Pande, *Origins of Buddhism,* 321–38.

51. Olivelle, *Buddhist Monachism,* 1.

52. See Sukumar Dutt, *The Buddha and Five Centuries After* (London: Luzac, 1957), 32–35.

53. "Discourse to Sandaka" (Sandakasutta), in I. B. Horner, trans., *Middle Length Sayings (Majjhima Nikāya)* (London: Pali Text Society, 1957), 2:192. Subsequent citations of Horner's translation are referenced with the abbreviation *MLS.*

54. "Greater Discourse to Sakuludāyin" (Mahā-Sakuludāyisutta), in *MLS,* 2:203.

55. "Discourse to Vacchagotta on the Threefold Knowledge" (Tevijja-Vacchagottasutta), in *MLS,* 2:159. The name of the park could also be translated as "single white lotus park."

56. "Discourse to Samaṇamaṇḍikā('s Son)" (Samaṇamaṇḍikāsutta), in *MLS*, 2:222.

57. "Discourse on the Ariyan Quest" (Ariyapariyesanasutta), in *MLS*, 1:214. There is a beautiful description of caste convention at a first meeting and the Buddha's criticism of it in "Pūralāsa Sutta" of the *Sutta-Nipāta* when a Brahmin goes up to the Buddha and says, "What caste are you?" After giving several examples of the qualities of a sage, including his homelessness, the Buddha responds, "Your question about caste is irrelevant." The Brahmin retorts, "But, Sir, when Brahmins meet they always ask one another whether or not they are Brahmins." For the full text see H. Saddhatissa, trans., *Sutta-Nipāta* (London: Curzon Press, 1987), 51–55. For another translation of this important text see K. R. Norman, *The Rhinoceros Horn and Other Early Buddhist Poems (Sutta Nipāta)* (London: Pali Text Society, 1985), 76.

58. "Greater Discourse to Sakuludāyin" (Mahā-Sakuludāyisutta), in *MLS*, 2:204.

59. F. L. Woodward, trans., *The Book of the Kindred Sayings (Saṃyutta Nikāya)* (Oxford: Pali Text Society, 1990), 5:60.

60. For a good discussion of this issue see Wolfgang Schlucter, "The Paradox of Rationalization," in *Max Weber's Vision of History,* by Guenter Roth and Wolfgang Schluchter (Berkeley: University of California Press, 1979), 11–64.

61. Deussen, *Philosophy of the Upanishads,* 11–12.

62. See Emile Durkheim, *Sociology and Philosophy,* trans. D. F. Pocock (New York: Free Press, 1974), 35–62; esp. 37–38.

63. Max Weber, *The Religion of India,* trans., Hans H. Gerth and Don Martindale (Glencoe, Ill.: Free Press, 1958), 209.

64. "The Book of the Great Decease" (Mahā Parinibbāna Sutta), in *Dial.*, 2:121.

65. "Discourse on the Ariyan Quest" (Ariyapariyesanasutta), in *MLS*, 1:211–12.

66. Ibid., 211–13.

67. Sister Vajira and Francis Story, *Last Days of the Buddha (Mahā Parinibbāna Sutta)* (Kandy, Sri Lanka: Buddhist Publication Society, 1988), 35. These translators and others have used the phrase "the evil one" for Māra; because I doubt that Buddhism has a theory of "evil" in the monotheistic sense, I have retranslated this phrase as "the malignant one."

68. Ibid., 43.

69. Mohan Wijayaratna, *Buddhist Monastic Life,* trans. Claude Grangier and Steven Collins (Cambridge: Cambridge University Press, 1990), 21.

70. Weber, *Religion of India,* 206.

71. Weber, *The Sociology of Religion,* trans. Ephraim Fischoff (Boston: Beacon Press, 1963), 46. Subsequent quotations from this work are cited in the text with the abbreviation *SR*.

72. Arthur Mitzman, *The Iron Cage* (New York: Grosset and Dunlap, 1971), 203.

73. R. C. Zaehner, *The Dawn and Twilight of Zoroastrianism* (New York: G. P. Putnam, 1961), 44.

74. Quoted in ibid., 38.

75. See, e.g., Trevor Ling, *Buddhism and the Mythology of Evil* (London: George Allen and Unwin, 1962); James W. Boyd, *Satan and Māra* (Leiden: Brill, 1975).

76. Walter Kaufmann, *Critique of Religion and Philosophy* (New York: Anchor Books, 1961), 403.

77. Jaspers, *Vom Ursprung und Ziel der Geschichte;* Eisenstadt, "Axial Age," and "Fundamentalism."

78. See Kosambi, *Indian History,* and Kosambi, *Ancient India.*

79. Debiprasad Chattopadhyaya mentions a second-century Sanskrit Buddhist text, *Avādana Sataka,* that refers to them: "A group of merchants of the Middle Country of Northern India . . . went to the Deccan. The king of the Deccan asked them, 'Gentlemen-Merchants, who is the king that rules over there?' 'Your Majesty, some areas there are under the rule of *gaṇa*s while others are under the rule of monarchs'" (Debiprasad Chattopadhyaya, *Lokāyata: A Study in Indian Materialism* [New Delhi: Peoples Publishing House, 1973], 467).

80. Kosambi, *Ancient India,* 111–20, 124–26; see also Kosambi's map on caravan routes, 136–37.

81. Ibid., 101–3.

82. See Emile Durkheim, *Suicide: A Study in Sociology* (New York: Free Press, 1966), 248–54.

83. Max Weber, "Social Psychology of the World Religions," in *From Max Weber,* ed. Hans Gerth and C. Wright Mills (New York: Oxford University Press, 1976), 293–94. Weber added: "Rationality means another thing if we think of the methodological attainment of a definitely given and practical end by means of an increasingly precise calculation of adequate means" (293).

84. See Weber, *Sociology of Religion,* 58–59.

85. Another great Indian philosophical system, Sāṃkhya, exemplifies beautifully what I have called "conceptualism," but this philosophy is outside the purview of my book.

86. The *Abhidhamma* is part of the canon. The first part of the canon comprises the discourses attributed to the Buddha, or the *Sutta Piṭaka;* its second is the rules of monk discipline, the *Vinaya Piṭaka;* and its third is the *Abhidhamma,* effectively philosophical and psychological monastic commentaries with an obsessively classificatory thrust.

87. "Brahmajāla Sutta" (The net of Brahma), in *Dial.,* 1:1–55.

88. See Fritz Staal, *Exploring Mysticism* (Berkeley: University of California Press, 1975), 61–63.

89. Albert Keith Whitaker, trans., *Plato's "Parmenides"* (Newburyport, Mass.: Focus Publishing, 1966), 55, 89.

90. Braudel, *On History,* 31.

91. James Paul McDermott, *Development in the Early Buddhist Concept of Kamma/Karma* (New Delhi: Munshiram Manoharlal, 1984), 2.

92. "Cūlakammavibhānga Sutta" (The shorter exposition of action), in Ñāṇamoli and Bodhi, *Middle Length Discourses,* 1053; see also McDermott, *Development,* 9.

93. T. W. Rhys Davids, trans., *The Questions of King Milinda* (New York: Dover, 1889), 1:9.

94. I am aware that the term *aporia* has several meanings: in the ancient Greek, in contemporary phenomenology and hermeneutics, and in deconstruction theory. *Aporia,* plural *aporiai,* generally refers in Greek to a condition of "not knowing where to turn next" or more broadly "puzzlements" or simply "questions." I use it broadly to designate existential puzzles that defy easy resolution or existential dilemmas that people confront as a result of contradictions, or seeming contradictions, in their thinking or lifeways (culture).

95. Paul Ricoeur, *Interpretation Theory: Discourse and the Surplus of Meaning* (Fort Worth: Texas Christian University Press, 1976), 87.

96. This whole section is derived from my early article "Theodicy, Sin, and Salvation in a Sociology of Buddhism," in *Dialectic in Practical Religion,* ed. Edmund R. Leach (Cambridge: Cambridge University Press, 1968), 21–22.

97. Ittepāna Dhammālankāra, *Venerable Balangoda Ananda Maitreye: The Buddha Aspirant* (Dehiwala, Sri Lanka: Sridevi Press, 1996), 121. The same point was made by Dandris de Silva Gooneratne in a pioneering article published in 1865:

> [E]very Buddhist priest admits, in a spirit of compromise, as it were, that many of the calamities or turns of good fortune, which befall men, do take place according to which the planets must move; that the planets are only sort of intermediate agents, serving merely as blind instruments in the hands of *Karma,* to prefigure to the world the various changes of fortune, which must come upon each man according to his *Karma,* that is, according to his good or bad deeds in a former life; and that no propitiation of the planets, or of any power whatsoever, in the whole universe, can ward off calamities, or hinder happiness and prosperity, deserved by a man on account of this inexorable *Karma.*

Gooneratne adds that in spite of the monks' view of karma ordinary people continue to believe in the planets along with other forms of "demonism." See Dandris de Silva Gooneratne, "On Demonology and Witchcraft in Ceylon," *Journal of the Ceylon Branch of the Royal Asiatic Society* 4, no. 13 (1865–66): 7–8.

98. Many of my publications deal with this issue, but see particularly *Cult of the Goddess Pattini,* 50–70.

99. The *Bhūridatta Jātaka* is number 543 of the compendium; see Cowell, *Jātaka,* 6:110.

100. For authorizing discourses in Christianity see Talal Asad, *Genealogies of Religion: Discipline and Reasons of Power in Christianity and Islam* (Baltimore: Johns Hopkins University Press, 1993), 37–39. The examination of such discourses is outside the scope of this project.

101. "Mahākammavibhaṅga Sutta" (The greater exposition of action), in Ñānamoli and Bodhi, *Middle Length Discourses,* 1058–65.

102. See Nyāṇatiloka, *Buddhist Dictionary: Manual of Buddhist Terms and Doctrines* (Kandy, Sri Lanka: Buddhist Publication Society, 1980), 92–95, for a good discussion of the various types of karma. Here is his view of *ahosi-karma:* sometimes karma may not have a result "if the circumstances required for the taking place of the Karma-result are missing, or if, through the preponderance of counteractive Karma and their being too weak, they are unable to produce any result. In this case they are called lit. 'Karma that has been,' in other words, ineffectual karma" (93).

103. Meditation comes last here because it is the true path of the Buddhist ascetic, and it does not involve the accumulation of good deeds. As the royal road to salvation it is a way of overcoming the accumulation of good deeds; those engaged in the latter continue to be reborn in good spheres, whereas the abolishing of rebirth is the goal of the salvation seeker. See "Padhāna Sutta," in Saddhatissa, *Sutta-Nipāta:* "I do not need the least merit you speak of, O Māra, you should preach about merits to those who need them" (48).

104. E. M. Hare, trans., *Gradual Sayings (Anguttara Nikāya)* (Oxford: Pali Text Society, 1989), 4:161–63. A similar sentiment is expressed in the "Māgha Sutta" of the *Sutta-Nipāta,* where the Brahmin Māgha asks the Buddha, "Which people are gift worthy?" The Buddha responds at great length, beginning with: "There are people who wander around in this world, without attachments, possessions, with nothing. They are whole and complete and they have control of the self" (Saddhatissa, *Sutta-Nipāta,* 56).

105. Hare, *Gradual Sayings,* 36–37.

106. McDermott, *Development,* 41.

107. Ibid., 38.

108. For a good discussion of this issue see Richard F. Gombrich, *Precept and Practice* (Oxford: Clarendon Press, 1971), 214–43; for the omnipresence of merit transfer in South and Southeast Asia see Charles F. Keyes, "Merit-Transference in the Kammic Theory of Popular Theravada Buddhism," in *Karma: An Anthropological Inquiry,* ed. Charles F. Keyes and E. Valentine Daniel (Berkeley: University of California Press, 1983), 261–86; for an interesting debate see G. P. Malalasekera, " 'Transference of Merit' in Ceylonese Buddhism," *Philosophy East and West* 17, nos. 1–4 (1967): 85–90; and the response by Richard Gombrich, " 'Merit Transference' in Sinhalese Buddhism," *History of Religions* 11, no. 2 (1971): 203–19.

109. Saddhatissa, *Sutta-Nipāta,* 23. I have substituted "wild goose" for "swan" because that is what the word *haṃsa* literally means, and the literal meaning is most appropriate in this context.

110. H. Saddhatissa, *Buddhist Ethics: Essence of Buddhism* (London: George Allen and Unwin, 1970), 87; see also S. Tachibana, *The Ethics of Buddhism* (Colombo: Bauddha Sahitya Sabha, 1943).

111. Saddhatissa, *Buddhist Ethics,* 100–101; Tachibana, *Ethics of Buddhism,* 43.

112. Saddhatissa, *Buddhist Ethics,* 106; Tachibana, *Ethics of Buddhism,* 43. Vasubandhu, the fifth-century Buddhist scholar who was very much interested in sexuality, has this to say about the precept on sexuality: "Sexual misconduct is much censured in the world because it is the corruption of another's wife, and because it leads to retribution in a painful realm of rebirth." It is clear that Vasubandhu is narrowing "sexual misconduct" to mean adultery. He then adds: "It is easy for householders to abstain from it [adultery], but it is difficult for them to abstain from all sexual activity: householders do not leave the world because they are not capable of difficult things" (Louis de La Vallee Poussin, *Abhidharmakośabhāṣyam,* trans. Leo M. Pruden [Berkeley: Asian Humanities Press, 1988], 2:604).

113. "Sigālovāda Sutta" (Sigāla homily), in Rhys Davids, *Dial.,* 3:167. The fifth precept reads as follows in the Pali: *surā meraya majjha pamādaṭṭhānā veramaṇī sikkhāpadaṃ samādiyāmī.* It is interesting that middle-class people, sometimes seriously and sometimes jokingly, give their own slant to "majjha pamādaṭṭhānā" to mean *mada pamanin* (in moderation), whereas the Pali meaning clearly refers to "strong drinks causing intoxication or sloth."

114. For the doctrinal statement regarding the Jaina precepts see Jaini, *Jaina Path,* 157–85; for their role in contemporary practical religion see Laidlaw, *Riches and Renunciation,* 173–89. Laidlaw, however, suggests that in reality Jaina *vratas* permit a great deal of ethical leeway; thus the distinction between lay and ascetic religiosity can be blurred in practical Jainism, although not to the same degree as in Buddhism.

115. For a discussion of the incorporation of hunters into agricultural society see Obeyesekere, *Cult of the Goddess Pattini,* 301–6. See also my review article "Avalokiteśvara's Aliases and Guises," in *History of Religions* (1993): 372; and my E. F. C. Ludowyk memorial lecture, 2000, "Voices from the Past: An Extended Footnote to Ludowyk's 'The Story of Ceylon.'" For a sophisticated discussion of similar processes in Tibetan Buddhism, especially the historical dialectic between Buddhism and shamanism in respect to animal sacrifices, see Stan Royal Mumford, *Himalayan Dialogue: Tibetan Lamas and Gurung Shamans in Nepal* (Madison: University of Wisconsin Press, 1989), 31–33.

116. Weber, *Religion of India,* 215.

117. "Mahā Parinibbāna Sutta," in Walshe, *Long Discourses,* 236–37; see also "Mahā Parinibbāna Sutta," in *Dial.,* 2:91.

118. Walpola Rahula, *History of Buddhism in Ceylon* (Colombo: Gunasena, 1966), 251.

119. Ibid.

120. I. B. Horner, trans., *Vimānavatthu: Stories of the Mansions,* Minor Anthologies of the Pali Canon, vol. 4 (London: Pali Text Society, 1974).

121. See Tachibana, *Ethics of Buddhism,* 56–62, for a brief account.

122. Rhys Davids, *Questions of King Milinda,* 2:244–60.

123. The forest-dwelling *vanavāsins* have been designated the inferior sect in some historical texts, but these texts have been composed by the temple-dwelling *grāmavāsins.*

124. See Michael Carrithers, *The Forest Monks of Sri Lanka* (New Delhi: Oxford University Press, 1983); and S. J. Tambiah, *The Buddhist Saints of the Forest and the Cult of Amulets* (Cambridge: Cambridge University Press, 1984).

125. I have seen this in an archaeological site at Rajagala in the Eastern Province of Sri Lanka.

## CHAPTER 4. THE BUDDHIST ASCESIS

1. See Marcel Griaule, *Conversations with Ogotemmeli* (London: Oxford University Press, 1975).

2. These are, broadly speaking, the views of scholars such as Rhys Davids, Hermann Oldenberg, E. J. Thomas, and, more recently, distinguished Belgian

scholar Etienne Lamotte; they are also the views of Western monks, of Theravada expatriate monks in Western nations, and of returning expatriate monks who are attempting to reproselytize native Buddhists in the "rational" Buddhism of the West.

3. See "Discourse on Wonderful and Marvellous Qualities" (Acchariyabbhutadhammasutta), in *MLS,* 3:163–69.

4. Ibid., 165. I have changed Horner's translation in order to make it more intelligible to an audience unfamiliar with Sanskrit and Pali. Horner's translation reads "surpassing even the *deva*-majesty of *devas,*" which I have rendered "surpassing even the divine majesty of the gods."

5. G. P. Malalasekera, *Dictionary of Pali Proper Names* (1937; reprint, New Delhi: Oriental Books Reprint Corporation, 1983), 2:610.

6. J. J. Jones, trans., *The Mahāvastu* (London: Pali Text Society, 1976), 2:3.

7. N. A. Jayawickrama, trans., *The Jātaka Nidāna* (The story of Gotama Buddha) (Oxford: Pali Text Society, 1990), 69.

8. Heesterman, *Inner Conflict,* 65.

9. "Mahāpadāna Sutta" (The sublime story), in *Dial.,* 2:4–41.

10. E. H. Johnston, trans., Aśvaghoṣa's *The Buddhacarita or Acts of the Buddha* (1936; reprint, New Delhi: Orient Reprint Corporation, 1972), 39; Jayawickrama, *Jātaka Nidāna,* 78.

11. Hermann Oldenberg, *Buddha: His Life, His Doctrine, His Order,* trans. William Hoey (London: Williams and Norgate, 1882), 104; see also Jayawickrama, *Jātaka Nidāna,* 82.

12. Jayawickrama, *Jātaka Nidāna,* 83–84; for a discussion of the significance of the number eighteen in Buddhism see Gananath Obeyesekere, "Myth, History, and Numerology in the Buddhist Chronicles," in *The Dating of the Historical Buddha,* ed. Heinz Bechert (Gottingen: Vandenhoeck and Ruprecht, 1989), 152–82.

13. "Mahāsīhanādasutta," in *MLS,* 1:103–4. This text should not be confused with another text with the same title in the *Dīgha Nikāya;* the latter is better known as the *Kassapa-Sīhanāda Sutta.*

14. One text, "The Bodhi Tree," has it that the theory of conditioned genesis was discovered in the first watch of the night. This is the first text in the *Udāna* of the *Khuddhaka Nikāya* (Minor collection) containing the "inspired utterances of the Buddha." This text, however, does not say that the discovery was made while the Buddha was in deep concentration; quite the contrary, it states that the Buddha emerged from concentration "and gave well-reasoned attention during the first watch of the night to dependent arising." See John D. Ireland, trans., *The Udāna* (Kandy, Sri Lanka: Buddhist Publication Society, 1990), 11.

15. It seems that among English-speaking Buddhists, scholars and laypersons alike, the conventional translation of the Buddha's powerful experience as *Enlightenment* has come to stay. However, there have been both European and Sinhala translators of the Pali, such as I. B. Horner and N. A. Jayawickrama, who have generally used *Awakening* even though they have missed the deep experiential significance of that "Awakening."

16. See Ireland, *Udāna,* 26. This short text tells of a lay follower who be-

cause of his business entanglements had no time to see the Buddha but at long last had a chance. The Buddha then makes this verse comment:

> Blissful indeed it is to own nothing
> When one is learned and has mastered the Dhamma.
> See how people who own things are afflicted.
> Bound to others by their obligations.

The same verse is repeated in the very next text, "The Pregnant Woman," 26–27.

17. Emile Durkheim, *The Elementary Forms of the Religious Life,* trans. J. W. Swain (1912; reprint, London: George Allen and Unwin, 1954), 316, my italics.

18. F. L. Woodward, trans., *The Book of Gradual Sayings (Anguttara Nikāya)* (Oxford: Pali Text Society, 1989), 1:190–91.

19. Ibid., 192.

20. For recent interest among Buddhists of past life identities, see chapter 2, note 35.

21. "Mahāpadāna Sutta" (The sublime story), in *Dial.,* 2:4.

22. Ibid. This appears elsewhere also. In the "Pāṭika Sutta" of the *Dīgha Nikāya,* the Buddha tells an interlocutor: "I know it [what would happen to an adversary] in my own mind, and I have also been told by a deva." In Walshe, *Long Discourses,* 376; "Pāṭika Suttanta," in *Dial.,* 3:17.

23. "Janavasabha Sutta," in *Dial.,* 2:237.

24. Ibid., 237–38, my italics. Popular texts are also full of references to the Buddha's referring to the past lives and postmortem destinies of lay folk. This theme appears in the justly famous "Mahā Parinibbāna Sutta," which deals with the death of the Buddha and his final passing away into nirvana. Here, as often elsewhere, Ānanda, the cousin of the Buddha and his personal attendant, is the mediator between the world-renouncing Buddha on the one side and the world-involved laity on the other. Ānanda wants to know what happened to certain monks and lay folk after death. The Buddha mildly chastises Ānanda for asking questions that are not conducive to salvation: "Now there is nothing strange in this, Ānanda, that a human being should die; but that as each one does (dies) so you should come to me, and inquire about them in this manner, that is wearisome to me" ("Mahā Parinibbāna Sutta," in *Dial.,* 2:99).

25. Mircea Eliade, *Shamanism: Archaic Techniques of Ecstasy* (Princeton: Princeton University Press, 1972), 5; see also Mircea Eliade, *Yoga, Immortality, and Freedom,* 2d ed., trans. Willard R. Trask (New York: Bollingen Foundation, 1969).

26. See I. M. Lewis, *Ecstatic Religion* (London: Penguin Books, 1971).

27. Eliade, *Shamanism,* 417.

28. "Mahāpadāna Sutta," in *Dial.,* 2:7.

29. M. M. J. Marasinghe, *The Gods in Early Buddhism* (Kelaniya: Vidyalankara University Press, 1974), 91.

30. "Ariyapariyesanasutta" (Discourse on the Ariyan quest), in *MLS,* 1:214.

31. "Sakkapañha Sutta" (Sakka's questions), in Walshe, *Long Discourses,* 321–22.

32. "Cūḷa-Sakuludāyisutta" (Lesser discourse to Sakuludāyin), in *MLS,* 2:234. Some texts of the *Sutta-Nipāta* mention the standard position of respect the gods and lay folk take when conversing with the Buddha. "Then, as night was passing away, a deity of surpassing brilliance, came up [to] the Blessed One and stood on one side after saluting him. Standing there the deity addressed the Blessed One in verse" (Norman, *Rhinoceros Horn,* 44; see also 17).

33. "Sāmaññaphala Sutta" (Fruits of the life of a recluse), in *Dial.,* 1:90–91.

34. *Kevaddha Sutta,* in *Dial.,* 1:278.

35. Ibid., 277.

36. Ibid. For another text that deals with this issue of supernormal powers, and with less ambivalence, see "Sangarava" (Discourse to the Brahmin Sangarava), in Woodward, *Gradual Sayings,* 1:151–56.

37. A. L. Basham, *The Wonder That Was India* (New York: Grove Press, 1959), 242.

38. Ibid.

39. These ideas are employed by I. M. Lewis in *Ecstatic Religion* (London: Penguin, 1971).

40. Elsewhere I have suggested that the hostile attitude to spirit possession is true of Christianity and other Axial Age religions. It is the seeming abdication of self-control that is at the heart of the conflict. In the monotheisms it is impossible not to define possession as the work of the devil and, consequently, as "evil," whereas Buddhism, in accordance with its soteriological stance, left spirit possession alone as long as it did not engage in animal sacrifices. Monks, however, were not permitted to witness these; such actions fitted the Vinaya rules that enjoined the monk to abstain from witnessing shows. I also pointed out an important psychological dynamic, namely that celibate monks cannot be confronted with the orgiastic—and sometimes orgasmic—convolutions of the body of female possessees. The possession condition not only undermines the clerical view of "rationality" and control but also threatens to undo the control of their own drives and loosen their own precarious repressions, especially those of sexuality. Even when there is no institutionalized celibacy, priestly orders, like many brands of Protestantism, have a rigid ethicization of sexuality that is threatened by possession trances. For details see Gananath Obeyesekere, "Despair and Recovery in Sinhala Medicine and Religion: An Anthropologist's Meditations," in *Healing and Restoring: Health and Medicine in the World's Religious Traditions,* ed. Larry Sullivan (New York: Macmillan, 1989), 127–48.

41. Henri Bergson, *The Two Sources of Morality and Religion,* trans. R. Ashley Audra and Cloudsley Brereton (New York: Henry Holt, 1935), 181.

42. "Janavasabha Sutta," in *Dial.,* 2:242.

43. *Koṭi* is most widely recognized as ten million, occasionally as ten lakhs (one million).

44. "Janavasabha Sutta," in *Dial.,* 2:250.

45. "Devadūtasutta" (Discourse on the divine messengers), in *MLS,* 3:223–24.

46. "Mahāsīhanādasutta" (Greater discourse on the lion's roar), in *MLS,* 1:95–100.

47. In all there are thirty-one otherworldly abodes. For a good description

of these abodes, see Marasinghe, *Gods in Early Buddhism,* 43–64; and Walshe, introduction to *Long Discourses,* 40–46.

48. Marasinghe, *Gods in Early Buddhism,* 49.

49. "Devadūtasutta," in *MLS,* 3:225.

50. John S. Strong, *The Legend of King Aśoka: A Study and Translation of the "Aśokāvadāna"* (Princeton: Princeton University Press, 1983). Subsequent quotations from this work are cited in the text with the abbreviation *LKA.*

51. This version is not found in the "Bālapaṇḍita Sutta" of the Theravada canon, but there are stanzas that come close to it.

52. "Bālapaṇḍitasutta," in *MLS,* 3:209–11.

53. "Kakacūpama Sutta" (Simile of the saw), in Ñānamoli and Bodhi, *Middle Length Discourses,* 223.

54. I must emphasize, however, that such breaks between the thought of the specialist and that of the ordinary citizen are by no means confined to Axial religions but exist in every sophisticated religious tradition, posing serious problems in determining the relevant level of ethnographic interpretation in which the scholar is engaged. For a discussion of this problem see Obeyesekere, *Work of Culture,* 225–36.

55. T. W. Rhys Davids says, "Sanaṃkumāra means 'ever-virgin.' According to the legend—common ground to Brahmans and Buddhists—there were five 'mind born' sons of Brahma, who remained always pure and innocent, and this Brahma was one of the five" (*Dial.,* 1:121n1).

56. For a brief and succinct account of the Brahma-worlds see Malalasekera, *Pali Proper Names,* 2:336–38.

57. "Tevijja Sutta" (On knowledge of the Vedas), in *Dial.,* 1:300–320.

58. Ibid., 301–3. In this regard note that the Pali word *sahavyata,* translated as "union" by Rhys Davids, could better be translated as "fellowship" according to Walshe (see Walshe, *Long Discourses,* 43).

59. Ibid., 304–6. The Buddha then gives a series of analogies that depict the folly of asking meaningless questions. For example, what if Vāseṭṭha were to love the most beautiful woman of the land and people ask him "whether that beautiful woman is a noble lady or a Brahman woman, or of the trader class, or a Sudra"? The answer, replies Vāseṭṭha, is obviously "no." And so would the answer be if people were to ask him the foolish question, whether you could love her whom you had not known or seen. Hence, the Buddha says that the Brahmins, or their pupils, or their predecessors even to the seventh generation and "even the Rishis of old" could not possibly "point out to a union with which they know not, neither have seen!" (308). The dialogue then proceeds with the Buddha making Vāseṭṭha admit that whereas Brahma is pure of mind, chaste, without possession of wives and wealth, free of malice and anger, full of self-mastery (all virtues of the Buddhist arahant), Brahmins themselves possess those very vices and lack those virtues. "Verily, good Vāseṭṭha . . . that these Brahmans versed in the Vedas, who live married and wealthy, should after death, when the body is dissolved, become united with Brahma, who has none of these things—such a condition of things can in no wise be!"(308).

60. These crucial terms are variously translated. Nyāṇatiloka's translation is

perhaps satisfactory. *Brahma-vihāra* are "the four sublime or divine abodes," also known as "the four boundless states" *(appamañña)*. These are *mettā* (loving-kindness), *karunā* (compassion), *muditā* (altruistic or sympathetic joy) and *upekkhā* (equanimity). See Bhikkhu Nyāṇaponika, *Buddhist Dictionary,* 44.

61. "Kūṭadanta Sutta" (Discourse on the Brahmin Pointed Tooth), in *Dial.,* 1:173–96. The Brahmin was called "pointed tooth" because he filed his teeth or one tooth, either as a personal idiosyncrasy or, more likely, because it was a custom of his group.

62. A good example of a revaluation of the Brahmanic fire ritual comes from the *Mahāvagga* of the *Vinaya Piṭaka* (Book of the discipline), where the Buddha converts matted-hair ascetics to his way of knowledge. See I. B. Horner, trans., *The Book of the Discipline* (London: Pali Text Society, 1982), 4:37–45.

63. For a good account of *sapiṇḍīkaraṇa* and the establishment of the relationship between the living and the dead see David M. Knipe, "*Sapiṇḍīkaraṇa:* The Hindu Rite of Entry into Heaven," in *Religious Encounters with Death,* ed. Frank E. Reynolds and Earle H. Waugh (University Park: Pennsylvania State University Press, 1997), 111–24; for a discussion of Hindu pretas and their conversion into ancestors in contemporary Banaras see Jonathan P. Parry, *Death in Banaras* (Cambridge: Cambridge University Press, 1994), 75–80.

64. "Sigālovāda Sutta" (The Sigāla homily), in *Dial.,* 3:173–84.

65. In a footnote to this passage Rhys Davids says: "The symbolism is deliberately chosen: as the day in the East, so life begins with parents' care; teachers' fees and the South are the same word: dakkina; domestic cares follow when the youth becomes man, as the West holds the later daylight; North is 'beyond,' so by help of friends, etc., he gets beyond troubles."

66. One of the fascinating changes in modern Buddhism is the reaxiologizing of the "Sigālovāda Sutta": thus the leader of the contemporary Buddhist reform movement known as Sarvodaya says that the wife should "consider one's husband a god and do herself everything to look after him"; and the late president Premadasa, influenced by Sarvodaya ideas, led a campaign to make children worship their parents (and teachers) every day. Both leaders assume that these are "traditional" Buddhist values. Much of this is a deliberate rereading of the "Sigālovāda Sutta," or an ignorance of it: it is presumed that the Buddha told Sigāla not to worship the six quarters but to worship one's husband, parents, and teachers instead (conveniently forgetting women, children, slaves, and servants)! For details of this issue see Richard Gombrich and Gananath Obeyesekere, *Buddhism Transformed: Religious Change in Sri Lanka* (Princeton: Princeton University Press, 1988), 249–52. The *Sutta-Nipāta* has much more interesting texts on popular ethics than the "Sigālovāda Sutta," especially the texts entitled "Failure" and "The Outcaste," in Norman, *Rhinoceros Horn,* 17–23.

67. Because many Indologists translate *varṇa* as caste, I use these two terms interchangeably; I use the term *jāti* to refer to the multiplicity of hierarchically graded groups in the operative stratification system, conventionally referred to as "caste" by anthropologists.

68. These outsiders are for the most part referred to as "caṇḍālas" in Buddhist texts.

69. "Vāseṭṭha Sutta," in Saddhatissa, *Sutta-Nipāta,* 71.

70. "Madhurāsutta" (Discourse at Madhurā), in *MLS,* 2:273–78.

71. "Ambaṭṭha Sutta," in *Dial.,* 1:121.

72. Ibid., 114–15; see also "Agañña Sutta," in *Dial.,* 3:77–94.

73. Buhler, *Sacred Laws of the Āryas,* 2:147–48. In this text Baudhāyana refers to the country of the Āryas, or Āryavartha, which "lies to the east of the region where (the river) Sarasvati disappears, to the west of the Black Forest (Kālakavana), to the north of the Paripatra (mountains), to the south of the Himalayas."

"Some (declare) the country between the (rivers) Yamunā and Ganges (to be the Āryavartha)."

"The inhabitants of Avanti, of Anga, of Magadha, of Surashtra, of the Dekhan, of Upavrit, of Sindh, and Sauviras are of mixed origin." The countries beyond that are much worse and if one travels there (such as Vanga [Bengal] and Kālinga [Orissa]), one must perform an act of purification.

74. K. R. Norman, trans., *Therigāthā* (Elders' verses), vol. 2 (London: Pali Text Society, 1971), 26. See also the translation and rendering into English verse by C. A. F. Rhys Davids, *The Psalms of the Early Buddhists* (1908; reprint, London: Pali Text Society, 1980), 116–19.

75. Louis Dumont, *Homo Hierarchicus: The Caste System and Its Implications,* trans. M. Sainsbury, L. Dumont, and B. Gulati, rev. ed. (Chicago: University of Chicago Press, 1980).

76. Patrick Olivelle, "Caste and Purity: A Study in the Language of the Dharma Literature," *Contributions to Indian Sociology,* n.s., 32, no. 2 (1988): 189–216.

77. These Buddhist texts seem to justify Dumont's position that Brahmins did make a claim for "intrinsic purity," and this observation is reinforced when the claim is made that the Buddha's lineage maintained its own purity through sibling marriage. This does lend some force to Dumont's argument, although it would be difficult, at least for the period of the Buddha, to use these somewhat ambiguous texts on intrinsic purity for formulating his general thesis that hierarchizing in Hindu society is based on the omnipresence of purity-impurity, with the former represented in the Brahmin and the latter in the untouchable. However, Dumont's vision of "homo" being entirely "hierarchicus" in the ordinary sense of that term seems validated by the texts, both in the Dharmasūtras and in the counterresponses of the Buddhists of this period. One could argue of course that the Brahmin position in the "Vāseṭṭha Sutta" is not about the intrinsic purity of the Brahmin class but about their having to safeguard themselves against wrong marriages that in turn might lead to impurity of a somewhat enduring sort. But one cannot get away from the fact that according to the "Vāseṭṭha Sutta" correct marriages preserve Brahmin purity. A similar situation arises in the case of women. A woman's menstruation is polluting, but from the point of view of her own ritual status the elimination of bad blood through the menstrual flow renders her pure. But how is this possible if she is not impure to begin with? If her impurities have to be siphoned off through the menstrual flow, then it must mean that she is already an impure being. It seems that at the cessation of the menstrual flow the woman becomes pure for a fleeting moment; the impurities of the body then must build up, and she becomes more and more impure. This comes close to the idea of a woman as "intrinsically impure" in the Dharmasūtra scheme of things.

78. For the most recent critique of Louis Dumont's thesis and an evaluation of scholarly arguments for and against it see Nicholas B. Dirks, *Castes of Mind: Colonialism and the Making of Modern India* (Princeton: Princeton University Press, 2001).

## CHAPTER 5. ESCHATOLOGY AND SOTERIOLOGY IN GREEK REBIRTH

1. Plato, *Phaedo* 114b; for the context of this expression see the discussion of the myth of Er below.

2. My ideas of history and storytelling come from Paul Ricoeur and Michel de Certeau, among others. See especially the section "History and Narrative," in Paul Ricoeur, *Time and Narrative,* vol. 1, trans. Kathleen McLaughlin and David Pellauer (Chicago: University of Chicago Press, 1984), 95–230; Paul Ricoeur, *Time and Narrative,* vol. 3, trans. Kathleen Blamey and David Pellauer (Chicago: University of Chicago Press, 1988), esp. sec. 2, "Poetics of Narrative: History, Fiction, Time," 104–240. For a neat early version of history as story see "The Narrative Function," in Paul Ricoeur, *Hermeneutics and the Human Sciences,* ed. John B. Thompson (Cambridge: Cambridge University Press, 1981), 274–96. For de Certeau see Michel de Certeau, *Heterologies: Discourse on the Other,* trans. Brian Massumi (Minneapolis: University of Minnesota Press, 1989); Michel de Certeau, *The Writing of History,* trans. Tom Conley (New York: Columbia University Press, 1988).

3. Edwin Minar, *Early Pythagorean Politics* (Baltimore: Waverly Press, 1942), 2–8. For specific details see M. L. West, *The Orphic Poems;* M. L. West, *Early Greek Philosophy and the Orient* (Oxford: Clarendon Press, 1971); and Kingsley, *Ancient Philosophy.*

4. For a good account of Pherekydes see Herman S. Schibli, *Pherekydes of Syros* (Oxford: Clarendon Press, 1990), esp. 104–27; see also Kirk, Raven, and Schofield, *Presocratic Philosophers,* 51–71; West, *Early Greek Philosophy,* chaps. 1 and 2, esp. 60–61.

5. David Grene, trans., *The History: Herodotus,* 2.123 (Chicago: University of Chicago Press, 1987), 185.

6. Long, *Doctrine of Metempsychosis,* 22–23.

7. *Herodotus* 2.81 (Grene translation), 164–65; for another translation see West, *Orphic Poems,* 16.

8. Diogenes Laertius, *Lives of the Philosophers,* cited in Jonathan Barnes, ed., *Early Greek Philosophy* (London: Penguin, 1987), 82.

9. Peris, "Greek Teachings," 58–61.

10. The ridiculing of Pythagorean beliefs went down to the middle comedy of the fourth and early third centuries B.C.E. "Some suggest that these had taken a leaf out of the Cynics' book (or that the comic poets chose to bait them by maliciously making the confusion), caring nothing for appearances but going about unwashed in filthy rags. They include, however, digs at their vegetarianism, for example, the obvious joke: 'The Pythagoreans eat no living thing.' 'But Epicharides the Pythagorean eats dog!' 'Only after he has killed it'" (Guthrie, *Earlier Presocratics,* 187).

11. Guthrie, *Earlier Presocratics,* 164, my italics; for an excellent discussion of Pythagoras's former birth as Euphorbus and the various later refractions of that story see Peris, "Of Euphorbus, Pythagoras' Prior Incarnation," *Sri Lanka Journal of the Humanities* 14, nos. 1 and 2 (1988): 61–94.

12. Guthrie, *Earlier Presocratics,* 164.

13. Ibid., 160–61; see also Kirk, Raven, and Schofield, *Presocratic Philosophers,* 219. For Iamblichus's version see Taylor's *Iamblichus' "Life of Pythagoras,"* 35.

14. Clark, *Iamblichus,* 26.

15. Ibid., 74.

16. This crucial passage was translated for me by Professor Merlin Peris. See also Guthrie, *Earlier Presocratics,* 186, where Guthrie renders the key phrase as "nothing is new in an absolute sense."

17. Cited in Peris, "Greek Teachings," 153–54.

18. Plato, *Meno* 81c, in G. M. A. Grube, trans., *Five Dialogues: Euthyphro, Apology, Crito, Meno, Phaedo* (Indianapolis: Hackett Publishing, 1981). Unless otherwise noted, all quotations from *Meno* are from this translation.

19. However, what seems like a soteriological account of life after death is provided by Ion of Chios, born c. 490 B.C.E., perhaps not long after the death of Pythagoras, and Diogenes refers to Ion's references to Pythagoras. "So he, endowed with manliness and modesty, has for his soul a joyful life even in death, if indeed Pythagoras, wise in all things, truly knew and understood the minds of men" (Guthrie, *Earlier Presocratics,* 158). Both Keith Guthrie and Hugh Tredennick think this passage refers to a doctrine in which a "good man will be rewarded after death," but this reading typically injects ethical notions that do not emerge from the text itself. See Guthrie, *Earlier Presocratics,* 158; Hugh Tredennick, "Pythagoreanism," Appendix A in *The Ethics of Aristotle,* trans. J. A. K. Thomson (London: Penguin, 1976), 345–46. Tredennick thinks Pythagoras subscribed to a karma-like system of rebirth: "since all life is one, souls are subject to transmigration, sin in one life being punished by downgraded reincarnation in the next" (345). All the text tells us is that Ion thought that Pythagoras's soul would have a delightful existence after death, a likely reference to his soteriology rather than to afterlife rewards in heaven and earth. It seems that those who have written about Greek rebirth share some of the prejudices of early Indologists, namely, that a systematic soteriology must also entail a systematic ethicization. It seems that in the Herodotus-Porphyry model, as we have it in existing accounts, there is no intermediate otherworld in which the soul temporarily sojourns, nor is there any reference to such places in Heraclides. Thus, step 1 of the ethicization process simply did not occur: there is no heaven and no Hades as realms of compensatory reward and punishment.

20. Aristotle, *De Anima* 407b 20, cited in Guthrie, *Earlier Presocratics,* 306; or as Kirk and Raven say "for any chance soul to enter into any chance body." See their *Presocratic Philosophers,* 261.

21. A strong case for Indian influence was stated very early by L. von Schroeder in *Pythagoras und die Inder* (Leipzig: O. Schulze, 1884). Schroeder's argument was refuted in Arthur Berriedale Keith, "Pythagoras and the Doctrine of Transmigration," *Journal of the Royal Asiatic Society of Great Britain and Ireland* 41 (1909): 569–606; see also Keith's chapter "Greece and the Philoso-

phy of India," in *Religion and Philosophy,* 1:601–13. This controversy is far from settled. For a detailed account of the diffusion of ideas from the ancient Near East, Iran, and India see West, *Early Greek Philosophy;* and the important study by W. Burkert, *The Orientalizing Revolution: Near Eastern Influences on Greek Culture in the Early Archaic Age* (Cambridge: Harvard University Press, 1992).

22. E. R. Dodds, *Greeks and the Irrational* (Berkeley: University of California Press, 1951), 150.

23. Ibid., 151.

24. Paul Radin, *Crashing Thunder: The Autobiography of an American Indian* (1920; reprint, Lincoln: University of Nebraska Press, 1983).

25. See esp. Kingsley, *Ancient Philosophy;* Burkert, *Orientalizing Revolution;* and West, *Early Greek Philosophy.*

26. T. J. Dunbabin, *The Western Greeks: The History of Sicily and South Italy from the Foundation of the Greek Colonies to 480 B.C.* (Oxford: Clarendon Press, 1948); Edwin L. Minar, *Early Pythagorean Politics in Practice and Theory* (Baltimore: Waverly Press, 1942).

27. Charles H. Kahn puts it well: "There seems to be no doubt that he [Pythagoras] used this powerful charisma to build a most unconventional social institution in Croton, with a structure that was capable of being reproduced in other cities." See his essay, "Pythagorean Philosophy before Plato," in *The Pre-Socratics: A Collection of Critical Essays,* ed. Alexander P. D. Mourelatos (Princeton: Princeton University Press, 1993), 168.

28. Kirk, Raven, and Schofield, *Presocratic Philosophers,* 225–27; see also 222–25 for other political conflicts.

29. For a detailed account of Pythagorean politics see Minar, *Early Pythagorean Politics,* 36–94; for stories of the death of Pythagoras see Taylor, *Iamblichus,* chap. 35, 127–36. Some sources say that Pythagoras died of starvation or committed suicide, but these claims might be later hearsay or denigration. Walter Burkert makes the following point: "In southern Italy around the middle of the fifth century political upheavals took place in the course of which the assembly houses of the Pythagoreans were set on fire, and Pythagoreans were massacred in large numbers" (*Greek Religion,* 303–4). See also, Kirk, Raven, and Schofield, *Presocratic Philosophers,* 222–25.

30. See, e.g., Kurt von Fritz, *Pythagorean Politics in Southern Italy* (New York: Columbia University Press, 1940), esp. chap. 5, "The Character of the 'Pythagorean Rule' in Southern Italy," 94–102.

31. Ibid., 30.

32. Burkert, *Ancient Mystery Cults,* 32.

33. See Taylor, *Iamblichus,* 203–52; for a more recent translation of *Protrepticus* see T. N. Johnson, trans., *The Exhortation to Philosophy* (Grand Rapids, Mich.: Phanes Press, 1988). See also Kirk, Raven, and Schofield, *Presocratic Philosophers:* "The existence of *hetaireiai* as religious bodies committed to a particular and exclusive way of life helps to account for such diverse phenomena as the form and substance of the *acusmata,* the secrecy adherents were reputed to maintain, and the evidence of distinctive Pythagorean ritual" (228).

34. Taylor, *Iamblichus,* 28.

35. Clark, *Iamblichus,* 17.

36. Ibid., 28–29.

37. Burkert, *Greek Religion,* 303; see also Clark, *Iamblichus,* 32.

38. This is spelled out in great detail by Walter Burkert in *Lore and Science in Ancient Pythagoreanism* (Cambridge: Harvard University Press, 1972).

39. See Burkert, *Lore and Science,* 142–45.

40. Taylor, *Iamblichus,* 72.

41. Ibid.

42. See Friedrich Nietzsche, *The Birth of Tragedy,* trans. Douglas Smith (New York: Oxford University Press, 2000). The Apollonian and intellectualized portrait of Pythagoras that I have drawn contrasts sharply with the more Dionysian version of his teachings presented by Kingsley in *Ancient Philosophy.* Admittedly, my version of Pythagoras has been influenced by Aristotle's discussion of his "mathematics," but I am not willing to dismiss Aristotle's arguments as Kingsley does.

43. Dillon and Hershbell, *Iamblichus,* 93. See also 195: "And he also ordered abstinence from living beings for many reasons, but mainly because the practice tended to promote peace. For once human beings became accustomed to loathe the slaughter of animals as lawless and contrary to nature, they would no longer make war, thinking it even more unlawful to kill a human being." I wonder whether at this time the Greek construction of Pythagoras was influenced by the Buddhist.

44. Ibid., 123, 133.

45. Clark, *Iamblichus,* 48.

46. See Burkert, *Greek Religion,* 302, where Burkert refers to the mythic murder of Dionysus by the Titans: "Only lifelong purity can eradicate the guilt, in particular abstinence from everything in which there is soul, *empsychon.*"

47. Guthrie, *Earlier Presocratics,* 188.

48. Ibid., 188.

49. Taylor, *Iamblichus,* 45.

50. Ibid., 81.

51. Marcel Detienne and Jean-Pierre Vernant, *The Cuisine of Sacrifice among the Greeks* (Chicago: University of Chicago Press, 1989).

52. Taylor, *Porphyry on Abstinence,* 123, 131. Subsequent quotations from this work are cited in the text with the abbreviation *PA.*

53. See ibid., 116, 137.

54. The tradition of Pythagorean vegetarianism was so strong that Porphyry in his *Life of Pythagoras* refers to "Eudoxus in the seventh book of his Description of the Earth [who] says that he [Pythagoras] exhibited such purity and such abhorrence of killing and killers that he not only abstained from animal food but would have nothing to do with cooks or hunters" (cited in Guthrie, *Earlier Presocratics,* 187).

55. Guthrie, in *Earlier Presocratics,* sums up neatly this overdetermined character of beans in the symbology of Pythagoreanism:

> Beans resembled testicles: they resembled the gates of Hades, or the whole universe (all these were recorded by Aristotle . . . ): their stems were hollow throughout and unjointed. . . . Porphyry connected this fact with the return of souls from beneath the earth. . . . [T]hey are of a windy or breathy nature and hence full of the life-

> force. . . . [T]hey contain the souls of the dead. . . . When in the creative chaos at the beginning of the world life arose out of the primeval slime, beans and human beings had their origin from the same form of primal matter. There were strange superstitions about the metamorphoses which a bean would undergo if buried in earth or dung. Heraclides Ponticus [a Pythagorean] is reported as saying that it would assume human shape. From later writers we learn that it would be assimilated to a child's head or the female pudenda. Porphyry and others adduced the belief that if chewed and left in the sun a bean would give off an odour of semen. (184)

56. Ibid.

57. Kirk and Raven, *Presocratic Philosophers,* 228. This important observation is missing in the second edition of this book.

58. Ibid.

59. Carl Huffman, "The Pythagorean Tradition," in *The Cambridge Companion to Early Greek Philosophy,* ed. A. A. Long (Cambridge: Cambridge University Press, 1999), 78–85.

60. Kirk and Raven, *Presocratic Philosophers,* 229; Guthrie, *Earlier Presocratics,* 225.

61. Kirk, Raven, and Schofield, *Presocratic Philosophers,* 329.

62. Guthrie, *Earlier Presocratics,* 225.

63. Ibid., 240.

64. Kirk and Raven, *Presocratic Philosophers,* 245.

65. Ibid., 243; Guthrie, *Earlier Presocratics,* 242–43; see also John Burnet, *Early Greek Philosophy* (London: Adam and Charles Black, 1958), 102–3.

66. Numbers, however, are not abstractions according to these thinkers. Aristotle says, perhaps with some exaggeration, that numbers for Pythagoreans are real things, having substance and magnitude and consequently occupying space. Thus, what we now think of as abstract conceptions—such as justice, goodness, opportunity, or even marriage—were characterized by substantiality and associated with numbers. Whereas Buddhist thinkers could postulate totally abstract conceptions, not so with the Pythagoreans, and it is with Plato and Aristotle that ideas could exist outside space and substantiality. Aristotle was understandably critical of this philosophical orientation. "The Pythagoreans also recognize a single type of number, mathematical number, but not as existing apart from sensible things which they regard as being composed of it. They in fact construct the whole universe out of numbers, not however truly monadic [incorporeal] numbers, for they suppose the units to possess magnitude" (Aristotle, *Metaphysics* 1080.b16, in Guthrie, *Earlier Presocratics,* 234).

The fundamental dualism of the limited and the unlimited on which everything else rested also shared this characteristic of substantiality. The dualism implied, according to Aristotle, that "contrarieties are the principles of things," and he presented the well-known table of opposites constituting ten principles arranged in two columns of cognates, thus:

| | |
|---|---|
| limited | unlimited |
| odd | even |
| one | plurality |
| right | left |
| male | female |

| | |
|---|---|
| at rest | moving |
| straight | crooked |
| light | darkness |
| good | bad |
| square | oblong |

Although Aristotle thought the table of opposites was a fixed scheme for Pythagoreans, he qualifies himself by saying that Alcmaeon of Croton (also a Pythagorean) adds notions of "chance contrarieties," such as sweet and bitter, white and black, great and small. It seems likely that the table constituted the basis for the formation of other dualisms also, as for modern-day structuralists. I also think Guthrie is wrong to ethicize the whole table on the basis of the dichotomy of good (the left column) and bad (the right column), although it is indeed true that, according to Aristotle, "evil belongs to the Unlimited and good to the Limited." Although the interpenetration of the two is crucial for the constitution of the world, the limited and the unlimited are much wider than good and evil. The latter is more Zoroastrian, and it is true that Greeks of the fourth century B.C.E. saw a parallelism between Zoroastrianism and Pythagorean religion, even stating that the founder himself visited Zoroaster. But Pythagorean impersonal dualism is not to be equated with Zoroastrianism's personalized deities Ahura Mazda and Ahriman. Good and bad are merely one function in the table. For example, when we go down the table of opposites we see that woman is on the unlimited side. This is not because she is "bad" but because she creates progeny, and that function expresses the unlimited; so is it with square and oblong (Guthrie, *Earlier Presocratics,* 245–46). Kirk, Raven, and Schofield, *Presocratic Philosophers,* 339, voice an unfavorable view of the table of opposites as having had too little to do with "original Pythagorean ideas" and as containing little internal structure, but these criticisms seem to me unfounded.

67. Francis Cornford, "Mysticism and Science in the Pythagorean Tradition," *Classical Quarterly* 16 (1922): 137–50; and *Classical Quarterly* 17 (1923): 1–12; see also Kahn, "Pythagorean Philosophy before Plato."

68. Kirk, Raven, and Schofield, *Presocratic Philosophers,* 343.

69. Guthrie, *Earlier Presocratics,* 285.

70. For a detailed examination of Philolaus's thought see the excellent account in Kingsley, *Ancient Philosophy,* 172–213; see also the older account by Kahn, "Pythagorean Philosophy before Plato," 169–80; and more recently Huffman, "The Pythagorean Tradition," 78–85.

71. Kahn, "Pythagorean Philosophy before Plato," 170.

72. Quoted in Kirk, Raven, and Schofield, *Presocratic Philosophers,* 345.

73. J. G. F. Powell, trans. and ed., *Cicero's "Laelius, on Friendship" and "The Dream of Scipio"* (Warminster: Aries and Phillips, 1990), 141.

74. Ibid., 143.

75. Inwood, *Poem of Empedocles,* 75.

76. Clark, *Iamblichus,* 27.

77. Ibid.; see also Taylor, *Iamblichus,* 32–33; Dillon and Hershbell, *Iamblichus,* 91.

78. Dillon and Hershbell, *Iamblichus,* 137; Taylor, *Iamblichus,* 61.

79. Guthrie, *Early Presocratics,* 202–3.

80. Burkert, *Lore and Science,* 363.

81. Burnet, *Early Greek Philosophy,* 197–99; Guthrie, *Presocratic Tradition,* 131–32. For details see Dunbabin, *Western Greeks,* especially, 301–25.

82. Burnet, *Early Greek Philosophy,* 203–4; Kirk and Raven, *Presocratic Philosophers,* 322.

83. For an excellent review of this issue see Peris, "Greek Teachings," esp. 525.

84. Guthrie, *Presocratic Tradition,* 125–26.

85. For an interesting interpretation of Empedocles' suicide, which he committed by jumping into the crater of Etna, see Peter Kingsley, *Ancient Philosophy,* chaps. 15–18. On the basis of his far-reaching research into West Asian, Orphic, and other mystery religions Kingsley has shown the widespread distribution of this myth. However, I doubt one can, on the basis of mythic evidence, infer that the historical Empedocles actually jumped into the crater, as Kingsley argues. This is too literal an interpretation. As I understand it, the crater is the womb that leads to the underworld, the very world from which Empedocles is going to resurrect the dead. If so, and here Kingsley is right, death has a symbolic meaning; in initiation rites it must lead to a rebirth and an emergence. Thus the reference to his jumping into Etna might be a *dromenon,* an awesome enactment, well known in Orphic mysteries, rather than a literal act of suicide.

86. Guthrie, *Presocratic Tradition,* 138; Kirk and Raven, *Presocratic Philosophers,* 322.

87. Guthrie, *Presocratic Tradition,* 137.

88. Wright, *Empedocles: The Extant Fragments,* no. 102 (112). For the reader's convenience I will for the most part refer to Wright's edition of Empedocles. I find many of Wright's interpretations of Empedocles' thought hard to accept, however, because of their literal-mindedness. For this reason I will also include in parentheses the fragment numbers from Hermann Diels and Walther Krantz, trans., *Die Fragmente der Versokratiker,* 10th ed., vols. 1 and 2 (Berlin: Weidmann, 1961).

89. See Guthrie, *Presocratic Tradition,* 137.

90. See, e.g., Kingsley, *Ancient Philosophy,* 363–70; Brad Inwood, *Poem of Empedocles,* places this fragment in the beginning as no. 15.

91. Empedocles frag. 101 (111).

92. Ibid., 102 (112).

93. Kahn, "Religion and Natural Philosophy in Empedocles' Doctrine of the Soul," in Mourelatos, *The Pre-Socratics,* 429.

94. Kenneth G. Zysk, *Asceticism and Healing in Ancient India* (New York: Oxford University Press, 1991).

95. Empedocles frag. 7 (6); for other translations see Kirk, Raven, and Schofield, *Presocratic Philosophers,* 286; Guthrie, *Presocratic Tradition,* 141.

96. Empedocles frag. 14 (21); I have capitalized *Love* and *Strife*, but Wright does not.

97. In Empedocles *Sphere* refers to something like a divine, although not anthropomorphized, cosmos. In fact, the Empedoclean cosmos stands in contrast to the human model. It is rounded and a near-perfect Being, ultimately consti-

tuted of the four elements, or roots. "For two branches do not spring from his back, he has no feet, no swift knees, no organs of reproduction, but he is equal to himself in every direction, without any beginning or end, a rounded sphere, rejoicing in the encircling stillness" (Empedocles frag. 22 [29]). One interpretation, favored by Guthrie (*Presocratic Tradition,* 168–71) and many early commentators, is that in Love the Sphere is in perfect harmony, and in Strife it disintegrates and reverts to chaos, but this interpretation seems to me faulty. Love and Strife are never in their pure state but reflect degrees of interaction. A. A. Long puts it thus in his interpretation of frags. 16 (26) and 26 (29): Stage A, where there is a movement from weakening Strife toward maximum Love; then B, a movement from maximum Strife to incipient Love; then C, a stage where all things are one and at rest. This is the Sphere. And D, "Love's loss of power to unite the Sphere and the development of Strife within it. At a precise moment Strife utterly shatters the Sphere, which brings the cycle to B. So we have this circular movement: C-D-B-A" (A. A. Long, "Empedocles' Cosmic Cycle in the Sixties," in Mourelatos, *Pre-Socratics,* 406). This too seems to me as controversial as the traditional view Long criticizes, especially the idea that the Sphere is shattered at a "precise moment," but it has the virtue of focusing on the discontinuous and changing view of the cosmos that is at the heart of Empedocles' thought. It seems to me that the Sphere is a "blessed god" but not a perfect Being; it must share the quality of becoming that is central to Empedocles' worldview.

98. There are many new approaches to Empedocles, but I have used primarily Long, "Empedocles' Cosmic Cycle," 397–425; Kahn, "Religion and Natural Philosophy," 426–56; and Wright, *Empedocles.*

99. Sigmund Freud, *Beyond the Pleasure Principle,* in vol. 18 of *The Standard Edition of the Complete Psychological Works of Sigmund Freud,* ed. James Strachey (1920; reprint, London: Hogarth, 1981), 44–62. Freud adapts Empedocles' dualism as the life instinct, or Eros, and the death instinct, or Thanatos.

100. Empedocles frag. 50 (57).

101. See also Burnet, *Early Greek Philosophy,* 215. The term *sterile,* which Burnet uses, is apparently Hermann Diels's speculative rendering; other sources suggest *shadowed.*

102. Jacques Lacan, "Aggressivity in Psychoanalysis," [1948] reprinted in *Écrits: A Selection,* trans. Alan Sheridan (New York: Norton, 1977), 11.

103. Jacques Lacan, "The Mirror Stage as Formative of the Function of the I as Revealed in the Psychoanalytic Experience," [1949] reprinted in *Écrits: A Selection,* trans. Alan Sheridan (New York: Norton, 1977), 4. I personally find Lacan's early work, which develops these ideas of the mirror stage and the illusory self, much more persuasive than his later, highly formalistic, work on the symbolic and the real.

104. See, e.g., Wright, *Empedocles,* 215.

105. Quoted in Guthrie, *Presocratic Tradition,* 208.

106. Kirk, Raven, and Schofield, *Presocratic Philosophers,* 304. Our contemporary metaphor of trees possessing "limbs" obviously did not make sense to Empedocles.

Although the extant fragments do not refer to any other "whole-natured" form, there is a beautiful example in Plato's *Symposium* that anticipates our own human prototype. Plato's Aristophanes describes the original human condition, when "we used to be wholes in our original nature . . . but now the god has divided us for the wrong we did him" (Plato, *Symp.* 193a, trans. Alexander Nehamas and Paul Woodruff [Indianapolis: Hackett Publishing, 1989]). This was the hermaphrodite, unfairly vilified today but once a holistic creation in which the sexual features of both genders were unified:

> Each human being was completely round, with back and sides in a circle; they had four hands each, as many legs as hands, and two faces, exactly alike, on a rounded neck. Between the two faces, which were on opposite sides, was one head with four ears. There were two sets of sexual organs, and everything else was the way you'd imagine it from what I've told you. They walked upright, as we do now, whatever direction they wanted. And whenever they set out to run fast, they thrust out all their eight limbs, the ones they had then, and spun rapidly, the gymnasts do cartwheels, by bringing their legs around straight. (*Symp.* 189e–90a)

Here also is a creature very much like a tree, although the manner of reproduction is not clear from Aristophanes' account. One cannot discount the idea that the primal hermaphrodite of the *Symposium* is based on Empedocles' view of whole-natured forms.

107. Although "unassisted," the four elements still constitute the atomic principles, or "roots," of all existence.

108. Peris, in "Greek Teachings," defines Empedocles' use of *psyche* thus: "the totality of the psychological functions when they are activated in the body by the presence in it of the daimon" (533).

109. See Inwood, *Poem of Empedocles,* 78–82, for a discussion of these controversies.

110. Kahn, "Religion and Natural Philosophy," 434.

111. Empedocles frag. 107 (115). Unfortunately, this text is not clear, particularly the crucial section that deals with "daimons." See Inwood's translation in *Poem of Empedocles,* 12.

112. Kirk and Raven, *Presocratic Philosophers,* 352.

113. We cannot altogether reject the idea that Love and Strife in the cosmos are refracted within the individual as two souls (daimons). We know from cross-cultural evidence that there are cosmologies that posit multiple souls within a single body; in the later Platonic eschatology itself the soul is constituted of three separate parts located in different areas of the body—which in effect means that humans have three souls. More significant, the early-third-century Neoplatonist Porphyry refers in his text on vegetarianism to Greeks "who assert that we have two souls" but does not develop this idea. Moreover, if the two daimons within the body possess the features of Love and Strife within the cosmos, then they, like the Pythagorean dualisms, must interpenetrate, in which case it is possible for the daimon of love to succumb to strife and vice versa.

A similar argument was made much later by another physician, Eryximachus, in Plato's *Symposium.* When the four elements are in right proportion, says Eryximachus, life is bound together in an orderly and harmonious love in humans and in nature; but when this balance gets upset because of seasonal conditions, there is "inordinate love" or a "vicious love." Thus, in the Greek medical tradition, of which Empedocles was a formative influence, it is possible to think of a form of love that "pollutes." However, the preceding arguments are very speculative, and these issues remain unresolved. For another insightful view of Empedocles' worldview and rebirth eschatology see Peris, "Greek Teachings," 522–609.

114. Kahn, in "Religion and Natural Philosophy," makes the case that "daimon" is the soul personified as Love itself; but I think this is a Christianization of Empedocles. Yet Kahn admits that "there is no clear statement of this link between Love and the daimon in any extant fragment, and no ancient author ascribes such a view of the soul to Empedocles" (450). My notion of the oppositional nature of Love and Strife, both as cosmos and as constituents of the soul, is consistent with Empedocles' own oppositional thought and similar thought among Pythagoreans. It also helps to reconcile the two key concepts, "psyche" and "daimon."

115. Empedocles frag. 120 (139); Guthrie, in *Presocratic Tradition,* translates the key phrase as "the impious food" (249).

116. Empedocles frag. 124 (137).

117. Nevertheless, a later tradition believed that Empedocles "on his Olympic victory sacrificed a bull made of barley and honey." See Peris, "Greek Teachings," 546. Peris thinks this claim is not true but invented to justify Empedocles' vegetarianism because the Olympic victory was not his but that of his grandfather, also known as Empedocles. Nevertheless, the doxographers who mentioned or invented this account did make a powerful, symbolically "true" statement.

118. Once again I prefer Burnet's translation in spite of its Victorianisms because it captures the emotional feel better than Wright's (Burnet, *Early Greek Philosophy,* fragment 136 [225]).

119. Hence fragments 127 (140) and 128 (141): "to keep completely from leaves of laurel"; and "wretches, utter wretches, keep your hands from beans." Wright has little understanding of the nature of taboo and considers the latter fragment an "appalling line" and not Empedocles' own (Wright, *Empedocles,* 289). But given the fact that beans are so significant in Pythagorean esoteric symbology, it is not surprising that Empedocles himself would share that view.

120. Empedocles frag. 108 (117).

121. Empedocles frag. 115 (120). Wright, as well as early commentators, is not able to explain what I think is a widespread symbol of birth or rebirth in a womb.

122. Empedocles frag. 112 (118). Plutarch says that the "unfamiliar place" is this world (Wright, *Empedocles,* 278).

123. Empedocles frag. 114 (124).

124. Empedocles frag. 113 (121). Here also I am reading against the grain of conventional interpretations of this fragment.

125. Burnet, *Early Greek Philosophy,* 223n2. The relevant fragments are 116 (122) and 117 (123).

126. Empedocles frag. 131 (127).

127. Cited in Guthrie, *Presocratic Tradition,* 250. Long, in *Doctrine of Metempsychosis,* makes the following reasonable argument regarding the hier-

archy of life-forms: "All animal life is divided by Empedocles into four categories: plant, animal, man, god. Within each of the three lower categories there is a gradation of members: the laurel is the highest plant; the lion, the highest animal; and soothsayers, singers, physicians and princes are the highest men" (61). But then, what about the categories of bird and fish?

128. Empedocles frags. 132 (146) and 133 (147). Kingsley, in *Ancient Philosophy,* 344–45, shows how this idea of gradations is picked up later in the Hermetic text *Kore Kosmou,* which says that the most just, before being transformed into divinity, will enter into human bodies to become just kings, true philosophers, authentic prophets, and genuine root-cutters (healers). This also echoes Pindar, as I show later.

129. Long, *Doctrine of Metempsychosis,* 54–55; see also Empedocles frag. 110 (126): "clothing (the daimon) in an unfamiliar garment of flesh." Wright (119) interprets this as a reference to Ananke.

130. Hesiod, *Works and Days,* in Dorothea Wender, trans., *Hesiod and Theognis* (London: Penguin, 1973), 62.

131. Empedocles frag. 118 (128).

132. See Detienne and Vernant, *Cuisine of Sacrifice.*

133. Ibid., 133; see also Detienne's discussion of the name "Bees," given to the faithful of Demeter Thesmophorus: "the Bee Woman can be recognized by a pure and chaste life based on a strictly vegetarian diet. She puts the hunt and the carnivorous life behind her with the invention of honey, which wrests humanity from its cannibalistic fate" (145).

134. In his old age Plato also seems to have idealized this era. In book 6 of the *Laws* he makes the Athenian say:

> We observe, of course, the survival of human sacrifice among many people today. Elsewhere, we gather, the opposite practice prevailed, and there was a time when we didn't even dare to eat beef, and the sacrifices offered to the gods were not animals, but cakes and meal soaked in honey and other "pure" offerings like that. People kept off meat on the grounds that it was an act of impiety to eat it, or to pollute the altars of the gods with blood. So at that time men lived a sort of "Orphic" life keeping exclusively to inanimate food and entirely abstaining from eating the flesh of animals. (Plato, *Laws,* trans. Trevor J. Saunders [London: Penguin, 1970], 264)

It is also possible that Empedocles derived his model of the ideal age from a prior Orphic source, or the reverse might also have been the case.

135. Empedocles frag. 119 (130).

136. Again, I think Burnet's translation in *Early Greek Philosophy,* although not literal, has a better feel: "From what honour, from what height of bliss have I fallen to go about among mortals here on earth?" (223).

137. Wright, *Empedocles,* 227–28.

138. Ibid., 177.

139. See Freud, *Beyond the Pleasure Principle,* 45–48.

140. Burkert, *Ancient Mystery Cults,* 79–88. Burkert, who was unfamiliar with Indic religions, thought that stable congregations developed only with Judaism and Christianity. It is surprising that he ignores Zoroastrianism.

141. Long, *Doctrine of Metempsychosis,* 39.

142. Frank J. Nisetich, trans., *Pindar's Victory Songs* (Baltimore: Johns Hop-

kins University Press, 1980), 89–90 (lines 54–75). A more literal translation of lines 56–77 is provided by Kirk, Raven, and Schofield, *Presocratic Philosophers,* 236:

> Those who are lawless in mind pay the penalty straightaway here [*sc.* on earth]—but the sins committed in this realm of Zeus are judged below the earth by one who pronounces sentence with hateful necessity. The good, upon whom the sun shines for evermore, for equal nights and equal days, receive a life of lightened toil, not vexing the soil with the strength of their hand, no, not the water of the sea, thanks to the ways of that place; but in the presence of the honoured gods, all who rejoiced in keeping their oaths share a life that knows no tears, while others endure labour that none can look upon. And those who, while dwelling in either world, have thrice been courageous in keeping their souls pure from all deeds of wrong, they traverse the highway of Zeus to the tower of Kronos, where the ocean-breezes blow around the Island of the Blest; and flowers of gold are blazing, some on the shore from radiant trees, while others the water fosters; and with chaplets they entwine their hands, and with crowns, according to the righteous councils of Rhadamanthys—for he sits ready with advice beside the great Father, the lord of Rhea with her throne exalted over all.

143. This part of the Pindaric ode is not clear, and I present West's opinion from *Orphic Poems:* "There is judgement of the dead (56–60), a pleasant existence for the good with those gods who have not perjured themselves (61–67), a hell for the wicked, presumably with the perjurer gods (67), repeated reincarnations with the possibility of final escape to the Isle of the Blessed where the heroes live" (110n82).

144. "Rhadamanthys with his un-Greek name, the ancient king and lawgiver of Crete who was believed to be the son of Zeus by Europa, seems to appear in . . . the *Odyssey* . . . ; but in the fifth century myths were certainly current which made him continue for the dead the offices of lawgiver and judge, which had made him famous during his ordinary life" (W. K. C. Guthrie, *Orpheus and Greek Religion* [1952; reprint, Princeton: Princeton University Press, 1993], 152).

145. Cf. Guthrie, *Orpheus and Greek Religion,* 152; I. M. Linforth, *The Arts of Orpheus* (Berkeley: University of California Press, 1941); Gunter Zuntz, *Persephone: Three Essays on Religion and Thought in Magna Graecia* (Oxford: Clarendon Press, 1971).

146. See West, *Orphic Poems,* 68–69. Subsequent quotations from this work are cited parenthetically in the text with the abbreviation *OP.*

147. West also provides an imaginative reconstruction of an Orphic-Bacchic initiation (163).

148. Plato, *Gorgias* 493, trans. Walter Hamilton (London: Penguin, 1977).

149. Long and many others make the point that the texts written before *Phaedo* make no reference to rebirth, the critical event being Plato's visit to Italy, where presumably he was converted to Pythagoreanism. It is equally likely that it was after this visit that Plato went public with his erstwhile private beliefs in rebirth.

150. Nevertheless, Plato was sympathetic to Pythagoras and the sodalities he created. In the *Republic* he is critical of Homer, who he says neither did public service nor founded a school for those who did public service. "That was how Pythagoras got his great reputation, and his successors still talk of a Pythagorean

way of life which distinguishes them in the eyes of the world from other people" (Plato, *Republic* 10.600b, trans. H. D. P. Lee, rev. ed. [London: Penguin, 1987]). Subsequent quotations from the *Republic* are cited in the text with the abbreviation *Rep.*

151. All references to the myth of Er are from Plato, *The Republic* (Lee translation, 10.447–55).

152. Plato, *Gorgias* 523 (Hamilton translation). Subsequent quotations from this translation are cited in the text with the abbreviation *Grg.*

153. Francis Cornford, trans., *The "Republic" of Plato* (New York: Oxford University Press, 1977), 351n1.

154. Plato, *Republic* 10.614b.

155. Guthrie offers a good interpretation of the judges described in this passage. "The place where judgment takes place as described in the *Gorgias* as being 'in a meadow, where there is a fork from which lead the two roads, the one to the Islands of the Blest, the other to Tartaros.'" The names of the judges are given as Minos, Rhadamanthys, and Aiakos, sons of Zeus. Guthrie says that although not explicitly stated, this form of judgment is implied in the *Republic* account also. As in the *Gorgias,* the road that the just take after judgment is described as leading "to the right and upwards to the heaven," the other road to "the left and downwards." See Guthrie, *Orpheus and Greek Religion,* 168. Subsequent quotations from this work are cited parenthetically in the text with the abbreviation *OGR.*

156. Buhler, *Sacred Laws,* 2:101.

157. The idea that those who are reborn tend to follow what they have been in the previous life is notably absent in Buddhism. As far as I know, the only Buddhist theorist who combined this idea with that of karma in a highly elaborate thesis is Vasubandhu (see Vallee Poussin, *Abhidharmakośabhāṣyam,* 91–92).

## CHAPTER 6. REBIRTH AND REASON

1. Plato, *Phaedo* 81a. The edition of *Phaedo* I use is Hugh Tredennick's translation, which appears along with other of Plato's works in *The Last Days of Socrates* (London: Penguin, 1969), 99–183. Unless otherwise indicated *Phaedo* refers to this edition. Subsequent quotations from the *Phaedo* are cited in the text with the abbreviation *Phd.*

2. For a detailed argument of the genesis and significance of Plato's cosmogeography see Kingsley, *Ancient Philosophy,* 79–95.

3. Hugh Tredennick uses the phrase "a life of surpassing holiness," which I think is overdone. I prefer Grube's translation: "those who are deemed to have lived an extremely pious life are freed and released from the regions of the earth as from a prison" (Grube, *Five Dialogues,* 152).

4. Plato, *Phaedrus* 244, in Walter Hamilton, trans., *The Phaedrus and Letters VII and VIII* (London: Penguin, 1973). Unless otherwise noted, quotations from the *Phaedrus* are taken from this translation. Subsequent quotations are cited in the text with the abbreviation *Phdr.*

5. This quote and the one immediately following are from Harold North Fowler, trans., *Plato: Euthyphro, Apology, Crito, Phaedo, Phaedrus* (London: William Heinemann, 1960).

6. The eleven bands along with Hestia are called the ruler gods; they are simply the traditional twelve Olympian deities. Plato incorporates them into his illustrative myth; in the more serious cosmological statement in the *Timaeus* they are ignored.

7. For a definition of these terms see W. K. C. Guthrie, *Plato: The Man and His Dialogues,* vol. 4 of *A History of Greek Philosophy* (Cambridge: Cambridge University Press, 1975), 510.

8. There is considerable controversy regarding the nature of this Transcendental Reality. Later Platonism formulated a Reality beyond that of the Demiurge, a Reality identified with the One, or the Good, which I examine at length later, in my discussion of Plotinus. The *Timaeus* refers to an "unsayable father," but "whether this unsayable father is identical with the good or with the *demiourgos* remained a much discussed problem of Platonism: Plato kept his secret" (Burkert, *Greek Religion,* 327).

9. Plato, *Timaeus* 3.29, trans. H. D. P. Lee (London: Penguin, 1965). Subsequent quotations from the *Timaeus* are cited in the text with the abbreviation *Ti.* See also W. K. C. Guthrie, *The Later Plato and the Academy,* vol. 5 of *A History of Greek Philosophy* (Cambridge: Cambridge University Press, 1978), 251.

10. A. E. Taylor, *A Commentary on Plato's "Timaeus"* (1928; reprint, New York: Garland, 1987); F. M. Cornford, *Plato's Cosmology: The "Timaeus" of Plato* (London: Kegan Paul, 1937).

11. Cornford, *Plato's Cosmology,* 24.

12. Sameness and difference are for Plato, as with Greeks in general, the characteristic forms of reasoning, that is, affirmation and negation.

13. Cornford, *Plato's Cosmology,* 103.

14. Ibid., 105.

15. There are references to the mixing bowl or "krater" in other Platonic texts. See, e.g., *Phaedo* (111d) and *Philebus* (61b–c).

16. Parker, "Early Orphism," 486.

17. Other contradictions in Timaeus's thought are mentioned by Leonardo Taran, in "The Creation Myth in Plato's *Timaeus,*" in *Essays in Ancient Greek Philosophy,* ed. John P. Anton and George L. Kustas (Albany: SUNY Press, 1971), 372–407.

18. See *Timaeus* 44–46.

19. Claude Lévi-Strauss, "The Structural Study of Myth," in *Structural Anthropology,* trans. Claire Jacobson and Brooke Grundfest Schoepf (New York: Basic Books, 1963), 206–31.

20. West, *Orphic Poems,* 70.

21. Unlike Pythagoreans and Empedocles, Plato seems to have had a harsh view of fish reincarnations.

22. Cited in D. A. Rees, "Platonism and the Platonic Tradition," in *Encyclopaedia of Philosophy,* ed. Paul Edwards (New York: Macmillan, 1972), 6:334. Taylor's own famed commentary on the *Timaeus* is vitiated by his Christian prejudices. Plato would find any form of Christianity, Neoplatonist or otherwise, quite abhorrent.

23. In his famous commentary on *Timaeus* Taylor is dismissive of Timaeus's whole cosmology as Pythagorean; he is equally so for the myth of Er. Taylor thinks

that Plato did not believe in reincarnation and that the *Timaeus* is an account of a certain strand of Pythagoreanism of the fifth century. He adds that "the system expounded by Timaeus, though in general Pythagorean, does not agree with any known Pythagorean theory" (*Commentary on Plato's "Timaeus,"* 19, 48). Taylor does not explain why Plato goes through all this bother to depict an un-Pythagorean Pythagorean theory that he was not interested in. Equally problematic is Taylor's urging us not to take the reincarnation theory seriously in the concluding section of *Timaeus*. Reincarnation is such a "questionable point" for Taylor that his rationalist Plato could not possibly have taken it seriously (635).

24. For a provocative and controversial study of Greek homoeroticism see David Halperin, *One Hundred Years of Homosexuality* (New York: Routledge, 1990). See also K. J. Dover's classic study *Greek Homosexuality* (Cambridge: Harvard University Press, 1978).

25. This is not the kind of purity and virginity in women that Freud notes in respect to men's fears of incest. In Freud there is the idealized virgin and the despised harlot. I am suggesting a totally different dynamic: the woman's need for sexual passion is denied, and she is neither virgin nor harlot but one whose task is the very opposite, namely, child bearer. I suspect that this dynamic is found among homoerotic monks also.

26. Plato, *Symposium* 180e, trans. Walter Hamilton (London: Penguin, 1951).

27. See ibid., 206d.

28. Plato, *Symposium* 207b (Nehamas and Woodruff translation).

29. Ibid., 208b.

30. Ibid., 208e.

31. Ibid., 209a. The second quote is Hamilton's translation.

32. Plato, *Symposium* 210b–12b (Nehamas and Woodruff translation).

33. Ibid., 219d.

34. See Plato, *Republic* 10.402c–3c.

35. Ibid., 5.451d–57b.

36. For a discussion of the continuity of Pythagorean mathematics and physics in Plato see Dominic J. O'Meara, *Pythagoras Revived: Mathematics and Philosophy in Late Antiquity* (Oxford: Clarendon Press, 1989), 179–92.

37. Hamilton, trans., *Gorgias,* 142n2. For Hades as a place of punishment in the Philolaic scheme see Kingsley, *Ancient Philosophy,* 205.

38. *Phaedo* 114e. Earlier in the same text he says that "in despising the body and avoiding it, and endeavouring to become independent—the philosopher's soul is ahead of all the rest" (65c–d).

39. I have already discussed these "higher ethics" in some detail. Cornford, in *Plato's Cosmology,* neatly summarizes Plato's soteriological ethics: "The kernel of Plato's ethics is the doctrine that man's reason is divine and that his business is to become like the divine by reproducing in his own nature the beauty and harmony revealed in the cosmos, which is itself a god, a living creature with soul and body and reason in soul" (34).

40. See Guthrie, *Plato,* 515.

41. Guthrie, *Earlier Presocratics,* 160–61.

42. Ibid., 164.

43. Ibid., 165.

44. Perhaps this is what in fact Porphyry attributed to Pythagoras—that nothing is *altogether* new or nothing is new in an *absolute* sense, as against Eudemus's more simplified view.

45. Here I have used Grube's translation of *Meno* (81c) in *Plato: Five Dialogues* (120) because Tredennick translates "the gods" as "God," a conception alien to Plato.

46. "Brahmajāla Sutta" (The perfect net), in *Dial.,* 1:28.

47. Jayawickrama, *Jātaka Nidāna,* 24.

48. See, e.g., Michael Harkin's "Person, Time, and Being," a study of the Northwest Coast Heiltsuk Indians: "For the Heiltsuk, deathbed prophecies of rebirth into the dying one's own family set the stage for further evidence of reincarnation, once the presumptive reincarnate is born. Such evidence includes scars and other physical signs, as well as precocious behavior, especially the early acquisition of language. The reincarnated child is thought to be aware of his or her own previous life and thus possesses private knowledge" (198).

49. Kingsley, *Ancient Philosophy,* 129.

50. See the address to the "new colonists" in *The Laws* 4.716–18 (Saunders translation).

51. Ibid., 10.884–910.

52. For a clear exposition of the *Enneads,* see Dominic J. O'Meara, *Plotinus: An Introduction to the "Enneads"* (Oxford: Oxford University Press, 1996); for a more specialized account see Gerson, *Plotinus.*

53. See *Republic* 507b; *Parmenides* is entirely devoted to a discussion of the One, and although Plotinus takes his bearing from this text, his is a much more sophisticated and meaningful discussion. For a brief account of the sources for Neoplatonic ideas see Wallis, *Neoplatonism,* 32–36.

54. *Enneads* 5.1.6 (MacKenna translation). Subsequent quotations from MacKenna's translation of Plotinus' *Enneads* are cited in the text with the abbreviation *Enn* and in the notes as "MacKenna, *Enneads.*"

55. MacKenna, *Enneads,* xxxiii.

56. O'Meara, *Plotinus,* 36.

57. See Ennead 2.3.7. Armstrong puts it thus: "All things must be joined to one another; not only must there be in each individual part what is called a single united breath of life but before them, and still more, in the All. One principle must make the universe, a single complex living creature, one from all; and just as in individual organisms each member undertakes its own particular task, so the members of the All, each individual one of them, have their individual work to do" (2:71). Citations from A. H. Armstrong's translations of the Enneads appear in the notes as "Armstrong, *Plotinus,*" with the specific Ennead cited.

58. MacKenna, *Enneads,* xxxiv.

59. O'Meara, *Plotinus,* 43.

60. Ennead 3.4.2 (Armstrong, *Plotinus*).

61. Ibid.

62. Ibid., 3.4.3–8.

63. Ibid., 3.4.3.

64. This point is made by John Dillon in his summary of Plotinus's "Our Tutelary Spirit," in MacKenna, *Enneads,* 166.

65. I have used MacKenna's very readable translation of this passage from Ennead 3.2.13. For a more accurate translation the reader may wish to consult Armstrong. For example, MacKenna's translation that deals with "a woman wronged" is perhaps more accurately rendered "one who has raped a woman will be a woman in order to be raped" (Armstrong, *Plotinus,* 3:83). Yet I believe that MacKenna captures the spirit of Plotinus.

66. Wallis, *Neoplatonism,* 3.

67. See *Enn.* 6.9.7, 6.9.10.

68. O'Meara, *Plotinus,* 49. See 44–53 for a detailed exposition of this theme.

69. Ennead 6.9.8 (Armstrong, *Plotinus*).

70. Ibid., 6.9.9.

71. Ibid., 6.9.10.

72. Ibid., 6.9.9.

73. Quoted in MacKenna, *Enneads,* civ. See also Wallis, *Neoplatonism:* "On leaving Ammonius in 243, Plotinus joined the emperor Gordian's expedition against the Persians, perhaps as a member of the scientific staff that often accompanied armies in ancient times, hoping to make contact with the sages of Persia and India" (39). The expedition itself was a failure; but it does indicate Plotinus's interest in Indian ideas.

74. "Plotinus, by his use of negative language, stresses the transcendence of the One to an extreme degree" (Armstrong, *Plotinus,* 1:xvii).

75. Thus, reminiscent of contemporary obscurantist writing, Plotinus says:

> It is now Intellectual-Principle since it actually holds its object, and holds it by the act of intellection: before, it was no more than a tendency, an eye blank of impression: it was in motion towards the transcendental; now that it has attained, it has become Intellectual-Principle: always implicit (in the Transcendent), it now, in virtue of this intellection, holds the character of Intellectual-Principle, of Essential Existence, and of Intellectual Act where, previously, not possessing the Intellectual Object, it was not Intellectual Perception, and, not yet having exercised the Intellectual Act, it was not Intellectual-Principle. (*Enn.,* 5.3.11)

76. There are several discussions of the limitations of astrology. See Armstrong, *Plotinus,* Ennead 2.3, "On Whether the Stars Are Causes," and Ennead 3.1, "On Destiny."

77. Wallis, *Neoplatonism,* 70–71.

78. Porphyry, "Life of Plotinus," in Armstrong, *Plotinus,* 1:35.

79. Armstrong says that the closest that Plotinus came to describing the One in "positive" terms is in Ennead 6.8, "On Free Will and the Will of the One," where the One is endowed with some seemingly theistic qualities that surely appealed to Christians and later Muslim theologians. See Armstrong, *Plotinus,* 6:223–24.

80. Wilferd Madelung, "Shiism: Ismā'ilīyah," *Encyclopedia of Religion,* 13:250. Madelung has an excellent summary of the main Plotinian concepts taken over by the Ismā'īlī:

> In this cosmology Kuni and Qadar [the male and female principles] were replaced by the Neoplatonic Universal Intellect and Soul. God [One], who is beyond any attribute and name and even beyond being and non-being, has originated *(abda'a)* the Intellect through his divine order or volition *(amr)*. The Intellect is described as the first originated being *(al-mubda'al-awwal)* since the *amr* has become united with

it in existence. The Universal Soul emanated from the Intellect, and from the Soul in turn issued the seven spheres of the heavens with their stars. These spheres revolve with the Soul's movement, producing the mixture of the four single natures—dryness, humidity, cold, and warmth—to form the composites of earth, water, air, and ether. Out of the mingling of the composites arise the plants with a vegetative soul, which in turn give rise to the animals endowed with a sensitive soul. Out of the animal realm arises the human being with a rational soul which seeks to ascend through the spiritual hierarchy and to rejoin its origin in the Intellect.

81. Ibid., 253.

82. Porphyry, in his *Life of Plotinus,* says that Plotinus never talked about his life except for one event, when "at the age of eight, when he was already going to school, he still clung about his nurse and loved to bare her breasts and take suck: one day he was told he was a 'perverted imp,' and so was shamed out of the trick" (MacKenna, *Enneads,* ciii). Freud would have loved to relate this experience to Plotinus's later "oceanic feeling" of mystical identity with Being. Yet it is much more sensible to see this early erotic nurturance at the root of Plotinus's own ecstatic experience but transmuted into something vastly different through various degrees of symbolic remove from that primal experience. Unfortunately, we do not know enough of Plotinus's life to even guess at the manner in which the symbolic transformation of affects took place in his unconscious thought processes.

83. O'Meara, *Plotinus,* 83; see also Armstrong, *Plotinus,* Ennead 1.8.7.

84. O'Meara, *Plotinus,* 87.

85. Cited in ibid., 85.

86. This idea of the universe having always existed is mentioned in Ennead 3.2.1, in the famous essay "On Providence": "we affirm that the universe is everlasting and has never not existed" (Armstrong translation); the idea is also discussed in great detail in Ennead 5.31.7.

87. For the Alevis see Ian Stevenson, "Characteristics of Cases of the Reincarnation Type in Turkey and Their Comparison with Cases in Two Other Cultures," *International Journal of Comparative Sociology* 11, no. 1 (1970): 1–17.

88. I use several sources: the excellent overview by M. G. S. Hodgson, "Durūz," in *The Encyclopaedia of Islam* (Leiden: E. J. Brill, 1965), 2:631–34; Betsy Strick, "Ideology and Expressive Culture in the Druze Family" (Ph.D. diss., University of California, San Diego, 1990); Theodore Besterman, "Beliefs in Rebirth of the Druzes and Other Syrian Sects," *Folklore* 39, no. 2 (1928): 133–48 (reprinted in *Collected Papers on the Paranormal* [New York: Garrett, 1968], 1–11 [my page citations are to the reprint edition]); Sami N. Makarem, *The Druze Faith* (New York: Caravan Books, 1974); Jonathan W. S. Oppenheimer, "'We are born in each other's houses'": Communal and Patrilineal Ideologies in Druze Village Religion and Social Structure," *American Ethnologist* 7, no. 4 (1980): 621–36; and the important work of Ian Stevenson, *Cases of the Reincarnation Type,* vol. 3, *Twelve Cases in Lebanon and Turkey* (Charlottesville: University Press of Virginia, 1980).

89. Hodgson, "Durūz," 632.

90. Ibid.

91. Strick, "Ideology and Expressive Culture," 37. When subsequent quo-

tations from this work are cited in the text, they are referenced parenthetically with the abbreviation IEC.

92. Ibid., 40. Although Strick's account is consonant with what we know about the Druze in general, Oppenheimer's account in " 'We are born in each other's houses' " seems to contradict this for the Druze village in which he worked.

93. See Strick, "Ideology and Expressive Culture," 56.

94. Hodgson, "Durūz," 633–34.

95. Nura S. Allamuddin and Paul D. Starr, *Crucial Bonds: Marriage among the Lebanese Druze* (New York: Caravan Books, 1980), 12 (cited in Strick, "Ideology and Expressive Culture," 45).

96. Hodgson, Durūz," 634.

97. Stevenson, *Twelve Cases in Lebanon and Turkey,* 4. When subsequent quotations from this work are cited in the text, they are referenced parenthetically with the abbreviation *TC.*

98. Ibid., 13. Indeed Stevenson thinks that rebirth "forms a larger part of the whole religion of the Druses than it does of the religion of any other group believing in reincarnation" (13).

99. Besterman, "Beliefs in Rebirth," 11. When subsequent quotations from this work are cited in the text, they are referenced parenthetically with the abbreviation BR.

100. See Hodgson, Durūz, 634. Besterman, in "Belief in Rebirth," 9, gives some examples of animal reincarnation from ordinary Druze and reviews travelers' accounts of such beliefs. However, Ian Stevenson, in his extensive interviews, did not find a single instance of animal reincarnation; nor do Strick's Israeli Druze seem to acknowledge such beliefs (see Strick, "Ideology and Expressive Culture," 47). Yet it is indeed possible that some Druze did hold such unorthodox ideas.

101. Besterman, "Beliefs in Rebirth," 5–6. One does not know, of course, whether the old Nuṣayrīyah was taking his interlocutor for a ride!

102. Stevenson, *Twelve Cases,* 6 (citing Makarem, *Druze Faith*).

103. Besterman, "Beliefs in Rebirth," 6. Besterman is citing A. A. Paton, *The Modern Syrians; or, Native Society in Damascus, Aleppo, and the Mountains of the Druses* (London: Longman, Brown, Green, and Longmans, 1844), 277–78.

104. Herodotus, *History,* bk. 2, in Grene, *Herodotus,* 131–210; see also the map on p. 674 of Grene. For a further defense of Herodotus in this regard see Peris, "Greek Teachings," 52–56.

105. The features of Ismā'īlī rebirth that resemble the Greek might be summed up as follows:

1. Rebirth eschatology, bypassing the otherworld
2. Initiation into a special class of virtuosos, male and female
3. Secret knowledge and esoteric symbology shared by virtuosos alone
4. Cross-species reincarnation on the popular level as a possible pre-Islamic and pre-Ismā'īlī feature but only existing occasionally among contemporary sects

5. Purification of the soul through successive rebirths
6. Astral immortality

The first three features are also shared by Pythagoreans but not Platonists, whereas feature 4 is shared by both Pythagoreans and Platonists. Feature 5 fits with Plato, although it is not alien to Pythagorean thought and is consonant with Empedocles' view of the fallen daimon. Feature 6 alone seems exclusively Platonic. However, as I mentioned earlier, astral immortality also might have belonged to a broad stream of Pythagorean beliefs. The critical difference between Platonic eschatology on the one hand and Pythagoreanism and the Ismā'īlī sects on the other is that Plato envisions heaven and hell as places of reward and punishment. Pythagoreanism has no concept of heaven or hell as places of reward or punishment, and in Ismā'īlī thought these realms of punishment are only available at God's judgment.

106. In "Greek Teachings" Peris sums up the Christian resistance to reincarnation:

> Among individual Christian philosophers and theologians a belief in reincarnation was attributed, and sometimes carelessly, to Origen of Alexandria, Nemesius, Synesisus, Bishop of Ptolemais, to Hilarius, Boethius, Psellus of Andros and a few others. Often they subscribed to the belief in reincarnation as a corollary to the tenet of preexistence, which they invariably held to account for the fall of man, but as often they only preached the latter. Exegeses of the fall from grace and the return to grace, with reincarnation providing a fallback for those still not ready to recover the lost estate, were variations played upon the Platonic theme. That such a doctrine did have a strong appeal to Christian thinkers until growing Western influences frowned upon it is to be inferred from the out-and-out declaration of the teaching of preexistence (generally linked with the doctrine of preexistence in the Platonic tradition) as anathema by the Fifth Ecumenical Council, the Second Council of Constantinople, in A.D. 553. Five years later Justinian was to support this anathema with one of his own declaring: "Whosoever says and thinks that human souls pre-existed—i.e., that they had previously been spirits and holy powers, but that satiated with vision of God, had turned to evil, and in this way love in them had died out and that they had therefore become souls and been confined to punishment in bodies—shall be anathema." (37–38)

## CHAPTER 7. IMPRISONING FRAMES AND OPEN DEBATES

1. Slobodin, "Kutchin Concepts of Reincarnation," 138.

2. Edmund R. Leach, "Virgin Birth," *Proceedings of the Royal Anthropological Institute of Great Britain and Ireland for 1966* (1967): 39–49; Melford E. Spiro, "Virgin Birth, Parthenogenesis, and Physiological Paternity: An Essay on Cultural Interpretation," *Man,* n.s., 3 (1968): 242–61.

3. David. M. Schneider, "Virgin Birth," *Man,* n.s., 3 (1968): 126–29.

4. Guemple, "Born-Again Pagans," 120–21.

5. See, e.g., Jones, *The Mahāvastu,* 2:131–34.

6. My information is culled from Goulet, "Contemporary Dene Tha," 156–76. When subsequent quotations from this work are cited in the text, they are referenced parenthetically with the abbreviation CDT.

7. Ibid., 165; square brackets are the author's.

8. Malinowski, "Baloma," 195. Malinowski thinks that the goal of the ethnographic enterprise is to "give an organic account of their beliefs, or to render the picture of the world from the native perspective" (211).

9. Leach, "Virgin Birth," 41.

10. See M. F. Ashley Montague, *Coming into Being among the Australian Aborigines* (London: Routledge, 1937), 228–32.

11. Leo Austen, "Procreation Beliefs among the Trobriand Islanders," *Oceania* 5 (September 1934): 102–13. When subsequent quotations from this work are cited in the text, they are referenced parenthetically with the abbreviation TI.

12. Ibid., 110, my italics.

13. See Malinowski, "Baloma," 192, where an informant says that the spirit enters only during the ceremonial bathing of the child and not during pregnancy or before.

14. Ibid., 195. Malinowski's views on orthodox beliefs appear in many places. See, e.g., *Magic, Science, and Religion,* where he talks of an "orthodox and definite doctrine" and "speculations not backed up by orthodox tradition" (145); see also section 7 of "Baloma," esp. 226.

15. Malinowski's erotic fantasies and ambivalent attitude to his informants are scattered throughout his *A Diary in the Strict Sense of the Term* (New York: Harcourt, Brace and World, 1967).

16. "Mahāsīhanādasutta" (Greater discourse on the lion's roar), in *MLS,* 1:97–98; this might be a development of Upanishadic ideas, as in *Chāndogya,* 6.4.3, in Olivelle, *Upaniṣads,* 148.

17. For the roots of Ayurveda in Buddhism see Zysk, *Asceticism and Healing;* for Ayurvedic experimentation see Gananath Obeyesekere, "Science, Experimentation, and Clinical Practice in Ayurveda," in *Paths to Asian Medical Knowledge,* ed. Charles Leslie and Allan Young (Berkeley: University of California Press, 1992), 160–76. For an important critique of Zysk's ideas see Hartmut Scharfe, "The Doctrine of the Three Humors in Traditional Indian Medicine and the Alleged Antiquity of Tamil Siddha Medicine," *Journal of the American Oriental Society* 119, no. 4 (October–December 1999): 609–29.

18. James Paul McDermott, "Karma and Rebirth in Early Indian Buddhism," in Doniger, *Karma and Rebirth,* 169–70.

19. Vallee Poussin, *Abhidharmakośabhāṣyam,* 2:395.

20. Ibid.

21. "Desire is the state of one who desires pleasure and sexual union," says Vasubandhu (Vallee Poussin, *Abhidharmakośabhāṣyam,* 2:403), anticipating Freud's idea of the pleasure principle. The identification of sex with *taṇhā*, or craving, is further expressed in Vasubandhu's interpretation of the Buddhist myth of human evolution, the "Aganna Sutta," in the section on the development of the organs of excretion and sex: "Beings with sexual differences, by reason of their previous habits, were seized by this crocodile which is wrong judgement; they conceived an active desire for pleasure and so had sexual intercourse. It is from this moment on that the beings of Kāmadhātu were possessed by the demon which is craving" (ibid., 488). *Kāmadhātu* can be loosely translated as the "world of lust" and consists of "hell, the Pretas, animals, humans and six [classes of gods]" (365).

22. Wilhelm Geiger, trans., *The Mahāvaṃsa* (Great chronicle) (London: Pali Text Society, 1980), 149.

23. Ibid.

24. Ananda W. P. Guruge, trans. and ed., *Mahāvaṃsa* (Colombo: Associated Newspapers, 1989), 875.

25. Malalasekera, *Pali Proper Names,* 1:155.

26. *Mūga Pakkha Jātaka,* Jataka no. 538, in Cowell, *Jātaka,* 6:2.

27. Montague, *Coming into Being,* 131.

28. Obeyesekere, *Cult of the Goddess Pattini,* 80–82, 121–27, 230–37.

29. Angela Hobart, Urs Ramseyer, and Albert Leemann, eds., *The Peoples of Bali* (Oxford: Blackwell, 1996); see especially the essay "Religion and Beliefs in Practice" (98–136), which totally ignores reincarnation.

30. The sources I refer to are James Boon, "Incest Recaptured: Some Contraries of Karma in Balinese Symbology," in Keyes and Daniel, *Karma,* 185–222; Linda H. Connor, "Contesting and Transforming the Work for the Dead in Bali: The Case of Ngaben Ngirit," in *Being Modern in Bali: Image and Change,* ed. Adrian Vickers, 179–211 (New Haven: Yale Southeast Asia Studies, 1996); and Connor's Ph.D. dissertation for the Department of Anthropology, University of Sydney: "In Darkness and Light: A Study of Peasant Intellectuals in Bali" (1982). See also the more accessible study by Linda H. Connor, Patsy Asch, and Timothy Asch, *Jero Tapakan, Balinese Healer: An Ethnographic Film Monograph* (Los Angeles: Ethnographics Press, 1996).

31. Boon, "Karma in Balinese Symbology," 187.

32. *Leluhur* could also simply mean deities, whether ancestors or not.

33. Connor, "Darkness and Light," 3. When subsequent quotations from this work are cited in the text, they are referenced parenthetically with the abbreviation DL.

34. Ibid., 130–31. The other categories are illness of a relative (49 percent); cause of someone's death and/or instructions for mortuary rites (18 percent); household strife and misfortune (10 percent); and other (16 percent).

35. This kind of experience is described beautifully by Connor (see ibid., 47); for a detailed examination of cases from Sri Lanka that describe this "dark night" see Obeyesekere, *Medusa's Hair,* 53–66.

36. Connor, "Darkness and Light," 204. Although Connor rightly says that *taksu* is an indigenous Balinese concept, the idea is widely known in popular mediumistic discourses in many parts of the world in the notion of a guardian spirit. In Indic thought also it appears in both popular and classic texts as the *iṣṭa devatā,* the spirit protecting the individual.

37. *Pitaraḥ* is the Sanskrit word for the ancestral spirit of Vedic religion adopted by Balinese Hinduism.

38. Connor, "Darkness and Light," 207. Connor is not clear on whether God can change one's karma, but it does not seem likely according to the tenor of her argument.

39. F. L. Bakker, *The Struggle of the Hindu Balinese Intellectuals* (Amsterdam: VU University Press, 1993).

40. Ibid., 72.

41. Ibid., 169.

42. Hildred Geertz, personal communication. For accounts of the Eka Dasa Rudra see Connor, Asch, and Asch, *Jero Tapakan,* 62–63; Bakker, *Hindu Balinese Intellectuals,* 236–37.

43. Lévi-Strauss, *Structural Anthropology,* 48.

44. See Rodney Needham, "Polythetic Classification: Convergence and Consequences," in Rodney Needham, *Against the Tranquility of Axioms* (Berkeley: University of California Press, 1983), 36–65.

45. Friedrich Nietzsche, *Beyond Good and Evil,* trans. Walter Kaufmann (New York: Vintage Books, 1966), 27.

46. A quotation from Wendy Doniger, cited in Boon, "Karma in Balinese Symbology," 187.

47. James Boon, *Other Tribes, Other Scribes: Symbolic Anthropology in the Comparative Study of Cultures, Histories, Religions, and Texts* (Cambridge: Cambridge University Press, 1982), 180.

48. For a discussion of multiple forms of karma in village India see C. J. Fuller, *The Camphor Flame: Popular Hinduism and Society in India* (Princeton: Princeton University Press, 1992), 245–52.

49. Nietzsche, *Beyond Good and Evil,* 27. This brilliant sentence, I think, neatly summarizes much of Foucault's early thought!

50. Friedrich Nietzsche, *Thus Spoke Zarathustra,* trans. Walter Kaufmann (London: Penguin, 1978), 17.

# BIBLIOGRAPHY


Alderink, Larry J. *Creation and Salvation in Ancient Orphism.* Chico, Calif.: Scholars Press, 1981.

Allamuddin, Nura S., and Paul D. Starr. *Crucial Bonds: Marriage among the Lebanese Druze.* New York: Caravan Books, 1980.

Armstrong, A. H., trans. and ed. *Plotinus.* 7 vols. Cambridge: Harvard University Press, 1966–88.

Asad, Talal. *Genealogies of Religion: Discipline and Reasons of Power in Christianity and Islam.* Baltimore: Johns Hopkins University Press, 1993.

Austen, Leo. "Procreation Beliefs among the Trobriand Islanders." *Oceania* 5 (September 1934): 102–13.

Bakker, F. L. *The Struggle of the Hindu Balinese Intellectuals.* Amsterdam: VU University Press, 1993.

Barnes, Jonathan, ed. *Early Greek Philosophy.* London: Penguin, 1987.

Basden, G. T. *Among the Ibos of Nigeria.* Philadelphia: Lippincott, 1921.

Basham, A. L. *History and Doctrines of the Ājīvikas.* London: Luzac, 1951.

———. *The Origins and Development of Classical Hinduism.* Boston: Beacon Press, 1989.

———. *The Wonder That Was India.* New York: Grove Press, 1959.

Bateson, Gregory. *Naven.* 2d ed. Stanford: Stanford University Press, 1965.

Bechert, Heinz, ed. *The Dating of the Historical Buddha.* Gottingen: Vandenhoeck and Ruprecht, 1989.

Bergson, Henri. *The Two Sources of Morality and Religion.* Trans. R. Ashley Audra and Cloudsley Brereton. New York: Henry Holt, 1935.

Besterman, Theodore. "Beliefs in Rebirth of the Druzes and Other Syrian Sects." *Folklore* 39, no. 2 (1928): 133–48. Reprinted in *Collected Papers on the Paranormal,* by Theodore Besterman, 1–11. New York: Garrett, 1968.

Boas, Franz. *Kwakiutl Ethnography.* Ed. Helen Cordere. Chicago: University of Chicago Press, 1966.

———. *The Religion of the Kwakiutl Indians.* 2 vols. New York: Columbia University Press, 1930.

———. *The Social Organization and the Secret Societies of the Kwakiutl Indians.* Washington, D.C.: Smithsonian Institution Press, 1897. Reprint, New York: Johnson Reprint, 1970.

Bodewitz, Henk W. "Hindu *Ahimsa* and Its Roots." In *Violence Denied: Violence, Non-Violence and the Rationalization of Violence in South Asian Cultural History,* ed. Jan E. M. Houben and Karel R. Van Kooij. Leiden: Brill, 1999.

———. "The Hindu Doctrine of Transmigration: Its Origin and Background." In *Professor Gregory M. Bongard-Levin Felicitation Volume,* in *Indologica Taurinensia,* vol. 23–24. Torino, 1997.

Boon, James A. "Incest Recaptured: Some Contraries of Karma in Balinese Symbology." In *Karma: An Anthropological Inquiry,* ed. Charles F. Keyes and E. Valentine Daniel, 185–222. Berkeley: University of California Press, 1983.

———. *Other Tribes, Other Scribes: Symbolic Anthropology in the Comparative Study of Cultures, Histories, Religions, and Texts.* Cambridge: Cambridge University Press, 1982.

Boyd, James W. *Satan and Māra.* Leiden: E. J. Brill, 1975.

Braudel, Fernand. "History and the Social Sciences: The *longue durée.*" In *On History,* trans. Sarah Matthews. Chicago: University of Chicago Press, 1980.

Buhler, Georg, ed. and trans. *The Sacred Laws of the Āryas.* Vol. 1. Oxford: Clarendon Press, 1879.

———. *The Sacred Laws of the Āryas.* Vol. 2. Oxford: Clarendon Press, 1882.

Burkert, Walter. *Ancient Mystery Cults.* Cambridge: Harvard University Press, 1987.

———. *Greek Religion.* Oxford: Blackwell, 1996.

———. *Lore and Science in Ancient Pythagoreanism.* Cambridge: Harvard University Press, 1972.

———. *The Orientalizing Revolution: Near Eastern Influences on Greek Culture in the Early Archaic Age.* Cambridge: Harvard University Press, 1992.

Burlingame, E. W., trans. *Buddhist Legends (Dhammapada Commentary).* 3 vols. London: Pali Text Society, 1979.

Burnet, John. *Early Greek Philosophy.* London: Adam and Charles Black, 1958.

Burton, Robert. *The Anatomy of Melancholy.* Vol. 1. 1621. Reprint, London: Dent, 1964.

Carrithers, Michael. *The Forest Monks of Sri Lanka.* New Delhi: Oxford University Press, 1983.

Chattopadhyaya, Debiprasad. *Lokāyata: A Study in Indian Materialism.* New Delhi: Peoples Publishing House, 1973.

Clark, Gillian. *Iamblichus: On the Pythagorean Life.* Cambridge: Liverpool University Press, 1982.

Collins, Steven. *Selfless Persons: Imagery and Thought in Theravada Buddhism.* Cambridge: Cambridge University Press, 1982.

Cone, Margaret, and Richard F. Gombrich, trans. *The Perfect Generosity of Prince Vessantara: A Buddhist Epic.* Oxford: Clarendon Press, 1977.

Connor, Linda H. "Contesting and Transforming the Work for the Dead in Bali:

The Case of Ngaben Ngirit." In *Being Modern in Bali: Image and Change,* ed. Adrian Vickers, 179–211. New Haven: Yale Southeast Asia Studies, 1996.

———. "In Darkness and Light: A Study of Peasant Intellectuals in Bali." Ph.D. diss., University of Sydney, 1982.

Connor, Linda H., Patsy Asch, and Timothy Asch. *Jero Tapakan, Balinese Healer: An Ethnographic Film Monograph.* Los Angeles: Ethnographics Press, 1996.

Cornford, Francis. "Mysticism and Science in the Pythagorean Tradition." *Classical Quarterly* 16 (1922): 137–50; and 17 (1923): 1–12.

———, trans. *Plato's Cosmology: The "Timaeus" of Plato.* London: Kegan Paul, 1937.

———, trans. *The "Republic" of Plato.* New York: Oxford University Press, 1977.

Cowell, E. B., ed. *The Jātaka; or, Stories of the Buddha's Former Births.* 6 vols. London: Pali Text Society, 1981.

D'Anglure, Bernard Saladin. "From Foetus to Shaman." In *Amerindian Rebirth: Reincarnation Belief among North American Indians and Inuit,* ed. Antonia Mills and Richard Slobodin, 82–106. Toronto: University of Toronto Press, 1994.

Dasgupta, Surendranath. *A History of Indian Philosophy.* Vol. 1. Delhi: Motilal Banarsidass, 1988.

de Certeau, Michel. *Heterologies: Discourse on the Other.* Trans. Brian Massumi. Minneapolis: University of Minnesota Press, 1989.

———. *The Writing of History.* Trans. Tom Conley. New York: Columbia University Press, 1988.

de Laguna, Frederica. "Tlingit." In *Handbook of North American Indians.* Vol. 70, edited by Wayne Suttles. Washington, D.C.: Smithsonian Institution Press, 1990.

———. "Tlingit Ideas about the Individual." *Southwestern Journal of Anthropology* 10, no. 2 (1954): 172–91.

———. *Under Mount Saint Elias: The History and Culture of the Yakutat Tlingit.* Washington, D.C.: Smithsonian Institution Press, 1972.

Detienne, Marcel. *Dionysus Slain.* Baltimore: Johns Hopkins University Press, 1979.

Detienne, Marcel, and Jean-Pierre Vernant. *The Cuisine of Sacrifice among the Greeks.* Chicago: University of Chicago Press, 1989.

Deussen, Paul. *The Philosophy of the Upanishads.* 1906. Reprint, New York: Dover, 1966.

———. *The System of the Vedanta.* New York: Dover, 1973.

Dhammālankāra, Ittepāna. *Venerable Balangoda Ananda Maitreye: The Buddha Aspirant.* Dehiwala, Sri Lanka: Sridevi Press, 1996.

Diels, Hermann, and Walther Krantz. *Die Fragmente der Versokratiker.* 10th ed. Vols. 1 and 2. Berlin: Weidmann, 1961.

Dillon, John, and Jackson Hershbell, eds. *Iamblichus: On the Pythagorean Way of Life.* Atlanta: Scholars Press, 1991.

Dirks, Nicholas B. *Castes of Mind: Colonialism and the Making of Modern India.* Princeton: Princeton University Press, 2001.

Dodds, E. R. *Greeks and the Irrational.* Berkeley: University of California Press, 1951.

Dover, K. J. *Greek Homosexuality.* Cambridge: Harvard University Press, 1978.

Dumont, Louis. *Homo Hierarchicus: The Caste System and Its Implications.*

Trans. M. Sainsbury, L. Dumont, and B. Gulati. Rev. ed. Chicago: University of Chicago Press, 1980.

Dunbabin, T. J. *The Western Greeks: The History of Sicily and South Italy from the Foundation of the Greek Colonies to 480 B.C.* Oxford: Clarendon Press, 1948.

Durkheim, Emile. *The Elementary Forms of the Religious Life.* Trans. J. W. Swain. 1912. Reprint, London: George Allen and Unwin, 1954.

———. *Sociology and Philosophy.* Translated by D. F. Pocock. New York: Free Press, 1974.

———. *Suicide: A Study in Sociology.* New York: Free Press, 1966.

Dutt, Sukumar. *The Buddha and Five Centuries After.* London: Luzac, 1957.

Edgerton, Franklin. *The Beginnings of Indian Philosophy.* Cambridge: Harvard University Press, 1970.

Eisenstadt, Shmuel N. "The Axial Age: The Emergence of Transcendental Visions and the Rise of Clerics." *European Journal of Sociology* 23 (1982): 294–314.

———. "Fundamentalism, Phenomenology, and Comparative Dimensions." In *Fundamentalisms Comprehended,* ed. Martin S. Marty and R. Scott Appleby. Chicago: University of Chicago Press, 1995.

Eliade, Mircea. *Shamanism: Archaic Techniques of Ecstasy.* Princeton: Princeton University Press, 1972.

———. *Yoga, Immortality, and Freedom.* 2d ed. Trans. Willard R. Trask. New York: Bollingen Foundation, 1969.

Emmons, George Thornton. *The Tlingit Indians.* Ed. Frederica de Laguna. Seattle: University of Washington Press, 1991.

Field, M. J. *Religion and Medicine of the Ga People.* London: Oxford University Press, 1937.

Fienup-Riordan, Ann. *Boundaries and Passages: Rule and Ritual in Yup'ik Eskimo Oral Tradition.* Norman: University of Oklahoma Press, 1994.

———. *The Nelson Island Eskimo: Social Structure and Ritual Distribution.* Anchorage: Alaska Pacific University Press, 1983.

Fowler, Harold North, trans. *Plato: Euthyphro, Apology, Crito, Phaedo, Phaedrus.* London: William Heinemann, 1960.

Frauwallner, Eric. *History of Indian Philosophy.* Vol. 1. Translated by V. M. Bedekar. Delhi: Motilal Banarsidass, 1973.

Freud, Sigmund. *Beyond the Pleasure Principle.* 1920. Reprinted in vol. 18 of *The Standard Edition of the Complete Psychological Works of Sigmund Freud,* ed. James Strachey. London: Hogarth, 1981.

Fritz, Kurt von. *Pythagorean Politics in Southern Italy.* New York: Columbia University Press, 1940.

Fuller, C. J. *The Camphor Flame: Popular Hinduism and Society in India.* Princeton: Princeton University Press, 1992.

Geiger, Wilhelm, trans. *The Mahāvaṃsa* (Great chronicle). London: Pali Text Society, 1980.

Gerson, Lloyd P. *Plotinus.* London: Routledge, 1998.

Gñānavimala, Kiriällē, ed. *Pūjāvaliya* (Garland of offerings). Colombo: Gunasena, 1986.

Goldman, Irving. *The Mouth of Heaven: An Introduction to Kwakiutl Religious Thought.* New York: Wiley, 1975.

Gombrich, Richard F. *How Buddhism Began: The Conditioned Genesis of the Early Teachings.* London: Athlone Press, 1996.

———. "'Merit Transference' in Sinhalese Buddhism." *History of Religions* 11, no. 2 (1971): 203–19.

———. *Precept and Practice.* Oxford: Clarendon Press, 1971.

Gombrich, Richard F., and Gananath Obeyesekere. *Buddhism Transformed: Religious Change in Sri Lanka.* Princeton: Princeton University Press, 1988.

Gooneratne, Dandris de Silva. "On Demonology and Witchcraft in Ceylon." *Journal of the Ceylon Branch of the Royal Asiatic Society* 4, no. 13 (1865–66): 7–8.

Goulet, Jean-Guy. "Reincarnation as a Fact of Life among Contemporary Dene Tha." In *Amerindian Rebirth: Reincarnation Belief among North American Indians and Inuit,* ed. Antonia Mills and Richard Slobodin, 156–76. Toronto: University of Toronto Press, 1994.

Grene, David, trans. *The History: Herodotus.* Chicago: University of Chicago Press, 1987.

Griaule, Marcel. *Conversations with Ogotemmeli.* London: Oxford University Press, 1975.

Grube, G. M. A., trans. *Five Dialogues: Euthyphro, Apology, Crito, Meno, Phaedo.* Indianapolis: Hackett, 1981.

Guemple, Lee. "Born-Again Pagans: The Inuit Cycle of Spirits." In *Amerindian Rebirth: Reincarnation Belief among North American Indians and Inuit,* ed. Antonia Mills and Richard Slobodin, 107–22. Toronto: University of Toronto Press, 1994.

Guruge, Ananda W. P., trans. and ed. *Mahāvaṃsa.* Colombo: Associated Newspapers, 1989.

Guthrie, W. K. C. *The Earlier Presocratics and the Pythagoreans.* Vol. 1 of *A History of Greek Philosophy.* 1971. Reprint, Cambridge: Cambridge University Press, 1992.

———. *The Later Plato and the Academy.* Vol. 5 of *A History of Greek Philosophy.* Cambridge: Cambridge University Press, 1978.

———. *Orpheus and Greek Religion.* 1952. Reprint, Princeton: Princeton University Press, 1993.

———. *Plato: The Man and His Dialogues.* Vol. 4 of *A History of Greek Philosophy.* Cambridge: Cambridge University Press, 1975.

———. *The Presocratic Tradition from Parmenides to Democritus.* Vol. 2 of *A History of Greek Philosophy.* 1971. Reprint, Cambridge: Cambridge University Press, 1995.

Haimendorf, Christoph von Furer. *Morals and Merit: A Study of Values and Social Controls in South Asian Societies.* London: Weidenfeld and Nicholson, 1967.

Halbfass, Wilhelm. "Vedic Apologetics, Ritual Killing, and the Foundation of Ethics." In *Tradition and Reflection: Explorations in Indian Thought,* by Wilhelm Halbfass, 87–129. New York: SUNY Press, 1991.

Halperin, David. *One Hundred Years of Homosexuality.* New York: Routledge, 1990.

Hamilton, Walter, trans. *Gorgias.* London: Penguin, 1977.

———. *The Phaedrus and Letters VII and VIII.* London: Penguin, 1973.

———. *The Symposium.* Harmondsworth: Penguin, 1951.

Hare, E. M., trans. *Anguttara Nikāya* (Gradual sayings). Vol. 4. Oxford: Pali Text Society, 1989.

Harkin, Michael E. "Person, Time, and Being." In *Amerindian Rebirth: Reincarnation Belief among North American Indians and Inuit,* ed. Antonia Mills and Richard Slobodin, 192–210. Toronto: University of Toronto Press, 1994.

Heesterman, J. C. *The Inner Conflict of Tradition: Essays in Indian Ritual, Kingship, and Society.* Chicago: University of Chicago Press, 1985.

———. "Non-Violence and Sacrifice." In *Indologica Taurinensia* 12 (1984): 119–27.

Henderson, Richard N. *The King in Every Man.* New Haven: Yale University Press, 1972.

Herskovits, Melville J. *Dahomey: An Ancient West African Kingdom.* New York: J. J. Augustin, 1938.

Hertz, Robert. *Death and the Right Hand.* Trans. R. Needham and C. Needham. Glencoe, Ill.: Free Press, 1960.

Hobart, Angela, Urs Ramseyer, and Albert Leemann, eds. *The Peoples of Bali.* Oxford: Blackwell, 1996.

Hodgson, M. G. S. "Durūz." In *The Encyclopaedia of Islam.* Vol. 2. Leiden: E. J. Brill, 1965.

Horner, I. B., trans. *The Book of the Discipline.* Vol. 4. London: Pali Text Society, 1982.

———. *Middle Length Sayings (Majjhima Nikāya).* Vols. 1 and 2. London: Pali Text Society, 1957.

———. *Middle Length Sayings (Majjhima Nikāya).* Vol. 3. Oxford: Pali Text Society, 1990.

———. *Vimānavatthu: Stories of the Mansions.* Minor Anthologies of the Pali Canon. Vol. 4. London: Pali Text Society, 1974.

Huber, Hugo. *The Krobo: Traditional Social and Religious Life of a West African People.* St. Augustin near Bonn: Studia Instituti Anthropos, 1963.

Huffman, Carl. "The Pythagorean Tradition." In *The Cambridge Companion to Early Greek Philosophy,* ed. A. A. Long, 78–85. Cambridge: Cambridge University Press, 1999.

Inwood, Brad, trans. *The Poem of Empedocles.* Toronto: University of Toronto Press, 1992.

Ireland, John D., trans. *The Udāna.* Kandy, Sri Lanka: Buddhist Publication Society, 1990.

Jaini, Padmanabh. *The Jaina Path of Purification.* Berkeley: University of California Press, 1979.

Jaspers, Karl. *Vom Ursprung und Ziel der Geschichte.* Zurich: Artemiss-Verlag, 1949.

Jayawickrama, N. A., trans. *The Jātaka Nidāna* (The story of Gotama Buddha). Oxford: Pali Text Society, 1990.

Johnson, T. N., trans. *The Exhortation to Philosophy.* Grand Rapids, Mich.: Phanes Press, 1988.

Johnston, E. H., trans. *The Buddhacarita or Acts of the Buddha.* 1936. Reprint, New Delhi: Orient Reprint, 1972.

Jones, J. J., trans. *The Mahāvastu.* 2 vols. London: Pali Text Society, 1976.

Kahn, Charles H. "Pythagorean Philosophy before Plato." In *The Pre-Socratics: A Collection of Critical Essays,* ed. Alexander P. D. Mourelatos, 161–85. Princeton: Princeton University Press, 1993.

———. "Religion and Natural Philosophy in Empedocles' Doctrine of the Soul," In *The Pre-Socratics: A Collection of Critical Essays,* ed. Alexander P. D. Mourelatos, 426–56. Princeton: Princeton University Press, 1993.

Kamenskii, Archimandrite Anatolii. *Tlingit Indians of Alaska.* Trans. Sergei Kan. Fairbanks: University of Alaska Press, 1985.

Kan, Sergei. *Symbolic Immortality: The Tlingit Potlatch of the Nineteenth Century.* Washington, D.C.: Smithsonian Institution Press, 1989.

Kaplan, Flora *Edouwaye* S. "Some Thoughts on Ideology, Beliefs, and Sacred Kingship among the Edo [Benin] People of Nigeria." In *African Spirituality: Forms, Meanings, and Expressions,* ed. Jacob Olupona. New York: Crossroads Press, 2000.

Kaufmann, Walter. *Critique of Religion and Philosophy.* New York: Anchor Books, 1961.

Keith, Arthur Berriedale. "Pythagoras and the Doctrine of Transmigration." *Journal of the Royal Asiatic Society of Great Britain and Ireland* 41 (1909): 569–606.

———. *The Religion and Philosophy of the Veda and Upanishads.* 2 vols. Cambridge: Harvard University Press, 1925.

Keyes, Charles F. "Merit-Transference in the Kammic Theory of Popular Theravada Buddhism." In *Karma: An Anthropological Inquiry,* ed. Charles F. Keyes and E. Valentine Daniel, 261–86. Berkeley: University of California Press, 1983.

Kingsley, Peter. *Ancient Philosophy and Magic: Empedocles and the Pythagorean Tradition.* Oxford: Clarendon Press, 1995.

Kirk, G. S., and J. E. Raven, eds. *The Presocratic Philosophers.* Cambridge: Cambridge University Press, 1957.

Kirk, G. S., J. E. Raven, and M. Schofield, eds. *The Presocratic Philosophers,* 2d ed. Cambridge: Cambridge University Press, 1983.

Knipe, David M. "*Sapiṇḍīkaraṇa:* The Hindu Rite of Entry into Heaven." In *Religious Encounters with Death,* ed. Frank E. Reynolds and Earle H. Waugh, 111–24. University Park: Pennsylvania State University Press, 1997.

Kopytoff, Igor. "Ancestors as Elders in Africa," *Africa* 41 (1971): 129–42.

Kosambi, D. D. *The Culture and Civilization of Ancient India in Historical Outline.* New Delhi: Vikas Publishing, 1976.

———. *An Introduction to the Study of Indian History.* Bombay: Popular Book Depot, 1956.

Lacan, Jacques. "Aggressivity in Psychoanalysis." 1948. Reprinted in *Écrits: A Selection,* trans. Alan Sheridan, 8–29. New York: Norton, 1977.

———. "The Mirror Stage as Formative of the Function of the I as Revealed in the Psychoanalytic Experience." 1949. Reprinted in *Écrits: A Selection,* trans. Alan Sheridan, 1–7. New York: Norton, 1977.

Laidlaw, James. *Riches and Renunciation: Religion, Economy, and Society among the Jains.* Oxford: Oxford University Press, 1995.

Leach, Edmund R. "Virgin Birth." *Proceedings of the Royal Anthropological Institute of Great Britain and Ireland for 1966* (1967): 39–49.

Lee, H. D. P., trans. *Republic.* Rev. ed. London: Penguin, 1987.

———. *Timaeus.* London: Penguin, 1965.

Lévi-Strauss, Claude. "The Sorcerer and His Magic." In *Structural Anthropology,* trans. Claire Jacobson and Brooke Grundfest Schoepf, 167–85. New York: Basic Books, 1963.

———. "Structural Analysis in Linguistics and Anthropology." In *Structural Anthropology,* trans. Claire Jacobson and Brooke Grundfest Schoepf, 31–54. New York: Basic Books, 1963.

———. "The Structural Study of Myth." In *Structural Anthropology,* trans. Claire Jacobson and Brooke Grundfest Schoepf, 206–31. New York: Basic Books, 1963.

Lewis, I. M. *Ecstatic Religion.* London: Penguin, 1971.

Linforth, Ivan M. *The Arts of Orpheus.* Berkeley: University of California Press, 1941.

Ling, Trevor. *Buddhism and the Mythology of Evil.* London: George Allen and Unwin, 1962.

Long, A. A. "Empedocles' Cosmic Cycle in the Sixties." In *The Pre-Socratics: A Collection of Critical Essays,* ed. Alexander P. D. Mourelatos, 397–425. Princeton: Princeton University Press, 1993.

Long, Herbert Strainge. *A Study of the Doctrine of Metempsychosis in Greece from Pythagoras to Plato.* Baltimore: J. H. Furst, 1948.

Lowenstein, Tom. *The Things That Were Said of Them: Shaman Stories and Oral Histories of the Tikigaq People.* Berkeley: University of California Press, 1992.

MacKenna, Stephen, trans. *The Enneads.* Abr. ed. London: Penguin, 1991.

Madelung, Wilferd. "Shiism: Ismāʾīlīyah." In *The Encyclopedia of Religion.* Vol. 13. New York: Collier Macmillan, 1987.

Makarem, Sami N. *The Druze Faith.* New York: Caravan Books, 1974.

Malalasekera, G. P. *Dictionary of Pali Proper Names.* 2 vols. 1937. Reprint, New Delhi: Oriental Books Reprint, 1983.

———. " 'Transference of Merit' in Ceylonese Buddhism." *Philosophy East and West* 17, nos. 1–4 (1967): 85–90.

Malinowski, Bronislaw. "Baloma: The Spirits of the Dead in the Trobriand Islands." In *Magic, Science, and Religion and Other Essays,* by Bronislaw Malinowski, 125–227. 1916. Reprint, Boston: Beacon Press, 1948.

———. *A Diary in the Strict Sense of the Term.* New York: Harcourt, Brace and World, 1967.

———. *The Father in Primitive Psychology.* 1927. Reprint, New York: Norton, 1966.

———. *The Sexual Life of Savages in North-Western Melanesia.* London: George Routledge, 1929.

Marasinghe, M. M. J. *The Gods in Early Buddhism.* Kelaniya: Vidyalankara University Press, 1974.

Matlock, James G. "Alternate-Generation Equivalence and the Recycling of Souls." In *Amerindian Rebirth: Reincarnation Belief among North American Indians and Inuit,* ed. Antonia Mills and Richard Slobodin, 263–83. Toronto: University of Toronto Press, 1994.

———. "Of Names and Signs: Reincarnation, Inheritance, and Social Structure on the Northwest Coast." *Anthropology of Consciousness* 1 (1990): 9–18.

Matlock, James G., and Antonia Mills. "Appendix: A Trait Index to North American Indian and Inuit Reincarnation." In *Amerindian Rebirth: Reincarnation Belief among North American Indians and Inuit,* ed. Antonia Mills and Richard Slobodin, 299–356. Toronto: University of Toronto Press, 1994.

Matory, James Lorand. "Vessels of Power: The Dialectical Symbolism of Power in Yoruba Religion and Polity." Master's thesis, University of Chicago, 1986.

Mauze, Marie. "The Concept of the Person and Reincarnation among the Kwakiutl Indians." In *Amerindian Rebirth: Reincarnation Belief among North American Indians and Inuit,* ed. Antonia Mills and Richard Slobodin, 177–91. Toronto: University of Toronto Press, 1994.

McDermott, James Paul. *Development in the Early Buddhist Concept of Kamma/Karma.* New Delhi: Munshiram Manoharlal, 1984.

———."Karma and Rebirth in Early Indian Buddhism." In *Karma and Rebirth in Classical Indian Traditions,* ed. Wendy Doniger O'Flaherty, 165–92. Berkeley: University of California Press, 1980.

McHugh, Ernestine. "Reconstituting the Self in Tibetan Tradition: Models of Death and the Practice of Mourning in the Himalayas." In *Tibetan Studies: Proceedings of the Seventh Seminar of the International Association for Tibetan Studies.* Vol. 2, ed. Ernest Steinkeller. Vienna: Austrian Academy of Sciences, 1997.

Menovschikov, G. A. "Popular Conceptions, Religious Beliefs, and Rites of the Asiatic Eskimoes." In *Popular Beliefs and Folklore Tradition in Siberia,* ed. V. Dioszegi, 433–49. The Hague: Mouton, 1968.

Mills, Antonia. "A Comparison of the Wet'suwet'en Cases of the Reincarnation Type with Gitksan and Beaver." *Journal of Anthropological Research* 44 (1988): 385–415.

———. Introduction to *Amerindian Rebirth: Reincarnation Belief among North American Indians and Inuit,* ed. Antonia Mills and Richard Slobodin, 3–14. Toronto: University of Toronto Press, 1994.

———. "Reincarnation Belief among North American Indians and Inuit: Context, Distribution, and Variation." In *Amerindian Rebirth: Reincarnation Belief among North American Indians and Inuit,* ed. Antonia Mills and Richard Slobodin, 15–37. Toronto: University of Toronto Press, 1994.

Mills, Antonia, and Richard Slobodin, eds. *Amerindian Rebirth: Reincarnation Belief among North American Indians and Inuit.* Toronto: University of Toronto Press, 1994.

Minar, Edwin. *Early Pythagorean Politics in Practice and Theory.* Baltimore: Waverly Press, 1942.

Mitzman, Arthur. *The Iron Cage.* New York: Grosset and Dunlap, 1971.

Montague, M. F. Ashley. *Coming into Being among the Australian Aborigines.* London: Routledge, 1937.

Mourelatos, Alexander P. D., ed. *The Pre-Socratics: A Collection of Critical Essays*. 1974. Reprint, Princeton: Princeton University Press, 1993.
Müller, Max. *The Upaniṣads*. 2 vols. 1879. Reprint, New York: Dover 1962.
Mumford, Stan Royal. *Himalayan Dialogue: Tibetan Lamas and Gurung Shamans in Nepal*. Madison: University of Wisconsin Press, 1989.
Ñāṇamoli, Bhikkhu, and Bhikkhu Bodhi, trans. and ed. *The Middle Length Discourses of the Buddha*. Boston: Wisdom, 1995.
Needham, Rodney. "Polythetic Classification: Convergence and Consequences." In *Against the Tranquility of Axioms,* by Rodney Needham, 36–65. Berkeley: University of California Press, 1983.
Nehamas, Alexander, and Paul Woodruff, trans. *Symposium*. Indianapolis: Hackett Publishing, 1989.
Nietzsche, Friedrich. *Beyond Good and Evil*. Trans. Walter Kaufmann. New York: Vintage Books, 1966.
———. *The Birth of Tragedy*. Trans. Douglas Smith. New York: Oxford University Press, 2000.
———. *Thus Spoke Zarathustra*. Trans. Walter Kaufmann. London: Penguin, 1978.
Nisetich, Frank J., trans. *Pindar's Victory Songs*. Baltimore: Johns Hopkins University Press, 1980.
Noon, John A. "A Preliminary Examination of the Death Concepts of the Igbo." *American Anthropologist* 44, no. 3 (1942): 638–54.
Norman, K. R., trans. *The Rhinoceros Horn and Other Early Buddhist Poems (Sutta Nipāta)*. London: Pali Text Society, 1985.
———. *Therigāthā* (Elders' verses). Vol. 2. London: Pali Text Society, 1971.
Nuttal, Mark. "The Name Never Dies: Greenland Inuit Ideas of the Person." In *Amerindian Rebirth: Reincarnation Belief among North American Indians and Inuit,* ed. Antonia Mills and Richard Slobodin, 123–35. Toronto: University of Toronto Press, 1994.
Nyāṇatiloka, Venerable. *Buddhist Dictionary: Manual of Buddhist Terms and Doctrines*. Kandy, Sri Lanka: Buddhist Publication Society, 1980.
Obeyesekere, Gananath. "Avalokiteśvara's Aliases and Guises." *History of Religions* 32, no. 4 (May 1993): 368–73.
———. *The Cult of the Goddess Pattini*. Chicago: University of Chicago Press, 1984.
———. "Despair and Recovery in Sinhala Medicine and Religion: An Anthropologist's Meditations." In *Healing and Restoring: Health and Medicine in the World's Religious Traditions,* ed. Larry Sullivan, 127–48. New York: Macmillan, 1989.
———. *Medusa's Hair: An Essay on Personal Symbols and Religious Experience*. Chicago: University of Chicago Press, 1981.
———. "Myth, History, and Numerology in the Buddhist Chronicles." In *The Dating of the Historical Buddha,* ed. Heinz Bechert, 152–82. Gottingen: Vandenhoeck and Ruprecht, 1989.
———. "The Rebirth Eschatology and Its Transformations: A Contribution to the Sociology of Early Buddhism." In *Karma and Rebirth in Classical Indian Traditions,* ed. Wendy Doniger O'Flaherty, 137–64. Berkeley: University of California Press, 1980.

———. "Reincarnation Eschatologies and the Comparative Study of Religions." Foreword to *Amerindian Rebirth: Reincarnation Belief among North American Indians and Inuit,* ed. Antonia Mills and Richard Slobodin, xi–xxiv. Toronto: University of Toronto Press, 1994.
———. "Science, Experimentation, and Clinical Practice in Ayurveda." In *Paths to Asian Medical Knowledge,* ed. Charles Leslie and Allan Young, 160–76. Berkeley: University of California Press, 1992.
———. "Theodicy, Sin, and Salvation in a Sociology of Buddhism." In *Dialectic in Practical Religion,* ed. Edmund R. Leach, 7–49. Cambridge: Cambridge University Press, 1968.
———. "Voices from the Past: An Extended Footnote to Ludowyk's 'The Story of Ceylon.'" E. F. C. Ludowyk memorial lecture, University of Peradeniya, Sri Lanka, October 24, 2000.
———. *The Work of Culture: Symbolic Transformation in Psychoanalysis and Anthropology.* Chicago: University of Chicago Press, 1990.
Oldenberg, Hermann. *Buddha: His Life, His Doctrine, His Order.* Trans. William Hoey. London: Williams and Norgate, 1882.
———. *The Doctrine of the Upaniṣads and the Early Buddhism.* Trans. Shridhar B. Shrotri. Delhi: Motilal Banarsidass, 1991.
Olivelle, Patrick. "Caste and Purity: A Study in the Language of the Dharma Literature." *Contributions to Indian Sociology,* n.s., 32, no. 2 (1988): 189–216.
———. *The Origin and Early Development of Buddhist Monachism.* Colombo: Gunasena, 1974.
———. *Rules and Regulations of Brahmanical Asceticism.* New York: SUNY Press, 1995.
———, trans. *Saṃnyasa Upaniṣads: Hindu Scriptures on Asceticism and Renunciation.* New York: Oxford University Press, 1992.
———. *Upaniṣads.* New York: Oxford University Press, 1996.
O'Meara, Dominic J. *Plotinus: An Introduction to the "Enneads."* Oxford: Oxford University Press, 1996.
———. *Pythagoras Revived: Mathematics and Philosophy in Late Antiquity.* Oxford: Clarendon Press, 1989.
Oppenheimer, Jonathan W. S. "'We are born in each other's houses'": Communal and Patrilineal Ideologies in Druze Village Religion and Social Structure." *American Ethnologist* 7, no. 4 (1980): 621–36.
Ottenberg, Simon. "Reincarnation and Masking: Two Aspects of the Self in Afikpo." Unpublished ms., 1992.
Pande, G. C. *Studies in the Origins of Buddhism,* 1st ed. Allahabad: University of Allahabad, 1957.
———. *Studies in the Origins of Buddhism,* 4th rev. ed. Delhi: Motilal Banarsidass, 1995.
Parker, Robert. "Early Orphism." In *The Greek World,* ed. A. Powell, 483–510. London: Routledge, 1995.
Parkin, Robert. *The Munda of Central India: An Account of Their Social Organization.* Delhi: Oxford University Press, 1992.
Parry, Jonathan P. *Death in Banaras.* Cambridge: Cambridge University Press, 1994.

Patai, Raphael. *Druze*. In *The Encyclopedia of Religion*, ed. Mircea Eliade. Vol. 4. New York: Collier Macmillan, 1987.

Paton, A. A. *The Modern Syrians; or, Native Society in Damascus, Aleppo, and the Mountains of the Druses*. London: Longman, Brown, Green, and Longmans, 1844.

Peris, Merlin. "Of Euphorbus, Pythagoras' Prior Incarnation." *Sri Lanka Journal of the Humanities* 14, nos. 1 and 2 (1988): 61–94.

———. "Greek Teachings of Reincarnation from Orpheus to Plato." Ph.D. diss., University of London, Queen Mary College, 1963.

Powell, J. G. F., trans. and ed. *Cicero's "Laelius, on Friendship" and "The Dream of Scipio."* Warminster: Aries and Phillips, 1990.

Radcliffe-Brown, A. R. "The Mother's Brother in South Africa." In *Structure and Function in Primitive Society*, by A. R. Radcliffe-Brown. New York: Free Press, 1965.

Radhakrishnan, S., trans. and ed. *The Principal Upanishads*. London: George Allen and Unwin, 1953.

Radin, Paul, ed. *Crashing Thunder: The Autobiography of an American Indian*. 1920. Reprint, Lincoln: University of Nebraska Press, 1983.

———. "The Reincarnations of Thunder Cloud, a Winnebago Indian." In *Amerindian Rebirth: Reincarnation Belief among North American Indians and Inuit*, ed. Antonia Mills and Richard Slobodin, 55–66. Toronto: University of Toronto Press, 1994.

Rahula, Walpola. *History of Buddhism in Ceylon*. Colombo: Gunasena, 1966.

Rasmussen, Knud. *Across Arctic America: Narrative of the Fifth Thule Expedition*. New York: Putnam, 1932.

Rees, D. A. "Platonism and the Platonic Tradition." In *Encyclopaedia of Philosophy*, ed. Paul Edwards, 6:333–41. New York: Macmillan, 1972.

Reynolds, Frank E., and Earle H. Waugh, eds. *Religious Encounters with Death*. University Park: Pennsylvania State University Press, 1997.

Rhys Davids, C. A. F. *The Psalms of the Early Buddhists*. 1908. Reprint, London: Pali Text Society, 1980.

Rhys Davids, T. W. "The Buddhist Theory of Karma." In *Lectures on the Origin and Growth of Religion*, by T. W. Rhys Davids, 73–121. London: Williams and Norgate, 1881.

———, trans. *Dialogues of the Buddha (Dīgha Nikāya)*. 3 vols. London: Pali Text Society, 1977.

———. *The Questions of King Milinda*. 1889. Vol. 1. Reprint, New York: Dover, 1963.

Ricoeur, Paul. *Interpretation Theory: Discourse and the Surplus of Meaning*. Fort Worth: Texas Christian University Press, 1976.

———. "The Narrative Function." In *Hermeneutics and the Human Sciences*, ed. John B. Thompson, 274–96. Cambridge: Cambridge University Press, 1981.

———. *Time and Narrative*. Vol. 1. Trans. Kathleen McLaughlin and David Pellauer. Chicago: University of Chicago Press, 1984.

———. *Time and Narrative*. Vol. 3. Trans. Kathleen Blamey and David Pellauer. Chicago: University of Chicago Press, 1988.

Roth, Guenter, and Wolfgang Schluchter. *Max Weber's Vision of History.* Berkeley: University of California Press, 1979.

Rubel, Paula, and Abraham Rosman, "The Evolution of Exchange Structures and Ranking: Some Northwest Coast and Athabaskan Examples." *Journal of Anthropological Research* 39, no. 1 (1983): 1–25.

Ruegg, D. S. "Ahiṃsā and Vegetarianism in the History of Buddhism." In *Buddhist Studies in Honour of Walpola Rahula*, ed. Bālasūriya Sōmaratna et al., 234–41. London: Frazer, 1980.

Saddhatissa, H. *Buddhist Ethics: Essence of Buddhism.* London: George Allen and Unwin, 1970.

———, trans. *Sutta-Nipāta.* London: Curzon Press, 1987.

Saunders, Trevor J., trans. *The Laws.* London: Penguin, 1970.

Scharfe, Hartmut. "The Doctrine of the Three Humors in Traditional Indian Medicine and the Alleged Antiquity of Tamil Siddha Medicine." *Journal of the American Oriental Society* 119, no. 4 (1999): 609–29.

Schibli, Herman S. *Pherekydes of Syros.* Oxford: Clarendon Press, 1990.

Schluchter, Wolfgang. "The Paradox of Rationalization." In *Max Weber's Vision of History*, by Guenter Roth and Wolfgang Schluchter, 11–64. Berkeley: University of California Press, 1979.

Schmidt, H.-P. "The Origin of *ahiṃsā*." In *Mélanges d'Indianisme à la mémoire de Louis Renou.* Paris: E. de Boccard, 1968.

Schmithausen, Lambert. *The Problem of the Sentience of Plants in Earliest Buddhism.* Studia Philologica Buddhica Monograph Series 6. Tokyo: International Institute for Buddhist Studies, 1991.

Schneider, David M. "Virgin Birth." *Man*, n.s., 3 (1968): 126–29.

Schroeder, L. von. *Pythagoras und die Inder.* Leipzig: O. Schulze, 1884.

Slobodin, Richard. "Kutchin Concepts of Reincarnation." In *Amerindian Rebirth: Reincarnation Belief among North American Indians and Inuit*, ed. Antonia Mills and Richard Slobodin, 136–55. Toronto: University of Toronto Press, 1994.

Spiro, Melford E. "Virgin Birth, Parthenogenesis, and Physiological Paternity: An Essay on Cultural Interpretation." *Man*, n.s., 3 (1968): 242–61.

Staal, Fritz. *Exploring Mysticism.* Berkeley: University of California Press, 1975.

Stevenson, Ian. *Cases of the Reincarnation Type.* 4 vols. Charlottesville: University Press of Virginia, 1975–83.

———. "Characteristics of Cases of the Reincarnation Type in Turkey and Their Comparison with Cases in Two Other Cultures." *International Journal of Comparative Sociology* 11, no. 1 (1970): 1–17.

———. "Cultural Patterns in Cases Suggestive of Reincarnation among the Tlingit Indians of Southeastern Alaska." In *Amerindian Rebirth: Reincarnation Belief among North American Indians and Inuit*, ed. Antonia Mills and Richard Slobodin, 242–62. Toronto: University of Toronto Press, 1994.

———. *Twelve Cases in Lebanon and Turkey.* Vol. 3 of *Cases of the Reincarnation Type.* Charlottesville: University Press of Virginia, 1980.

———. *Twenty Cases Suggestive of Reincarnation.* New York: Society for Psychical Research, 1966.

Strick, Betsy. "Ideology and Expressive Culture in the Druze Family." Ph.D. diss., University of California, San Diego, 1990.

Strong, John S. *The Legend of King Aśoka: A Study and Translation of the "Aśokāvadāna."* Princeton: Princeton University Press, 1983.

Sullivan, Lawrence, ed. *Healing and Restoring: Health and Medicine in the World's Religious Traditions.* New York: Macmillan, 1989.

Tachibana, S. *The Ethics of Buddhism.* Colombo: Bauddha Sahitya Sabha, 1943.

Tahtinen, Unto. *Ahiṃsā: Non-Violence in Indian Tradition.* London: Rider, 1976.

Tambiah, S. J. *The Buddhist Saints of the Forest and the Cult of Amulets.* Cambridge: Cambridge University Press, 1984.

Taran, Leonardo. "The Creation Myth in Plato's *Timaeus.*" In *Essays in Ancient Greek Philosophy,* ed. John P. Anton and George L. Kustas, 372–407. Albany: SUNY Press, 1971.

Taylor, A. E. *A Commentary on Plato's "Timaeus."* 1928. Reprint, New York: Garland, 1987.

Taylor, Thomas, trans. *Iamblichus' "Life of Pythagoras."* Rochester, Vt.: Inner Traditions International, 1986.

———. *Porphyry on Abstinence from Animal Food.* London: Centaur Press, 1965.

Thapar, Romila. "Renunciation: The Making of a Counter Culture?" In *Ancient Indian Social History: Some Interpretations,* by Romila Thapar. Delhi: Orient Longmans, 1978.

Tredennick, Hugh. "Pythagoreanism." Appendix A in *The Ethics of Aristotle,* trans. J. A. K. Thomson, 345–46. London: Penguin, 1976.

———, trans. *The Last Days of Socrates.* London: Penguin, 1969.

Tull, Hermann W. "The Killing That Is Not Killing: Men, Cattle, and the Origin of Non-Violence *(ahiṃsā)* in the Vedic Sacrifice." *Indo-Iranian Journal* 39 (1996): 223–44.

———. *The Vedic Origins of Karma.* New York: SUNY Press, 1989.

Turner, Edith. "Behind Inupiaq Reincarnation." In *Amerindian Rebirth: Reincarnation Belief among North American Indians and Inuit,* ed. Antonia Mills and Richard Slobodin, 67–81. Toronto: University of Toronto Press, 1994.

Uchendu, Victor. *The Igbo of Southeast Nigeria.* New York: Holt, Rinehart, and Winston, 1965.

———. "The Status Implications of Igbo Religious Beliefs." *Nigerian Field* 29 (1964): 27–37.

Upatissa Thera. *The Path of Freedom.* Trans. N. R. M. Ehara, Soma Thera, and Kheminda Thera. Maharagama, Sri Lanka: Saman Press, 1961.

Vajira, Sister, and Francis Story, trans. *Last Days of the Buddha (Mahā Parinibbāna Sutta).* Kandy, Sri Lanka: Buddhist Publication Society, 1988.

Vallée Poussin, Louis de La. *Abhidharmakośabhāṣyam.* Vol. 2. Trans. Leo M. Pruden. Berkeley: Asian Humanities Press, 1988.

Walens, Stanley. *Feasting with Cannibals: An Essay on Kwakiutl Cosmology.* Princeton: Princeton University Press, 1981.

Wallis, R. T. *Neoplatonism.* 2d ed. London: Gerald Duckworth, 1995.

Walshe, Maurice. *The Long Discourses of the Buddha.* Boston: Wisdom, 1995.

Weber, Max. "The Logic of the Cultural Sciences." In *The Methodology of the Social Sciences,* ed. Edward A. Shils and Henry A. Finch. New York: Free Press, 1949.

———. "Objectivity in Social Science and Social Policy." In *The Methodology of the Social Sciences,* ed. Edward A. Shils and Henry A. Finch. New York: Free Press, 1949.

———. *The Religion of India.* Translated by Hans H. Gerth and Don Martindale. Glencoe, Ill.: Free Press, 1958.

———. "Social Psychology of the World Religions." In *From Max Weber,* trans. and ed. Hans Gerth and C. Wright Mills, 267–301. New York: Oxford University Press, 1976.

———. *The Sociology of Religion.* Translated by Ephraim Fischoff. Boston: Beacon Press, 1963.

Wender, Dorothea, trans. *Hesiod and Theognis.* London: Penguin, 1973.

West, M. L. *Early Greek Philosophy and the Orient.* Oxford: Clarendon Press, 1971.

———. *The Orphic Poems.* Oxford: Clarendon Press, 1983.

Whitaker, Albert Keith, trans. *Plato's "Parmenides."* Newburyport, Mass.: Focus Publishing, 1966.

Whitney, W. D. *Oriental and Linguistic Studies.* New York: Scribner, Armstrong, and Co., 1873.

Wijayaratna, Mohan. *Buddhist Monastic Life.* Trans. Claude Grangier and Steven Collins. Cambridge: Cambridge University Press, 1990.

Woodward, F. L., trans. *The Book of the Gradual Sayings (Anguttara Nikāya).* Vol. 1. Oxford: Pali Text Society, 1989.

———. *The Book of the Kindred Sayings (Saṃyutta Nikāya).* Vol. 5. Oxford: Pali Text Society, 1990.

Wright, M. R., trans. and ed. *Empedocles: The Extant Fragments.* London: Bristol Classical Press, 1995.

Zaehner, R. C. *The Dawn and Twilight of Zoroastrianism.* New York: G. P. Putnam, 1961.

Zuntz, Gunter. *Persephone: Three Essays on Religion and Thought in Magna Graecia.* Oxford: Clarendon Press, 1971.

Zysk, Kenneth G. *Asceticism and Healing in Ancient India.* New York: Oxford University Press, 1991.

# INDEX

114; Pindaric scheme of, 234–36, 401nn143,144; Platonic exclusivity of, 270–72, 274–75, 348–49; Plato's memory thesis on, 277–81; Plotinian quest for, 298–302, 406nn73,79,80; prophecy's role in, 116–17; Pythagorean notion of, 198, 210–14, 288, 391n19; Upanishadic paths to, 9–12, 85–86, 100–102, 112–13, 364n22
*Samādhi* (enstatic state), 165–66, 386n32. *See also* Enstasis
Samanic religions: aporia of, at ethicization, 95–96; defined, 88; inherited features of, 88–89; shamanism of, 167–68; species sentience beliefs of, 91, 376n14; without ethicization, 102–6. *See also* Ājīvikaism; Buddhism; Jainism
"Sāmaññaphala Sutta" (Fruits of the life of a recluse), 102–3, 104–5, 166
*Sammuti sacca* (conventional truths), 249
*Saṃnyāsin* (ascetic renouncer), 109
*Saṃsāra. See* Rebirth cycle
*Saṃsāra suddhi* (samsaric purification), 108. *See also* Purification
Sanaṃkumāra, Brahma, 163, 169–70, 177, 387n55
*Sanghas* (or *gaṇas,* assemblies), 121, 122, 380n79
Sanskrit transliteration, xxiii–xxiv
*Sapiṇḍīkaraṇa* (a food offering), 181
Sāriputta (Buddha's disciple), 138, 142–43, 156
*Sarvodaya* (Buddhist reform movement), 388n66
*Sassata-vāda* (Buddhist eternalism), 281
*Śatapatha Brāhmaṇa* (Brahmanic text), 100
Schmithausen, Lambert, 96–97
Schneider, David, 320
Schroeder, L. von, 391–92n21
Self, the. *See* Individuality
*Seṭṭhis* (traders/bankers class), 121
Sexual intercourse: as aporetic dilemma, 319–20; Buddhist conception with, 331; Buddhist conception without, 331–34; Dene Tha conception with, 322–23; Trobriander conception without, 33–35, 324–26
Sexuality: Buddhist repression of, 140, 171–72, 382n112; of Platonic creation myth, 264, 266–67, 320, 404n25; of possession trances, 386n40; and primal hermaphrodite, 267, 397–98n106; salvific sublimation of, 267–69
*The Sexual Life of Savages* (Malinowski), 29
Shamanism: *axis mundi* of, 243–44; and Buddhist enstasis, 163–68; defined, 164; of Dene Tha spirit helpers, 322; and Dionysian cults, 239–40, 286; and Empedoclean ascesis, 233; empiricism of, 286; of Er narrative, 241, 243–44; funeral rituals of, 370n60; Plato's belief in, 284–85; and Pythagorean miracles, 203–4, 393n42; and rebirth doctrine, 200–201; structural utility of, 346; third gender of, 47; of Tlingit, 55–56, 371n77; transpeciation ritual of, 61–67, 373nn103,106,116
*shaykhs* (Druze leaders), 310
Shi'ite Alevis (southern Turkey), 308, 316
Shi'ite Nuṣayrīyah (western Syria), 315
Siamese fraternity (Sri Lanka), 146, 147
Siddhārtha (Buddha's personal name), 154, 156. *See also* Buddha
Sigāla (a Brahmin youth), 181
"Sigālovāda Sutta" (The Sigala homily), 142, 181, 388nn65,66
*Sīla* (morality). *See* Morality
Silence: muni cult of, 13, 167; of Pythagorean sodalities, 192, 196, 202, 203, 210, 392n33; as symbolic language, 94, 168
Simmias (Socrates' friend), 278
Sin, 78, 132–33
Slaves: among Amerindians, 51, 65, 66; in Plato, 184; as Vedic *dasyus,* 184
Slobodin, Richard, 37, 319
Small-scale societies: otherworld features in, 74; rebirth without karma in, 14–15, 17; secular morality of, 74–75; structural approach to, xiii–xiv, 345–46; without universalizing religious forms, 122, 174–75. *See also* Amerindians; Igbo; Inuit; Trobrianders; West Africans
Smartha Brahmins, 358
Social morality. *See* Morality
*The Social Organization and Secret Societies of the Kwakiutl Indians* (Boas), 61
Society. *See* Laity
Socrates, 253, 258, 276; on choosing life-forms, 244–45; and Diotima, 267–68; on divine madness, 254; Er narrative of, 241–44, 402n155; ethical stance of, 248, 270; homoeroticism of, 269; memory thesis of, 277–80; on nature of soul, 250–51, 254–55

Designer: Nola Burger
Compositor: Integrated Composition Systems
Text: 10/13 Sabon
Display: Sabon
Printer and binder: Maple-Vail Book Manufacturing Group